PEOPLE, STATE, AND WAR UNDER THE FRENCH REGIME IN CANADA

MCGILL-QUEEN'S FRENCH ATLANTIC WORLDS SERIES

Series editors: Nicholas Dew and Jean-Pierre Le Glaunec

The French Atlantic world has emerged as a rich and dynamic field of historical research. This series will showcase a new generation of scholarship exploring the worlds of the French Atlantic – including West Africa, the greater Caribbean region, and the continental Americas – from the sixteenth century to the mid-nineteenth century. Books in the series will explore how the societies of the French Atlantic were shaped and connected by trans-oceanic networks of colonialism, how local and indigenous cultures and environments shaped colonial projects, and how the diverse peoples of the French Atlantic understood and experienced their worlds. Especially welcome are histories from the perspectives of the enslaved and dispossessed. Comparative studies are encouraged and the series will accept manuscript submissions in English and in French. Original works of scholarship are preferred, though translations of landmark books in the field will be considered.

Le monde atlantique français est devenu un domaine de recherche riche et dynamique au sein de la discipline historique. La présente collection a pour vocation d'accueillir une nouvelle génération d'ouvrages explorant les espaces de l'Atlantique français – y compris l'Afrique de l'Ouest, la grande région des Caraïbes et les Amériques continentales – du début du XVIe siècle jusqu'au milieu du XIXe siècle. Les œuvres qui y sont publiées explorent de quelles manières les sociétés de l'Atlantique français sont façonnées et reliées par les réseaux transocéaniques issus du colonialisme, de quelle manière les cultures locales et leurs environnements influencent les projets coloniaux, et comment les divers peuples de l'Atlantique français comprennent et expérimentent leurs mondes. Les ouvrages donnant la parole aux esclaves ou aux acteurs traditionnellement dominés sont particulièrement bienvenus, tout comme les recherches comparées. La collection est ouverte aux manuscrits rédigés en anglais ou en français, de préférence des monographies originales, ainsi qu'aux traductions de livres ayant marqué le domaine.

PEOPLE, STATE, AND WAR UNDER THE FRENCH REGIME IN CANADA

LOUISE DECHÊNE

Edition prepared by Hélène Paré, Sylvie Dépatie,
Catherine Desbarats, and Thomas Wien

Translated by Peter Feldstein

McGill-Queen's University Press
Montreal & Kingston • London • Chicago

© McGill-Queen's University Press 2021

Originally published in French as *Le Peuple, l'État et la guerre au Canada sous le Régime français* © Éditions du Boréal 2008

ISBN 978-0-2280-0676-3 (cloth)
ISBN 978-0-2280-0677-0 (paper)
ISBN 978-0-2280-0721-0 (ePDF)
ISBN 978-0-2280-0722-7 (ePUB)

Legal deposit third quarter 2021
Bibliothèque nationale du Québec

Printed in Canada on acid-free paper that is 100% ancient forest free (100% post-consumer recycled), processed chlorine free

This book has been published with the help of a grant from the Canadian Federation for the Humanities and Social Sciences, through the Awards to Scholarly Publications Program, using funds provided by the Social Sciences and Humanities Research Council of Canada.

We acknowledge the financial support of the Government of Canada through the National Translation Program for Book Publishing, an initiative of the *Roadmap for Canada's Official Languages 2013–2018: Education, Immigration, Communities*, for our translation activities.

We acknowledge the support of the Canada Council for the Arts.
Nous remercions le Conseil des arts du Canada de son soutien.

Library and Archives Canada Cataloguing in Publication

Title: People, state, and war under the French regime in Canada / Louise Dechêne.
Other titles: Peuple, l'État et la guerre au Canada sous le Régime français. English
Names: Dechêne, Louise, 1928–2000, author.
Series: McGill-Queen's French Atlantic worlds series ; 6.
Description: Series statement: McGill-Queen's French Atlantic worlds series ; 6 | Translation of: Le peuple, l'État et la guerre au Canada sous le Régime français. | Includes bibliographical references and index.
Identifiers: Canadiana (print) 20210160411 | Canadiana (ebook) 20210160497 | ISBN 9780228006763 (cloth) | ISBN 9780228006770 (paper) | ISBN 9780228007210 (ePDF) | ISBN 9780228007227 (ePUB)
Subjects: LCSH: Canada—History—To 1763 (New France) | LCSH: Canada History, Military. | LCSH: Canada—Militia—History. | LCSH: Militia movements Québec (Province)—History. | CSH: Canada—History, Military—To 1800. | CSH: Canada—Social life and customs—To 1763.
Classification: LCC FC226 .D4213 2021 | DDC 971.01—dc23

This book was typeset in 10.5/13 Sabon.

Contents

Tables and Figures

TABLES

FIGURES

Foreword to the French Edition

Thomas Wien

Louise Dechêne did not live to see this book to completion, for she died on 1 July 2000 at the age of seventy-one. Three days before that, she was still dictating the broad outlines of the conclusion to her daughters, Geneviève and Julie. *People, State, and War under the French Regime in Canada* is part of a broader study of relations between the Canadian colonists and the Ancien Régime adminis-tration. She had embarked on the project after completing her dis-sertation, submitted in 1973 and published the following year as *Habitants et marchands de Montréal au XVIIe siècle.*[1] In the course of the professorial career she was then, in her mid-forties, just begin-ning, Dechêne collected data, wrote index cards, and produced a sequence of drafts. In 1994, she published a book about one aspect of these relations: *Le Partage des subsistances au Canada sous le Régime français* (*Power and Subsistence* in its English translation) deals with administrative control over the grain trade under the French regime.[2] The next task was to complete another (in her mind, much more important) part of the analysis, concerning the military sphere. In retirement, this became the focus of her incessant labours. She had become, in her words, a "homebody," a euphemis-tic reference to being confined to her apartment by emphysema. And so the dining room became her point of departure for a series of archival journeys, back in time to the French regime, and this book was the result.

If she had had a few more months, Dechêne would have further revised certain chapters, especially the last, which was left in draft form. She would have added material to the historiographic portion of the introduction and written a lengthier conclusion than the ones found in her earlier works.[3] All these "would haves" should not, however, distract us from her substantial accomplishment: finishing the book's twelve chapters and its introduction. Their contents encompass nearly the sum total of her thinking about the colonial society of early Canada and the pervasiveness of military logic in its governance, and they go far in altering our perspective on the subject. A central theme that comes up for reconsideration is that of the colonial militias. For successive generations of historians brought up on the military annals and the ensuing historiography, the early Canadian militiamen all followed a single, undifferentiated trajectory, from the beginning to the end of the colonial era. For Dechêne, this reduction of the Canadians who set upon Anglo-American villages at the turn of the seventeenth century, or fought the invader in 1759, to the status of a symbol – of bravery, indiscipline, "Canadianness" – was problematic. One of her key goals with this book was to do justice to the complexity of these militiamen by debunking, or at least problematizing, the myth of the "warrior people." This she achieves by paying some attention to early military missions, before war utterly transformed this corner of the continent, but by devoting much more to a rereading of the militias' experience on the basis of recent advances in social history (in the broad sense of the term).[4]

But the scope of the study goes beyond the militiamen to include the whole population of a colony at grips with perpetual war and its exigencies. Even when the enemy was not at the remote outposts, let alone at the city gates, defending the colony imposed a burden in terms of work brigades (*corvées*) and various other obligations. In this regard, *People, State, and War* expands the study, begun in *Power and Subsistence,* of the sacrifices and commitments demanded of Canadian subjects by virtue of their fealty to the royal state. Dechêne's meticulous account does much to change the traditional portrayal of a carefree colonial population pampered by a faraway king. In its place, what we get is documentation and critique of a government given to arbitrary measures, with an increasing propensity to rule on an ad hoc basis.

The broader context for this history (as was true of the previous book) is, ultimately, the Ancien Régime itself, as observed from one of its remotest reaches.[5] The author's strategy of presenting Canada as an integral, if peripheral, part of the realm reminds readers that the ocean separating colony from mother country was not some unbridgeable chasm. Her analysis of the ambiguous relations between the two – between colonists and continentals – casts new doubts on past historical methods of interpretation marked, to varying degrees, by anticolonialism and nationalism.[6] Coming in for particularly harsh criticism is the thesis according to which two pre-Conquest groups in North America, the Canadians and the French, had practically arrived at a state of civil war.[7] The author counters this notion by rooting her analysis in relationships of domination and subordination that were only secondarily influenced by geographical origin. Adopting the perspective of peasants and working-class townspeople, she takes a close, cold-eyed look at how exactly the powerful – in Canada and, to a lesser extent, France – did the work of governing in the interests of the privileged. To this end, she fleshes out the practices associated with the colonial Ancien Régime – a notion that historians have too often merely brandished as an epithet.

In what follows, I discuss Dechêne's trajectory over a period of more than two decades as she homed in on the subject of her study and hammered out the content of what ultimately became two books. I then follow her from chapter to chapter as she unspools the argumentation of this second work. Finally, in the third part of this foreword, I dwell briefly on certain avenues for further research on the history of the colonial and European Ancien Régime as it was lived *and* written. I do so with the knowledge that the author, always impatient with the fripperies of historiographical debate, would have been briefer still.

I. THE PROJECT

Louise Dechêne had little to say about how this long project took shape. She was not partial to conference papers or articles giving tentative or fragmentary glimpses of a larger project – the typical trial balloons of the profession. On the contrary, prior to the publication of *Le Partage des subsistances* in 1994, her papers were devoted to other topics.[8] That book, on subsistence crops (mainly wheat) and their administration by the state, limned many of the themes that would be addressed in the present major work while also clearing the way for her to focus more or less exclusively on military affairs. She concluded it by saying no more of her research and writing process than that it had been long and of the initial project that it had unexpectedly become much broader in scope due to "the pleasure of teasing out and elucidating problems I had not originally thought about."[9] In the absence of a more in-depth study of the historian's working documents, a few scattered clues enable us to get incrementally larger glimpses into how the work proceeded and what her intellectual trajectory consisted of.

It might be said that a clue to the origins of this book is to be found in its first chapter. Consider the first witness called to the bar, the young Jérôme de Pontchartrain. One could not, he wrote to Vauban in 1699, rely on the Canadians for guard duty at the colonial forts, as one could on the French. In Canada, "it is a wholly different mentality, with other customs, other sentiments, a love of liberty and independence, and an insurmountable ferocity."[10] Dechêne devotes much of this chapter to an analysis of the successive avatars of this stereotypical image, scrolling through the ways in which the French perceived the colonists. The importance she accords to this aspect of colonial history makes sense, for this shifting image is the foil for not only *People, State, and War* but for all of her thinking about the French regime.

To see this, we must go back to the mid-1960s when she was in Paris. Working for the Archives du Québec, she produced an inventory of the correspondence of Vauban, along with other official documents of potential interest to historians of New France. At the same time, she frequented the seminars of Robert Mandrou, Pierre Goubert, and others. This work introduced her to the writings of the Annales School and the historiography of the French Ancien Régime, which was then undergoing a thorough overhaul. Where once she had considered the era uninteresting, overly familiar, she now, all at once, realized that it offered plenty of food for thought. Indeed, it soon supplanted the history of nineteenth-century Lower Canada as her primary focus[11] and induced her to change course.[12] How did this come about? Some clues can be found in a radio interview she gave a few years later in which she returned to the question of stereotypes. What she had realized was that the methods of the Annales School might prove useful in validating the received images of the French regime, derived from "the writings of observers who had spent a bit of time in New France and said one thing or another, characterized the habitants' behaviour as such-and-such."[13]

This generic image of the Canadian was indeed to play a paramount role in Dechêne's work. The first two books, *Habitants and*

Merchants and *Power and Subsistence*, problematize different facets of this image: respectively, the *coureur de bois* and the "rebellious" habitant. This third book methodically critiques two other facets: that of the "warlike" Canadian, always primed for battle with the enemy, and that of the Canadian *as* Canadian, as someone who gives lip service to his French identity but feels distinct. Dechêne strives to discern the extent to which, and under what circumstances, these images accurately describe the colonial population (including, in some instances, its female members): in other words, how well the stereotypes fit.

The foregoing discussion is intended to limn the common thread running through the three books. From here, we move on to a closer reading of the author's thought and work with an eye to discerning some of its complexities. The genesis of the original project – the author's inquiry into the relations between the colonial population and the royal state – is coterminous with the end of her dissertation, in 1973. *Habitants and Merchants* was a reaction not only to the hackneyed image of the colonist but also to its progress from trope to unquestioned fact in the historical literature.[14] Previous historians had tended to take at face value the official sources – in which the bias of the state or the church always lurks under the surface – and what resulted was a largely hagiographic approach to the governors and the intendants. These men had come to be depicted, alongside the bishops, as the architects of colonial development. By the same token, the historians had implicitly endorsed the criticism directed by these powerful men at a seemingly recalcitrant, even rebellious, populace. By contrast, Dechêne took deliberate distance from the official discourse, the better to "examine the evolution of this society step by step."[15] Her goal was, in some sense, to tune out the noise of events, thus laying bare the underlying or nascent structures of this society. Her method, albeit simple in appearance, presupposed an in-depth study of the colonial economy and social structure and how they came into being.[16] To get at the real lives of the colonists, she would have to make meticulous use of notarial and judicial documents found in the archives and read between the lines of the official sources as necessary.

In this initial phase of the research, Dechêne thus made a point of keeping the state marginal to the discussion. The idea was not to deny the influence of the state or of institutions more broadly; on the contrary, she devoted close scrutiny to its interface with the seigneuries and the fur trade. Nevertheless, the bulk of *Habitants and Merchants* was taken up with broad socioeconomic aspects. The book delves into the lives of ordinary people, paying little or no attention to the administrators and how they governed. As she wrote in its conclusion, the economy "had an autonomous existence ... it evolved according to its own rhythms, and the manner in which it interacted with the rest of the [colonial] system was neither pre-ordained nor pointedly dictated by the authorities."[17] Now, while this may hold true for the gradual, longer-range evolution – the plate tectonics, as it were – of the colony's history, it remained to be demonstrated for the shallower zones of that history and even for its economic history. The author knew this, noting in the same breath that her rereading of colonization necessitated a reconsideration of "what effect government has on development, and the effectiveness or pertinence of regulation."[18] That being the case, she called for renewed study of the colonial government, but this time with a fuller awareness of the specificities of colonial society.

The project arising from this line of thinking was, in 1973, still rather circumscribed, its outlines hazy. The author wrote no more than that "[a]n analysis of the public sector would demonstrate the financial links between the government and the private sector" while also highlighting "the nature of social relations." Such an analysis "would not, however, change the main trends delineated in [*Habitants and Merchants*]."[19] This outline presaged a study whose scope would have been circumscribed by the limited influence that the historian initially conceded to the state. But she would, in the next few years, come face to face with the need to integrate govern-mental action into her analysis, and when she did, the project was to be greatly broadened.

A brief review of the historiography of New France that she published in the French journal *Canadian Studies* in 1977 augurs this shift in emphasis. Although most of the paper deals with the durable features of colonial development and the "zones of rel-ative inertia" characteristic of its economy,[20] an abrupt, surpris-ing change of register toward the end points the way toward the author's future concerns:

It is possible, in France, to write a history of socioeconomic structures with almost no reference to the political sphere. Given the torpid pace of political change, historians can ignore decisions that barely grazed this society, faraway events with little (and always indirect) impact on it. By contrast, New France was "all surface" (*sans épaisseur*), its economy beholden to its politics. The colony's economic development was continually buffeted and shaped by administrative decisions, military strategy, and other factors.[21]

Was the state about to become a crucial part of Dechêne's analysis? So it seemed from these remarks.

A late-1970s notebook titled "Problèmes," in which the historian sets down her thoughts about the course of colonial and Quebec history, sheds further light on the path she was to follow after this shift of focus.[22] It begins with an analysis of the broader transition, in world history, from feudalism to capitalism. For the author, the most promising approach to this question in European historiography is to allow for the persistence of older structures, including governmental structures, even after capitalism was well on the way to dethroning feudalism. But for New France and other colonies, most authors had interpreted this transition as a function of one of three different models, centring around either mercantilism, markets and factors of production, or the ravages of colonialism. All three tended to classify modern colonies as capitalist, even though archaic structures were sometimes included in the analysis. "In each of these models, *economic production is the driver*," she concludes. "[Institutional] structures are ill-equipped to assist the growth of these economies, so they function as hindrances to their progress."[23] But in her view, these models had got Canada wrong; like Europe, Canada (and probably the other French colonies as well) had not skipped the stage of feudalism; rather, "it had to exhaust [feudalism] before it could make the transition to capitalist forms."[24]

So far, Dechêne had not ventured far from the interpretive framework of *Habitants and Merchants*. Her next step, however, was to further the analysis by addressing the question of the state more specifically. She found that the feudal mode of production had taken a peculiar form in Canada, where the colonial state enjoyed unusual margins of autonomy and power. What followed was a description of a full-fledged research project:

What I want to show is how, in Canada, the monarchy took on "the trappings of a class," in the sense that, in pursuing its

struggle to dominate the Indigenous nations, the "peoples,"
those who would become its vassals, it acted independently of
the other classes. This state was not in any sense stagnant, or an
impediment to progress; nor was it a proto-modern monarchy
(viz. Poulantzas, etc.).[25] Rather, it was an almost purely feudal
state, represented [in the colony] by military officers and nobles;
a state that deployed an anti-mercantilist policy (with increasing
firmness from 1700 [to] 1760) while keeping a nascent seigneurial nobility in check.[26]

In short, the state, unfettered by checks and balances, became central to the workings of the colony. In addition to overtaxing trade
(which is how "anti-mercantilist policy" must be construed here)
and coddling the nobles while keeping them on a leash, it nurtured
an atypical relationship with the population at large, who were
largely exempt from taxation in the narrow sense of the term. This
did not mean, however, that ordinary people had no obligations to
the state. In Canada, "people paid, gave, and contributed *in labour*
instead of *property*. The habitants could be drafted into work brigades and militia duty at will, but only by the state. To ensure their
availability, the authorities had to prevent the seigneuries from consolidating their power."[27] And so "the military context ... meant
that the exploitation of persons (work brigades, militia duty, etc.)
took precedence over the taking of surpluses (rents, usury, etc.)."[28]
State power engendered a lack of solidarity between social groups; it
continually provoked class conflict even as it obscured the relations
between classes. In short, the "monarchy in arms ... distorted the
whole society."[29]

At this stage of her thinking, Dechêne's emphasis was on the monarchy's capacity to influence (even as it obscured) social relations
in the colony. No surprise, then, that the list of "specific studies"
immediately following this research outline[30] draws diagonal lines,
as it were, between state activity and the different social groups in
the colony. Dechêne planned to "take inventory" of the colony's
nobles, studying their cohesion and ideology; analyze the clergy and
church finances for what they might reveal of church–state relations; study the complex of problems subsumed under the heading
of "merchants/purveyors"; and, finally, consider the population at
large through the lens of its obligations to the state (work brigades,
requisitions, militia duty). In short, the state was to be analyzed in

terms of its relations with various societal groups. Only one item on the list, concerning the intendancy (never to be developed, as it happened), refers to the state as a structure in and of itself, and on this score, the 1977 paper cited above gives a glimpse of a tentative research hypothesis, drawing on the work of other historians. One is tempted to see this research program as an application of the overarching theme of *Habitants and Merchants* to the governmental sphere. It may be recalled that the historian had written in her dissertation of "a traditional society [that] reformed spontaneously" in Canada.[31] Here, what reformed was an Ancien Régime state, and it lost no time in complicating the lives of its colonial subjects:

> There is no doubt that [the Ancien Régime] sought to simplify, to improve local [colonial] justice and government, and there was no obvious impediment to achieving these aims in the colony, since it was a blank slate, unburdened of the weight of customs and venal offices. But to succeed, it would have been necessary for these administrators to have a clear awareness of what stood in the way of good administration in the mother country. Instead, they often recreated problems that could easily have been avoided in this new land, such as the superimposition of civilian and military powers, and other convoluted arrangements that gave rise to infighting, confusion, and nuisances for the public.[32]

Here is a glimpse of the concept of arbitrary rule that will become a key theme of both *Power and Subsistence* and *People, State, and War*. The military aspect was already well represented in the author's research plan by the studies she planned to conduct on the purveyors and the militias. This aspect would become increasingly prominent as time went on. In the 1981 radio interview discussed above, Dechêne said that the study in progress dealt with the impact of political and wartime decisions on everyday life.

> What I want to do now, and I've already started working in the archives, is to delve further into the study of social relations, but that work takes me straight back into the eighteenth century. I don't want to produce any more full-length books – one monograph, that's enough for one lifetime. What I want to do instead is [devote broader study] to social relations in the latter days

of the French regime, by drawing (as before) on more general sources. And also, to try to see the influence of political aspects. Because, in the eighteenth century, you've got the wars ... Maybe also an aspect that I downplayed in [*Habitants and Merchants* but] one that shouldn't be forgotten: ... the extent to which ordinary people's lives were affected by political decisions, wars, the form taken by the administration.[33]

By this time, the research was well underway. Dechêne could draw on notes she had taken for *Habitants and Merchants* from the judicial archives of Montreal and from other sources. Meanwhile, she had combed through the files of other colonial courts, read the main series of official correspondence, and begun a detailed study of the Archives de la Guerre, which she had visited during her years in Paris. What remained was to complete this last task, read the manuscripts in the Baby collection and those in the Archives du Séminaire de Québec, and continue with her reading of the printed sources.

In the early 1980s, Dechêne's role as co-editor on the first volume of the *Historical Atlas of Canada* greatly slowed the pace of her work on this project. Still, the content of a 1984 grant proposal shows that while her research had made little headway, her thinking had evolved. Now narrowed down from the six decades of French domination in the eighteenth century to the years 1737–60, the analysis focused on three themes: the near-omnipotence of the royal officers and the spirit of the government they inhabited, between official discourse and practice; the military logic guiding state intervention in the colony, as opposed to the fiscal logic that prevailed in France, lending credence to the notion of a "garrison colony" peopled by land clearers who doubled as soldiers; and the attitudes of the public toward the "system of control" imposed on them, wavering between resistance on the one hand, "compliance and obedience" on the other. Dechêne had refined her conceptual framework so that it now revolved around the notions of authority, paternalism, subordination, and insubordination. The cornerstone was still "the monarchy in arms that distorted the whole society," but attitudes and discourses had now become as central to the analysis as acts, behaviours, and structures. And she now had a tentative outline consisting of at least seven chapters: the archival sources and the discourse characteristic of them; the hierarchy and workings of the administration and the symbolic representations of royal power; the colonial troops as "auxiliaries of the administration"; the recruitment, duties, and performance of the colonial militiamen; restrictions on the movement of persons; the social aspects of taxation and currency circulation; and the controls exerted over grain and its movement.[34]

Sidewise (after the fashion of our discipline, perhaps?), via a combination of deletions, additions, and extensions, the project had morphed into something new.[35] On the one hand, Dechêne steadily abandoned certain aspects of the initial program, realizing that it was too big, that other historians had made advances on some of these questions, and that her own priorities had evolved. There was less need now to devote in-depth study to the nobility, the church, and its servants, and the concept of the "merchant/purveyor" became incorporated into a more ambitious study of grain that would lead the historian to renew her acquaintance with rural history. On the other, the quest for explanations necessitated a return to the end – and soon even to the beginning – of the seventeenth century. Meanwhile, since about 1980, her readings had encouraged her to devote further (and more anthropological) study to various aspects of the exercise of power: hegemony, public opinion, political intermediaries, the conduct of war, and also, the pervasive fears experienced by all social strata, privileged and underclasses alike.[36] The "burden borne by the people," previously just one among many aspects of the research program, was now given pride of place.

Documentation is lacking for the late 1980s when the author was finalizing her research, writing new material, and revising the chapters already written. It became clear around 1990 that one book would not be enough to contain the whole study, even if the planned chapter on the movement of persons, and most of the one on currency, were eliminated. The study of grain, initially the subject of a single chapter, would ultimately take up the whole of *Power and Subsistence*, the book published in 1994. Subsequently, the manuscript published here as *People, State, and War* would take on unforeseen scope as well: during a marathon retreat taken by the author, the eight initially planned chapters would become twelve. Grappling until the very end with structural problems, Dechêne would repeatedly complain about the difficulty of reworking chapters written several years earlier – she never entirely succeeded – and of finding the right proportion of well-established factual matter to guide readers through her various studies.

During these years, her primary interest was in the *subjective* experience of early Canadians: their experience of war and, increasingly, of identity. Although she had touched on this theme in her examination of the terms in which the colonial population was typically described, she would now address it head on. What one assumes to have been a response to the vogue for subjectivism in Western historiography was also – as regards collective identity – a response to the intense debate taking place in Quebec around a redefinition of nationalism, if not the Québécois people as such.[37] Many of these thinkers posited that a key historical source of the Québécois identity was the one that the early colonists are asserted to have developed: a Canadian identity, in contradistinction to that of continental French subjects. In the last part of *People, State, and War*, Dechêne challenges this idea.

In short, the path taken by this long-aborning book was a singular one. The book took shape gradually – over the course of half a lifetime, if Pontchartrain is taken as the starting point. And it took place in step with the maturation of the author's thought process as she navigated both the archival sources and the changing political and intellectual context of her own day. A detailed study of these influences, as fascinating as it might prove, is beyond the scope of this foreword, yet another aspect of the book's genesis deserves a brief description: the writing process itself. In her explanatory note, editor Hélène Paré discusses the concentric geography in which the author worked: before her on an old pine table, lined paper and pen; a little further away, notes, index cards, and a few books; banished to another room, the computer she almost never used; towering above the abhorred machine, and in an adjoining corridor, her bookshelves. Corresponding to this arrangement of tools and materials was a distinctive approach to the construction of the narrative. To wit, information from books and archival documents arrived at her work table in the form of index cards, but it then underwent a final, even more profound transformation involving cutting and pasting of transcribed text with scissors and glue. Dense and sparing in its deployment of direct quotes, the author's prose belies the mountain of interpreted evidence underlying it, and increasingly so over time, as her annotations became more laconic. The resulting analysis seems all the more condensed, chock-full of authoritative judgments, in that a good deal of the source material is hidden from view. Insistent on persuading readers with sound argument, Dechêne asks no less of us than that we put our trust in her.

And now to the culmination of all this work: the book itself. Its complex structure and density attest to its long gestation and unfinished character, the feel of a work in progress, but also its ambition to grasp an entire field of historical experience. What the author wrote about its twin sister, *Power and Subsistence*, applies to this book as well: "Occupying a middle ground between the social and the political, between structures and the events that disrupt them, this study of an administration seeks to elucidate the thought patterns of a government and the people it governed – to understand the specific cultural whole that was theirs."[38]

2. THE STUDY

People, State, and War is divided into four parts of unequal length. Chapter 1, and the introduction in its way, focus on the problem of the "warrior-colonists": where the image came from and how it evolved into the modern era. They are followed by the main body of the work, divided into three asymmetrical sections comprising the remaining chapters. The next two of these (2–3), devoted to a prehistory of sorts, cover the period of familiarization and experimentation in the early seventeenth century. The next four (4–7) discuss the gamut of military operations, interventions concerning public order, and levies put in place between 1687, when a quarter-century of conflict began, and 1744, when the North American phase of the War of the Austrian Succession got underway. Finally, chapters 8 to 12 discuss, from different angles, the period of hostilities set in motion by this conflict, ending with the Conquest of 1760.

Haunting the introduction is the captivating image of Anne Edmond, a peasant girl willing to risk everything to prevent her brother and other young men from being sent off to war. Skillfully exploiting a legal document, Dechêne shows that the rural population was following the war, as far away as it seemed, with a mixture of fascination and worry. Seizing the opportunity to present a rare female figure, albeit in drag,[39] the author uses this episode as a way of introducing her central thesis: that not all Canadians went off to war enthusiastically, as the shopworn image conveyed by traditional and military history would have us believe. Furthermore, she contends, a species of social history that "pretend[s] that war did not exist" (p. 8)[40] has neglected to rectify this image. To know the circumstances under which Canadians participated in war, and to follow the traces left by war in colonial life, a nexus between the two historiographies would have to be established. And so begins the journey of this book.

Chapter 1 delves further into the genesis of these images of the war-hungry colonist – indeed, the colonist as such, the colonial population as a whole. The author's efforts to trace the genealogy of this constellation of metropolitan representations lead her back to the early voyages of discovery and to European perceptions of their outcomes. The idea of the colonist would thenceforth take on enduring criminal associations, mingled with refracted memories of forced emigrations. All this also reflected the European elites' persistent difficulty in imagining that a well-ordered society could exist so far away from the reassuring framework of the old institutions and so close to the "Savages." Dechêne strives to anchor the images of actual combatants emerging throughout the seventeenth century in the emerging social structure of the colony. As a counterpoint to these metropolitan aperçus, a different image comes into focus: a self-portrait, as it were, of a population desirous of building its colony in peace. Implicit if not subversive, this popular vision brings us full circle to the argument of the introduction.

The author then moves on to military affairs. The period ranging from the beginnings of the colony to the 1660s provides the subject matter of chapter 2. During this period, the French immigrants gained a growing, terrifying awareness of what war in the Americas would be like. They were from varying social backgrounds, but all harboured memories of the all-but-endemic conflict that had raged in the mother country. In North America, the scourge of war wore a different face. In the ensuing two decades, discussed in chapter 3, the colony's still-informal military organization was transformed, in the face of successive emergencies, into a more durable structure. The 1669 founding of the militia, placed for all intents and purposes under the discretionary power of the commandant, was followed by the arrival, in 1683, of naval troops from France, who would become the colonial regulars. The challenges of mobilizing for the (relatively fruitless) anti-Iroquois campaigns of the 1680s were an early sign that the minister's dream did not jibe with colonial realities. The hope that the colonists would spontaneously form militias in their own defence, on the Roman model, was an illusion. And so the regulars arrived on the scene. Their mission was to settle in the colony and serve as the foundation of a newly created military nobility in Canada, some of its members born there, many others adoptive residents. By the end of this period, the significant actors of the subsequent one were all present: the administration, contending with the circumstances but retaining a great deal of discretionary power; the "militarized" colonial elite (p. 79), and the people. The male colonists, divided into a majority of land clearers and a minority of *coureurs de bois*, were less willing than officer-nobles to take up arms unless faced with an unambiguous threat.

At first imminent, the threat receded over the ensuing years, which come in for more detailed treatment. Still invasive at the time of the Augsburg League (e.g., the Lachine massacre of 1689, the Phips expedition of 1690), the war was confined to frontier raids during the next conflict and, after 1713, became a matter of sporadic campaigns mounted to overcome Amerindian resistance deep in the hinterlands.[41] This sixty-year period (1687–1744) is examined from widely varying vantage points in chapters 4 to 7. Chapter 4 deals with the various types of operations, most notably the defensive manoeuvres of the late seventeenth century, some of them designed to fend off an invader who never materialized, and the major offensives, most of them targeted at the Amerindians and few of them effective. However, most of its length is devoted to the partisan warfare waged against the Anglo-American colonies prior to 1713. Arguing that such raids (*coups de main*) by small mobile units were not unknown in Europe, hence not an innovation in the eyes of French strategists, Dechêne situates them within the North American context where a partial fusion of military traditions took place. She stresses that while participation by the Amerindians was critical, few of the colonists possessed the necessary endurance to contribute much to these campaigns. Indeed, the majority of these small war parties were made up exclusively of Amerindians. Joint enterprises, in which the two groups worked together despite the vast differences between their military cultures, sometimes proved much deadlier, as witness the "total war" (p. 98) waged against Corlaer (Schenectady) in 1690.

The author's meticulous study of participation in these incursions culminates in an analysis of the "barbarity of the colonial conflicts" (p. 103). Here, we come close to the crux of Dechêne's argument. Giving careful scrutiny to the customs associated with scalping and the taking of prisoners, she identifies the categories of people involved in trade in these commodities and the circumstances under which it occurred. And then, the *cui bono*: Since the practice proved effective, authorities on both sides of the Atlantic were not much perturbed by the carnage wrought by intercolonial warfare. The colonists, she suggests empathically, had more doubts.

"Who Fought the Wars?" is Dechêne's straightforward title for chapter 5. She begins by stressing that the Amerindians – especially, for Canada, those who were known as *domiciliés* for having settled close to the French in the St Lawrence Valley – were "the principal military force of New France" during this period (p. 117). In this regard, she takes issue with the primary sources and, in their wake, the historians. The invaluable collaboration of these allies, whose military culture she briefly discusses, was subject to continual renegotiation. Combatants of French extraction were less effective, and of these – notwithstanding an enduring tendency on the part of historians to shroud the militiamen in myth – it was the colonial regulars who made the most substantial contribution.[42] The importance of the militia is further diminished by the presence of an elite composed of combatants from various strata of the population: volunteers, paid in cash or loot, who took part in parties or in the raids of Iberville and others. Last comes the militia, little used in the frontier incursions of the 1690s and 1710s. The authorities gradually – albeit more quickly than the historians, it seems – arrived at a more realistic assessment of these men's military potential. A few remarks in the official sources on the "flabbiness" (*mollesse*) of this group, purportedly once a paragon of bravery, would persist into the eighteenth century as the last trace of Versailles's hopes for this corps.

Henceforth, the militia's role was to keep the population in line. This observation prepares the groundwork for the ambitious chapter 6, whose main concern is local government in the colony, and here Dechêne grapples with a fundamental question about the nature of power in Canada. Taking distance from the standard generalizations about how French autocracy was either stripped to its essence, weakened, or achieved its full flowering in North America, she descries a historical process in which power in the colony became progressively militarized. There follows a fascinating comparative discussion in which she contrasts the case of the metropolis with that of the colony, where peculiar, war-driven conditions held sway; these, she argues, translated into significant deviations from the path taken by the mother country. In the colony, power was centralized around the royal commissaries – the governor and the intendant – at the expense of the courts, most of which were soon brought to heel: a governor with real power, thanks in part to a military nobility answerable, in the absence of venal offices, to him alone; an intendant resembling an army intendant more than a provincial one, as the classic historiography would have it, and forced to work with the governor to advance a common military agenda.[43]

Such was "military power" as seen from the top.[44] It was extended to encompass the people through the use of subalterns such as the intendant's subdelegates, who were very active in the towns, and through other intermediaries as well. The most important of these was the militia captain of the rural parishes. The rural militias were a far more important component of this society than the town militias. The author continues by analyzing the structure of these militias and of their officer corps, which became increasingly dominated by men from farming backgrounds as time went on. The militia captain's job was a hard one, particularly when the time came to assign the unpleasant work of road building (examined here in detail) and other hard labour to his fellow parishioners. The (largely intangible) emoluments associated with this position included a degree of local power. The upshot of this situation was that the peasants of Canada were a far weaker sector of society than their counterparts in France. The people's role in this rather authoritarian system of government and this infant society – one that apparently exuded hierarchy through its pores – was that of a foil, throwing the elite into relief.

Chapter 7 discusses another crucial aspect of how power was wielded in the colony: taxation, particularly in the form of compulsory labour and services. Once again, the approach is diachronic: the author probes how the system of personal service was initially implemented and how the attitudes of the men pressed into service changed over time. The first component studied is that of the military brigades created for the construction of the urban fortifications. Dechêne reviews the phases in the implementation (and ultimate abandonment) of this obligation and analyzes how the burden was shared between city and country dwellers. Her survey moves on to the billeting of soldiers, another burden unequally shouldered both within and between social groups. As an illustration of the tensions created by this forced cohabitation, the historian shows her sensitivity to social issues with a lively retelling of the legend of the "golden dog."[45] The chapter ends with an unusual and subversive question:

Wouldn't the colonial population have preferred to pay a head tax in order to be freed from all these other obligations? Her answer is qualified: While certain groups might have benefitted, the administrators never consulted them on the subject, seeing no advantage in such a course of action.

The last five chapters cover the final phase of the French regime in Canada (1744–60).[46] While in Europe the period consisted of seven years of peace sandwiched between two wars, the colony endured a single "long, hard war."[47] Much of the author's analysis here focuses on how generations of historians have dealt with the primary sources. In contrast to their Anglo-American counterparts, Canadian militiamen left very little in the way of a written reco;[48] as a result, the historiography has devoted too much scrutiny to the squabbles that took place within the general staff. Dechêne, suspicious of the defence of the Canadians proffered by Governor Vaudreuil, himself born in the colony, gives greater credence to the remarks of the French officers, albeit with caveats. The acerbic General Montcalm, that Turk's head of French-Canadian nationalist historiography, gains in stature from this rereading. Disappointed with the performance of the Canadian militiamen, he and his officers were ill-inclined to rethink the utility of irregular tactics, which had already proved their worth in Europe, and instead accused the officers of the colonial regulars of having trained them inadequately. After recapitulating the major engagements of this long final conflict, the author re-emphasizes the critical importance of the Indigenous allies, even while devoting much of her attention to the militia. A great many colonists did serve in these militias, at the remote outposts and elsewhere, and their absence from the colony weighed heavily upon it. Little by little, these difficulties wore down the people's patience.

Chapter 9 deals with an aspect previously given little study: the conditions under which the militiamen served – more specifically, the procedures by which they were recruited, trained, equipped, and commanded. Particular emphasis is placed on the near-absence of militia officers during the campaigns, at least prior to the war's final engagements, and the hardships of life in the camps. Chapter 10 homes in on the 1750s, the decade when the colony's very existence was in peril. In the rural parishes, families, and especially women, were coping with the men's increasingly frequent and prolonged absences; indeed, and as the author had previously documented in *Power and Subsistence*, a whole rural economy found itself disrupted as a result of labour shortages, poor harvests, and government requisitions. The chapter moves on to the military camps, where much has been made of alleged scuffles between French and Canadian soldiers.[49] Dechêne's close analysis of the documents leads her to regard the disputes as being more limited in scope, essentially pitting officers from different social backgrounds against one another. She draws an unflattering portrait of Vaudreuil, who has often been assumed to have had specific and valid reasons for accusing the French officers of mistreating the heroic Canadian militia, not to mention the Indigenous allies. A look at the militia's conditions of deployment shows this to be an untruth: the "Canadians" were, for the most part, commanded by colonial regular officers, nearly all of them born in the colony. Largely unaware of these internecine disputes and divided by a significant social gap from their officers and their champion Vaudreuil, the militiamen apparently got along fairly well with the French-born soldiers. Nor did the conflict between officers pit two monolithic "ethnic" blocs against each other. Ultimately, what the author evocatively discusses is the militiamen's experience of battle: exploratory journeys and patrols on the frontiers, the "workaday fear" (p. 271) of these poorly guided and trained men, which mounted as their participation in major engagements drew closer. In spite of it all, they would learn to "conduct themselves as soldiers" before the end came.[50] Evoking these scenes of carnage, Dechêne observes that the demographic history of the wars has largely ignored militia mortality, Indigenous mortality even more so. Back in the parishes, the men's families were perfectly capable of counting their dead and, in some cases, spending years awaiting the return of loved ones taken captive.

As to the final chapters, their intended organization is not entirely clear. Dechêne indicated toward the end of the writing process that they were in need of substantial restructuring, but ran out of time before this could be done. The notes she dictated on 28 June 2000 called for material to be moved around among chapters 11 and 12 and the conclusion, which thereby acquired the status of a thirteenth chapter. These changes were never made, yet even as it stands, chapter 11 is a long and cohesive account of the 1759–60 invasion of Canada. Chapter 12 is different in nature: it is part of a first draft written in the early 1990s, or even earlier, and then set aside, apparently never to be revised subsequently.[51] The historian had, moreover, incorporated one of its passages into the section of chapter 11 devoted to the spread of rumours during the invasion. The remainder contains a sequential analysis of certain phenomena of increasing interest to her at the end of her life: namely, identity, religion, and fear. These themes take us full circle to the preliminary discussion of popular subjectivity and the colonists' desire for peace, in chapter 1 and the introduction, giving the work a degree of symmetry.

Having led us, at the end of chapter 10, to the experience of war in the parishes, the author thus devotes the next chapter to the invasion. Avoiding the heavy emphasis placed on the Plains of Abraham in historical writing, Dechêne puts the focus on the misunderstood experience of the rural colonists.[52] The British invasion, as she depicts it, was at first met with overweening confidence on their part – for this attitude was not the sole preserve of the officers or the elite but shared by a large part of the population. Vaudreuil spearheaded the defence with ineptitude. The author's presentation of a series of topics – the lives of women, children, and old people in the woods; the scorched-earth strategy of a brutal invader; the militiamen's worry that they would not be granted the honours of war; the agonizing decision of whether to fight or desert – attests to her acute awareness of the suffering experienced by the Canadians, both those in arms and those who took refuge, during those terrible months. "Nothing is known about how this population survived the winter [of 1760]" (p. 298), she writes with some bitterness, setting the tone for a chapter packing a considerable emotional punch. The few pages describing resistance in the parishes no doubt make up only one portion of a section that would, according to the notes dictated in June 2000, have devoted more scrutiny to the period after September 1759. After that, the resistance became covert; the tension between these holdouts and those who abided by their oath of neutrality was clearly very strong. By May 1760, the British were the unchallenged masters of the colony: "Resistance was at an end now, for there was great fear, caused by the [British] victory: fear of the English, fear of the Indians, *panic* toward the end."[53]

Chapter 12 is essentially taken up with the following question: if most of the militiamen were not warlike by nature, why should they have agreed to fight? The search for an answer to this question eventually leads Dechêne to some striking conclusions. She begins by ruling out pecuniary gain as a likely motivator of participation in war. For most men, she reasons, the hope of sharing in the manna derived from war prizes, for example, was slim, and the actual distribution of these prizes, over time and among social classes, bears out this conclusion.[54] Intangible factors must therefore have played an important role. The remainder of the chapter goes on to address, from different angles, the interface between popular sentiment and the discourse of the powerful. In one of the book's most captivating passages, the author trains her disciplined imagination on the question of identity as construed by Canadians in this pre-national era. Weighing up what the accounts say and what a rigorous contextual analysis suggests they are knowingly omitting, she rejects the idea of a feeling of "Canadianness" that united colonial-born militiamen and officers (led, as we have said, by Vaudreuil). She likewise rejects the idea that any special antipathy toward the French officers might have had a demobilizing effect. In short, she doubts "the existence of a shared colonial identity transcending social divides and pitting the Canadians against the French" (p. 314). Patriotism certainly existed among the lower classes; it demanded no cognitive dissonance for them to feel both a Canadian identity and an allegiance to the king of France. On the whole, this patriotism must have favoured, not sapped, the mobilization.

Undoubtedly contributing to the same result was the encouragement of the clergy, for whom New France and its wars were blessed by God.[55] However, with the series of setbacks starting in 1758, the bishops' official message underwent a radical change: God had now forsaken the colonists and was punishing them for their many sins. Dechêne is careful not to invoke an instance of "treason of the clerics," for she is unable to rule out that the parish priests may have tried to soften the blow of the message. It remains that this dismaying announcement necessarily accentuated the people's fear of meeting the same fate, at the hands of the British *and* Indigenous enemy, that they had inflicted on their Anglo-American adversaries during sixty years of frontier war. This nagging fear of reprisals, she argues, was what led to the panicked stampede of the summer of 1760.

Louise Dechêne did not, in the end, write the conclusion to this book. It was completed by Sylvie Dépatie and Catherine Desbarats from three pages of notes written by the author around 1996, titled "General conclusion of the study," to which she added some verbal clarifications in June 2000. In this process, the identity question and the religious dimension – neglected components of the colony's identity – came in for some additional development. This portion of the book also serves as an opportunity for a last return to the historiography as

it bears on the notion of the collective memory. Dechêne felt it important to stress that the idea, dear to Quebec historiography, of a colonial
population that had turned hostile toward its ungrateful parent well
before the decisive battles came from a surprising source: the propaganda of the British invader![56] Then, in the aftermath of the French
regime, the painful collective memory of war had been obliterated by
a Church at pains to avoid "reopening the wound,"[57] and neither historians nor folklorists had revisited the matter since then. Central to
their vision of the past, and serving as the point of departure for this
study, was the image of a socially indistinguishable mass of Canadians
ever ready to fight for their Laurentian homeland.

3. THEMES AND AMBIVALENCE

In May 1760, the end was at hand. The last chapter of *People, State,
and War* ends with a distressing evocation of an exhausted people
wracked by the fear of their invaders. According to the bishop, and
perhaps his parish priests too, God had abandoned this people,
meting out a punishment commensurate with its sins. At first sight,
the notion of a colony abandoned to its fate in the final years of the
Seven Years' War, if not sooner, is rather reminiscent of the topos
(and pathos) of nationalist historiography. The difference is that in
the latter, as in the pro-British historiography, it was not God but
France that had left the colony in the lurch. This view of things has,
of course, been influenced in hindsight by the imminence of the colony's outright abandonment by France with the cession of 1763.
Also relevant was these historians' conviction that the colonial
population – sorely tried, no question, yet securely ensconced within
its Laurentian landscape – had for some time exhibited a dwindling
attachment to the mother country. On this view, it might be said that
the abandonment was mutual.[58]

Expressing her irritation at these historians' desire to hasten the
birth of the "Canadian nation," Dechêne underscores the strength
of the ties that bound the colonists to France and their king.[59] At
the same time, she takes note of their profound distress in the aftermath of the decisive battles, which was a reflection of their experience of wars recent and past. In this way, she does not so much
toss out the shopworn images of the Canadian and his distinctive,
war-hardened identity as allow them to dissolve into the complexity of colonial history.

Dechêne's method of reconstructing this complexity calls for a few remarks in closing. "Each war, in its fashion, is atrocious ... it was ever thus and still is today" (p. 103), she writes, expressing a little of the affliction she felt at the endless news coverage of the barbarity of her day, when the Rwandan and Yugoslav conflicts were raging.[60] Siding with war's victims and involuntary participants, whoever they may be – in the case at hand, primarily Canadians but also others, of European or Indigenous descent – Dechêne wrote a book that is both about war and against it; a book taking issue with a school of Canadian historiography that has tended to give short shrift to the horrors of the intercolonial conflicts; a book traversed by relentless moral doubts that are central to its intrigue.[61] For, in her way, she comes around to the position stated by the colonial Church hierarchy in its diatribes about how the colonists had been punished: not, of course, by a divine power angered at the people's blasphemy or lechery but by the invasion itself and all that surrounded it. The enemy, not God, was taking revenge for the havoc that the "French and Indians" had long been wreaking on the Anglo-American frontier. By the close of the turn-of-the-century wars, observes the author, the colonists were conscious of having had a close shave, but they also "evinc[ed] feelings of superiority and complacency, even contempt for the English colonists; most fatefully, they underestimated the hatred growing faster than fear, like a poisonous plant, under their own soldiers' boots" (p. 96). The store of hatred built up would be unleashed on Canada in 1759. Having lost their excessive confidence in British military incompetence, the Canadians feared, among other things, that it was their children's turn to be taken captive by the enemy and his Indigenous allies.

If any Canadians other than the elites had had the freedom of action of an archetypal character whose vanity makes him responsible for his own downfall, then the foretold punishment of the people's hubris might have given this drama the trappings of a Greek tragedy. This book can be read as a meticulous audit of sorts, whose purpose is to ascertain the extent to which the Canadians were responsible for their own fate. Dechêne precisely marks out the sphere of consent, and hence responsibility, with a finely calibrated analysis of the various categories of colonial combatants, the system of recruitment, and ultimately the whole military government, as well as by examining the colonists' attitudes toward war, the enemy, and the king. She comes to no final assessment but would presumably not have placed the full burden of collective responsibility on a population literally overtaken by events. This does not mean, however, that the people's malaise – transformed into terror as of August 1759 – was groundless. On the contrary, what followed would prove their fears to have been partly justified.[62]

One aspect of the colonial drama was the precarious situation of Canada, a sparsely populated settlement divided by an ocean from the metropolis. For the strategists (as for the colonists), this relative weakness dictated that warfare against the neighbouring colonies would have to take the form of lightning raids. Another of the colony's vulnerabilities is equally evident: namely, that its remoteness and relative underpopulation, but also its status *as* a colony, meant that metropolitan support was always conditional; a transaction like that of 1763 was always a possibility for Canada as it could never be for, say, Brittany. The fundamental asymmetry of colonial history is reproduced in this book, which works its way through the often unflattering metropolitan representations of the colonists, and the ways in which the Ancien Régime was denatured in its overseas incarnation, to arrive at a depiction of a colonial population evincing an apparently unshakeable loyalty to His Most Christian Majesty until the very end and even afterward. There is no necessary contradiction between these portrayals: just one more perspective on early Canadians doing their best to interpret the peculiar historical circumstances in which they found themselves.

Another vulnerability takes us from Greek tragedy to Kafka (one of whose protagonists has his sentence carved into his back): this population would experience, in most concrete fashion, the process whereby a discourse – or rather, an image, that of the generic colonist – takes on a life of its own. For might it not be said that the decision at the negotiating table in 1763 to cede Canada to the British flowed in part from the stereotype of the rebellious Canadian – a second-class citizen with vaguely criminal associations?[63] It may be that the invaders who streamed into the parishes also harboured a distorted image that was bound to make the punishment more brutal. Who were they expecting to encounter? Consider the remarks of a British observer writing in 1757 when the wind was just about to shift:

[The Canadians] are not only well trained and disciplined, but they are used to arms from their infancy among the Indians; and are reckoned equal, if not superior in that part of the world to veteran troops. These French are troops that fight without pay – maintain themselves in the woods without charges – march without baggage – and support themselves without stores, and magazines.[64]

It had been decades since the French authorities believed in this utopia of the peasant in arms raised Amerindian style, but it subsisted – with what consequences on the ground? – among the British officers (including Wolfe), who had their own gripes about their colonial troops.[65] Later, as we have seen, it would nestle down in the historiography for the long run.[66]

Then came the Conquest. The historian's insistence on the Canadians' loyalty in spite of everything attests to her rigorous imagination and affords a glimpse of her larger ambivalence about the prospects for the Ancien Régime. For the spirit of Tocqueville pervades this book: the old regime got older, or rather, more arbitrary, when it crossed the Atlantic. At first sight, the colonists' submission, inculcated by long, hard experience, perfectly corresponds to this view of the regime. Yet the historian offers a less mournful perspective on the long-term dynamic of the colonial government, evoking an elite that could have ultimately been less divided and less dependent on France, along with a people that could have embarked on the societal learning process leading to democracy under more favourable auspices. This projection is predicated on the comparable cases of other colonies: those of the English-speaking Americas and, rarely cited in the Canadian historiography, those of the French Caribbean.[67] The Conquest obviously turns these reflections into a counterfactual thought experiment, interrupting or at least delaying any such political maturation and causing the Canadians to miss the rendezvous of 1789. History had other plans for Canada; as Dechêne points out in her notes for the conclusion, it was to inherit "a tradition of obedience ... of which the British and the Catholic Church would take advantage."

In closing, one final ambiguity, emerging from the author's manifest antipathy to nationalist interpretation. Where did her attitude come from? It must have been due to a number of factors, including the deep ambivalence with which she lived her Quebec identity, no doubt making her particularly sensitive to how the people of an earlier era lived, or doubted, various identities ascribed to them. Inevitably, in a book that alternately rejects and adopts the metropolitan perspective, this ambivalence spills over onto France. The author critiques nationalist history for its tendency to ignore the relations of domination that existed within colonial society but were largely obscured by the elitist discourse of the sources and to project blame elsewhere – onto the conqueror and, especially, onto an ungrateful France. Melding empathy with sensibility to social concerns, Louise Dechêne undertakes to reconstruct the perspective of the dominated. Rejecting a historiography that takes the distinctive, warlike character of the colonists as an article of faith, she strives to restore to this colonial condition a portion of its dangers and ambiguities – and to restore to the people a voice. As she herself wrote, in the telegraphic style of her notes: "Direct testimony lacking; had to reconstruct the context."[68]

Thomas Wien
Professeur agrégé
Département d'histoire
Université de Montréal

Foreword to the English Edition

Thomas Wien

Reviewer Christopher Church writes that Peter Feldstein's recent translation has given Louise Dechêne's *Le Partage des subsistances* (1994) a chance to make a welcome "reappearance in the scholarly conversation."[1] Now, some dozen years after its posthumous publication in 2008, Feldstein and McGill-Queen's University Press offer the same opportunity to that book's sister volume, *Le Peuple, l'État et la guerre*.[2] As the original foreword shows, by the time of her death in 2000 Dechêne had nearly completed this much longer study. It, too, had been in the works since the mid-1970s.[3] Since appearing in print, *Le Peuple* has found a place in scholarly conversation in its turn. Following this discussion closely would make the second foreword even longer than the first and only try readers' patience further. In the following pages, I shall touch upon the book's initial reception, c. 2009 or 2010, and offer some impressions of what it might tell us, c. 2021, in the light both of recent historical work and of the *moment présent*. The exercise may provide some clues about how studies age – and how changing circumstances endow them with new meanings. After all, one never reads the same text twice.

Presenting *Le Peuple* to Anglophone readers shortly before its launch, Catherine Desbarats and Allan Greer pointed out that Dechêne was nothing if not determined to "rattle the larger-scale narratives that troubled her."[4] Rereading her book a dozen years on, and twenty after she put down her pen, only strengthens this impression.[5] While she of course took recent monographs into account, it was older work that provided her with her animus (merging the word's two meanings felicitously yields "motivating object of displeasure").[6] She was at odds with the long and contentious historiographical tradition extending back to Garneau and Parkman in the nineteenth century (if not to Charlevoix in the eighteenth) and forward at least as far as Guy Frégault and W.J. Eccles in the twentieth. At every turn, her arguments pointed to the received wisdom they sought to correct. She called into question (French) Canadian settlers' martial vocation – their "military ethos" (Eccles)[7] – and their cultural proximity to Indigenous allies, articles of faith for many of her predecessors; cast autonomous Indigenous combatants and not the militia or the troops in the role of the colony's principal military force; argued that historians had made too much of tensions between metropolitan French and Canadians and too little of conflict and solidarity along other, social lines; portrayed Canadian identity not as allegiance to a new American nation but, for the moment at least, as a transatlantic form of French subjecthood; saw the state as tightening its grip rather than letting colonial society escape into proto-national orbit; offered a contrast to the traditional, by turns romantic and instrumental, the-ends-justify-the-means view of warfare by empathizing with victims of all origins, including Anglo-American targets of "total war" (p. 103) *and* Indigenous allies doing the bulk of the fighting.

In several respects, then, the book occupied a narrative terrain all its own. Dechêne staked it out not just with evidence and argument but with a particular sensibility that seems even more evident now than at first reading: mistrust of rulers and their discourse; seeing French colonies as an (analytically) inseparable part of the transatlantic Ancien Régime; sensitivity to "[war's] tragedy rather than its glory."[8] Also striking is her sense of history's *direction*, her critique of the familiar teleologies that gave a centrifugal spin to colonial destiny (colonists were *fated* to escape from metropolitan control and indeed from much of their Frenchness, although opinions diverged as to the extent of Indigenous influence on the process). She invited her readers to imagine French settlers who had not been informed that they were recruits for a new nation and for a transformative experience on the banks of the St Lawrence. Arguably, it was her social historian's identification with *le peuple* (in the sense of "ordinary" colonists) that provided her with a vantage point from which to question such accepted inexorabilities.

Those who published an opinion in the wake of publication in the spring of 2008 tended to see the book as timely, if not overdue.[9] The 250th anniversary of the Seven Years' War, which seemed to drag on for at least seven years and dredged up much familiar material, may have made Dechêne's re-examination of colonial military history from a sociocultural perspective seem especially welcome.[10] More generally, the book's sweeping, provocative character struck early readers. Take this comment from the Canadian Historical Association, which bestowed on the work one of two distinctions it was to receive, an honourable mention for a prize then still commemorating Sir John A. Macdonald:

> *Le Peuple, l'État et la guerre* offers a reinterpretation of the history of New France by placing military conflict at the heart of the lives of the peoples and society of [Canada], as well as at the heart of state strategies, and by placing that society at the center of her description of fighting, the military and war ... Dechêne leaves few historiographical claims about New France unexamined in this magisterial reinterpretation of the French Regime in Canada.[11]

Alongside such praise, the reservations of two otherwise admiring commentators are particularly revealing; they, too, give a sense of the historiographical moment, c. 2010. Digressing from a survey of Native peoples' role in the Seven Years' War that relied heavily on *Le Peuple* for contextual information, ethnohistorian Denys Delâge argued that by 1759, the Canadians were well on their way to forming a nation; this they had achieved by striking root in the colony and, just as much, by frequenting Indigenous North Americans for generations. In his view, Dechêne's emphasis on colonists' essential Frenchness left them with "neither an identity, nor a country."[12]

In formulating his version of the Canadian-to-nation narrative, Delâge saw Dechêne's reading of colonial history as not traditional enough. Preoccupied by Indigenous peoples' place in history more generally, Allan Greer perceived it as *too* traditional: he cited *Le Peuple* as an example of recent work that treated First Nations "as an external factor in what remains basically a settler-national narrative." While acknowledging that "Natives were deeply and crucially involved" in the history of war in New France, Dechêne still "focuse[d] exclusively on the French."[13] From the perspective of an emerging history of *all* the region's peoples, her recognition of Indigenous combatants as the colony's "elite troops"[14] and as war victims no longer seemed remarkable. Rather, since colonists remained her true protagonists, it now appeared paradoxical: she appeared to place Native people both at the centre and at the edge of her story.

How has the historiography of the past decade digested this singular study? The book's paper trail – now increasingly an electronic one – of textual references and footnotes leaves the impression of a work that is widely cited but rarely explicitly challenged or endorsed, even by authors whose arguments bear directly on Dechêne's. Dialogue has in this sense been halting. Historians' uneven citation practices, sometimes inadvertent, sometimes not, make incorporation of new work into the shared narrative less than systematic at the best of times. Possibly silence signifies consent – and in *Le Peuple*'s case, what limited discussion may have been posthumous publication, or, for debates in English, the uncertain status of studies written in another language, often read but rarely engaged with (translations are important!). The scattered reception provides all the more reason to *create* a conversation of sorts by following some of the book's themes through the historical work of the past decade. Three seem the most resonant: violence, power, and colonial ways of being.

Violence, be it enacted, threatened or feared, was obviously a central preoccupation in this book on war. Characteristically, Dechêne gave the subject an Atlantic dimension. And, as a guiding principle, she refused to make a fundamental distinction between "North American barbarity" on the one hand and an enlightened European way of war on the other, encouraging her readers to see both as part of the "ordinary violence" of the day. Stressing transatlantic continuities, she viewed irregular warfare on two continents as variations on a common theme and pointed to a certain hybridity of strategy and tactics in the colonial marchlands even on the occasions when large numbers of regular soldiers from France joined the hostilities.[15] It followed that evolving "attitudes, or sensibilities ... among different social groups and across successive generations" regarding different forms of warfare were at least as interesting as the forms themselves (p. 103). Here, New France's offensive/defensive strategy of terrorizing British American frontier settlements, indispensable for authorities in Versailles and in Quebec but (she argued) troubling for many ordinary Canadians, preoccupied her most, the more so since it raised the issue of colonists' role in those raids.[16] The question of terror has since surfaced in studies of French administrators' and officers' writings during the Seven Years' War. Dechêne read skeptically Montcalm's and some of his French colleagues' expressions of dismay with Native allies' supposedly indiscriminate use of violence, bluntly concluding that "Indigenous-style warfare ... was condemned as a matter of humanitarian principle but encouraged for military reasons" (p. 268 and 515, n. 114).[17] Others have since seen these pronouncements as an expression of the officers' visceral fears of being associated with or even drawn into dishonourable ways of war.[18] This reading situates the rhetoricians in uniform even more clearly among the Europeans brought face to face, in Dechêne's ironic phrase (p. 10), with the "troubling fragility" of their civilization – or, in this case, with the anxiety underlying the European military enlightenment's notions of "civilized" warfare.[19] Recent examinations of the British invasion of the St Lawrence Valley, the subject of Dechêne's climactic chapter, raise similar issues. Here the irony of James Wolfe's punishing the "savagery" of Canadian irregular combatants by sacking the Quebec region and bombarding the town's refugee-filled outskirts is the centre of attention. Taking note of this violence against non-combatants and the high level of colonists' mobilization, at least two authors have situated the episode in a transatlantic genealogy of total war.[20] A third has viewed it as one of the manifestations of the brutality rippling out from British repression of the Jacobite rebellion in Scotland in the 1740s.[21] Since the desire to provoke Montcalm into joining battle helps to explain Wolfe's campaign of destruction, this gives sobering colonial relevance to Hervé Drévillon's caustic remark on "enlightened" European warfare in the eighteenth century: "the more civilians' lives were valued ... , the more profitable it became to threaten them."[22]

Particularly tangible in her rendering of the war's last phase, which depicts colonists in fear not just of redcoats and rangers but also of the Indigenous allies of both sides rumoured to have come together to support the British, a sense of vulnerability is at the heart of the colonial predicament for Dechêne. It underlies her central thesis, her characterization of settlers as anything but militaristic and, consequently, of their militia as being unable to defend the colony unaided.[23] She saw this vulnerability as the essential background to the exercise of power in the colony, our second theme: she concluded that "the need for order and safety impelled both city and country to cooperate with the military" (p. 192) and, one might add, with authorities in general. In a kind of tacit entente worked out over time, the population was brought to accept military service and other exactions in return for some form of protection from external foes. The situation enabled as much as it obliged successive colonial intendants and governors to construct, piece by ad-hoc piece, their arbitrary colonial "quasi-state."[24] At first glance, Dechêne's submissive colonists seem antithetical to the colourful, diversely privileged individuals whom recent work depicts as using their official functions in the colony or in Indigenous lands for personal gain, simultaneously flaunting and executing royal policy. Once portrayed as "rogues" symbolizing all that was ineffectual and corrupt in the French empire, they have since been persuasively described as linchpins of empires that, even more than monarchies at home, were defined by accommodation.[25] If empires are essentially "negotiated," as this line of argument runs, Dechêne's autonomous intendants and governors can take their place among the negotiators.[26] But she reminds us as well to take into account the geopolitical context weakening le peuple's bargaining position in the silent, eternal tug of war – negotiations of another sort – between rulers and ruled.

For Dechêne, colonists' assessment of their place in the world (our third theme) reflected their loyalty to a monarch who deigned to maintain troops in Canada. In this sense, the settlers' Frenchness was an epiphenomenon of their vulnerability. But in the end, Dechêne's saw settlers' attachment to France as a process bound up with colonization itself. Her observation on the colonial elite no doubt applied to much of the rest of the Creole population, if one removes the reference to "careers": "their attachment to the land where they had made their careers and raised their families did not vitiate [their] allegiance [to the king and to France]: on the contrary, it strengthened it" (p. 316). Much work since (and on other empires, before) has confirmed the tenacity of French and indeed other American Creoles' attachment to their respective metropoles and monarchs. But recent research on various French colonies also encourages us to read Dechêne's schema of mutually reinforcing allegiance to colony and metropole as an invitation to explore Frenchness's local content and, hence, its multiple forms.[27] In the case at hand, the eternal question of Indigenous influence on colonists has continued to attract scholars' attention, albeit increasingly in the context of reciprocal interaction. Concentrating on military matters, Dechêne carefully documented Canadian participation in joint expeditions with Indigenous combatants but did not see war as offering decisive opportunities for cultural contact to the ordinary settlers who

interested her. Seeking out precisely those contexts where such contact was likely to occur, research of the past quarter-century has projected a more mobile and finely grained image of cultural encounter,
within the colony proper and in the Indigenous interior of the continent. Zeroing in on specific forms of exchange, scholars have emphasized Indigenous influence not just on the usual suspects (*coureurs
de bois*) but also on less likely ones (Jesuits); they have brought to
the fore the Laurentian colony's Native inhabitants, be they domi-
cilié allies of the French or slaves who lived in close, often very close
(and in the latter case, involuntary) proximity to the colonists.[28]
Proximity, as Stephen Greenblatt reminds us, does not automatically
produce cultural mobility and indeed creates a dialectic of movement
and resistance.[29] But these studies are beginning to give us a sense
of the variety of cultural itineraries, whether under the umbrella of
Frenchness or more widely within the colonial contact zone.[30]

It is hoped that this brief exploration shows that for all its twenty
years, Louise Dechêne's book has not yet become what she dismissed as "literature," speaking of older studies that seemed to
have lost their relevance to ongoing discussions. Her proposition,
a "forward-looking" rather than a genealogical history, sought to
imagine a colonial horizon as yet uncluttered by the long nineteenth
century's preoccupations.[31] As such, it shares common ground with
that other critique of traditional history centred on Indigenous people and predicated on "denaturalizing" colonialism itself.[32] In either
language, the work's critique of classic historiography may save it
from classic status for some time yet.

Preface to the French Edition

Without question, it was the writing of this book that gave our mother, Louise Dechêne, the courage to face the final years of her life. Emphysema, a devastating disease, had confined her to the house. *People, State, and War under the French Regime in Canada* was the life preserver that made her days bearable. Even though it will soon be eight years since her death on 1 July 2000, we cherish the memory of our mother at work, forearms propped on her desk for easier breathing, surrounded by her notes, reference books, and the various sections of her manuscript, exulting over the progress made on it and describing the obstacles to its completion, such as elusive references still needing to be checked.

Since she was no longer mobile, it was at the same work table, amidst her papers, that she received the few relatives whom she still allowed into her space in spite of her illness. Her latest grandson was born just in time for them to get acquainted, but her last granddaughter, Sophie, arrived from Vietnam too late. Our mother would have loved to meet her.

This book was her last project, but our childhoods unfolded to the rhythms of her historical research. Louise Dechêne was a tireless researcher. After her day at the university, she would come home to her massive desk in the middle of the dining room and work on her doctoral dissertation, often with the children lending a hand. Geneviève and I organized the cards summarizing the notarized documents, while François drew maps. We had learned to play in silence so as not to disturb her concentration, and we all felt immensely proud when she earned her doctorate in Paris: It was the whole family's victory, under difficult circumstances.

Our mother was a remarkable and imposing woman, a feminist before the term became common. She raised three children by herself while carrying on a brilliant university career. In the 1960s, it was highly uncommon for a single woman of no means to pull up stakes and take all her children to Paris. She inculcated in us an ethic of impeccable work, an acute sense of responsibility, rigour, and constant striving to better oneself. Mediocrity and weakness were anathema to her, and living up to her expectations was not easy.

During her last hospital stay, when she knew death was near, she used what little energy she had left to instruct us on how to finish the manuscript. We had so many other things to tell her, but she chose how she wanted her life to end, just as she had always decided how to live it: not amid pity and tears but with us taking dictation while she, in a thin, barely audible voice, told us what would be needed to finish the work. In a real sense, this book was her last will and testament, and she made clear her commitment to having it published.

What we received from her, then, was a mission – but not one we could accomplish without help. To carry this book to completion took the assistance of a group of friends, colleagues, and former students. We must begin by paying special tribute to Hélène Paré, a great friend of our mother's, who took this long and difficult project in hand and never gave up hope. She was the chief organizer. Hélène worked in collaboration with Sylvie Dépatie, Catherine Desbarats, and Thomas Wien, professors in the history departments of the Université du Québec à Montréal, McGill University, and the Université de Montréal, respectively. We thank them with all our hearts.

Our sincere thanks go to everyone else who worked on this project as well: Christophe Horguelin, who worked with Hélène Paré to oversee the transcription of the manuscript; Isabelle Masingue, who helped to revise and proofread the text; Brigitte Caulier, Director of the Centre interuniversitaire d'études québécoises (CIEQ) at the Université Laval, who oversaw the cartography; and Philippe Desaulniers, a cartographer at the CIEQ, who produced the maps. We also wish to thank the Quebec Studies Program of McGill University, the institution where our mother spent the longest stretch of her career.

Finally, our warm thanks go to our aunts, Louise Dechêne's sisters Suzanne Saint-Jacques Mineau, who was highly committed to bringing this book to fruition, and Marie Saint-Jacques Clusy, who generously helped to fund the work.

We hope that the publication of this book, symbolizing persever-
ance in adversity, will serve as an example to our children, Camille,
Vincent, Jean-Marie, Laurent, and Sophie – that it will show them
the value of pursuing their ambitions as far as they can, just as their
grandmother did.

François, Geneviève, and Julie Miville-Dechêne

Compiling and Editing the Text

Hélène Paré

On the work table sits a blotter; arrayed around it, within arm's reach, are neat, moderately tall piles of documents and a few boxes of index cards, all relating to the last five chapters. Steps away from the table, near a door leading into the hallway, is a bench piled with file folders and several more shoeboxes of cards; under the bench, a box containing a transcription of the first seven chapters, in hard copy and on backup disk. In the corridor, a set of bookshelves filled with books and documents related to the ongoing project. Facing that, a door opening into another room with more piles of folders on a writing desk: old versions, handwritten text, and photocopies of the latter.

Louise Dechêne wrote by hand, then had several chapters transcribed at once. At the time of her death, the introduction and the first ten chapters had been transcribed. The eleventh was completed but not yet sent for transcription, since she felt it needed trimming. As to the twelfth, its component parts were in another folder along with reading notes and worksheets.

A quick glance at the folders was all it took to realize that some editing would be required and, more important, that we would have to take inventory of the documents relating to the book before anything was moved.

It was best to proceed as an archeologist would, so we drew a map of the work area and took initial inventory, assigning a number to each set of documents as a function of its geographical location. Once we were able to move the documents, we took a more in-depth inventory. This simple precaution was to spare us a great deal of effort when the time came to piece together certain sections and resolve various outstanding issues. We ensured that it would always be possible to retrace any given document to the precise folder and location it occupied in Louise Dechêne's work area, bearing in mind that the most important items were within arm's reach, on her work table or right nearby.

The next step was to combine all the transcribed chapters into a document that we called Text A. An examination of this text, the original manuscript, and the photocopies of the latter more or less pointed the way to completion of the work but also indicated the principles to be observed throughout the process.

These principles were simple: do our best to abide by Louise Dechêne's text and intentions, which could be discerned from her notes and from rearrangements of the text done at various times; resolve issues of chronology or unconfirmed fact; fill in a few gaps or supply indispensable additional information; and, finally, incorporate tables and maps in accordance with her intentions.

The method consisted in working out the final text of each chapter by comparing Text A with other versions of the same text: the original manuscript, its photocopy, and a copy of the transcription, these last two bearing the author's annotations. Our systematic reading of the original manuscript enabled us to restore some words and even a few passages that the transcriber had missed. This work was done by a team of two, one person reading the manuscript, the other checking the transcription. As to the photocopy of the original manuscript, the author had used it while the original was being transcribed, and she sometimes noted corrections and additions on this copy. Finally, when writing the last chapters, she occasionally returned to an early chapter to correct or modify it or to add or remove passages; she did this by writing on either a copy of the transcription or on the photocopy of the manuscript. Our methodical review of all these materials enabled us to determine with near certainty the final form she wished to give the text, at least as regards the introduction and chapters 1 to 11. It should be mentioned that chapter 11 was the only one of which she did not see the transcription, done in July 2000. All we know is that she would have liked to shorten it.

These verifications were augmented by others. We checked the accuracy of the citations and the bibliographic and archival references,[1] as well as that of the cross-references to other parts of the book or its appendices. We also referred to the sources and at times added a detail or two to dispel any possible confusion.

We also undertook to resolve various issues that the author had tentatively left hanging. These issues dealt with dates or specific terms and people's names but also brief passages in need of recasting, an idea wanting development, or a provisional conclusion. For example, on page 35 bis of the manuscript of chapter 1, Dechêne left a note in the margin of the last paragraph of the third section (74): "rewrite/look for other perspectives/counterweights." While dates and proper names are readily checked, it is a much more delicate matter to rewrite whole paragraphs or to fill sizeable gaps. We did not try to do this with the first eleven chapters, although we did at times include an editors' note indicating certain remarks left by the author. There were even cases in which we decided to bring to the reader's attention comments that Dechêne had deleted; some of these (e.g., ch. 3, note 126, and ch. 4, note 111) had even been inserted elsewhere and then deleted again. Finally, we reorganized the table of contents following her directions and assigned titles to the chapter headings and subheadings.

We kept a log of all this work, each of these interventions in Louise Dechêne's text, with the reasons for each edit. And this was how, little by little, a second version, Text B — that is, a more or less definitive version of the work — came into being.

THE FINAL CHAPTER AND THE CONCLUSION

Chapter 12 and the conclusion necessitated a different approach. For the first, the folder contained only segments of the chapter and a few notes; for the second, notes were all we had. Rather than leaving both chapter and conclusion unfinished, in the state in which we found them, we decided that it would be better to propose connections among the parts of chapter 12 and build a conclusion around the structure written or dictated by Dechêne – in short, to do a historian's job. See the editors' note at the beginning of chapter 12 and the text of the conclusion.

OTHER COMPONENTS

As a basis for her argumentation, Dechêne had compiled chronological tables of military movements from 1666 to 1760. A number of references to these tables, particularly in chapters 4 and 8, confirm that she planned to finish them and append them to the work.

The same rigour as for the rest of the text was applied to the transcription and editing of these appendices (A, B1, and B2) devoted to troop movements.

In addition to these chronological tables, the historian had sketched some maps, no doubt in order to better trace these movements, the recruitment of militiamen in the parishes of the colony and their comings and goings, as well as the notable events taking place simultaneously at great distances from one another. It seemed to us that these aids would be indispensable to readers as well. In conformity to the author's instructions, we settled on the content of five maps representing eastern North America and the St Lawrence Valley in the late seventeenth century and at the time of the Seven Years' War.

In chapter 1, Dechêne notes the similarities between two seventeenth-century engravings depicting combatants in Canada and the West Indies (19, 21). We chose to incorporate these two illustrations for visual clarification of the historian's point, which is that the well-known image of *Canadians Going to War on Snowshoes* bears not the slightest resemblance to the Canadian militiamen as they actually were.

The copious notes that we read through gave no indication of how the author wished the work to be titled. We needed a title that would serve as a good summation of her project and of the continuity among her different lines of research. Thomas Wien came up with this title during the writing of the foreword, and we agreed that the author would surely have approved.

Maps

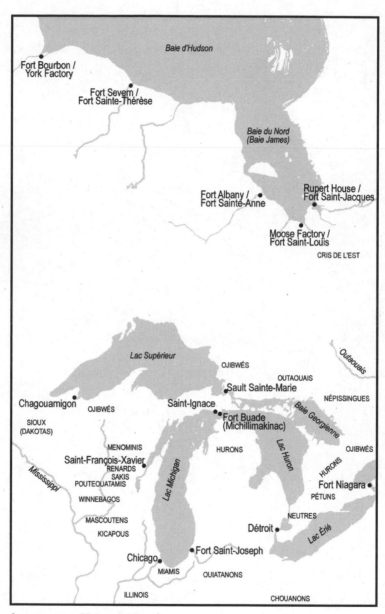

Source: CIEQ, Université Laval

Source: CIEQ, Université Laval

Map 1. Canada, Acadia, and Northern New England: 1660–1715. Based on:
R. Cole Harris and Geoffrey Matthews (eds), *Historical Atlas of Canada:*
Volume I: From the Beginning to 1800 (Toronto: University of Toronto Press,
1987), passim; Gilles Havard, *Empire et métissage: Indiens et français dans le*
Pays d'en Haut, 1660–1715 (Quebec: Septentrion, 2003), 438.

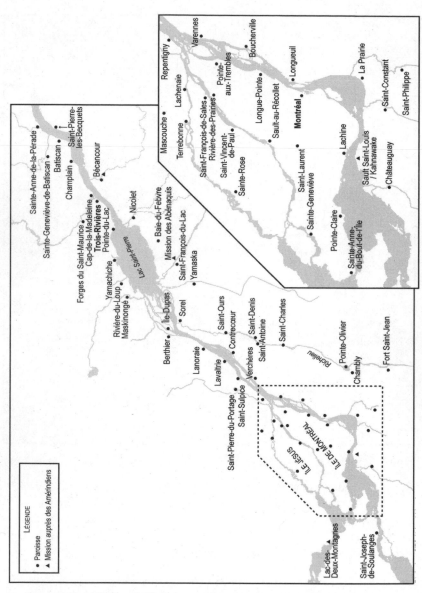

Source: CIEQ, Université Laval

Map 2. The parishes of the St Lawrence Valley around 1759
(southwest). Based on: R. Cole Harris and Geoffrey Matthews (eds),
Historical Atlas of Canada: Volume I: From the Beginning to 1800
(Toronto: University of Toronto Press, 1987), plate 46.

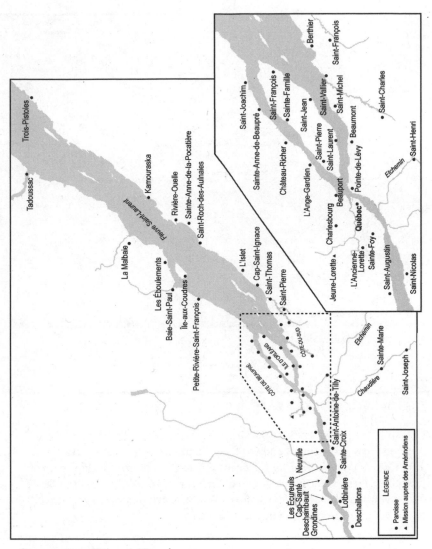

Source: CIEQ, Université Laval

Map 3. The parishes of the St Lawrence Valley around 1759 (northeast).
Based on: R. Cole Harris and Geoffrey Matthews (eds), *Historical Atlas
of Canada: Volume I: From the Beginning to 1800* (Toronto: University of
Toronto Press, 1987), plate 46.

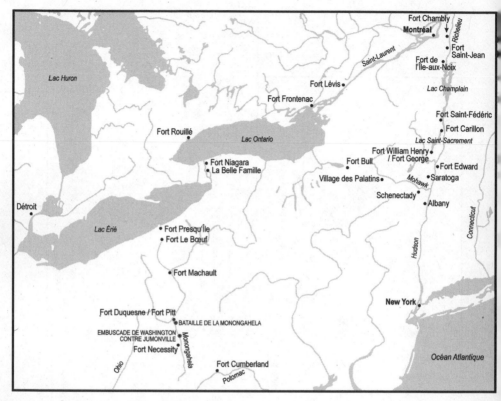

Source: CIEQ, Université Laval

Map 4. The region south of the Great Lakes during the Seven Years' War. Based on: R. Cole Harris and Geoffrey Matthews (eds), *Historical Atlas of Canada: Volume I: From the Beginning to 1800* (Toronto: University of Toronto Press, 1987), plate 42; Fred Anderson, *Crucible of War: The Seven Years' War and the Fate of Empire in British North America, 1754–1766* (New York: Alfred A. Knopf, 2000), map 4.

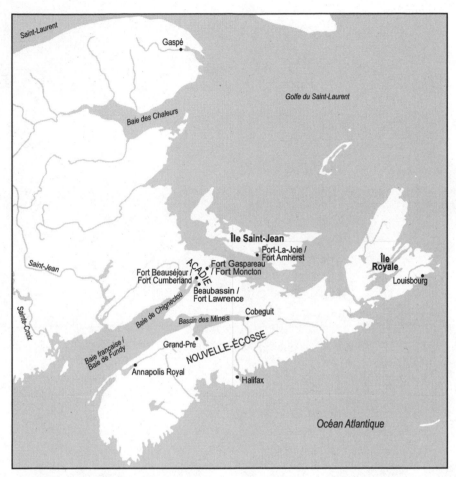

Source: CIEQ, Université Laval

Map 5. Acadia, Île Royale, and Nova Scotia during the Seven Years' War.
Based on: R. Cole Harris and Geoffrey Matthews (eds), *Historical Atlas of Canada: Volume I: From the Beginning to 1800* (Toronto: University of Toronto Press, 1987), plate 42.

PEOPLE, STATE,

AND WAR UNDER

THE FRENCH

REGIME

IN CANADA

Introduction

As winter approached in 1696, the governor of New France decided to assemble a large corps of soldiers, militiamen, and *domiciliés* (Christianized Indigenous people who had settled in the St Lawrence Valley in proximity to the French) for an attack on the Onondaguas in their territory south of Lake Ontario. Quebec and its region were to make a sizeable contribution of 400–500 men. An initial call for militiamen went out in January, but the expedition was then put off until the summer.[1]

On 13 June, the day the recruits were leaving their parishes, an extraordinary rumour spread through the city like fire through a haystack: An English fleet of at least forty ships and 10,000 men was about to invade the colony. Four enemy frigates had already sailed up the river to Tadoussac. The news was brought by a young stranger who had just set foot on land and was headed for the fortress, flanked by a curious crowd. His story went on: He had escaped, so he said, from the prisons of Boston, where he had witnessed the enemy readying for war; he had watched gunpowder being loaded onto a ship for four days straight. And if that was not bad enough, Pierre Le Moyne d'Iberville, then on a privateering expedition near Boston, had been captured by the English and burned alive on the town square; the prisoner had witnessed this, for he and others had been forced to participate in the execution. Iberville's second ship had sunk, and his brother, its captain, had gone down with it. As to the 300 Frenchmen who made up their party, they had gone over to the enemy; now, these men – "meaner than the English themselves," said the informant – were on their way with the British army to lay waste to the colony. From Boston, the prisoner had gone to Acadia, where there was more tragic news. Quebec privateer Joseph Guyon had died at the hands of the English, while his captain, Joseph Robinau de Villebon, had died of an illness. His lieutenant, Jean-Vincent Abbadie de Saint-Castin, had provided the messenger with a canoe and an Indian guide, which was how he had managed to reach Quebec. To those who asked how it was that he had been spotted arriving on the barque of a resident of Île d'Orléans named Dorval, the traveller explained that after making camp on the northern tip of the island, he had awoken to find his canoe stolen during the night. There had been no choice but to take leave of his guide and walk along the coast in search of a ferryman.[2]

More than these remarks, what seems to have aroused suspicion was the messenger's appearance. At the fortress, where the guards invited him to eat something before entering the governor's chambers, several observers had begun to have doubts. Suddenly, a man named Lacroix thrust an impudent hand down the boy's shirt and cried out, "It's a girl!" She – for a girl it was – pluckily objected. When "pressed to reveal herself" in the presence of Governor-General Louis de Buade, Comte de Frontenac, his secretary, and the town major, she burst into tears and admitted the deception – but not without attempting one more. She had not come from Boston, she claimed, but from Grande-Anse (Saint-Roch-des-Aulnaies) in the Côte-du-Sud (the string of settlements on the south shore of the St Lawrence downriver from Quebec). While crossing the river to Île d'Orléans, she had spied four frigates blocking the river, clearly English although flying white flags. It was no use: Her lies had been found out, and the militiamen's departure for Montreal and Iroquois territory proceeded as planned.

The intendant, who was to join them on this journey, confided the information to his subdelegate, who doubled as lieutenant of the provost court. A trial took place promptly the next morning and continued into the following day, with the assistance of three witnesses: a secretary to the governor who had witnessed the scene at the fortress, the accused's brother, and the credulous ferryman. Found guilty of cross-dressing for the purpose of "spreading impostures and falsehoods, thereby disturbing the peace and seeking to impede the advance of the king's armies in this land," sixteen-year-old Anne Edmond of the seigneurie of Argentay (on Île d'Orléans) was sentenced to being caned, bare-shouldered, by the public executioner on the accustomed corners and places of the city and then delivered to her parents, who were cautioned to do a better job of minding her. The sentence included a fine of 250 livres payable to the king, an enormous sum for these peasants, and the forfeiture of the brother's clothing (brown greatcoat, white shirt with lace cuffs, black hat, breeches, socks, and gloves) to the hospital poor. The mortifying sentence was executed two days later. Anne's brother and the three other youths implicated in the affair were to be tried on their return from the war, but no record of these later trials has survived.[3]

It was not the first time that rumours of invasion by sea had disturbed the tranquility of Quebec's residents, nor was it a novel idea to spread such rumours deliberately in an attempt to interrupt an expedition of the regional militia to the Great Lakes region (then known as the *pays d'en haut*). If the enemy was at the gates, why would the capital let its defenders leave? Thus, for example, in June 1673 someone attempted to interrupt Frontenac's journey to Fort Cataraqui (Fort Frontenac, at present-day Kingston, ON) with a large contingent of colonists, claiming that a Dutch fleet was advancing toward Quebec after having taken Boston.[4] And this corps was not even battle-bound: the men were on their way to build a fort, and there was little or no chance of a military clash. The truth is that the downriver residents of the colony were, for the most part, at little risk of an Iroquois incursion. They had no desire to court danger, not to mention the accidents and diseases that might befall them during movements of troops to remote and inaccessible places. Nevertheless, they had often been pressed into service far from home, and some of these campaigns remained fresh in memory, along with the casualties and unpleasant memories that had resulted.

The elder Edmond son, mobilized in January 1693 to march against the Senecas in the Lake Champlain region, thanked God for sparing his life during his detachment's dreadful retreat.[5] Three years later found him married, and it was his nineteen-year-old brother René's turn to be recruited along with Joseph Gaulin, a boy of twenty who had his eyes on Anne. The Edmond and Gaulin families had crossed the river from Château-Richer around 1666. They were among the pioneers of the Sainte-Famille and Saint-François parishes at the northeastern end of Île d'Orléans. The Edmonds were fairly representative of the average colonist, while the Gaulins, with several plots of land and numerous well-established relatives in the region, were a notch above them; they even had one son, Antoine, studying theology at the seminary in Quebec. Another, Robert, took over the family farm at Sainte-Famille, while Joseph, the youngest, lived on the land at Saint-François, of which he had received a share.[6]

One Sunday in May found these three boys – Joseph and Robert Gaulin and René Edmond, along with a fourth named Jean Laviolette, whose particulars are more obscure – plotting in the bushes behind the Saint-François church in the presence of Anne, "the girl who will keep us from going to war." The long interval following the initial call for militiamen, in January, had strengthened their resolve and given Joseph time to work out his plan. René didn't want anything bad to happen to his sister, but the objection was weak, for they were all persuaded that a "poor little girl" was not likely to be severely punished in the event that the ruse was discovered. Anne shared this illusion, arguing at trial that her sex and age shielded her from responsibility; "I was told to say ...," she kept repeating. Asked why she had followed this bad advice – did she not know that to disobey the commands of persons vested with the king's authority was one of the gravest crimes one could commit? – she responded that she could hardly have refused when the brothers Gaulin and the two others had drummed it into her "that she would never see them again, that they were being taken to the slaughter."[7]

Of the various unusual features of this story, the most notable is the surprising knowledge of current events on which these young peasants' fabulations were predicated. They had perhaps exaggerated the threat, laid on the reversals of fortune too thick, yet each episode in the saga was plausible on its own. Iberville's ships are known to have left France in the spring for the coasts of Acadia and Maine, so there was no reason that they could not have been attacked and defeated north of Boston.[8] Likewise, the chain of command on the Saint John River was very much as Anne described it, and since no one contradicted the news of Robinau de Villebon's death, it can be deduced that the government had had no recent news of Acadia and that the plotters had foreseen this. As for Joseph Guyon, his was a household name in a city with few privateers. Everyone knew that he was currently on a ship at the mouth of the gulf; he could have spotted the enemy ships, announced their arrival, but failed to intercept them. The idea of having him die in battle was both plausible and canny.[9] Nor was French desertion improbable: there had been much talk, three years earlier, of two turncoats who had attempted to assassinate Saint-Castin in Acadia on the orders of the governor of Boston.[10]

In short, cut from whole cloth as it was, the story remained believable enough to trouble the authorities – so much so, in fact, that they suspected Joseph Gaulin and his friends of doing the bidding of higher-calibre conspirators. "Who put you up to this?" asked the judge repeatedly. In the end, he had to accept that the conspiracy went no further than the story concocted by these young peasants, implicitly acknowledging that they were well-informed and capable of acting out of a desire for self-preservation.[11]

Claude-Charles Le Roy Bacqueville de la Potherie included this item in his *Histoire de l'Amérique septentrionale* but treated it as a romantic entertainment, a tale of a girl who cross-dressed and told tall tales to keep her lover by her side. Is this how the story was related to him, or did the author of a work devoted in large part to Canadian heroism and military feats leave out the boys' role as being extraneous to his narrative?[12] For that is the long and the short of this anecdote. What the trial reveals is an essentially trivial fact rarely discussed in the context of New France: that not every colonist went cheerfully off to war with a flower in his gun. There were men in the colony, as there are everywhere, who would do anything to escape being sent off to die in some remote, terrifying land. More surprising is their fear of the groups of volunteers – their own compatriots – who accompanied military officers such as Iberville.[13] What we glimpse here is a traditional, rather European vision of war in which the demarcation is not between "our" army and the enemy's but between peasants and bands of soldiers, regardless of origin.

This was assuredly not the attitude prevailing throughout the colony; still, it did exist at a certain time and place, and that is what matters. Without question, war occupied a predominant place in this society, and the purpose of this study is to mark out that place with reference to the diversity of circumstances, of social and individual situations, found in the colony. Stereotypes run roughshod over time and social divides; they ascribe behaviours, qualities, and failings to a whole population instead of noticing their uneven distribution among social groups and from one time period to another. And of all the stereotypes bound up with the history of New France, the most durable has been that of the Canadians as natural soldiers. These were fierce, formidable men, goes the legend, men inculcated in the art of war at an early age who learned how to live and fight as the Indigenous peoples did. Moreover, their mediocrity as farmers and labourers is said to have led them to prefer war to other occupations, and this allegedly explains their continual victories over British colonists too preoccupied with the success of their own enterprises to defend themselves. Social history has made strides, but these canards have not been debunked. Studies of the family, agriculture, commerce, and lifeways in early Canada pretend that war did not exist, while both military historians and the authors of grand syntheses continue to see the militiamen through the eyes of Charlevoix and the other observers of his day.[14]

1

Representations

In response to a long letter from French military engineer Sébastien Le Prestre de Vauban sketching out a plan for the military colonization of Canada, Jérome Phélypeaux de Pontchartrain wrote:

As to the castles and citadels which you propose to build in the cities as they become powerful, I do agree even now that they will usefully serve to defend us from the enemies; but, who will you assign to guard them, and how will you guarantee the loyalty of the men to whom you assign this task? For we must not regard the Canadians as we do here the Frenchmen; it is a wholly different mentality, with other customs, other sentiments, a love of liberty and independence, and an insurmountable fierceness, acquired through continual interaction with the Natives.[1]

This amicable exchange – between a young man about to replace his father as secretary of state for the navy and an old officer who had once mentored him in the art of building fortifications – occurred in January 1699. Pontchartrain had been associated with the work of the navy for four years; this correspondence, addressing various aspects of foreign trade and colonial affairs, shows that he was well acquainted with the work and attentive to any advice that might prove helpful. Vauban's proposal was clearly unhelpful, so he did not deign to rebut it point by point but instead laid the matter to rest by reaching for the first idea that came to mind. This representation of Canadians as barbarians and renegades must have been quite widespread at the turn of the century – but where did it come from?

For many years, the colonists had been saddled with an unfavourable image in Europe. The sense of wonder following the discovery of the Americas had barely worn off before the classic figure of the colonist began to coalesce out of a set of vexed, conflicting representations: He became the personification of the savage lurking within the civilized man. Christian Europe had a fatalistic conception of human nature. Freed of the traditional strictures that kept them honest, mere mortals would be unable to resist the temptations of evil. Their passions, their lust and greed, would inexorably lead them to cruelty. Over time, this initial belief was shored up by various scientific explanations. The Black Legend of Spanish atrocities in the Caribbean and on the continent did much to link barbarity with colonization in the European mind, but the association extended to other nations – England, France, Holland – regardless of their relations with the American Indigenous peoples. For what was at issue here was not the fate of the latter so much as the nature of civilization and its troubling fragility.

Why make such a detour before coming to the image of the Canadian soldier? Because his allegedly bellicose temperament is not an isolated trait whose validity can be measured by historians against a set of feats or defeats. It is part of a larger portrait of the French colonists in North America, dovetailing with other factors relating to their origins, their environment, and a collection of behaviours. It is necessary to revisit and re-evaluate the interlinkages among these various factors, along with the models on which these authors drew in constructing this portrait.

To this end, I have relied on a group of "literary" sources published in the era of New France, as well as another group circulating in manuscript form then but published later. Around this corpus, I have assembled other accounts that were not intended for public consumption, such as those found in official or private correspondence. It should be realized that none of these sources was hermetically sealed off from the others. Administrators, officers, priests, and merchants wishing to learn something of what awaited them across the Atlantic read travel diaries and other works about the colony before making the crossing. They also read them in Canada, where – *pace* certain historians – people did indeed have access to books.[2] Conversely, authors in New France often had access to official correspondence or to the manuscript memoirs of missionaries and merchants. Michèle Duchet's discussion of the spread of information during the mid-eighteenth century is at least partly relevant to the prior period as well.[3] At Quebec as at Versailles, colonial documents were fairly easy to obtain with the approval of the minister, the intendant, or a helpful clerk.[4] The image of the colonist is reflected from one account to another, as in a hall of mirrors, and its source is not always easy to trace.

The authors in question came from diverse walks of life. There were administrative and combat officers, churchmen, sailors, merchants who had lived in the colony briefly or their whole lives, and a few men of letters who had never been there. The seventeenth century is overwhelmingly dominated by the voices of clerics, while those of officers become more prominent subsequently. From source to source, the importance accorded to the population of French origin varies. Historical narratives always place this population at the centre of the action, while contemporary accounts, travel diaries, and other descriptive texts place the primary if not the sole focus on the Indigenous people. These emphases are worth noting, since the collection of brief, scattered references to the colonists' character that I present here might tempt readers to give them more importance than is warranted by the contexts in which they appear.

1. GENEALOGIES

Historians generally believe that the social origins and moral qualities of pioneers are important factors in the history of colonies, and genealogical explanations for the behaviours exhibited by early Canadians are common currency in the historiography. One of the most frequently heard theories explains the fabric of this colonial society as having been woven from threads traceable back to the poorest subjects of the realm; another highlights the military antecedents of these individuals.

a) Low-born progenitors

The first explanation finds its source in popular fears of forced embarkation, in endless schemes hatched with the goal of ridding France of its poor while populating the colonies at a single stroke. Perhaps this notion dates back to the spring of 1541 when locals at Saint-Malo witnessed the arrival of groups of chained prisoners bound for Canada, as per the commission given to Jean-François de

La Rocque de Roberval, "whom the King did send to that land ...
with great company of people of good spirit, both gentlemen and
others, and with them a large number of degraded criminals, to
inhabit the country."[5] Or perhaps its roots are to be found in Rouen
in May 1598, the day that its parliament published:

> an order, to the sound of fanfare, to assemble, from all corners
> of the city, each and every pauper, able-bodied beggar, whether
> man or woman, and to choose from among them up to two
> hundred men and fifty women to be sent to Canada, according
> to the king's wishes and intentions, and to this end handed over
> to the Marquis de La Roche, and, while awaiting the occasion
> of the said voyage, to be chained two by two and employed in
> public works and fed on bread and victuals, and enjoined, the
> said paupers, to obey and no longer roam or beg in the streets,
> on pain of the lash.[6]

More than 800 showed up, coming from the outskirts and the neighbouring towns and villages, and when the magistrate explained to
them that the strongest would be chosen for Canada, some said
they would rather go home, while others "were pleased to go on the
voyage" and would do "whatever they were asked, as long as they
were fed."[7] Over the following century, ships bound for the Caribbean, Guiana, or New France continued to arouse disturbances in
the cities of northwestern France, as at La Flèche in 1653 when riot-
ers objecting to the departure of three nuns for Canada, allegedly
against their will, had to be dispersed at swordpoint[8] or at Angers on
1 May 1662, when the news that men were being recruited for Plaisance (present-day Placentia, NL) touched off such a panic among
the indigent persons assembled for that purpose that more than
thirty people perished under the heels of the madding crowd.[9] The
resumption of more systematic deportations in the 1680s, and with
even greater vigour under the Régence, revived these old fears, particularly in the capital, further solidifying the association between
colonies, criminals, and forced embarkation in the public mind.[10]

As for enlightened opinion, if it wanted to conclude that all the
colonies had begun as places of exile for the undesirable elements of
the realm, it could look to treatises of political economy such as those
of La Popelinière (1582), Turquet de Mayerne (1611), Du Noyer
de Saint-Martin (1616), or Montchrestien (1615); the numerous

memoranda on file at the naval ministry (Secrétariat d'État de la Marine); or certain shipping company charters.[11] What did it matter that the government, despite all these enticements, had no genuine relegation policy until the eighteenth century, that many such plans came to nothing, or that the governor of Canada took the trouble, in 1658, of sending a pregnant girl back to La Rochelle "to restore the reputation of this colony, which is confounded with that of the Saint Christopher Islands"? By now the pall of disrepute hung over the colonists and could not be easily dispelled.[12]

Thus, even if Louis XIV's minister of finance Jean-Baptiste Colbert had not decided in 1669 to take girls out of the general hospital to hasten the peopling of Canada, Louis-Henri de Baugy would have expected to find "ladies of good humour" there as surely as snow and mosquitoes. Nor did he have any doubt as to the origins of Quebec's little merchant society: "They are all bankrupts or people who have had shady dealings ... in a word, scoundrels, almost to a man."[13] During the long crossing to Canada, which they reached in September 1682, Baugy and new intendant Jacques de Meulles were at leisure to reinforce each other's prejudices. Several times during his brief mandate, de Meulles sought to throw his own talents into relief by evoking the colonists' criminal past. "It is not so easy ... to govern these people," he wrote, "for they are made up of all sorts of characters, and vice obliged most of them to seek out this country as a refuge, a place to hide from their crimes."[14] Antoine-Denis Raudot made similar remarks in his *Relation par lettres*, written in the early eighteenth century.[15] Bertrand de Latour, who observed well-organized parishes and well-educated, upright, courteous Christians during his stay in Quebec (1729–31), was at pains to stress the contrast with the crowd of adventurers who had gone to Canada in the early days "to seek impunity ... legions of rebels, libertines, and nonbelievers: worse than Rome at the arrival of St. Peter."[16] This idea of a colonial birth defect of sorts also turns up in the writings of French officers who served in Canada during the Seven Years' War (1756–63).[17]

In the interim, literary parodies gave the conventional wisdom a second life and a kindlier spin − or, alternately, a more sexist one. Robert Challes, arriving after the Baron de Lahontan had brought marriages in Canada into fashion,[18] took advantage of a layover in Martinique in 1691 to melt at the sight of a certain Miss Fanchon and other women of the island: "Three fourths of these women still feel coursing through them the blood of Mother Eve, who brought them here by authority of justice, or brought their mothers here." Challes mentioned New France while stopping at the Cape Colony and commenting on the vagrants whom the States of Holland were planning to send there. "We could do the same: Paris alone could supply more than 50,000 scoundrels who do nothing but tempt the hangman. This vermin, living in the heart of the realm, would meet their punishment in necessary labour; their children would no longer be infected by their parents' crimes, and they would gradually be turned into honest men. This was seen at the founding of Rome and is still seen at Quebec, whose first inhabitants were nothing but a handful of bandits and whores."[19] *Les Avantures de Monsieur Robert Chevalier* (see p. 22), a biographical novel published in 1732 by French writer Alain-René Lesage, introduces social distinctions into this anonymous group of deportees. Lesage's characters – the Comte de Monneville and the wise Miss Du Clos in particular – are depicted as the scions of great families who have been unjustly punished by their cruel parents.[20]

b) Religious and military origins

A contrasting narrative tradition, dating back to the beginnings of the colony and developing in isolation from some of the malicious remarks cited above, credits the Canadians with exemplary origins. Finding expression in the first Jesuit *Relations*, the annals of the religious communities, and the annals of Montreal written by the Sulpician François Dollier de Casson, it construes emigration as a mark of divine election.[21] According to this tradition, those Frenchmen who left their homeland to go and assist the missionaries in creating Christian communities amid barbarity were people of great devotion, many descended from old lineages, deriving from them their noble hearts and manly courage. Even people of modest background arrived in a halo of virtue. Nearly a century later, an echo of these exalted images is found in *History and General Description of New France*, a work by the Jesuit Pierre-François-Xavier de Charlevoix. Charlevoix's description of the pilgrims to this new Jerusalem mixes evocations of ancient texts with polemical intent.

> All know how most colonies in America were formed; but we
> must do this justice to New France, that the origin of almost
> all the families still subsisting there is pure, and free from those

stains which opulence effaces with difficulty. Its first settlers were either mechanics, who were always engaged in useful labors, or persons of good family, who emigrated with the sole view of living there in greater quiet, and preserving more certainly their religion; a thing impossible then in many provinces of France, where the Huguenots were very powerful. I fear contradiction on this point less, as I lived with some of these first settlers, then almost centenarians, their children, and many of their grandchildren, all most worthy people, estimable for their probity, their candor, and the solid piety which they professed, as well as for their whitened locks and the remembrance of the services which they had rendered the colony.[22]

After Charlevoix, the religious dimension of emigration fell into oblivion. From the late seventeenth century onward, emphasis was placed on the colonists' military background. "I am not surprised, Madame, if the Canadians are so brave," wrote Bacqueville de La Potherie, "for most of them descend from officers, and from soldiers who emerged from one of the finest regiments of France."[23] The Sieur de Rémonville, a Nantes-based shipowner who had invested heavily in the Mississippi country before the time of Antoine Crozat (the first owner of French Louisiana), proposed a military settlement on the Canadian model: "Ten thousand of the finest men and brave as Caesar, which the Carignan regiment produced there, where there was nothing before the arrival of that regiment."[24] With time, the memory of the first generation of gentlemen faded, and subsequent authors tended to portray the nobility of New France as having descended in its entirety from the officers left behind by the Carignan-Salières regiment in 1688.[25]

c) Mere mortals

Between scoundrels and heroes, was there no room for the ordinary immigrant, the person who was neither angel nor beast? Pierre Boucher, a merchant and officer of the Compagnie des Cent-Associés (officially, the Compagnie de la Nouvelle-France) who grew up in Canada, thought so. The *Histoire véritable et naturelle ... de la Nouvelle France* that he published in Paris in 1664 sought to "undeceive" honest people of their poor opinion of Canada and, in particular, to reassure those who wondered whether the people going there were all rascals and girls of ill repute.[26] But his plea had little impact, no more than did that of the Récollet Chrestien Le Clercq, who was still arguing this point thirty years later. With the exception of a handful of gentlemen, wrote Le Clercq, "other heads of families who passed to Canada were in France good city bourgeois pretty well off or mechanics of different trades, farmers not very well off or soldiers, but all honest folk, having probity, uprightness, and religion, and, although reverse of fortune may have induced the emigration of a few, they were nevertheless men of honor in their state and condition."[27]

2. PORTRAITS OF MEN OF WAR

a) Early heroes

To those who criticized him for putting his life in danger, Raphaël-Lambert Closse, the town major of Montreal, responded: "Sirs, I came here only to die for God, by serving him in the profession of arms. If I did not believe I would die, I would leave this country to go and fight the Turk, and not be deprived of that glory."[28] His conduct, like that of Paul de Chomedey de Maisonneuve, Charles Huault de Montmagny, Claude de Brigeac, François Hertel, and other early Canadian officers was characterized by self-mastery and by the discipline, patience, care, and prudence they knew how to instill in their subordinates. When the time came for action, they were ready to sacrifice themselves. "Retreat and save your lives, while I bear the brunt of the fight, dying for you," said the captain of Tadoussac to his men.[29] Glory was not to be found in victory – a rarity in any case – so much as in the courage and serene acceptance of death that won respect even from enemies.[30] When twenty-six Montrealers survived being surrounded and fired on by 200 Iroquois while each of their own shots hit its mark, this was not set down to their marksmanship but to "the visible protection of the Mother of God."[31] To believe these accounts, these epic heroes faced enemies who could only win by outnumbering or tricking them. And if the same authors were at pains to praise the physical qualities of the Amerindian, to a man they condemned his style of warfare, marked, they said, by indiscipline, recklessness, a momentary flush of excitement, and cowardice. Their criticism and sarcasm was directed at not only the enemy Iroquois but also the Hurons and other French-allied Indigenous groups.[32] The man of war described in the pages of the missionaries and other annalists of early colonial days is an unambiguous figure, embodying valour in the full sense of the term, with all the moral and physical virtues combined in a single person.

b) The new warrior

In the last third of the seventeenth century, this figure underwent an abrupt metamorphosis. Subsequent representations are not uniform, but they do have two points in common: the primacy of physical attributes and the coalescence of a single colonial identity in which social differences are obscured.

Where the warrior of old had distinguished himself by his moral virtues, the new one owed his reputation to his physical attributes. The accounts are numerous, and unanimous: Canadians were robust, indefatigable, and the world's best shots. Antoine-Denis Raudot described the incredible difficulties of the military campaigns. Soldiers travelled on snowshoes or by canoe depending on the season, hunted their food, and carried their wounded with the enemy in hot pursuit.[33] The colony's inhabitants were inured to "forced marches through the woods for three or six months at a time, withstanding the rigours of the cold, living from the barrel of a gun," wrote the engineer Louis Franquet.[34] According to Charlevoix, "the most skillful Natives do not steer their canoes any better through the most dangerous rapids, nor do they shoot any straighter," and the idea that the Canadians outdid the Amerindians at paddling and portaging also appears in Pehr Kalm's journal.[35]

Such feats were the preserve of sons of the land. While a few French-born officers were able to withstand the rigours of the Canadian environment, the mass of immigrants were implicitly excluded, and it is hard to find a single positive reference to the colonial regulars who took part in even the most hazardous campaigns. Franquet, an officer of this corps, went as far as to assert that these soldiers had never been to war.[36] And to what should the Canadians' endurance and skill be ascribed? The answers are vague and unconvincing. There is talk of hunting being learned "in tenderest youth," of the "roving life" to which "they early became accustomed." Elsewhere, the colonists' physical attributes are presented as innate or as gifts acquired effortlessly, "insensibly," assimilated with their mother's milk or the air they breathed, to mention two recurring metaphors.[37]

Such explanations were bolstered by the climatic theory according to which physical strength and bellicose temperament are linked to cold weather.[38]

While the colony's first soldiers had always been clearly identified by status and condition – their chroniclers never confused the attributes of leaders with those of subordinates – the identity of these "new warriors" was nowhere near as specific. Indeed, it tended to be obscured by the use of the word "Canadians," which had become generalized by the end of the century. Observe, for a moment, the well-known engraving found in Bacqueville de La Potherie's *Histoire de l'Amérique septentrionale* (figure 1); titled *Canadians Going to War on Snowshoes*, it is intended as an illustration of Iberville's campaign to Newfoundland in 1696.[39] The figure is lightly dressed: a justaucorps cut above the knees, with tasseled sleeves and short tails, thin socks revealing the curve of the man's calves, boots, and snowshoes. Neck and nape are uncovered, and the hands are bare. Hostile nature is represented by snowy mountains in the background, the warrior's ferocity by the hatchet hanging from his sash. Who is this Canadian? The pipe, a popular habit, might suggest that it is a lower-ranking soldier, but the relative elegance of the attire contradicts this impression, implying instead one of the numerous officers or cadets who took part in the expedition. Now compare this portrait with that of Pierre Le Grand, the buccaneer of Saint-Domingue (figure 2), found in the French translation of Alexandre-Olivier Exquemelin's *Bucaniers of America* (published in 1686 and reprinted many times).[40] There is a family resemblance of sorts between these two fresh-faced, curly-haired figures with their long muskets and pipes, each of them uneasily situated in a different exotic decor. Reminiscent of medieval sculptures, they are expressionless, devoid of any character of their own; their identity is portrayed by symbolic objects. Yet the emblematic snowshoes refer to more than one social class: to both the independent fur trader (*voyageur, coureur de bois*) who defied authority and the militiaman marching docilely to war, or to both the commandant and the man who obeyed his orders.

The same can be said of most of the texts that deal with the character and behaviour of an idealized Canadian, abstracted from his time and place. "Who exactly are we talking about?" asks the perspicacious reader. Readers attentive to nuances of vocabulary and ideology get an occasional glimpse of the real person lying behind the generalization.

Figure 1. This engraving, titled *Canadians Going to War on Snowshoes*, is found in Claude-Charles Bacqueville de La Potherie, *Histoire de l'Amérique septentrionale* (1: 51). Reproduction: Library and Archives Canada, C001854.

c) Bacqueville's hero

Bacqueville de La Potherie's book does not pose such difficulties. He does, of course, claim to discuss all social groups involved in military efforts:

> I generally report all the feats of war ... I thought that if I had diminished this work, several officers of Canada would have had reason to reproach me, for having consigned them to oblivion. The war which we had with that terrible [Iroquois] nation is too cruel not to mention every last subaltern and habitant who took part in it. It is right to set down for posterity what each of them did and withstood for the glory of the King.[41]

But make no mistake: The "Canadian" glorified on each page, the one who "loves war more than any other thing," is an officer, a member of the colonial military nobility.[42] Combatants of modest origin, like the French-allied Amerindians, are barely present in the narrative, while the regulars, who did not know how to walk on snow, are disqualified outright. "One had to be a Canadian, or have a Canadian's heart, to see such an enterprise through," wrote the author about the Hudson Bay campaigns, putting these words in the mouth of the governor to give them more weight.[43]

Bacqueville was the son of a Guadeloupe planter, a scion of an old family of lawyers intermarried with the Phélypeaux family, some of whose members were high-ranking government officials under the Ancien Régime. Starting his career as a purser on board the *Pelican* during Iberville's 1697 campaign to Hudson Bay, he returned to Canada the following year as a naval comptroller and departed in 1701 to pursue a new career as a regimental officer in Guadeloupe, a job more to his liking.[44] The capture of Fort Nelson under extraordinarily harsh and hazardous circumstances was his baptism by fire; it serves as the point of departure for a thrilling narrative of all the other engagements, which make up the bulk of the work. The tone contrasts sharply with the dryness of earlier military accounts or with Lahontan's ironic precision. Apart from the chapters devoted exclusively to the Indigenous people, which are derived from the memoirs of the merchant Nicolas Perrot, *Histoire de l'Amérique septentrionale* is a celebration of the Creole officer, his endurance and bravery: a luminous, unsubtle portrait into which the author injects

Figure 2: This engraving of a "Bucanier of Saint-Domingue" is taken from Exquemelin, *Bucaniers of America*. Reproduction: Bibliothèque et Archives nationales du Québec.

a great deal of himself. For, as he constantly repeats, Bacqueville is an *Amérikain,* "a man of the New World." His marriage to the daughter of a captain in the Carignan regiment, which boasted 500 years of unshakeable nobility (as he pointed out), consummated the identification of a gentleman "born in the torrid regions" with one skilled at winter warfare.

This portrait is surely the one that best corresponds to the colonial elite's image of itself, as is corroborated by remarks recorded by the Swedish botanist Pehr Kalm during his 1749 stay in the colony. Kalm never had an opportunity to observe Canadians on manoeuvres, at war, or involved in military drills, and he had no preconceived notions. His travel diary contains careful observations of his hosts' and travelling companions' boasts about the extraordinary talents and endurance of the colony's intrepid inhabitants, their exemplary observance of their generals' orders, their ability to sing on an empty stomach and to smile at death. In a word, Canada was a budding Rome, the British colonists its Carthage. In Kalm's description of the latter as people softened by comfort, their officers drunkards and incompetents, his views on American degeneracy (with New France excepted) are mingled with the prejudices of his hosts.[45] The War of the Austrian Succession (1740–48) had just ended, yet despite adverse conditions, Canada had not suffered much. Abundant self-satisfaction wafted through the drawing rooms of the colony, and it was echoed by the distinguished visitor.

In the early eighteenth century, extraordinary adventures such as pirate stories enjoyed an unprecedented vogue. In 1732, Alain-René Lesage capitalized on this phenomenon with *Les Avantures de M. Robert Chevalier, dit de Beauchêne, capitaine de flibustiers dans la Nouvelle-France*, a biographical novel presented as the hero's posthumous memoirs. The novel is well enough documented to seem plausible to anyone unfamiliar with the nature of colonial society.[46] Beauchêne was a Canadian who returned to the colony after spending some of his childhood among the Iroquois. He went on to participate in a few military campaigns before joining some privateers he had met in Acadia and sailing the Caribbean with them. Lesage leaves him in the Gulf of Guinea and takes up the story of one Comte de Monneville, alias Monsieur Le Gendre, a man deported from his homeland only to be promoted to captain in the colonial army. In this compendium of clichés, three in particular stand out: the fierceness of the Canadian, the warrior society, and the subjugation of the Indigenous people or the subversion of power.

"I was," writes "Beauchêne," "a cruel, violent child who accepted no form of authority and drove my mild-mannered French parents to despair." An admirer of the Iroquois, he arranged to be adopted by them so that he could bear arms and join raids. After six years of this life, the vicissitudes of war drove him back to his birth family. "I long regarded myself as just another Iroquois. It took me several years, I will not say to vanquish, but only to mollify somewhat the ferocity which those men instilled in me." The battle and torture scenes with which the novel is peppered seem to imply that all Canadians went to the same school. When not at war, they were out hunting and bringing back furs, just as the Indigenous people did. If an account like this is to be believed, there was no commerce, no division of labour, no real social demarcation between soldier-colonists and the men chosen for their bravery to serve as their officers – as if this society of warriors functioned rather like the Brethren of the Coast on Tortuga.[47] Authority was negotiated, war was a lifestyle, and notions of duty and loyalty to the king went unmentioned. Finally, Beauchêne never went anywhere without "his Natives," who followed him blindly and would have defended him at the cost of their lives. Their willing participation in any given military campaign was predicated on their love for him, and their presence was enough to make anyone think twice before attempting to order the hero around.[48] In short, the Amerindians were in thrall to the adventurer, who decided their fates as he saw fit.

d) The rebel in fiction

When not forced to confront reality, the French imagination remained captivated by the figure of the rebel. Thus did Robert Challes fancifully portray the Acadians in his Mémoires, with the boundary between reality and fiction becoming indistinct. "It was essential that the governors sent to Acadia ... be gentle and well-loved men, so as to gradually win over these habitants, weaned as they were on the independence they acquired with the Natives among whom they were raised ... Quite the opposite was done. To Port-Royal [present-day Annapolis Royal, NS] they sent mimics of royalty, who all at once demanded blind obedience, who forbade the colonists from all commerce with the English, without bringing them what they needed." The result was that trade continued in secret. The authorities ordered a few colonists to be hanged, "outraging all the others, who did, in large part, take to the woods, enraged by the cruelty of their own nation. In concert with the Natives, they set upon any Frenchman from Europe ... who dared set foot in the forest, or wander away from the settlements."[49]

The theme of the fierce European finds its clearest expression in writers such as these, who were not bound by the conventions of military narrative. Unlike other authors who mentioned European atrocities in passing, matter-of-factly, as if par for the course in this setting, the novelists dwelled on them, likening them to acquired traits. There is, in this literature, a peculiar fascination with cannibalism, perceived not as an Indigenous ritual but a common habit, one that the colonists acquired during military campaigns when provisions ran low.[50] The reader will have recognized, in the writings of Challes and Lesage, the same disquieting figure of the rebel, the fierce soldier whom Pontchartrain had in mind when he took charge of the naval ministry. It is a caricature, of course, but one that is much closer to authoritative historical accounts than one might suppose, for scholarly observation and faithful narrative often evoke the same clichés, the same mythology.

e) Charlevoix's ambiguous hero

We now come to the figure of the man of war as he appears in Charlevoix's *History and General Description of New France*, published in its original French in 1744.[51] The figure is ambiguous, especially when compared with the preceding three stereotypes of the saint, the hero, and the rebel. Charlevoix built his portrait of the Creole, or rather the Creole officer – for that is whom the text is really about – in imitation of the bifurcated descriptions of Indigenous traits and customs to be found scattered throughout the accounts of missionaries and other observers: positive attributes on the one hand, shortcomings on the other, with the latter unequivocally outweighing the former.[52] This stereotyped officer has all the admirable physical qualities discussed so far and is sharp-witted and civilized besides, making him very agreeable in the commerce of life. He is brave, yet bravery is in him a sort of instinct, not a firmness of soul; he is said to be fickle and inconstant. Being impetuous, he is incapable of sustained, concerted action; being undisciplined, he generally knows neither how to obey nor how to command. Having compared Iberville to Caesar leading the Tenth Legion into a rout, the author then feels obliged to preserve the hero's reputation by specifying that "the late Monsieur d'Iberville ... had all the good qualities of his Nation and none of its faults."[53] Pessimistic about the future of the colony, Charlevoix remained optimistic as to the potential of these brave, adroit men, good Christians into the bargain, who could render great service to their sovereign abroad, for, curiously, their defects vanished when they left the colony.[54]

To grasp the meaning of these remarks, one must carefully peruse the first two volumes of the *History* and their repeated denunciations of the independent fur trade (*course des bois*), whose function in the narrative is that of a local curse, the source of all ills. The fur trade renegades had rendered the French contemptible in the eyes of the Indigenous peoples; the industry had contaminated the colony's youth and spoiled the character of its nobles. "They would be perfect men if, alongside their own virtues, they had retained those of their ancestors."[55] This is the theme of the book: a moral regression, a malady of the soul. In Charlevoix, this plague is alleged to have halted the progress of the Gospel among the heathen and hindered the settlement of the colony.[56]

Charlevoix did not dream up his Creoles' faults; his was no more than a compilation of scattered accounts found in previous works, the correspondence of the late seventeenth-century administrators in particular. What he did do was to give them a particular meaning by incorporating them into the weft of his narrative,[57] and this procedure is what we must analyze. Charlevoix's moral depiction may strike one as rather distant from the military sphere, yet that is what it circles back to, for the trope of degeneracy figuring so heavily in the writings of these authors assigned such men the warring life as their default condition.

3. VIRTUES AND SHORTCOMINGS OF THE CREOLE

The case file is voluminous but repetitive. The Creoles are blamed for three dominant faults – laziness, independence, and improvidence – and one great attribute, the love of war.

a) Laziness

Under the impetus of the Reformation, the modern era had rehabilitated work, stripping it of its medieval association with divine punishment and suffering. Work was now synonymous with virtue, discipline, and wealth. This idea, put forward by sixteenth-century economists Barthélémy de Laffemas and Antoine de Montchrestien among others, was reiterated and put into practice by Colbert.

"Abundance always proceeds from labour, and poverty from idleness," he wrote to the mayor and aldermen of Auxerre.[58] The weaknesses (or the nature) of the economy were not the cause but the consequence of unemployment and vagrancy. The people's natural idleness had to be counteracted; they had to be prodded into contributing to the enrichment of the country and the consolidation of the social order. In a well-ordered society, each individual does the work determined by his station: the ploughman in the field, the craftsman in his shop, the merchant on the roads and in the marketplaces, the officers in the higher spheres of justice and arms.

Colbert had internalized this idealized model by the time he took over the administration of New France. He deplored that the Compagnie des Indes Occidentales had given up its monopoly over fur trading in the interior, "for it is to be feared that fur trading will keep the inhabitants in a state of idleness for much of the year, whereas, if they were not at liberty to do so, they would be forced to apply themselves to the proper cultivation of their lands."[59] In the minister's eyes, the *engagés* (contract labourers) and soldiers had been sent to Canada to clear and work the land; this was in the natural order of things, and any occupation diverting them from these tasks was pure laziness. Subsequent alarmist reports from clergymen and administrators would help to spread the idea that the whole colonial population had turned its back on agriculture and headed off into the woods. Here is the genesis of the generalizations found in the official correspondence of the late seventeenth century, and later creeping into Charlevoix's writings, about the Canadians' taste for easy living and their aversion to hard work.[60] Although the existence of sedentary peasants in this colony was eventually acknowledged, the prejudice persisted: How hard-working could they be if they paid no taxes and sat idle during six-month winters?[61]

Others, like Raudot, ascribed the habitants' laziness to their origins. "The Canadian ... has great difficulty settling anywhere and resembles the Native in his love for independence and idleness ... but ... what else could be expected from people born of idle fathers and mothers? The soldiers populated this land with those girls who, having lived wayward lives in France, instilled in their children not love of labour but pridefulness and laziness."[62] In contrast to Lahontan and Challes, this intendant meant no irony, no more than did previous administrators who had ascribed the colony's disorder and poverty to women's laziness, from which all other vices were said to spring. In some accounts, these attacks were directed at female artisans; in others, they targeted the daughters of nobility. In 1710, Louise-Élisabeth de Joybert de Vaudreuil, the governor's wife, declared war on "idleness" in the countryside: men who refused to go anywhere on foot and had thus sacrificed their virility, women "who do nothing most of the time" and ought to be put to work making tow for the king's stores or some such task.[63] The question of women's work arises again in the journal of Pehr Kalm, who presents a considerable number of contradictory observations, his own and other people's, on the idleness and vanity of Quebec and Montreal women. This, it seems clear, must have been a topic of conversation in the drawing rooms of the colony.[64] Equally germane in this connection is the praise expressed in 1688 by the young bishop of Quebec, Jean-Baptiste de La Croix de Saint-Vallier, for Madame Denonville, the governor's wife, who spent her life visiting the sick and devoted any spare time to raising a family and working with her hands, "teaching even more by her example than by her words, to all who pay a visit, that a Christian woman of whatever rank must never remain idle; that the moment she finds herself doing nothing, she is well placed to do great evil."[65] There is, of course, nothing novel in such normative discourse; still, the negation of women's toil seems more insistent here than elsewhere.[66] In any case, these remarks, in combination with the criticisms directed at the men of the colony, reinforce the prevailing image of indolence.

b) Independence

In the writings of the period, the critique of laziness is often closely associated with a critique of willful independence. This argument gestures toward the submissiveness said to be shown, in a well-ordered society, by people of lower rank to their superiors. The Indigenous people were invoked as a bogy, as people to whom the principle of hierarchy was alien: "They are unchallenged lords of themselves and are beholden to no law, so the willful independence in which they live subjugates them to the most brutal passions ... From such independence, all manner of vices are born."[67] That the fur traders' insubordination should draw ire, or that Governor Philippe de Rigaud de Vaudreuil should excoriate "the spirit of mutiny and independence" that had taken up residence among country folk allegedly living too comfortable a life, should come as no surprise. Such accusations,

alongside inevitable references to the air and the natives, are typical
of those heard wherever masters and servants, lords and peasants,
governors and governed are found. What is striking is that these
accusations were also directed at the nobility.[68] Nobility and independence would seem to lie at opposite poles from one another.
In principle, commandments and punishments are needed for the
rabble, who cannot control their impulses, not for the upper classes,
who are supposed to have learned to govern themselves, to internal-
ize moral constraints, and to assimilate social constraints marked by
respect and submission where due, in increasingly dense networks
of interdependence.[69] Yet the nobles induced by the monarchy to
go to New France with the idea of somehow perfecting the organization of colonial society found themselves in difficult straits from
the moment of their arrival. Having no initial fortunes with which
to finance the development of their land while patiently waiting for
rents to rise, often lacking all but military skills, certain gentlemen –
demobilized and left to themselves under precarious circumstances
– began defaulting on their duty of exemplary dignity. Before the
resumption of war rechannelled their energies and revived their
career prospects, the colonial nobles and their delinquency took
up much space in the correspondence of the administrators, who
were distressed by these disorders, much as if their own families
were involved:

> I ordered the arrest of two sons of Sieur Damours, one of our
> councillors, who have concessions in Acadia. I locked them in a
> room with darkened windows, cut off from contact with their
> father and friends, for having ignored the warnings I instructed
> their father to convey to them, that if they continued to live in
> the woods in a disorderly state of savagery and drunkenness, I
> would punish them ... I only let them out after the whole family
> gave public assurances that they would change.[70]

Such waywardness was ascribed to lapses of parental authority.
Children did not go to school and were not disciplined at home.
As they grew up, they were said to take on "a hard, fierce character reflecting – indeed often – on their fathers and mothers, to
whom they show as much disrespect as to their superiors and priests,
thus also rendering them incapable of any honesty in their dealings
with one another."[71] Charlevoix took up the same theme of the

"wrong-headed gentleness" displayed by parents toward their children and the latter's "surliness" toward their parents. "The Natives are prey to the same failing," he intoned, ignoring all the paeans to the filial piety of the Indigenous people, as if their supposed vices were expected to stand surety for the credibility of similar accusations against the colonists.[72]

c) Improvidence

What patterns of thought underlie the repeated complaints of Canadians' improvidence, greed, and propensity to squander all they had earned on frivolities, with nary a thought to tomorrow or their children's welfare? One should not be too hasty in positing that these critics partook of an emerging bourgeois ethic of moderation and rational accumulation. To take one illustration, the banter that Kalm heard at the governor's table on the subject of Quebec merchants' sumptuous tables, their wives' expensive taste in clothing, flowed naturally from a traditional conception of the sumptuary order in which each person should dress and eat as befits his station.[73] In the mid-eighteenth century, these customs were undergoing profound transformations in both France and Canada, yet such transgressions still offended the sensibilities of observers on both sides of the Atlantic – perhaps especially in the colony, where the privileged were more vulnerable and hence more sensitive.[74]

However, most of the accusations of improvidence leveled at the Canadians went deeper, revealing a profound contempt for the fur trade that formed the basis of the colony's development. To Lahontan, the fur trade was epitomized by the debauchery of the *coureurs de bois* when they returned to Montreal after a long sojourn in the Great Lakes region: "they Lavish, Eat, Drink, and Play all away as long as the Goods hold out; and when these are gone, they e'en sell their Embroidery, their Lace, and their Cloaths. This done, they are forc'd to go upon a new Voyage for Subsistence."[75] Lahontan disliked merchants but was well aware of their role as managers of trade, so he treated the carefree behaviour of the voyageurs as nothing more than a picturesque detail.[76] For Charlevoix, in contrast, it was the main "reason for the decline of trade in Canada." Grasping for easy money, the "Canadians" – here a synecdoche for the *coureurs de bois* – had failed to foresee that by bleeding the Indigenous people dry, they would destroy the trade. What was bound to happen, happened, and "the fur trade [was] now almost exclusively in the hands of the English."[77] The profits had evaporated, yet Canadians still took to the woods – for the sole pleasure of the wandering life and the glory they acquired by overcoming the attendant perils.[78]

d) "The youth ... detest peace"

Yet, for the Jesuit historian, the vanity and frivolity that prevented the Canadians from building anything durable were not without their good side, for as deplorable as these vices were from other points of view, they conduced to the military vocation in Canada. In a passage titled "Difference between the English and French Colonies," Charlevoix contrasts the rusticity of the English, which kept them from profiting from their opulence, with the civilized manners of the French nation and its prodigal spending. The English fortified themselves through trade and agriculture, building up assets with which to settle their heirs, while the French left theirs penniless. It followed that

> The North American English seek to avoid war, for they have much to lose; they are hard on the Natives, thinking they have no need of them. For contrary reasons, the French youth detest peace and want to live with the Natives, whose esteem they readily garner during wartime, and whose friendship they ever enjoy.[79]

For readers of today, as for people of the Enlightenment who prized order and peace, the pursuit of happiness, and bourgeois enterprise, this judgment was damning for Canada. But Charlevoix saw things differently. First, he disliked the English as much as the merchants. "They were almost always men of fortune," he wrote in regard to the English governors, "ignorant of war, never even in service, whose sole merit was their accumulation of wealth by means that did not presuppose qualities necessary to uphold the rank to which they were raised, qualities which such men never acquire."[80] In these lines, as in the rest of the book for that matter (but not always as clearly), the author's fundamental perspective is readily recognizable. The ideal society is the one with a military and aristocratic hierarchy.[81] New France, thinks Charlevoix, had come near to adopting such a structure, and thus he remains attached to the French Canadians – indulgent of their lapses, aware of how far they had fallen from their original state of grace. The important thing was that they feared God and were good at fighting wars; that they had failed to grow wealthy was only a venial sin in his eyes.[82]

But for his many readers, this observation was important indeed. In the decade following the publication of the *History*, Charlevoix's consecration as the great, if not the only, specialist on New France became a fait accompli.[83] A veritable *vade mecum* for the officers of the eight battalions that went to Canada between 1755 and 1757, the book was often the source of their "observations" on the state of the colony and the customs of its inhabitants. Sub-lieutenant Louis-Guillaume de Parscau Du Plessis noted in his journal, after a two-week stay in Quebec in 1756, that the Canadians raise their children "like the Natives," without any discipline, and added other clichés of the sort. Did he get this information directly from reading Charlevoix? From a conversation with another officer who had read him?[84] For unlike the other authors discussed in this chapter, who were all conversant with the documentary sources touching on Canada, the French witnesses to the Seven Years' War knew next to nothing about the colony. All they had were a few received ideas, plus whatever they had just finished reading in one or two selected books: perhaps Lahontan, more often Charlevoix, or sometimes Abbé Prévost's *Histoire générale des voyages*, which derives its information on Saint-Domingue and Canada from Charlevoix. "A most truthful man," wrote Voltaire about the man who had been his prefect of studies, and this opinion was shared by Mirabeau, Raynal, and Diderot.[85] New France took up little space in their writings on trade and on the colonies in general; a well-documented, limpidly organized work like the *History* offered these busy, prolific authors just about everything they needed. One day someone ought to broaden the analysis of Charlevoix's oeuvre, situating his historical works on Saint-Domingue, Japan, New France, and Paraguay within the intellectual landscape of the eighteenth century and focusing on their conception and reception in that context.[86] For the time being, it must suffice to note the popular success of the *History* even as we wonder whether this success might have done Canada a disservice. Since the French no longer had any trade there and had become "the *coureurs* of North America," in Mirabeau's phrase, what was the real value of this colony?[87] The Canadians' sole asset – their talent for warfare – offered little of interest to the Encyclopédistes.

For French military men, however, the portrait of a population that loved nothing so much as war, and was so good at it, must inevitably have aroused inflated expectations and ultimately disappointment.

> If the Canadians had only been farmers and manufacturers, they would yet subsist ... But, ruined by the mother country, having almost no notion of property, finding that their only aptitude was for war, they sought to destroy the English by way of the Natives and the Natives by way of the English, and fate had it that they were themselves destroyed, if only to make them right once.[88]

These remarks by Michel-René Hilliard d'Auberteuil of Saint-Domingue clearly evoke the warlike image of the Canadians that would linger in the public mind, becoming solidly entrenched over a hundred years of literature devoted to the heroism of missionaries and soldiers. Like the discourse on the Indigenous people, the discourse on the Creole tells us more about its authors' concerns. This leads me, in concluding this chapter, to a discussion of the concerns of those who left neither journals nor memoirs.[89]

4. A DIFFERENT VIEW

Readers who delve into the literary sources of British colonial history are inevitably struck by the abundance, and especially the diversity, of authors and opinions. There too they find generalizations about the colonists' criminal background, clichés about the influence of Indigenous culture, considerations about moral degeneracy and the advance of indolence, extravagance, and corruption. At the other extreme, they find writings by proponents of settlement: praise heaped upon generous nature, celebrations of material success and social mobility, exhortations from those who dreamed of building the city of God, lamentations about cultural impoverishment or the deleterious effects of the environment. American and European voices mingle in this discordant choir, and the dividing line between favourable and unfavourable judgments is not necessarily congruent with the one separating colonists from Englishmen. Colonial writers, aware of America's poor reputation in England, are at pains to improve it, yet they are frequently also the harshest critics of their own society. Diversity of status, profession, intellectual background, and purpose contribute to the diversity of the discourse found in these works.[90]

Although relatively numerous and extremely valuable in ethnographic terms, the literary sources on the history of New France do not offer the same diversity. These authors are almost exclusively priests and officers, and this overrepresentation of church and nobility is just as important as their belonging to the metropole, if not even more so. The Canadians discussed in these texts are Others in two ways: bound by their fate to that of the colony and – regardless of their status as peasants, artisans, or merchants – dependent on the continual improvement of trade networks and on peace with their neighbours for their success and the security of their families. They know this, and presumably repeat it often, but rarely write about it.

The only two extant works advertising New France, published a few years apart in the third quarter of the seventeenth century, have several points in common: aversion to war; sensitivity to the beauty and bounty of the land and its promise for the future; faith in the harmonious association of trade and agriculture; finally, no attempt to take distance from the colonists by discoursing on their character or the influence of the environment.[91] Pierre Boucher and Nicolas Denys were merchants who wrote of the colonies in terms of investment and profit, "the primary motive of men of all stations."[92] Boucher began as a clerk and interpreter for the community of habitants of Trois-Rivières before being appointed governor of the same post. Denys represented the Compagnie des Cent-Associés in Acadia for a time, dedicating most of his life to the establishment of sedentary fishing posts in that colony.[93] Boucher played an active role in the defence of French settlements during the French and Iroquois Wars but derived no glory from it, and where he briefly mentions these hardships, it is only to stress that they are now in the past.[94] On the savoir-faire of the Iroquois warrior he is laudatory, but he has nothing to say about the military experience acquired by the French or even his own. The king had promised to send an army to destroy the enemy, and now the colonists were free to go about their business, having been delivered from the danger and their military responsibilities. That is the essence of his message.[95]

At the moment when these books went to press, the development of New France, long stalled by war, was on the point of taking off. Two or three generations later found the colony having made genuine progress, albeit not as spectacular as in the neighbouring colonies. Said an old man in 1749, "Where there are now houses and splendid farms, where the fields stretch out to the horizon, there was [in my childhood] nearly nothing but forest" and hardly any habitants outside the cities.[96] He would surely have been amazed to learn that a scholarly Jesuit had called the country he had built a failure. The habitants had conquered the forest, attained food self-sufficiency, and made improvements in construction, heating, transportation, parish planning, and community life. The man spoke of these things proudly, as evidence of success, and yet no other words of his were ever copied down. The fur traders, too, had good reasons to congratulate themselves. Trade had been restructured and consolidated after the turbulence at the turn of the century; the volume of fur exports from New France now stood at thrice what came from the Hudson Bay posts and all the British colonies combined, and this despite the hindrances put in their way by the government.[97] Voyageurs and purveyors in pursuit of profit had created, consolidated, and extended their network of alliances with the Indigenous nations. As Bruce Trigger reminds us, the trading companies and their clerks were the initial architects of goodwill, the true "founders of New France," but since they did not leave accounts of their activities, history has retained only their adversaries' published accusations against them.[98] So too has the voice of subsequent generations of fur traders largely been erased. One of them, Nicolas Perrot, wrote a history of these nations based on their oral tradition and his own experience of thirty years of travel in the Great Lakes region, working both for himself and as a government agent and interpreter. These unpublished memoirs were extensively relied on for their documentary content by Bacqueville de La Potherie, Michel Bégon de la Picardière, and Charlevoix, but the author's name was not revealed until their publication in the nineteenth century.[99] Modest, brusque, lacking deference to his compatriots and the Indigenous peoples, Perrot believed that the French wars against them, and in particular the Foxes, could and should have been avoided.

Might the desire for peace so clearly stated in Boucher, Denys, and Perrot in fact have been a constant across certain strata of society? Research in the archives would have to continue in an effort to find texts written by merchants and others who did not have military or religious careers.[100]

Beginnings of the Colonial Military, 1608–69

By 1665, the year the king sent a regiment to subdue the Iroquois, Canada's generally hostile relations with the Indigenous peoples dated back almost half a century, from distrust and isolated attacks in the early days to outright war in the early 1640s. Thanks to the work of anthropologists and a few historians, the complex nature of the relations between the Five Nations and the peoples to their north, in which conflicts the French had been inextricably involved since their arrival, is starting to be understood. In a war that gradually became theirs, the colonists never had the upper hand; given their numerical and military weakness, they could easily have been expelled or exterminated if their enemies had so desired.[1] But they did not, for that sort of determination was quite foreign to the Indigenous cultures of North America. Military action against the French took the same form as ordinary intertribal warfare: prolonged conflict punctuated by battles with intervening lulls. Extending over about twenty-five years, this conflict compromised the settlement of the colony, delayed the development of agriculture, and often interrupted the fur trade, the only source of financing for the French enterprise. In 1665, Canada's population stood at a mere 3,500 people dispersed among three fortified towns and several rural settlements.

I. THE IROQUOIS WARS

a) A special period

According to one widely espoused interpretation, the Canadians' aptitude for low-intensity warfare dated back to this initial period. In the course of these terrible clashes with the Iroquois, they had adopted their enemies' tactics; they had learned to fight fiercely, with the energy of despair, preferring to die with weapon in hand than to suffer the thousand tortures reserved for captives.[2] Long after these events, this notion remained current in the writings of the memorialists of the French regime.[3] An "obsession with origins"[4] – a tendency to look for explanations of present behaviour in the distant past – appears to have been operating, for cursory examination shows that the early seventeenth-century military experience had little in common with the military practices of subsequent years. Two sets of factors distinguish this period from later colonial military history. The first relates to the circumstances of the colony, the fact that the colonial forces were outmatched, the French positions extremely vulnerable and continually on the defensive. The second relates to the circumstances of the metropole: the profound changes taking place in the structure of the army, and the changes in the relationships among state, war, and society, from the France of Henry IV to that of Louis XIV.

"Our familiar distinction between soldiers and civilians did not have the same meaning in the first half of the seventeenth century,"[5] writes André Corvisier, and his remark is especially applicable to this colony. The first Europeans to endure the winter were sailors, farmers, and merchants with their clerks and valets. Most of them knew how to wield a sword and an arquebus, and in this sense one could say that they all doubled as soldiers. This is the proper interpretation of the surrender of Quebec in 1629, when the few Frenchmen to be repatriated were divided into two groups: people of quality, who were authorized to keep their weapons and personal effects, and "soldiers" – everyone else – who were disarmed.[6] Three years later, Samuel de Champlain, who arrived to officially retake possession of New France in the name of the Compagnie des Cent-Associés, marched to the fort accompanied by the beat of a drum at the head of a squadron of pikemen and musketeers.[7] From then on, soldiers formed a separate category, at least in the company's accounts. There cannot have been many of them – at most a few dozen between 1633 and 1643 – since the company of sixty soldiers that arrived in 1644 was greeted as a powerful reinforcement.[8] According to Marcel Trudel, if those recruited by the Société Notre-Dame de Montréal are added, the total then becomes 100 men divided among Quebec, Trois-Rivières, and Montreal, plus Huronia and Fort Richelieu on a temporary basis, all of them for the express purpose of defending the colony. In 1648, the Communauté des Habitants, a subcontractor to the Cent-Associés, produced a lower figure of twenty-four garrisoned soldiers distributed among the three towns, plus forty more gathered into a flying column whose job was to secure navigation on the St Lawrence and to protect the settlements dispersed throughout the côtes (rural settlements along the St Lawrence) by means of incessant patrols.[9]

The war had the effect of decreasing the fur exports that generated the Communauté's revenues. The greater the frequency of attacks, the less money there was to protect the settlements. To come to the aid of the Huron mission that was in the process of being annihilated by Iroquois attacks, the administrators resorted to an expedient that would make frequent reappearances in the colony's history, with variable results: They recruited volunteers, who were remunerated by being allowed to trade with goods advanced by the Compagnie and retain a share of the proceeds. The few relevant notarized contracts mentioned by Marcel Trudel indicate that these volunteers included soldiers but were made up of a majority of servants (sixty in 1649 and around thirty the following year) who were willing to face danger in the hope of earning profits normally beyond their reach.[10] They did not see military action, but the first contingent brought back furs.[11]

The administrators took advantage of the fragile peace achieved in 1653 to deal with their financial difficulties by breaking up the flying column and eliminating the Trois-Rivières garrison and perhaps the Montreal garrison as well. For the next nine years, the colonists would have to "fend for themselves."[12] In 1662, with a recrudescence of hostilities and insistent requests for reinforcements, the colony received a new contingent of 100 soldiers.[13]

The soldiers of this period did not belong to any regular formation. There is almost no information concerning the method of recruitment, but it may be assumed to have been no different from the one used for ordinary labourers. The recruit committed to a fixed period of service, usually three years, in exchange for annual wages; the company paid for passage to North America, living expenses in the colony, and return to France at the end of the contract. Unlike the labourers whom recruiters resold to colonists and religious communities, arquebusiers and soldiers remained in the employ of the Compagnie, unless, of course, the parties agreed to cancel the contract. We do not know, for example, what agreement there was

between the Communauté des Habitants and the seventy soldiers
of the flying column dismissed in 1653 for lack of funds.[14] It may
at least be affirmed that the status of these first soldiers was as precarious as that of the other engagés. The men in charge of training
and commanding these young recruits had some military experience,
although what it consisted of is difficult to specify in most cases. It
was reported that Maisonneuve, the governor of Montreal, had first
gone into battle in Holland at the age of thirteen, that another soldier had fought the Turks or the Spanish on the Mediterranean, that
still another had joined the Swedes in Germany or "held some position of command in the French army."[15] These were rather ill-defined
careers. Two governors and several gentlemen had acquired their
ranks in the king's regiments or on his ships, but the other commissioned and non-commissioned officers had no ranks per se; their
titles merely corresponded to their duties in the colony. There were
commandants (sometimes referred to as captains), their adjutants
(lieutenants), and a relatively large number of sergeants and corporals. Many of them were educated, well-born people who had come
as volunteers, or soldiers without contract, to whom the authorities
entrusted responsibilities.[16]

Some of the archaic features of this small military organization
were its private rather than governmental character, absence of
professionalism, brief enrolments, and lax command. Furthermore,
there was no clear hierarchical distinction between commissioned
and non-commissioned officers. Accentuated by remoteness, these
features remind us that the military institutions of the Baroque were
still in a period of transition.[17] But whatever their real worth, the
mere presence of these troops afforded reassurance. "We have here
many fine and determined soldiers," wrote the Jesuit Paul Lejeune in
1636. He continued:

> It is a pleasure to see [our soldiers] engage in their warlike
> exercises during the calmness of peace, to hear the noise of
> muskets and of cannon, only in rejoicing, our great forests and
> mountains responding to these reports by Echoes rolling as inno-
> cent thunders, which have neither bolts nor lightning. The Diane
> wakens us every morning; we see the sentinels resting upon their
> arms. The guardhouse is always well supplied; each squad has its
> days of sentry duty. In a word, our fortress at Kébec is guarded
> in time of peace as is an important place in the midst of war.[18]

But the following year, when he tried to overtake some Iroquois warriors who had intercepted a fur-laden Huron convoy, the governor relied on the residents of Quebec as much as on the garrison.[19] Circumstances dictated that the colonists be on a war footing, and they were at least mentally prepared, to a degree. Two-thirds of them had come from Normandy and the western provinces, which had been regularly disrupted by all sorts of violence. They had all turned twenty sometime between 1628 and 1655, which meant that the first to arrive in Canada had witnessed the last of the Huguenot rebellions. They had all been affected to some extent by the rebellions in the countryside and the urban periphery and by the terrible repression that ensued. Several had seen the *bandes françaises*, the first standing French infantry units, at work in Caen, Avranches, or Rouen, the principal ports of embarkation for Canada.[20] Those who had grown up along the Loire or on Île-de-France still remembered the riots and the severe punishment meted out in their wake or the looting by the Prince of Condé's army during the Fronde.[21] *La doulce France* was laid waste. War was part of daily life; arms had the run of the city; townspeople were accustomed to guard duty and patrols; the littlest town had its defence strategy; and until 1660, the urban militias retained their military role, since the protection of property and the security of militiamen's families depended on it. The bearing of arms was not reserved to the elite. The communes had their companies of arquebusiers, and holidays were occasions for shooting contests and warlike excesses in which the entire population took part.[22]

b) A colony on the defensive

In Canada too, war was the business of all; the main difference between soldiers and civilians was that one group was paid to fight while the other was not. And since the first group was very small, the colonists had to cobble together their own system of defence from the outset, re-creating forms of association and collective discipline inherited from tradition and revived during the troubles that had marked their youth. We know a little about the prevailing forms of organization at the start of the 1650s in the town of Trois-Rivières, where 100 Frenchmen lived alongside a group of Algonquins and other Indigenous neophytes, to whom the Jesuits ministered in a separate chapel. The town was surrounded by a new, eleven-foot-high stockade with a redoubt serving as a guard house for the three squads that kept watch on a rotating basis. Several pieces of artillery filled out the defence. Every Frenchman between the ages of sixteen and sixty, whether "habitant, soldier or journeyman," was required to serve. An ordinance reminded all concerned that journeymen must not keep watch more often than their share and that servants on night watch must be allowed by their masters to sleep until nine o'clock the next morning.[23] The ordinances of the time make no distinction between soldiers and civilians: Both were under the authority of the town captain, who acted as the local merchant and judge, ordered reviews and target practice, organized guard duty, and fined offenders.[24] Thus, the abolition of the small garrison in 1653 changed nothing. It is important to note that here as elsewhere in the colony, compulsory service did not extend to patrols conducted beyond the town limits, which consisted of volunteers. The Indigenous people did not do regular duty but did provide volunteers for combat, as during the disastrous sortie of 19 August 1652.[25] The following year, several hundred Iroquois massed for another attack on Trois-Rivières. Although the habitants were incapable of chasing off the enemy and preventing him from ravaging the nearby fields and herds, they did manage to withstand a nine-day siege, indicating that the conventional military drills to which they had been subjected had not been useless.[26]

Next to nothing is known about the defence measures adopted for Quebec and environs. There were reorganizations in 1653 following the abolition of the flying column, among others the selection of eight townspeople to supervise the habitants from the urban outskirts and the more distant côtes.[27] The speed with which newly arrived governor Pierre de Voyer d'Argenson gathered 160 men in July 1658 to chase a party of Iroquois suggests the existence of a fairly effective mobilizational structure.[28] In Montreal, the most exposed post, the order of patrols was adjusted in 1653 to incorporate 100 new engagés. There was also a religious component of this military organization in the form of the brotherhood or "devotion of soldiers to the Holy Virgin" that is mentioned by the annalist of the Hotel-Dieu.[29] One of Maisonneuve's ordinances from 1658 reiterates the watchwords: never leave home unarmed, never work the fields alone, and barricade yourself indoors as soon as the curfew sounds. No one was to hunt beyond the cleared area or to fish further away than the bank of the St Lawrence.[30] The thirty-six after-death inventories drawn up during this period show that the regulations concerning arms were largely obeyed and suggest the existence of a varied and considerable arsenal.[31] Nearly all the deceased owned at least one musket or arquebus, often several, and the four who did not were servants who had access to their masters' weapons.[32] Pistols – easy to hide and useful in responding rapidly to an attack – are found in only five inventories, but more than two-thirds include a good sword in a leather scabbard. And if artisans and land clearers possessed such a weapon, it means that they knew how to wield it and expected they would sooner or later have to face the enemy.[33] Sword bearing, later to become an honorific practice reserved to the elite, had an important utilitarian role here.

The colony's forts were precarious refuges with inadequate control over the surrounding countryside and the sources of supply. To get closer to their land, the colonists built houses outside the stockades but within sight of one another. The ones in Montreal were built "in the manner of redoubts," with iron braces. When attacks intensified, those who had settled in the isolated seigneuries downriver from Trois-Rivières had to abandon their houses and seek refuge in the fortress. Conditions of confinement were not as harsh in the Quebec region, which avoided the worst, but there too the habitants had a suffocating feeling of being held prisoner.[34] They had been "held captive for eighty years by the great wars waged by the Iroquois, their most dangerous enemy," wrote a French officer in 1669, who was obviously ignorant of the history of the colony he had come to rescue yet must have heard those words somewhere.[35] Such a long ordeal can cause one to lose the notion of time.

Every governor had dreamed of leading a powerful army to attack, subdue, and if necessary exterminate the Iroquois in their territory. Champlain thought that 100 carabineers, pikemen, and halberdiers "accompanied by three or four thousand allied Natives" would suffice. "We would go to the Iroquois's land in twelve days; with petards, mines, granades, and horsemen, we would make them surrender their principal villages without a fight, and we would lay down the law to them. We would then be feared by the enemy, we would be feared and loved by our allies, and all would know the valour of the French when they are given offence."[36] Overconfidence in the real and symbolic power of French arms, ignorance of the forces and politics of the allied nations, underestimation of enemy resistance: These were enduring features of colonial military discourse and are found, in mildly attenuated form, in the early-1660s invasion plans of governors Voyer d'Argenson and Pierre Dubois Davaugour.[37] While waiting for the king to give them the means to put these plans into action, the French remained on the defensive. Very rarely did they take the initiative to harass the Iroquois parties prowling around the settlements. The Jesuit *Relations* and *Journal*, as well as the other sources, mention only nine such "offensives" over a period of thirty years. The vehicles used were usually flag-flying barques equipped with small artillery. In half of these cases, the detachment returned without having seen the enemy. When the men threw caution to the wind and set foot on land, the enemy found them and inflicted heavy casualties.[38] The Battle of Long Sault (near present-day Saint-André-d'Argenteuil, QC), one of the offensives that went awry, was a truly exceptional case of recklessness.[39] Ordinarily, colonists died or were taken prisoner not during guerrilla operations in the woods but in their fields, a musket shot away from their houses, surprised in the course of routine activities despite whatever precautions they had taken. The alarm would be sounded, and a few of them would try to intercept the enemy convoy and free the captives, most often without success. The dead would be buried and the prisoners' fate entrusted to God.

John Dickinson has established that this war caused relatively few casualties among the French. One could probably quibble with the accuracy of his sources, but the numbers remain low even if one factors in those anonymous individuals, whether soldiers or servants, whose death or capture was not reported. Depending on the period, deaths and prisoners together accounted for 5 to 7 per cent of the population, with peak casualties occurring in the 1650s.[40] In comparison, the epidemics of 1687 or 1703 carried off up to 8 per cent of Canadians in just a few months.[41] These numerical comparisons have their limits, however, and cannot fully account for a historical phenomenon as real as that of demographic losses: the climate of terror described by the annalists as reigning in the colony. If there has been any exaggeration, the historians have had nothing to do with it. What must be interrogated is the colonial mind, how contemporaries perceived the situation.

It has often been noted that the violence associated with early seventeenth-century European military movements was the equal of that deployed by the Amerindians. In Europe too, townsmen were seized from meadows and peasants from their fields; cottages were burned, cattle slaughtered, prisoners ransomed.[42] But this is beside the point, for it was not how the colonists reasoned. They were plunged into a world whose signs they could not read. What happened to them was always unpredictable and incomprehensible. The same could be said of torture, which, in France, served to extract confessions or to deter from crime those to whom it was presented as spectacle. But what meaning could anyone find in the tortures inflicted by the Amerindians, and why were certain captives released while others were killed?[43] That the situation was subject to sudden change must also have been hard on the colonists. No sooner had they celebrated a truce with two of the five Iroquois League nations than a third sent 600 warriors to harass their settlements.[44] Another region, believing itself safe, might discover to its astonishment that the enemy had just carried off a woman and her four children, as happened in the Côte-de-Beaupré in June 1660.[45] And while it is true that attacks against the French were intermittent, the war itself – i.e., the one waged between different Indigenous groups – never ceased. The whole occupied land and far beyond was constantly crisscrossed by bands of warriors pursuing objectives and strategies that European observers often struggled to grasp. This climate of war exacerbated the sense of danger.

Were the French involved in intertribal clashes? Was this how they learned the art of low-intensity war – by fighting alongside the Montagnais, the Algonquins, the Hurons, and the Ottawas?[46] So the historians assert, yet this statement is premised on a second postulate: that there were, early on, a large number of *coureurs de bois* in the western and northern reaches of the colony for whom military activity was just one of several marks of acculturation. The fact is, though, that the number of Frenchmen who ventured outside the colony before the peace of 1667 was very small. In an average year prior to 1629, the interpreters and trading company agents who wintered with the Huron, the Algonquin, or the Nipissing could be counted on the fingers of one hand.[47] Subsequently, their presence was no longer strictly necessary, since the Hurons took charge of gathering the furs and delivering them to the colony's stores. The Jesuits kept an eye on their mission staff, and the *Relations* do not mention the passage of independent traders who might have sowed disorder among the catechumens.[48] It was only in 1653, after the network built by the Hurons was dismantled and the truce with the Iroquois reached, that the French started to visit the Ottawas.

From then on, there was regular movement of traders through the northern territories between the Saguenay and Lake Superior, but its importance must not be exaggerated – a few dozen men, perhaps, in peak years. These were extremely dangerous voyages undertaken in groups, avoiding the most dangerous areas as much as possible.[49]

Regardless of the number of these bold traders, one thing is certain: They did not go to war with the Indigenous people. To affirm the contrary, it would first have to be shown that there was a rationale for French participation, that it was required. This was true in the early days when musketeers had only to open fire in order to scare off the enemy. The familiar engravings immortalizing the defeats of the Iroquois in 1609 and 1615 thanks to the presence of Champlain and his men are well known. The Hurons continued to appreciate the presence of the armed traders who wintered in their villages and invited some of them to join their expeditions. Military aid was a key feature of the alliance for the Hurons, and they were dismayed to receive missionaries instead of soldiers.[50] In short, this was a short-lived experience limited to a handful of individuals and did not live on with the colonists who began settling in the colony after 1633.[51] After a momentary lull, the Amerindian wars resumed with greater intensity, but the French took no part in them unless they themselves were threatened. They denied assistance to the Algonquins and the Montagnais, and it appears that the Hurons too could no longer rely on it.[52] One can be sure that no Frenchmen joined their raiding parties against the Iroquois, for the Jesuits, who recounted such movements quite faithfully, would surely have mentioned French involvement if it had occurred. Moreover, when the Indigenous people acquired firearms in the 1640s, French soldiers ceased to be a boon to this kind of warfare and could even be a burden.

We shall return to the apprenticeship and discipline required in order to master the Indigenous style of warfare. However, the account of Pierre-Esprit Radisson must be mentioned here because it falls within this initial period and apparently contradicts my remarks. He whom history has designated the *coureur de bois* par excellence recounted that during his captivity among the Iroquois, around 1653, he joined them in battle against some southern nations. The boy (he was then about thirteen) showed such bravery that the village welcomed him as a returning hero.[53] This last detail should suffice to establish the unlikelihood of the episode in which the narrator asserts possession of a natural superiority enabling him to assimilate and surpass the techniques of his hosts.[54]

While the French did not help their allies much, the latter were often mobilized for defensive operations around Quebec, Trois-Rivières, and Montreal and on rare occasions fought alongside the colonists. Not all the commentary is full of praise and gratitude – far from it! Can popular sentiment be glimpsed in the writings of the Jesuits, whose distrust and contempt for military conduct they considered cowardly and disorganized continually pokes through their prose? How are we to know?[55] Recall that no trace is to be found during this period of the privileged relations that would later be established between certain Frenchmen and one or more Indigenous groups, becoming one of the colony's key strengths. Before making war as allies, they had to get to know each other, evaluate each other's strengths – a process that had barely begun. Before going on raids and laying ambushes for the enemy, the colonists had to learn to navigate forests and rivers; in 1666 few of them possessed such skills. In short, if the people were crying out for support from the king's army, it is because they felt utterly incapable of defending themselves alone and did not trust their allies.

c) Carignan and the campaigns of 1666

French troops – the Carignan-Salières regiment and four more infantry companies, for a total of 1,310 men – arrived in the summer of 1665 on a mission to exterminate the Iroquois "in their homes."[56] Until their departure three years later, they were put to work fortifying the colony's borders in the Richelieu River and Lake Champlain region and manning the garrisons in the three towns and at the new forts. Military expeditions took place in 1666. The first campaign, lasting ten weeks, from 9 January to 17 March for the men who started from Quebec, was a failure that turned tragic. The detachment of 500 soldiers got lost and wandered for weeks on empty stomachs, decimated by the cold, before reaching the Anglo-Dutch settlement of Schenectady, which they took for a Mohawk settlement. The return was even harder. The second campaign, led by Alexandre de Prouville de Tracy, turned back after meeting some Iroquois ambassadors who were bringing back prisoners and coming to offer peace guarantees. Dissatisfied with the ensuing negotiations, the authorities launched a major offensive in the fall. This time, the

1,300-strong army went deep into the territory of the Mohawks, who did not wait for drumbeats to sound before leaving the area. After finding and demolishing four fine deserted villages, and with winter approaching, the French headed home.[57] Was the Iroquois League as intimidated by this military deployment as preening contemporary accounts suggest? One thing is certain: the League was momentarily exhausted and sought an accord with the French so that it could rebuild its forces.[58] This was signed on 10 July 1667 and gave the French twenty years of peace.

In these campaigns, colonists served as both soldiers and fort builders. Versailles insisted that the expeditionary corps be supported by soldiers supplied by the colony "who know how to fight these savage peoples."[59] The only extant data with which to take the measure of this participation are found in the Jesuit *Relations*, which mention 200 "volunteers" out of a total of 500 men for the January detachment and 600 out of 1,300 for the autumn detachment.[60] The estimate is certainly greatly exaggerated, for 600 corresponds to 43 per cent of the total male population over the age of fifteen in that year.[61] Such a high level of participation would not be found until 1759; the average normally hovered around 20 per cent. Let us therefore assume that fewer men participated in the Tracy campaign, albeit still in significant numbers, for so they appeared to the chroniclers. But was their participation purely voluntarily? Here too, doubts are in order. In each year of the 1660s, Canada received several hundred engagés. In 1666, many of the colony's youth – perhaps a third – were not emancipated and had little experience of the country.[62] Doubtless some more war-hardened colonists fought alongside them, but apparently none of these engagés was able to make his way through the forest without Indigenous guidance. Dollier de Casson's praise for the notable conduct of the Montrealers in these campaigns must be taken with a grain of salt,[63] for these rather inglorious campaigns gave no one an opportunity to show off his skill or courage.

But for the first time, the French dared to march outside the narrow, relatively well-protected confines of the colony and took great pride in doing so. This sentiment is palpable, despite the conventions of the genre, in the long burlesque poem composed by the young René-Louis Chartier de Lotbinière during the winter campaign, from which he miraculously returned unharmed. There was obviously no question of transforming such a miserable adventure into an epic, but neither did the author resign himself to ridiculing the army and its commander. He reserved his barbed remarks for the enemy, and, as for the rest, the parody remains good-natured, superficial, rhyming *guerriers* (warriors) with *lauriers* (laurels) and *jeunesse* (youth) with *prouesses* (feats of bravery). The debacle took on an air of victory,[64] and the colony unhesitatingly greeted the following autumn's campaign as a resounding success. Far from being discouraged by the Iroquois's flight and the impossibility of winning a contest of arms, the commander of the Quebec militiamen at this battle, Jean-Baptiste Legardeur de Repentigny, saw the hand of God in the outcome. As he told Marie de l'Incarnation, he had witnessed a miracle with his own eyes: Climbing up on a hill to observe the scene, the troops below had suddenly appeared to him so numerous "that he believed the angels had joined them, which made him ecstatic with joy." The enemies, who took in the same trance-like scene of a 4,000-man army from another height of land, decided against pursuing a siege for which they were quite well prepared.[65]

"Divine intervention" had been a regular occurrence in a colony that had, since its origins, been carrying on a holy war against those who would impede the spread of religion among people considered heathens. This was the Catholic Church's view of the situation, and the colonists were only too willing to subscribe to it: Those who carried out the designs of providence surely could not be forsaken by it. Such assurance helped to keep fear at bay. The remarks of Repentigny, one of the colony's oldest and most illustrious inhabitants, afford a good reflection of the public state of mind. But after 1667, this type of account grows scarcer because the sources become more secular, even if the corresponding mentality remains unaltered. On the one hand, the Jesuit *Relations* and the other religious annals ceased to play the role of colonial gazettes, focusing instead on the missions and convents of the religious orders; on the other, the new sources, including administrative correspondence and military journals, have their own conventions, according to which details with no direct bearing on the outcome of a campaign are excluded. Military history is enriched, while cultural history grows impoverished. The religious dimension is an important element of the colonial wars that I shall attempt to analyze within a long-term perspective at the end of this study.[66]

Finally, it is worth noting the discretion observed by witnesses in regard to the victims of the January–March 1666 campaign. The

Jesuits, ordinarily so precise in their estimates of numbers killed or captured by the Iroquois, become laconic: more than sixty dead. How many more? "We lost ... four hundred men, who dropped dead from the cold as they marched," wrote one infantry officer in his journal, still shaken by the experience.[67] Nothing more, apart from a vague reference by Dollier de Casson to the sick and wounded members of Governor Daniel de Rémy de Courcelle's army who were treated at the Hotel-Dieu "after this terrible winter war."[68] A ten-week march, including five weeks through uninhabited lands, in the depths of winter, by malnourished men, must certainly have produced many casualties. No doubt fewer among the colonial volunteers, who were fitter to march and more warmly dressed than the French soldiers; still, some of them – perhaps forty, according to one conservative estimate – lost their lives or came home invalids. If so, then this one campaign produced as many casualties as the previous five years of Iroquois attacks.[69] The bias shown by such sources when they ignore or downplay casualties is another constant in the military history of the colony, as are the resupply problems that sorely plagued the campaigns of 1666 and would rear their heads each time the authorities sent large contingents off to war.

2. MILITARY FOUNDATIONS

a) A failed military settlement plan

Under the initial plan, the Carignan-Salières regiment's sojourn in Canada was not intended to be lengthy. In 1668, three years after its arrival, it returned to France, leaving behind a series of small posts where the colonists could seek refuge in the event of a never-to-be-discounted resumption of hostilities, as well as some 400 soldiers and thirty officers who accepted the licence (*congé*) offered and became colonists.[70] Bonuses had been offered and heavy pressure applied, but no more could be persuaded to stay. To comprehend how the king and his minister perceived the Canadian militia, the illusions they entertained on this score, it is necessary to dwell on the military settlement plan that was the cornerstone of the sociopolitical regime they sought to establish in the colony. Under the plan, officers would receive a seigneury and would encourage the soldiers of their company to occupy plots of land on it.

This manner of apportioning a newly conquered country corresponds to the erstwhile custom among the Romans of distributing to soldiers the fields of the subjugated provinces, known as *paedia militaria,* and the practice of these political peoples and warriors could, in my estimation, be judiciously introduced into a country a thousand leagues removed from its monarch, which, by reason of this remoteness, may often be reduced to the necessity of providing for its own subsistence. It seems to me all the more foreseeable that it will one day supply the king with a corps of venerable troops capable of preserving this nascent State of Canada against the incursions of the Natives. This is why the first of our kings, greater statesmen than we might have realized, introduced into newly conquered lands men of war, born their subjects, whose loyalty was well known to them, to confine the inhabitants to their duties within and, without, to keep their common enemies at bay. To maintain them and look to their subsistence, our ancient kings granted, within those very lands, plots that they would cultivate, affording them, by their own produce, all that was necessary to life; this being both an economical and a political policy, since it spared the finances of the public treasury on the one hand and involved the officer and the soldier in the preservation of the country, as that of their own heritage, on the other.[71]

This document by Intendant Jean Talon faithfully reflects the thinking and intentions of Versailles. While allusions to Rome were commonplace in the early days of the reign, the idea of connecting the conquest of the Americas to a legendary account of national and monarchic origins was less so; this latter allusion clearly shows the importance accorded to this new extension of the Merovingian kingdom.[72] Yet despite a few small, scattered successes, military colonization did not go as planned. On the one hand, less than a third of the officers agreed to settle in Canada, compromising the operation from the outset. On the other, the soldiers were for the most part young recruits who had not been associated with their officers long enough to follow their lead. Instead of company-by-company disbandment, what took place was a series of individual decisions. The future farmer-soldiers settled wherever they wished, often close to town in the places where they had been quartered. They dispersed, mixing with the pre-existing inhabitants and with the hundreds of militarily inexperienced engagés also recruited in the 1660s.[73] The officers-turned-seigneurs waited in their more distant fiefs for *censitaires* (subordinate landholders who paid seigneurial dues) to arrive, but in vain. Since they lacked the capital necessary to develop their domains, they soon went looking elsewhere for the income denied them by the land.[74] Historians have laid bare the internal logic of settlement, which, as long as people remain free, eludes the designs of planners: Colonists' decisions are guided by land quality, market proximity, kinship, and material constraints. Not only did the men not group together around their former officers, but they preferred to live in their own habitations rather than in village agglomerations. This typically North American form of dispersed habitat, though rational and advantageous in many respects, was unconducive to the creation of an easily defended colony based on a network of fortified residential-cum-military settlements of the kind Europe had been building since the great migrations of the first millennium, which it hoped to recreate in the colony.[75] Did the first royal administrators realize that their recommendations were futile and would not prevail over agricultural and domestic exigencies or over the optimism of habitants who were counting on peace to let them resume their lives? Perhaps, but few – certainly not Jean Talon, the courtier's courtier – took the additional step of telling the minister that he had misunderstood the context and ought to rethink his plan. Thus, the king's instructions of 1669 concerning military organization presupposed shorter distances, a much denser population than actually existed, and the presence of former officers capable of instilling military discipline in each côte.

My intention is that you divide up all those of my subjects living in said land by companies, having regard to their proximity to one another; that, having divided them thus, you establish captains, lieutenants and ensigns to command them; that where all members of said companies can assemble and return home in one day, you give orders for them to assemble once a month to conduct the exercise of handling their weapons; and where they are too far remote, that you subdivide the companies into squads of 40 to 50 men and have them do the exercise as indicated hereinabove; and, as regards the full companies, that you assemble them once or twice a year.

And you shall take care that they are all well armed, and that they always have enough powder, lead, and fuse to use their weapons where there is occasion for it.

And you shall visit the squads and companies often and have them conduct the exercise in your presence.

And, insofar as possible, you shall, once yearly, assemble the greatest possible number of these habitants and have them perform the exercise as a corps, taking care, however, not to make them walk exceedingly long distances, and leaving it to your discretion to assemble only those who can do so and return home in two days' time, so that any extra time does not use up the time they must devote to looking after their business and cultivating their land. I leave it to your discretion to consider whether it would not be more advantageous to the good of my service and the increase of the colony to assemble one thousand to twelve hundred well-armed soldiers every two or three years, and conduct a march through the territory of the Iroquois and the other Nations, so as to keep them always mindful of the power of my arms and to contain them within their due obedience to me.[76]

b) The enabling text of the militia

The foregoing text, in essence the enabling act of the Canadian militia, is taken from a letter from the king to Governor de Courcelle – that is, from private correspondence. There would be no subsequent public act sanctioning, complementing, or detailing these instructions so that the people would know what was expected of them. When wars broke out, the administrators published one-time ordinances forcing the habitants to obtain guns, erect forts in their parishes, or take charge of signal fires; an ordinance of 1710 gives pride of place to militia captains over church wardens in processions. But there is no point in searching for the general regulation governing the operation of the militia, the selection criteria for recruits, the choice of militia officers, their rank and powers during campaigns, the holding of assemblies and the drawing up of rolls, the sanctions applied to offenders, and so forth: It does not exist. To issue an ordinance enumerating the colonists' duties would have circumscribed them, by the same token. In the era of the trading companies, the governors' orders regulating guard duty implicitly acknowledged that compulsory service stopped at the doors of the fort.[77] By virtue of their secrecy, the royal instructions of 1669 did away with these older customs, effectively instating an unlimited regime of military and paramilitary service.[78]

It is my belief that this way of governing was peculiar to the colonies, and particularly to New France, for the naval bureaucracy did not have as free a hand in the Caribbean. The governor-general of the West Indies simultaneously received similar instructions to put his people on a war footing, yet the extent of these instructions was revealed and clarified by subsequent ordinances.[79] The absence of general regulations governing various branches of the administration was in fact to become a principal grievance of the Caribbean colonists in the latter half of the eighteenth century. It was claimed that Versailles avoided laying down the law to its colonies so that its representatives would not be bound by it.[80] When the Conseil de la Marine (a body that replaced the Secrétariat de la Marine under the Régence) asked the intendant of Quebec to take inventory of the titles and texts of Canada's legislative acts, including directives taken from ministerial correspondence, it consecrated the existence of a dual repertoire, one public and duly recorded, the other hidden.[81] Thus, the case of the militia is not exceptional, yet it is nonetheless surprising that such an important institution should have remained in administrative limbo until the end of the regime without this void attracting attention. It is, of course, quite possible that such criticisms were voiced but have been lost to history.

c) An attempted definition

The major features of the militia can only be understood as a function of both ministerial directives and customs, which – as the remainder of this study will demonstrate – departed from the directives on several points. This initial definition is necessarily incomplete yet necessary as a point of departure. In early Canada, military service was an obligation of a personal and universal nature. The burden rested on each individual, not on the group, parish, or family. Service was, in principle, compulsory for all able-bodied men, regardless of marital status, family responsibilities, or social position. The ability to bear arms was deemed to be acquired by a youth when he reached the age of fourteen, according to a decree of 1686 and a governor's memorandum of 1716, which also set the upper limit at sixty.[82] In the mid-eighteenth century, annual censuses set the boundary between younger and older children at age fifteen and between adults and the elderly at age fifty.[83] The question is largely moot, as we shall see, for adolescents and older men were unlikely to be recruited. Although civil status was never mentioned, Versailles liked to remind administrators that social or occupational status did not exempt anyone from militia duty. Administrators were to ensure "that no habitant, servant, or labourer be exempted and that if there be gentlemen who do not wish to hold the position of officers, they must serve as soldiers." Only officers possessing a royal warrant were exempt.[84] Militia officers were chosen and their commissions were signed by the governor-general, seconded by the two local governors for matters under their purview. Nowhere in the extant correspondence are there more specific instructions as to selection criteria. Versailles held that these responsibilities naturally rested with the nobility, who were duty-bound to accept them. Militia companies did not form regiments but were grouped by government, with commandants, town majors, and their assistants – whose jurisdiction was not always clear – in Quebec, Trois-Rivières, and Montreal.[85] Militia officers had no rank in the regular troops; that is, they ranked no higher than soldiers in the military hierarchy. Militia recruitment and command were the responsibility of the governor and his general staff or *état-major* (consisting of the local governors, king's lieutenants, town majors, and their assistants distributed among the three urban centres). As time went by and as circumstances dictated, militiamen were commanded to go to war, perform paramilitary tasks, carry supplies, or work on fortifications. In every case they were expected to serve without pay and to provide their own weapon – a musket with a quantity of powder and lead – at their own expense.[86] The militia was a military institution, governed by military rules and military justice. Any disobedience or criminal act committed in the service, whether this involved corvées or military operations as such, was beyond the bailiwick of the ordinary judges and courts and has thus been lost to history, for little trace persists of the military courts.[87] Again, this concise description of the militia is intended as a provisional starting point; the goal of the remainder of this study is to complete the picture, insofar as possible.

d) A novel institution

Unlike the other colonial institutions, which resembled those of the realm to a greater or lesser extent, the militia was a novel creation. Of the two basic systems of military recruitment – conscription or voluntary enlistment – the monarchy had, since the sixteenth century, chosen the latter for the reorganization of its army. However, volunteerism in France went along with various forms of compulsory service that can be divided into three categories. The first consisted of forms handed down from medieval tradition, such as the *ban* and the *arrière-ban* – royal proclamations summoning all the king's vassals to war – or the obligation of personal service attaching to the possession of a fief. Seigneurs with the power of *haute justice* were required to attend the summons with their arms and those of the peasants who accompanied them, but they had been remunerated for this task since 1483. Tours of duty lasted three months within the country or forty days outside its borders. The military value of this formation was nil, yet the monarchy carried it on throughout the seventeenth century and, most importantly, levied a heavy tax on those who sought exemptions – which explains why it outlasted its usefulness.[88] Urban militias, too, had a very old history. Traditionally, townspeople served without pay and equipped themselves at their own expense. All citizens of arms-bearing age were required to participate in defence under the command of their magistrates. Cities claiming the privilege of self-defence had their own artillery and did not allow royal troops to enter. In the seventeenth century, the monarchy had no interest whatsoever in the military power of cities, and soon their militias were reduced to a nominal existence. They took part in ceremonies and had some limited participation in keeping watch.[89]

Thus, all these old forms of defence and compulsory service had either disappeared or were in decline at the time Colbert founded the colonial militias. The second, more modern category of compulsory service consisted of coast guards and "land" or provincial militias, of which only the first already existed in the colony. Created in the sixteenth century to perform the work of a navy and reorganized several times subsequently, the coast guard comprised all men ages eighteen to sixty living within two leagues of the coast. It played an essentially passive role, keeping watch and maintaining fortifications, but had to be ready to fend off an enemy landing. The service was made more orderly and efficient in the eighteenth century with the introduction of wages and conscription by lottery.[90] Compulsory service was imposed throughout the realm by an ordinance of 1688 creating the provincial militias. Parishes had to supply a certain number of men, chosen by lot from among unmarried men under the age of forty, equip them, and pay them an enlistment bonus and a wage as long as they remained in the province. Officers, chosen by the intendant from among the gentlemen of the colony, received a royal commission and a salary. While peace persisted, these two-year tours of militia duty amounted to little, but in wartime the institution functioned as an army reserve, with longer periods of service. A large proportion of militiamen – up to 46 per cent during the War of the Spanish Succession (1701–14) – were incorporated into the regiments. As necessary, they served at the king's expense and held the same status as regulars. Militia duty was scary, and parishes were willing to finance a volunteer at considerable expense if it meant they could keep their sons from being drafted. Recruitment into the active army became less intense as the eighteenth century progressed, concentrating on the cities so as not to interfere with agriculture. While in the service, recruits were exempted from the land tax on the peasantry (the *taille*). As a final note, the details of militia recruitment were not handled by military officers but by the intendant and his subdelegates, assisted by community-elected syndics.[91]

The third category of compulsory service consisted of in-kind contributions for military purposes. Peasants were requisitioned in unequal fashion to provide carts and labour for transportation and earth-moving operations, and these exactions weighed more heavily on the frontier provinces. The conditions under which these tasks were to be performed were not well defined, leading to abuses; nevertheless, the custom of remunerating pioneers or corvée members appears to have become the norm by the end of the seventeenth century. It is not impossible that peasants enlisted of their own accord when the season and the wages suited them, as they did during the construction of the fortress of Ath in 1668. Intendants retained the right to oversee recruitment and execution of the corvées.[92]

Let us now attempt to see the big picture emerging from this inventory of the various forms of compulsory service in France. Unpaid military duty all but disappeared. Recruitment weighed upon only a small fraction of the population, sparing farmers and heads of households. And enlistment of these auxiliary troops was a matter for the civilian authorities. How strikingly different from the system implemented by Louis XIV and Colbert in their colonies! While it did bear some resemblance to one or another metropolitan organization, the coast guard in particular, the latter was solely devoted to local defence, while the colonists were forced to take part in offensive expeditions.[93] Quite clearly, the colonial model was not French;

rather, it was inspired by ideas circulating since the Renaissance about the Greek phalanges, composed of farmer-soldiers who fitted themselves out at their own expense; the free soldiers of ancient Rome; the superiority of subjects in arms over a mercenary army.[94] It was the dream of a perfect society in which individuals could replace one another interchangeably in a continuous rotation between productive occupations and military activities with no impact on the performance of either. By then ancient, the theme of the citizen-as-soldier was to be very popular with the Encyclopédistes: "Every citizen, of every condition, ought to have two attires: the attire of his station and military attire."[95]

In Colbert's time, the colonies offered an ideal terrain on which to put these theories into practice. After the experience of military colonization by the Carignan-Salières regiment came the creation of civic militias made up of sturdy, well-trained peasants who owned their own land and were, as such, perfectly capable of bearing the cost of their equipment and food when going to war. The determination to refrain from all future spending on the defence of the colonies thus gave wings to utopian thinking.[96]

The absence of the word *milice* in the instructions given in 1669 to Courcelle is significant, although this may not be obvious without briefly retracing the history of the word.[97] In its older, rather long-lived meaning, emerging in the sixteenth century, *milice* designated soldiers in general, and this was how it was used by the chroniclers of New France in the early seventeenth century. "Our French soldiers are so fervent," wrote Marie de l'Incarnation in regard to the Carignan regiment and the colonists, "that they fear nothing ... This whole militia appears to believe that it is going to lay siege to Heaven and expects to capture it, and enter it, since it is for the good of the faith and religion that it is going off to fight."[98] The religious reference is not accidental. Under the influence of ecclesiastical Latin, *milice* was often an allusion to the heavenly host. Perhaps this fact explains the popularity of the term among clerical historians of old who, to enhance the valour and saintliness of the first colonists, replaced the words "soldiers," "warriors," "men," "French," or "volunteers," used indiscriminately in the sources, with the word *milice*. Thus, for example, we have the founding of the "Militia of the Holy Family" by the governor of Montreal in 1663 – a pious invention that still lingers in our textbooks.[99] The word also has a more modern sense that gradually spread during the seventeenth century: It designates a corps of citizens armed for the defence of a territory and assisting the regular army.[100] But that is not at all what Louis XIV and his minister had in mind. The word *milice* does not appear in the instructions of 1669 because what was being created was not an auxiliary corps but a bona fide colonial army.

Restructuring the Military (1667–87)

During two periods, the wars that punctuated the history of the French regime were interrupted long enough for the colony to take advantage of the lull, leave the danger behind, and carry on its activities relatively untroubled. The thirty years' peace following the Treaty of Utrecht (1713) was one of these key periods that offer historians an opportunity to turn their attention away from the procession of events and take stock of the general climate of the colony.[1]

a) Agricultural progress

By contrast, the twenty years of peace that followed the signing of the accord with the five Iroquois nations in 1667 is rarely identified in the historiography as a lull, for it is obscured by the hubbub of conventional sources, namely, the administrative correspondence and the religious and judicial archives. While the authorities feuded bitterly and accused the colonists of all manner of disruptions, the majority of the latter were working to provide for their families. Land clearing and development was the immediate task demanding all their energy. It was during this period that agriculture on the island of Montreal made its greatest strides, as shown in an earlier work in which I analyzed censuses, parish registers, and notarial acts, and the same was doubtless true in the other seigneuries, such as those in the vicinity of Quebec.[2] But as solid as my demonstration may have been, it did not succeed in dispelling the conventional wisdom, including the allegedly sharp opposition between commerce and agriculture. More recent works of synthesis have carried on the broad-brush depiction of seventeenth-century Canadians as fur traders, situating the thrust of "colonization" as such in the following century.[3] I must therefore re-emphasize that the militias being formed in the 1680s were largely composed of peasants, two-thirds of whom lived in the government of Quebec, far from the temptations of the Great Lakes region.[4]

b) Consolidation of the fur trade and alliances

Just as the lens must be turned on the countryside if one is to assess the progress of agriculture, one must look to the situation of the Indigenous peoples in the western part of the colony to understand the evolution of the fur trade. Seen from Chequamegon Bay (on Lake Superior), Frontenac's squabbles, the struggles to control the fur trade, and the cascade of regulations against the *course des bois* were of little or no importance. Richard White's approach in *The Middle Ground* goes to the heart of the matter. Decimated and dispersed by intertribal war and European diseases, the Indigenous peoples or fragments thereof that settled around the Great Lakes and their tributaries had two priorities: subsistence and safety. The latter was far from assured, and suspicion reigned. When not threatened by famine or enemies, some of these people were willing to undertake the long and arduous journey to Montreal with furs for trade, but they would abandon such plans at the slightest alarm.[5] In order to continue exporting furs, the French needed men on the ground to encourage the suppliers to come down into the colony or, if they refused, to carry goods up to them and bring furs back, and the Indigenous suppliers often demanded the latter. In short, commercial practices largely depended on circumstances and individual decisions by the Indigenous groups with which the French traders were continually renegotiating agreements.[6]

Versailles had yet to grasp the complexity of its relations with the remote nations. It wrongly believed that the French were free to organize the fur trade as they saw fit and that only libertinism and looting attracted Frenchmen to the Great Lakes region. Everything would fall into place if the fur market were regulated according to the model of public contracts used in the realm. These were the assumptions set out in the royal edict of 15 April 1676, which abolished the permit system for fur trading in the deep woods.[7] As

Colbert explained to the intendant of Quebec, the king's intent was for weekly markets to be set up in the main towns of the colony for public trading of furs. Two or three times a year there would be fairs on the same sites, bringing together a larger number of visitors.[8] Versailles was sure that the ban on trading in the interior would induce the Indigenous traders to come down to the colony, docilely, as did the peasants of the decommercialized zones of France's large cities, who were disallowed from selling their grain anywhere but on the market square.[9] One smiles at such ignorance of the land, the distances, the shifting of hunting and trapping areas, the culture of the suppliers, and the diplomatic dimensions of the fur trade. Colbert was no straitjacketed thinker, incapable of imagining what he did not know; nevertheless, he was kept ill-informed by administrators annoyed at their own powerlessness in the absence of military or police support and seemingly incapable of quelling their rancour long enough to articulate the problems and propose reasonable solutions.

Between 1672 and 1681, no fewer than seven regulations of royal origin, plus twenty more of local origin, were issued in an attempt to rein in the *coureurs de bois*. They were backed up by threats of death, whipping, galley slavery, fines, and confiscation, yet their only effect was to exacerbate the phenomenon.[10] The denunciatory fever running through the administrative correspondence culminated in 1679–80 with Intendant Jacques Duchesneau's accusation that the governor preferred to ship pelts to the English, coupled with his assertion that 800 Frenchmen had lived in the woods for years while their lands, cattle, and wives had been left to fend for themselves.[11] The creation of a system of licences covering voyages to the west, along with an amnesty for violators, decriminalized the interior fur trade and helped to impose discipline on the voyageurs. Moreover, Duchesneau's recall in 1682 helped to restore a sense of proportion to the administration – for in actual fact, there had never been 800 or even 600 colonists in the Great Lakes region, the colony's farmland was being steadily planted, its livestock were multiplying, and women were having children with their husbands.[12] But the number matters less than the characteristics ascribed to the men designated as *coureurs de bois*. The phrase first appeared in the official texts in 1672 as a catchall for all sorts of individuals: former engagés of no fixed address; criminals who took advantage of the Indigenous people; young Montrealers who intercepted furs bound for the fairs and merchant-outfitters; and a majority of voyageurs who did not deserve to be lumped together with such bad elements.[13] As they pursued their interests, these traders became, along with the missionaries, the first architects of the alliance to which New France was to entrust its destiny.

The diplomacy learned by voyageurs in the Great Lakes region made many of them good soldiers, although there were no guarantees. To begin with, the men who practised this trade were sturdier than the common run of colonists. They had acquired an estimable knowledge of forests, lakes, and rivers, knew how to sleep outdoors, could walk long distances on an empty stomach, and could carry heavy loads. But these choice members of war parties were often harder to mobilize than peasants. They belonged to no militia and, when joining military campaigns, did so as volunteers because of the advantages they could derive from the enterprise.

c) The colony left to its own devices

In 1670, after the withdrawal of the Carignan-Salières regiment, Colbert sent five new companies to Canada along with funding to maintain them until 1 July of the following year. Pursuing his military settlement plan, he enjoined the captains and the intendant to do everything in their power to settle and marry off these new arrivals.[14] The administrators begged the minister not to send the regiment away so soon, arguing that the absence of regular troops would encourage Iroquois "insolence," but in vain: The decision was irrevocable, and the colony would have to look to its own defence.[15] But neither Courcelle nor Frontenac, who succeeded him in 1672, accepted this. From the moment of his arrival and for the next ten years, Frontenac tirelessly argued the point. Without soldiers, he wrote, it would be impossible to keep the enemy at bay and to preserve public order.[16] In 1682, newly arrived Governor Joseph-Antoine Lefebvre de La Barre took up the call for help in marching against the Iroquois, who were stepping up their attacks on the allied nations: "I cannot subdue or ruin them with the colony alone."[17]

What strikes the reader of the correspondence from these years is the scarcity of specific references to the colonial forces that were, in principle, there to signify the power of the king's arms to the Indigenous peoples. In 1667, Intendant Jean Talon wrote that the peoples of Canada, being "naturally warlike," would quickly form a nursery of soldiers capable of defending both the southern and northern colonies of the Americas.[18] But after the royal instructions of 1669 to form the habitants into companies and prepare them for war, the administration tended to avoid the subject. The governors' loud calls for deployment of regulars were tantamount to an admission that they did not trust the colonists; being personally responsible for their military training, however, it would have been bad form to stress the point. Instead, they wrote of the habitants' negligence in obtaining guns, thus diverting attention away from more fundamental problems, such as the lack of officers in the côtes to train soldiers. When Frontenac wrote in 1673 that he had "begun" to raise a colonial militia in anticipation of a Dutch attack on Quebec, one might have expected a pointed reaction from Versailles: Why had the militarization program been delayed so long?[19] But the admission went unnoticed. One senses that Colbert had lost interest in the matter. During the Franco-Dutch War (1672–78), the correspondence takes on an enduring routineness, the minister or his assistant mechanically repeating that the habitants must be armed and trained while ignoring the subtext and the worry looming behind the repeated requests for troops. For the colonists had yet to be put to the test. Only once had they been mobilized during these truce years: in 1673 for the construction of Fort Frontenac (Cataraqui) at the entrance to Lake Ontario, an arduous operation requiring the men to carry matériel, including six small cannons, over the rapids.[20] It provoked much grumbling in Montreal, but the governor was pleased to report that some 400 men recruited into the corvées had shown good will and extraordinary endurance.[21] War would demand more.

At long last, in 1683, Versailles consented to send troops. Three naval infantry companies arrived at Quebec that year, and others followed, reaching a total of thirty-five companies or 1,750 men in 1688.[22] The hiatus following the end of the Franco-Dutch War and the Truce of Ratisbon (1684) justified the sending of reinforcements, even if they were perceived as a temporary measure. "Make sure the soldiers and officers understand," wrote the new secretary of the navy, Jean-Baptiste Colbert, the Marquis de Seignelay, to the intendant at Rochefort, "that they were not sent there on a permanent basis, but only to provide prompt relief at the present time, so that La Barre is given the means with which to promptly prevail in the war with the Iroquois."[23] In June 1689, with the outbreak of the Nine Years' War (War of the League of Augsburg), the minister reminded Governor

Frontenac of the militias' importance in the defence of the colony. They must be capable of defending themselves, "especially given that His Majesty wishes to withdraw the troops stationed there as soon as can be managed."[24] Ten years would pass before Versailles implicitly acknowledged that the troops were in Canada to stay, and even so, whenever war gave way to peace, the idea that the colony should take charge of its own defence reappears in the correspondence.[25] Still, no further illusions were harboured. The word *milice* that entered common parlance with the arrival of the regulars reflected the reality of a local reserve corps subordinated to the army.

2. TO HUMILIATE THE IROQUOIS

The two expeditions launched against the Iroquois nations in 1684 and 1687 marked the end of the truce and the official entrance of the militias onto the military stage. These relatively well-documented expeditions will serve to identify certain characteristics found in subsequent campaigns that were also based on the mass mobilization of colonists.

a) The invasions of 1684 and 1687

The 670 men at Fort Frontenac in 1684, and the 804 there in 1687, represented about 21 per cent and 24 per cent, respectively, of the male population aged fifteen and over.[26] Let us be clear: this was not one-fourth of the militia, since neither boys nor old men nor the infirm went to war; it is an abstract measure based on the census categories. In lieu of a precise definition and militia rolls, it allows for comparison of rates of participation from one campaign to the next.[27] The rates for these years were about average. In 1684, the distribution of recruits between city and country accorded with that of the population at large: slightly over three-fourths of them were rural. Men from the government of Montreal were somewhat over-represented at 32 per cent – by the same criterion, they should have supplied one-fourth of the troops.[28] For men from the government of Quebec, who had to travel a longer distance to join the rest of the army, the first campaign lasted two and a half months; the second, three months. The campaign of 1684 took place at harvest time, while the campaign of 1687 encroached on planting time. The intendant thought he could easily solve these problems by forcing those left behind to harvest their neighbours' crops, on pain of prison. The corresponding ordinance of 10 July 1684 was very poorly received in the government of Montreal; a month later, Intendant Jacques de Meulles had to relax the conditions imposed on the harvesters. They would be supplied with tools and provisions out of a fund into which the wealthier townspeople and peasants were expected to pay.[29] From this maladroit intervention emerged what apparently became a well-accepted principle: that non-recruits were expected to bear the cost of absent soldiers' agricultural labours. But this work was not limited to planting and harvesting, as the intendants seemed to have believed. To accomplish everything that needed doing, it would be necessary to find replacements for the absentees and to pay them out of contributions from all residents of the côte. Aside from two later examples, such arrangements have left no traces;[30] they were, however, predicated on the existence of well-established and sufficiently prosperous parishes, which were few in number in the seventeenth century. Finally, an essential piece of information is missing: How many heads of households were among the recruits? If all were single young men still living with their parents, as was to be the case in the mid-eighteenth century, then the rural communities would have fulfilled their obligation at a lower cost.

Every colonial census from 1681 on had a heading for firearms; from 1692 on, there was also one for swords. Although these figures indicate that the parishes had more than enough guns to arm the men who went to war, they may be misleading. In 1682, the governor ordered men without guns to purchase them from merchants; the following year, weapons were ordered from the king and made available at a lower price. Yet despite these precautions, some militiamen showed up at the July 1684 review empty-handed; they were lent weapons that had to be returned after the campaign or paid for within six months if kept or lost. And this intendant was at great pains to recover his advances, as shown by the ordinances of October 1684 and August 1685, backed up by fines and threats of seizure.[31] This scenario repeated in 1686–87, with an order of 500 muskets to be sold on credit before the campaign began; here again, and to the minister's exasperation, recovery of the advances was delayed.[32] This ill will, evinced by the peasants until the very end of the regime, was not engendered by being forced to own a musket – they all had guns at home for hunting and self-defence – but by having to purchase a weapon for use in the king's faraway wars.

To move 1,000 men over a distance of more than 600 kilometres, with the munitions and provisions necessary to maintain such an army, must certainly have been an expensive operation, yet the ministerial correspondence does not address this issue until the campaign of 1684. The unspoken assumption seems to have been that the colony would defray any expenses unconnected with the maintenance of the regular troops.[33] The cost of the Anse à la Famine expedition was 45,368 livres, a trifle compared to later campaigns but an enormous sum from the standpoint of contingency spending.[34] And yet the intendant had made efforts to minimize the king's outlay. There was no question of handing out shoes, shirts, puttees, or other clothing, as would be done systematically after 1744. The militiamen went off to war with the clothes on their backs, and lucky were those who had blankets when the cold September nights rolled around. The intendant also expected them to provide for their own subsistence; if he was not exaggerating, most "had made private arrangements for their provisions."[35] The policy remained the same in 1687, but the recruits apparently showed less willingness to comply in the matter of provisions. Their expenses were ultimately borne in part by the king and in part by the colonists left behind, who were required to contribute to the expedition in one way or another.[36] This typically seventeenth-century approach to war financing is so poorly documented that it has eluded historians. It is not known, for example, how the intendant went about extracting provisions from those who remained in the parishes. He did ask each of the colony's largest merchants to fit out one militiaman at their expense, a procedure that has left no traces, with one apparent exception. On 5 July 1684, a few days before the departure of the Quebec detachment, a merchant of that city named François Hazeur contracted before a notary with a habitant of Grondines named Lavallée, evidently a former soldier, to go to war in place of the man whom his mother-in-law, a Montreal merchant, was "obligated to send." In addition to his equipment – a musket, a blanket, a minot of biscuit, and a jug of aqua-vitae – Lavallée was to receive 250 livres in colonial currency on his return. If rejected on any grounds at the review to be held in Montreal, he would receive only forty livres in compensation for the round trip.[37] These conditions were notably generous. Volunteers could be found for much less, as evidenced by the contracts of replacement signed by two Montreal recruits that same month.[38] This form of taxation of merchants, introduced in

1684 and 1687, appears to have remained in effect until the end of the century and to have been extended to the religious communities. "We were obliged to supply two men, and fit them out and pay them to go to war, and there was no avoiding this," wrote one Ursuline nun about the campaign of 1696.[39] These practices seem to have vanished subsequently.

b) Hardships of the military campaigns

After several years of tranquility, did the population readily accept the resumption of war against the Iroquois? Did Iroquois acts of hostility against the Illinois allies and a few French traders justify, in the eyes of habitants from Beauport or Longueuil, the risk that these offensives might boomerang back against the colony? This seems doubtful, since none of the reasons put forward by the partisans of war affected them directly. In 1684 as in 1687, the announcement of imminent mobilization was coolly received, and the authorities had to publish ordinances – "a manifesto of sorts," as the governor put it – to explain the issues and squelch unrest.[40] The Church's assistance was needed. "We have deemed the success of this enterprise to be of the utmost consequence, not only for the preservation of the colony, but for the good of the religion and the conversion of all the Natives of Canada," explained a pastoral letter of 24 April 1687 ordering the Forty Hours' Devotion and the holding of processions for the success of what the ecclesiastical authorities considered a holy war.[41] Their authors reported that these interventions had a good effect and that the men showed their good will. It would always be thus in campaigns of this type: an initial timid and easily quieted protest movement, after which it was up to each man to make the best of the situation. As everywhere, this colony comprised a minority of boys attracted by war and adventure and by the rigours and prizes that they promised. They would, in subsequent decades, be found among those volunteers who set off in small bands to raid the English settlements. The large militia contingents deployed against the Iroquois gave a rank-and-file fusilier no chance to show off his talents and offered him little opportunity for profit, so these contingents generally consisted of those who would have preferred to stay home. But in 1684, the distinction had yet to be made; the French had yet to embark on partisan warfare, and illusions could still be harboured.

Indeed, there was room for such illusions in the last clause of the contract between Hazeur and his stand-in: "The parties understand that if Mr Lavallée should make any profit or derive any fortune from this voyage, they [Hazeur and Soumande] shall let him have it, Mr Hazeur claiming nothing more than half of one slave, in case Mr Lavallée should succeed in bringing any back."[42]

As may be seen in Appendix A, the militia still accounted for only one part of the colonial armies, which also included the regulars, the domiciliés and Indigenous allies, and sometimes, as in 1687, a battalion of volunteers from the Great Lakes region.[43] The 142 soldiers who took part in the expedition of 1684 and the 843 enumerated in the army of 1687 had just arrived in the colony. Having been recruited in the weeks and months preceding embarkation, they possessed little more military experience than the majority of the colonists. For both groups, the voyage into Iroquois territory proved a nightmare. Very few, most certainly not including the Quebec militiamen, knew how to steer a canoe through rapids; they came in for constant dunkings as a result of their clumsiness, caught fevers, and lost guns and supplies whenever their boats capsized.[44] The losses were so great that the general staff became accustomed to entrusting the king's supplies to experienced, well-paid canoeists. Transportation between Montreal, Fort Frontenac, and the other Great Lakes forts accounted for a large share of the extraordinary expenses incurred by the colonial wars.[45] Another consequence of this practice was to deprive the militia of its most capable men, the ones from Montreal and environs, who would always arrange to be exempted in order to work on the convoys. To avoid drowning, inept canoeists stayed close to the forested bank where the enemy might well lie in ambush. Fear set in as soon as Lake St Louis was crossed.[46] The campaign of 1684 was marred by an illness that put half the militia out of commission and killed eighty, as well as by a shortage of provisions, and both of these eventualities were to recur.[47] As thoroughly as the intendant saw to making provisions, the logistical problems involved in getting them to the army and conserving them would never really be solved. Disease befell the troops again in 1687, the men returning from Niagara specifically, with several being buried along the way.[48] There were also combat casualties: 100 Frenchmen and a dozen Amerindians according to Lahontan, a mere six Frenchmen and five Amerindians according to the official report.[49] Uncertainty and contradictions in the counting of casualties were other constants. The tendency was to amplify enemy casualties and gloss over one's own. Historians have no way of deciding between these conflicting accounts.

c) Militia performance: A training problem

Lieutenant Louis-Henri de Baugy, aide-de-camp of Governor-General Jacques-René Brisay de Denonville, left a journal from the 1687 expedition that was published in 1883 with appendices including the marching orders, and Lahontan inserted into his *Nouveaux voyages* a map of the army's position just before a Seneca ambush threw Denonville's regiments into disorder. Only the major battles of the Seven Years' War are as well documented. These accounts clearly show what could already be surmised from the administrative correspondence: that the militiamen had not, on the whole, received any military training before being sent out. They had not been taught to worm out their muskets; to fire on command and in order, one row or column at a time; to refrain from firing their guns without reason while on the march or encamped; to be silent; to stay clean; to repair their shoes; to ration provisions and munitions – in short, to obey orders. A 50,000-man army would make less noise, wrote Baugy.[50] Since the regulars were just as hopeless, the enemy had only to fire off a few musket shots in order to send the 1,600 men scattering in all directions. The vanguard of Amerindians and voyageurs stood fast, making it possible for the commander to reassemble his troops. Meanwhile, the Iroquois, in a characteristic tactic, had speedily given up the fight and abandoned their positions after burning their village; the French set about destroying their corn, beans, and squash with great swipes of their swords and ravaging two other equally deserted villages.[51] It was an on-the-job apprenticeship, coming rather too late to transform a crowd of stirred-up peasants into a disciplined army.

By the end of the seventeenth century, it had long been standard wisdom that the military art is a technique of subordination. The purpose of drills – repetition of ostensibly pointless exercises – is to instill reflexes of automatic obedience. Every officer knew the value of this. Poorly drilled men who thought before acting could make the best enterprise, even one carried out in the deep woods, go awry.[52] And by all accounts, exercises designed to teach the colonists to maintain their muskets and to avoid firing on each other while advancing in formation would not have been pointless either. The Carignan men of earlier years were aging and surely accounted for only a small minority of militia battalions in the 1680s; these battalions were largely composed of colonial-born young men along with immigrants hired as servants in the preceding decade. The gap between this militia and the colonial army of Versailles's dreams was considerable, and the governors who began by sharing those illusions were soon disabused of them. No sooner had he arrived at Quebec than La Barre found himself setting out with 1,200 seasoned colonists to winter in Iroquois territory. A year later he was calling for soldiers: "I need a corps of men who obey, whereas the youths of this land are neither drilled in war, nor capable of the obedience they could acquire through a bit of service and experience." In the aftermath of the sorry expedition of 1684, which ended in talks with the enemy, barely a shot having been fired, he thought it would be better to scrap the militia altogether.[53] Denonville, drawing on his predecessor's experience, was more realistic from the outset, opting to leave the habitants on their land, use only those with canoeing skills for the transports, and reserve war for the soldiers.[54]

To explain the absence of a military drill system, one might be tempted to invoke the dispersed nature of the inhabited area and the difficulties associated with conducting drills in the countryside, but since the urban militias were apparently no better prepared, another explanation must be found. The real question is undoubtedly: How many hours per week and days per year of training did a reserve corps need in order to be ready to move at the first alert? The answer falls within the domain of military specialists, but the drills prescribed by the minister's instructions surely did not suffice. This leads to a second, crucial question: How much was the administration willing to spend in order to keep the colonial population on a war footing? To this we know the answer: not a penny.

d) The invasions of 1693 and 1696 and the peace of 1701

Twice more would French arms invade the Iroquois towns. The offensive of 1693 against the Mohawks (Agniers) took place from January to March. Three hundred militiamen, most of them recruited from the Quebec area, made up half the contingent. The general staff did not unanimously approve of such winter campaigns, which demanded uncommon endurance, thus limiting the number of men who could participate. Moreover, the assailants were all but certain to find none but women, children, and old men in the Indigenous villages, since this was hunting season. That being the case, historians face a choice between two hypotheses as to why winter was chosen for these campaigns: so that prisoners could be taken without doing battle or, as Bacqueville believed, because the warriors would be forced to come home and fight to protect their families.[55] This is indeed what happened in 1693, but there is no evidence that the colonial strategists expected such a fierce riposte. On the run, caught off-guard by the thaw, famished, the troop abandoned most of its captives along the way and reached Montreal more dead than alive. The "limited success" (to use a typical euphemism) of the venture was blamed on the domiciliés among the party.[56] The hardships endured, not to mention the numberless victims, left bitter memories in the côtes of Quebec in particular, where the plot described in the introduction to this book was dreamed up by a group of youths during the recruitment campaign of 1696.[57] This campaign, targeting the Onondagas and Oneidas, comprised more than 2,000 men, including 800 militiamen. Although taking place earlier in the season, it followed the general pattern of the Tracy campaign of 1666: exhausting efforts to reach villages abandoned by their inhabitants at the approach of the French; a few days to ravage crops and burn what had yet to be burned; a generally uneventful return voyage; no unpleasant surprises like those that had occurred in 1687. In short, a success that "even exceeded my expectations," wrote the governor, who had not set the bar very high.[58]

Although the first French attack against the Iroquois, that of the autumn of 1666, had surprised and marked the Mohawks, subsequent invasions did not have the repercussions attributed to them by certain contemporaries and by historians in their wake.[59] In the aftermath of the 1687 expedition, the Iroquois resumed their offensive against the colony, regularly ravaging its western reaches for the next ten years. The French defended themselves as best they could, several times beating back their bands of warriors, as we shall see. But neither were these small campaigns decisive. The circumstances that forced the Five Nations to give up on their ambitions and sign an enduring peace treaty in 1701 are multiple and complex; nevertheless, recent scholarship has demonstrated that what drove the Iroquois to this extreme was not the colony's military power but rather the sustained harassment and stinging defeats inflicted on them by French-allied peoples from the Great Lakes region. At the end of the day, the French victory over these long-standing adversaries was diplomatic more than it was military.[60]

3 . A CAREER PATH FOR THE NOBLES

Gentlemen had long been welcomed with open arms in the colony, their presence imparting an aura of respectability and permanence to these faraway trading posts. Most of the first to arrive had been merchants and sailors. They took the reins of the colony's nascent commerce and government and derived enough material and intangible benefit to want to settle for good, even if they did not amass large fortunes. Later on, Seignelay would put pressure on the officers of the Carignan regiment to stay in New France. Until the 1670s, the administration likewise sought to augment the colonial nobility by encouraging well-born individuals to emigrate and by granting letters of nobility to six or seven old residents of the colony. Historians have descried in these decisions a desire to solidify the social order by expanding the seigneurial class at its apex, but this would appear to be a confusion of means with ends.[61] This policy was inspired by more immediate practical concerns having to do with the military thrust that the minister wanted to impart to the colony. In exchange for favours granted, the nobility would make itself useful by overseeing the colonists in their role as soldiers. Each seigneury would form a military unit, and the seigneurs would regain, in Canada, their traditional role as warlords. Valour being the natural mark of their station, every noble – even one who had not passed through the ranks of the king's armies – was thought capable of taking on this responsibility.[62] In 1671, Intendant Talon was pleased to note the arrival at Quebec of five gentlemen of Poitou, Saintonge (present-day Charente and Charente-Maritime), and Normandy: "If people of this quality readily take this route, Canada will soon be filled with persons capable of sustaining it."[63]

The enthusiasm soon dimmed. Duchesneau, Talon's successor, was the first to raise the alarm, in 1679, and for the next decade the poverty and delinquency of the nobles took up considerable room in administrative correspondence: they were incapable of subsisting on their seigneuries, too poor to do honour to their station; they had large families that let their sons run wild in the woods and associate with the common people, sowing disorder in the colony. Blatant examples do exist, but until a comprehensive study of the status and behaviour of this social group has been completed, prudence must be observed.[64] The malaise was real but not universal. Certain nobles were high-ranking members of the commercial elite; others did good business as fur traders; a few found jobs as military or court officers. However, such positions were few, most of the seigneuries had yet to produce income, and the small favours meted out by the king to those who gave up their commissions in order to do his bidding were not enough to raise children and earn a living.[65] Beyond their immediate money problems, those who had a name to lose were inhabited by the fear of watching their families disintegrate through mediocre marriages and menial labour, their good names besmirched if it was impossible to preserve them with some form of public distinction. Nobility requires public repute, tangible signs of distinction, broader societal acknowledgment than what the seigneury offered, and in 1680 its existence in the colony looked to be compromised.

Officer positions in the militia – lacking royal commissions or wages – were no solution, not least because as long as peace prevailed between Canada and its neighbours, there were no opportunities for these men to distinguish themselves. Well aware of the needy nobles' lot, Intendant de Meulles, and subsequently Governor Denonville, proposed remedies that were favourably received by Versailles. The king awarded scholarships in the Gardes-Marine (the Ancien Régime's naval officer school) at Rochefort to two young colonial gentlemen each year, a measure that did not resolve the problem of the sons' education at a stroke but did hold out a semblance of hope to these families.[66] A gateway to a naval career, away from the colony, it broke their isolation and strengthened their ties to France. Another proposal was for the formation of a Canadian volunteer corps to discipline "the children of our nobility" and give them the means to earn a living.[67] Although approved in principle in 1686, the plan was for some reason modified along the way: The company formed in the autumn of 1687 was not composed of idle young colonial gentlemen but of 120 voyageurs of various backgrounds living in the Great Lakes region. They earned a soldier's pay, six sols per day, while the four lieutenants who led them earned twenty-four sols. The fund was not renewed, and the company was disbanded after a year; an attempt by the governor of Montreal to revive and expand the project in 1690 proved abortive.[68]

Too brief to be conclusive, the experience is interesting in and of itself, for it shows that the colonial military system was still capable of evolving toward new forms of participation, as occurred in the neighbouring English colonies. In New England – Connecticut, for instance – the militia functioned mainly as a defensive force and a reserve army. For scouting and intelligence purposes, the provincial assemblies preferred to raise and pay for volunteer companies led by notables, which were demobilized at the end of each campaign. Elite ranger companies, such as the one that was to acquit itself well during the Seven Years' War, fall into this category, but other units distinct from the militia proper came into existence from the seventeenth century onward.[69] In Canada, the presence of regulars impeded the militia from evolving toward more onerous forms that would have been more efficient in terms of recruitment.

a) Rescuing the Canadian nobility: The clamour for commissions

The third proposal for saving the Canadian nobles was to offer them commissions in the colonial (naval) regulars. The suggestion was made and approved, at least in principle, with the arrival of the first companies. Since these companies arrived with their own officers, local candidates would have to wait for spaces to open up in the wake of departures, deaths, and promotions, auguring a gradual, limited integration of a few selected subjects. But the colony was impatient and it had the governor's ear, and he proceeded to accelerate the process by using his power to fill vacant positions. One gets the impression that the minister, who had certainly not foreseen the importunity, more or less adopted a hands-off stance, even if it meant reclaiming this authority after the war.[70] In sending these new troops to Canada, Seignelay was attempting to repeat the Carignan experience, and he gave orders for soldiers who wished to marry and settle in the colony to be discharged with a year's salary.[71] These departures, added to deaths and to invalids sent home to France, added up to a deficit of 450 men for the thirty-five companies in early 1689. Versailles decided to reduce this latter number to twenty-eight, meaning, in principle, the elimination of twenty-one officer positions (three per company), a measure that threatened to jeopardize the integration process.[72] But the governor kept these reformed officers in the service and, by doubling each rank in the hierarchy, managed to retain and even increase the number of these positions for more than ten years. Soldiers now rose from the rank of half-pay ensign to ensign, from half-pay lieutenant to lieutenant, and from half-pay captain to captain.[73] The path was long but open to a larger number of people. To justify his system, Frontenac argued that war as practised in the colony – by small, widely dispersed units – dictated a higher officer-to-soldier ratio than in the European armies, which fought in battalions, and that the larger number of ranks through which the men had to pass gave officers a better opportunity to learn their profession.[74]

Despite the influx of a thousand recruits, the number of soldiers dwindled during the Nine Years' War, and when peace returned, new discharges of soldiers wishing to settle in the colony gave the coup de grâce to the companies.[75] Around 1699, troop numbers stood at 800 instead of a nominal force of 1,400, and Versailles ordered another reform, letting Quebec choose the method. Opinions were divided. Some, like the intendant, proposed to reduce the number of companies even further, but the general staff imposed another solution: The twenty-eight companies would each now comprise thirty soldiers instead of fifty, thus leaving the officer corps untouched.[76] This structure was to remain in place until 1750. At the turn of the century, the number of supernumerary officers decreased. Appointments of half-pay captains and lieutenants ceased, but Vaudreuil insisted on retaining the half-pay ensigns, then called *petits enseignes*, to facilitate the integration of officers' sons into the corps. Versailles eventually gave in and in 1722 created the rank of second ensign to regularize their status, bringing the number of officers to four per company, for a total of 112, to which a few staff officers must be added.[77] The gentlemen of the colony were well represented in the officer corps, which had offered positions to fifty-five of them by 1695, not counting those who served in other colonies or on the king's ships. From 30 per cent, the proportion rose to 45 per cent in 1722 and to 75 per cent in the 1750s.[78] By 1700, officers were largely being recruited within the colony, and it was only a matter of time before the first contingent sent from France began to fade in importance.

Although awarded to a small group of individuals, the fifty or so commissions doled out between 1685 and 1695 did not meet all expectations. Those who had to wait, the youngest men in particular, were authorized to serve in the corps as cadets. In the French army, cadets were sons who held the rank of soldiers without making a commitment or receiving any pay; they could resign whenever they wished.[79] Naval cadets enjoyed the same privilege and received wages into the bargain.[80] A list of cadets from this period would undoubtedly reveal a large, shifting, multifarious group, for until the end of the War of the Spanish Succession, admittance was an informal and rather haphazard procedure. The commissary at Montreal, François Clairambault d'Aigremont, wrote in 1715 that more than ninety cadets had been admitted into the companies in recent years; he requested a regulation to fix the number of candidates and oblige them to do an ordinary soldier's work.[81] Under pressure to prove themselves, the cadets were continually being detached from the corps to accompany war parties. While valour was an undeniable factor in obtaining a commission, birth and well-connected patrons were at least as important. Be that as it may, the seventeenth century was a time when many less-favoured candidates also had a chance. If one considers, for example, that 54 per cent of the officers on Louis XIV's ships were commoners by birth, there must surely have been some hope for young colonial townspeople.[82] At this remove, however – and contrary to the conventional wisdom – it can be seen that commoners' chances were smaller in Canada and that for want of high birth, these cadets must have comprised a large number of officers *manqué*.[83] In the eighteenth century, the group averaged even younger, and its ranks closed even more. Versailles had given in and lowered the age of eligibility from sixteen or seventeen to fifteen, so the governor proffered reassurances. He was being quite exacting in his choice of candidates, he wrote to the minister, offering these spaces to officers' sons as a form of recompense. "This succession in military positions from fathers to sons is the source of nobility; it is what improves families and, for the king, trains men on whom he can rely."[84] The royal ordinance of 1731, in creating the rank of gentleman cadet (*cadet à l'aiguillette*), consolidated these provisions. Selection henceforth took place at the time of admission rather than at the end of the apprenticeship, and the number was set at two cadets for each of the twenty-eight companies.[85] A young recruit began by serving as a junior cadet (*cadet-soldat*) before being promoted to gentleman cadet, assuring him of a second ensign commission at some future point.[86] The way was long, but the goal would eventually be reached. The fast track – direct accession to a commission after a brief sojourn in France, in the Gardes-Marine, for example – was reserved for a few privileged souls. Since opportunities to go to war had dwindled, the governors learned to use cadets in other capacities: as informants to warn of plotting or sedition among soldiers and as garrison adjutants.[87] In this latter capacity, they often commanded the militias in carrying out various and sundry tasks.

Before the regulars opened their ranks to them, the nobles of the colony served as volunteers on various expeditions, including those of 1684 and 1687. Subsequently, those who had not been selected during the first wave of promotions, and who did not wish to relin- quish their liberty by joining the troops, continued to volunteer for war parties and other campaigns in the hope of one day having their worth recognized. When the volunteers were "persons of quality," they appear in the military accounts alongside officers and cadets, and their deaths or injuries were reported. Several saw privateering as a means of gaining access to a commission of some sort, with the navy if possible or in the infantry companies failing that.[88] Few succeeded. Several eighteenth-century officers sent their sons to fight the Foxes and the Chickasaws as volunteers so that they would gain preferential admission to the cadets.[89] With such a rigid, competitive corps, no illusions subsisted as to the possibility of circumventing channels of promotion.

The officer-to-soldier ratio in the autonomous naval infantry units maintained in Canada (known as the *franches compagnies*) grew constantly between 1689 and 1750 as the size of the corps dwindled, rising from one officer per thirteen soldiers in 1690 to one for every eight soldiers in 1700; from 1720 to 1750, it held steady at around one to seven. And if cadets are counted among the officers – since they did, after all, fulfill the same functions – then the ratio was only one to five, or even fewer, during the first half of the eighteenth century.[90] With a few exceptions, these officers and aspiring officers were scions of the four dozen noble families that had settled in New France between 1636 and 1668 or the nine families ennobled after their arrival by Louis XIV, or else they were naval officers who had arrived after 1683, a hundred of whom put down roots in the colony. (Circa 1700, this social category may have accounted for 3 per cent of the population, a proportion that declined subsequently.[91]) As soon as the door opened a crack, the colonial nobles hurled them- selves into the race to earn a commission. Such unanimity is rather rare; noblemen elsewhere might harp on their war experience and demand a monopoly on higher-ranking military positions, but they had long since learned to diversify their activities. In Canada, the nobility, who had emerged from motley origins and did not have to scour the past to find merchants among their ancestors, went about transforming themselves into a military order of sorts. Consider the case of Charles Legardeur de Tilly, whose nobility dated back to

1510. He held lands and titles in the côte of Caen and possessed the enthusiasm for maritime speculation that characterized Norman gentlemen at the start of the modern era. In 1636, Charles went to Canada with nine other members of his family and went on to play an important role in the colony's commerce and government. Having retired from business in 1663 without having made his fortune, he sat on the Conseil Souverain and attempted to find situations for his fifteen children. Six of the seven boys embraced soldiering, half in France in the navy, the other half in the colonial troops.[92] This was far from the only such case. The sons of ennobled merchants Le Moyne, Boucher, and Denys all sought military employment. Officers arriving from France as members of the Carignan regiment or the naval troops were often the younger sons of old families of the robe in which the office passed to the eldest. For them, Canada was the starting point of a new family tradition in which older sons were preferentially destined for a military career, as Jean Chagniot notes.[93]

As long as the history of the Canadian nobility remains to be written, such observations will have to remain much too vague. If a survey of the genealogical works could serve to reconstruct families and help to identify those sons who opted to pursue a different career, then it would be possible to determine the exact proportion of nobles in military employment from 1684 to 1760 and thus to decide whether there is reason to believe that this proportion peaked at the start of the period.[94] It was then that circumstances aligned to spur the nobles along this path. In the background were poverty, isolation, and demoralization, the circumstances sketched out above; in the foreground were continual war and the constantly expanding employment options it offered.[95] The striving for material security was at least as important as the honour attaching to service to the king. An officer's commission did not bring riches, but it did offer a somewhat better-than-average living and the satisfaction of being able to settle at least one son.[96] In the eighteenth century, circumstances were different. Increasingly attractive agricultural and seigneurial revenues, new commercial opportunities, and the development of governmental and religious services gave rise to new options. The connection between nobility and military service became looser, but the pressure to obtain commissions did not let up, for the size of the noble class increased with each generation and peace time yielded very few new positions. This state of affairs led Intendant Gilles Hocquart to opine in 1737 that every gentleman or officer's son wished to enter the service, which is laudable, but that many sought this employment for the salary it afforded, which is less so. "We have nothing to offer those who do not succeed," he wrote, suggesting that they be allowed to serve in France.[97] In fact, the gentleman cadets and ensigns had grown weary of waiting and had already begun fanning out to the other colonies, where they had better chances of rising quickly through the ranks; first to Île Royale and Louisiana and somewhat later to the West Indies.[98] Incapable of supplying the colonial army of Talon's dreams, one that could come to the rescue of the southern Americas, Canada became a breeding ground for officers.[99]

b) Criticism

The integration of colonial nobles into the regulars took place to the detriment of the militia, depriving it of the leaders it was initially supposed to have received. This was as plain as day to those who felt stymied in their aspirations and afforded a good pretext for complaining of the governors' powers. Following the Peace of Ryswick (1697), the rumour of an imminent reform of the troops gave the officers a shudder. If the companies were cut down by half, which of them would lose their jobs? For François Lefebvre Duplessy Faber, who had come to Canada in 1687 at the head of a naval infantry company, the answer was clear. He confided his "feeling" to his supporter, Sébastien Le Prestre de Vauban: "They should begin this reform with all the officers who cannot but be regarded as militiamen." He clarified his thinking as follows:

> The governors never did worse than to pack the king's troops with such a large number of Canadian officers; besides, they weakened the forces of the colony in this manner by adding to them families of all sorts, parts of which were assigned to the defence of the colony and other parts, as needed, to lead the militias; and, by having made them regular officers, we weakened these forces by as many men of quality or duty as would have been sent from France to fill these positions and who might have settled in the colony, thus contributing to its increase.[100]

The "Canadians" he meant were not necessarily natives of the colony but two specific groups: the descendants of old merchant families such as the Le Moynes, who had had time to acquire some

wealth, and the Carignan officers, who had been given "very fine
seigneuries on which they can live in luxury."[101] These confidential
remarks betray the bitterness of an aging officer who had come to
Canada in the hope of rapid advancement and had been unsuccess-
fully requesting an officer position for ten years.[102] But beyond his
personal grievances, Duplessy Faber was expressing a feeling of
injustice no doubt felt by every one of the naval officers who had
married and settled in the colony in the late seventeenth century
without receiving any enticement or quid pro quo, be it land or grat-
ification, as their predecessors had. Not counting five gentlemen who
had arrived as soldiers or cadets, forty-two of the 105 officers who
came between 1683 and 1688 (40 per cent) would remain in the
colony, as compared to 30 per cent of the Carignan officers, and the
needs of the naval officers were just as pressing, for in many cases
venality had forced them to give up the army for unpaid positions in
the ports and colonies.[103] Between 1690 and 1749, fifty more officers
of the naval troops would augment this contingent of émigrés. Most
of them being mere youths when they arrived, they were obliged to
get in line with the other local candidates and settle in for a long
wait.[104] The opposition between local officers and officers arriving
from France did not last long: the two groups were soon melded by
marriage, and only individual and familial rivalries persisted in this
increasingly homogeneous assemblage.[105]

The militarization of the colonial elite elicited other, much more
perfidious remarks. In the late seventeenth century, there was a pervasive rumour to the effect that certain people did not want the war
against the Iroquois to end for fear of losing their place if the king
were to withdraw his troops. Neither, it was said, did the governor
long for peace, since he would lose his authority over "the good
families" along with the right to make military appointments.[106]
François-Madeleine-Fortuné Ruette d'Auteuil, the disgraced former
attorney general of the Conseil Souverain, took as a given that military power hindered the colony's peaceful development. Nothing
obliged the king to maintain troops at such great expense during
peace time, he wrote in 1719, were it not for the willfulness of the
governor, the intendant, and the officers, who each had their motives
and interests. On these grounds, he suggested a general reform "as
was done for the Carignan regiment, provided that the soldiers settle
and marry in the colony, and the officers are put on half-pay as
and when they are required to discipline the militias where they are

quartered." These militias would then be able to defend the colony effectively in case of attack. Ruette d'Auteuil further proposed to abolish the Montreal and Trois-Rivières officer positions, shorten the governors' mandates so as to curtail favoritism, and halt the construction of forts that the king and the population neither needed nor could afford.[107] His was a lone voice, no doubt, for the Canadian context, unlike that of the Caribbean, was unconducive to the emergence of such unabashedly anti-militaristic views.[108] Nevertheless, his opinion, like the others cited above, reminds us that the colonial officers' interests must not be conflated with those of society at large and that contemporary observers knew the difference.

Years ago, W.J. Eccles stressed the importance of what he called the military "establishment" of New France and summarized the stages in its formation.[109] I have drawn in part on the same data in order to shed light on two peculiarities. The first is that this officer corps was relatively hermetic from the outset: as an entrance criterion, birth trumped merit. The nine titles of nobility awarded in the colony during the seventeenth century rewarded an initial generation of merchants who had done their part for settlement and the rise of commerce, and it was their sons who later obtained officer commissions. The Hertels – the last to be ennobled, in 1716, for their military exploits – were not representative but rather the exception to the rule.[110] While commissions did not create nobility, they consolidated it; they served to erect clearer boundaries around a group that, without this tangible recognition, would have swelled to such an extent as to lose all specificity. The ultimate effect of these commissions was to bind together all the old and new families who had access to them. The second peculiarity is that more than the urge to serve or the military ethos evoked by Eccles, what impelled the nobles to join the troops was the striving for employment – thus their relative disinterest in the unpaid positions initially set aside for them in the militia.

c) Militia officers in the seventeenth century

In the 1670s and 1680s, the social divide that would come to separate regular officers from militia officers in the eighteenth century was not yet in place. There are essentially two sources, neither of them satisfactory, that can offer some insight into militia organization and hierarchy during this period: the battalion reviews for the campaigns of 1684, 1687, and 1696 and references to militia officers in notarial acts.[111] There were thirteen companies in 1684 and sixteen in 1687, each comprising two commissioned and two non-commissioned officers. The former's names appear on the 1684 roll, while the 1687 roll only mentions captains' names. These companies were regional formations comprised of militiamen from a single urban parish or a few adjacent rural parishes. They were grouped into three or four battalions approximately corresponding to the same geographical divisions.[112]

Let us begin with a consideration of the urban militias, whose prestige and tradition, inherited from the era of the *franches compagnies*, were not shared by the rural militias. Before the arrival of the naval regulars, the captains of Quebec, Trois-Rivières, and Montreal had been invited to participate in various consultative assemblies and even to sit on councils of war alongside the five staff officers when necessary to achieve quorum.[113] When he travelled to Lake Ontario in June and July 1673, the governor went as far as to entrust the "command of the fort and city of Quebec, and of the surrounding habitations," as well as of "all the habitants and militias to be found in the said expanse," to Charles Legardeur de Tilly, who had been appointed "colonel of the first regiment of the militia of this colony" for the occasion.[114] Even though the militias were not then formed into a regiment, the rank was flattering and was to endure. René-Louis Chartier de Lotbinière, councillor and lieutenant-general of the provost court, who succeeded Tilly, commanded the "Quebec regiment" in the campaign of 1684. The lieutenant of "the first company [*compagnie colonelle*] of the Quebec town militia" was a merchant, Antoine Gourdeau *dit* Beaulieu, who also took part in the 1684 expedition and no doubt the 1687 one as well. Paul Dupuy de Lisloye, an ensign from the Carignan regiment who had become special lieutenant to the provost court, served as a major in the two campaigns.

The officers of Trois-Rivières and Montreal also belonged to the local nobility, derived equally from commerce and law. The captain of the Montreal militia was for many years Charles Le Moyne, a rich merchant ennobled in 1668 for his success as an interpreter and as the governors' principal negotiator with the Five Nations. He commanded his company in the expeditions of 1666 and again in that of 1684.[115] His brother-in-law Michel Messier, a merchant of lesser stature, was a lieutenant in the 1670s. The bailiff of the seigneury,

Jean-Baptiste Migeon de Branssat, replaced him in the following decade but did not participate in the 1684 campaign.[116] Another gentleman and officer of justice, king's prosecutor Jacques-Alexis de Fleury Deschambault, was a captain later promoted to colonel in the Montreal militia at the end of the century. He had taken part in the 1684 campaign as an adjutant of the Quebec "regiment" and commanded the Montreal battalion in the expedition of 1696.[117] Trois-Rivières was the home of another ennobled merchant family, the Godefroys, who headed up the local militia. It seems clear that commissions in the urban militias stroked the vanity of the colony's well-established families during this period. Those who could did not hesitate to accompany their men to war, confident that their services would be recognized. Yet in the early eighteenth century – suddenly and as if by mutual agreement – the nobles ceded these posts to the merchants, and from then on the honorific dimension of the institution took precedence over the military dimension. How can this turnabout be explained, other than as the result of a defensive reflex? The nobility sought to distance themselves from the militia so as not to afford any justification to those who might have wanted to confine them to it. They wanted to assert their right to military positions more firmly at a time when there was talk of their being deprived of them.

Nor did the nobles ever evince the same interest in leading the rural militias. Many of them did not live on their own land, and those who did took little interest in offering military training to their *censitaires*. The formation of officer-led militia companies began in 1673 with the looming threat of a Dutch attack.[118] The first mentions of militia officers in the notarial records date from 1676, and the rarity of these references in subsequent years indicates that the institution had yet to be entrenched in all the côtes before the end of the century.[119] Nevertheless, the social profile of these officers had already taken on what would be its characteristic eighteenth-century form: Most were pioneering peasants of the parish or merchants, while a few were owners of seigneuries and arrière-fiefs from the same social stratum. Most had no military experience. During the expeditions of 1684 and 1687, governors La Barre and Denonville called on erstwhile Carignan officers, and other nobles familiar with the profession of arms, to lead the habitants from the côtes to war. Two-thirds of them did not live in the same parish or seigneury as the men in their company. One such was René Legardeur de Beauvais of Montreal, who headed the Batiscan militia; another was Pierre-Noël Legardeur de Tilly of Quebec, who substituted for Étienne Lessard, its nominal captain, as commander of the Beaupré militia.[120] Only three seigneurs belonging to the colonial elite – Boucher, Juchereau, and de Suève – marched with their *censitaires*, and this does not imply that they shouldered the responsibilities of militia officers at other times.

Officers in the côtes were not, however, absent from the campaigns of the seventeenth century and as junior officers were entitled to recognition from the general staff; thus, for example, the troop review of 1684 includes the militia lieutenants' names. Some, like the captain of the Côte-de-Beaupré, took their role as military leaders seriously. The account book of the Sainte-Anne church contains the following text: "Received, the sum of 40 [livres] from Sieur Noel Gaignon and other youths who accompanied him during the campaign of sixteen hundred ninety-six, after a solemn thanksgiving mass in honour of St. Anne, which they asked to be sung in this Church."[121]

These characteristics were already fading in importance. After the turn of the century, militia officers appear to have ceased to hold any rank during military operations. In wartime, they served as soldiers alongside all the other habitants under regular officers, cadets, and sometimes noncoms. Intendant Jacques Raudot, wishing to enhance the institution's military character and the militia captains' authority, proposed in 1707 that they be made sergeants and paid the salary commensurate with this rank. Like similar suggestions in later years, this one met with opposition from the regular officers and came to nothing.[122] Deprived of their structural autonomy when the time came to go to war, these militias ceased to function as geographical formations and became an undifferentiated pool of recruits. Instead of departing and returning with Sieur Gaignon, the youths of Sainte-Anne-de-Beaupré would be scattered into various units of shifting dimensions, commanded by men they did not know.[123] The genesis of this development was the decision to recruit officers for the *franches compagnies* in the colony itself. The policy was different in the Caribbean, where an effort was made to keep a barrier between the French regulars and colonial society – by forbidding officers from owning homes, for example. Even if these rules were indifferently obeyed, the principle remained. As a result, the militias of the "islands" retained their primitive territorial organization and came to be perceived, under the control of the large planters, as the defence arm of civil society.[124] In the English colonies, long bereft of regular troops, the militia represented a local force with which governors had to reckon.[125] Canada stood in stark contrast as a place where the militia did not form an autonomous military corps and had no political existence of its own.[126]

4

Three Wars (1687–1744)

Before the summer 1687 campaign against the Senecas, Louis Ataria, an Iroquois from Sault-Saint-Louis (present-day Kahnawake, QC) and the godson of Louis XIV, warned Denonville that he who pokes around in a wasp's nest must crush them all at once or risk being stung.[1] No sooner had the troops returned to their homes than reports were received of attacks on the scattered settlements in the government of Montreal. In the years to come, not one but three wars, each with its own history and chronology, would overlap in northeastern North America: the one beginning in 1688 between the New England colonists and the French-backed Abenaki confederacy, which ended with a precarious peace in 1699, only to resume in 1703; the one pitting the Iroquois confederacy against the French-allied Algonquin nations and against the French directly as of 1687, which ended with the Great Peace of 1701; and the Nine Years' War, or the "English War" as it was called in the colony, which obeyed the European calendar.[2] During these years, defensive manoeuvres in the towns and rural areas of New France bled into offensives against the Iroquois and the English settlements of Newfoundland, Hudson Bay, and to the south of the colony. The treaty of neutrality signed by the Five Nations gave the next war, that of the Spanish Succession, a different feel; it was slower, more mercantile, and more concentrated on the maritime frontiers. While nearly every spring arrived with rumours of invasion, the Canadians got off with no more than a good scare, and those with a taste for adventure travelled far in search of it. After Utrecht, war receded even further. The occasional detachment sent by the colony to put down Indigenous revolts along the Mississippi barely disturbed the tranquility that had set in along the St Lawrence.

The list of military movements presented in the appendices to this book reflects the bias of my sources, which boil down to the governors' and intendants' correspondence augmented by the occasional first-hand account.[3] In their reports to Versailles, the administrators emphasized those engagements in which regular officers and other people of rank were involved. The most inconsequential engagement merited a detailed account as long as Sieur So-and-So had been there and not disgraced himself. Meanwhile, a clash involving only peasants, so many of which occurred in the colony in the early 1690s, got no more than a vague mention in passing: "The enemy made numerous incursions into our côtes." The bias is even more blatant with regard to the majority of detachments of Indigenous people, whether domiciliés or allies, who were not accompanied by officers; all these merited no more than "Our Natives continued to harass the settlements" of Boston or Orange (present-day Albany, NY). The authorities knew full well that these movements were both the shield and the spearhead of the colony, and they did everything they could to foster the warriors' loyalty and ardour. But when the time came to recount "the most notable happenings in Canada since the departure of the ships," Indigenous operations formed an indistinct backdrop, a side note to French exploits. Moreover, a choice had to be made among the many military events taking place in Acadia, Newfoundland, Hudson Bay, and Louisiana: In general, only those to which Canada contributed, plus those that were part of a single strategy and had direct and immediate repercussions for the colony's security – for instance, the attacks against New England by the Penobscots and the Kennebec Abenakis – were retained.

Nor was there any kind of standard format in which to present operations that attracted the administrators' attention. In some instances, there are precise figures for each well-identified category of participants, while in others there is only a round number of soldiers, officers, and militiamen combined: "a party of 200 Frenchmen and Natives." The stereotype of the greatly outnumbered heroes – a handful of brave warriors against hundreds of foes – is typical of the era's military discourse. The usual procedure was to exaggerate the number of adversaries, but it cannot be ruled out that French forces, and particularly Indigenous contingents, were underestimated as well.[4] The English sources are even less reliable: They too tend to overstate the enemy forces and to blur the distinction between French and Indigenous attackers.

The chronological lists presented in the appendices, with all their gaps and imperfections, serve as the basis for the analysis that follows, which distinguishes among three types of military operations: defensive manoeuvres carried out around the towns and in the rural areas of the colony, small detachments or parties sent to attack the enemy on his territory, and larger-scale offensives.

1. DEFENSIVE MANOEUVRES

a) Iroquois attacks and life in the forts

In the decade from 1687 to 1697, the inhabitants of the western part of the colony were the target of a sequence of raids that interrupted communication and farm work, producing many casualties and a great deal of material damage. The number of Iroquois incursions rose to a peak between 1689 and 1692 and declined after that. The parishes took advantage of a lull in 1694 to disinter bodies from their temporary resting places and give them proper burials.[5] The failure of peace talks in 1695 led to a recrudescence of hostilities, but attacks dwindled. Enemy bands generally made their appearance around planting time and remained in the vicinity of the côtes until autumn. True to tradition, they did not make war in winter. In addition, their warriors were no longer as advantageously positioned. Fifty years earlier, they had all but had the run of the St Lawrence, whereas now they had to take the colony from behind by more circuitous routes, walking longer distances at greater risk. To enter the colony, they had to follow the Richelieu, Saint-François, and Ottawa rivers and their extensions into the Rivière-des-Mille-Îles and the Rivière-des-Prairies. This constraint limited their ability to manoeuvre, and people living downriver of Trois-Rivières slept soundly. But upriver, the situation was critical, and the colony's defences were far from adequate.

To understand why the colony had been slow to mount a defence, it should be recalled that land development had thus far been left to private initiative by seigneurs and later by colonists. They had, of course, heard stories of the old Iroquois wars and the dangers experienced by the previous generation but refused to believe that history might repeat itself. Most seigneurs were not men of great means; many did not even live on their land. Few took the trouble to protect their property. Montreal offers a good illustration of this state

of mind. The post had turned into a large, sprawling town facing
the river and the surrounding countryside. The Sulpician seminary,
assisted by its bailiff, concerned itself with the planning of streets and
buildings, ignoring security issues almost entirely.[6] In former times,
the Sulpicians had granted a group of arrière-fiefs around the western
perimeter of the island that were expected to serve as a rampart for
the most exposed part of the seigneury.[7] The owners installed rather
makeshift palisaded stores for the Indigenous clientele, but these
lacked enough employees and arms to defend themselves, much less
prevent the enemy from entering. A store as fortified as the one built
by Charles Le Moyne in his Chateauguay seigneury on the south
shore of Montreal – a post-and-beam structure with two thicknesses
of mortar-filled boards, set within a two-arpent enclosure – was very
much the exception.[8] Not far from there, Kahnawake, the region's
second-largest agglomeration, nearly as populous as Montreal, sat
poorly guarded behind a dilapidated stockade. Most exposed were
the peasants: The houses ranged along the St Lawrence or one of its
tributaries were at least 120 metres apart, and distances increased
where concessions were wider or land clearing not as far advanced.
The danger always came from the forest, which began just in back
of the cultivated land. Wooden houses and barns did not withstand
attacks; their thatched or boarded roofs caught fire in less time than
it took to run away.

The royal administration, now more conscious of the perils to
which it was subjecting the colony, took matters in hand. The governor of Montreal put the habitants to work, expediting the process by
augmenting them with soldiers. The fifteen-foot-high stakewall completed in 1688 delimited a wide area around the city to accommodate encampments of refugees in their hundreds. The stockade was
protected by a moat and reinforced by guard houses and a number
of platforms for what appear to have been considerable quantities
of artillery. The construction of a wooden redoubt on a small hill in
1693, later to be contained within the expanded palisade, completed
the defences.[9]

The rural reconfiguration raised more difficulties and demanded
heavy sacrifices from the peasants. They were asked to build a fort
or cabin in the centre of the parish, around the church for example, large enough to shelter all the families with their provisions of
grain, feed, and animals, plus a small garrison. The work and all the
activities at the fort were under military command. The owners of

the site and surrounding land were ordered to cede their rights to
the buildings, woodlots, and cultivated acreage to the community
of habitants on a temporary basis under arrangements varying from
one parish to another. The assessment of levies and damages was
delayed until the end of the war, at times giving rise to intermina-
ble trials.[10] But these protected plots would not suffice to feed the
population. At planting, ploughing, and harvest time, the peasants
assembled to go off to work on remote plots, in principle under the
protection of soldiers.[11] Living conditions within the forts were miserable. Alongside the guard house and one or two suitable houses
made available to the officers, habitants and soldiers were housed
in makeshift shelters such as bark-covered log cabins and slept on
straw.[12] The houses they had been forced to leave, however rustic,
evoke images of comfort by comparison.

At first the people refused to move, and some openly refused to
work on the forts. "Each habitant would like his own house to have
a citadel and no one wants to leave it, much less to build villages,"
wrote Denonville in August 1687. But "once the enemy has broken
a few heads, they will resign themselves to it."[13] The prejudices harboured by this governor in regard to peasants did not help him to
understand their anxiety at the idea of giving up everything they
owned and on which they subsisted.[14] It would take more than a few
scattered attacks to make them move. The habitants of Lachine, with
three nearby forts in which to seek protection, did not feel threatened enough to move away from their land once the harvest had
begun. It may be surmised that the sacking of this parish of some
sixty families on 5 August 1689 put an end to resistance throughout
the region.[15]

In all, about thirty forts or enceintes were erected or consolidated
in the government of Montreal. Some, on the margins of the inhabited area – at Chambly and Chateauguay or near the Lake of Two
Mountains – were mere military outposts. Several, such as the ones
at La Prairie, Sorel, and Pointe-aux-Trembles and two or three others similarly erected at strategic sites, housed both refugees from the
côtes and a permanent garrison. The rest did no more than provide
safe harbour for the local population.[16] Of the two planned methods
of communication, signal fires and cannon shots, only the second
worked at all well. Each fort received a cannon with which to alert
its neighbours, who in turn passed along the alarm to their neighbours, and the closest garrison sent a detachment to the place where

the enemy had been reported.[17] At the outset, the bulk of the troops were quartered in the city, but it was soon decided to multiply and enlarge the garrisons in the *plat pays*, the lower-lying areas outside the walls, for quicker response to distress calls.[18] The detachments patrolling the countryside were commanded by regular officers and composed of soldiers and habitants from the fort, at times joined by domiciliés if any were in the vicinity. By the time they arrived at the site of an attack, the assailants had run away, taking several captives with them. If pursued too closely, they might kill the captives to lighten their load, but since they usually had a good lead, the French rarely faced this dilemma.[19] On a few occasions, the governor assembled a few hundred soldiers, militiamen, and domiciliés, either to fend off an enemy raid, as in August 1693, or to give vigorous chase to the fleeing enemy, as at Long Sault in July 1692. Ordinarily, however, the riposte (like the attacks) took place in piecemeal fashion, using small detachments put together in haste. The recruits sometimes marched grudgingly, discipline was often lacking, and successes were few. Gédéon de Catalogne, an officer who left a highly detailed chronicle of these operations, reproached the French, and especially their officers, for their cowardice. A little more aggressiveness, he felt, would have put an end to these incursions, for the Iroquois, he claimed, were cowards – a dubious opinion easier to express on paper than to defend on the ground.[20]

Most of the forts, particularly those that had no garrisons, little artillery, and no moat or fill to protect the stockade, would not withstand an attack by a small, moderately determined band. And the prospect was not unthinkable, for the Iroquois – who lived in fortified villages themselves – knew full well how to conduct a siege and force a barricade. In earlier days, they had been known to attack even a well-defended French fort.[21] But they had grown more cautious as a result of political and military setbacks as well as demographic losses. More than ever, they avoided battle and limited their attacks to isolated, defenceless groups, families who straggled behind in their homes or returned to them too soon, exposed harvesters and labourers, canoeists separated from a convoy, etc., retreating as soon as the raid was over. No Iroquois attacks on forts are reported for this period, no attempts to besiege habitants taking refuge there. This brings us to a digression on the subject of the exploits of Madame de Verchères (Marie Perrot) and her daughter Madeleine, a national heroine for posterity.

The story, first told by Madeleine herself in a letter of 1699 to the Comtesse de Maurepas, was repeated by Bacqueville de La Potherie, a family friend who arrived at the end of the war. The two versions differ so little that it is hard to know whether the writer dictated the text to the heroine or vice versa.[22] According to the legend, the Verchères fort, which served as a stronghold for the seigneurial family and their peasant neighbours, was attacked twice by the Iroquois: In 1690, Madame de Verchères repulsed an assault for two days, with the attackers lifting the siege shortly before the arrival of relief, while on 22 October 1692, fourteen-year-old Madeleine commanded the fort in her parents' absence after having a escaped a band of forty Iroquois by the skin of her teeth. On the second occasion, the assailants continued to prowl around the fort even after they had captured twenty colonists while they worked the fields. Alone with a few children, a soldier, and "weeping," whimpering women, the girl held off the enemy for several hours by dint of cleverness and courage, loading the cannon herself and firing off a shot. The alarm having been relayed from fort to fort as far as Montreal, the governor sent a barque with a hundred-man detachment, but the Iroquois had slipped away with their prisoners by the time help arrived. As an epilogue, Bacqueville adds that they were overtaken and defeated at Lake Champlain by a party of domiciliés, an episode borrowed from the previous year's annals that had nothing to do with the habitants of Verchères.[23] Indeed, almost everything about this tale strains credibility, including the terror allegedly sown among the Iroquois by the cannon shot, as if they had not had fifty years to become acquainted with such weaponry. Furthermore, events so surprising, so contrary to military practice, involving one of the colony's most distinguished families, should have been reported and attracted some comment from the governor and the intendant, yet not a whisper is to be found in the official correspondence of 1692 and 1693. As to the official journal, it offers another version of what happened at Verchères that fall: namely, that Governor Louis-Hector de Callière decided to resupply the forts of the lower Richelieu after the Iroquois's passage and sent a canoe to ascertain whether the water was high enough for a barque to pass. "On its return, this canoe learned that the enemy had killed or taken prisoner several individuals at Verchères, drove the animals off into the forest, and scalped one soldier at Saint-Ours. It was said that this must certainly have been a small party separated from the larger one."[24] Thus, as elsewhere in the western portion of the colony, the habitants of this seigneury lived in fear and suffered human and material losses. In their ill-defended fort, the women of Verchères may well have succeeded in keeping a cool head at these times, but all the rest was just a pious invention.[25]

b) Victories and reprisals

The casualties of this war have yet to be tallied. The pattern among recent Quebec historians and demographers has been to minimize the losses and to reject all higher-than-average contemporary estimates. A recent article reduces the 200 dead or disappeared in the sacking of Lachine to a couple of dozen, neglecting to mention war as one factor explaining the systematic underestimation of deaths that occurred throughout the colony in the seventeenth and eighteenth centuries.[26] Is there any need for a reminder that those who died in wars were almost never buried in parish cemeteries and that the victims of Iroquois raids were no exception? For a more accurate count of these missing people, historians can rely on a number of sources, beginning with the figures mentioned by witnesses of the day, which need to be compiled and analyzed as John Dickinson did for the period 1608–66.[27] The Quebec genealogy database of the Programme de recherche en démographie historique (PRDH) might also offer clues, such as remarriages in the absence of a death certificate for a first spouse or children of all ages who vanish from the registers.[28] More conclusive is the information contained in the judicial archives and the notarial records, such as community inventories, estate divisions, agreements, and contestations. After the death of René Huguet, killed and buried at Lachine in June 1691, the inventory of his possessions tells us that his wife and two children were "captured by the Iroquois" on the same occasion. An inventory from 1697 then reports that the mother returned, the older child André had died in captivity, and eleven-year-old Françoise was still being held captive.[29] Relatives' petitions and data from successions reveal the fate of Jean Lelat of Montreal, killed north of the island while returning from an escort; that of a husband and wife by the name of Faye from La Prairie, kidnapped in 1690 and released before 1695; that of another couple, the Estiers of La Chesnaye, who died while being marched away to captivity; and that of their two-year-old daughter, who was raised by the Onondagas.[30] The number of victims revealed by such a survey would not likely be very great; be that as it may, the perception of casualties is relative to the size of a population, and such a small one would have keenly felt even limited losses. A loss of 250 or 300 men, the most exposed group, would have represented one-tenth of the adult male population, a proportion as large as the one recorded in New England during King Philip's War (1675–78), considered especially bloody by historians.[31]

Such a survey could serve other purposes as well. Americans have reverently compiled the names of victims of the "French and Indian" wars since the eighteenth century, and these lists have contributed more recently to the study of Indigenous cultures. Who, among men and women, adults and children of all ages, was most likely to be killed on site or taken captive? The answers vary according to eras and circumstances and also according to the assailants' identity.[32] A study of Canadian victims in the years 1687–97 could supplement this work and shed light on the behaviour of the Five Nations at a critical moment in their history; by the same token, it might elucidate the colonists' reactions.[33] The official reports are ordinarily quite discreet as to the fate of Iroquois individuals who fell into French hands. The captors were required to deliver prisoners to the governor or the commandant of the fort, and custom had it that they were then turned over to the Indigenous allies, who did as they pleased with them – a convenient way for the French to wash their hands of any barbaric acts that might ensue.[34] Executions took place in Indigenous villages or at times in colonial towns before a crowd of onlookers. Lahontan, with a mixture of humour and indignation, described one such spectacle that took place at Quebec during the winter of 1692, with the Hurons in the role of executioners.[35] Things were different in the government of Montreal. On two occasions, the habitants themselves apparently demanded and lit the pyres. In October 1689, three Iroquois prisoners were brought to Montreal "where the whole populace and the domiciliés demanded, by right of reprisal, that they be burned." The second episode took place in June 1691 as the French returned from a rather chaotic pursuit in which they defeated the enemy but lost several men. The four prisoners they took were shared out among the members of the detachment and brought back to their respective parishes – Repentigny, Boucherville, Pointe-aux-Trembles, Montreal – for public burnings there. The officers, including Gédéon de Catalogne, who witnessed and chronicled these events did not just tolerate this conduct, they approved of it.[36] How can such eruptions of popular violence be understood without taking the measure of the fears they were meant to exorcise?

c) Confronting the invader: Intoxication and complacency

The mass mobilizations provoked by the announcement of an English invasion stood in marked contrast to the tensions engendered by confinement in the forts and by continual surreptitious attacks and small, scattered, futile troop movements. When assembled to fight off an enemy army or fleet of known size and location, habitants and soldiers alike suddenly felt inspired by a heroic mission, and a feeling of excitement pervaded the rallying sites. The crowds and ceremonies associated with these troop movements – the speeches, cries, raised flags, priests' blessings, and so on – intoxicated the troops as much as the wine and aqua-vitae that were also part of the ritual. On 17 October 1690, 800 soldiers and militiamen from the government of Montreal entered a besieged Quebec to the sound of fifes and drums; "the noise of these bellicose youths, who came bounding in with great demonstrations of joy," must certainly have disconcerted the enemy, wrote Jeanne-Françoise Juchereau de la Ferté, author of *Les Annales de l'Hôtel-Dieu de Québec, 1636–1716*.[37] Again in 1707, 1709, and 1711, troops and militias coming to the relief of Quebec celebrated, laughed, and danced all night in the streets of the city while awaiting the British.[38] The faces of those assembled shone with determination and gaiety, as the officers often noted on such occasions.[39] Such accounts describe a phenomenon well known to specialists of military history: that of pre-battle confidence and enthusiasm, which is particularly acute when the troops are preparing to defend their own patch of ground.[40] In New France, however, these good intentions were rarely put to the test, since only two out of a total of nine or ten apprehended invasions, whether by land or by sea, ever took place.

The first time, in 1690, the habitants of the government of Quebec played an active part in the defence. For two months, in the absence of the troops and the governor, whose main concern at that time was an attack in the Lake Champlain region, town militias under the command of the fort major were entrusted with keeping order in the town and supervising its continued fortification. With the approach of William Phips's fleet, the habitants of the Côte-du-Sud, Pointe-Lévy, and Île d'Orléans received orders to fend off an attempted landing; this was accomplished so well that the Bostonians arrived at Quebec on 16 October without having been able to resupply. During the ensuing two-day siege, the habitants of Beaupré and Beauport showed presence of mind and resolve.[41] Although not decisive, these actions showed that parish militias commanded by their officers were, when threatened, capable of acting as a corps and on their own initiative. Yet this autonomy would subsequently be denied them, as the sequence of events associated with the false alarm of 1709 illustrates. The colony was again living under the threat of two coordinated attacks, by river and by land. Governor Vaudreuil decided to order the evacuation of the countryside and concentrate all his forces in the cities. Further to an assembly held in Montreal in June, to which the urban and rural militia officers were not even invited, the habitants were ordered to retreat into the city with their families, possessions, grain, and animals as soon as the enemy crossed the border. The following month, the governor himself travelled through the côtes of the government of Quebec enforcing the new strategy. "I even increased the number of militia officers so as to instill in the habitants what I wanted them to do": that is, send their women, children, animals, and other possessions into the woods and "hurry" into Quebec, bringing their provisions with them.[42] The plan elicited strong opposition. The habitants apparently feared for their families; they were convinced that they might succeed in preventing the enemy from landing by staying put, as they had in the past. The alarm was sounded anew two years later, in 1711, and Vaudreuil resumed his tours through the côtes downriver of Quebec to encourage the habitants "to abandon everything for the common cause." After some deliberation, he wrote, the assembly of priests, militia officers, and other principal habitants of the five parishes on Île d'Orléans finally agreed to the evacuation.[43] With Sir Hovenden Walker's fleet shipwrecked in the fog off Sept-Îles, no one could say whether this complicated plan, which clashed with the colonists' spontaneous reactions, could have improved the colony's readiness. The real test would come much later, in 1759.

One by one, English attempts to invade the colony via the Richelieu River prior to 1712 proved abortive. The small armies awaiting them at La Prairie or Chambly would break camp after a few days or weeks in response to intelligence of enemy movements, although this was always slow in coming and often erroneous. Only once, on a rainy night in August 1691, did a party of English and Amerindians commanded by the mayor of Albany surprise the camp at La Prairie, taking advantage of defection by militiamen who had left their positions to seek shelter. After a deadly engagement at the door of the fort, the English beat a retreat. A group of scouts caught up with them, and the long ensuing battle produced many casualties on both sides.[44]

On the whole, it may be said that Canada enjoyed incredible good luck during these two wars. Quebec was never in a position to withstand a bona fide siege, and defences were just as fragile further upriver. But circumstances smiled on the French. Even as they thanked the heavens for the blessings they had received, they were capable of evincing feelings of superiority and complacency, even contempt for the English colonists; most fatefully, they underestimated the hatred growing faster than fear, like a poisonous plant, under their own soldiers' boots.[45]

2. PARTISAN WARFARE

The words used by historians to describe the kind of offensives launched by New France against English settlements starting in the late seventeenth century – raids, guerrilla or petty or commando warfare – belong to the vocabulary of the modern day. Only the phrase "petty warfare" (*petite guerre*) is of distant origin, but it rarely appears in colonial texts because of its long association with marauding. Its usage spread during the eighteenth century as European strategists began seeing value in positioning specialized mobile units on the flanks of the army and assigning them various diversion, reconnaissance, and other high-risk missions. While the officers detached to Canada during the Seven Years' War often used it in a more general sense, the phrase remains ambiguous. Even more ambiguous is the term "guerrilla warfare," brought back from Spain by Napoleon's armies and heavily laden with political meanings, while other terms that entered the language later take us even further from the context.[46] One might be tempted to infer from the use of these neologisms that this form of warfare was so alien to the seventeenth-century French that they had no words to describe it. This would be a mistake. The language of the classical era had all the words needed to designate bold, swift, ad hoc attacks, scattered manoeuvres with no bearing on a larger strategy. Terms such as *coup de main*, *incursion*, *course* (on land or at sea), and especially *parti* are commonly found in the writings of that time.[47] As the *Dictionnaire universel* (1690) explains, a *parti* was a small offensive military formation acting on orders, thus distinguishing it from groups of brigands. These ancient words remind us that while this species of warfare owed much to the Indigenous people, it also had European antecedents. The French did not just imitate Indigenous tactics: They combined them with their own military traditions, and the complementarity often played to their advantage. Still, it must be recalled that the majority of the parties were made up of Indigenous people travelling in small bands of six to twenty warriors, rarely more, so that they could take isolated colonists by surprise and ravage the *plat pays*. The sum total of these campaigns cannot be quantified, but the figures compiled by Richard Melvoin for the Connecticut Valley give an idea of their magnitude. Between 1688 and 1698, the domiciliés attacked this highly vulnerable region, readily accessible from the north, on thirteen separate occasions, yet the scope of these operations cannot be grasped from French sources. The War of the Spanish Succession saw a total of twenty-nine attacks, only two of them joint initiatives.[48] These latter involved larger numbers of men and ordinarily caused more destruction and casualties in a single incident than several Indigenous incursions combined. Although relatively rare, joint French-Indigenous parties attracted much attention, whether from the colonial government, which justified its policy and expenses by boasting of its performance and results, or from its English neighbours, shocked that Christians could orchestrate and take part in such cruel campaigns.

a) Two models: The campaigns of 1686 and 1690

The colony discovered its talents in 1686 on the occasion of an expedition to James Bay in the guise of a police operation, which took control of three fur trading posts belonging to the Hudson's Bay Company. "A quarrel between merchants," wrote Governor Denonville, for France and England were not at war, although this had not prevented the minister and his local administrators from supporting a campaign undertaken and paid for by the Compagnie du Nord.[49] A hundred volunteers chosen from among colonists and naval regulars trekked two and a half months under incredibly harsh conditions to cross the drainage divide and three weeks more to reach the back of the bay, where they made an initial attack on a tiny fort that surrendered after half an hour. They proceeded to board an English ship, using this to take over two more forts. Lost and isolated in these deserts of mud and ice, the merchants did not stand to gain by holding out too long, and it was in the interests of the French to preserve the posts so that they could be occupied and run for French benefit. The operation killed only three or four Englishmen and brought in tidy profits in beaver furs for its backers after deduction of outfitting costs, wages, and the participants' share in the booty. "There, Your Excellency, are the first efforts of our Canadians," wrote the vicar-general, who, like the rest of the colony, thrilled to the audacity and undeniable success of the enterprise.[50]

The three parties sent by the governor against the English colonies four years later, in the winter of 1690, were also learning experiences but on another order, for they were experiences of total war. The first 200-man detachment, composed of French and Indigenous volunteers in equal numbers, headed off in the direction of Corlaer (Schenectady), the Anglo-Dutch town upon which Courcelle's frozen, hungry, disoriented troops had stumbled a quarter-century earlier.[51] In the interim, trade and good neighbourliness had blazed trails between the two colonies, and the French had learned much. It was a matter of twelve hours or so – a carbon copy of an Indigenous action, excepting the season – to fall upon a sleeping, undefended village, massacre a good part of the population, reduce the fort and the houses to ashes, keep a few able-bodied prisoners, and claim whatever prizes could be easily carried away. The parties organized out of Trois-Rivières and Quebec had a harder task. Even for well-trained men, the march from Saint-François or La Chaudière to the inhabited villages of New England was long and exhausting. The residents of Salmon Falls put up no resistance. Those of Casco (Falmouth), at war with the Abenakis for two years and more on their guard, had time to take refuge in a large fort with a garrison and eight cannons. René Robinau de Portneuf and Jean-Baptiste Hertel de Rouville, who had joined forces and were commanding 300 men, mostly Amerindians, laid siege to the fort using classical methods. But that was the extent to which they drew on European lessons: Having accepted the English surrender in exchange for safe conduct for the prisoners, the two officers let the Abenakis deal with them as they saw fit. The death toll was large: nearly 125 men, women, and children killed on site; 150 prisoners, of whom very few survived; kilometres of land burned.[52]

Joint actions of the same kind were repeated several times during the War of the Spanish Succession. The other parties, comprising several dozen colonists or soldiers, sometimes mingled with Amerindians, stuck to manoeuvres more akin to that of 1686 at Hudson Bay and to contemporary military practice, privateering especially. Some of these incursions are scarcely mentioned in the official annals; my information is derived from about twenty feats of arms that were highly publicized in their day and have been tirelessly reprinted by historians, for it is on these that the fame of the Canadians rests.[53] A review of them will help us to comprehend the behaviour and mentality of the small numbers of men from different backgrounds who voluntarily joined war parties.

These detachments rarely numbered more than 100 participants of French origin and were often much smaller. Men willing to join a party were not legion, since even a bare-bones contingent sent to Acadia or elsewhere aroused immediate fears for Canada's safety and its capacity to recruit for other enterprises. The local authorities particularly resented Iberville, who was able to attract the best men by offering attractive conditions. All it took for Callière to cancel a planned expedition to Fort Frontenac, for instance, was for Iberville to recruit 110 Canadians for a campaign to Hudson Bay. The year 1696 found the governor again putting up resistance to recruitment for Newfoundland.[54] Good soldiers were unquestionably a scarce resource, to be used sparingly; at century's end they numbered perhaps 200–300, or 10 per cent of men of arms-bearing age – a sizeable proportion, all things considered.[55] Historians have tended to posit higher figures by conflating physical strength, fur trading savvy, and military engagement. Yet trade does not predispose one to violence – quite the contrary. From the number of voyageurs in the Great Lakes region, one would have to begin by subtracting all those who had not the slightest interest in warmaking[56] and then those who, due to their age, were no longer fit to join a party. Fur trading had become a well-organized activity in which tasks could be assigned unequally to accommodate beginners and weaker individuals. Canoe brigades moved serenely from one landmark to the next. Men took time to sleep and did not lack for food. When they reached Michilimackinac (now Mackinaw City, MI) or Detroit, they could rebuild their strength before continuing or embarking on the homeward journey. Finally, traders did not travel out of season. By contrast, war parties took tortuous, often impassable roads. The length of a journey was not always predictable: It might extend to a few weeks or to several months. Provisions were limited so as to lighten loads, and hunting was unreliable; men on the march were guaranteed to experience hunger at some point. And there was no respite after the attack but rather a hasty return, often with the enemy in pursuit. In winter, all these difficulties were multiplied tenfold. In short, only young, hearty, highly motivated men were of any use in such parties.

Since the Indigenous people were fitter for such ordeals, the question becomes: Why did the colonial government insist on including Frenchmen at all? Its reasoning was laid out in the early days, at the start of the 1690s, before the custom of small mixed parties was adopted. The primary reason was psychological. The administration had to prove to its allies that the French knew how to wage their kind of war and, in so doing, erase the bad impression apparently created by the setbacks and passivity of previous years. Is this how the allies saw things? Did they need such a demonstration in order to embrace the cause of Onontio (the governor)? A difficult question. Nevertheless, the argument offers a good reflection of the feeling of insecurity in the colony, its mistrust of its allies. The second reason was tactical. Indigenous raids were not enough, it was said, to terrorize the English, to keep them shut up in their forts and prevent them from taking the offensive. The presence of Frenchmen alongside the Amerindians was claimed to introduce "resolve and leadership" into the enterprises and was necessary to paralyze the enemy.[57] This argument is easy to see through. For our purposes, it may be noted that the French were not there to temper their partners' cruelty – quite the contrary.[58] Frenchmen accounted for half of many parties, much smaller proportions of others, and often just a single individual.[59] The general staff pushed future officers, whether cadets or volunteers, to join Indigenous parties in order to learn the corresponding techniques and pass them on to their own soldiers.[60] But while a French presence was optional, Amerindians were indispensable when penetrating into enemy territory. They alone could guide the troops, hunt noiselessly if necessary, correctly identify the enemy's comings and goings on the forest floor – not to mention their military talents as such and the fright induced by the sight of their war-painted bodies. Expeditions composed entirely of Frenchmen, such as that of 1686 to James Bay, the winter privateering expedition to the Newfoundland fisheries in 1697, and other more maritime than land-based enterprises, were exceptions to the rule.[61]

The French and their allies learned to share knowledge in order to improve their war efforts, but the two groups still diverged on the essential matter of authority and how one should relate to it. For a seventeenth-century European, these chiefs who "commanded no one at all," who lacked the power of reward and punishment, never ceased to be objects of amazement. "They simply say that a certain thing must be done, and then the others do it if they want; since there is no punishment between them, there can be no subordination."[62] Claude Sébastien de Villieu, who did not command as much as accompany 200 Abenakis from Acadia to the New England coast, described the procedure. After several councils to decide where to strike, the opinion of younger warriors prevailed over that of older ones, and the former took charge of leading the party. Throughout the mission, they took time to deliberate as to whether the initial plan ought to be modified. The opinion of the chiefs they had chosen might ultimately win out, but everyone had the right to speak and shared decisions were respected.[63] It was another form of submission, to custom rather than to people, and one that the men of the Ancien Régime could barely recognize. In less homogeneous parties than this one, comprising Frenchmen and warriors from different nations, the series of councils could go on even longer.

With the French, everything was tidier: The commander gave orders and the men obeyed. A distinction must be made here between training-based discipline and mere obedience – to God the father and to all representatives of legitimate authority, which constituted the fundamental law in this society.[64] Boys who volunteered for parties out of ambition, interest, or a taste for adventure were no doubt more brutal, cocky, and unruly than average, yet these small formations functioned with order and efficiency. Ever-present hierarchy, backed up by force as necessary, kept the group together. Its cohesion relied on vertical personal ties built by the leader with his men, the loyalty he inspired in them. On the expedition to Hudson Bay in 1686, its commander Pierre de Troyes had to lay down the law several times, squelching quarrels and incipient mutinies that he attributed, in keeping with the preconceived notions of the time, to the Canadians' "nature." The real lesson, however, was simply that these barque captains and fur traders were not soldiers. The long voyage was an initiation in military discipline. If adroitly meted out, punishment put each man in his place and reminded him of his duty to obey, even if it could not replace the training that none of them had received. The lessons seem to have borne fruit, for, in spontaneous acknowledgment of their acceptance of his leadership, the corps proceeded to plant the maypole by the tents of the captain and his lieutenants.[65] Family, friendship, and community relations played an important role in party composition. The majority of the twenty-four Frenchmen who accompanied François Hertel to Salmon Falls in 1690 were related to him in one way or another. Larger detachments presented themselves as an assemblage of three concentric circles: in the centre, the commandant with a few family members and companions; in the next circle, ordinary volunteers whom he had managed to attract and who had remained loyal to him from one campaign to the next; in the last circle, new arrivals who had yet to be broken in.[66] Iberville is the best example of a leader surrounded by loyal soldiers who were willing to follow him anywhere – to Schenectady, the Maine coast, Newfoundland, and ultimately the Gulf of Mexico. The private character of such engagements strengthened bonds. The men who went from Canada to Plaisance in 1696 at the behest of Iberville – the "sole master of winter warfare," as they repeatedly described him – refused to attack St John's if he did not lead them into battle.[67] Among the military leaders of that generation were another privateer, Pierre Denys de Bonaventure, and regular officers Nicolas d'Ailleboust de Manthet, Jacques Testard de Montigny, and the Hertel de Rouvilles, Jean-Baptiste and his father Joseph-François. A commandant had to show considerable flexibility, respecting the dynamics of the Amerindian group by taking care not to impose his will on them, at least overtly, while at the same time asserting his authority over the soldiers and colonists and building esprit de corps among these individuals, a feeling of solidarity not present at the outset. Hertel de Rouville the younger, for example, won the entire confidence of the Abenakis in his party and asked the "hundred chosen soldiers and Canadians" to embrace and make peace before leading the attack on Haverhill.[68]

b) Ordinary barbarity

Haverhill (then called Hewreuil by the French) is a Massachusetts town on the Merrimack River. On 29 August 1708, the French "entered sword and axe in hand and set it afire." At least a hundred people were massacred, not counting those burned alive in their homes, and "the number of prisoners was considerable." Charlevoix, our narrator, contented himself with a succinct account of the affair derived from Vaudreuil's correspondence. But he added: "I was at Montreal, at the very port, when the party landed there about the middle of September. Great praise was given especially to the Sieur Dupuys, son of the Lieutenant Particulier of Quebec, who had carried his humanity so far as to carry the daughter of the King's Lieutenant at Hewreuil, a good part of the way, the girl being almost unable to walk."[69] This passage from the *History and General Description of New France* affords a good summary of the colony's official stance vis-à-vis the barbarity of its partisans. Mingled with the crowd of onlookers, Charlevoix watched the arrival of the Haverhill party, but instead of describing the scene, the historian – whose choices were rarely innocent – digressed to mention this one young officer's goodheartedness in the face of danger. While French sources recount Iroquois attacks against the colonists in minute detail – babies ripped from their mother's bosoms and roasted on spits, etc. – they wrap the deeds of the French and the domiciliés in a veil of modesty, offering only toned-down accounts and shopworn phrases – "they gave no quarter," "the enemy was cut to ribbons" – whose real meaning was surely obvious to contemporary readers.[70] To find appalling images of women eviscerated and children's heads crushed against tree trunks, one must turn to the English sources, where they abound.[71] Traditional history has contrasted the total war practised in the Americas with the increasingly circumscribed, orderly war typical of Europe. More recent attempts have been made to put North American barbarity into perspective, but the truth is that such comparisons lead nowhere. Each war, in its fashion, is atrocious, regardless of the methods with which the carnage is inflicted; it was ever thus and still is today. What do change are attitudes, or sensibilities, and it is their evolution, among different social groups and across successive generations, that historians must strive to grasp. Likewise, they must work to draw the outlines of ordinary violence with greater precision. Unlike American historians, with their incessant interrogation of their nation's relationship to war, historians of New France have not generally dwelt on the barbarity of the colonial conflicts.[72] Those who have done so, such as Cornelius Jaenen, tend to exaggerate the problem by confounding common military practices with rarely observed rites such as torture and cannibalism, which the domiciliés, for example – the closest allies of the French – had long since abandoned.[73] By contrast, scalping and prisoner-taking were forms of violence closely associated with partisan warfare and must be studied over the long term; that is, beyond the time frame covered by this chapter.

c) Scalping

All European writers observed with fascination the Indigenous custom of flaying the scalps of dead enemies, painting and decorating them as trophies, and triumphantly parading them around the village. For lack of a better word, the French used the term *chevelure* to denote these strange skins until the word *scalp* replaced it in the late eighteenth century.[74] From Samuel de Champlain to Joseph-François Lafitau, many observers described the practice, but always within the context of intertribal warfare, never giving much thought to the ways in which it was transformed by European influence. The English colonies, in their wars with various Indigenous nations, had been quick to adopt the practise of placing bounties on their enemies' scalps. At first employed as a means of whipping up the allies' ardour for war, the bounties became coveted by militiamen and frontier villagers, who began scalping the corpses of their Indigenous (or at times French) assailants. The amount of the rewards, published in newspapers and on placards, varied from one colony and period to another, trending strongly upward in the mid-eighteenth century as attacks proliferated. By then, as James Axtell explains, the custom had entered the colonial culture. Scalps adorned the Salem court and were flown as banners by provincial militia companies parading in the streets of Boston and New York. Following the English example, the Indigenous nations apparently began to consider scalps as a source of profit rather than a symbol of individual prowess and community cohesion. Instead of keeping them to adorn their villages, they brought them to the authorities to earn the reward and were even accused of cutting them in half to double the amount paid.[75]

The situation and the policies were different in the French colonies, yet some historians, particularly specialists of American colonial history, believe that New France, too, systematically handed out rewards to headhunters, with the same consequences: perversion of the colonists and weakening of Indigenous traditions.[76] Convinced of what they set out to prove, these authors read things into their source texts that are not there. It is known, for example, that Amerindians typically presented their trophies to the governors or fort commanders before taking them back to their villages. The ceremony was surely not entirely disinterested, but the fact that the Abenakis presented Denonville with "seven or eight blond scalps" in 1688 is insufficient to conclude that the governor had offered to buy them.[77] In fact, only the following year did the French begin to hand out presents to the Abenakis to induce them to make war on the English, and only in 1690 did the king authorize, in vague terms, "assistance" to allies who joined parties against the Iroquois.[78] Bounties were mentioned for the first time in a letter dated 1692 in which the intendant explained that he and the governor had agreed to pay domiciliés and allies thirty livres per scalp and sixty livres per prisoner, a practice I believe to have been initiated around the end of 1690.[79] It did not last long, for Versailles immediately objected – not out of scruple but because of what was seen as the overly high cost. The administrators insisted. At thirty livres per head, they argued, they could wipe out the Iroquois warriors for only 30,000 livres or even less, since the bounties were paid in goods "valued at high prices." But the king persisted in his refusal, and the question of scalps vanished from the official correspondence for many years.[80] When the Abenakis went to Quebec in 1706 to complain that "their houses were filled with English scalps flapping in the wind and you do not even seem to notice," Vaudreuil took pride in reminding them that he had never, not since the beginning of the war, paid for scalps – too inhuman a practice – but was willing to pay a good price for prisoners.[81]

The rewards took another, less precise, more haphazard form, one more in keeping with the spirit of the regime. As Catherine Desbarats explains in a study on the distribution of presents to Indigenous people, Versailles preferred to speak of free gifts, royal charity, rather than to admit that the king was paying for services rendered.[82] When commencing a campaign, the French offered feasts in exchange for war chants. Each time warriors joined a party, they were outfitted anew. Provisions were distributed to their families during their absence, and they received rations on their return, plus replacements of whatever had been broken or lost. Scalps were generally paid for in this way, without demanding a precise accounting or requiring the warriors to leave their trophies in the king's stores. Long afterward, in 1741, the intendant proposed to dispense with this notion by putting a price on Chickasaw scalps, confirming that the practice was not routine.[83]

It certainly took on new importance during the War of the Austrian Succession; nevertheless, careful study of party movements and accounting documents is insufficient to conclude that it was a regular procedure. The main reference appears in a partial statement of expenses incurred at Montreal between 1 September 1746 and 31 August 1747: 1,867 livres and ten sols in payment for fifty-six scalps.[84] It happened that François-Pierre de Rigaud de Vaudreuil (Rigaud), the governor of Trois-Rivières, had reported the return of some Abenakis detached from his army on 22 September with precisely fifty-six scalps.[85] This appears, then, to have been a special award, a sort of bonus, since this number was unquestionably much smaller than the total number of victims and scalps brought back during this twelve-month period. A few other scattered references in the accounts from Acadia and the Great Lakes solidify the impression that the rewards (the word *primes*, bounties, is for that matter never found in the texts) were more ceremonial than commercial in nature. "For two scalps given by them for Monsieur Le Général, 61 l. 13 s.," reads one statement of goods supplied to the Wea (Ouiatenon) people in 1744.[86] The Montreal offices left detailed documentation of departures and returns of parties as well as of foodstuffs and other goods supplied. Scalps and prisoners are mentioned in these series but not included in the accounting; moreover, there is no apparent correlation between the number of scalps declared and the value of the supplies.[87] As a final note, the unit price paid was still thirty livres, as it had been in 1690, despite the galloping inflation of the 1740s and 1750s, a fact that should dispel the idea that this was any sort of market. Indeed, the real value of these rewards had become almost symbolic. Nor does the practice appear to have gained ground during the Seven Years' War. The account books are lacking, but the silence of the numerous military journals on this score is one clue and certain isolated accounts provide others. The French do not pay for scalps, declared both a British prisoner at Detroit and a French prisoner at Albany.[88] When Major Robert Rogers's men entered the Abenaki village of Odanak (Saint-François-de-Sales) on 4 October 1759, they found hundreds of scalps hanging above doors and elsewhere, proving that these were not items of commerce.[89]

In partisan war, New France was the aggressor, and its allies were more numerous than those of the British colonies; hence the differences between the two sides in terms of how violence was dealt with. At no time, for example, was there any talk of offering rewards for scalps to French partisans, who would have been disinclined to adopt a custom that earned them nothing. This does not rule out the occurrence of isolated gratuitous acts. If a cadet named Raimbault did in fact take a scalp during the expedition of March 1747, what that proves, if anything, is that war can drive men mad.[90]

d) Ownership of captives

At Trois-Rivières in 1644, Governor de Montmagny wanted to ransom three Iroquois prisoners whom his allies had just captured. The Algonquins agreed to give him their prisoner, but the Hurons refused to hand over the other two. "I am a man of war and not a merchant," said their leader; "I have come to fight, not to do business; my honour is to go back to my land not with presents but with captives; so I will not touch your axes or your kettles."[91] Fifty years later, the domiciliés of Iroquois origin had become more conciliatory; the purchase of captives still nonetheless posed many difficulties, and while Algonquin tradition was less rigid in this regard, the Abenakis too sometimes proved intransigent. In all these cultures, prisoners, whether European or Indigenous, had real and symbolic importance for the community and the warriors who had captured them and to whom they belonged. Those eventually released, for ransom or barter, had taken part in welcoming ceremonies, occupied the role assigned to them in the village for a period of time, and lived with their owner or adoptive parent. Once these customs had been observed, ransom negotiations could begin.

French sources are stingy with information about movements of prisoners between the colony and the Indigenous peoples. Contemporary authors such as Bacqueville, Raudot, Lafitau, and Charlevoix studiously avoided the matter; their works talk of traditional forms of war and prisoner treatment before modification by the presence of Europeans and the spread of Christianity. The official correspondence is silent, and the transactions were conducted in private. What is known comes mainly from stories of captivity reverently preserved in the English colonies and inserted into their pastors' sermons. Several became bestsellers in their day. The documentary value of these works is inseparable from their ideological content. In Puritan culture, captivity is a spiritual experience, a passage from sin to redemption – from Babylon, personified by the French colony, to Israel, or deliverance.[92] The manner in which the facts are presented – to wit, as an illustration of the Lord's greatness – does not lessen the value of these accounts; still, it should incline historians to prudence. They can be marshalled to bolster any stereotype: e.g., the existence of a unique Franco-Indian culture, as imagined by Cotton Mather or more recently by Alden Vaughan and other American colonial historians.[93] It follows for these authors that European conventions concerning prisoners of war in existence since the sixteenth century were not observed in New France and that French partisans were allowed to capture enemies for ransom.[94] In sum, the colonial administration is said to have become so acculturated that it ignored the royal ordinance of 1654 stipulating: "It is for the king alone to dispose of prisoners, whether liberally, by exchange, or by ransom, and to put a price on them as he sees fit."[95] It need hardly be specified that while the Indigenous people did not acquiesce to French laws, the colonists were governed by them and could not take prisoners for their own gain.

In principle, the government of the colony had to purchase all prisoners that the allies were willing to hand over and bear the costs of feeding and housing them, which would be repaid along with the ransom when they were repatriated.[96] But delays were long, prisoners were numerous, and public finances did not allow for such expenditures, so the governor – to use an anachronism – contracted these functions out to the private sector. Encouraged by the authorities and the Church, any convents, merchants, or civilian or military officers who had the means to do so made it a duty to ransom captives and then recoup the money without delay, by employing them as servants for example.[97] When the time came for prisoner exchanges, the representatives of Boston or New York found themselves negotiating the terms of release with these entities or individuals. There is no indication that a lucrative trade involving specialized resellers and auctions on the market square is hidden behind such arrangements, as John Demos concluded too hastily with reference to the testimony of Elizabeth Hanson, captured in 1724 by the Abenakis.[98] Regular officers and privateers brought back more prisoners, who were most often housed in habitants' homes at the king's expense, driving the intendant to despair.[99] From 1745 on, the cities of the colony and the surrounding parishes were filled with prisoners of many origins.

These clarifications represent a digression from my original point concerning the Indigenous attitude toward prisoners. On the battlefield itself, at the moment of victory, ownership of captives was non-negotiable. Warriors who joined parties with Frenchmen did not share their prisoners with the king's officers. Nor did they accept European conventions such as ultimatums and conditional surrenders, which frustrated their desire for glory and their community's expectations.[100]

When a party succeeded in surprising the enemy, overrunning a fort before resistance could be organized (as at Schenectady in 1690 or Deerfield in 1704), the issue of prisoners raised no difficulties. At a certain point, the attackers interrupted the carnage, assembled the survivors, and divided them up among the warriors for the return voyage. The French had no role to play. Things became complicated when the English fort was alerted and resolved to defend itself, as at Casco in 1690 and Pemaquid (present-day Bristol, ME) in 1696. The first summons issued by the French commander ordinarily took the form of blackmail: If the enemy refused to lay down its arms, then he could not answer for what the Indigenous members of the party might do. Did the commander honestly believe he had the power to hold them back in any case? After rejection of an initial ultimatum and a five-day siege, Fort Loyal (at present-day Portland, ME) capitulated with the honours of war, consisting of a promise of safe conduct to the nearest English post for all its occupants – seventy men plus a large number of women and children. But the Abenakis moved in, killed all who resisted, and took the others back to their villages.[101] The conquest of Fort William Henry at Pemaquid began similarly. The garrison surrendered after a single day's siege on the condition of protection from the Amerindians. This time, Frenchmen made up a larger proportion of the detachment and were backed by two ships at anchor, so they were able to uphold the terms of surrender. The disarmed prisoners were placed on an island in view of the ships before being carried to Boston and Mount Desert Island for exchange.[102] But few commanders enjoyed such leeway. The military history of New France is replete with unkept promises, humiliating surrenders. The massacre of the garrison at Fort William Henry (rebuilt as Fort George, at present-day Lake George, NY) in 1757, which caused a scandal in its day, was the last in a long series.[103] European and Indigenous rules of war were irreconcilably different in their approaches to human life and captivity.[104] Since the colony had placed its fate in the hands of its allies, the latter's rules prevailed. Where material destruction was concerned, however, European tradition took precedence: Expeditions with large contingents of colonists were characterized by looting and scorched-earth tactics. Since the partisans did not occupy the field after victory and did not have to worry about their own subsistence, they wholeheartedly indulged in the systematic destruction of resources.

e) French and colonial sensibilities

Did partisan war, and the violence that it oozed, meet with unanimous approval, or was there any reticence in certain circles, any action taken to limit or temper these acts of aggression? One thing is certain: The criticism did not come from Versailles. One combs in vain through the king's memoranda and the ministerial correspondence for the slightest hesitation to arm the allied warriors, the most timid remonstrance against cruelties visited on civilian populations, or any allusion at all to the moral responsibilities of officers or to the honour and reputation of France, as if wars taking place outside Europe fatefully eluded all of its conventions.[105] The reactions elicited by a letter from the governor of Acadia to Pontchartrain might seem to invalidate this observation, but let us look closer. "It is claimed," wrote the governor of Acadia, Daniel d'Auger de Subercase, in 1708, "that a party of Canadians and Natives entered the Mazamet river and cut the throats of 4 to 500 persons, giving no quarter to women or children, and that this is what stopped the English." The Marquis de Chevry, who had an interest in Acadian commerce and advised the ministry, wrote in the margin: "These cruel actions should be moderated. We must fear a riposte." Someone else, the minister or a clerk, added: "Good. Forbid it. Write to Monsieur de Vaudreuil to find out the truth of the matter and the reasons."[106] By conveying the news without altering the words in which it had come to him, Subercase inadvertently touched off a malaise, a jolt of concern. The image of cut throats – coming straight out of the popular imagination – and the displeasing reference to women and children contrasted sharply with the neutrality of the official reports, ruffling bureaucratic indifference for an instant. But the affair was soon forgotten without Vaudreuil having to explain himself.[107] When strategic differences arose, as during the War of the Spanish Succession, Versailles urged that raids be stepped up while Quebec recommended prudence.[108] Small parties did not cost much, and this advantage won out over other considerations.

There is no indication that the governors of this period attempted to rein in the behaviour of the warriors they sent to attack English

villages. How indeed could they have asked them to spare English prisoners while urging them to kill without mercy any Iroquois enemies
who fell into their hands or rebuking them for "foolish pity" if they
decided, as in February 1693, to spare a few?[109] Was there even the
mildest scruple? When cruelty was evoked, as in the correspondence
exchanged with the governors of the English colonies, it was always
the other side's cruelty.[110] Canada was no Tortuga. Commandants were
not mavericks but regular officers who obeyed orders and looked to
their own advancement. Campaigns, even when financed by private
interests, were governed by a plan worked out between Versailles and
Quebec.[111] In short, this was a just war, a war desired by the king and
necessary to avert a greater evil, a war claimed to be defensive because,
by terrorizing civilians, it forced the enemy to disperse its forces to
protect them, rendering it unable to attack New France. Such was the
principle underlying the strategy: often belied by facts on the ground
but continually adhered to for lack of an alternative.

Were the people just as certain that war had to be made elsewhere
in order to preserve peace at home? We will never know. As long as
the colony lived under the Iroquois threat, it may be supposed that
popular resentment extended to the people of New York, who were
accused of arming the assailants – but did it also extend to those living in faraway New England? Were partisans given the same endorsement when the threat was more remote? From the standpoint of the
Abenakis of Odanak, the 1704 attack on Deerfield was fair revenge
for the treason committed by Major Richard Waldron against their
people thirty years earlier.[112] But what were the thoughts of the colonists, to whom that event was just old history, as they watched
the victors parade by with their scalps and captives? The surviving
accounts of captivity tell us that they showed compassion toward
English prisoners. When Englishmen travelled in the colony, country people offered them shelter and at times a pallet by the fire to
alleviate the hardships of the journey, if the seigneur permitted.[113] In
my view, what motivated high-born people to ransom captives and
treat them decently was pity much more than self-interest: that, plus
the hope of getting them to abjure heresy. Such charitable acts had
the effect of preserving the colonists' good conscience and kept them
from wondering as to the source of the misfortunes they were trying
to alleviate. It might be added that the fear of reprisals, which can
beget wisdom, was insignificant here, since Acadia and not Canada
bore the brunt of the Bostonians' raids.

Even though the war receded from the St Lawrence Valley after 1696, each gloriously returning party brought it home and put it on display. The scene was played out in one port, then in another, but it was always the same.[114] At Quebec on 25 July 1745, about twenty Lorette Hurons returned from Annapolis Royal with three prisoners and some scalps. They had camped on the northern tip of Île d'Orléans to prepare for a grand entrance, with heads shaved, faces (theirs and their prisoners') painted, and scalps hung show-ily on hooks in the centre of their canoes. Their antiphonal cries, announcing the numbers of dead and prisoners, could be heard the next morning as they paddled along the island toward Quebec. Fifty metres from the bank, the canoes stopped and the warriors waited in silence, immobile as statues, while people gathered. At a signal, they grabbed their paddles and rushed in to shore, where other Hurons took charge of the prisoners and administered the usual tortures. Then, escorted by the crowd, they climbed up to the governor's cha-teau to report on their campaign, joining the officers of the party who had preceded them.[115] There was no one in this colony who was unable to interpret a death cry, who had not at some point stopped scything, hammering, or sewing to listen to the toll produced by one of these faraway campaigns being relayed from one bank of the river to the other. Many people, not really knowing whether the foretold victory might also be a threat, must have crossed themselves before resuming their work.[116]

To keep anachronism at bay, we should not forget the political and cultural context of the age of Louis XIV, the revocation of the Edict of Nantes in 1685, the backing given to James II in 1689, the repression of peasants in the Cévennes from 1702 to 1709, and other acts decried abroad but largely accepted within the realm.[117] Why would French colonists have let their consciences be troubled by the barbarities visited on the English, who were not only heretics but also upstarts against their own legitimate prince?[118]

3. MAJOR ENTERPRISES

In July 1704, a detachment of 800 men en route to attack several English villages was sent scattering in utter confusion before even reaching enemy territory. The governor was blamed for having poorly planned the operation, the domiciliés for having succumbed to panic.[119] In July 1709, a small army of 1,500 men who had gone off to destroy military storehouses on the frontier "scattered like partridges" upon learning that a large enemy force was headed toward them. Blame was laid on the scouts for letting themselves be seen, the messenger who had relayed the false report, the officers for disobeying the commander, and the Kahnawake warriors for abandoning the army.[120] The site known thereafter as Pointe de la Peur (Point Fear) preserved the memory of this cowardice for posterity.[121] In 1715, an expedition against the Foxes that was supposed to have assembled 1,100 voyageurs and warriors from the Great Lakes region disintegrated in the face of resupply and indiscipline problems as it departed Michilimackinac.[122] It was the first in a series of six major offensives against this upper Mississippi nation over a thirty-year period. Some of them turned catastrophic; all were military failures. In 1728, for example, 400 militiamen and 800 domiciliés, in concert with men from the Great Lakes region, were mobilized to exterminate a group of "rebels"; the latter managed to flee at the approach of the expeditionary corps, which had to rest content with burning villages and destroying cornfields after the fashion of long-ago operations in Iroquois territory.[123] But what had been presented as a near-success in the seventeenth century was now perceived as a shameful campaign, with each man trying to elude blame by shifting responsibility for the torpor and chaos onto his subordinates.[124] The disastrous campaigns of 1736 and 1739 against the Chickasaws, conducted as joint efforts between Louisiana and Canada, concluded this first cycle of military fiascos running from 1666 to 1740.[125]

In all, there were a total of about fifteen campaigns, with two commonalities distinguishing them from ordinary parties: the troops were more numerous, and the colonists did not participate freely. Since these campaigns were expensive, demanded lengthy preparations, and did not fulfil all expectations, they were always widely written about, and what was said tended to mask the real problems at the root of these repeated failures or semi-failures. Until the early eighteenth century, the colonial administrators' rhetorical style was ostentatious, as if imbued with the triumphalism typical of the reign. When results were disappointing, they did not abandon hyperbole but used it to cast the undisputed aspects of the initiative in a positive light. Instead of writing, "the corps let the enemy run away and did nothing to stop them," they wrote, "the corps frightened the enemy away and so had no occasion to demonstrate its valour."

When the men's resolve and bravery under enemy fire was not noteworthy, the texts spoke of "immense" fatigue, "incredible" endurance, and the officers' "miraculous" zeal. And to dispel the idea that a campaign had been futile, it was described summarily using euphemisms, only to dwell on the great long-term advantages it had procured: the way it had consolidated alliances, for example, or its implications for the enemy's strategy. The accounts of the expeditions of 1696 and July 1704 are exemplars of the genre.[126] The tone changes with the advent of the Régence. To curtail the logorrhea of the colonial officers and expedite the service, the Conseil de la Marine demanded brief letters dealing with a single matter in which ostentation had no place.[127] Subsequent reports, although less grandiloquent, still avoid shining a bright light on military calamities – for there is a second line of defence, more opaque than euphemism, and that is baseless accusation. As a general rule, the governors preferred to harass the enemy with small parties rather than to order large contingents into battle. Aware of the difficulties and liable to be blamed for any failure, they turned a deaf ear to contrary advice as long as it did not gain Versailles's favour.[128] Thus, debate over the major offensives did take place, but it concerned the personal will of the governor and the commandants, not the military merits of the endeavour. No one asked whether Frontenac was capable of surprising and vanquishing the Onondagas and the Oneida in 1696, or whether Constant Le Marchand de Lignery could crush the Foxes in 1715, but only whether either of them wanted to achieve this goal. No, answered the accusers: These officers had sacrificed victory to their private interests. In the little world of royal servants in exile, of stalled careers and wounded ambitions, malice triumphed, and in the back-and-forth between Quebec and Versailles, suspicion took on the strength of conviction. It was said, for example, that Frontenac needed the Iroquois threat in order to hold onto power and that he went easy on them by deliberately abandoning an offensive in the summer of 1696.[129] When Vaudreuil delayed raising an army to exterminate the Foxes, he was accused of arming them to destroy the Illinois and, by the same token, the Louisiana trade that could compete with Canada's, in which the governor had a personal stake. That a seventy-eight-year-old officer whose sons had made careers in the navy could have hatched such a byzantine plot seems to have gone unquestioned by all concerned: The case was heard, without a scrap of evidence to support it.[130] These intrigues have found an echo in the historiography, boxing it into narrow chronologies, brief explanations, while continuing to mask the functional aspect of governmental and military affairs. In this respect, Dale Miquelon's enlightening synthesis stands apart. Leaving the many spurious accusations in the background, he studies what actually happened on the ground and draws the requisite conclusion: that ambitious military expeditions with undisciplined troops and weak logistical support were destined for failure.[131]

When volunteers showed up for parties, they did so with weapons and baggage in hand. They knew how to travel with a minimum of provisions, relying on trapping, hunting, and looting to complement their supplies. The king's stores surely supplied much of their provisions, but the demand was spread out over the year and was not big enough to cause problems, as attested by the silence of the intendants' correspondence on this score. Things became complicated when the time came to command hundreds of troops. The torpid pace of mobilization was compounded by the equally slow preparations: construction or requisition of canoes to carry the men, stockpiling of guns to arm all those who came to the review empty-handed, provisions of wheat and lard in sufficient quantities to feed everyone throughout the entire expedition.[132] The chief weapon of partisan war – surprise – was out of the question here. The whole colony, its allies, and its enemies knew weeks if not months in advance that a campaign was underway. Unlike parties, these small armies could not live from the barrel of a gun; the organization of convoys of provisions and matériel through forests and across rivers posed insurmountable problems and undermined morale. Finally – and this was surely their main weakness – such large enterprises relied upon men who lacked military training and had never seen battle. Only those colonists in the government of Montreal who had repulsed the Iroquois in 1689 and 1696 possessed such experience, but they accounted for just a quarter of the colony's militias. The young men mobilized during the War of the Spanish Succession were of a new generation; from one end of the colony to the other, inexperience reigned supreme. Each large militia moving at great expense between Quebec, Montreal, and Chambly was taking its first steps. As may be seen in Appendix A, the composition of these small armies varied. Militiamen ordinarily made up 30 to 50 per cent of the corps, while the rest consisted of soldiers from the *compagnies franches* and hundreds of Indigenous fighters. While these last joined small parties spontaneously, they had to be begged to participate in larger operations and often deserted along the way, not on a whim, as the officers claimed, but out of prudence. They were not the leaders of the operation; the troops' noisy, unpredictable conduct was bound to compromise the outcome and put their lives in danger.

The first people recruited to march against the Foxes were not habitants of the côtes but professional fur traders, for it was believed that these men were inured to fatigue and would make good soldiers. The plan was hatched at Versailles in the aftermath of Utrecht. Since this rebel nation had to be subdued and His Majesty lacked the means to pay for it, the expedition would be transformed into a commercial affair in which all participants played the role of privateers in search of profit. The 200 voyageurs operating illegally in the Great Lakes region were offered an amnesty, or the possibility of returning to the colony without prosecution, in return for their participation. They were augmented by 200 official fur traders, who would be permitted to do business provided that they first joined the army assembled at Michilimackinac. All these men, like the officers leading the expedition, were to supply provisions, munitions, canoes, and everything else needed at their own expense, placing a liability on their balance sheet before they set out.[133] The abolition of trading permits since 1696 facilitated negotiations. Voyageurs who had no choice but to accept the governor's offer if they wished to trade legally cannot be considered volunteers, especially given that many of them discharged their military obligation by proxy, with engagés or valets taking their places.[134] Compelled by circumstances to enlist, they dragged their feet and challenged orders; in spite of their vigour and knowledge of the terrain, they proved no more worthy than the parish militias and were less docile to boot. Thanks to their privileged position in the allied villages, some voyageurs rendered great services to post commandants, but these traders did not add up to a military force on which the colony could rely.[135] The Fox Wars dispelled any remaining illusions.

Who Fought the Wars?

This chapter spells out what the foregoing analysis of war movements has already strongly suggested. Those who went to war were mainly Indigenous allies, soldiers, officers and aspiring officers of the colonial regulars, and volunteers. We shall briefly explore the contours of these groups and their motivations for going to war. Unlike those who chose to serve and risk their lives, militiamen only went to war when ordered to do so. Two rather hazy portraits emerge from the foregoing pages: one of habitants in the government of Montreal vigorously defending their territory in the 1690s and one of multiple battalions recruited from all over the colony being sent into Iroquois territory and New York. The paucity of available documentation makes it impossible to bring these two portraits into sharp focus. While the militias had a fairly low profile on the ground during this era, they loom large in the plans of the general staff and in the administrative discourse in general, and it is on these sources that I have focused. This approach highlights the authorities' enduring illusions vis-à-vis the military capacities of the habitant-soldiers, as well as the more realistic vision that finally took hold in the early eighteenth century.

I. THE COLONIAL FORCES

a) The Amerindians

The Amerindians were the principal military force of New France. This point must be stressed, for past historians have been slow to acknowledge it. In the works of William J. Eccles, for example, the Indigenous allies are presented as third in importance after the militias and the *compagnies franches*. They are depicted as auxiliary forces – skilled, no question, but fickle, in need of Canadian supervision.[1] This was not the opinion of the colonial government, although its discourse might give the contrary impression. Beyond all the references to the allies' inconstancy and deceit, the putatively high costs of their cooperation, what must be noted is the increasing amount of room taken up by Indigenous policy in the official correspondence, the gradual appropriation of diplomatic initiative that had for so long been left to the Jesuits. In 1666, it was believed that one good regiment would serve to quell the Iroquois and bring the other nations to heel. The events of the last two decades of the century undermined this rosy confidence. Little by little, the administration lost sight of the religious aspects of the mission; it came to view these people as a source of warriors overseen by priests in the service of the king.[2] By the outbreak of the War of the Spanish Succession, the primacy of the alliance had become taken for granted – in the colony, at least, for it took Versailles longer to understand and accept the consequences of its dependency.[3] To employ Richard White's Janusian metaphor of the "middle ground," of interest here is the eastern side of the alliance, the one that served French interests and translated militarily into a preponderance of harassment tactics over other troop movements.[4] War parties retained their tactical hegemony; they were still the fulcrum of French strategy and composed of majorities of Indigenous people. The data collected in Appendix A (1666–1740) present a far from complete picture of this reality, since contemporary sources counted Indigenous troops only on those rare occasions when they marched with the French.[5] But it does offer clues that, when combined with counts of total population and combatants, help to put approximate numbers on the Indigenous forces engaged alongside New France from one year to the next.

As mentioned in the introduction, contemporaries used the term *domiciliés* to refer to those Indigenous groups that had converted to Catholicism and taken up permanent domicile in the colony amid the French settlements. These communities had often been moved since the time of the earliest missions. In the early eighteenth century, the Hurons were gathered at Lorette, the Abenakis at Bécancour and Odanak, and the Iroquois at Sault-Saint-Louis, with all these villages being served by the Jesuits. Another Iroquoian group settled on Montreal Island by the Sulpicians would be relocated to the seigneury of Lac-des-Deux-Montagnes in 1721, along with the Algonquins of Île-aux-Tourtes (off the west end of Montreal Island at the junction of the Ottawa and the St Lawrence) and several Nipissing bands.[6] The distinction between allies and domiciliés has no political connotation. The French had had to give up the idea of converting these neophytes into subjects of the king, subject to the same laws and obligations as colonists, for the domiciliés expected to be treated like the other allies. Officers went to their villages to sing the praises of war, and the governor offered a feast – fatted calves, chickens, pigeons, sugar, wine, etc.[7] At the close of lengthy ceremonies, the council agreed to offer its assistance and stated its conditions. Continual migration of Indigenous people between missions and their home territory, like the adoption of captives, could abruptly change the number and composition of a population, and these changes would affect its degree of participation in military campaigns. The total population was relatively stable, standing at 2,000 in 1680 and about 2,500 in the first third of the eighteenth century before climbing to 4,000 in the two subsequent wars.[8] The official correspondence sometimes provides the number of warriors for one or other of these villages; John Dickinson and Jan Grabowski juxtaposed these figures with those found in the censuses and established a very high ratio of warriors to total population, on the order of one-fifth to one-fourth.[9] Thus, according to contemporary estimates, the domiciliés may have supplied as many as 500 warriors between 1687 and 1740, and the analysis of military engagements shows that these estimates square with the facts. Year after year, this little population produced hundreds of good soldiers who were dispersed among the war parties or, on occasion, assembled to participate in the defence of the colony or in a few large expeditions.

It is hard to provide precise estimates for the participation of the more remotely situated allies. The Abenakis on the Saint John and St Croix rivers and on the Maine coast seem to have been able to send 400–500 men. In 1736, after heavy migration toward the St Lawrence, there were still 350 warriors along the Saint John River.[10] The Mi'kmaq, who were to play an important role in the mid-eighteenth century wars, rarely became involved in French operations prior to that time. Iberville appreciated their skills as sailors and hired thirty Mi'kmaq from Cape Breton Island for the Siege of Pemaquid in 1696. Circumstances alone prevented him from enlisting the La Hève (LaHave) Mi'kmaq for the Newfoundland campaign.[11] During

the War of the Spanish Succession, the governors of Plaisance called
on the Mi'kmaq several times for navigation along the coasts, and
the latter captured a number of good prizes at sea on their own
initiative.[12] In the Great Lakes region, nations were too numerous
and changing for any estimates to be hazarded. It is not known, for
example, how many Hurons, Ojibwas, Ottawas, Illinois, Miamis,
Sakis, and other allies regularly harassed the Iroquois in the 1680s
and 1690s before the latter were forced to accept peace with the
French: thousands, no doubt, for the size of the population was considerable.[13] The figures in Appendix A account for only those groups
who lent their assistance to the French in the colony or who took
part in joint manoeuvres against the Foxes and the Chickasaws.
Pressure sometimes had to be applied in order to obtain their help, as
with the 400 warriors recruited by Denonville in 1687 or the 400–500
recruited by Vaudreuil in 1711. In other instances, men who had come
to Montreal to deliver furs were asked to participate in a raid before
returning home and could have asked for nothing better. In this way,
warriors from the Great Lakes region took part in seven campaigns in
the southern part of the colony between 1687 and 1711 in numbers
ranging from 200 to 500.[14] The Ojibwas, and especially the Ottawas
and the Michilimackinacs, were the most loyal.

It is beyond the scope of this book to address a question that has
held the attention of Native Americanists: Why did these peoples
fight on the French side? In their emphasis on the allies' importance
to French strategy, the foregoing pages might lead readers to believe
that the colony had 1,500 warriors at its beck and call. Quite the
contrary: These alliances were fragile in the extreme, subject to continual renegotiation. Relations between New France and its allies
were never easy, and they were particularly tense with the Iroquois
domiciliés, the most numerous of the Christianized Amerindians,
who remained attached to their Five Nations brethren and their
ancestral New York homeland.[15] It is of course well understood
that the Indigenous people were not mercenaries or puppets whose
strings the Europeans could pull. But beyond their immediate reasons for accepting the hatchet of war from the French – a desire for
vengeance, a search for captives to replace the casualties of a previous war, religious loyalty, trade issues – beyond all the explanations
offered by the course of events, is there not a more fundamental
question: Why was war so prominent, so integral to the workings of
these societies? Pierre Clastres's theory perhaps provides an answer.

Among stateless peoples, he writes, war obeys a logic of differentiation. Each small community puts a priority on preserving its identity and political independence with respect to the others. The dynamic of war, the alternation between alliance and discord, is their way of perpetuating dispersion and plurality, preventing the absorption of one group by another.[16] Certainly, all the groups under discussion here weathered terrible disruptions during the seventeenth century. They were communities reconstituted from fragments torn out of their territories of origin – communities of refugees and not as homogeneous as they might have wished.[17] Under such circumstances, the quest for identity and differentiation might be experienced as an emergency and quasi-permanent war as the only way to cement the new community.

b) The colonial regulars and their officers

Neither their contemporaries nor subsequent historians have recognized the contribution of the *compagnies franches* to the wars of New France. In the colonial tableau coming into view in the first half of the eighteenth century, dominated by the admirable and troubling figure of the Canadian, these men are nowhere to be found.[18] Commentators celebrated the Carignan regiment, which had spent three years in Canada without distinguishing itself in war, but ignored the naval regulars stationed in the colony and involved in most of its military operations for nearly ninety years. "It is most vexing for the poor habitants to be continually ordered off to war when the majority of the soldiers are not," wrote Intendant Jean Bochart de Champigny in 1691. Half a century later, a naval engineer passing through the colony sounded a similar note: "In wartime, none but habitants can be armed for the defence of the colony and to assault and harass the English." There follows the classic portrait of the Canadian living by the gun and the French soldier incapable of marching in summer, let alone winter.[19] Shut out of the narrative by Bacqueville, Raudot, and Charlevoix, conflated with the colonists by certain observers, the colonial regulars are confined to the role of the foil in period writings.[20]

Although overflowing with military events, traditional history has not accorded them any greater importance. It is hardly surprising that this tack should have been taken by French-Canadian historians whose primary goal was to demonstrate that Canada owed nothing to France; for less obvious reasons, Anglophone historians have devoted little or no attention to the regulars either, other than to emphasize their inadequacies.[21] A few more recent articles on social profile, dress, or delinquent behaviour leave unchallenged the previous generations' judgment of this corps as militarily useless.[22] Only Jay Cassel's thesis finally provides some precise data on the subject, thereby adding nuance to this interpretation.[23]

Yet one need only read the chronicles of the war years 1689–97 to discover that the *compagnies franches* played a very important role in the defence of the colony. The thousand soldiers quartered at Montreal and nearby forts were constantly on the move, pursuing the enemy or accompanying convoys. Colonists, too, were members of such detachments but in smaller numbers, and nothing suggests that they performed any better than the regulars – quite the contrary.[24] Official troop registers (*contrôles de troupes*) have not survived, and the references found in the administrative correspondence are contradictory; military mortality during this period is therefore clouded in uncertainty, although there is every reason to believe it was very high.[25] Moreover, the regulars did more than just patrol the côtes of the colony to protect and assist habitants, taking part in major campaigns as duty demanded: A minority of them joined war parties as volunteers. They accounted for one-third of the detachment that captured the English forts at James Bay in 1686, about half the French troops involved in the attack on Schenectady in February 1690, and two-fifths of the men who sacked the Newfoundland coasts with Iberville in the winter of 1697. They were present at Deerfield in 1704, in Newfoundland with Montigny in 1705, and at Haverhill in 1709, and doubtless participated in other less-documented parties. At the end of the Nine Years' War, an intendant counted 300 soldiers able to join a party, or two-fifths of the corps – an honourable proportion, whatever he may have thought.[26] In short, these French soldiers supplied their complement of hale and hearty young volunteers eager for action, just as the colony did. In their case, it was adventure for adventure's sake, since the clamour for commissions was much too strong for a soldier of modest background to expect to rise through the ranks.[27]

The active duty officers, supernumeraries, and cadets, a group of 150–200 men, made the renown of New France. They acquitted themselves well in the defence of the territory and especially in war parties, leading small motley formations rather than their own companies. Several factors converged in the late seventeenth century to favour their outstanding individual feats, beginning with the young age of this officer corps. The *compagnies franches* were a recent creation, and the officers arriving from France between 1683 and 1687 were not much older than the young people of the colony jostling one another to gain access. Youth was an asset, since what counted in this type of military endeavour was boldness more than experience. The presence of war on the territory for nearly ten years left no role for idlers – those who found the service too hard went home, leaving the stronger-willed ones in the colony.[28] Another momentary advantage: The weakness of the command structure and the lack of troop cohesion gave the officers great freedom of movement. Finally, their ardour was stoked by fierce competition for commissions. Colonial youths had no option other than to throw themselves headlong into war if they hoped to carve out a niche in the profession. This whole situation was to change in the eighteenth century as the danger receded, the corps aged, priority was assigned as a function of seniority, and easy wins nurtured complacency, but for the time being the officers spared themselves no hazards: twenty-seven, or about one-fifth, were killed during the Nine Years' War, as many as during the Seven Years' War.[29]

And it was not just a matter of striving for a job or a promotion, as stressed at length in the previous chapter. Officers and cadets fought for the honour of serving the king, for personal glory, for pleasure, often for the spoils of war, to uphold or glorify the family name: indeed, for so many closely intertwined motives that they themselves would have been unable to distinguish between duty and interest.

c) Volunteers

Enough data exist to sketch a portrait of the men – grouped here into the category of volunteers – who followed their officers into war parties.[30] Historians have always conflated them with the militias, despite obvious differences: for these men, there was no coercion or predetermined geographical origin. The expedition commander possessed the *sine qua non* of official authorization to take a certain number of men with him and chose them at his discretion from among those who offered their services.[31] The private nature of this word-of-mouth recruitment explains why members of the commander's community or extended family accounted for so many of the recruits. He expected volunteers to turn up well armed and, in many cases, to bring along the rest of their kit as well. Only steadfast, motivated, and, if possible, experienced men were taken. They were young – in their early twenties, for most of those that I identified – and generally from urban backgrounds. Quebec produced far more than Montreal, largely reflecting the demographic weight of the two towns or the officers' domicile and especially the maritime venue of a large number of the corresponding operations.

Beyond these general characteristics, it is possible to discern an upper crust composed of sons of nobles and townspeople, plus members of seigneurial families. Volunteering served as a springboard for aspiring officers and enabled certain commoners of honourable background to eventually obtain a commission in the colonial regulars. Daniel Migeon de la Gauchetière, son of a Montreal bailiff, invoked his service on Iberville's ships to obtain a naval commission, and it was for having participated as volunteers in the expeditions to Hudson Bay (1686) and Schenectady (1690) that Jacques Testard de Montigny and Zacharie Robutel de la Noue, merchants' sons related to the Le Moynes, were admitted to the officer corps.[32] But these successes were too exceptional to sustain the ambitions of the many other volunteers who came from the same social class. We will never know exactly why Louis Crevier, the son of the seigneur of Saint-François, was to die at Salmon Falls or why the sons of notary François Genaple de Bellefonds lost their lives in Acadia, at Fort Bourbon (York Factory, on Hudson Bay), or in Louisiana.[33] There was never much cultural distance between such volunteers, who earned an epitaph in the military chronicles, and the troop of partisans. Proximity favoured bonds of camaraderie, or at least acquaintance, among these sons of a single generation of immigrants who had grown up side by side in these small towns and the countryside around them. But whereas such friendships cannot be easily measured, family ties are unmistakeable and were just as strong among sons of artisans, or members of the working class in general, as among sons of the elite. A list of sixty-seven Canadian volunteers awaiting a Mississippi-bound boat at Rochefort contains seven pairs of brothers, a remarkably high proportion.[34] The three sons of the arquebusier René Fezeret were killed in action in Louisiana at the turn of the century, and three of the four sons of a former Carignan officer lost their lives as volunteers in the campaign against the Chickasaws.[35] This is to say nothing of the ripple effects among

extended families, the best example being that of the Le Moyne
brothers, who could count on the loyalty of a large number of relatives to support their enterprises.[36]

Among the many motives that drove young people to join war parties, wages, or the promise of participation in looting and ransoms,
often proved decisive. In the case of expeditions financed by private
interests, the conditions are fairly well known and were at times
generous. In 1686, the Compagnie du Nord offered 100 volunteers
willing to travel overland to Hudson Bay and harass the English a
monthly wage of thirty livres or more as a function of each one's
talents, with three months paid in advance, "apart from their share
in any profits which it may please God to bestow." It surely took no
less to attract people capable of bearing up under the rigours and
risks of such a voyage, including indispensable tradesmen, sailors,
ship's carpenters, gunsmiths, and others.[37] The troops who took part
in the Newfoundland campaign with Iberville in 1696–97 invoked
their charter party in claiming half the prize captured at St John's, on
which they had received an advance when departing from Canada.[38]
The conditions and vocabulary – the contract reads, "prizes taken, be
it on land or at sea," for example – reflect the influence of the privateering that was taking hold in Quebec around this time. According
to maritime custom, shipowners retained two-thirds of prizes, and
the crew shared the remaining third; this was divided into a certain
number of lots, with each member getting one or more of them as a
function of rank and merit. Advances were sometimes extended, but
wages were rarely paid.[39] The Newfoundland campaigns of 1704,
1705, and 1709, the Port-Royal campaign of 1707, and the Hudson
Bay campaigns of 1694, 1697, and 1709 were private enterprises
that conformed, in most particulars, to this model of distribution.

Nothing is known about how much was actually earned, and
Carbonear was no Cartagena. Still, the profits must have been sufficient, for the organizers never lacked for volunteers.[40] But it took
time to convert prizes – principally furs and cod – into money, so volunteers had to settle in for a wait. Almost two years after their 1686
expedition, five volunteers of the Chevalier de Troye's party waived
their rights and actions against the Compagnie du Nord in exchange
for a lump sum of 400 livres.[41] The distribution of the prizes taken
at St John's in 1709 was still wending its way through the courts
in 1716. Half the sums "from the spoils and ransoms" owing to
the combatants, officers, soldiers, and habitants of Plaisance went

unpaid by the parties in question, Philippe Pastour de Costebelle and Joseph de Monbeton de Brouillan (*dit* Saint-Ovide), governor and king's lieutenant, respectively, at the time of this expedition. They contended that the bills of exchange drawn on London to cover a portion of the "ransoms" had not been honoured.[42] What is meant by the term "ransoms" here is far from clear. It can only have covered the enemy's property, not his person, for this latter would have been an illicit transaction that could never have been mentioned in court. The Newfoundland campaigns yielded hundreds of prisoners who, for lack of funds, were often abandoned in their devastated villages after being disarmed. Even those who went to prison were ordinarily released quickly as a cost-saving measure, so the release itself could not have been a source of much profit. Did French officers acquiesce to sparing certain property, certain shipments, in exchange for a monetary contribution? Perhaps, but the explanation sits uneasily alongside the systematic tactics of burning, looting, and destruction described in the military accounts. What, for example, was the object of the 260 pounds sterling remitted by the merchant George Skeffington to Lieutenant Testard de Montigny in conjunction with the capture of Bonavista in 1705? This post was destroyed forthwith and its inhabitants, Skeffington chief among them, transported to the prisons of Plaisance.[43] In contrast to privateering, which was strictly regulated and watched by the admiralties, these "prizes captured on land," governed by private agreements alone, eluded investigation, leaving backers and commanders all the latitude they needed to deprive the men of their fair share of the profits. The 1744 expedition against the port of Canso, financed by Louisbourg merchants and officers, offers a good example of misappropriation: The garrison members who had volunteered apparently received none of the promised booty.[44]

Finally, there was always the risk of defeat, as in 1709 at Fort Albany on Hudson Bay, where there was nothing to share other than debts and humiliation. This case is particularly interesting for its illustration of Versailles's ambiguous attitude toward such campaigns: benevolent when they succeeded, contemptuous when they failed. You claim, wrote the minister to Vaudreuil, that it would be easy to chase the English out of James Bay with 100 men, "offering the spoils, or a share of them, in recompense." If this could be done at no cost, "His Majesty ... would find it well that you undertake it." The governor and the intendant hastened to grant this wish. They founded and personally invested in a corporation to set an example and were then harshly rebuked for having acted according to their "private interest."[45]

Nevertheless, the operations just discussed offered a major benefit that attracted both investments and participants: These coastal villages had stocks of cod and furs, as well as boats with which to carry these items to their destination. Parties targeting New York and New England did not offer these advantages and were always at the king's expense, which was no impediment to the participants' sharing in the spoils but limited their share to what they could personally carry off. The chances of finding money or valuable objects in these frontier towns were all but nil; still, in a world of scarcity, anything was fair game. After sacking Schenectady in February 1690, the partisans took off with fifty horses loaded with booty. With the adversary on their heels, they abandoned most and then ate some in order to survive. Louis Descarri nonetheless succeeded in bringing two horses back to the family home in the Montreal suburb of Saint-Joseph.[46] Men ordinarily weighed themselves down for the return voyage, lightening their loads when difficult passages had to be negotiated; fortunate were those who had anything left after a four-to-six-week trek through the woods. As Harold Selesky has observed in regard to a dragoon company raised in Connecticut, the promise of booty in this kind of warfare was just smoke and mirrors – repeated with every campaign, revealed as largely empty in practice.[47] The disappointment proved less bitter for English volunteers, who were paid by their provincial assemblies, whereas Canadians recruited by the king were not, in principle, entitled to a salary.

The absurdity of this principle certainly did not escape contemporary observers. The intendant might offer 300 livres to volunteers for an expedition to Michilimackinac because of the risks inherent in the voyage, yet not a penny for those who escorted them or joined a war party.[48] At Quebec, adventuresome youths, who were far from legion, could choose from among three employers: fishing and trading companies at twelve to thirty livres per month, depending on the job; privateers and the officers recruiting for them, who told of fabulous profits and often paid advances; and the governor, who offered nothing but an unlikely shot at the spoils. Could he have been so ignorant of supply and demand? Did he really think such conditions were enough to recruit good men for war parties? The intendant explained in 1692 that he had been obliged to pay twelve livres per month to sixty volunteers who had gone to Acadia, and it is a good bet that every call for volunteers gave rise to similar negotiations, as well as compensation kept secret so as not to annoy the minister.[49]

The competition between paid voyages and free military service is a problem that would recur during the mid-eighteenth century wars but in another context. The context we have just glimpsed – maritime campaigns largely backed by private capital and close ties between Quebec, Plaisance, and Port-Royal – was fast disappearing. Not enough attention has been paid to this short-lived phase of New France history. For France and its colonies, the years 1690–1713 were the golden era of privateering. Port-Royal, quite reasonably nicknamed the "Dunkirk of the Americas," was an important staging point for privateers, although far surpassed by Plaisance in terms of the number of prizes.[50] The north Atlantic witnessed the adoption of the Caribbean technique of buccaneering, involving the use of small boats (often under thirty-five tons) armed with a few cannons and demanding minimal financing.[51] Buccaneers relied on surprise and flexibility to attack fishing boats and merchant ships along the coasts of Newfoundland and New England. These waters were plied by English privateers as well, which made the work dangerous but did not deter small investors. In 1704, Quebec merchant baker Louis Prat built a schooner, christened the *Joybert* in honor of the governor's wife, for his business supplying flour to Newfoundland and "for fitting out ships as privateers to fight the state's enemies"; on the prow was an image of St Michael crushing the dragon of heresy. Prat's zeal eventually won him a harbourmaster position.[52] Encouraged by the authorities, Quebec's largest traders and many of its officers were involved in outfitting privateers during this period, almost always working in partnership to diminish the risks.[53] Canada could overcome its two main handicaps – the interruption of river navigation in winter and an initial shortage of good 75- to 100-ton ships – by relying on the ports of Newfoundland and Acadia, where ships were exchanged and sailors could carry their prizes to shelter at all seasons. Quebec, however, held an asset with respect to the neighbouring colonies: a larger population from which to constitute or fill out privateer crews, which demanded many more men than ordinary navigation.[54] Since no studies have been done on the subject, there is no way to tell whether Canada took advantage of this complementarity. From an economic standpoint, and despite the enthusiasm aroused by a few successes (e.g., the buccaneer Jean Léger de

Lagrange's 1704 expedition against the English in Newfoundland), it is quite possible that there were more failures than successes.[55]

But the point of the discussion is not to measure success or failure but to observe that these maritime activities had undeniable repercussions for volunteer reserves. Combined with engagements for the gulf fisheries, privateering used up the best sailors, the most resolute young men – more than 100 in some years, many of whom were on one-way trips. It was commonly believed that, from one voyage to the next, a portion of the Canadian crews had been lost "in the hot countries."[56] The "Beauchesne" character created or embellished by Alain-René Lesage in 1732 – a Canadian who swapped his snowshoes for a cutlass and died in France after buccaneering in the southern seas – belongs to the same tradition.[57] Volunteers did in fact move from one theatre of war to another. No sooner had he returned from his "expedition against the Iroquois" than Jacques Dain hired on for Hudson Bay and set off westward the following year, eventually meeting an unknown death. Three notarized donations so that his friends would "remember him in their prayers" punctuate his ill-starred path.[58] Raids on English villages, clashes with the Iroquois at the Ottawa rapids, a winter on Hudson Bay between two battles, a sea campaign: all these were employment possibilities for men who made war an occupation, a way of life. After a few years of danger, privation, killings, ravages, and meagre prizes, some returned to settle in the colony, but they were ill prepared for the dull life and labour awaiting them. War wrecked bodies and souls. To be a good partisan, one had to join every party. The colony's peasants and labourers were poor soldiers because they rarely went to war. Nothing could be more obvious. To put it bluntly, and *pace* theoreticians of the farmer-soldier, these two occupations are incompatible.

Circulating along with rumours of military actions on the frontiers were disturbing stories of young men who roamed the woods and the waters and guarded the forts: for example, the killing of the chaplain of Fort Albany by young Guillory, son of a Montreal gunsmith.[59] Such stories heightened the people's mistrust of volunteer bands, widening the gap between them. Recall the fear aroused by Iberville's comrades in arms, "meaner than the English themselves," among the young men of Île d'Orléans recruited as militiamen in 1696.[60] No better illustration of the difference between the two military corps can be found; it was perceptible to contemporaries, even if historians have chosen to ignore it.

2. THE MILITIA AS SEEN BY THE ADMINISTRATION

In the early eighteenth century, when the Treaty of Utrecht had just put an end to intercolonial hostilities, the Canadian population of men aged fifteen to fifty stood at around 4,000. The survivors among the upriver habitants who had fended off Iroquois incursions for ten years were now in their forties or even older and only accounted for a small proportion of the total. The same was true of the volunteers, never very numerous, some of whom had dispersed outside the colony in the course of their distant engagements. The majority of militiamen had never been to war. Although frequently mobilized, they had faced enemy fire only four times: in 1687 and 1693 in Iroquois territory, in 1690 at Quebec, and in 1691 at La Prairie. They had been mobilized several times during the War of the Spanish Succession but never saw battle. There is a sharp disconnect between this limited experience and the enduring generalizations about the military performance of this population. At the beginning of this study, I traced the idealized images of soldiers and militiamen through the relations, accounts, historical memorials, and literature of the era. I will now proceed to consider whether these discourses influenced the course of events: whether colonial administrators shared contemporary opinions as to the value of the militias and whether their policies reflected this confidence.

a) Manhattan and Boston as targets of conquest

An analysis of plans to conquer Manhattan and Boston answers the question. It shows that many early administrators – with notable exceptions – believed the militias to be war-hardened enough to carry such campaigns to successful completion. But the jaded remarks proliferating in the early eighteenth century mark the end of this blithe assurance and the beginning of a more realistic vision of the colony's military potential.

In the latter third of the seventeenth century, the naval ministry considered a dozen initiatives for conquest of the English colonies and twice gave the go-ahead. The annexation of New Netherland to Canada was in itself an excellent idea. It would force the Iroquois to surrender their weapons, give the French colony a second outlet to the sea and a monopoly on furs coming from inland, and keep New England "contained within its borders." The raid on Manhattan and the Hudson River posts instigated in 1664 by the Duke of York, the brother of Charles II, combined with the presence of the Carignan regiment, seemingly boded well for this plan. Intendant Jean Talon believed that after having subdued the Mohawks, it would be necessary to attack Fort Orange (today Albany, NY), where the Dutch were bound to join the French in an effort to shake "the insupportable domination of the English."[61] Appearing here for the first time is the idea that various groups oppressed by the English colonies – Flemish, Irish, Catholics, African slaves – would hail the French army as liberating heroes; it gave licence to all manner of bold schemes and was to be repeated often. The king, continued Talon, could also opt for a diplomatic solution that forced England to restore the colony to the Dutch, after which a purchase agreement with the latter could be reached. In 1681, Talon's successor Jacques Duchesneau still believed that the Duke of York would willingly relinquish his American domain to France for the right price. It would then be a mere matter of conquering Boston by force of arms – child's play – and so consolidating the colony's acquisition.[62] This was the second assumption: that England was not particularly attached to its colonies and would not intervene to drive out the French the day they captured them.

The mediocre campaigns of 1684 and 1687 did not pour cold water on these schemes of conquest – on the contrary, they revived them. The argument was simple. Since the Iroquois could not be defeated militarily, the French would have to begin by dislodging their English protectors with a two-pronged attack, by sea and by land. In the fall of 1688, Louis-Hector de Callière, governor of Montreal and representative of Governor-General Denonville, proposed this plan to Versailles, which decided to put it into action but with considerable modifications. Canada would secretly assemble 1,000 soldiers and 600 habitants to march on Fort Orange and then on to Manhattan, which would already be under siege from two frigates. The minister put the governor in charge of the operations. The bulk of the instructions concerned the disposition of prizes, the occupation of the conquered land, and the fate of its population.[63] The decision to undertake this campaign and the optimism emanating from the instructions were not unrelated to recent events in England: William's landing in November, the flight of James II to France, the crowning of the "usurper" in February 1689. The colonies would surely revolt against the representatives of their legitimate sovereign, it was believed in Quebec and Versailles alike, and the disorder would inevitably favour French arms.[64] The rebellions of New York and Boston with the announcement of the glorious revolution gave credence to these long-standing prejudices. A "popular government" like that of New England, which did not recognize the royal representatives' authority, was an aberration that would eventually sink into total anarchy. In the minds of contemporary administrators, Boston was little more than a haven for bandits that would disintegrate with the first attack, for – and this was the fourth assumption – its residents were only interested in commerce, knew nothing of warfare, and were incapable of defending themselves.[65]

Sieur de la Coffinière's frigates reached Chedabucto (present-day Guysborough, NS) on 12 September 1689, too late to assemble the colony's troops and send them off to attack New York, as Frontenac chose to explain the matter to the minister.[66] The idea of a land invasion did not in fact enjoy unanimous support, the new governor being one of those who thought it unfeasible. He ardently hoped that the king would send a fleet to strike "those old parliamentarians of Boston ... and those of Manhattan in their lair" but did not think Canada's assistance ought to be counted on. The distance was an insurmountable obstacle, he said, as were the difficulties associated with the journey and the transportation of provisions and munitions.[67] But others continued to believe in the plan. Iberville, for one, had the ear of Pontchartrain and Jean-Baptiste de Lagny, the intendant of commerce, who was in charge of Canadian affairs for the naval ministry.[68] A new attempt at a joint expedition was launched in 1697, with Boston as the first target. Following the orders received, Frontenac gathered 1,500 men in late May and ordered canoes, arms, and provisions to be prepared for the voyage to Fort Pentagouet (present-day Castine, ME), where they would embark on André de Nesmond's battlefleet, consisting of eleven ships carrying 300 soldiers plus four fireships. An Indigenous advance guard reinforced by 100 Canadians would travel on foot to paralyze Boston's defences before the landing. After taking the city, the troops would follow the coast to New York, destroying everything in their path. The question of booty takes up much space in the memoranda and instructions surrounding the enterprise, and it is clear that the minister was counting on the lure of "immense riches" to cover his costs.[69] But once again, winds and other factors thwarted this plan. After three months of waiting at Quebec, the militias were demobilized and sent back to their parishes, while Nesmond embarked on the return voyage to France having accomplished nothing.[70]

Four years later, Iberville tried to revive the enterprise with a new strategy. Since coordination between naval and land forces seemed impossible, the colony would act alone, with the help of a single ship to supply provisions along the coast. Secrecy being the key to success, the 1,800 troops (1,000 Canadian militiamen, 400 regulars, 400 Amerindians) would take the more direct and concealed route along the Chaudière and Kennebec rivers instead of the usual route via the Rivière-du-Loup and the Saint John River, where they would have been spotted at once. The campaign would take place in winter when Boston Harbor was deserted and only indigents unsuited to military duty were present. He predicted it would take a few hours to capture the city, or at most a few days, and the rest of the winter to devastate the countryside all the way to the gates of New York, forcing the population to take refuge in Pennsylvania. A similar expedition could be launched against New York the following winter. Flush with confidence from the decade's triumphs, Iberville was ready to take command of it. This time, however, his proposals were not entertained.[71]

Following in Charlevoix's footsteps, historians have ascribed the failure of these schemes of conquest to external circumstances, never considering whether the colonial troops were actually capable of accomplishing the mission if only Versailles had deigned to give them better support, if the ships had made haste.[72] That is highly doubtful. These enterprises were not really planned. The attendant logistical problems, such as the lack of stores of provisions along these routes, were not even discussed. The colonial strategists seemed to believe that an army of recruits could function like a party of a hundred determined French and Indigenous volunteers; that like them, it could reach the Atlantic coast within a month; that the tactics used to sneak up on a town of 300 or 400 such as Schenectady could be reproduced with the same efficacy to subdue cities of 5,000 to 7,000 such as New York and Boston. Iberville's final schemes, the most unrealistic by far, were modelled on Portneuf's January 1690 raid, which had nonetheless taken more than three months to reach its target by following the Chaudière River upstream, an all but impassable route.[73] The numbers betray the same blithe imprudence. The plans for the 1689 campaign had largely been predicated on the colonial regulars, who were then numerous. But war had decimated their numbers, so the number of militiamen was increased for these faraway expeditions without considering the repercussions this would have on the colony.

These schemes reveal the attitude prevailing in the colony in the late seventeenth century. They were, as we have said, rooted in ignorance of the English colonies: Every strategist underestimated the adversary's political will and capacity to resist. Most striking is the abiding but outsized confidence placed in the officers' talents and the habitants' military capacities on the strength of a few fresh exploits. The defence of Quebec in 1690, at which the militias performed well, did much to lend credence to the idea that, where military prowess was concerned, the colonists could do everything without having learned anything. Was the euphoria confined to a small circle of officers, or had it pervaded public opinion to a large extent? There is no way to tell, but we know for a fact that it evaporated after 1700, when such plans for conquest were consigned to oblivion.[74] From then on, the boldest plans hewed to modest objectives more in keeping with the practices of partisan war: sacking the target and retreating at once. In response to the minister's rebuke for failing to capitalize on the militias' good will and organize a large expedition to New England, as the governor of Montreal had proposed, Vaudreuil explained that it might be easy to mobilize the habitants to defend Quebec, "a common cause" and a two-week journey, but that the same was not true of a months-long party. Furthermore, he wrote, "not everyone is capable of it"[75] – an obvious statement, yet one that colonial administrators had yet to clearly articulate. In 1709, the militias' reputation took a beating: that July, they gave in to panic along the shores of Lake Champlain and in September put up resistance when asked to defend Quebec from another impending invasion.[76] It is no surprise to find enthusiasm for their prowess waning.

b) The militia: Not what it used to be

The government's attitude toward horses, which deserves to be highlighted in the annals of administrative idiocy, illustrates this turnabout. Until then very rare in the colony and practically absent from the countryside around Montreal, horses began to make their appearance in the early eighteenth century, thanks in particular to intercolonial trade conducted by a few Englishmen in the interwar period.[77] The authorities immediately asserted a connection between peasants who travelled by carriage and sled on the one hand and the military disappointments of recent years on the other. "It has been noticed," wrote the governor's wife and spokesperson, "that since the arrival of so many horses in Canada, the youth are no longer as vigorous as when they were obliged to travel on foot in summer or on snowshoes in winter, so that … if a few winter parties need to be organized, one is hard-pressed to find people who can travel on snowshoes as they used to." In a word, the Canadians had become "effeminate."[78] Also mentioned was the threat posed by an abundance of horses to the raising of livestock. Versailles found the first of these arguments persuasive and demanded harsh measures to prevent the habitants from leading an easy life, which was claimed to diminish their strength, tear down their courage, and erode their superiority over the English.[79] From 1710 to 1713, the destruction of horses was a central theme of the annual memorandum from the king to his administrators, and the latter never failed to respond with respect that they were doing their best to curtail the problem. In reality, they were doing nothing at all, since the problem did not exist and they soon realized it. When an ordinance forbidding ownership of more than two horses was published, only a minority of peasants owned even one, and the legal threshold was attained in the ensuing decades by a tiny proportion of the peasantry – 3–10 per cent, depending on the seigneury.[80] The ministry thought the matter buried for good, yet no sooner had Jean-Frédéric Phélypeaux, Comte de Maurepas, become secretary of state than he saw fit to reopen it. Maurepas denounced horse-owning as a disastrous custom that would make the colonists "unfit to serve as their fathers did" in the wars to come.[81] Intendant Gilles Hocquart struggled to convince the minister that horses were useful for agriculture and transportation, that the proposed plan to export them to the West Indies was unprofitable, and that the taxes and fines to be levied against horse owners were unviable. This curious obsession dragged on into mid-century in the king's memoranda, spurred on by criticism levelled by colonial officers at the campaigns against the Foxes and the Chickasaws.[82] If it was true that the Canadians were "not as fit for war" as they once had been, an explanation had to be found, and this one, which presented the situation as readily reversible, retained favour.[83]

The militia, as a specific corps in need of training and discipline, occupies an increasingly prominent place in the official correspondence from 1710 on. Formerly all but absent, references to troop reviews in the côtes, weapons inspections, the selection of officers, and the overall organization of the corps multiplied during this period. The governor wrote that they had to be taught "to march and form ranks as much as is necessary for them to obey a command, and everything having to do with military discipline."[84] At first sight, this sudden interest, coming at the very end of the war, seems paradoxical. Why this concern with military discipline, hitherto given short shrift, when the colony was no longer in danger? The answer is that the militia had, over the years, become much more than a reserve of recruits. It organized and structured the lives of the habitants in their parishes and already played the role of rapidly mobilizing corvées to build fortifications. By coincidence, just as the administrators were becoming fully aware of the institution's usefulness in relaying commands and maintaining public order in the côtes, a series of small, scattered disturbances and seditious remarks uttered on the king's work sites revealed a need to reinforce the hierarchy and inculcate obedience. What better than to subject the colonists to military discipline?

Yet, for lack of resources and will, the program never amounted to anything. Although it did please the ministry, the Quebec town major's annual tour to the parishes of that government had no effect in practice. When war resumed in 1744, the habitants were still unable to move as a unit or tell left from right.[85] But they had undergone another form of discipline, one that assured their docile acceptance of the continuous mass mobilization that would prevail from then on. Note that this was not an abrupt conversion to obedience, since this population had never in fact refused to serve. What had changed was the context and with it the demands of the military government. These demands increased considerably in the mid-eighteenth century and might have provoked resistance if the conditions for obedience had not long been in place.

Public Order and Military Power

Historians of New France have devoted hardly any attention to the nature of the colonial government. Scholarly work on its public institutions is lacking, and nearly everything written has dealt with the individuals who directed them rather than with the long-term workings of the administration. The general idea emerging from these portraits, and from the descriptions found in works of synthesis, is that the Ancien Régime became less autocratic – some would say weakened – when it crossed the Atlantic. For the authoritative historian William J. Eccles, the government of New France was an improved version of the government of a French province, the result of an enlightened policy that strove to neutralize privileges or private interests for the benefit of the colonists' common good. He argues that the extreme centralization of power, the absence of any form of representation, afforded guarantees of equity and efficiency.[1] Contrasting with this is Alexis de Tocqueville's criticism in a footnote to his work on the Ancien Régime, which is never so much as mentioned in Canadian historiography.

> The physiognomy of governments can be best detected in their colonies, for there their features are magnified, and rendered more conspicuous. When I want to discover the spirit and vices of the government of Louis XIV, I must go to Canada. Its deformities are seen there as through a microscope.
>
> A number of obstacles, created by previous occurrences or old social forms, which hindered the development of the true tendencies of government at home, did not exist in Canada. There was no nobility, or, at least, none had taken deep root. The Church

was not dominant. Feudal traditions were lost or obscured. The power of the judiciary was not interwoven with old institutions or popular customs. There was, therefore, no hindrance to the free play of the central power. It could shape all laws according to its views. And in Canada, therefore, there was not a shadow of municipal or provincial institutions; and no collective or individual action was tolerated. An Intendant far more powerful than his colleagues in France; a government managing far more matters than it did at home, and desiring to manage everything from Paris, notwithstanding the intervening eighteen hundred leagues; never adopting the great principles which can render a colony populous and prosperous, but, instead, employing all sorts of petty, artificial methods, and small devices of tyranny to increase and spread population; forced cultivation of lands; all lawsuits growing out of the concession of land removed from the jurisdiction of the courts and referred to the local administration; compulsory regulations respecting farming and the selection of land – such was the system devised for Canada under Louis XIV: it was Colbert who signed the edicts ...

In the United States, on the contrary, the English anti-centralization system was carried to an extreme. Parishes became independent municipalities, almost democratic republics. The republican element, which forms, so to say, the foundation of the English constitution and English habits, shows itself and develops without hindrance. Government proper does little in England, and individuals do a great deal; in America, government never interferes, so to speak, and individuals [join together to] do everything. The absence of an upper class, which renders the Canadian more defenseless against the government than his equals were in France, renders the citizen of the English colonies still more independent of the home power.[2]

This long quotation is not superfluous, for it gets to the heart of the problem, which has to do with governmental centralization and the respective importance of political will and historical context as factors of change. Tocqueville encourages us to study the facts of the colony from a comparative perspective and to acknowledge that which divides and distinguishes them from those of the metropole. To begin with, an incontestable fact: Whereas everywhere else in the realm, the monarchy had to come to terms with local power, in the colony it met with few obstacles and made short work of snuffing out the few institutions that might eventually have interfered with its administrators. Tocqueville observed colonial legislation at a time when the "obsession with governing" (Mirabeau) was at its height, and one can only agree with him as to the foolishness of certain edicts or draft edicts to encourage settlement (*peuplade*) and organize life in the colony.[3] But the ministerial directives do not explain everything. At first equally lacking in administrative checks and balances, Canada and the West Indies shared the same administrative system, and yet, in one case, royal representatives were able to wield power without serious opposition for more than a century, while in the other, the threat of unrest repeatedly forced them to back down.[4] At the very least, the contrast casts doubt on the vigour of the Ancien Régime bureaucracy, suggesting that individuals' capacity to band together when their interests are threatened should not be underestimated. It is well, wrote Colbert to the governor of New France, that "each person speak for himself, and that none speak for all," yet even in the colonies, even in the absence of bona fide institutional support, new communities sprang into being and at times spoke with a single voice.[5] Moreover, it is clear that factors other than those singled out by Tocqueville – economics, and especially war, that powerful driver of state growth – influenced political and administrative development.[6]

While in France war engendered fiscal crisis, demanding more complex and centralized financial management and, paradoxically, consolidating the pre-eminence of the civilian sphere over the military, in Canada it set in motion a contrary process: the progressive militarization of power. The future was not, after all, a foregone conclusion in 1663. The two-headed administration implemented by Colbert in the American colonies – the king's commissioners on the one hand, a sovereign court entrenched in the colony on the other – reflected the weight of French tradition more than it did the secretary of state's centralizing designs. And since the powers and responsibilities of both were rather ill-defined and overlapping, the power dynamics between them had yet to ossify.[7] They soon would. The Conseil Supérieur was quickly shorn of the broadly defined administrative jurisdiction found in its enabling edict, becoming little more than a closely supervised tribunal. Even its right of registration (the power to ratify or modify royal ordinances) was severely limited in the eighteenth century, and the powers and discretion of the three royal trial courts were likewise eroded. A study of these institutions and the major modifications they underwent between 1663 and 1760 remains to be done.[8] It suffices to point out this tendency and situate it in the military context that served as its justification, although a final observation about the absence of venal offices in the colony must be added. This was progress, say the historians, a gauge of competence and honesty, since magistrates who did not give satisfaction could be revoked. But revocations were rare and always for insubordination, never for incompetence. As a general rule, the insecurity of their positions made these individuals fearful, highly vulnerable to pressure from the governor and the intendant, at times torn between the two, and incapable of defending their institutions.[9]

The governor, the one always called "Monsieur le Général," was the embodiment of both dignity and authority. Unlike the provincial governors, who possessed only the first – "ado, trumpets, violins, an air of royalty," wrote Madame de Sévigné – the governor of Canada played a leading role.[10] The fact that justice and, at least in principle, policing were the bailiwick of the intendant did not alter the real and very broad powers of the king's representative, which would remain intact until the end of the regime.[11] The frequent quarrels between seventeenth-century governors and intendants ought not to obscure the fact that in the final analysis, military priorities took precedence over all other aspects of the administration and demanded cooperation on essential matters. Moreover, these rivalries subsided after 1715.[12] The intendants' involvement in military administration was not an original feature, since their jurisdiction in this area was considerable in France as well, particularly in frontier regions and conquered lands, but it was even more marked in Canada.[13] By virtue of his training in the offices of the navy as much as his duties and affinities, the intendant – who sat on war councils and whose principal task was to manage finances, essentially the military budget – more closely resembled an army intendant than a provincial one. Intendant Champigny, for one example, went to Fort Frontenac in June 1687 and ordered the "arrest" of some Iroquois on Lake Ontario;[14] Intendant François Bigot, for another, left the capital in the colony's final days to live in the army camp at Beauport: two isolated acts, yet nonetheless suggesting the value of studying areas of agreement instead of seizing upon every dispute, of not falling for facile interpretations such as the cliché that the balance of power was maintained by the opposition between the robe and the sword.[15]

The colony's military orientation was also reflected in the nature of taxation. The population was subjected to a series of direct, in-kind levies: militia duty, corvées for the forts, billeting of soldiers, and requisitions of labour, carts, and grain. The general staff oversaw recruitment in each of the three governments. We saw earlier how the integration of the colonial nobility into the regulars reinforced an inegalitarian social structure that might otherwise have faded away. As partners of royal power, the military nobility became a vehicle for its entrenchment in the colony.

In sum, the continuous presence of troops, the primacy of the Indigenous alliance, and incessant wars were some of the unforeseen developments that accentuated centralization and made administrative practices more rigid. In the last two decades of the French regime, Canada looked more and more like a big garrison, commanded more than it was governed. "This administration, the most absolutist there ever has been, will hear nothing of representations, nor difficulties, nor delays, nor refusals," said one colonist and former employee of the king at the end of the regime.[16] This introduction forms the backdrop to the following chapters, and to this one in particular, which takes a close look at local governmental organization – in particular, the role of the urban and rural militias in community formation and the maintenance of public order.

I. URBAN POLICING AND TOWN MILITIAS

a) Closely watched towns

In the 1670s, Canadian towns were characterized by an absence of municipal organization. The colonists of Quebec, Trois-Rivières, and Montreal had formerly had general assemblies on the model of French villages, composed of free, domiciled men who elected a procurator-syndic each year to administer the community's affairs and property on their behalf.[17] Marcel Trudel, a historian of this period, linked the presence of the syndics to the council established in 1647 to administer the colony, on which they had a consultative and later a deliberative voice, but he ignored the local duties that were the original reason for these officials' existence.[18] To plan, organize, and protect the first settlements, habitants had no choice but to gather in communities under the authority of the governor, even before the creation of the Conseil de Québec (1647). Excluded from this, and from colonial administration generally after 1657, the three syndics continued to be in charge of municipal policing until Colbert ordered their positions abolished in 1673. Four years later, they had ceased to exist.[19] The withdrawal of this privilege apparently did not cause a stir, and the memory of the institution, which had existed for thirty years, soon faded. The big losers were the artisans and small merchants, the middle (and majority) fraction of the urban population from whose ranks most of the syndics had come; put bluntly, they lost the people who looked after their interests. The abolition of the town assemblies seems to have left the elites indifferent; were it not so, the official correspondence would contain some record of protest on their part. Nobles and larger merchants were regularly consulted by the authorities anyway; they saw no need to make common cause with the lower classes in a fight to preserve the right to administer their own affairs. The communal tradition that had crossed an ocean was not strong enough to withstand the will of the central power, and the nature of the taxes levied in the eighteenth century was not conducive to the revival of that tradition. Town dwellers were aware that there was "no syndic or public person to represent the public interest" but grew inured to this reality.[20]

Starting in 1663, the body rechristened the Conseil Souverain, along with the king's commissioners, issued general regulations concerning public order while the lieutenant-general for civil and criminal affairs or the local judge was in charge of local policing, or the enforcement of these regulations in the towns.[21] In the course of exercising their administrative duties, the magistrates found themselves in continual competition with the king's representatives, so much so that there can be said to have been two or even three levels of urban government. The intendants, whether directly or through their subdelegates, intervened regularly in policing and frequently in judicial proceedings. Relations were always tense between the naval commissary – the ex officio subdelegate in Montreal – and the officers of that jurisdiction. Clashes between them multiplied in the 1740s, for Lieutenant-General Jacques-Joseph Guiton de Monrepos was less tolerant than his predecessors of encroachment on his jurisdiction or acts that besmirched the dignity of his office.[22] Quebec and Trois-Rivières were unaffected by such conflicts; perhaps out of necessity, and certainly by clever design, it was the royal attorneys and judges who acted as subdelegates in those jurisdictions. By consenting to their total subordination to the intendant, these colonial officers contributed to the erosion of their own powers.[23] In gradually increasing measure, the administration of the city – involving such matters as the regulation of trades, the supplying of markets, and the taxation of goods – eluded the power of the courts.[24] The latter did remain partly responsible for roads and cabaret policing and could still prosecute various petty offenders but had to report to the intendant all weightier matters "that could relate in any way to property, public safety, or regulation of the troops" – which is to say, nearly everything.[25]

Local governors, staff officers, king's lieutenants, and town majors and their assistants represented the third tier of authority. Where law enforcement was concerned, they sat above the civilian authorities, who lacked the resources to preserve law and order. The entity officially responsible for this was the marshalcy, a body of military origin dedicated chiefly to the pursuit of brigands and deserters in the French countryside, which was introduced at Quebec in 1677 to mete out the same rough justice to vagrants and to assist with ordinary policing.[26] But vagrants were too few to justify an ad hoc tribunal, and the arrival of the naval troops a few years later further deprived the marshalcy of its utility. Instead of being abolished, however, it was left to languish. The provost at Quebec had just one exempt cleric (*exempt*) and four court officers (*archers*) at his command, while another small brigade composed of a lieutenant and three court officers was established at Montreal in 1711, supposedly to arrest drunken Indigenous people.[27] In both cities, the marshalcy assisted law officers and king's commissioners in enforcing ordinances and escorting convicts to their public tortures and executions. But it was too weak, for example, to pursue wrongdoers and deserters beyond town limits, especially since it had no horses to devote to this task. It occasionally rented horses but almost never went out without reinforcement by the regulars.[28]

In the first half of the eighteenth century, from November to April of each year, the Quebec garrison numbered a little under 200 soldiers and non-commissioned officers, the Montreal garrison nearly 500, amounting to one soldier per 2.5 inhabitants in 1700 or one per six or seven inhabitants in the 1740s.[29] The rest of the year saw some soldiers deployed to remote outposts, although an attempt was made to keep the urban garrisons at sufficient strength to command respect and preserve public order. Court officers who risked provoking violent reactions or resistance when making arrests, serving summons, or seizing property were accompanied by a sergeant and a few soldiers. Similarly, the court never travelled to investigate crimes committed in the countryside without a military escort. But the general staff did not just lend its soldiers for law enforcement duty; as the parties responsible for keeping the peace, and keeping watch in particular, the troops intervened on their officers' orders whenever crime or unrest was reported. If the persons apprehended were civilians, the ordinances dictated that the matter be heard by the judge as soon as he took cognizance of the arrest,[30] but this rule seems to have been largely ignored. Frequent scuffles between soldiers and colonists often resulted in the latter being summarily jailed for lengthy periods. When men rebelled against being recruited to build forts, regular officers did not hesitate to imprison them without appeal to the court. The magistrates complained, the officers were blamed, but the practice continued.[31] Even when right was not on their side, the general staff could resort to intimidation. Having decided, for example, to convert Montreal's marketplace into a parade ground, the officers repeatedly harassed peasants and the public to expel them from the site. The intendancy did not encourage these abuses – no more than many other manifestations of arrogance – but often opted to turn a blind eye to them.[32] It chimed in with the governors to demand an increase in troop numbers, for the preservation of law and order as much as the safety of the colony.[33]

For the urban population, the military represented a burden, a source of noise and disorder, but also conduced to the security of their property and persons, and this second consideration seems to have won out over the first. The people did not trouble themselves with jurisdictional conflicts; they recognized authority by its capacity to intervene, spontaneously running to the guard house when in need of protection.[34] This confidence could take surprising forms. In 1728, Montreal's artisans and merchants, worried about the price and scarcity of wheat, addressed a petition not to the competent authorities – the judge and the subdelegate – but to the local governor: in their minds, he alone could take effective action against hoarders.[35] Besides a few similar documents scattered in other fonds, the general staff and subdelegation archives are lost,[36] and a whole vista on urban life is closed off to historians. We have little or no knowledge of cases pitting colonists against Indigenous people or civilians against soldiers; of various societal movements that may have existed but had been nipped in the bud; of mutterings, minor unrest, repeated complaints, or other provocations, which, if better known, might shine a light on latent hostilities, unexpected socio-cultural divides.[37] Urban policing was not just a matter of sweeping chimneys, cleaning streets, and keeping cabaret owners in line, as the slim extant documentation from the ordinary jurisdictions might lead one to believe. Not easily separable from justice, policing concerned everything that stood to threaten public order. If Canadian towns were relatively peaceful after the late seventeenth century, it was surely thanks to the development of self-restraint, as André Lachance notes, but also, and especially, to the strict governance and close surveillance to which they were subjected.[38]

b) The town militias

The town militias sat in the shadow of the military, as the scarcity of references to them attests. A few times – in 1714, for example, and again in 1727 – Versailles asked that a roll of the colonial militias and their officers be drawn up, and the governor-general complied.[39] None has survived. All that remains is a summary from 1744 and a "recapitulation" for the year 1750, giving the number of companies per parish, their composition, and the captains' names in the case of urban companies. A search for militia officers in the judicial and notarial sources yields a few mentions for the first third of the eighteenth century, and this data is presented in Tables 6.1 and 6.2.

The Montreal companies were smaller and more numerous. There were five by 1721 and twelve in 1750, with numbers ranging from thirty to 110 men. Quebec, though more populous, had only two companies at the turn of the century and seven in 1750, with an average of 103 men, or twice that of Montreal. As in the home country, town militias were in charge of artillery, and young men from the cities were invited to learn how to fire a cannon on Sundays and holidays so that they could defend their towns when the moment came.[40] But as long as the naval troops detached to Canada did not have their own artillery company – which they would not until 1750 – the governor relied on the master gunners of Quebec and Montreal to teach the trade to soldiers, thus limiting the time devoted to militiamen-in-training.[41] It appears that their training continued to be neglected after 1750, since the city's officers, and even its master gunners, were doing continual duty at the posts and with the army.[42]

During this period, the infantry companies were led by four officers or even, in Montreal, by five, all of them merchants, some among the colony's most prominent.[43] Commercial success undoubtedly expedited one's rise from the rank of ensign to that of senior captain (*premier capitaine*), and seniority was equally important. The governors had to respect these criteria and resist the temptation to parachute a new, more militarily experienced arrival to the head of the pack. Pierre Guy, who immigrated to Canada shortly before 1725, rose through the four ranks within thirteen years. A small businessman at the time of his first commission in 1730, he quickly carved out an enviable reputation as a supplier to the king's Montreal stores and a purveyor to the fur trade.[44] Others, after less illustrious careers, languished in the rank and file, leaving the corps before they could obtain the social recognition accorded to captains. The title of colonel crowned the *cursus honorum*. At the turn of the century, it was still reserved for law officers, such as Jacques-Alexis de Fleury Deschambault and François-Marie Bouat, successive lieutenants-general of the jurisdiction of Montreal, and Conseil Supérieur member Jean Crespin, who succeeded lieutenant-general of the Quebec provost court René-Louis Chartier de Lotbinière. Note that these magistrates were also merchants. Subsequently, the rank of colonel was awarded to the most senior captain.[45] In 1750, merchants Jean-Baptiste Neveu and Joseph Fleury de la Gorgendière, both aged seventy-four, were militia colonels at Montreal and Quebec, respectively. Even captains were rarely in the flower of youth – their average age at the same date was forty-five. The names of the three or four sergeants who filled out each company are unknown, and one can only suppose that they were artisans or in some cases ex-soldiers. Only one thing is certain: as in the regulars, a social barrier separated them from the officer corps, to which they had no access.

When Louis Charly Saint-Ange, captain of a militia company in 1752, asked the governor of Montreal for permission to leave the service while retaining "the ranks, honours, exemptions, and prerogatives attaching to said rank," he was mainly referring to the exemption from housing soldiers, an imposition abhorred by the townspeople.[46] The other advantages were less clear. Urban officers were not entitled to particular distinctions in churches and processions as were their rural counterparts. If they attended police assemblies or were invited to other consultative meetings, it was on a personal basis as notables or merchants, not as militia captains.

But this did not affect the prestige associated with the rank in their eyes, as witness the stiff competition and the striving for precedence within the corps. At one general assembly, an officer from the côtes claimed to have priority over the Montreal officers; the latter immediately brought the matter to the governor's attention and recorded his response, which confirmed that city officers had precedence over country officers and those from the capital over those from the other two cities.[47] At his investiture, a colonel would present his commission to the commandant of the fortress and in turn received that of the government's new militia officers; these little ceremonies legitimized his title and confirmed the others in theirs.[48]

It may be supposed that each militia company consisted of men from the same vicinity. Since socio-occupational segregation was not yet highly developed, the geographical organization of the militias meant that people from diverse backgrounds would serve side by side. Landlords, accounting for the majority of heads of households, made up the stable core of the company; tenants, who came and went between town and country and from one neighbourhood to another, the unstable fringe.[49] Youths engaged for seasonal voyages, apprentices, and indentured servants represented another group of virtual militiamen. The company was also expected to incorporate as ordinary fusiliers those gentlemen who lacked royal commissions in the regulars or other employment, but there is good evidence that they did not acquiesce to this directive.[50] In short, problems of mobility, availability, and social susceptibility made militia duty less than universal in the urban context. But what sort of duty was this? Were militia companies anything more than a registration system in which lists were hastily revised before each new round of recruitment? Did the companies have any permanent existence on the ground? Were rolls kept up to date? Were drills held once or twice a month and weapons inspections in accordance with recommendations? Were there durable ties between the men and their officers? Did these companies represent an urban police force, and were particular duties assigned to them? The administrative sources provide few answers: on the question of military training, none at all. If town dwellers were better trained and armed than peasants, why does the correspondence with Versailles – which never ceased to inquire about such matters – contain jaded comments about the militias in general and no praise for their zeal? And if the urban companies did not assemble for regular drills, what else was there to establish the internal relations of authority and solidarity on which esprit de corps depends?

In Canada, as we have seen, night watch and gatekeeping – the two traditional functions of French town militias – were fulfilled by the colonial regulars in all but exceptional circumstances, as at Quebec in 1690 and Montreal in 1692 and during the War of the Austrian Succession.[51] In 1744, the Montreal garrison, reduced to fewer than 200 men including the sick and injured, no longer sufficed to guard the 3,500 metres of fortress walls. The first step taken was to block off eight of the fifteen gates and entrust some guard duty to militia officers under military command. Guard duty at that time was largely directed toward the outside to avert an ever-impending enemy raid and to prevent Indigenous people, particularly allies from the Great Lakes region, who were living in a shed outside the walls, from moving about town after dark.[52] Lacking so much as a guard house for its sentries, the militia's involvement in urban policing was only a temporary arrangement, one that became superfluous after the troops were augmented in 1750. It was even less frequent in Quebec. In 1742, to curtail a wave of robbery, the governor assigned militiamen to patrol the town every night for two months. Ordinarily, however, the marshalcy and the troops were enough to accomplish the task, even in wartime.[53]

There were also ceremonies. In November 1686, to inaugurate a bust of Louis XIV, the townspeople of Quebec had been ranged around the Lower Town square when one of them withdrew, leaving behind a gun borrowed for the occasion. His neighbour, who could not find his own, picked up that one – unaware that it was loaded with lead shot – and fired in fun on a passerby, who died of his injuries. After the trial, the Conseil Souverain banned militiamen from carrying loaded weapons at assemblies and from firing them, except into the air and on command.[54] In a significant detail, the court did not hold the militia officers responsible for the accident and did not even subpoena them as witnesses. The *compagnies franches* that had recently arrived in the colony did not take part in this ceremony but were always on prominent display in the ones that followed, impeccably decked out for battle in their blue and white uniforms, with fifes and drums, insignias bearing gold *fleur de lis*, and the full arsenal of pikes, halberds, swords, and Tulle muskets. Quebec spared no powder in celebrating the arrival of a new bishop, governor, or intendant with pomp and circumstance: the dignitary would be welcomed on the riverbank by the officers of the provost court, replacing the municipal politicians for the occasion. The other members of the official procession for these arrivals, and the order in which they were arranged, varied according to the figure in question, but militia officers were not among them; with their companies in arms, they lined the way. The dignitaries' first visit to Trois-Rivières and Montreal likewise took place to the sound of bells, cannons, and drums, flanked by soldiers and citizens in arms.[55]

In comparison to the regulars, the urban militias cut a sad figure at these ceremonies. They lacked uniforms and flags and possessed only assorted muskets, plus a drum with which to beat out a marching rhythm. "It was perhaps the thing that most elicited the loyalty of the militiamen," wrote Médéric Louis Élie Moreau de Saint-Méry in reference to the sumptuous, colourful uniforms of the companies of Saint-Domingue, which had become objects of pride and emulation on the island over the years.[56] The fact that Canadian town militiamen made do with showing up in their Sunday best, their officers adorned only with gorgets or metal ornaments, is not purely anecdotal.[57] The institution's marginal role in the urban community did not justify vestimentary displays, and the companies lacked the cohesion that might have led them to seek to differentiate themselves at great expense. Bonds between militia captains, who had neither powers nor responsibilities, and these unstable urban groupings appear to have been quite loose. Occasions to act as a corps were so rare that it is hard to see how the militia could have served to reinforce neighbourhood bonds or contribute to the construction of an urban identity. Quite the reverse was true in the rural parishes.

2. GOVERNING THE COUNTRYSIDE

General and special policing of the countryside was the direct and exclusive responsibility of the intendant and his subdelegates in each government, except in a few places where a well-established seigneurial court assisted in prosecuting offenders.[58] Sidelined from the administration of the côtes, the royal courts of Quebec, Trois-Rivières, and Montreal continued to deliver justice in their jurisdictions, concurrently with the intendant and his representatives, including various rural notables, priests, notaries, and seigneurial officers who were awarded provisional commissions to investigate or rule on specific cases.[59] Research in the series of intendants' ordinances shows that their personal interventions in the judicial sphere were more limited than they sometimes claimed: an average of about fifty cases a year before 1748, the majority of them arising out of rural parishes in the government of Quebec.[60] They took the lead on litigation relating to property and seigneurial privileges as well as many family disputes, but it may be that not all summary cases – particularly those ending in out-of-court settlement – left documentary traces. Elsewhere in the colony, the subdelegates heard litigants who preferred to avoid ordinary justice, and records of these cases have not survived, as we have seen.

Militia captains were in charge of publishing and enforcing policing ordinances in their parishes, enforcing judicial orders by the king's commissioners, and enforcing court orders when there was no court officer nearby. They filled an institutional void. To make up for the scarcity of seigneurial judges and the absence of legally constituted rural communities, the authorities made the militia – again, a military organization – into an essential cog in the administration of rural areas. They arrived at this state of affairs not as the result of a decision and a specific plan but little by little, from one experience to the next, until the practice had proved itself efficient enough to be extended to the whole colony, apparently not before the early eighteenth century.[61] The consequences of this policy for rural communities were significant. Thus transformed into local police forces, the militias offered habitants a hierarchical structure within which relations among neighbours could be organized and consolidated, common interests defined and managed through a series of conflicts and compromises, and relations between the parish and the outside world mediated. I shall begin by describing their overall organization and by homing in on the individuals known as the *capitaines des côtes* as they went about learning how to wield power.

a) Rural militia officers

The general census of the militias taken in 1750, which I used earlier to describe the urban militias, constitutes the only statistical portrait of this institution in its rural setting.[62] It gives the number of companies per parish and the number of men and officers per company, but no names. To study the organization of the institution before this date and identify militia officers, it was necessary to resort to other sources. A 1721 survey of parish boundaries affords a fairly close

Table 6.1 | Militia censuses, 1744 and 1750

	Urban militias				Rural militias				Combined total
	Quebec	Trois-Rivières	Montreal	Total	Quebec	Trois-Rivières	Montreal	Total	
1744									
Companies	7		12		42		55		
Total men	1,245		871		4,775	1,150*	4,220		12,261
1750									
Parishes or seigneuries	1	1	1	3	46	16	40	102	105
Infantry companies	7	1	12	20	60	16	67	143	163
Artillery companies	1		1	2					2
Officers	32	4	64	100	310	63	251	624	724
Sergeants	21	3	41	65	245	35	179	459	524
Soldiers	807	63	570	1,440	5,226	888	4,127	10,241	11.681
Total men	860	70	65	1,605	5,781	986	4,557	11,324	12,929

* The census of 1744 does not give the number of companies in the government of Trois-Rivières, and the number 1,150 covers both the city and the côtes.

Sources: AC, CIIA, 81: 177, "Recensement des milices du Canada en 1744"; 95: 344–9, "Récapitulation des milices du gouvernement général du Canada, 1750."

Table 6.2 | Identified militia officers, 1710–29

	Urban militias				Rural militias				Combined total
	Quebec	Trois-Rivières	Montreal	Total	Quebec	Trois-Rivières	Montreal	Total	
1721									
General staff					5	1	1	7	7
Captains	1	1		2	21	8	19	48	50
Lieutenants					23	4	5	32	32
Ensigns					16	2	2	20	20
Sergeants					3	4	8	15	15
Total	1	1		2	68	19	35	122	124
1710-29									
General staff	1			1	4	1	3	8	9
Captains	1	1	6	8	9	5	10	24	32
Lieutenants	1	3		4	5	2	4	11	15
Ensigns		3	1	4	6	4	5	15	19
Total	3	7	7	17	24	12	22	58	75
Combined total	3	8	8	19	92	31	57	180	199
Companies*	(2)	(1)	(5)	(8)	(32)	(8)	(22)	(62)	(70)

* Approximate number.

Sources: RAPQ (1921–22): 262–380, report of survey of parish boundaries by Mathieu-Benoît Collet, 1721; BAnQ-CAQ, TP1–S777/1: 175–226, grain survey, 1729; other officers identified in the Parchemin notarial database. A total of 149 officers were identified in this last source, including seventy-four who are duplicated in the 1721 document and were therefore deleted from the table.

estimate of the number of companies in each of the three governments and serves to identify 124 officers and noncoms who testified.
I have drawn up a second list of officers from the titles of notarial
acts dated 1710 to 1729, as retranscribed in the Parchemin notarial
database.[63] Added to this are a dozen names taken from the 1729
survey of wheat provisions. Table 6.2 amalgamates the quantitative
data from these documents.[64] Half of the 149 persons identified in
the notarial acts also appear in the 1721 list, leaving seventy-five
new names (fifty-eight in the côtes) to fill out the sample. With a
total of 180 individuals, this list must certainly contain the majority
of the rural militia officers of the first third of the eighteenth century.

In this era, there was approximately one company per parish, its
size varying widely according to the size of the settlement. As soon
as a côte had thirty families, the governor appointed a captain and,
soon after, a lieutenant and an ensign to assist him. Each company
comprised one or two sergeants, very probably named by the militia
captain. By this time solidly rooted in the government of Quebec,
the institution lagged behind in Montreal, which had fewer companies and officers as a proportion of its population. To oversee the
companies in each region and coordinate their operations, town
majors and assistant town majors were appointed for the Côte-du-
Sud, Île d'Orléans, the Côte-de-Beaupré downriver of Quebec, and
the seigneuries of Beauport and Charlesbourg combined, as well as
a major-generalship in each government. Thirty years later, the number of men fit to bear arms had doubled, but the number of rural
officers had nearly quadrupled.[65] This inflation resulted from both
a gradual upward trend and an abrupt increase during the War of
the Austrian Succession. The case of La Prairie will serve to illustrate
these patterns. The seigneury possessed a single company and three
officers in 1721, four companies and seventeen officers in 1745, and
six companies and twenty officers in 1750. A second captain had
been added to certain companies, plus a major for the whole seigneury. Meanwhile, the number of households had risen from 100
to 300, faster growth than elsewhere but not by itself sufficient to
justify the increasing top-heaviness.[66] The greater civilian responsibilities imposed by the administration on the rural officers, as well as
the personal benefits they derived from their positions, also boosted
the numbers of commissions. Many of the companies counted in
the government of Quebec in 1750 were quite large, with up to 170
militiamen and six to eight officers. The average was ninety-one men

and 5.2 officers per company, as compared with sixty-four men and 3.7 officers per company in the government of Montreal.

To keep the country people in line, the governors stressed the importance of choosing good militia officers, wise individuals who knew how to assert their authority.[67] Priests' and seigneurs' recommendations were helpful, especially when the latter belonged to the military elite, but the agreement of the existing officers in the parish weighed more heavily in the decision. Vaudreuil, accused of favouritism for having appointed a militia captain unworthy of the position at Portneuf, defended his choice as follows: "In this I followed custom; not only is he the best habitant of this seigneury, but his father-in-law held this position for twenty to thirty years, and it would have seemed an injustice not to give it to the son-in-law; Messrs. Portneuf and Dejordy, the seigneurs in this time and place, had insistently requested this."[68] By the turn of the century, the hereditary character of these positions had been cemented: sons, or sons-in-law in their stead, succeeded fathers, and since the same family often provided the officers of new companies, kinship networks in many cases extended over several neighbouring parishes. In this system of disguised co-optation, the governor's commissions ratified the choices of the "old and principal habitants." It follows that there were few new arrivals among militia officers. Of the sixty officers counted in the 1721 survey for the government of Quebec, only seven had been born in France. The phenomenon was less marked in the Montreal region, fed by a continual stream of migrants from the rest of the colony and from the regulars; there, the proportion of militia officers born in France was seven out of twenty-seven.[69] Old families still succeeded in wresting away some militia positions, but by and large, immigrants had easier access to such positions in the western part of the colony.

The long-standing controversy among historians as to the social background of militia officers rests on the erroneous postulate that the militia was the die in which Canadian society was cast. Historians seeking to prove that the society was egalitarian and democratic have stressed the working-class background of militia captains: the fact that a mere habitant could assert himself vis-à-vis his seigneur, the government, and the men of the parish who followed him to war.[70] Fernand Ouellet, attempting to make the contrary proof that the society was in fact "feudal," regarded these officers as gentlemen, seigneurs, or townspeople willing to betray their station, to embrace the military values of the nobility in the hopes of gaining access to it.[71] It is, to be sure, a sterile debate. Suffice it to say that the profile of the militia officers reflected the local socio-occupational structure, not the social order in general. Between 1710 and 1729, the population of the côtes consisted almost entirely of peasants, and so it was peasants, chosen from well-to-do pioneering families, who made up the majority (about 75 per cent) of militia officers.[72] There were also a dozen merchants, navigators, or former voyageurs, and two notaries. The seigneurial group, the second largest, comprised twelve seigneurial employees, receivers, managers, seigneurial attorneys, and judges, as well as fifteen seigneurs or seigneurs' sons. Many of these last owned only a portion of a fief or an arrière-fief. Some were natives of the area, hence of peasant stock; others were merchants who had left the city to live on land they had purchased or inherited. Five seigneurs or members of seigneurial families appear among the fourteen staff officers. As the responsibilities of militia captains increased, it became advantageous for seigneurs to leave this job to their *censitaires* and hold onto the more prestigious, less demanding major or commandant positions. If this hypothesis is correct, then there were even fewer seigneurs among militia captains at mid-century.

The direct or indirect seigneurial presence among officers was particularly visible in the Côte-du-Sud downriver of Quebec and in the government of Trois-Rivières. The plate illustrating the seigneuries in the *Historical Atlas of Canada* shows that these regions shared two features: the humble origins of many concession holders and the small size of their properties.[73] And indeed, seigneurs I found among militia officers were not members of the colonial nobility, who had received the lion's share of the land and were making careers in the regulars. Names such as Costé, Fortin, Guimont, Petit, Lefebvre, Jutras, and Brunet corresponded to families much lower in the social hierarchy, very close to their *censitaires*, which did nothing to facilitate the exercise of authority. It was no accident that disputes between militia captains and seigneurs broke out specifically in the government of Trois-Rivières, where the seigneurs demanded that the captains show them all orders from the central administration before publishing them. The case was considered serious enough to be brought in 1711 to the attention of the minister, who ruled against the seigneurs.[74] After all, the best way to avoid these problems was for them or their family members to apply for jobs in the militia.

This type of conflict was less likely to occur in the government of Montreal, dominated as it was by large properties owned by the Church and the nobility.[75] By virtue of their social status, priests and nobles had other ways of intervening in parish affairs, and they were the first to be apprised of ordinances concerning them (since they had been consulted prior to publication). During the period from 1710 to 1729, the proportion of peasants among militia officers in the western part of the colony was already somewhat higher than elsewhere: as high as 90 per cent, according to a cursory list of 100 names gathered from the judicial and other archives between 1740 and 1755. Peasants could boast of a stable existence lacked by other occupational categories – rural merchants, for example, who were numerous in the region but rarely appear on my lists.[76]

The analysis of the social background of militia officers confirms the conclusions of chapter 3: namely, that in setting their sights on the regulars, the colonial gentlemen as a bloc – including those who pursued other careers – turned their backs on the militia positions offered by Versailles as if to accept would have been tantamount to renouncing their nobility.[77] Nor was there any movement in the opposite direction. The militia was not a springboard to employment in the regulars or a route to ennoblement. On the contrary, the rural militia is congruent with the outlines of another social category: that of notables whose prestige and influence stopped at the parish limits.

Military experience did not figure among the selection criteria for militia captains, and apart from a handful of demobilized soldiers among the minority born in France, these men did not possess any. Indeed, they were not counted on to dispense military training to the peasantry, at least until 1750. Moreover, their advanced age meant that they would not be very useful in war. In 1721, the average age of captains was fifty, that of lieutenants and ensigns forty-seven.[78] A few surveys at mid-century show that the officer corps had not been rejuvenated. For example, the average age of eleven La Prairie captains and lieutenants in 1745 was fifty-two.[79] In a small group of twenty-five rural officers summoned as witnesses in court cases between 1743 and 1758, six were over the age of sixty-five. The deans Prisque Lessard of Sainte-Anne de Beaupré and Jean-Baptiste Quenel of Lachine were seventy-six and seventy-four, respectively.[80] Evidently, this society believed that wisdom was the privilege of age. There is the occasional case of a "former militia captain" who gave up his place before dying, but on the evidence, nothing forced them to do so; meanwhile, the other officers grew old in the lower ranks. Furthermore, age did not prevent captains from carrying out their duties, since they could always delegate a man to do the work. The problems posed by illiteracy could also be circumvented. Antoine Bazinet, a peasant and militia captain in Pointe-aux-Trembles, relied on a merchant of the parish to publish ordinances on the forecourt of the church for people to read as they emerged from Sunday mass.[81] Although not exceptional, such cases were less frequent than one might believe in these school-less villages, where at most a tenth of peasants could sign their names. Of the rural officers who testified in 1721 and 1729, three-fifths (seventy-two out of 116) signed their depositions, indicating a clear effort to do honour to their position.[82]

b) Local affairs, royal affairs

The initial circumstances of settlement – low rates of immigration, dispersed habitat, agrarian individualism – were not conducive to gatherings of colonists. Beyond the urban perimeter on either side of the St Lawrence, there was something desolate, troubling, about the landscape stretching out before the traveller, with shacks sticking out of fields still occupied by tree stumps and separated from one another by wide bands of forest. The colonists lived deep in the woods to hide from the authorities, wrote Governor-General Denonville and Intendant de Meulles, for it eluded the comprehension of such observers that the solitude of the pioneer was not desired so much as inscribed in the North American frontier.[83] The first manifestation of community, a step toward the breaking of isolation, occurred when habitants assembled and pooled their resources to build a church. They would chose a syndic or receiver of alms and promise (each according to his ability) to contribute labour or materials. Shortly afterwards, the church was consecrated, and the missionary priest inaugurated the registers, followed by the vestry accounts once church wardens were elected. This first page of parish history generally took place in isolation. Since there was as yet no resident priest, the seigneurs were often absent, and the colonial administration had no other intermediaries or antennae in the countryside, the first parishioners quietly handled their own affairs.[84] Twenty years later, "the little ramshackle wooden church" had to be replaced, and wrangling commenced between older habitants who wanted a nice new stone church as a mark of their success and newer, poorer colonists who did not contribute their fair share. This time, everyone got involved – priest, seigneurs and co-seigneurs, bishop, judges, subdelegates, and intendants: whence the dozens of eighteenth-century ordinances bolstering the authority of the assembly and wardens, sanctioning the division of labour and capital, and fining holdouts. In many cases, the militia captains were in charge of overseeing the procedures and enforcing labour contributions. In principle, these were freely given donations commensurate with the donor's income. But in the heat of habitants' assemblies, social pressure was such that many offered too much and later found themselves incapable of honouring legally binding promises, thus giving rise to the court cases.[85] While many parishes retained the traditional procedure, others replaced the optional offering with a mandatory contribution calculated according to the amount of land owned: the same rigid but convenient system already in effect for road work.[86] This replication is understandable, since a single group of notables presided over both vestry affairs and land use planning.

In the seventeenth century, the building and maintenance of the roads leading to the church and the mill were collective tasks that eluded the gaze of the central administration and hence the historian as well. We do know how things were done in Montreal, a well-managed seigneury from which archives survive. As elsewhere in the colony, *censitaires* were bound by their deeds of grant to cede the land required for public roads. It was not long before the bailiff was ordering them to clear and drain the section of the cart track that passed in front of their houses and the seigneurial attorney was taking deadbeats to court.[87] But results were poor, so the assembly of habitants decided in 1680 to chip in on making the roads passable and building the necessary bridges. The taxpayers, divided into four classes according to their means, paid a total of 1,625 livres; the seigneurs paid 430 livres, and four trusted citizens took charge of collecting the money, organizing the work, hiring labourers, and so forth.[88] The method was equitable and effective, and yet it was not used in other seigneuries, where the corvée method was chosen: individual corvées for the main road, collective corvées for frontage along ungranted lands or lands with absentee owners and for harder jobs such as bridge building. If the work demanded a contractor, contributions were made in money instead of labour but always pro rata to property holdings.[89] Since plots of land along a watercourse were nearly all the same size, the division was about equal.

Yet, as Roland Sanfaçon has observed, this system did not work well – in fact, without coercion it would not have worked at all.[90] Two factors underlay the difficulties: climate and the taxation system. Once built, tracks demanded extensive, quasi-annual repair because of the damage caused by frost heave. This onerous work (which must have taken at least a week in the case of a main road, given the primitive techniques in use) always conflicted with the demands of agriculture. Winter being what it was in this colony, farmwork could not be put off until the slow season as it could in France.[91] As to taxation, colonists found it hard to conceive of a piece of land they had been granted, and were solely in charge of working, as public property. The temptation was great to skimp on the statutory width or block the way in order to protect one's livestock: in short, to treat the track as an extension of one's own land. Most were nonetheless willing to do their part, since they needed the track for their own purposes – but what was the good of working on a segment of a road that was only going to vanish into the forest, the brush, or the sloughs of an absent or negligent neighbour's land? The inaction of a few cancelled out the efforts of the many. Moreover, in spite of appearances, the division of labour was far from equitable, since, especially in the early days of the colony, the area of a land grant did not reflect the wealth of its owner. Corvées exacted a heavier toll from those who had only a few acres of crops, and had to hire themselves out to feed their families, than from well-established peasants with sons and indentured men in their employ. There may not, perhaps, have been a better choice for the construction and maintenance of the main road, but why not redress the injustice when the collective corvées rolled around by demanding less of the poor and more of the well-off? Whose interests were served by establishing and maintaining this regressive levy?

The seigneurs' interests, to begin with, for the road increased the value of a seigneury, and it may be presumed that seigneurs played an important role in the organization of the work, either personally or through the agency of their representatives. Good princes, they set an example by putting in the work where the road bordered their own cultivated land; this, however, did not generally extend beyond the width of one *censive*, and they had no intention of doing any more.[92] A distribution of labour that took personal wealth into consideration, or the profitability of establishments such as mills, ferries, fisheries, or woodlands, would have inflated the seigneurial contribution, as was observed in 1681 on Montreal Island, where the seigneur bore 20 per cent of the cost of public works – an instance that must have given pause. Very soon, the custom of apportioning corvées pro rata to land-holding was adopted, with the corresponding seigneurial exemption.[93] This exemption did not go unnoticed. At the request of the *censitaires* of Rivière-Ouelle, Intendant Raudot tried in 1709 to reverse the trend with an ordinance making Henri-Louis Deschamps de Boishébert liable for the cost of the road running through the ungranted part of his seigneury; this, however, was an isolated measure that did not create a legal precedent.[94] No other rural community, it seems, protested the privilege that the seigneurs were in the process of establishing. This does not mean that they all accepted it, but it does mean that they rarely formed a common front against a seigneur. When a right was deemed abusive, *censitaires* resisted, after their fashion, with inertia and disobedience.[95] Thus, the seigneurial exemption was certainly one of the factors that fed into chronic bad will on the part of the men required to participate in corvées. For their part, the "oldest and most considerable habitants," those who always participated in the assembly and spoke on its behalf, faced a dilemma: While they would have liked the seigneur to do his fair share, they were not keen to change the division of labour, which also worked to their advantage. A product of local power relations, the corvée system was adopted wholesale by the intendancy when it embarked on major road building projects in 1706.

At that point, the work was assigned to militia officers in each parish, working under the authority of the roads superintendent (*grand voyer*). The job required a great deal of time and skill. The captain had to check regularly whether the residents had cleaned out and repaired the ditches, cleared and surfaced their portion of the road; in winter, that all waymarks were still visible after each snowfall; and at all times, that violators were reported and fines collected. For collective work, it was his duty to publish the orders, convene the assembly, draw up the tax rolls, collect money to pay the fees of the road surveyor[96] (and the contractor, if there was one), assemble the work crew, survey the site, note absences, report progress to the roads superintendent (or the intendant if necessary), and justify delays. A militia captain who did not acquit himself of these tasks was responsible for the poor condition of the roads, at least on paper, but it cannot be told from the documentation whether punishment ever went beyond a warning.[97] A clever captain used denunciation only sparingly, when his powers of persuasion failed to secure obedience. In parishes where webs of kinship, dependency, and clientele were dense, he could not denounce anyone he wished. One would have to comb through the records of each parish to discover the social context and strategies behind these petitions, ordinances, and assembly minutes and, more particularly, the degree of influence wielded by seigneurs over these matters. A militia captain representing the habitants' interests who clashed with a seigneur over the route of a road, or a right to use communal land, was the same one who provided him with the certificates necessary to adjoin to the domain the lands of vagrant concession holders who paid no rent.[98] This too was part of his job, as was the surveillance of cabarets and the obligation to report to the intendant the names of people who sold liquor without a permit,[99] held unauthorized assemblies, sold salt or wheat above the official price, "presumed" to teach children to read and write without the bishop's approval, and so on.[100]

When the penal emigration program announced under the Régence began to take on certain proportions, control over people entering and exiting the colony, or moving from place to place within it, became a matter of great concern to the authorities. Canada at first received criminals for incorporation into the troops, then salt smugglers to serve as servants or soldiers, and then sons exiled from their families by *lettre de cachet* (an order bearing the seal of the sovereign), who were more difficult to settle.[101] Some of those who had been involuntarily expatriated sought to return to France, particularly married men who had left families behind. The task of scouring the territory to prevent clandestine embarkations or flight through the woods toward the British colonies was entrusted to the militia. Its officers were under orders to arrest all soldiers or other individuals not carrying a travel permit or a certificate of freedom signed by the governor, and habitants who housed foreigners were required to report their departure, or presumed desertion, to the militia captain within twenty-four hours, with the latter immediately organizing a posse. The directives were backed by heavy fines, prison terms, and revocation of officer's commissions for anyone who abetted an escape.[102] Desertions were more frequent in the Montreal region, where garrisons were numerous and the path leading to British territory could be quickly travelled. Vigilance was in order downstream of Quebec as well, where the militias also had to keep an eye on naval deserters seeking to enter the colony rather than leave it.[103]

In 1741, the habitants of Kamouraska refused to obey their captain and help the commandant of the *Imprévu*, en route to Le Havre, to capture sailors who had taken advantage of the stopover to run away.[104] That same year, militia officers in Terrebonne and environs were cashiered for failing to assist the sergeant of the marshalcy in pursuing two soldiers convicted as counterfeiters and, in one case, for having offered them safe haven.[105] But one could just as well adduce the example of the Chateauguay captain who, with his sons and three other militiamen, brought back to Montreal an unfortunate soldier who had knocked on the door of a parish resident after spending a week lost in the woods and "living on morels,"[106] or the successful dragnet operation launched in 1742 to capture vagrants and bandits in the Quebec region, which led to thirteen arrests,[107] or the statement of Jacques Lebault, a Boucherville militia officer who, "having found the said Desse ... at the home of Captain Quintal, where he had been taken by some habitants of Chambly ... took charge of him and escorted him to the royal prison of the city of Montreal, assisted by Jacques Dulude and Louis Joachim, militiamen of Boucherville, for which purpose we have made and drawn up this report of capture."[108] Here were militiamen who took their policing responsibility seriously – the attitude I found most commonly in the archives but not necessarily the most representative, since others who did not report illicit activity, who did not systematically track down foreigners, attracted no notice unless caught disobeying *in flagrante delictio*.[109] Furthermore, deserting soldiers did not generally take refuge in the parishes but went over to the British colonies as fast as they could, often aided by Indigenous guides. Arrests were rare, then, but – contrary to the assertion of one governor – there was no way for militia officers to improve their performance.[110]

A lawman within the parish, the militia officer was responsible, as the leader of his men, for accompanying court officers to serve seizure notices, expulsion orders, and other documents apt to provoke violent reactions.[111] He was asked to escort or arrange for escort of witnesses or suspects to court, make judicial sales, and, in short, assume all the court officer's responsibilities in his absence or assist him in all manner of circumstances. In trials heard by the intendant, the captain often acted as an investigator, appraiser, or arbiter.[112] When a criminal case came to light in the parish, he was on the front lines, uncertain of what he should do, frightened of the consequences. Law officers from Montreal took two days to reach Terrebonne after the killing of Jean-Baptiste Truchon, a poor habitant of Côte-Sainte-Marie. While waiting, Captain Jacques Brière lacked the authority to arrest the man's wife, to all appearances the murderer, who took the opportunity to flee. But he had the presence of mind to post guards at the door of the house to preserve the damning evidence against her.[113] To go down to Kamouraska and arrest Joseph Ouellet, accused of making counterfeit card money, Conseil Supérieur member Joseph Perthuis was accompanied by a military detachment, as custom dictated. But the news travelled faster than the lawmen, who learned on arriving that Ouellet had vanished two days earlier. The crime, punishable by the gallows – graver indeed than murder in the eyes of the administration – barely excited the peasants' ire, since they were not personally harmed. When the suspect was one of their own, the parish closed ranks and kept quiet. Maybe the Kamouraska militia officers knew nothing, thought Pertuis; still, he had their houses and barns searched like those of any other habitant, without regard for their commissions, since they had not reported the crime and might well be accomplices.[114] For the law, the militia captain was a useful auxiliary yet nonetheless to be mistrusted. The incidents that I found mentioned in the archives do not suffice to tell whether this mistrust was justified.

The remaining responsibilities related to military and ceremonial service. In wartime, militia captains designated men to participate in campaigns, an important task to which we shall return in our study of the mobilizations of the 1740s and 1750s. These men were in charge of assigning housing to soldiers passing through or billeted in the parish, and they organized compulsory corvées of men and horses from rural areas for the construction of urban fortifications (see chapter 7). Officers in the Montreal region also commanded corvées for the stake fences that had to be rebuilt whenever war loomed.[115] Those who lived downriver had to look out for the arrival of the king's ships and send replenishments aboard, Quebec being still a good way off.[116] When "Le Général" travelled in the colony, custom had it that the militias render military honours to him on his arrival in the parish and that twenty men keep watch all night around the house where he slept. The job of organizing the welcoming ceremony and the watch, billeting or finding suitable billets for the official guests and their retinue, and, in winter, packing down the roads and preparing the sequence of horses and drivers fell to the local captain. On their seasonal journeys between Quebec and Montreal, intendants and governors were usually flanked by a sizeable group. Fourteen officers or officers' wives accompanied Intendant Bigot to Montreal in February 1753, with the group being augmented by at least forty servants. In addition to personal belongings, the party carried everything needed for sleeping, cooking, and eating – a tremendous load. At two horses per sleigh for the main party, one each for the sleighs carrying the servants and for the baggage sleds pulled behind, the captain of Cap-Santé or Saint-Sulpice would have to gather forty fresh horses and nearly as many coachmen to carry the dignitaries to the next stage of their journey. Coachmen were paid for their services, and habitants surely did not have to be begged to lend their teams and drive the travellers, but the militia captain, on whom the success of the operation depended, worked for free.[117]

The only surviving rural officer's commission emphasizes the military training of the habitants:

> Philippe de Rigaud, Marquis of Vaudreuil, Commander of the Military Order of St. Louis, Governor and Lieutenant-General for the King and all of New France.
>   ... having knowledge of the experience, good conduct, and loyalty in the king's service of Sieur Pierre Dupré, habitant of Baie Saint-Paul ... We have appointed and established him, and by these presents appoint and establish him captain of the militia company of the habitants of Baie Saint-Paul, Éboulements, Île-aux-Coudres, and Petite Rivière in order that he act in that capacity to keep the peace and unity among them; that he oversee their practice in the handling of arms from time to time, so that they are capable of defending themselves in case of enemy attack; that he ensure that the said habitants keep their arms in good condition, and do not part with them, and that he enforce such orders as we may convey to him, and we do hereby order the habitants ... to acknowledge the said Mr. Dupré as their captain, etc., etc.[118]

The text dates from 1717. It is not known whether the governor always used this boilerplate or whether subsequent commissions continued to stress fictitious military duties and gloss over the many civilian tasks imposed by the intendant. For this was indeed a fiction. Militia captains were often threatened with punishment if they delayed in carrying out road work or attending to other matters of policing, but at no time were they held responsible for the chronic lack of weapons in the countryside. Furthermore, all the staff officers admitted – in 1717 as in 1744, on the eve of the new war – that the peasants were not trained to handle weapons. Still, none of them rebuked the militia officers for this state of affairs, for they all knew it was no longer their responsibility.[119]

3. AUTHORITY OF THE MILITIA CAPTAINS

The responsibilities of the militia captains grew progressively heavier between the beginning and the middle of the eighteenth century and also varied according to how busy or close to the city each parish was. On the whole, the record is impressive, especially when one considers that these local agents were not remunerated for their services. In 1707, when the administration was only just beginning, reluctantly, to use them for the enforcement of its ordinances, Intendant Jacques Raudot expressed concern about this state of affairs. He suggested that they be given an annual salary of 100 livres and decorated with the rank of sergeant in the colonial regulars. He also proposed that appointments be made jointly by the governor and the intendant, since the rural police reported to the latter.[120] These were costly suggestions that offended military sensibilities and had no chance of being adopted. Raudot had to content himself with an arrangement with the clergy: The militia captain would have his seat marked in the country church – the most honourable pew after the seigneur's – and would receive the holy bread, the holy water, the peace and incense, the altar candles, the ashes, and the branches in season after the seigneur and the wardens but before the rest of the congregation. He would march at the head of processions with the other rural militia officers.[121] There would be no more talk of salaries, and the small gratuities doled out by the intendant in the form of powder and lead to a few zealous officers in the early 1740s were largely symbolic.[122] Note that travel costs incurred by soldiers and militia officers when travelling to the city on duty were reimbursed. Minor profits may lurk within such errands and tasks, but material benefits were assuredly not what made commissions attractive to peasants and induced them to take so much time out of their ordinary occupations. What is certain is that the ones who did so must have had time to devote; hence, their status must have been above that of the average habitant, always hurrying to finish the farmwork before winter closed in. This was a well-off minority of people who, as they aged, derived income from lands they were not alone in working.[123] While captains could plan bridge and road work, demands from the central administration might come at any time and required generous availability. To hold this position, one had to have sufficient finances and, most important, a striving for power, a desire to be the leading citizen of the parish, or one of them.

Social recognition was the most important reward. When habitants of the côtes spontaneously called on the captain to help them resolve disputes or to do what was necessary and inform the persons concerned in the event of misfortune, he reaped the fruit of his labours.[124] A commission from the governor did not by itself create such confidence and authority; before that could happen, the institution had to take root in the community. The more important the militia officers' role, the more valued they felt and, I believe, the greater was the propensity to cite their titles in official acts of private life: children's marriages, wills or donations, real estate transactions, and so on. In this regard, the parishes in the governments of Quebec and Trois-Rivières had a good lead over those of Montreal, where the rural officers' silence on their positions extends into the second decade of the eighteenth century.[125] Thus, for example, Jacques Richaume, the militia captain of Repentigny as of 1706, did not mention this position when he went to the notary, nor did his family mention it at his death in 1713.[126] After 1720, the institution was imposed from one end of the colony to the other, and the corresponding titles proliferate in the archives. Personal capabilities mattered, of course; some militia officers had more trouble making others do their bidding, especially where roadwork was concerned. Others were so visibly dedicated to private interests – the seigneur's interests, for example – that their every intervention in parish life was looked at askance.[127] A good militia captain was a minor strategist who presented himself as a mediator between local factions. His powers were of two kinds. There were powers granted to him by the intendant for the fulfilment of a specific, time-limited mandate, such as the power to fine individuals whose participation in a given road crew was delinquent, a power that did not extend to other roads at other times. Without an explicit order, he could not arrest a suspect or take initiative more generally.[128] The other type of power was indefinite, discretionary. It flowed from the regulatory void surrounding the selection of participants for military campaigns, the members of fort construction corvées, or the quantities of grain owed by each habitant in response to requisitions. As long as he fulfilled the quotas set for the parish, the militia captain could, as an administrative matter, designate anyone he wanted while exempting his relatives. His leeway was narrower than it seems, however, for he had to contend with the tacit rules of his community, which tempered favouritism even if they did not forbid it outright.

Over time, the system proved effective and relatively conflict-free. It gave parishes an illusion of autonomy. By choosing one of their own to carry out its orders, the colonial administration made sure that these men would be better received than if they came directly from the outside. Pierre Paris, of the seigneury of Saint-Sulpice, refused to receive a naval soldier who arrived at his home with a billet issued by Sieur Duvivier, captain of the company. He had "no power over the habitants," pled Paris, imprisoned for disobedience, "for this right [to assign billets] rests only with the militia captain."[129] There was, of course, well-chronicled hostility in France surrounding the figure of the gabelman and the collector of the land tax or *taille*, those outsiders who personified state authority. In the colony, the power dynamic between centre and periphery was very real, if less visible; indeed, it was woven into the very fabric of the community.

Since most extant information about policing in rural New France comes from intendants' ordinances, it is easy to believe that all of public life bent to their will; however, rural communities had other options besides acquiescing to or resisting orders: They played an active part in the development of institutions. For example, and as noted earlier, the customs governing road and church construction had taken shape well before any intendant took an interest in these matters. The organization of the militia, too, illustrates the play of local interests. It was not the governors who imposed these rigid frameworks – the heritability of titles, the primacy of seniority, the clear demarcation between commissioned and non-commissioned officers, the obscure role of the latter. The habitants could have adopted a more flexible, less status-centred system, one more open to individual merit, instead of reproducing the hierarchical values of the wider society as they did. From the standpoint of Ancien Régime history, there is nothing surprising about what they did: The conservatism of rural societies, and notables in particular, is a ubiquitous historical observation.[130] But in the context of New France, this conformism may come as a surprise to those who believe that the colonists rejected the world view and norms of France in their efforts to build a new egalitarian, individualistic culture – an American culture.[131]

Eighteenth-century Quebec rural history has made great strides in recent years. Studies of population and property trends, marriages, inheritance, agricultural and commercial practices, the composition of fortunes, and material culture have been published. But rural community studies are still lacking. Louis Lavallée is the only historian to have addressed the question; we owe to him an excellent description of the assembly of habitants of La Prairie, its skirmishes with the seigneurs, and its struggles to retain its communal property. Perceived essentially in its institutional form, this community, which "did not regulate farm life or levy taxes," is concluded to have been weaker than its French counterpart.[132] Just so – or rather, it was a different sort of community, with no legal existence, hence not readily comparable.[133] Furthermore, we still know little about the informal community to which this chapter has accorded a presumption of existence: that is, the relations among habitants of a given place and between them and outsiders, whereby a community of residence became a community of belonging that placed constraints on its members. Demographic statistics and land occupancy maps do not answer all the questions. Contrary to expectations, intense community spirit can still coalesce out of an area of dispersed habitat, as T.J.A. Le Goff observed about the Breton rural experience, and social relations are not always as we imagine them to be.[134] Seen from the inside, divisions between rich and poor, or between old habitants and new settlers, may have seemed less significant than they do when analyzed by historians. The contrary situation, which would have posed an obstacle to solidarity, is also possible. The only way to know the thoughts of rural people is to listen to them: to dig through the jumble of judicial archives and find their words buried within, to chance upon a revealing account, to grasp the meaning of a word or incident, and so to elucidate the weaknesses and strengths of rural communities.[135] This approach would undoubtedly reveal that the family or familial clan took precedence in the hierarchy of identities, followed by the parish, which gathered together the men and the women, the living and the dead. It would flesh out the role of the militia company hiding somewhere below the surface in the tangle of local rivalries and solidarities, in the dissemination of information and the construction of a local vision of public order and military affairs.

The Question of Taxation

The alleged contrast between the French peasant, smothered under the weight of seigneurial dues and government taxes, and the free and independent Canadian is a commonplace that has withstood the progress of knowledge. Research on the seigneury and, to a greater extent, the vogue for the concept of "feudalism" in the 1970s and beyond, have dulled this contrast somewhat, yet it is still widely believed that the government demanded nothing of the colonists apart from some small duties on trade and that they lived out of sight of the central authority in their parishes if not deep in the woods, paying no taxes at all.[1] Militia duty is not presented as a public office, and the other obligations, including military corvées, requisitions, and billeting of soldiers – the subject of this chapter – are seldom mentioned. A good description of them is therefore in order. But my main interest has less to do with the onerousness of the charges than with the implementation of a system of personal services that kept the population closely tied to the military government. Contemporary reactions to these obligations clarify this society's vision of itself, the social divides that it was trying to entrench. Different tax regimes for city and country exemplify the divide between them. Whatever historians may think, contemporaries from the top to the bottom of the social hierarchy never doubted that payments in services and labour were very much a form of taxation.

I. MILITARY WORKS

The militiaman was both a soldier and an earthmover. There had been some military campaigns devoted to construction and excavation during the seventeenth century, but the oscillation between the two roles was even more marked during the mid-eighteenth-century wars. An engraving depicting a Canadian with a gun slung over his shoulder and a shovel in his hands would faithfully reflect the experience of the years 1744 to 1760. Furthermore, the work parties for the Quebec and Montreal forts were a natural extension of the free and compulsory service provided by the militia. A lot of building was going on in this colony. The initiative usually came from the general staff, who wanted strongholds to intimidate the enemy, slow him down if he should invade, reassure the people, and render them more submissive.² Others countered that the colony's best defence was its geography; that forts attracted British attention rather than deterring an offensive; that the garrisons were insufficient to defend these sites; that no one wanted to be shut up in them; and that public funds could be more profitably spent on port facilities and other projects. The administrators condemned such arguments as "seditious speech," "cabals"; they proceeded without public assent and without taking the time to assess the actual cost of these works.³ Versailles gave its approval, only to express indignation later on that cost overruns were drawing down the colony's finances. The work was frequently interrupted by shortages of funds, and the perception that taxes were being levied in the form of money and labour caused tongues to wag.

a) The urban contribution

Forts made of stakes were temporary affairs, said the pessimists: made to last three or four years at best. The colonists had built dozens of them since 1608 – hundreds if all the times each had had to be rebuilt from scratch were counted. Settlements contributed to their own security as circumstances dictated, supplying stakes, teams, and men to erect these palisades and embankments. Besides a small bonus for infantrymen of the *compagnies franches* who occasionally pitched in, these structures had yet to cost the king a penny.⁴ But carpentry and masonry cost money, whether contracted out or directed by the engineer, for such tradesmen did not work for free. In the 1680s, the minister agreed to disburse a few thousand livres to repair the walls of the Château Saint-Louis (the governor's official residence) and to build a powder magazine and a warehouse, but there was no money in the budget for the line of defence that the capital began hastily building in 1690 as an English fleet loomed on the horizon.[5] That same year and at least once more that decade, Quebecers were taxed to cover the most pressing expenses. These were small sums up against the contribution of the naval treasurer, which ballooned in spite of remonstrances: from 15,000 livres for the year 1690 to 80,000 livres for 1697.[6] The money was used to build redoubts and batteries, and more was needed for materials, tools, and supervision of the work crews employed on the embanked palisades. These men came primarily from the country, for Quebec was still only a small town of under 2,000 with a paltry garrison. Lacking sources besides the vague information contained in the official correspondence, historians have no way to determine just how town dwellers were taxed during this initial phase of the work. It may have been a tax in the form of labour that was convertible into cash.[7] After 1702, the situation becomes clearer. The minister had decided to devote an annual sum to fortifying the capital, and all urban contributions would henceforth be made in man- or cart-days as a function of each person's abilities. Those who could not or would not move earth had to hire someone to do it for them unless they preferred to supervise the construction corvées. Although the rolls have disappeared, certain clues suggest that the average contribution was five man-days.[8] There were no exemptions – a principle the religious communities and the military, court, and militia officers found unacceptable. Good will on the work site soon gave way to grumbling, especially by the elite, who criticized the plans and the conduct of the work and who invoked their privileges as a reason not to contribute. "If things continue in this way, Your Excellency," wrote the engineer to the minister, "only the poor will bear the burden of this labour, which is causing such muttering among the habitants as may lead them to revolt."[9] To do away with these annoyances and solve the underfunding problem, he proposed to replace the work crews with new import duties, or better yet a property tax, a solution viewed favourably by Versailles but energetically rejected by the colonial administrators on the grounds that the population was too poor.[10] The work progressed in fits and starts and in different directions; when it was finally abandoned in 1720, Quebec remained ill-fortified.

Until the end of the War of the Spanish Succession, Montrealers maintained their three kilometres of fencing at the rate of a thousand new stakes a year, supplied by different habitants in rotation as determined by the court.[11] The decision to replace the palisade with a masonry enceinte, dating to 1712, was published in November 1714. The intendant assembled the militia captains and principal habitants of the town and the côtes, in the presence of the general staff, to draw up lists of man- or team-days that each would have to supply and to form corvées. The average burden represented by the work crews, based on status and abilities, varied from four to six days or eight to twelve livres.[12] Corvée members had to supply their own food. In contrast to the system operating at Quebec, the tax could be paid in cash instead of labour, and the administration even relied on this revenue to pay the contractor, since Versailles refused to subsidize the project.[13] But a year later, the intendant proposed a new arrangement. Only rural residents would have to join the corvées, while the city would pay an annual tax of 6,000 livres until completion of the enceinte, to which the Sulpician seminary, seigneur of Montreal Island, would make a one-third contribution. A Conseil d'État decree of 5 May 1716 confirmed these arrangements.[14] The reasons for this turnabout are unknown. There had been no popular rebellion against the corvées; perhaps the administration had been obliged to consider opposition from the religious communities and notables. Clearly, the money from conversion of the corvées into monetary contributions would not have sufficed to complete the work – but then why had the colonial administrators professed to believe the contrary in 1714? Had it been a stratagem, later deemed pointless, to force the minister's hand?[15] Whatever the case, the seminary was satisfied, and Montrealers had every reason to be as well. The new tax was modest, in fact lower than the value of the work days it replaced, and the average assessment was to decline with growth in the urban population.[16] According to French custom, each group of taxpayers – officers, seigneurs, religious communities, merchants, and artisans – was represented in the assembly by one or more members who, in addition to the responsibility of drawing up the rolls, had a say in how these revenues would be spent.[17] Yet it was precisely the use of these funds that was to provoke discontent among town residents, paralyzing for ten years a project initially greeted with favour. Once again, the resistance came from the elite. In the early days, to diminish the costs of defence, townspeople had been encouraged to purchase land along the St Lawrence and build houses there, and this line of houses was to form the southern flank of the city. But the plan approved in 1718 opted for a continuous rampart. The residents found themselves holding land that was devalued by being partially expropriated to make room for the enceinte. The seigneurs, for their part, felt wronged by the expropriations, which were more extensive than planned.[18] The masons had their own reasons for being angry. The bidding took place in Quebec, not Montreal, and the contractor who won each year, despite his exorbitant price, was reputed to be a favourite of the administration, a "foreigner," a "shoddy mason from the capital."[19] In 1720, an impasse was reached. The assembly refused any further contribution, charging that the tax was being misused, and the king's prosecutor in charge of seizing property from a few high-profile citizens begged the intendant to dispense him from this task, "which has brought upon him the cries, grumblings, and enmities of an entire people."[20] The crisis was resolved the following year by a fire that destroyed much of the city. From then on, home reconstruction monopolized workers and resources. Work on the enceinte progressed at a snail's pace with funds borrowed from other colonial budget items, and the administration delayed collecting the tax until the minister got impatient. By the early 1730s, opposition had faded, contributions began coming in regularly, and the pace of work increased.[21] By 1737, the city was enclosed, and a 1743 decree by the Conseil d'État took stock of the experience. To that time, the tax had brought in 115,524 livres, meaning that according to the agreement of 1716, the Montrealers still owed 46,476 livres. But the rules had changed along the way. The king charged the city for the real cost of the enceinte, nearly half a million livres, and maintained the annual 6,000-livre tax indefinitely to provide for repairs and reimbursement of the debt.[22] The decree must have come as a surprise, although it did not cause an uproar. No one wanted to resume the battle over a charge they had got in the habit of paying, one that had decreased over the years with the doubling of the population between 1714 and 1760.[23]

The military administration often invoked public opinion – e.g., "The whole colony is of this view" – in its justifications of troop movements or of defensive structures built in the heat of the moment, without the ministry's express authorization. This final clash over the fortifications serves as a reminder of the meaning of the notion of public opinion under the Ancien Régime. It did not mean a majority of individual opinions, as it would today, but a majority of opinions among persons considered loyal and enlightened, whatever their number.[24] The onset of war in 1744 revived the Quebec work site;

the batteries were restored, and a palisaded entrenchment was built along the Saint-Charles River. The news of the siege of Louisbourg, received 21 June 1745, more than a month after the Bostonians had disembarked, compelled the governor to build a masonry wall around the city. He was forced to do this, he explained, by the residents of Quebec, who were trembling with fear and demanding that he take action.[25] The engineer went further, writing that "the whole colony has demanded it."[26] An assembly – something of an expanded council of war – ratified the decision. Twenty-one of the thirty-one individuals consulted belonged to the general staff or the regular officer corps. The administration and judges had four representatives between them, the Church three, and the merchants three, including Pierre Trottier Desauniers, their syndic, who was assigned the contract the very same day without tender. Only the intendant disagreed, although he downplayed this in the interests of order.[27] The work proceeded apace until it was abruptly interrupted on 10 July 1746 by the arrival of a letter from the minister, who did not see the utility of the fort; if the habitants did, it was up to them to pay for it. The governor was asked to convene a new assembly that would have to choose between demolishing or continuing the work and to decide on a tax scheme if it opted for the second.[28] Recalled in haste, the previous year's council hesitated, requesting a few days in which to deliberate. When next it met, the deputation of merchants and law officers had grown from five to forty-four. Governor-General Charles de la Boische, Marquis de Beauharnois began with a corporate vote (*vote par corps*), but since the merchants had given him two contrary opinions in writing, he went to an individual vote (*vote par tête*). The builders won by a slim margin.[29]

Dissidents were treated with disrespect, as foreign hawkers (*forains*) in large part, devious shipowners, traitors in the making who had been seduced by English liberties, or cowards who would rather hide out in the woods than confront the enemy from within a well-defended fort.[30] Besides, it was well known that "everyone" supported the decision, "except for a small number of foreigners, or commoners whom one might have refrained from including in such a deliberation."[31] The hawker was the prime scapegoat in this colony. In reality, almost all the twenty-four townspeople who opposed the fortification were Quebec residents of long standing, if not by birth, who belonged to the commercial elite. The intendant was more lucid. The townspeople, he wrote, had voted for demolition. "If I am

Table 7.1 | Composition of the assembly and breakdown of votes in favour of the fortifications (Quebec, 30 July 1746)

Group	Representation		Votes in favour	
	Number	*%*	*Number*	*(% of group)*
Military	32	38	31	(97%)
Clergy	4	5	4	(100%)
Administration	4	5	2	(50%)
Justice*	14	16	5	(36%)
Merchants	30	36	6	(19%)
Total	84	100	48	or 56% of votes

*The councillors are in the "justice" category even when they also held a post in the administration. There were two who were undecided, one councillor and the new syndic of the merchants, plus one abstention (the intendant).
Sources: AC, F3, 13: 225–8; C11A, 85: 76–8.

not mistaken, that is rather the general opinion of all the habitants of this colony."[32] They feared the tax, certainly, and had moreover lost their belief in the invulnerability of fortresses, particularly since the capitulation of Louisbourg. To the military command, the most shocking aspect of this story was that the population had suddenly begun discussing in public the merits of strategies worked out in the privacy of war councils. The giddiness had even infected the militia officers: among the eight invited to the assembly, four sided with the city against their colonel.[33]

The majority group did not resolve the question of financing. It is clear, however, that the administration would not countenance a direct tax like Montreal's that would be limited to the city of Quebec. Starting from the principle that the whole colony must contribute to the security of the capital, it opted for indirect taxes on trade. Versailles adopted the proposal, not to go easy on city residents but because customs duties brought in much more money. Taxes on spirits were increased the following year, and the edict of 1748 introduced a general duty of 3 per cent on other imports as well as an export duty of 3 per cent on primary products.[34] The possibility of imposing corvées on the Quebec population as a form of taxation was not even evoked during the assembly and the ensuing negotiations.

b) Peasant corvées before 1745

Insofar as they created many jobs, military works were a stimulus to the urban economy. When town dwellers were required to work for nothing, as Quebecers had been at the turn of the century, only a small group of skilled construction workers benefitted.[35] In Montreal, whose residents were not subject to corvées, the job offer was extended to all carters, labourers, and others available for transport and earthmoving work, as long as corvée members from the countryside and soldiers could not be found for the big jobs. In short, the advantages to be derived by town residents were often less enticing than has been believed, but they did exist, whereas for rural residents these projects represented a dead loss, a considerable waste of time. The peasants in the government of Quebec bore the biggest burden. In the autumn of 1702, before returning to France, Intendant Champigny explained the procedures to his successor. To get the men to work quickly and efficiently, corvées were treated as piecework; more specifically, each participant was required to carry a given volume of earth, normally amounting to two weeks of work.

> It has happened on occasion that they finished the work sooner, working at night so that they could return home. Only half the habitants of a parish are drafted at any one time and only after the planting is done, toward the end of May, until harvest time. These habitants are given two pounds of bread a day, [one pound] of lard, and a good quantity of aqua-vitae, and every other day a plug of smoking-tobacco. The Engineer oversees the work and the Intendant sends a scrivener to keep the rolls for him.[36]

Similarly, the king's memoranda of 1706 and 1707 recommended apportioning the work by the piece and appeasing the habitants by feeding them.[37] The administrators responded that these instructions were being followed, yet at the same juncture the military commandant of Quebec was writing that the length of the corvée composed of rural people had been set at two weeks for those who accepted the king's provisions and ten days for those who brought their own.[38] Whether modified or not, the work remained onerous from the opening of the work site in 1692 to its closing in 1720. From Batiscan upriver to Port-Joli downriver, some twenty-nine parishes, representing a reserve force of 1,500 to 2,500 men, each supplied two contingents of workers nearly every summer.[39] When rumours of invasion arose and the work was stepped up, habitants (undoubtedly from the closest parishes) might be called back to the site a second time and in other seasons. In that case, they were paid wages or given an exemption from participation in the following year's corvée.[40]

The officers often complained of the town dwellers' ill will but never the peasants'. Must it be concluded that the latter were more docile? No, for the difference mainly consisted in the administration's attitude toward the two groups. If it treated the townspeople, court officers, and clergy members too harshly, it might be reproached for it. Since it could not bring them to heel, it would denounce others who refused to obey. Prudence vis-à-vis the working classes was well advised too. Urban riots remained a keenly apprehended threat, even though this colony had never experienced them. In contrast, there was no impediment to employing strong-arm tactics with country dwellers, strangers in the city who were fragmented into small local bands lacking ties of solidarity. They protested often and violently, but ineffectively, and punishment rained down on them, as shown by the following incident, the only one to have left traces in the archives.[41] One July morning in 1695, two corvées, one from the seigneury of Lauzon, the other from Beaupré, were working under the supervision of Jean-Baptiste Bécart de Granville et de Fonville, the king's attorney in the provost court, who struck a boy named Comtois from Lauzon. His comrades "took revenge on Mr. Fonville" and were sent to prison forthwith, while the habitants of Beaupré, who observed the scene, pelted them with cries of "Cowards!" for giving up so easily. François Chauveau, a boy from Lauzon, recounted the events at the supper table that evening at the home of a cooper named Jorian where he was living. Still fuming, he did not hide his feelings: The habitants were fools for letting themselves be mistreated, and "when they should decide to revolt ... he would join them." At the table was one of the king's gunsmiths, a man named Thibierge, who lectured him: "[You] should not say such things ... What if Monseigneurs the governor and the intendant were to send troops to your house to subdue you and cut your throat?" To which the young man replied "that they might be very surprised themselves to have their throats cut by the habitants." The gunsmith ran to the authorities to report these seditious remarks, and Chauveau was sent to join his fellow parishioners in prison.

Peasants in the government of Montreal were accustomed to military corvées, but until the early eighteenth century these were limited to building local enceintes for their own safety. The masonry fort built at Chambly in 1710–11 was the first project to mobilize all the habitants of the côtes.[42] The subdelegate allotted tasks and material supply obligations among the parishes, and taxpayers who so desired could pay their share in cash to an employee expressly in charge of this revenue.[43] Four years later, a similar system was used for the new enceinte in Montreal. Rural contributions were allotted on the same basis as urban ones, by land area and property value. According to the tax rolls drawn up between December 1714 and April 1715, the average length of service in the côtes was about four days, representing a monetary value of eight livres, and more than a quarter of peasants owed only two days or less.[44] The tax came at a time when inflation and the excesses of the grain police had provoked a rural rebellion.[45] Why, asked the habitants of Pointe-aux-Trembles, should they help the locality build its fortress when its merchants charged high prices for everything and the administration forbade the habitants from transporting and selling their grain as they wished?[46] Trusting that such a modest tax would eventually be accepted, the governor of Montreal let the protest run its course – at which point a further decision to levy a money tax in the city sowed new uncertainty. Yet the decree of 1716 did not mention the rural people. As the procurator of the Sulpician seminary explained in Paris, "The Conseil did not see fit to compel the habitants of the côtes to contribute to the town fortifications because they have forts of their own to maintain, but the Governor promised to cajole them into bringing cartloads to speed up the work ... not a word of this to anyone."[47] The tax roll seems to have been set aside. One thing

is certain: Corvées would no longer be convertible into cash payments. The peasants would have to gather materials, stones, sand,
etc., in the fall and carry them to the work site in winter. It is not
known whether these requests were frequent or how many days of
work they amounted to.[48] Thus, it is hard to know what could have
aroused the ire of the people of Longueuil in August 1717. It all
began with a tumultuous assembly at the seigneurial manor, which
the governor-general decided to attend personally in an attempt to
smooth things over. It did not go well. The habitants proved inso-
lent, one of them being so bold as to touch his necktie, and were
consequently roughed up by the guards. Others came to their aid, in
arms, and Vaudreuil thought it safer to leave with his retinue. The
rumour then spread that the domiciliés were coming to pillage and
burn the parish on his orders, and for two days the men of Longueuil
kept watch. The governor was on the point of sending in troops
to disperse them when the priest and several notables came to beg
for clemency, having succeeded in reassuring the rebels.[49] In short, a
hastily convened assembly in the middle of harvest season, clumsy
words, and a false rumour that spread panic had transformed a mere
hue and cry of the kind one might find anywhere into an uprising
– the gravest incident of its kind in the history of the colony. The
peasants of the government of Montreal had not taken up arms to
evade their work obligations; the collective corvée system came to
an end with the last cartloads for the Montreal enceinte. The construction of the new Quebec fort that began in 1745 relied only
on salaried workers, both urban and rural, and, in a few instances,
manpower supplied by the militia companies stationed in the capital
for its defence.[50]

There was, to sum up, no colonial system of military corvées:
practices varied according to circumstances and the administrators'
views. When Intendant Champigny imposed a two-week stint on
the residents of the colony's eastern côtes, they were living in peace,
whereas the population in the west was continually besieged by the
Iroquois and had long been on a war footing. To contemporaries, the
burden may have seemed comparatively equitable – provided one
did not pay too close attention to the divide between this uniform
obligation and the one applicable to the town, only a third as onerous and varying according to each person's abilities. It is hard not
to read into these practices the prejudices of the era, the prevailing
contempt for the peasantry – the "lazy, stubborn" colonial peasantry

in particular.[51] Whereas corvées in the Quebec countryside resembled military service in their arbitrariness, the one established in the côtes of the government of Montreal in 1715 adhered to the procedures of a well-regulated tax: parish assemblies, tax rolls drawn up by leading citizens, contributions according to the habitants' means. Since the criteria for town and country were the same, the less well-off country people were taxed less. Governor Claude de Ramezay seems to have invested a great deal in this arrangement, "a thing ... well deliberated and resolved," as he wrote.[52] The influence of the Sulpician seminary, which always adhered to tradition and regulations, may have been felt. And times had changed, perhaps mentalities to some extent as well. At mid-century, a logic of war once again ruled decision-making but differently from that of 1690. The militia had priority. Youth had to remain available for military operations and garrison duty. Large numbers were recruited each year in all the parishes, and it was henceforth as militiamen that they went to dig and fill in the outermost reaches of French-defended territory. The time for economy had passed, and those who did not go to war could profit from the military works and transports underway in the vicinity.[53]

2. REQUISITIONS AND BILLETING

a) Requisitions of workers and supplies

In addition to the corvées, the administration often requisitioned workers for fortification and other tasks related to the king's service. Even if remunerated, these exactions could become insupportable when they were too frequent and prevented the colonists from going about their business. Two examples follow. Whenever the royal shipyard was short of manpower, the intendant sent his court officers (*hoquetons*) to "requisition workers" in the côtes of La Canardière, Beauport, Île d'Orléans, and elsewhere.[54] These workers were not labourers and carters only too happy to earn a few pennies but small businessmen who, with the journeymen carpenters they employed, had contracts with shipowners, deadlines to meet: in short, professional obligations that were jeopardized by these forced interruptions. The Saint-Maurice Ironworks, another royal enterprise, regularly mobilized habitants from the surrounding côtes for hard work, in particular the felling of trees to make charcoal. "They resist going on the pretense that they have their land to cultivate," wrote Louis

Franquet. "Violence is at times used to force them, and it has happened that one or another has opted to leave the area and settle elsewhere rather than submit."[55] But this conflict should not be overdramatized. If labour requisitions fell outside the farming season, they were well received: better, certainly, than wheat requisitions, which were always hated because they prevented the best farmers from taking advantage of high prices and could even eat into family reserves. Wheat requisitions were used during the shortages of 1737–38 and 1742–44. After having paralyzed the trade and set the price of wheat below its market value, the intendant had it seized from the peasants' barns "for the subsistence of the troops and the city poor." As we shall see, these brutal methods were to reappear, this time on a regular basis, during the regime's final war.[56]

b) Billeting of soldiers, 1665–1748

Billeting was another onerous public charge to which historians have paid little attention.[57] Contemporaries in France all but unanimously denounced this obligation, which was all the more onerous in that the well-off often secured exemptions and all the more hateful in that the troops' indiscipline and the obstacles to obtaining justice exposed hosts to all manner of abuses. Often, when the men to be billeted were not numerous, municipalities rented, set up, and maintained houses at their own expense while awaiting the construction of barracks. Barracking in France was considered necessary to appease the people and reinforce military discipline, but it was costly and made very slow progress throughout the eighteenth century.[58] The same customs, abuses, and remedies are found in Canada with a few original features as a bonus, although these did not improve matters – quite the contrary.

When the 1,300 men of the Carignan-Salières regiment disembarked at Quebec in 1665, the colony had no more than 500 houses, 100–120 at best in its western region where the largest numbers of troops were stationed. They spent three winters there in unimaginably crowded, uncomfortable conditions.[59] The experience left a few bad memories that induced the habitants of Montreal Island to tax themselves for the money to rent the building serving as a guard house for the small garrison. During the assembly of 3 December 1673, the syndic reminded those present, in veiled language, that rape is a hazard of billeting: If the habitants did not respond, he said, then he would have to house soldiers for three-month periods in the townspeople's homes, cheek by jowl with their women and children.[60] The threat had its effect: The 327 livres collected that year were used to pay the arrears and to start a maintenance fund, and fifty livres continued to be collected year after year to cover rental charges.[61] If, as may be supposed, the Quebec garrison lived in the Château Saint-Louis at the king's expense, then the capital must have been entirely spared this expense until the arrival of the first contingent of 1,750 naval troops in 1683. At that point, the colonists went back to preparing straw pallets, providing spoons and pots, and making room at the hearth for the soldiers to make their lard soup. Although less glaring than before, the disproportion between the number of soldiers in the colony and the space in which to billet them remained high. The majority of the soldiers roomed in rural parishes near the towns; on several occasions, during the Nine Years' War and afterwards, peasants were paid to feed the soldiers they billeted, either because the intendancy was short of provisions or, at other times, out of convenience.[62] In the government of Montreal, the troops lived for a time in small forts with colonists whom the war had forced to evacuate their homes.[63] After the Peace of Ryswick in 1697, a decline in troop numbers coupled with urban growth made it possible, until the mid-eighteenth century, to billet all soldiers in the cities for the winter, an undeniable advantage for the service.[64] Each autumn, Montreal received nineteen companies, or more than 500 men when the companies were full, amounting to two soldiers per household at the start of the period, only one per household fifty years later. But since the companies generally were not full and married noncoms who had their own homes must be subtracted, the actual burden was lower. With seven companies, or at most 210 men, for 461 households in 1716 and 1,055 in 1744, Quebec was to a large extent spared.[65]

Is there reason to believe that the billeting of officers was peculiar to the colony and that they paid their own housing costs in France? The absence of any reference to this practice in the general regulations would appear to confirm this hypothesis. The method was used for the Carignan officers and thereafter for all officers, whether from France or elsewhere in the colony, who did not reside in the town where they were stationed.[66] The host was required to provide them with a heated private room and a candle. This duty, then, rested with the most well-off townspeople, and even some of them lacked the requisite space. For this reason and, above all, because a stranger's presence could easily become intolerable, most preferred to rent a room at the inn or in a private home for their assigned officer.[67] The expense could exceed 100 livres and was more or less frequent depending on the period. In the first half of the eighteenth century, the majority of officers resided with their families in the town where they were garrisoned. Few, that is, found themselves dependent on the community, and if the judge established a fair rotation among the hosts in this category, their turn did not come every year. But the multiplication of troop movements with the war, and the augmentation of the *compagnies franches* in the 1750s, would increase the burden.

As regards exemptions, the colony obeyed the customs of the realm, according to which the list of privileges, defined in particular by the regulations of 1651 and 1678, was very long. Religious communities, nobles, military and law officers, seigneurs, a notary, a surgeon, and the syndic of the habitants appear on a list of persons exempted from the tax levied in 1673 to billet the Montreal garrison.[68] Intendants readily granted billeting exemptions as a reward or as a bonus for unpaid or poorly paid work; thus, one finds on the list the names of clerks of the roads superintendent and the Domaine d'Occident, special syndics of the convents, fine collectors, and a carpenter responsible for fire prevention.[69] The Sulpician seminary managed to obtain exemptions for its millers, tenant farmers (*métayers*), and other tenants.[70] The urban militia captains – wealthy traders for the most part, who would have been obligated to billet an officer – had "always," they said, been dispensed from billeting.[71] All these latter exemptions would be abolished after 1748 in order to better allocate the barrack tax in Quebec and accommodate the surfeit of soldiers in Montreal. But the restrictive measure was more symbolic than practical, for it did not affect the majority of exempt persons belonging to the Church, the nobility, or those members of the military and administrative officer corps who held royal commissions.[72]

The police magistrate kept a list of available dwellings and another of soldiers staying in the city for even one night, and he handed out billets for the soldiers to present to their hosts. "The mason Sarot shall, until further notice, billet a soldier from the company of Saint-Ours who has arrived at Fort Saint-Frédéric. Done at Montreal, this 24th day of May 1740."[73] The lists have not survived. The sample of billeters of soldiers and non-commissioned officers that I have collected from scattered occurrences in the Montreal judicial archives offers no surprises:[74] Of a total of 156 cases, seventy-one (45 per cent) were artisans, 13 per cent innkeepers, and 13 per cent merchants. Were the innkeepers obligated to accommodate this many soldiers, or were they paid to take soldiers off billeters' hands? Impossible to know. The urban elite is nearly absent here, since they were either exempt or responsible for officers, and the lower stratum made up of labourers and carters is also underrepresented (4 per cent) because the accommodations they could offer were inadequate. One should therefore not take at face value the remarks of the engineer who, to promote the barracks project, stated that only "the poorest are billeting."[75] The tax actually fell on middle-income townspeople living and working in heated but cramped apartments, where the presence of a soldier (or two) represented an added encumbrance when winter kept everyone indoors.

The ordinary disputes, damages, and brutalities associated with this forced cohabitation fell under the jurisdiction of the fort major or the company captain, with whom hosts filed their complaints. The procedure was not such as to earn their trust. Grievances came to the attention of the court, where the historian finds them, only when the soldier was accused of a criminal act such as theft or assault, as happened at the home of a butcher named Bolvin [*sic*] in Trois-Rivières. One evening, in the parents' absence, a quarrel broke out between their daughters and one of the two naval regulars billeted there. Alerted by the noise, a neighbour entered, tried to intervene, and was stabbed in the abdomen during the ensuing altercation. Without this injury, nothing would be known of the girls' exasperation and the soldier's cursing of the "good-for-nothing Canadians."[76] Elsewhere the cohabitation was better tolerated, even appreciated, when the host acquired a good servant or journeyman, as did Pierre Lenclus, a Quebec shoemaker, who billeted two apprentice shoemakers doing military service in 1738.[77] The general staff recommended that soldiers be placed in homes where they could practice their trade, if any, but the absence of such cases in my sample of Montreal hosts shows that they were infrequent. Recall that the troops were garrisoned at remote posts for half the year, which did not favour such arrangements and made it difficult to form attachments. In short, while there were good sides to billeting, on the whole it represented a burden, a source of vexation and conflict, even between people of the same social stratum.[78] When rank entered into it, exacerbating tensions and humiliating hosts, it became insupportable. Only one townsman in the sample was killed in a quarrel with an officer billeted at his home, but this incident remains exemplary in terms of the attitudes it reveals: the officer's arrogance, the quiet assurance that the authorities would always find in his favour, the victim's impotent fury. On 17 January 1748, merchant baker Nicolas Jacquin *dit* Philibert was shocked to find Lieutenant Pierre-Jean-Baptiste-François-Xavier Legardeur de Repentigny at his door with a billet. It was a mistake, he said, abruptly turning the officer away: He supplied soldiers' bread and ought therefore to be exempted. Repentigny ran to tell the governor, who ordered the judge to uphold the billet. Two days later, the officer had his things brought to the baker's house with an order to get the room ready. When he arrived that evening, a furious Philibert told him he had sent his things to the previous host and would go there the next day to agree upon a price. During this second encounter, the quarrel resumed with greater intensity, until Repentigny, according to his petition, drew his sword to avenge his honour after this terrible slander. The baker had the time to file a complaint before dying of his injury. Protected by the governor, the intendant, the bishop, and the whole officer corps, "the unfortunate Mr. Repentigny" took shelter at Fort Saint-Frédéric (now Crown Point, NY) while the provost court heard his case and sentenced him *in absentia* to be beheaded. Letters of mercy were published the following year, but the governor saw fit to send the lieutenant to Île Royale for a time out of consideration for the Philibert family and public opinion.[79]

c) Barracking at Quebec, 1748

No sooner had he arrived at Quebec in the fall of 1748 than François Bigot, the new intendant, ordered the garrison to be barracked. It seems unlikely that the drama of the previous January had influenced his decision. The question is, rather, why such a decision had been so long in coming, since the capital had had a building for its troops since 1717. At that earlier time, Vaudreuil and Bégon had proposed this reform for the good of the service; the Conseil de la Marine – while warning them of the taxpayers' likely reaction – had given them carte blanche to replace the billeting obligation with an annual tax to defray the cost of maintaining and heating the barracks.[80] But they dithered, and the project was shelved until 1726 when a new governor briefly revived it. To instill discipline in the troops, wrote Beauharnois, they ought to be rapidly removed from the habitants' pernicious influence. Two years later found him deeming the project premature.[81] These thirty years of procrastination are explained by a convergence of specific interests. The administrators ultimately opted to let things go, to refrain from "troubling the townspeople," rather than be forced to grapple with the difficulties inherent in a new tax, one that would invite criticism and put a bad mark on their service records.[82] For as long as billeting affected only a small number of homes – one in ten in Quebec circa 1744 – the majority of city dwellers, especially the most well-off, had no greater interest in favouring a more equitably apportioned tax.[83] The hosts may have had a different opinion, but they were never consulted. Less craven than his predecessors, Bigot also had the task of preparing for increases in troop numbers. Already, some 300 soldiers bound for Île Royale had been added to the small local garrison between 1747 and 1749. The following year, the colony received more than 1,000 recruits and redistributed its forces, with thirteen companies of fifty men at Quebec and Montreal and four at Trois-Rivières.[84] In this last, two companies had hitherto been accommodated in a guard house, apparently at the king's expense; the doubling of the garrison would thus initiate the practice of billeting here.[85] It remained customary in Montreal, where the number of soldiers grew from 410 to 650.[86] The big changes took place at Quebec, with an immensely increased military presence and higher taxes than anticipated, startling the townspeople. Furthermore, the procedure that was followed violated all the established rules of the realm, as noted by the city's merchants on 30 April and 2 May 1750.

> They have the honour to represent to the honourable governors and intendant that all perpetual taxation and urban charges, of the sort intended, can only be applied by virtue of a decree of the King's Council of State and a declaration by His Majesty registered with the Conseil Supérieur de Quebec; that the minister's letter cannot be regarded as a declaration by the King, to whom the said habitants are willing to submit when His Majesty so orders.[87]

Bigot rejected both the legal argument and the plea to diminish the tax, set at 13,491 livres and payable retroactively. The syndic was asked to participate in the apportionment assembly; if he did not, it would go ahead without him. Versailles had at first blamed the intendant for barracking the garrison without authorization; however, a Council of State decree ratifying the procedures was subsequently issued, on 1 June 1753.[88] The previous administrators' fears had proved unfounded: After initial protests, the city paid willingly. The tax roll of January 1756, for example, shows only a small outstanding balance for the six previous rolls. On that date, the average contribution of the 1,003 taxed households was thirteen livres and six sols, with amounts varying from three to sixty livres.[89]

The tax was actually quite onerous, but its effect was that Quebec escaped the billeting that would become a crushing burden elsewhere in the colony, with the subsequent arrival of army battalions and a second naval troop increase.[90] In 1755, Montreal households that had not yet been chosen to billet officers were ordered to widen their pallets and bedsteads to accommodate two men, offer utensils for two meals, and receive not only soldiers stopping briefly en route to the camps but also those quartered in the city for the winter.[91] During the first half of the century, the rural parishes had been relatively spared. They were accustomed to billeting soldiers travelling between Quebec and Montreal, while people living near Quebec received newly arrived recruits from time to time. From 1755 on, their billeting responsibilities became far more onerous, as we shall see.

3. WHO'S AFRAID OF CAPITATION?

"Albeit these corvées are a form of taxation, the name is not hateful in this land, for the people have long since grown accustomed to it."[92] "Accustomed" is the key word. Contemporaries knew that where taxes were concerned, the old methods, such as the *taille*, were better tolerated than an innovation such as the *dixième*, or later the *vingtième*, even though these methods were fairer and more rational.[93] The Canadians had supplied their labour to build churches and rectories, roads and bridges, stake forts around their parishes; the administrators thought they would put up no fuss about also working on the Montreal enceinte, and despite an initial row or two they were proved right. However, to say that the colonists were accustomed to giving free labour does not mean that this system was a sort of colonial victory with respect to the tax administrations in the metropole. In the first place, they had not chosen it over a different system; they had never been given an opportunity to reject a uniform tax commensurate with income and payable in cash or kind. The administrators had rejected Versailles's tax schemes on three occasions, claiming to speak for the people without even consulting them as had been recommended. "As you have remarked, we did not think it wise to communicate our views to several notables. We know that they regard the matter in question less favourably than the people, and prudence demanded that we act with this restraint."[94] A laboured, ambiguous phrase leaving open the possibility that the people – those who provided the labour – might have preferred a different form of contribution. In the second place, and regardless of popular opinion, it is plausible that far from being unfair, uniform taxation would have fostered the political maturation of the colonists and might also have allayed the farmers' fears.

Since duties on colonial products and other indirect taxes did not bring in enough money, in 1713 the king ordered the adoption of direct taxation in all his American colonies.[95] His finances were exhausted, and it was fair that their inhabitants, the Canadians among others, do their part, "since they had in no way contributed to the immense expenses of the war like the others of His Majesty's subjects, and yet they will enjoy, like the others, and even more usefully, the benefits of peace." It was up to them to choose the form of taxation and up to the governors and intendants to convene the assemblies and report their decisions.[96] Further to these instructions, Saint-Domingue consented to levy a head tax proportional to the number of slaves in the form of a city toll (*octroi*) administered by its Conseils Supérieurs.[97] At Quebec, the king's commissioners rejected the demand. Twenty years later, and again in 1743, Maurepas returned to the fray, only to be told that such a tax was impossible. The war that broke out the following year shunted aside the plan for some years until it was put forward again, with great insistence, by Secretary of State for the Navy Antoine-Louis Rouillé between 1751 and 1754. Quebec showed some semblance of going ahead with it but delayed until war once again interrupted any attempt at fiscal and administrative reform.

Arguments for putting off taxation varied from reasonable to implausible. After emphasizing that the Canadians had supplied labour for the fortifications and participated in several military manoeuvres, thereby going to considerable expense and inconvenience, Vaudreuil and Bégon felt it necessary to invoke the spectre of widespread defection if a tax were to be imposed and to stress "the restraint which should be shown the habitants of this colony, what with the English nearby."[98] Beauharnois and Hocquart shifted the emphasis to the colonists' poverty and above all the danger of insurrection. These men preferred to tax trade, but since the minister wanted a direct tax, they outlined a plan that could not be put into effect without a prior doubling of troop numbers. "And that is not an excess of caution," they wrote, given the Canadians' "spirit of independence," which they contrasted with the "perfect submission" of the French peasants.[99] It was not so much these threats, taken with a grain of salt anyway, that made Versailles back down as it was the ill will of its agents, ill-concealed under these sensationalistic arguments. The administrators subsequently gave up on these and fell back on the time-tested dilatory tactics favoured by the slowness of communication. And so it was that in 1754, three years after requesting a proper tax plan, Rouillé had received only vague proposals, and the colony still awaited his decision.[100]

The correspondence does not address the real problems. To begin with, would it have been possible to preserve the labour regime and the duty of free military service once the habitants started paying taxes? After all, the *taille* had initially been a way of "buying one's freedom from enlistment."[101] In the eighteenth century, the relationship between tax and labour, or between military service and taxation, was well-established in the minds of administrators and religious communities. The French militiaman was exempt from the *taille* while he served and for a year after his discharge or three years if he married. Above a certain level of *taille*, peasants eluded the drawing of lots.[102] To take a colonial example, Saint-Domingue consented in 1763 to pay the king a "free gift" of 4 million livres in exchange for abolition of the militia.[103] The Canadian administrators clearly had good reasons to fear that new taxes, however modest, would induce the population to question its labour obligations. To keep the people willing to "march on command," the administrators preferred to tax trade to the maximum supportable limit. Versailles, in contrast, wanted to go easy on trade and tax the habitants as a spur to production.[104] The latter position surely had greater economic merit – provided the taxpayers were allowed to go about their labours, a trade-off that the administration was unwilling to accept.

A second contradiction with local customs concerned the parish assemblies and syndic elections that would have had to accompany the introduction of a fiscal system such as the *taille* in a colony where the rural communities on whose collective responsibility such systems are based had no legal existence, where constraints and sanctions were only exercised against individuals. The Ancien Régime state had yet to resolve the technical problems of income tax as we know it today, such as how to verify each return so as to arrive at an accurate picture of the various sources of income. It also feared finding itself up against a mass of debtors, many of them insolvent, and having to undertake costly prosecutions and make do with uncertain revenues. Instead, it remained faithful to an "apportioned" tax determined in advance and allocated among communities as a function of their presumed resources. In each parish, the habitants were jointly and severally liable for the debt, so shares owed by indigents and other defaulters ultimately fell on solvent taxpayers' shoulders.[105] For the same reasons, and irrespective of the choice of tax base for Canada – whether it was the area of cleared land in Hocquart's plan or the more arbitrary criteria in Bigot's – debt collection, too, took a collective form.[106] Habitants subjected to labour obligations had always faced the authorities alone, and the authorities were not willing to give up this advantage in exchange for endless wrangling with rural communities consolidated by new procedures. Furthermore, in the cities, a head tax (*capitation*) in the form of a city toll would give the assemblies a say in the use of the funds.[107] The administrators knew how the Caribbean planters had availed themselves of this prerogative to reject military spending; closer to home, they were worried by Montreal taxpayers' protests over the use of the tax to build the enceinte.[108] The administrators knew too that they would be the first to be blamed if a confrontation with the colonists should take place. All these were good reasons to shy away from innovation.

The pressure to preserve the status quo also came from colonists, and in particular from churchmen, whose righteous anger was aroused whenever the idea of taxing property and income and competing with tithes was raised. In 1754, the minister demanded that the hitherto secret head tax plan be revealed to the bishop so that he could help to mould public opinion into approval. The two memoranda following this demand show that the clergy was not willing to rise above its own special interests.[109] The following year, the Abbé de l'Isle-Dieu, vicar-general of the French colonies in Paris, was pleased to announce to the bishop of Quebec that the tax had been set aside for the time being.[110] The other social groups did not have an opportunity to give their opinion publicly, but it may be supposed that most of the seigneurs – like other rural notables whose greater-than-average property holdings did not mean they had to supply more labour – concurred with the Church. The new taxes, progressive by nature, would have imperiled this misleadingly egalitarian system. They would not have spared the military nobility, who were well represented in the seigneurial group.[111] The nobles were close to the governors and must have been familiar with the decisions to tax and re-tax trade rather than income. For others, the new taxes would come on top of contributions already seen as too onerous. By means of licences, exclusive trading concessions, and privileges accorded to post commandants, the administration took a substantial share of the profits from the fur trade. There were also indirect taxes on foreign trade and long-term credit in the form of deferred bills of exchange and payment orders without fixed maturity, which the king's suppliers had to carry on their books.[112] Early eighteenth-century peasants who supplied two weeks of labour on the walls of Quebec and another ten days building and maintaining their parish roads – nearly a month out of a six-month agricultural season – could be forgiven for thinking that they were making a major contribution to public works. The same was true of the thousands of young men who, instead of helping their parents or preparing for their own settlement, served without pay during long military and paramilitary campaigns after 1744. It can be asserted without complex calculations that the burden was often much greater than the *taille*, the *aide* (indirect tax), and the *gabelle* (salt tax) paid by peasants in various regions of France.[113] The comparison rests on an acknowledgment of the value of farm labour, which historians who insist that Canadians were not taxed have chosen to deny or ignore, thus taking a position in opposition to enlightened eighteenth-century opinion. "To take the farmer's time, even if he is paid, would be the equivalent of a tax. To take his time without paying him is double taxation," reads the edict of 1776 abolishing the royal corvée system in France.[114] The colonists knew it, and ultimately accepted it.

There is no way to understand the ease with which the general staff was able to mobilize this population during the mid-century wars – to force them to carry out obscure and unpleasant tasks in remote, insalubrious places – without first having described the settings for public life and the various services they were already accustomed to providing, as I have done in the previous two chapters.

For coercion alone leaves a good deal unexplained. Beyond private interests, mundane complaints, and certain more critical opinions, the same need for order and safety impelled both city and country to cooperate with the military. Over the years, the habitants of the côtes learned to work together, to form earthmoving corvées or small police detachments, to obey and be obeyed. The government could draw on this discipline for its own purposes.

8

Sixteen Years of War (1744–60)

The war between the French and British colonies that broke out in May 1744 was to last sixteen years. In North America, the truce between the two European conflicts (1748–56) was a time of redeployment of forces along ill-defined borders, soon followed by armed attacks. By the end of these uninterrupted clashes, peace was barely a memory to a whole generation of colonists. Unlike the previous Franco-British wars, in which the militias had been spared to a great extent, the War of the Austrian Succession was marked by an ongoing mass mobilization of habitants, on the order of 2,000 each year. This activity briefly declined after 1748, only to rebound, reaching 4,000 in 1753 and 1754, nearly 6,000 in 1755, and then rising rapidly to 11,000 men – very probably corresponding to the near-totality of the male population fit to march – at the time of the invasion. The militia's increased participation in military operations was in part linked to the proliferation of strongholds in the colony, another novel feature with respect to the previous period. It took a great many men to build, arm, supply, heat, and protect the forts and to maintain contact between them and the centre of the colony. Even recruits lacking training and experience could help with paramilitary tasks. All these demands led to an increase in the number of young men who learned the art of war during these years.

1. SOURCES

For the study of recruitment methods, militia composition, and militia participation in campaigns between 1744 and 1760, the literature is ampler and more varied (at least at the outset) than for the seventeenth century. Given the ideological fog in which the end of the French regime is enveloped, some clarifications on this documentation are in order.

First, despite its volume, there are significant gaps. With a scant few exceptions, there are no journals kept by militia officers or soldiers, no private correspondence, or any trace of sermons delivered by chaplains to troops assembled in the camps and forts: the kinds of sources that make Fred Anderson's book about Massachusetts recruits during the Seven Years' War so valuable.[1] Widespread illiteracy among the Canadian peasants does not explain the rarity of accounts originating from other largely educated social groups, merchants and city artisans in particular.[2] As long as winter did not interrupt contact between Montreal and Lake Erie, Lieutenant Gaspard-Joseph Chaussegros de Léry and his wife wrote to each other every two or three days.[3] In 1754, the governor complained of the great many letters filled with what he described as false news coming from the Ohio garrisons.[4] The texts were once extant but have been lost. Recall that the local press in New France was nonexistent, whereas in the British colonies it did much to preserve people's stories. Different reasons explain the absence of genuine militia rolls giving names, ages, places of residence, trades, and dates of mobilization; here, the problem has to do with the negligence of the colonial general staff, not the vagaries of conservation. "The use of rolls is unknown here," wrote an investigator sent by the naval treasurer, an observation supported by the piteous state of the few subsisting lists of recruits.[5]

For 1744–48, a rich variety of accounting documents is available. Drawn up in the offices of the intendancy and the king's stores, these documents shed much light on military movements, the composition of parties and large detachments, the equipment and provisions given them, the diversity of jobs involved, and the question of wages and remuneration. The arrival of a new intendant in 1748 put an end to the proliferation of these partial statements of revenues and expenses filled with precise details. Subsequent statements obscure the realities lying behind the skyrocketing expenses. As in the past, the administration wrote an ongoing chronicle of military events titled "account of the most interesting occurrences" between two dates. This offers something of a backdrop to the governors' correspondence with Versailles and to the numerous campaign reports and journals written by regular officers and also sent to the minister.

The internal correspondence between the governor, his staff, and the commanders of the operations sheds a clearer light on the details of the service. Here, one finds more candour in addressing the difficulties and problems of discipline generally sidestepped in the official reports. This correspondence has almost entirely disappeared, but its value is known thanks to a few scattered letters and, above all, the valuable Contrecoeur and Léry papers.[6]

The colonial officers' accounts are particularly useful for my purposes, since they commanded the militias wherever they served, whether at the forts or in the army. Unfortunately, these accounts all but vanish after 1756.[7] If the contents of the colonial archives are to be believed, the ministry was down to a single correspondent in Quebec, Governor-General Pierre de Rigaud de Vaudreuil de Cavagnial, who had occupied the position since the previous summer.[8] He tells us that he forbade his officers from communicating with the minister directly; however, there is no way of telling whether this censure suffices to explain the void left by the other correspondents.[9] Vaudreuil's dispatches to the court – spread out over a period of several months, thanks to the couriers of Louisbourg – plus his partially preserved orders, manifests, and instructions, form a considerable corpus. The information is broken up into short missives; the language is clichéd, unabashedly bombastic. Sentence after sentence begins with the word "I," giving readers the impression that Vaudreuil himself saw to the completion of every task. Yet no other administrator lavished as much praise on his subordinates, albeit in abstract terms. Vaudreuil took pleasure in exalting the merits of the colonial troops, their officers, and, above all, the "Canadians resolved to spill their blood," who had a "passion for burning gunpowder" and asked only "to be put in the most exposed places," etc.[10] It goes without saying that this discourse – a strategic element in a power struggle – tells us nothing about the hardships small and large occasioned by the war or the morale of the militias. The governor-general almost never discussed the specifics of the service.

To know what happened on the ground during the Seven Years' War, one must draw on the accounts of the army officers who disembarked at Quebec in 1755 and afterwards. They left a huge quantity of documentation – memorials, campaign journals, correspondence with France and within the army – of which a small fraction was stored in the archives of the Ministry of War and another devoutly conserved by their descendents; some of these documents were later published.[11] In them, the outlook of the foreign traveller intertwines with that of the military man. The first puts the emphasis on picturesque details; one finds little essays on local customs that are more often derived from a few preconceived ideas or half-remembered books than on the author's own observations: He judges, passes sentence, and follows the traveller's natural inclination toward generalization. Not all the texts exhibit the same degree of candour. When François-Gaston de Lévis mentions the "alleged" assassination of Joseph Coulon de Villiers de Jumonville at the start of his journal, it is clear that the man holding the pen is not the brigadier of 1756 but the marshal of 1783, voicing the opinions of his day and those of his friend James Murray, governor of Minorca.[12] Many others, too, had the time to touch up their memoirs before giving them over to posterity, to say nothing of the alterations and deletions made later by their editors.[13] The journal of Louis-Joseph de Montcalm, commander of the French army expeditionary corps, is from this standpoint beyond reproach, and for good reason.[14] Dictated in large part to various secretaries, it is the cornerstone of this documentary apparatus for both its volume and its historical and literary interest.[15] With small sarcastic flourishes, Montcalm describes the quirks, loves, games, and schemes of the administration and the colonial elite. The writing – of the journal and of his private correspondence with second-in-command Lévis – was his way of coping with the long, monotonous Canadian winters and airing his frustrations with the conduct of the war. He had his figures of ridicule, such as the governor's brother, François-Pierre de Rigaud de Vaudreuil (Rigaud), and his protégé, the engineer François-Marc-Antoine Le Mercier. As a man of culture, Montcalm could not abide dull-wittedness and ignorance and was willing to overlook a witty man's faults. Frivolity and meanness cohabit with compassion, tenderness, and anguish, with life and death, in a tossed-off, chaotic, captivating chronicle very much of its time – which was not a time of respectful, charitable, or politically correct speech. That such a freewheeling style should have shocked Quebec historians of the past, those ardent defenders of the nation's glories and sworn enemies of the Enlightenment, is understandable. That it should garner the same disapproval today, as witness the section devoted to the writings of the Seven Years' War in *La Vie littéraire au Québec* or the articles on Montcalm in the *Dictionnaire des oeuvres littéraires du Québec* and the *Dictionary of Canadian Biography*, is more surprising.[16]

That said, what draws my attention is not the visitor's perspective but that of the soldier – the longest, dullest, and most solid part of this documentation. These authors note what they see and write what they know. They chronicle movements of partisans and scouts on the frontiers, marching orders, discipline in the camps, position and behaviour of combatants during sieges and battles, and so on. The idea – especially common in Quebec historiography – that the French officers could only conceive of war in terms of pitched battle and disdained the Canadians' and Amerindians' talents for petty warfare does not withstand a reading of these campaign journals.[17] We must first recall what several historians have established: that the officers who spent time in North America in the 1750s knew and appreciated the harassment and ambush tactics that the War of the Austrian Succession had helped to spread. Having defended itself in Bohemia against Maria Theresa's hussars, and having learned from its hard experience fighting the Turks and in Piedmont against Charles Emmanuel I, Duke of Savoy, the French army, under the impetus of Marshal Maurice de Saxe, had begun using light infantry units in 1743 to protect its flanks, perform dangerous reconnaissance missions, and take the enemy by surprise. Later on, these missions were preferentially entrusted to temporary formations or pickets made up of the best shooters, the most resolute men, from several regiments. And several of the expeditionary corps officers who arrived in Canada – such as Jean-Armand Dieskau, Saxe's aide-de-camp in the Bohemian army, or Montcalm and Lévis, veterans of the Piedmont campaigns – had acquired battlefield experience of these new tactics. These tactics are extensively discussed in military treatises published during that era and were included in the training of young officers.[18]

Everyone knew that this was how war was practised in New France, and if the commandants arrived with no knowledge of what the Amerindians had in store for them, they were sure of being able to rely on the colonial militias, renowned for their endurance, intrepidity, and ferocity. They expected, from the accounts of Bacqueville de la Potherie and Charlevoix, to find the small, compact, autonomous, highly mobile units that had been the strength of the Hungarians, the Serbo-Croats, and the Catalonian montagnards. We are back to the image of the Canadian man of war seen in outline at the beginning of this study; an image borne along by the literature for over a century, nurtured by the silences and euphemisms of the official reports; an image harboured by the newly arriving army officers and one that many of them proved unwilling to question when reality departed from their ideals. Instead of grappling with an inflated reputation, or misleading generalizations, they complained that "the Canadians have lost all their former fighting spirit."[19] These inexperienced, ill-dressed, poorly armed young men sent en masse to join the army at Fort Oswego (known to the French as Chouaguen) and Fort Carillon (later rebuilt as Fort Ticonderoga) in 1756 simply fell well short of expectations.[20] Still, the ensuing criticism did not target the militiamen, as has too often been written, but rather the government and the colonial officers in charge of recruitment and training, who were blamed for the resulting disorder. Once the initial disappointment had passed, the senior officers set about introducing discipline into the camps and using the irregulars to best advantage, with a better sense of their strengths and weaknesses.

No more or less reliable than the other sources, the documentation left by the French military men has the merit of highlighting certain details concerning the militia that were invisible to the colonial officers, so familiar had these details become. But since the militiamen were rarely under the army officers' direct command, these observations are not as numerous as one might have hoped.

2. MILITARY MOVEMENTS

As for the previous wars, the troop movements of the years 1744–60 are compiled in the appendix to this book.[21] The list is even more selective than the first one, and this time the sources are not at fault. It does not systematically include the hundreds of small parties mentioned by the Montreal storekeeper around 1745–47 or enumerated in the journals of the commandants at Carillon, Niagara, and elsewhere between 1755 and 1759. However, the excess detail would have added nothing without a bona fide analysis aiming to discover, for example, which groups among the domiciliés and the allies were the most active or what was the proportion of partisans among colonial regular officers, and these issues are beyond the scope of this study. So as not to overwhelm the reader, I proceeded in the traditional way, listing only the most decisive episodes, the ones that made noise in their day, as well as those in which the militia played a part, even if this means that the prominent Indigenous presence on all battlefronts is regretfully minimized. In the majority of cases, several convergent sources served to establish the numbers of participants in each category. Where they differ, the choices of other historians are considered. It is especially important to avoid taking ethnonyms at face value. In an oft-repeated formulation, expeditions are described as having consisted of, e.g., "100 Frenchmen and 200 Indians." Here the term "Frenchmen" does not serve to distinguish soldiers from colonists; rather, it is a generic term designating all men of European origin as opposed to Indigenous troops.[22] Similarly, until the early 1750s, the word *habitant* was regularly employed as a synonym for militiaman; a given detachment was said to consist of 300 habitants and 200 soldiers. Under the influence of the officers arriving from France, "habitants" became "Canadians." Thus, in addition to designating the colonists as a group, the name "Canadians" took on the more restrictive meaning of "militiamen": i.e., a social category as distinct from others. A detachment was composed of "Canadians and ... voyageurs from the Great Lakes region," reads one document; three officers "were killed along with three Canadians," reads another, even though all six were colonists.[23] Finally, the expression *troupes de la colonie* might very well designate a mixture of colonial regulars and militiamen. In short, the vocabulary of the time does not necessarily reveal the ethnic identities with which historians are obsessed.[24]

a) War of the Austrian Succession

In his instructions of 30 April 1744 following Great Britain's declaration of war the previous month, Maurepas opined that Canada had nothing to fear from the enemy, whether he arrived by sea, where British undertakings had never been successful, or from behind, where the forts of Montreal, Chambly, and Saint-Frédéric offered good protection. The colony could, and in fact should, act "offensively" on all fronts, against Oswego and the Hudson Bay and New England settlements, and should assist the forces of Île Royale in their reconquest of Acadia as soon as the order was received.[25] But the tone at Quebec was much less optimistic. Rumours of invasion by sea circulated all summer, whipped up by a false alarm during the night of 27 July. The signalling system entrusted to the riverside parish militias evidently needed some fine-tuning, and the city remained unfortified, to the despair of the general staff.[26] The year 1744 was also marked by an abrupt interruption of trade with France, Île Royale, and the other French colonies because privateers from the

Anglo-American ports had literally taken over the Gulf of St Law-rence.[27] Cut off from markets and suppliers, reeling from losses at sea, the large Quebec merchants demanded effective escorts for fish-ing and commercial vessels.[28] That autumn, the administrators had only one piece of good news to report to Versailles: that an abundant harvest, coming after three years of drought, would finally make it possible for war parties to be fitted out, once the Amerindians had been successfully mobilized. As to Acadia, Canada was willing to lend a hand, but not to the point of compromising its own security. With only about 500 regulars on hand, it was not about to let its militias and domiciliés go.[29]

At sea, nothing went as planned. An army of 4,400 Bostonian vol-unteers backed by an equal number of sailors and four British ships landed on Île Royale in April 1745. On 27 June, after a fifty-day siege and intense bombardment, Louisbourg, that famously impreg-nable fortress, was forced to surrender. The considerable efforts of the French navy to support the land operations in the region resulted in missed rendezvous, as at Port-Royal (Annapolis Royal) in 1744 and Louisbourg in 1745, or in deadly disasters such as those that beset the Duc d'Anville's expedition to recapture Louisbourg, Port-Royal, and Plaisance in 1746.[30] In May 1747, a convoy of thirty ships commanded by Admiral Jacques-Pierre de Taffanel de la Jonquière and bound for Quebec was attacked by the British off Cape Ortegal in the Bay of Biscay. The ships managed to escape and reach their destination but without the commandant and new governor-general, who had been taken prisoner.[31]

Canada supplied two detachments for the Acadian operations. The one commanded by Paul Marin de la Malgue, composed of 100 volunteers, eighty Hurons and Abenakis, and a dozen young officers and cadets, departed in late January 1745, with at least some of the troops following the portage route to the Saint John River and other Indigenous people augmenting their ranks along the way. First in the Minas Basin, then at the entrance to Annapolis Royal, Marin waited in vain for orders from Louisbourg. Were it not for the presence of two merchant ships detained in the harbour by bad weather, which the troops boarded, he would have accomplished nothing at all. The call to assist the commandant of the besieged fort did not arrive until 1 June. By the time Marin returned to Cobequid (now Truro) at the eastern tip of the Minas Basin, with men who had no desire to risk their lives on Île Royale, it was already too late, and the detachment returned to Quebec with its prizes and prisoners.[32] The second, much bigger detachment set sail for Acadia in June 1746 with orders to blockade Annapolis as soon as the French ships hove in sight. It consisted of more than 600 militiamen led by fifty officers and cadets while an additional 300 domiciliés travelled on foot, meeting an equal number of Abenakis and Mi'kwaq on arrival.[33] Stationed in the Beaubassin region at the back of Chignecto Bay, awaiting news of the Duc d'Anville's battle fleet, the little army had already used up its provisions and begun foraging for food when the governor decided that the men, especially the domiciliés, would be more useful on the Lake Champlain front where, he believed, an invasion was in the offing. But when the French fleet finally arrived at Chebucto (Halifax) after a long delay, it had been decimated by storms and hunger. Although the siege of Annapolis went ahead in late September with the dispatch of a reduced force weakened by hunger and disease, by 3 November it had been called off. The Canadians managed to return to the Isthmus of Chignecto thanks to a Louisbourg privateer and regain their strength before embarking on what would become the highlight of this arduous, as yet futile campaign. The attack, on the night of 11 February 1747 against a detachment of 500 men who had come from New England to chase them out of Acadia, had all the characteristics of the raids that had once made their reputation: a party of 200 colonists, sixty Mi'kmaq or Abenakis, and a few Acadian guides well commanded by officers and cadets; a march of almost 100 kilometres through the snow to reach Grand-Pré, where the Bostonians were housed; a surprise attack; many dead and wounded, nearly all of them on the enemy side.[34] But disease, carried to Chebucto by the unfortunate French fleet, took an ever greater toll on the ranks of the Indigenous allies and on the militiamen, who reached Quebec by summer in a pitiful state.[35]

In Canada, offensive operations did not really get underway until 1746. They were initiated by Paul Marin when, on returning from Acadia, he fell upon Saratoga with a troop of 500 men, including 300 domiciliés.[36] Until then, the latter had shown little haste to join such parties, and the colony had concentrated its forces on defending the territory: building the Quebec enceinte and installing a system to fend off an attack from the river; consolidating the network of forts in the government of Montreal; opening a road between La Prairie and the Richelieu River to expedite communication with Fort Saint-Frédéric toward the south end of Lake Champlain.[37] Since the

Iroquois League's neutrality guaranteed, for all intents and purposes, that the British would not attack via Lake Ontario, the colony could concentrate its forces on the southern frontier. Built between 1731 and 1735, Saint-Frédéric was the hub of the operations. A large, year-round garrison was kept there, providing workers for the construction of the fort as well as scouts to track the enemy's movements. Of the three large detachments sent to attack the British settlements on this frontier, the first two – Marin's and the one led by Rigaud in 1746 – won easy victories, since Saratoga and Fort Massachusetts were defended by just a handful of men.[38] The 1747 detachment, still commanded by Rigaud, stopped short of attacking Saratoga, by then equipped with artillery and a garrison of 300 men, and returned having accomplished nothing.[39] Still, the French forces had twice succeeded in moving several hundred militiamen deep into enemy territory, representing progress with respect to the abortive turn-of-the-century expeditions.[40]

Like its predecessors, this began as a partisan war waged principally by Indigenous people, and as in the past, the official reports do not evidence this reality: instead, they highlight the actions of the colonial soldiers. But in this case we also have the intendancy's bookkeeping, showing the number, makeup, and destination of the groups fitted out at the king's stores in Montreal and encompassing all operations to the south and west. My calculations cover only the parties returning from the British colonies, eighty-two in total for the year 1746.[41] These parties were small bands of ten to thirty men on average, with one exception numbering 100 men. The majority (seventy out of eighty-two) were composed of Indigenous fighters alone. In twelve cases, they were accompanied by colonial regular officers and cadets, at times by "volunteers" or "habitants." The breakdown is as follows: seven officers, eighteen cadets, and seven colonists for over 1,000 Indigenous partisans.[42] The Acadian campaign, by draining off fifty officers and cadets and 600 militiamen, was perhaps a cause of the dip in colonial participation that year. The numbers were a bit higher in 1747, with eleven officers, around thirty cadets, and 100 volunteers grouped into thirteen mixed parties of thirty, sixty, or up to 200 men. Since the store accounts stop in August before any items were returned, it is impossible to quantify the other parties, but all appearances are that they were just as numerous as they had been the previous year and that the numerical superiority of the Indigenous people was just as overwhelming.[43]

The local forces were augmented by about 500 allies from the Great Lakes region during the summer of 1746 and perhaps by as many the following summer. They took part in Rigaud's campaigns and in two or three mixed expeditions. However, almost all the small parties that I uncovered in the archives were made up of domiciliés. Thanks to a slight natural increase and the arrival of Abenaki and other refugees at the start of the war, the population of the Indigenous villages in the St Lawrence Valley stood at around 3,500, and they could supply up to 700 warriors.[44] Directly or through missionaries, the government exerted intense pressure on these people. No important expedition took place without their help. At the same time, it was expected that they would uninterruptedly carry on their raids against the British settlements, do garrison duty, and patrol around the forts.[45] But these services were never mentioned without a few unkind remarks being thrown in. Who but the Indigenous people – their whims, their "prodigious consumption" of provisions and munitions – was to blame for the skyrocketing military expenses? No matter that the store accounts belied these accusations, the notion stuck.[46] The colony had never been so conscious of its dependency, and perhaps this was what accounted for its ungratefulness and suspicion. The governor of Montreal made no bones about interpreting the unrest among Indigenous people of the Detroit region as a sign of a "general conspiracy of the redskin against the white" with which the domiciliés were allegedly complicit. "We are poorly served by them," he wrote, "and while they no longer strike at us, they encourage the enemy to do so and do not protect us."[47]

The population shared this feeling of insecurity, for it had lived for three years with the fear of an invasion. The militias in the western and central portions of the colony spent the summer of 1745 at Quebec awaiting the arrival of the British fleet with a mission to take the capital after having conquered Louisbourg. The following year, the riverside parishes remained on the qui vive, while upriver, 1,500 men stood ready to head off the enemy army in the Lake Champlain region. In the event, the only attacks, seven in total, were by small bands of Mohawks against isolated habitants. Awoken twice in the middle of the night to run after the assailants, the Montrealers became confused, fired on one another, and lost ten men in a drowning incident. The Iroquois of Sault-Saint-Louis showed more sang-froid and, to everyone's surprise, helped to repel the enemy, temporarily quieting accusations of treachery.[48]

It has often been said that the War of the Austrian Succession was merely a reprise of previous wars. Indeed, the strategy was the same: mount a large number of parties to sow terror among the enemy and keep him on the defensive. Fort Saint-Frédéric, serving as a stopover in both directions, enabled partisans to penetrate more deeply into the British countryside, where the peasants were less on their guard, producing more casualties and doing more damage.[49] But Saint-Frédéric, along with the warehouses and lesser forts spread out along this frontier, introduced a new dynamic into militia service, and from this point of view, this war diverged considerably from the turn-of-the-century model. The colonial regulars were not numerous enough to guard the forts. Colonists had to be mobilized according to rotations of several months, doing garrison duty and any other work for which they were required. The most zealous among them volunteered for scouting missions in the vicinity, occasionally joining a party bound for enemy territory. In former times, men had marched directly into battle and returned home when the campaign was done. Now, recruitment was done in stages, with a sojourn at Fort Saint-Frédéric or another outpost before or after the expedition. The length of duty increased, and the boundary between recruit and volunteer became blurred. The hundred "volunteers" who accompanied Marin to Acadia in 1745 had been recruited at great expense and some difficulty from twenty parishes in the government of Quebec.[50] This detachment bore no resemblance to the old volunteer corps made up of faithful companions with kinship ties who followed their chosen leader from one adventure to the next. A final distinction vis-à-vis the old days concerns the intensity of mobilization. When all militiamen who took part in military and paramilitary enterprises are counted, about 2,000 men left their parishes for prolonged periods each year from 1745 to 1748. Factoring in annual turnover, just about every colonial youth must have lived this experience.

b) From 1748 to the taking of Fort Necessity (1754)

Nobody believed that the Treaty of Aix-la-Chapelle (1748) was the prologue to the peaceful coexistence of the French and British colonies in North America. "God grant ... that we can get out of this country before war resumes," wrote Élisabeth Bégon from Montreal, a wish also expressed by several merchants who had suffered during the previous conflict.[51] Those who regarded the restitution of Louisbourg as a return to the *status quo ante* had only to look to Halifax to realize their mistake. Great Britain had just built this naval and military base with the firm intention of occupying the whole of Nova Scotia, which it claimed extended all the way to the St Lawrence estuary. France, which had definitively given up the reconquest of Acadia, wanted to confine the British to the peninsula.[52] Its declarations of principle were vigorous, but its on-the-ground resources were weak compared to the enemy's new power. France essentially fell back on the tortuous strategy deployed in this land since Utrecht: pressure the missionaries to secretly push the Mi'kmaq and Malecites to attack the British. This time it was also hoped to mobilize the Acadians: to convince them to leave their land and property and move their families into French-controlled territory where their numbers could then be drawn on for militia duty.[53] With a population of approximately 13,000, Acadia could supply more than 2,000 militiamen if only half its inhabitants agreed to emigrate to Île Saint-Jean (now Prince Edward Island) to the north of the Bay of Fundy and Chignecto. And since the Acadians did not respond promptly enough to the priests' and officers' solicitations, the latter incited the Indigenous people to burn their houses and transform the whole Beaubassin region (near present-day Amherst, NS) into a war zone.[54]

Several times during this period, Acadian groups asked for official authorization to settle in Canada, in places "suitable for farmers and fishermen," so as to escape from a threatening future, but each time their request was denied. "It would be better for them to stay where they are ... so as to set upon Nova Scotia if war should break out," wrote the intendant.[55] The plan was designed to minimize outside military relief. Quebec sent only four small detachments between 1749 and 1751, each in turn overseeing the "Acadian transmigration," fortifying the frontiers, and attacking enemy settlements in concert with the Amerindians.[56] Thus, some 100–200 Canadian militiamen, mingled with soldiers and domiciliés, were present in the region at any given time during these three years. After the completion of forts Beauséjour and Gaspareaux on the Isthmus of Chignecto in 1752, only officers and cadets remained there, with a garrison of about 150 colonial regulars, assisted in principle by the local militia. Composed of refugees from Beaubassin and elsewhere, with no military experience and often traumatized by events, this militia clearly could not replace the army demanded by such an exigency as the preservation of the corridor linking Canada to Île Royale and the Atlantic.[57] Ill-defended Fort Beauséjour surrendered on 16 June 1755 after a four-day siege, with the French immediately abandoning their positions on Baie-Verte and at the mouth of the St John River. In the months that followed, the British destroyed the Acadian villages of Nova Scotia and locked up their populations while awaiting the ships that would disperse them along the coast, from Boston to Savannah. By late autumn, the number of deportees had risen to 6,000 or 7,000; by the end of this cleansing operation in 1762, it had reached 11,000 and included those who believed they had found asylum on Île Saint-Jean or on the banks of the St John and Miramichi rivers. Among those who succeeded in escaping, about 2,000 took refuge in Canada without prior permission.[58]

In their opposition to the British occupation of Acadia, the Mi'kmaq and Abenakis carried on old wars related to the occupation of their land, and France readily took advantage of the convergence between their interests and its own. Nothing similar occurred in the western part of the colony, where the nations were numerous and divided and the British were not their enemy. The good relations between French fur traders and Indigenous clientele – the cornerstone of the alliance – were compromised at the onset of the war by the maritime blockade, and the situation remained tense even after the canoes resumed their journey into the Great Lakes region.[59] Forgetting that the allies had, in spite of everything, come in large numbers and on two occasions, in 1746 and 1747, to take part in its military campaigns, the colony believed that it was about to experience a general uprising fomented by the British. So great was the fear that it was all but impossible to recruit militiamen to escort voyageurs and supply the principal posts.[60]

Tensions subsided after the war, except south of Lake Erie, where the Indigenous peoples continued to receive merchants from Pennsylvania and stepped up their hostile acts against the French and their allies. A small detachment sent by the governor in 1749 to take stock of the situation and order the British to decamp was not well received.[61] Meanwhile, the Ohio country (known to the French as Belle-Rivière), hitherto a marginal territory claimed by both France and Great Britain but poor in furs and hence little frequented by French traders, became a major front overnight. In the plan produced by Governor Roland-Michel Barrin de La Galissonière in concert with Maurepas and Rouillé, the region was the indispensable link between Canada and Louisiana, forming, with Illinois, the barrier that would contain the British colonies to the east of the Alleghenies. The plan was to punish the rebels, drive the British back by force if necessary, and build a few forts to maintain order among the Indigenous peoples and defend the territory.[62] After three years of vacillation, the operation went off successfully. In July 1752, a detachment of Ottawas and Saulteaux led by Charles-Michel Mouet de Langlade, a cadet in the colonial regulars, destroyed Pickawillany, a village of British-aligned Miamis (near present-day Piqua, OH); the following year, more than 2,000 men were mobilized to build a fort at Presqu'île (Presque Isle) on Lake Erie, one on the Rivière-au-Boeuf (now French Creek, at present-day Waterford, PA), and Fort Machault (present-day Franklin, PA) to the south. On the British side, a group of investors to whom London had granted a wide strip of land along the Ohio for settlement of colonists decided to take action with the backing of the governor of Virginia. This incursion into French territory favoured a rapprochement between the local population and the French, and on three occasions they forced the Virginians to retreat without a fight. With the completion in April 1754 of Fort Duquesne, begun earlier by the British company at the confluence of the Ohio, Allegheny, and Monongahela rivers (present-day Pittsburgh, PA), the chain of French posts along this frontier was complete.[63] The first bloody skirmish took place a month later when a detachment of volunteers and Indigenous allies commanded by George Washington suddenly attacked the small troop that had come to serve them with another warning. Its commandant, Joseph Coulon de Villiers de Jumonville, was killed along with nine of his men, and the remaining twenty were taken prisoner. The affair was treated as an assassination and caused a tremendous stir in Canada and France.[64] It was followed almost immediately by a riposte whose command was entrusted to Jumonville's brother, which also succeeded in capturing the popular imagination. The French victory over the Virginian troops at Fort Necessity on 3 July 1754 marked the start of the Seven Years' War proper.

The pressure on the Canadian militias had not let up since 1748. It had first been necessary, for lack of soldiers, to use colonists for garrison duty in the Great Lakes region, a practice that continued even after the augmentation of the colonial regulars in 1750. They also provided the bulk of the manpower for construction of trading posts at Toronto, the Niagara portage, La Présentation, and Saint-Jean on the Richelieu River and for transportation of materials and artillery, clearing of land, and additions and repairs to the old forts – not to forget annual recruitment of 1,000–1,500 men to go to Acadia on postings that rarely lasted less than a year. Mobilization took a quantum leap with the Ohio campaigns of 1753–54, affecting 3,000–4,000 colonists.

What was the colony's view of such an aggressively expansionist peace time policy that deprived it of its youth and its subsistence? From the moment of its conception, the idea of reclaiming the Ohio country bumped up against opposition from the merchants. To gain the rebel tribes' confidence, the government forced purveyors to send trade goods to the region at low prices, to the detriment of their investments to the northwest of the Great Lakes where fur quality was higher and the terms of trade more advantageous. These directives were greeted unfavourably.[65] Taking a broader view, Canadian trade needed a durable peace to rebuild its strength, and the best merchants were bound to condemn anything that jeopardized it.[66] Nor did the plan meet with the officers' unanimous approval, for even though they agreed in principle, they would have preferred to proceed more slowly, with 500 men instead of 2,000, so as to go easy on the existing logistical resources on the one hand and the farmers on the other.[67] "You have no troops," not even for indispensable needs, wrote Captain Charles de Raymond to the minister. "Will you continue, as you are doing, to strip the fields of your habitants?"[68] He was certainly not the only officer to denounce a strategy the colony could not afford, but personal ambition and devotion to duty always won out over these men's hesitations. The whole population was afraid of dying of hunger if the habitants could no longer till their land, and when news of the recruits started filtering into the colony in the summer of 1753, worry turned to anger. The rumbling was even louder in the fall with the return of the sick. Satirical verses, seditious remarks, "foul rumours" about the officers who commanded the expedition were heard in the streets of Montreal and surely elsewhere too.[69] The people were on the verge of revolt, recounted a British prisoner, for their children had been arbitrarily snatched away.[70] But they did not go to that extreme, and the opposition appears to have died down by the following year – perhaps because war no longer looked like a choice but an inevitability.

c) 1755 to 1760

In early 1755, France and Great Britain sent reinforcements to their colonies. Combined with the units already there, the number of regulars recruited in Europe rose to 5,000 for each of the two camps.[71] The local forces of Canada comprised approximately 1,500 Amerindians and 10,000 colonists of arms-bearing age, half of whom were already serving regularly.[72] With a population twenty times larger, the British colonies enjoyed a considerable reserve that had barely been tapped. On the ocean, Britain started off strong by capturing two ships carrying troops to New France in June 1755 and more than 300 merchant ships in the following months. The French fleet was often pinned down in the ports; contact with the rest of the Americas, though not entirely cut off, remained risky and uncertain. In 1755, the enemy was pursuing a limited goal: to push back the Canadian frontier by destroying its four principal outposts, at Duquesne, Niagara, Saint-Frédéric, and Beauséjour. The year ended with the French defeat in Acadia, the destruction of Edward Braddock's army in Ohio by the Indigenous allies, and an indecisive engagement in the Lake Champlain region.[73] The gap between the French and British forces widened rapidly in the years that followed, despite the arrival of four more battalions along with recruits for the French colonial regulars. The British side saw a larger increase in troops from the metropole: the implementation of a unified command and a good organization of transports and supplies to the armies, and the creation of a light infantry unit, several provincial regiments, and a ranger corps, adding up to about ten 100-man companies well-versed in petty warfare tactics and making up for the shortage of Indigenous partisans.[74] New France found itself facing a much larger and better-organized army in a war that already, in 1756, promised a fight to the finish.[75] It did win the first few rounds, going on to victory after the Battle of the Monongahela at Oswego in 1756, Fort William Henry the following summer, and Carillon in July 1758. But these were provisional victories, for the adversary immediately retook its positions, built new forts on the ruins of the old and, far from exhausting itself, took advantage of delays to increase and improve its troops. The invasion began with the fall of Louisbourg on 26 July 1758, followed by the destruction of Fort Frontenac in August, the sacking of the Gaspé coast in September, and the abandonment of Fort Duquesne and the whole Ohio region in November as John Forbes's army advanced on this frontier. In 1759 and 1760, the British army reached the heart of the colony and completed its conquest.

These and other military incidents are a matter of history. Less known are the administration and operation of the militias on the ground, as well as the living conditions and morale in the camps and the threatened parishes. The following chapters turn to these matters.

9

Marching on Command

This chapter focuses on the administrative aspects of the military duty done by the militias. Make no mistake, this was a strictly military administration. Elsewhere, militias were also subordinated to civilian power. In the British colonies, for instance, maximum authority rested with the provincial assemblies. In France, intendants or subdelegates, assisted by local communities, were in charge of drawing up rolls, issuing exemptions, and administering lotteries.[1] In Canada, the intendant had no part to play in recruitment, his oversight being limited to spending on equipment and provisions, as with the regulars. The colonial militia was an incomplete organization; without a higher administrative structure of its own, it was essentially amalgamated with the colonial regulars, administered by the same general staff, commanded by the same officers. There were of course militia colonels in the cities and militia majors or commandants in the côtes, but it seems clear that these dignitaries had no useful function, and they are never mentioned in the archival texts.[2] Governors' orders and observers' criticisms were always directed at parish militia captains, confined for the purposes of duty to their role as recruiting agents.

Another singularity of the Canadian militia is that it was unregulated.[3] There are, for example, no military ordinances to guide my research. Nevertheless, by making cautious use of the available piecemeal documentation, it is possible to identify the customs or informal rules governing military duty done by colonists between 1744 and 1759. This chapter covers the major modifications introduced in the first two years of the war.

I. TRAINING

Responsibility for militia training had been entrusted around 1711 to the commandant and adjutant (*major des troupes*) of the colonial regulars, who were to conduct reviews twice a year, inspect weapons, and ensure that habitants were drilled and disciplined. This objective was perceived as a priority, and various suggestions were put forward to help achieve it.[4] After the commandant's death in 1714, interest waned and did not revive until the early 1730s, as rumours of war began to be felt.[5] At that point, a subaltern began visiting the côtes of Quebec to provide basic training, a job for which he was paid 200 livres a year to cover travel expenses. The smallness of this sum suggests that he did not spend every Sunday and holiday on the road and that the forty-five parishes in his jurisdiction, especially the most distant ones, did not often receive a visit. When war was declared in 1744, four officers instead of one were assigned to this task: one in Montreal, one in Trois-Rivières, and two in Quebec.[6] But these Sunday strolls were clearly insufficient. The administrators had to admit that most militiamen had no notion of military discipline and that 5,000 men, or almost half of them, were unarmed.[7] Townspeople, at least Quebecers, were no more ready. Two of them described what happened when the urban militia was asked in April 1747 to guard a group of British prisoners gathered on the square: The troops showed up pell-mell and torpidly went through the motions, with considerable difficulty telling left from right. Mortified by this miserable performance in front of strangers, the governor must have given orders, for Quebec's militiamen were convened for drills on every subsequent Sunday.[8]

None of these initiatives paid any attention to the militia officers, as if it were understood that they could not be relied on to instruct the men in their company. It is true that most of them, elderly peasants without military experience, would have been incapable of doing so and that appointments by heredity and co-optation did not favour veterans newly settled in the parishes. These latter were slightly more numerous in the government of Montreal, but not numerous enough to explain why little or no militia training had been done in the western part of the colony before 1744.[9] For lack of personnel, maybe? After all, the officers' tutelary role over the militia had long been generally accepted. It was only the press of events that finally forced the militia to take its own training in hand. On the one hand, regular officers became increasingly unavailable; on the other, after years of continuous duty, every parish had militiamen capable of conducting drills, not to mention all the regulars billeted among them who wanted to make themselves useful. Weekly exercises after high mass became a routine; youth going to war for the first time were somewhat better prepared than their elders had been.[10] Between the excited, inexpert Montreal Island troops who pursued Mohawk assailants in 1747 and the elite battalion of 1759–60, extensive, long-range training work had been done, in marked contrast to earlier neglect.

Historians of New France have not addressed this question, no doubt because they implicitly associated military training with the parades and pitched battles of European armies and believed that militias did not need drilling to be effective in the kind of war practised in North America. This is false. It is one thing to shoot straight, quite another to know *when* to shoot. Furthermore, these colonists were not leaving home to go on small raids with Indigenous allies; they were gathered in large numbers in camps for months at a time. And if they were serving as soldiers, it was only fair that they be taught how to survive in the army, how to avoid accidents: in short, all forms of discipline. The governors had always been aware of this, even though neglect had long prevented them from making good on their good intentions.

2. RAISING THE MILITIA

Once the number of men necessary for a given enterprise was determined, the governor and his officers allotted them to the parishes – or, more precisely, to the militia companies. There were generally four, ten, or twenty men per company, to be recruited from across the colony if the number was high, from a single government or a dozen contiguous parishes if fewer were needed.[11] The custom was to spread out recruitment to the greatest extent possible. To levy fifty men, at least twelve parishes were called on. Thus, the 204 militiaman who went to Fort Duquesne in 1755 under the command of Captain Daniel-Hyacinthe-Marie Liénard de Beaujeu had been recruited from twenty-eight parishes of the government of Montreal.[12] The choice of the company as the basis of recruitment, rather than the parish, went some distance toward accommodating demographic differences but not far enough, for the companies were

Table 9.1 | Rural militia companies in 1750

Government	Quebec	Trois-Rivières	Montreal
Number of localities	46	16	40
Number of companies	60	16	67
Number of soldiers and non-commissioned officers	5,471	923	4,306
Mean company size	91	58	64
Median	88	52	62
Minimum size	34	32	16
Maximum size	171	87	140

Source: AC, CIIA, 95: 344–9, "Récapitulation des milices du gouvernement général du Canada, 1750."

of unequal size. The militia census of 1750 enumerates 101 rural localities along with the number and size of the corresponding companies (Table 9.1).

Population and geography do not fully explain the differences, since they are also found in the cities. In the west, the tendency was to divide companies as soon as they reached sixty men, while in the Quebec region, old, populous parishes such as Château-Richer, Charlesbourg, Lévis, and the ones on Île d'Orléans had only one or two large companies of 120–160 militiamen.[13] Thus, an across-the-board number of, say, ten men per company would produce fewer recruits in this government than in Montreal, even though the latter was less populated. If rigorously applied, this method would have created absurdities, crying injustices for the new côtes, which were poor in men and resources, yet these injustices were to a great extent avoided, for rigour was not the military government's strong point. Nor was planning. By working out its needs at the start of the year, it could have rapidly mobilized all the recruits at any given moment during the campaign. For their part, the habitants would have been able to plan their work according to the date of their own departure or that of their sons, engagés, or neighbours; the task of the recruiting officers would have been simplified and the king's expenses reduced. But the general staff went about it haphazardly. The officers collected a few men at a time through tirelessly repeated visits to the same parish: five in May for garrison duty, three in June to form a convoy, eight in July to join a particular detachment, and so on. The habitants never knew what awaited them, and these ad hoc practices hindered operations.[14]

Yet the general staff was of no mind to change its practices, predicated on the idea that the population would be less alarmed, the danger of local insurrection averted, if only a small number of men were taken from a parish at once. As Governor-General Michel-Ange Duquesne de Menneville explained to one of his officers, the 1,400 militiamen who went to Lake Erie in 1754 would come from all over, "and the colony would hardly notice this recruitment."[15] It was only at the very end of the war, with the press of events, when the officers could no longer increase the number of visits to the côtes, that the men of entire parishes began marching off en masse to join the army, led by their militia officers. History has retained this image, but it was in fact the exception; the rule had always been dispersal of militiamen from a single company into different brigades operating at different places. The militia company was just a unit of recruitment and identification; it never had any genuine existence outside of parish borders.[16]

In the administration's mind, there was never any question of sparing farmers and heads of households, as was done elsewhere. In principle, all men were required to serve, regardless of social or marital status, and only physical aptitudes were to be taken into consideration. How did this actually work? Let us begin with the cities, where the number of exempt individuals was certainly much larger than that of "officers bearing commissions, warrants, or letters of service from His Majesty" – the only ones dispensed from militia duty under the official directives.[17] A comparison of the 1744 and 1750 numbers, as given in Table 6.1, affords an initial clue.[18] The Quebec militia census of 1744 coincides rather closely with the parish census taken the same year: 1,245 militiamen and militia officers versus 1,299 parishioners of ages fifteen to sixty.[19] The small discrepancy might correspond to persons exempted from this service, but in any case it corroborates the accuracy of the numbers. The census of 1750 is at first sight more problematic; it appears to underestimate the male population considerably. Note, however, that the rural militias exhibit a plausible growth rate of 15 per cent in the six years between the two censuses. In contrast, the Quebec and Montreal militias appear to have diminished during the same period. It seems, then, that undercounting only affected the urban militias, unless these figures reflect a genuine absence: the absence, that is, of all those who were not included in militia companies for various reasons. With urban population growth adding to the apparent deficit, this would be the case for about one-third of city dwellers. Before deciding that the proportion is too high, remember that there was a transient population of labourers, merchants, sailors, voyageurs, and engagés for the fur trade who easily eluded enlistment. Others were exempt by virtue of working for the king. Between 1744 and 1748, the intendant had eight ships built at Quebec, five with a capacity of over 500 tons. These high-priority projects occupied up to 200 workers.[20] All the artisans and labourers employed in the stores, shops, and transports must be added to this figure, for they were numerous during wartime and indispensable to the administration. The fact that the deficit is higher in Quebec, where the majority of these jobs were situated, buttresses this hypothesis. After 1750, military supplies were contracted out to purveyors. Quantities skyrocketed, as did the numbers of butchers, bakers, coopers, wheelwrights, gunsmiths, carters, and others who were exempted from militia duty by virtue of their work. Next came those who enjoyed personal favours. "Monsieur de Céloron's detachment is keeping him busy," wrote Mrs Bégon, "what with the clamour of women wanting their husbands and children exempted."[21] How many masters similarly sought exemption for a servant or apprentice?[22] Favouritism in the choice of recruits was often denounced but always in regard to the rural militias, as if special favours were unknown in the cities. Yet they were quite common – in fact inevitable. The authorities turned a blind eye because they knew full well that an egalitarian, universal military regime could not work perfectly in a society founded on precedence and privilege.

The bourgeoisie (in the broadest sense of the term) wanted to take part in the colony's defence but not as militiamen under military command. For all those who did not have a commission in the militia, the alternative was to volunteer. The cities were incubators of volunteers. Merchants stepped forward to organize guard houses and signal fires toward the estuary and on the Gaspé Peninsula, supervise the construction of fire ships on Île-aux-Coudres, carry messages to the governor, and other delicate missions.[23] Shopkeepers – persons situated barely a notch above the ordinary citizen – served as volunteers in the detachments rather than alongside the other habitants in the ranks.[24] In this, the townspeople were simply following the example of the nobles, who would have imagined themselves to be violating some rule by serving in the militia. The royal instructions on this score, albeit quite clear and tirelessly repeated, were never obeyed.[25] Members of the colonial nobility living as rentiers or practising a non-military trade were numerous by the mid-eighteenth century. They were concentrated in the cities or nearby. Many made it a point of honour to serve the king, provided that they could choose the occasion and the commanding officer. As volunteers they retained this pride and could be sure of receiving the esteem due their name.[26]

Around 1756, events conspired to forbid anyone from staying behind, and the elite regrouped to form "the company of gentlemen of the government of Montreal." Reformed regular officers and older urban militia captains joined its ranks.[27] Under this banner they took part in the Fort George expedition of February 1757, the defence of Île-aux-Noix in 1759, and perhaps other operations where their presence was not reported.[28] Far from attracting sympathy, the initiative was considered pretentious and greeted with mockery. The French army officers jeered at these "ridiculous gentlemen," these "so-called volunteers" whose sole aim, they said, was to avoid incorporation into the militia under unknown officers who would subject them to military discipline.[29] If Courville's memorial reflects the prevailing opinion in the colony, it was no kinder to those who, "shielded by their worthless titles," refused to serve like everybody else.[30]

It goes without saying that seigneurs who lived on their land, like other rural notables, are not found on the lists of recruits, for they too found less humiliating ways to serve when necessary. But rural habitants as a whole had even less leeway than their urban counterparts. Every new arrival was listed on the roll and known to his militia captain, and jobs providing a momentary exemption from going to war were rarer. It all depended on the location. Around Montreal, west of the city in particular, youths easily found an out by hiring on for the fur trade. Since the turn of the century, merchant-outfitters and voyageurs had been using paid labour to take goods up to the Great Lakes region and bring back furs. In the 1730s, the number of annual engagements ranged from 300 to 500. The city supplied 100, the rest consisting largely of rural youths who made a few journeys before settling on a piece of land and starting a family. A minority – one-third in the case of La Prairie – took it up as a career.[31] Since equivalent salaries were not to be found in rural parishes, engagements for the fur trade were highly sought after, and employers had their pick of applicants. The very high concentration in a dozen parishes, and in a few families within those parishes, clearly illustrates the extent to which labour supply exceeded demand.[32]

Apart from an interruption in 1745–46 due to the naval blockade and the resulting goods shortage, the fur trade seems to have been little affected by the war, judging at any rate by the number of engagements, which surpassed pre-war levels between 1748 and 1758.[33] By this means, each year saw some 500 sturdy young men placed off-limits to the militia, a fact that scandalized the French army officers. But the government had no way to stem this tide without dismantling both the alliance and the colonial economy. The personal interests held in this trade by certain staff officers, such as Rigaud, the last governor of Montreal and the concession holder at the Baie-des-Puants (Green Bay) post, made them even more tolerant.[34] However, not all these men were shielded from recruitment. An analysis of destinations for 1755 shows that 64 per cent of them went to the Ottawa Valley or toward Michilimackinac, La Baie, and the Lake Superior and Lake Winnipeg posts, far from frontiers and dangers. The remaining third, who travelled on the St Lawrence, Lake Ontario, Lake Erie, and down to the southern posts, stood to be impressed on the fly when commandants needed reinforcements, as was often the case.[35]

The colony's western parishes also supplied canoeists and boatmen to carry munitions and provisions to Saint-Frédéric, Frontenac, and Niagara. The contractors to whom the intendant entrusted this part of the service chose the best men, and the staff could not oppose this drain on the militia without compromising the security of the king's property and the supply lines to remote outposts.[36] Elsewhere in the colony – that is, in the vast majority of parishes – only highly privileged habitants could escape enlistment.

For recruits determined and wealthy enough to stay home, substitution offered a way out. In July 1758, within the space of a few days, Louis-Eustache Cousineau and Joachim Berthelet (*dit* Savoyard), habitants of the parish of Saint-Laurent on Montreal Island, each hired a substitute for

> any campaign to which the king's generals may see fit to assign them, for the places and posts and for the time they see fit, be it for Carillon or the Great Lakes region. The said Pierre Papineau, volunteer ... promises to obey, for the said king's service as a militia soldier, in everything licit and honest which he may be ordered to do, and shall do his duty continuously and without leaving the said service until the end of the campaign upon which the militia soldiers of the De Vertus company, the company of the said Mr. Savoyard, are to embark, in exchange for all expenses, damages, and interest.

The substitutes were city residents who received 200 or 150 livres, respectively, most of this payable on their return.[37] The judicial archives offer up two other cases. One is that of a vagrant, later hung as a thief, who took part in the 1756 campaign as a replacement for a blacksmith from Contrecoeur, the other that of a soldier who deserted his company to replace a habitant from Mascouche at Carillon, collecting fifty livres and a canvas shirt for his trouble. He saw no reason why he should be punished, he said, since other soldiers had done the same thing.[38] This story tells us much about the disorder reigning in the colonial regulars; like the other such accounts, it shows that rural people had to look for replacements among marginal city folk or in the troops, since their fellow parishioners had all been recruited or were required to be available. Thus, this procedure could not have been very frequent.

While substitution was not unfair to the other militiamen of the parish, special favours forced them to do more than their share in order to meet mobilization quotas. It is known that the militia captain had total authority over the choice of recruits. Recruiting officers, having neither the time nor the means to select men themselves, merely conveyed the orders to him. And since there were no regulations covering the matter, his power was discretionary. Did he abuse it as much as his contemporaries claimed? Prominent merchant Joseph Fleury Deschambault and Governor Vaudreuil, the principal accusers, had an interest in making the situation seem worse than it was. The first proposed in 1750 to draw up a detailed roll of militiamen, allowing the general staff to recruit those men most precisely corresponding to its needs. The militia captain's only role would be to gather the designated men, instead of sending the mediocre ones and sparing his relatives, as had been seen in the previous war. If he obtained a royal commission as colonel-general of the militias, he promised to draw up this roll and keep it up to date.[39] Having had no reply to his petition from the minister, Fleury took up the matter again in 1755, this time strongly supported by Vaudreuil, who denounced the anarchy and torpor affecting the mobilization; he ascribed this state of affairs to the "country captains, nearly all of them illiterate, who obey no orders and even, as is very common, neglect good subjects out of private considerations." Those who had occupied land were unable to clear it and were exhausted, he added, because they had always done duty while their well-heeled neighbours were spared.[40] The new governor had two good reasons to berate the militia captains in this way: to give more weight to Fleury's arguments and to blame his predecessor Duquesne for having tolerated these abuses. He himself would do nothing to correct them, however, and never brought the matter up again.

The army officers, too, criticized this selection method. "As long as the method of militia recruitment is not changed, no service will ever be derived from them," wrote Montcalm,[41] although he did not specifically mention the militia captains. The adjutant Jean-Guillaume Plantavit de Lapause (also spelled La Pause) was more explicit. "The manner in which they are enlisted to go to war is utterly haphazard; they take whomever they want, and it is always the same ones who pay, and the poorest; neither friends nor money can dispense them from marching." Like Vaudreuil, he had harsh words for the militia captains, "most of them as blinkered as they are biased in favour of themselves or their relatives, or those from whom they receive benefits," and he proposed a parish census method that would limit their role to that of obeying orders.[42]

Historians have no way of verifying these accusations. Favouritism certainly existed, but was it that widespread, and even if so, how should it be interpreted? As a reflection of the private interests of a petty local potentate or as the result of a certain conception of the good of the parish, shared by the community or the *senior pars* who represented it? This second hypothesis is more plausible.[43] The

habitants did not think they were interchangeable or that the best
lands and harvests could be entrusted to anyone in the absence of
their owners. They believed that subsistence and good order dictated that the best farmers, the heads of households, remain behind.
The age of the recruits, our only clue, partly reflects these choices. I
succeeded in identifying forty-three individuals on the lists of militiamen bound for the Ohio country in 1755. Nine-tenths of them
were under thirty, and the average age was twenty-three. The oldest,
aged thirty-seven, was also the only married man in this sample.[44]
An analysis of burials of militiamen at the forts of Saint-Frédéric,
La Présentation, Presqu'île, and Duquesne between 1753 and 1757
yields similar results. Of eighty-one known cases, the mean age is
twenty-three, the median and the mode twenty-two. To summarize
this data differently, let us say that only 10 per cent of the dead were
under twenty while 5 per cent were over thirty. It is no surprise, then,
to find only three married men and one widower in the group.[45] This
data contradicts two historiographic clichés: boys trained for military life as soon as they hit adolescence, colonists who abandoned
family and property to a soldier so that they could go to war. The
age of the recruits reflects the vision of human experience typical
of these peasant communities. They held their sons back until age
twenty and strove to protect fathers for as long as possible. I realize
that these observations are predicated on small numbers, but even
so they are representative, for men in their twenties were not more
vulnerable to disease, the main cause of death, than younger or older
men. The war would eventually overcome the militia captains' hesitations, and all habitants would be mobilized, irrespective of their
responsibilities. Among the fifty-eight people interred in the Hôpital
Général de Québec cemetery between 13 September 1759 and the
autumn of 1760, at least a third, and perhaps as many as half, were
older married men.[46]

3. MARCHING WITH THE REGULARS

Everywhere – on the move, at the forts, or on expeditions – the
militias were commanded by officers of the colonial regulars. That
which had formerly been an occasional duty brought about by
sporadic military campaigns became, as of 1745 – when hundreds
of habitants began to be recruited on a regular basis – an ongoing
responsibility, additional to the officers' responsibilities vis-à-vis the

men of their own companies. How did they acquit themselves of this task? What were the relationships between the militiamen and the officers who led them to war? Information on these questions is sparse and scattered, but a glance at the officer corps and its relations with the colonial regulars, a well-documented subject, suggests some answers.

It should be recalled that the colony had a dozen staff officers – local governors, king's lieutenants, town majors, and assistant town majors – distributed among the three cities, as well as 112 officers attached to the twenty-eight companies, consisting of one captain, one lieutenant, and two ensigns each. The reforms of 1750 and 1756 increased the number of men per company from thirty to fifty and then to sixty-five but did not affect the number of officers, unlike what had happened at the end of the seventeenth century.[47] This time the colony had no say in the matter, and the minister's intention, no doubt for the sake of economy, was to limit troop increases as much as possible.[48] Renewal came in the form of fifty-six cadets, two per company, who, although soldiers in rank, assumed many of the responsibilities normally reserved to their superiors while awaiting their first commission. The wait promised to be long, since officers did not start dying in war before mid-century and did not readily agree to take retirement. A look at the service records shows that access to promotion was blocked, so much so that a number of men in their forties had yet to rise above the rank of second ensign.[49] Talent and high birth could accelerate advancement, but no guarantees were to be had. Though the governor managed to sideline the infirm and the old before the War of the Austrian Succession, the image of an aging corps transpires from a list drawn up in 1748. The average age of these twenty-eight captains was fifty-one, and while some of them, such as Marion or Contrecoeur, were still hale and hearty, many more were getting long in the tooth – the seventy-one-year-old Charles Legardeur de Croisille, for instance, a veteran of Deerfield and Haverhill, or more mediocre subjects who, having risen through the ranks at a snail's pace, were no longer of much use.[50] The situation improved somewhat during the Seven Years' War but not so much as to obscure the torpid advancement characteristic of the preceding decades. It is still quite visible in the "General table of the various grades of officers of the regular troops serving in Canada, according to their rank and seniority" that was drawn up after capitulation.[51] Age was a matter of considerable friction between these men and the arriving French army officers, who averaged thirty-four years old for the captains and only twenty-six for the lieutenants.[52] There was talk of how "unpleasant" the colony's lieutenants and ensigns found it to be ordered around by much younger captains.[53]

"On 6 September, I attended the commissary's review, where I saw officers without soldiers and soldiers without officers, as usual," wrote Josué Dubois Berthelot de Beaucours, the governor of Montreal. His irony could not hide his exasperation. In the 1740s, he repeatedly denounced the negligence and complacency of the regular officers who did not look after the details of their company, who had "not even a trace of discipline and are unable to instill it in their soldiers."[54] The problem was not new: Intendant Champigny had noted as early as 1703 that numerous soldiers did not know their officers' names.[55] These observations were reiterated by Seven Years' War army officers such as Jean-Baptiste d'Aleyrac, Jean-Guillaume Plantavit de Lapause, and Pierre Pouchot, who noted that the colonial officers did not know the men of their company, left the details of the service to the cadets, and were incapable of giving a proper order. Consequently, they wrote, the soldiers were untidy and undisciplined.[56] The governors-general, Beauharnois in particular, were always tolerant, preferring to ascribe the problems of the troops to the poor quality of the recruits rather than to a lack of training and command.[57] In the officers' defence, it may be said that the colonial context was not conducive to company cohesion, that soldiers were dispersed to all sorts of garrisons and the officers assigned to remote outposts. The excuse is only partly valid, however, since only a minority of officers were permanently assigned to the Great Lakes region and the autumn found all troops returning to the cities for a six-month period – more than sufficient to get to know them.[58] Absenteeism had more to do with the slack attitude that had come to inhabit the whole corps during peace time, the custom of giving sergeants full responsibility for soldiers, the advanced age of many captains, the lack of consequences for rural rentiers who failed to report for duty, and the laxity and incompetence of many higher-ranking officers.[59] During his short mandate, Governor Duquesne used strong-arm tactics to change these habits. Sternly reminded of their duties, the officers would not forgive him and welcomed his successor Vaudreuil as a saviour.[60] The augmentation of the companies and the rapid incorporation of hundreds of recruits inevitably exacerbated the problems of discipline, disorder, and filthiness of the colonial regulars during the Seven Years' War.

The seventeenth-century officer corps had comprised a number of subjects who had served in Europe, in the king's regiments or on his ships, before distinguishing themselves in colonial wars and Indigenous tactics.[61] The same versatility is not to be found fifty years later, at least not in the higher ranks – a matter of concern to Intendant Hocquart at the outbreak of the War of the Austrian Succession: "There are [no officers] whose vision is not extremely narrow and whose knowledge is not limited in regard to military movements, other than those practised in the war with the Natives."[62] The colony was entering into conflicts that demanded more rigorous training, and this is why La Galissonière suggested in 1748 that officers be sent from France with the new companies, despite a plethora of local candidates.[63] One of them, Jean-Daniel Dumas, a young captain with several campaigns to his credit, arrived in 1750 and was soon recognized as one of the colony's best officers.[64]

Yet the abilities that had made the reputation of the Canadian officer – going on raids with the Indigenous people, marching in the forest, living by one's wits and attacking by surprise – should not be underestimated. Whatever the views of French observers, who were always looking for degeneracy and finding it, the colony probably had as many good officer-partisans as in the previous wars.[65] These officers had always been in the minority, and if they seemed less numerous in 1755–60, it is surely because the needs were greater. The word "officers" as used here encompasses cadets, who probably accounted for more partisans than all the other ranks combined. Custom had it that post commandants took their sons with them to learn the languages and customs of the allies. This early initiation sometimes preceded, and probably hastened, their obtaining a cadet position around age fifteen; thereafter, the boys served for long periods alongside their fathers.[66] "I still have two children who can replace me," wrote Claude-Pierre Pécaudy de Contrecoeur, the commandant of Fort Duquesne. The older one had left, he continued, but the younger one, still a cadet, had "always followed me in this engagement."[67] One striking example of family tradition was that of the six Coulon brothers who did their apprenticeship at the Miamis' Fort Saint-Joseph (near present-day Niles, MI), where their father was the commandant and where the older sons continued to train the younger ones after his death in 1733.[68] Another was that of

the Céloron brothers who followed their father on his various assign-
ments, such as at Fort Saint-Frédéric in 1747. "Ten days ago, my sons
went off to attack the English. The bad weather worsened the rigours
of the voyage, and it is causing me terrible worry. I do not think, if the
good Lord should return them to me, that I shall ever expose them to
so much hardship again."[69] They did return and went off again several
times, during this war and the next one. The necessity of increasing the
number of bold officers led the governors to open up the corps to the
sons of merchants settled in the Great Lakes region and living on the
margins of the military elite; men such as Paul Marin de la Malgue,
Charles-Michel Mouet de Langlade, Philippe-Thomas and Daniel-
Marie Chabert de Joncaire, and Michel Maray de la Chauvignerie
served as interpreters, diplomats, and soldiers.[70]

It is incorrect, explained the governor of Montreal in speaking of
the cadets, to call these young men "commanders of the Natives";
the latter do not let themselves be commanded, making war as they
please.[71] The whole art consisted in following the Native warriors
and subtly influencing them, an experience that did not prepare one
for leading inexperienced soldiers without much motivation and
incapable of functioning as a corps by themselves. In sum, the colonial regular officers formed neither a better nor a worse military
group than many others but one that ultimately could not live up
to its inflated reputation. There were many fatigued or unfit officers, especially in the higher ranks, many elite subjects accustomed
to petty warfare among the youth, and relatively few men capable
of commanding and transforming the French recruits and colonial
habitants into an orderly, effective corps. Beyond all these weaknesses, there simply were not enough officers to lead both the regulars and the militias.

4. STATUS OF MILITIA OFFICERS

a) Volunteers without a company

As we have seen, prior to the invasion of the colony, militia companies did not serve as a corps with their own officers.[72] Men went
to war individually, not initially as part of a company and not in
large numbers. Only fifty-one are identified, most by name, in the
detailed sources for the years 1744–48; this number must be fairly
accurate, since the administration made a point of mentioning their

presence. It may be recalled that the colony then had more than 700 militia officers.[73] The few available clues for the subsequent period suggest that militia participation remained low. Militiamen do not appear on the lists of recruits for the Great Lakes region drawn up in 1754 and 1756 and are rarely mentioned in campaign accounts.[74] Rural parish officers did not go to war, wrote a captain in the French battalions, but stayed in the village, where they fulfilled the duties of mayor and syndic.[75] With a few exceptions, the observation is accurate. Already demanding, the job of the militia captains and other officers had become more burdensome in wartime, with incessant recruitment, numerous wheat requisitions, and billeting of soldiers added to their list of responsibilities. Nothing prevented them from taking part in military expeditions if they so chose, but those who preferred to stay home – the immense majority – had a good excuse.[76] Their duties made them *de facto* exempt, and any who did go to war can be considered volunteers. Most of those who appear in my sources came from the Montreal region, and townsmen are better represented. These sons of merchants, notaries, or traders served as ensigns or lieutenants in the urban companies, and some fifteen of them regularly took part in operations during the War of the Austrian Succession.[77]

Unlike the volunteers of former times, who all came from the same social background, these militia officers knew that their zeal would not earn them a commission in the colonial regulars.[78] Perhaps they were aiming for other rewards – a supply contract, a job in the administration ... One thing is certain: The attractions of war must have overcome any reservations they may have had about the ambiguous and at times humiliating status reserved to them in the armed camps. Militia officers had no official rank there. Like mere militiaman, they fell under the authority of lower-ranking officers or even sergeants, corporals, or cadets. In fact, their duties in the detachments were left to the commanding officer's discretion. For the February 1757 expedition against Fort William Henry, Rigaud placed two regular officers, a cadet, and a militia officer at the head of mixed companies of fifty men (thirty-five militiamen and fifteen soldiers). Similar arrangements, no doubt worked out in advance, may be supposed for the eighteen militia officers he took with him to Fort Massachusetts in August 1746 or the fourteen who accompanied Ramezay to Acadia the same year.[79] With the duties of command came small perks, such as better-quality biscuit than what the soldiers got, a bearskin blanket, or wine like the regular officers and cadets. And like these last, men who embarked on the long Acadian campaign enjoyed relatively sizable gratifications in return. Custom had it that a militia officer, especially one of bourgeois background, be treated with consideration and incorporated into the chain of command at the commanding officer's pleasure. He had only to choose his campaigns and leaders and to show some aptitude. Thomas-Ignace Trottier Dufy Desauniers, a Montreal merchant and militia officer related to Vaudreuil, who was very active from 1746 to 1760, offers a good example of this sort of self-flattering military experience.[80] That of rural militia officers who led their own companies in the army during the invasion was entirely different. Holding no official status, easily confounded with their men, they stood to be shunted aside by the first soldier to appear or find themselves assigned to a picket if they did not wear their identifying medal or gorget.[81] Men who enjoyed a position of authority in their parishes were bound to be put off by this loss of status.

In other colonies, militia officers had demanded delineation of their status and rank with respect to the regular officers.[82] But their Canadian counterparts had asked for nothing since the arrival of the *compagnies franches* in the 1680s; they seem to have been satisfied with an unofficial place in the contingents and some small personal favours. It is no surprise, then, that the initiative to regulate and raise their status came from the ministry and not the interested parties. This initiative arose during the War of the Austrian Succession and answered to bureaucratic dictates. Why not give the Canadian militias regulations similar to those of the "islands," where the captains were entitled to royal warrants and ranked alongside regular officers?[83] The reform was to take place in two stages: immediately grant royal commissions to the most deserving subjects, and then, after having prepared the groundwork for acceptance and determined the necessary adjustments, publish ordinances to resolve the issue of precedence, among other matters. Militia officers would rank above regular sergeants, while captains honoured with a royal warrant would hold the rank of lieutenant.[84] Blocked by three successive colonial governors until 1760, the reform was never implemented. La Jonquière, who was supposed to designate several militia officers deserving, "by virtue of their status and the services they will have rendered, of being awarded a commission by His Majesty," proposed no one and avoided addressing the subject in his dispatches.

Duquesne, who received the same instructions, turned an equally deaf ear. Far from abandoning their plan, the ministers – Machault, followed by Moras – became more insistent, and Vaudreuil found himself forced to break the silence. Without openly opposing the reform, he managed to forestall it through continual procrastination until too late, thus depriving the militia captains of the honours that the court had intended to bestow.[85]

What explains this resistance? In a petition of 1755 to the minister, Joseph Fleury Deschambault, receiver for the Compagnie des Indes in Montreal and a relative of Vaudreuil, offers some hints.

> I make bold to assure you, Monseigneur, that the militia captains of the côtes of this colony are not at all deserving of the dignities which the king customarily grants to those of Saint-Domingue, since nearly all these officers have nothing above the militiamen in either fortune or talent; and when they have participated in war parties, they have always had a regular officer as commander. Experience teaches only too clearly that in three-quarters of the parishes, the captains are not even able to draw up the rolls of their companies, clearly demonstrating the utility of the desired position.[86]

Fleury was applying for a job as administrator of the militias and was not an objective observer.[87] Nevertheless, his dismissive remarks afford some insight into two realities. First, the rural militia captains had not been chosen on the basis of their military aptitudes but for whatever ascendancy they possessed in the parishes. Since the turn of the century, their role as agents of the administration had taken precedence over the initial function of the institution. Meanwhile, the court, which had never been informed of this deviation, remained under the impression that the militia captains were commanding officers of a sort. Neither had it been told that most of them were mere peasants, not seigneurs or other persons of higher social condition. This second fact, tardily revealed, gave rise to repeated recommendations to "choose subjects with care," for "their status" as much as their services.[88]

Fleury's remarks did not concern the urban militia captains. These well-born citizens might, like the planters of Saint-Domingue, have a better claim to royal dignities, provided that they took part in campaigns. But the men who held these now essentially honorary positions were getting on in years, and few of them were fit for war. In the last decade, efforts were made to rejuvenate the corps and choose candidates attracted by warfare. Hindered by the seniority rule, these efforts mainly concerned lower-ranking officers; few Quebec and Montreal militia captains would ultimately be eligible for royal commissions by virtue of their military service.[89] But there were some notable exceptions in the cities and also in the country, and there would surely have been more if it were known that the promise of royal commissions, or even pensions and the cross of the order of Saint-Louis, were attached to the offer. This is precisely what the colonial general staff, on behalf of all the regular officers, wanted to avoid. The proposed changes were minor, all things considered, yet the creation of a parallel military formation with leaders who would automatically be inserted into the chain of command was perceived as an attack on the established order. The officers had no use for a reform that might, in the long run, cut into their share of royal rewards and, in the immediate, subject their sons, who were ensigns and cadets, to the authority of a nobody. Thanks to delayed decision-making caused by frequent shuffles at the ministry and the urgency of the military problems, the officers had their way.[90]

5. EPHEMERAL REVIEWS AND FORMATIONS

Once the recruiting officer had passed through the parish, the recruits had to be "ready to depart on command, arms and baggage in hand." When the order came, they went to the gathering place on their own steam. Habitants in the governments of Quebec and Trois-Rivières first converged on the city, where they were met and taken upriver to Montreal under military escort. The general review took place at the point of embarkation. Those bound for posts in the Great Lakes region gathered at Lachine on a piece of land where as many as a thousand men might be encamped.[91] Those routed toward Lake Champlain assembled at Chambly, Saint Thérèse, or Saint-Jean-sur-Richelieu, depending on the year. Attendance was taken using the list of recruits provided, at least in principle, by the militia captain; absentees were reported and punished. Next came the arms inspection and a cursory appraisal of physical fitness. The outcome of this appraisal depended on the assignment. Great care was taken in picking and choosing the 162 militiamen sent to attack Fort Bull in February 1756, and officers commanding expeditions of this kind were well advised to participate in the review.[92] But most of the time, the contingent was sent for garrison duty or to join the army, and in that case, number mattered more than quality. Just about everyone who showed up was taken, and the officers who received them complained of being weighed down with useless men.

The review was an important moment for boys leaving their parishes for the first time. It always took on a solemn cast, at times heightened by the presence of the governor-general. It was an opportunity to instruct the recruits by reading them news of the war – the one raging in Europe, which was also their war – and to present it in such a way as to appeal to their good will. After the speech and several unison cries of "Long live the King!" or "Long live the King and our general!" this good will was momentarily acquired. The opportunity was also used to inspect the regulars taking part in the same campaign; however, Amerindians were not present. In August 1746, to add luster to his expedition against New England, Rigaud offered the entire corps, including 161 warriors from the Great Lakes region and perhaps a few domiciliés, a banquet at Chambly, with many glasses of wine and rum raised.[93] Such treatment was not customary. The Indigenous allies had their own departure ceremonies in their villages and were generally prepared in advance; they waited until the detachment neared the enemy frontier before joining it. Aquavitae may have been part of the assembly ritual, but this cannot be stated with assurance based on the sources.[94]

At the end of the review, the militiamen received their equipment and several days' worth of provisions. When departing on a specific mission, they were grouped into "brigades," or large, variously commanded units. The brigades that went to build forts in the Ohio country in 1753 and 1754, for example, consisted of eighty to 100 men, including a minority of regulars, a sergeant or corporal, and rarely more than one commanding officer.[95] Little more was generally done than to put the militiamen in boats and send them off to the posts, where they arrived pell-mell, often hundreds at a time. In one case, 1,200 men disembarked at Fort Frontenac before the siege of Oswego "without commanders or order, without lists of names, without arms, and nearly naked," related the army adjutant.[96] It was up to the officers who received them to organize this crowd into units suited to the army's needs and find leaders to command them. This procedure posed no great difficulty at posts with a small garrison, where recruits could quickly get to know each other, but in camps with large numbers, the system led to disorder for the army and demoralization for the militia.

Division of the soldiers into permanent companies of thirty to forty men led by three commissioned officers and several noncoms was a fundamental military principle long taken for granted in the European armies and observed in the troops of the British colonies.[97] The technique ensured that there would be solid command and discipline at all times, and it facilitated manoeuvres when the time came for battle. It offered individuals torn out of their social setting a new and stable environment in which camaraderie could flourish and subordination could be reinforced; it created a group dynamic that encouraged recruits to imitate exemplars of courage and avoid looking like a coward to their comrades and commanders. Military service was tolerable, writes André Corvisier about the eighteenth-century French army, when it preserved ties among men or allowed them to be rebuilt. Uncertainty and anonymity made it unbearable.[98]

The colonial general staff flouted this principle. It is true that Canadian recruits operated within a smaller area and for relatively short periods, but neither the familiarity of their surroundings nor the brevity of their tours of duty should be exaggerated. A boy from Pointe-à-la-Caille transplanted to Carillon in the midst of a 6,000-man army, or to Fort Duquesne among hundreds of warriors from various allied nations, was bound to feel disoriented. The length of postings varied from one place or year to another – rarely less than a year for posts in the Great Lakes region or Acadia, three to six months in the camps on Lake George (Saint-Sacrement) – but was never fixed in advance, and nothing guaranteed a militiaman sent home for the harvest that he would not be recruited again in the fall. Uncertainty was the rule, and, for that matter, so was anonymity. The fact that recruitment was spread out over a large number of parishes, as described above, made the presence of relatives, friends, and neighbours in a given contingent less likely. Incessant troop movements, accentuated during the 1750s, and the ephemeral nature of the brigades interfered with any new bonds of camaraderie that the recruit might have been able to form. Finally, the set of procedures used to levy a militia and order it off to war were incompatible with the establishment of personal relations between militiamen and their commanders. For a recruit from Mascouche or Lotbinière, officers came and went in a rapid succession of faces and names: the subaltern who recruited him in the parish; the officer who conducted the review; another who escorted him to the army; the sergeant who oversaw work around the fort; the captain responsible for the advance camp to which he had just been assigned without notice; the staff officers who made occasional appearances. Which of them called him by his name even once? Without question, this shifting, shapeless context could easily lead to discouragement and desertion.

As regards the conduct of the war, these practices underlay several defeats that a better organized army would have avoided. Lacking the stable armature of the company, militiamen were extremely vulnerable to emotions, unpredictable fears.[99] Finally, without sufficient training, militiamen did not learn the elementary rules of hygiene and nutrition, leading to wasted provisions and costly diseases that weakened the army. And how could it have been otherwise when officers who barely sufficed to command the regulars were also required to take charge of thousands of inexperienced country boys?

6. WAGES, EQUIPMENT, AND PROVISIONS

Militiamen who went to war served without pay; in contrast, those employed in transporting munitions or building defensive structures outside their parish were generally remunerated for their work. This dual system originated in 1744 when the general staff found itself forced, for lack of sufficient troops, to entrust the bulk of military and paramilitary tasks to the colonists. It will be recalled that the colony had previously had no strongholds to maintain outside of inhabited areas, where everything was done by corvées, war parties were largely composed of volunteers, and militias were only levied from time to time, always for a specific campaign, such as an expedition into Iroquois territory, the defence of Quebec, or that of the Richelieu River forts. The mass recruitment during the War of the Austrian Succession created a new situation that engendered new administrative problems, among other kinds. Could so much be asked of the habitants without offering anything in return? The governor and the intendant thought not, especially since they were not unaware that regulars had always received supplemental pay for their work.[100] Already convinced that the minister would not pay a cent for the militia, they arranged to bury the cost of its services amid the larger bulk of military spending, under the usual headings: forts, man-days, raids and voyages, or "contingencies." It would have taken a sharp eye to tease the militiamen's wages out of the accounts, and of course the subject was never mentioned in correspondence with Versailles. These payments did, however, leave traces in the local correspondence, a few surviving lists of workers, and the hundreds of payment certificates that circulated at the posts before being gathered in the treasurer's office.[101]

Within this motley collection of documents, the singular cases can be distinguished from those that appear to have been common practice. In 1749, for example, two men on duty at Detroit each received 100 livres "to do garrison duty with the Weas in their capacity as militiamen ... in lieu of pay and equipment."[102] The recent unrest in the region and the acute shortage of soldiers explain this momentary generosity. For the same reasons, sums varying from sixty to 100 livres were offered to the 206 militiamen who escorted canoes bearing goods to Detroit and Michilimackinac in 1748. Though less than the wages paid by merchants for these voyages, the remuneration was not negligible.[103] Custom dictated, however, that habitants not be paid a lump sum but rather wages for days of labour and raids that they performed during their stay at posts and camps. The transportation of provisions, munitions, and trade goods to remote outposts from Montreal was normally the role of private enterprise: voyageurs for the goods, the king's navigators for the military portion, with selected and relatively well-paid engagés in their employ.[104] The militia played only a complementary role in this regard, except during the Ohio campaigns of 1753 and 1754. In that instance, the expedited construction of four forts south of Lake Erie, three of them inland and hard to access by water, gave rise to a far-reaching transport operation requiring some 2,000 militiamen, guided by experienced voyageurs from La Prairie. The naval commissary mentions payments of fifteen and eighteen livres per voyage out of Lachine, and an officer explained that men had to be paid by the piece to get them to do the arduous work of portaging the bundles.[105] It is not known whether the whole corps received similar consideration. At that point, the garrisons at the new forts became the priority. The transportation of munitions and provisions in dugout canoes on tributaries of the Ohio River occupied a large proportion of the forces stationed in the region during the Seven Years' War. No doubt the custom continued of paying the men (whether militiamen or soldiers) for this kind of expedition, as attested by the 1749–50 accounts of Fort Miami (at the site of present-day Fort Wayne, IN).[106]

Construction work represented a much larger expense item. The first references date from 1745 with the opening of a road between La Prairie and Saint-Jean, as well as the fire ship and signalling services on Île-aux-Coudres and farther down the St Lawrence.[107] The rule adopted at the outset of the war seems clear: Local projects, such as repairing the old forts of the government of Montreal or surveillance and signal fires, were carried out by corvées, while projects taking place outside the parish were remunerated. For felling, clearing, digging, and other tasks related to fort construction and maintenance, militiamen generally received a daily wage of twenty sols or one livre, sergeant overseers thirty sols.[108] The scale is the same as that for soldiers working alongside them but lower than the going rate in the colony, where labourers ordinarily earned twenty-five to thirty sols per day. This observation is based on 615 certificates issued at the Fort Duquesne garrison for work done in 1754 and 1755, another certificate dated 1758, and the account of an officer who commanded workers at the Beauport camp before the siege of Quebec.[109] A regulation by Vaudreuil concerning work done by militiamen incorporated into the French battalions confirms, if more confirmation were necessary, that remuneration was common practice.[110]

Yet the unpaid status of militia service was never questioned. No wages were paid the 600 men who spent a year in Acadia in 1746–47, nor those who attacked Saratoga and other British settlements in those same years. They were fitted out for battle – which was not true of those who did garrison duty – and nothing more. Take, for example, a militiaman sent to Carillon in 1757. He received no wages for the six months spent standing guard at an advance camp and going on scouting missions or for his participation in the siege of Fort George in August. Only the firewood he was ordered to cut in the fall, before being sent home to his parish, earned him a few livres. This was an anomaly that eluded no one, but it could not be remedied without a sweeping reform of the militia. To introduce wages, it would have been necessary to fix the duration of duty and, above all, to implement a bona fide general staff for the militia, with responsibility for all aspects of the service. For lack of funds and time, improvisation was the only possibility, and contradictions built up as the war intensified.

The colonists' obligation to arm themselves at their own expense remained the rule, although it was increasingly difficult to enforce and soon overrun by exceptions. At the start of the War of the

Austrian Succession, one-third of militiamen did not own a musket, and perhaps as many again had poor-quality ones. With a certificate of poverty issued by the militia captain, those who could not, as ordered, afford to buy a gun from a merchant could borrow one from the king's stores or have their own gun refurbished for free in his shops.[111] The colony used two types of weapons in this era: a military musket (*grenadier*) equipped with a bayonet for the regulars[112] and a hunting musket specially manufactured at Tulle or Saint-Étienne, which the habitants, generally good hunters, appreciated for its lightness and sturdiness, even though it was smaller-calibre and less fit for war.[113] It cost about twenty livres, the price of a cow or two weeks of a harvester's wages. There was no advantage for militiamen to buy a military musket, which undoubtedly cost more and would be of little use back at home. It is probable, moreover, given the chronic shortage of military weapons, that the intendant reserved these for the regulars, although this did not rule out loans for important expeditions. Thus, for example, the 600 militiamen sent to Acadia in 1746 received *grenadiers* marked "property of the king," to be returned at the end of the engagement.[114] The king's stores also had large stocks of hunting muskets for Indigenous partisans and for militiamen who showed up for review empty-handed or with a broken gun. Some officers claimed they did this on purpose.[115] There was some exemplary punishment, but the administration soon had to give up and offer all recruits the measures initially put in place for the poorest of them. It had to lend them a gun, to be returned after the campaign or paid for if the person had lost it or wanted to keep it. Could the storekeeper keep accurate records of all these transactions? Surely not, and so the system became an invitation to fraud and waste. And it was costly, perhaps as much as if every militiaman had been given a good musket for which he then became responsible, as was done with the regulars. Indifferently maintained hunting muskets remained common in the militia until 1760; men learned to pare bullets down to fit the narrower barrel and to attach a knife to the end in lieu of a bayonet.[116]

The intendancy also handed out basic equipment to war-bound militiamen, consisting of munitions (firesteel, screw-wire, six gunflints, two pounds of shot and one of powder), tools (a tumpline, two knives, an awl for punching holes in leather, and a small hatchet known as a *casse-tête*), and clothing (a cotton shirt, a pair of puttees, a deerskin to make shoes).[117] If the campaign took place in the

cold months, these items were augmented by a woollen cap, a pair
of mittens, a greatcoat, and a blanket or bearskin for bedding, if the
nature of the expedition permitted.[118]

Recall that in the seventeenth century, the administration had
provided nothing but munitions and provisions to militiamen and
volunteers on their way to war. Clothing only began to appear regularly among the items supplied as of 1745. The intendant had these
items ready to hand, however, since they were part of the goods
bound for the Indigenous clientele at the king's posts. Shirts, greatcoats, and puttees were mass-produced by Montreal seamstresses
for the fur trade. Some articles of clothing are missing from this
assortment, such as breeches, which the Indigenous people always
rejected, finding that they hindered walking. The militiamen had to
wear out their own breeches or replace them with a breech-cloth – a
piece of cloth inserted between the thighs and held on with a belt,
after the fashion of canoeists who were constantly walking in water
and had adopted this convenient attire. During the Seven Years' War,
breech-cloths became standard equipment.[119] Some wore them even
in winter, observed a British prisoner returning from the expedition
against Fort Bull in March 1756.[120] Besides the greatcoat reserved
for winter parties, the king's stores did not offer vests or other pro-
tective clothing suited to rain and cold. At home, when not in their
Sunday best, Canadian peasants wore homemade cow's-leather
shoes. Relying on this know-how, the administration provided no
shoes when they went to war, but skins and an awl for them to
make their own as needed and make them for the regulars too. What
with delayed cargoes, losses at sea, and a leather shortage in the
colony, the administration increasingly relied on these rustic shoes
for the regulars.[121] Deerskin was abundant and cheap but fragile –
only good for walking on snow. And since campaigns generally took
place between spring and fall, the men had to bring their own shoes
or walk barefoot like the Indigenous people. Summing up, the militiamen's attire, a motley assortment of their own rags and a stock
of goods designed for other uses, owed more to the whims of the
administration than to cultural choices.[122]

Neither were they given any kind of sleeping shelter. They slept
on the ground, under the stars, in a crude hut made out of branches
or under an inverted canoe: whatever the circumstances required.
Alarmed by the large number of the sick, the intendant asked the
minister for 500 tents for the militiamen. "It is true," he explained,

"that they have never made use of them for ordinary manoeuvres, but when they are camping for seven consecutive months, as they have this year [1756], it is good to be out of the rain."[123] Nothing came of this request. In winter, a bearskin might be provided as a mat, with one skin for every one, two, or three men as circumstances allowed. The militiamen who went to Acadia had them, as did those who departed for Rivière-aux-Boeufs (now known as French Creek, a tributary of the Allegheny River) in January 1754. In the detachment commanded by Rigaud in February 1757, skins were provided to the regulars but not the 600 militiamen.[124] Bearskins were heavy, and a sled was needed to carry them. When the men had to haul everything on their backs, as was most frequent, all they carried was a wool blanket.

The foregoing description is derived from a small number of references relating largely to expeditions into enemy territory. Did militiamen who served in the colony also receive equipment? Apparently not, or at least, not systematically. It is known that men who did garrison duty at the posts were not equipped at departure.[125] All they received were provisions for the voyage, while they had to buy from the fort store, upon arriving at their destination, all the clothing and other items they would need during their sojourn. It may nonetheless be supposed that the commandant of a frontier post such as Fort Duquesne provided the essentials to men whom he sent out in parties or to work in exposed locations. The case of militiamen amalgamated with the army is less clear. Evidently, the 1,200 men who arrived "without arms and nearly naked" at Fort Frontenac in August 1756, before the siege of Oswego, received nothing, and it seems clear that the thousands of others who camped at Carillon during those years were no better equipped.[126] This was first and foremost an administrative problem, an incapacity to keep militia rolls up to date, and even more so to keep an accurate count of advances extended to each man so as to prevent recruits, who came and went between camps and their homes, from abusing their privileges.[127] For lack of resources, the intendancy used an arbitrary procedure that engendered waste on the one hand, hardships and insalubrious conditions for a large number on the other, and all on the pretense of saving money.

All militiamen who served outside their parish, regardless of assignment, received the soldier's daily ration. At the garrisons, this ordinarily consisted of a pound and a half of bread, biscuits, or the equivalent in flour; four ounces of dried legumes, and four ounces of salt lard or eight of beef. The intendancy made slight modifications as resources dictated. Garrisons at the remote posts often had ways of varying the menu, as we shall see. Neither tobacco nor aqua-vitae were dispensed automatically, although commandants had supplies that they doled out at opportune moments.

Rations were more substantial on the march: two pounds of biscuit and one of lard, to which a few ounces of peas were sometimes added.[128] The general staff was still grappling with the problems of transportation and conservation of provisions discussed earlier in connection with the large turn-of-the-century military enterprises.[129] Whether the party consisted of ten, twenty, or 800 men, it was always ideally the same method: each one carried his provisions on his back. Accounting for the weight of the musket and the rest of the equipment, a partisan could carry ten to fifteen days' worth of provisions, but beyond that, additional means of transport had to be provided for, slowing the pace of the detachment.[130] The men refused to take on excessive loads. An officer observed that militiamen travelling from Lake Erie to the Ohio River in dugout canoes carried the provisions necessary for the voyage but that those travelling on foot took as little as possible, fasted on the final days, and arrived famished at Fort Duquesne.[131] Such behaviour might compromise an expedition into enemy territory. It is true that the colony still had a minority of officers, cadets, and other partisans capable of accompanying Amerindians, travelling with a minimum of baggage, relying on game, fish, and berries, and moving on an empty stomach when nothing availed. Thus, the lack of provisions did not stop the party launched against the Palatine village of German Flatts in the autumn of 1757 (composed of 200 domiciliés, forty-four Canadians and volunteer soldiers, and twenty officers and cadets) from reaching its target.[132] Problems arose, however, with larger contingents of European origin and/or inexperienced participants. On 11 March 1756, a party of about 400 men, two-thirds of them militiamen and regulars, left the village of La Présentation with two weeks of provisions to attack Fort Bull. Two days before reaching their target, they were out of food: The provisions had been eaten too quickly, or the men had jettisoned them earlier in the voyage. A providential encounter with a convoy of enemy provisions saved the day, but the return was equally difficult because, "according to a foolish Canadian custom, they had eaten in four days the provisions given them for eight."[133]

On expeditions, colonial regular officers received a better-quality biscuit made with patent flour and a more varied diet including rice, beef tongue, pepper, chocolate, and wine. Cadets, militia officers, and volunteers shared this higher-grade menu but received the same equipment as the rest of the corps, including the tumpline. Only regular officers had tents and were assured of being given sled dogs in winter or horses for certain stages of journeys within the colony.[134] They were generally accompanied by a servant who carried their bags.[135] Such distinctions are a matter of course in any army and particularly in those of the Ancien Régime. It is worth mentioning them because they do not readily fit the stereotype of the Canadian partisan who, regardless of his social status, lived from the barrel of a gun, with a bit of flour and bear fat as his only reserve – an image whose dissemination was helped along by the colonial officers.[136] Without going as far as to agree with Montcalm's description of the benefits extended to the officers who accompanied Rigaud to war in 1757 as "Asiatic luxury," it must be admitted that what they received did nothing to set an example of austerity.[137] Finally, my sources contradict another of the era's widespread notions, to the effect that the Spartan habits proper to war "after the fashion of the Natives" continued until 1755, when the French regiments introduced their elaborate and costly methods.[138] Most of the examples used to describe Canadian practices date from the years 1745–48.

7. PUNISHMENTS AND REWARDS

Did the Canadian militiaman fall under military jurisdiction if he committed a crime while serving? The absence of a general regulation for the militia, and the thinness of the file on the corresponding penal practices, do not lend themselves to a categorical answer. It appears, however, that the general staff answered yes without hesitation. In 1751, when news arrived that the Fort Beauséjour garrison had assembled in arms to protest against a reduction of rations, the governor sent the following order to the commandant: in the future, every Canadian soldier or militiaman guilty of rebellion would be sent to Quebec to be judged by a council of war. Only Acadians not incorporated into the militia would be handed over to civilian justice.[139] The militiaman's military status was reaffirmed the following year by the procedure followed in a criminal case. During a brawl at the Wea (Ouiatenon) post, a soldier stabbed a militiaman to death. At first judged by a council of war held at Detroit, the soldier was taken to Montreal for a second trial. He must be tried in an ordinary court, contended the king's prosecutor in his petition to the governor, as required by the ordinances whenever a soldier injured a civilian. The judges (the subdelegate and a few regular officers) in charge of reviewing the point of law disagreed, concluding that the victim had to be considered a soldier.[140] Indeed, a militiaman needed not even be on duty to be treated as a soldier, a step that Governor Duquesne did not hesitate to take when, without so much as a summary trial, he banished a Detroit habitant guilty of a common-law crime from the colony. The incident was reported by the intendant, who was certainly not the only one to denounce the procedure.[141] Some claimed, for example, that since the Canadians served without pay, they should be regarded as volunteers and exempted from harsh military punishment. According to one memorialist, the argument was put forward by those who objected to the publication of ordinances "on pain of death" against militiamen who deserted during the invasion of 1759–60.[142] It could not have been a new argument, but neither does there seem to have been much in the way of protest until then.

Excessive punishment, more than the cutting of legal corners, had the potential to upset the population. On the whole, the general staff, so sure of its authority, proved quite hesistant when the time came to punish militiamen; it generally saved harsh treatment for the regulars. Military justice was not, in my estimation, particularly lenient in the colony. It is true that colonial regular officers were lax disciplinarians where their companies were concerned. Certain offences, such as negligence, inattention, uncleanliness, always punishable in a well-kept army, were tolerated in the colonial corps.[143] But this does not mean that these officers were more indulgent when soldiers defied their authority. Indeed, the reverse is more plausible, for indiscipline conduces to confrontation and engenders a desire to inflict exemplary punishment. Military justice has left few traces in the archives, apart from a series of prosecutions of deserters that reveals the existence of brutal practices, at least in the last decade of the regime. Fugitives were shot point-blank when caught, and those who went before councils of war were shown little or no clemency: no commutation of capital punishment into life in the galleys, for example, as was often the case in France.[144] A drunken soldier who insulted an officer was hanged after having his hand cut off, as per one ordinance, and a witness reported that three soldiers died after being caned.[145]

By comparison, the punishments inflicted on militiamen were moderate. For minor offences subject to summary punishment, the governor recommended that post commandants put the guilty parties in irons, on bread and water, for as long as they saw fit, rather than whip them, a punishment reserved for soldiers.[146] "The irons are always full," wrote one officer about men employed in transporting materials to Lake Erie in 1753 who dropped from exhaustion and refused to budge.[147] Because he put up resistance at the moment of departure, a certain Malouin was made to go to the commandant with a rope around his neck and beg to be taken back into the detachment.[148] Prolongation of duty, a disciplinary sentence typically meted out to militiamen, also seems to have been in common use. Four men were sentenced to spending three years at Fort Duquesne for showing up unarmed to a review at Lachine in the spring of 1755.[149] But a complete picture of the crimes and punishments that punctuated daily life in the camps is lacking. Military journals as detailed as those of Gaspard-Joseph Chaussegros de Léry or Nicolas Renaud d'Avène Des Méloizes do not mention any discipline problems among their troops. Militiamen who looted and stole the king's property while the transports were underway – a major crime under the ordinances – were almost never tried in civilian courts, nor were they court-martialed. Here again, punishment was at the behest of the post commandant.[150]

The offence typically giving rise to punishment was rebellion, also called "mutiny," a term given its broadest definition in that era. All individual or collective disobedience of a superior – a challenge to the hierarchical order – was considered mutiny. For having grumbled, disputed an order with a sergeant or officer, or outright refused to obey one, militiamen were put in irons, deprived of food, and forced to beg for forgiveness. At the start of the Ohio campaign, Governor Duquesne thought exemplary punishment would be more effective and deported two men named Desnoyers and Cardinal to Cayenne, deeming them "leaders of the riot" for having uttered seditious remarks. The minister strongly disapproved of the initiative and had the men sent home after a short stay on Île Royale to let the governor save face.[151] Collective rebellions were extremely rare outside of the mass resignation of militiamen at Quebec on 14 September 1759 and other episodes related to the defeat that were not strictly military.[152] In 1752, the habitants of Kaskaskia in Illinois demanded the release of a boy imprisoned for having refused to run after deserting soldiers; they told the local commandant that they no longer wished to take part in such pursuits. The power dynamics were not in the commandant's favour, and the uprising went unpunished.[153] Nothing is known of the circumstances that drove the habitants of Detroit, in 1756, to gather and call for the removal of Jacques-Pierre Daneau de Muy, the commandant of Fort Pontchartrain (Detroit). The governor summoned the guilty parties to Montreal, and sixteen of them were sentenced to prison and a hefty fine.[154] Beyond the turbulence typical of these outlying communities, the two mutinies attested to the cohesion of the militia company and its capacity for resistance on its own territory. Contrariwise, the dispersion of the companies stationed more centrally, or that of their members to several different forts, was not conducive to spontaneous alliances, as the absence of collective protests in the camps – or at least any deemed important enough to be reported – appears to illustrate.[155]

A few times, the administrators requested, for militiamen disabled in war, the same pension or half-pay that the king offered to soldiers who settled in the colony.[156] "Such mercy will stimulate the other habitants to serve zealously when called upon, in the hope of receiving similar treatment," they explained to the minister in regard to two young men wounded in the capture of Fort Massachusetts in 1746.[157] These proposals collided with bureaucratic reasoning: On the one hand, the militiamen did not possess the required seniority, and on the other, they had not paid into the pension fund, for they served without pay. In lieu of a pension, the decision was made to offer bonuses for the most deserving cases, a method that offered the great advantage of preserving the administration's discretionary power. The king remained free to decide just how far to extend his mercy. As an example, in 1747 the intendant was given the latitude to offer thirty livres to each of 200 militiamen returning "sick and nearly naked from Acadia as a reward and to procure new clothing," without creating a precedent, and to give gratuities of fifty to eighty livres to militia officers who took part in the same campaign.[158] Subsequent bonuses were largely reserved for war wounded who could no longer work to earn a living and for widows and orphans of militiamen who died while serving. These royal charity payments were limited by fluctuations in revenue from the posts in the Great Lakes region and by competition from privileged groups – churchmen and families of military nobles – who claimed the lion's share. The gratuities, also called alms, were never very sizeable: e.g., forty-eight livres for the widow of one habitant who had nine children. They may perhaps have been paid more than once, something that is impossible to verify given the absence of detailed accounts for the 1750s.[159] Duquesne secured nearly 3,000 livres for the victims of the Ohio campaign and the men wounded at the Battle of the Monongahela in 1755, but the revenue from the posts seems to have diminished after that.[160] To enhance the appeal of the 1757 distribution, Vaudreuil asked all the militia captains to draw up a list of subjects deserving royal mercy in their parishes. This unusual, unwise procedure – there was only enough money for twenty to thirty people – caused a real commotion. Believing they would finally be compensated for past service, the habitants raced to obtain certificates from the regular officers, who were forced to set them straight. The misprision left a bitter aftertaste.[161]

10

Jean-Baptiste Goes to War

This chapter will attempt to discern the military experience of colonists during the Seven Years' War by situating it in its context: that of the forts and armed camps where militiamen lived cheek by jowl with regulars. The parishes, which provided not only men but also provisions and housing for soldiers, are also part of the context; their difficulties had implications for the conduct of the recruits, and it is here that we shall begin.

I. UPHEAVAL IN THE PARISHES

Well before the enemy was at their door, Canadian rural people were squeezed from all sides by the war, depriving them of much of their manpower at the same time that they were forced to provide housing for soldiers, provisions, and draft animals for the needs of the service.

The early 1750s saw wheat requisitions become a routine occurrence. They provoked a considerable outcry, with many contemporaries seeing in them nothing other than a stratagem by the intendant and his cronies to corner the harvest for a pittance, then resell it at high prices to the king or foreign customers.[1] In reality, and whatever the profits concealed by the operation, the government had little or no choice if it wanted to pursue its military enterprises. My earlier book, *Power and Subsistence: The Political Economy of Grain in New France*, addresses the problem of how the harvest was allocated between city and country and between the army and the civilian population,[2] but I will reiterate its main points here. The grain balance was perpetually fragile. Canada generally produced enough wheat for its own subsistence and in good years exported its surplus to Île Royale and the West Indies, but when production so much as flagged, supplies to the cities and the troops could be jeopardized, causing panic. This vulnerability was due to three main factors. The first was the small number of farms, reflecting sluggish settlement of the colony: somewhat fewer than 7,000 at the start of the war, a third of which were still being cleared.[3] The rural population kept two-thirds of the wheat harvest for seed and food, resulting in a very limited marketable surplus that was highly sensitive to fluctuations in yield. The second factor was the harsh climate, which meant a very short growing season. The autumn was a busy time, in the Quebec region especially, where the season was three weeks behind Montreal's. Peasants there often struggled to finish the work before winter set in, and this constraint limited the area that could be planted, hence the volume of production.[4] Finally, climate and distance combined to isolate the colony for six months of the year, preventing it from receiving flour from overseas if provisions were insufficient to get through the winter. This third factor weighed heavily on the minds of townspeople and engendered a feeling of powerlessness and anxiety among administrators.

That was the situation while peace reigned: a vulnerable agriculture-based economy that nonetheless possessed the resources necessary to rebound after each crisis. The war destroyed these resources, at first slowly, then at an increasing pace. By the end, the whole farming system had been undone. The mobilization of young men had both short- and long-term effects. In the immediate, it occasioned a shortage of labour power at harvest time and when other time-sensitive work had to be done. The problem did not escape the notice of the authorities, who tried their best to discharge a portion of the militias in time for the harvest. The long-term effects were cumulative, hence more serious. Steady land clearing was the mechanism that allowed for production to keep pace with demographic growth. Yet clearing dwindled after 1745 when peasants' sons, the main category of land clearers, began to be employed outside the parishes for most of the year. After ten years of mass recruitment, farmland growth stagnated and production hit a plateau.[5] The war also interfered with the agricultural calendar by forcing habitants to thresh the wheat right after the harvest. This work ate into the time available for ploughing, reducing the area sown to wheat the following spring.[6] Lastly, France's maritime woes made the arrival of relief less predictable, and dependence on local agriculture more total, at the very moment when its growth possibilities had been exhausted.

Already large during the War of the Austrian Succession, the quantity of provisions required to support the military campaigns rose sharply around 1750 in step with troop movements in Acadia, the Great Lakes region, and the Ohio country a little later. The number of regulars shot up from 800 to 1,500 in 1750 and 7,000 in 1757. On this last date, there were perhaps 8,000 militiamen and 3,000 Amerindians under arms and receiving a soldier's ration. The transportation of foodstuffs over long distances under arduous conditions resulted in scandalous levels of waste, which would have to be added to real consumption to gain a better idea of the magnitude of the demand. To manage scarcity while prioritizing military resupply, the intendancy put in place a rigid system of control over wheat movement and processing, going as far as to put seals on bolters at all mills other than those producing flour for the king.[7] The requisitions introduced in the aftermath of 1751's poor harvest, and repeated annually thereafter, were the cornerstone of the system. Each autumn, the peasants were ordered to deliver a given quantity of wheat to the commissary, for which they were paid at a price set by ordinance. Further levies ordinarily took place in winter or spring when the rest of the harvest had been threshed.[8] How did the authorities go about determining the surplus that each producer could cede to the king without cutting into the seed reserve or jeopardizing his family's subsistence? The parish priests, who could judge the size of individual harvests by the volume of the tithe, were of no use in this matter because the main requisitions took place shortly after the harvest, while tithes were delivered many months later, around Easter. Instead, the commissaries went about it randomly, based on information obtained from the peasants themselves, their neighbours, and local notables. Once again, the militia captains served as convenient scapegoats. They were accused of going easy on certain families and letting the intendancy's agents take most of what was needed from those who had no surplus.[9] In fact, whatever the pool of people affected by the requisitions, they fell heaviest on the poorest fraction of the rural community, those who had yet to reach the threshold of self-sufficiency and who depended on wages and in-kind payments for their survival. By appropriating local surpluses and more, the military government destroyed the proximity- and kinship-centred network of exchange at the base of the rural economy and in so doing heightened social tensions.[10]

By 1757, purveyors were using beef, or even horsemeat, to replace salt pork in military rations. The new requisitions may have begun at that time, but only those of 1759 and 1760 left traces. Added to the rations was the demand for draft animals for artillery and the army's other requirements, along with mounts for the cavalry units.[11] The numbers taken from peasants' herds were so large that some feared for the survival of the animal populations. At the start of the invasion, the parishes downstream of Quebec were ordered to drive their animals in the direction of the Beauport army. During the summer, Captain Charles-François Tarieu de La Naudière, mockingly nicknamed "Cowherd-in-Chief" (*Grand Bouvier*), travelled through the upriver parishes as far as Trois-Rivières and brought back to the stores anything he could seize, having been ordered to leave no more than one draft animal and one cow for every two houses.[12] The next spring, the authorities searched the devastated countryside, desperately looking for a few horses and cows to pull the cannons and feed Lévis's army, which had come to attack the British at Quebec.[13] Considerable levies also took place in the government of Montreal in the fall of 1759. Much of the colony's land could no longer be cultivated for want of oxen, while everywhere the roads and adjoining fields had been ruined by the passage of the herds.[14]

The intendancy faced another dilemma in the early winter of 1757: The habitants' barns could not be emptied while at the same time asking them to feed soldiers billeted in their homes. Until then, billeting of the French battalions had gone off without incident. The cities being already occupied by the colonial regulars, most of the 1,700 army soldiers arriving in 1755 spent their first winter in the country around Montreal.[15] The next year, after the arrival of two new battalions, Quebec and the Côte-de-Beaupré were also brought into play.[16] Efforts were made to group the troops in the cities and their environs in order to facilitate the distribution of provisions and the service of the officers. The three barracks at Quebec could accommodate a thousand men, but soldiers were still billeted in Montreal, a city of around 4,000 that could not accommodate the same number without calling on 150 additional households in the surrounding rural area.[17]

The decision to eliminate rations in the country and to make the habitants responsible for the soldiers' subsistence disrupted these arrangements, especially since it coincided with a large increase in troop numbers, totalling a little more than 6,000 in November 1757.[18] As can be seen in Table 10.1, the number of households subjected to billeting grew considerably and even more the following winter. The

Table 10.1 | Winter housing of regular battalions

Place	Before 1755	Winter 1755–56	Winter 1756–57	Winter 1757–58	Winter 1758–59	Winter 1759–60
Government of Montreal City and suburbs	Colony	Colony La Reine (9)	Colony Languedoc (9)	Colony Béarn (7)	Colony	Colony
Lower Montreal Island		Guyenne	La Sarre (…)		Béarn	Béarn
Upper Montreal Island			La Sarre (…)	Béarn (6)	Colony	Colony
Contrecoeur/La Prairie		Béarn	Béarn	Roy Roussillon	Roy Roussillon Guyenne (…)	Roy Roussillon Guyenne
Fort Chambly/Richelieu River		Languedoc (9)	Roy Roussillon	Guyenne	Guyenne (…)	La Reine
Île Jésus				La Sarre	La Sarre (…)	La Sarre
Terrebonne/Repentigny						Berry
Saint-Sulpice/Berthier					Béarn	Berry
Government of Quebec City and suburbs	Colony	Colony	Colony, Guyenne	Colony, La Reine	Colony	
Beaupré and Beauport			La Reine (9)	Berry	Berry	
Île d'Orléans				Berry	Berry	
Côtes upstream of Quebec (north and south)				Languedoc	La Reine	
Côte-du-Sud, downstream						
Government of Trois-Rivières City	Colony	Colony	Colony	Colony	Colony	Colony

urban garrisons, still supplied by the purveyors, were diminished; all the rural parishes, including the most recent and the most remote, were pressed into service. Those in the Côte-du-Sud downstream of Quebec, which supplied the capital with some difficulty, were the only exceptions.[19] This dispersal was necessary because there was no question of assigning more than one soldier to each household, now that he had to be fed, and because a large proportion of peasants did not billet at all, being incapable of providing for themselves. Even though the eastern portion of the colony, occupied by the British, did not contribute to billeting in the winter of 1759–60, the overall burden on the rest of the colony was not heavier than in previous years, for troop numbers had plummeted during the last campaign. These procedures were neither planned nor coordinated. For three years, only the urgency of meeting immediate needs determined how wheat requisitions took place when the troops were on the march or moderated them when the men were billeted with peasants. And each year their stay in the parishes extended a little more beyond the regulation six months (November to April) so as to spin out the purveyor's provisions a little longer. One way or another, the peasantry was dispossessed and harried.

Note concerning Table 10.1

"Colony" denotes the colonial (naval) regulars (the *compagnies franches*). There were 1,500 of them in 1750, 1,950 in 1756, and 2,600 in 1757. The battalions are named according to the regiments from which they were derived. Each consisted of thirteen companies, totaling 525 men for those who came from France in 1755 and 1756, 540 for those arriving in 1757. Reduced to nine companies after losses to the British at sea, the La Reine and Languedoc battalions were not filled out until 1757. Parentheses indicate that the battalion had fewer than thirteen companies at a given place.

In the winter of 1756–57, sixteen companies were housed at Montreal, ten at Quebec, and four at Trois-Rivières. The allocation is presumed to have been the same before and after this date.

The number of soldiers billeted in the parishes was always lower than the official figures. One must take account of the spaces left by the dead and injured, which the year's new recruits did not always fill, as well as the pickets derived from different corps wintering at the forts – perhaps 5–10 per cent of the total.

Sources: RAPQ (1931–32), 19, 45 (Lapause); *RAPQ* (1944–45), 55, 75, 78, 109 (Doreil); Casgrain, ed., *Collection*, 1: 112–15, 121, 164, 231–2 (journal of Lévis); 2: 171–3, Lévis to the minister, 8 October 1757; 4: 296–7 (winter 1759–60); 6: 51–3, 54–7, Montcalm to Lévis, 9 and 14 September 1757; 7: 81, 313–14, 479–80 (journal of Montcalm).

But the peasants were paid for what was taken, so this raises the question: Did any rural people profit from the war? In the initial stages, and for one part of the population, the answer is yes. The colony enjoyed good harvests during the War of the Austrian Succession, and the king's stores offered advantageous prices for farmers' surpluses. Troop movements and expedition preparations also generated economic benefits in the form of wages, horse and cart rentals, and so on in the parishes located along the route of the convoys,[20] and these factors may have mitigated the negative impacts of militia recruitment to some extent. But the situation deteriorated rapidly: According to undoubtedly accurate contemporary accounts, sales and services ceased to be freely given or paid for at fair market value. Still, the absence of detailed public accounts, coupled with the rampant inflation of the time, makes it impossible to gauge the difference between the official price and the going rate. It is known, for example, that the purveyor paid habitants ten sols a day for billeting a soldier and sold his rations at a higher price, to the king and the public alike.[21] But at what markup? Did he really deduct up to thirty sols per ration from his employees' wages, as some observers remarked?[22] Scandalized by these monopolies, the irregularities plaguing the administration of the colony, the illicit profits they saw hiding behind every transaction, the memorialists often expressed the hardships of the day in monetary terms – and in so doing lost sight of the real problems. As one colonial officer wrote, the authorities seized all the animals at eighty livres a head "while the unfortunate Canadians, who shed their blood, could have sold their cows privately for 100 pistoles and 1,200 livres a head."[23] What caused the peasants' consternation in 1759 was not, however, the loss of potential profits: it was their inability to work the land, to produce wheat to feed their families for another year.

To make matters worse, the produce taken away was not paid for in cash but in "ordinances": government-issued bills that were legal tender in the colony. These bills depreciated day by day in the war's final years, making the requisitions even more insupportable. In the spring of 1759, cash was offered to habitants in the government of Montreal in exchange for what remained of their wheat reserves. But whatever the views of the intendant, who had put a priority on his own enrichment and painted the world in his own image, their fear of want was stronger than their lust for lucre.[24] They rejected money, we are told, and some "pushed insolence so far as to claim, when offered cash [for their wheat], that their horses would eat nothing else."[25]

In general, the chroniclers complained about the peasants at length but hardly ever listened to them. For each word reported, how many millions vanished into thin air? Is there any way to guess what the peasants were thinking based on the collective attitude toward the demands of the military government? Not easily. During these ten hard years, not a single rural assembly or protest movement is recorded. Yet the parishes had been driven to revolt over much less at the turn of the century.[26] The peasantry had been brought to heel in the interim, and as we saw earlier, the militia had done much to instill this obedience;[27] or rather, what had happened was that the peasants' methods of resistance had been transformed, from collective and at times obstreperous to individual and discreet. For there is no doubt that many habitants skirted the rules when they could get away with it. There must, after all, have been some motive for the strong-arm tactics employed: exorbitant fines and prison terms for those who sold wheat above the official price; military intimidation when visits to barns and stables were necessary; a sworn oath demanded in connection with the requisitions of January 1758.[28] Contrasting with the suspicions of the administration, some observers ascribed noble sentiments to the peasantry. "These good people, devoured by rapacious vultures, suffered these vexations in silence, saying each time their produce was taken, 'May the King [take] it all, as long as the colony is saved.'"[29] Between the two extremes of refusal and consent, the typical colonist bent his will to general, local, or familial circumstances, while the urgency – the very immensity – of the government's demand snuffed out protests before they could spread.

In this process of bringing the countryside to heel, priests played an important role. One should not imagine, as some "revisionist" historians would have us do, that the tight union between Church and monarchy did not survive the crossing of the Atlantic. These authors have made much of quarrels among the clergy, conflated bad conduct with irreligion, and taken the confessor's discourse at face value, and on these grounds have claimed that the Church was incapable of assisting the civilian authorities in overcoming the colonists' indifference, as it did in France.[30] More serious research on such subjects as parish assemblies, religious brotherhoods, alms, offertory donations, and the founding of parishes indicates a rather devoted populace that ordinarily accepted the Church's authority.[31] Its tutelage was certainly felt more strongly in the cities; nevertheless, in the second quarter of the eighteenth century, the majority of the hundred or so rural parishes had overcome initial difficulties related to their small and scattered populations and the shortage of priests. Most had a resident *curé* who worked hard to instruct and guide the faithful.[32] Upon arriving in 1741, the bishop of Quebec, Henri-Marie Dubreil de Pontbriand, worked vigorously – and successfully, it seems – on standardizing practices and disciplining the clergy. "You seem quite pleased with your parish priests," his vicar-general wrote to him in 1755.[33] Until late 1758, the bishop's loyalty, even devotion, to the king and his local representatives was unflagging.[34] It was reflected in a series of highly politicized pastoral letters paired with circulars suggesting points for celebrants to emphasize in their sermons. "On that point, you may say any number of things that will induce the habitants to pray God for His Majesty and his representatives in the colony, and you may take the opportunity to instill in them the feelings of respect, submission, and fidelity that they must have."[35] In 1755, the bishop recommended that they stay in their parishes. "Though the people must perceive that the raising of the militia was essential in the present situation, in which the English are attacking from all sides, I think it could incite some muttering to which a priest's presence might put a stop."[36] The sermons have not survived, but it may be assumed that the bishop's instructions were followed.

The annual wartime pastoral letters instituting public prayer served equally as calls for mobilization and exhortations to obedience. The bishop could also take advantage of the occasional ordinance, such as when celebrating a thanksgiving mass and a *Te Deum*, to remind the faithful of their duty.

> The militia which the illustrious general, who governs you with as much wisdom as strength, was obligated to levy for the good of the state leaves you with worries that are only too evident to others; and yet you should be rejoicing to see your kin busy working for the expansion and safety of the colony. We ask for their prompt return, as you do: but ask without grumbling, ask humbly; that is how you will obtain it, with gratitude to them and glory for the nation.[37]

The tone hardened from one year to the next, with the government's demands becoming more pressing and popular discontent on the rise. Compare the pastoral letter of the winter of 1756 with the one issued two years later. The first reads:

The muttering against the recruitment, the lies rehearsed in order
to outwit the recruiters, the unfair methods used to elude them,
are only too frequent, so much so as to annoy our Lord; and it is,
after all, impossible, Dearest Children, to prevent all abuses; and,
if any occur, it is contrary to the intentions of the first superiors.
You know the tender feelings of the illustrious General who
governs you, and his ardent wish to let you work your fields
in peace, enjoying the fruits of your labour. The troops he has
brought with him, the reinforcements he has requested from His
Majesty, justify his hope for the very best outcome; but now the
enemy is drawing near on all sides: Can he let him penetrate
into the heart of the colony, and would you wish to deny him a
final, generous effort? Surely not. Then obey the recruiters. Obey
the orders, which you must regard as sacred. God will bless this
obedience, and will find a way to repay you.[38]

In the 1758 pastoral letter, the bishop writes:

You must ... bear up under the hardships which Providence
sends your way, without muttering and with humility. The
patience of the unfortunate preserves him from the abyss:
patientia pauperum non peribit in aeternum (Ps. 9: 18). You
must go even further, and lovingly adore the hand that strikes
you. The slightest murmur against the punishment serves only
to irritate the law which orders it; humble and respectful resignation alone can stop it, and put mercy in its place: *patientia
lenietur princeps* (Prov. 25: 15). And make no mistake, Dearest
Brethren, to mutter against the orders of those who govern you
is to attack God himself: *qui resistit potestati, Dei ordinationi
resistit* (Rom. 13: 2); words of the Holy Ghost, words of truth,
which must guide our conduct in the present circumstances.
Opinions may be divided on the measures that could be taken;
where they differ, it is up to the authorities to command, and us
to obey: *obedite prepositis vestris* (Heb. 13: 17).[39]

Reiterated during Sunday sermons and inculcated through a
whole set of extraordinary ceremonies – processions, litanies, special orations, benedictions of the blessed sacrament – the Church's
lectures had their intended effect. But these were troubled parishes in
which life – particularly the lives of women who stayed home alone

on the land – took the form of an ongoing confrontation with the government, in a climate of dire poverty and suspicion mixed with worry about the fate of the absent men.

2. LIFE IN THE CAMPS

At Fort Frontenac, this 9th day of June 1757.
Dearest wife,
I cannot let this occasion go by without giving you news of me, and the news is good, thanks be to God. I pray the lord that the same is true for you. I will tell you that we are going to Fort Duquesne, where all indications are that we will be spending the winter. I recommend that you take every precaution for your own winter subsistence, for I expect to be on my journey for a long time. Our officers tell us that we will have to stay for a period of eighteen months. I will tell you that we arrived at the fort of Cataraqui [Frontenac] on 5 June in perfect health. I pray, dearest wife, that you will have a mass said for me so that God may preserve me during my journey. I also ask you, in regard to our labours, that you look after them faithfully in my absence. Kiss our little children for me; my regards to my uncle Bourassa and his wife and their whole family. Give my brother-in-law, the one living with us, my regards and tell him that I am relying on him to help you with the work. I can ask of you nothing else for the moment, until I arrive at the post where I am to stay, and I will write again from there. I forgot to tell you that there is a piece of land which belongs to you and which you have only to sell, should you find yourself in any sort of difficulty. Regards to my uncle Allée and his wife and their whole family. Adieu to my aunt Couture.

Dearest wife, I remain your faithful husband, Louis Alée.

I must tell you that I have not had any trouble since I left; I have been doing well the whole time.[40]

Louis Alée, a habitant of Pointe de Lévis, had been married for seven years and had fathered three children when he was sent to the Ohio frontier. He had joined a contingent of 400 militiamen from the government of Quebec bound for the Ohio country.[41] His family and in-laws were among the oldest residents of the parish, hence the presence of several relatives to take care of his family and land during his absence.[42] I have transcribed his letter in its entirety because, with its expressions of familial piety and religious devotion and its insistence on health, it seems to me the epitome of mundanity. Equally mundane must have been the worry peeking through these platitudinous, reassuring words. Louis Alée would not return home before the winter as he had anticipated, and the faraway Ohio country, ill-reputed since the campaign of 1753, was surely not the destination he would have chosen. What awaited him at Fort Duquesne in the months to follow? What was the daily life of a militiaman in the military camps? With the help of the army's orders of the day and a few colonists' journals and letters, Fred Anderson was able to reconstruct the experience of the Massachusetts militias stationed at Lake George during the Seven Years' War.[43] The historian of New France is less fortunate, for our sources offer up very few details about work and daily life at the armed camps.

Almost all the colony's forts had the shape of an irregular quadrilateral measuring fifty to sixty metres on a side, flanked by four bastions. In the eighteenth century, stakes were replaced or reinforced by masonry walls, squared-off pieces of oak, or a combination of the two. Within, ringing the place d'armes, were the guard house and the other military lodgings, storehouses of munitions and goods, sometimes a hospital, a powder magazine, a bakery, a forge, stables, and a garden. At some forts, merchants' shacks further encumbered this space.[44] Garrisons before 1753 were ordinarily small, consisting of forty soldiers or militiamen augmented by one or two carpenters, blacksmiths, and other tradesmen in the king's employ, a clerk, an interpreter, the commandant and his wife, and perhaps a few servants for his personal service and that of the fort in general.[45] Time glided by, punctuated by arrivals and departures of Indigenous allies or brigades of voyageurs; work proceeded at a leisurely pace. The subsistence of these small groups did not wholly depend on provisions supplied by the intendancy. They had their own garden produce, poultry, cows, and pigs and, most important, fresh fish and game sold to them by Indigenous neighbours. The officers and employees no doubt kept the lion's share of this, but the troops could supplement their diet by hunting, fishing, or trading. Some of these facilities persisted for a few more years,[46] but militiamen no longer lived inside the forts after the Ohio operation. They were now gathered in large numbers outside the walls, camping under harsh conditions and performing all manner of arduous and urgent tasks.

No fewer than 1,000 to 1,500 men were assigned to the defence and resupply of the Ohio country. The general staff had not foreseen, and never solved, the logistical problems posed by the occupation of a region that the French had taken by force instead of by diplomacy. Intimidated by the troop movements and the initial military successes, the mistrust of the local populations endured.[47] Provisions were needed for the Indigenous partisans and their families and far more for the men who carried these provisions to their destination. The vicious circle was obvious to all observers. When not busy making dugout canoes and hauling them along the muddy rivers running between forts Presqu'île, Le Boeuf, Machault, and Duquesne, militiamen were put to work completing defensive structures, keeping watch, and, more rarely, going on reconnaissance missions. In a 1757 deposition before a Pennsylvania judge, young Michel Maray de la Chauvignerie, son of the commandant at Fort Machault, used the word *journaliers* (labourers) and not *miliciens* (militiamen) to describe this army of workers.[48] Segregation was the rule: there were as many camps around Fort Duquesne as there were nations or bands represented among the warriors fighting alongside the French. Housed in huts and other makeshift shelters, the militia made up one or perhaps two of these camps. All were set up near the fort, within sight of one another, ready to intervene in case of attack.[49] At these outposts where war parties had to be supported year-round, it was in the interest of the service to keep the men as long as possible. Louis Alée's eighteen-month sojourn was perhaps the norm.

The campaign at Fort Carillon lasted about six months, often punctuated by return trips to the colony's downriver parishes for harvesting or fall ploughing. Since the fort was only a six-day river journey from the farms, the administration believed, or claimed to believe, that it could mobilize peasants without worrying about the fate of agriculture, even if it meant lending them a hand at times of urgent need. In reality, the comings and goings were a source of disorder that did little to meet the needs of agriculture while also hampering military operations.

While Fort Duquesne sat on an uncontested military frontier from Braddock's defeat in 1755 until the arrival of John Forbes in 1758, Fort Carillon was a different story: There, the enemy kept close watch on the French army from its stronghold at Fort George and might cross the lake at any time to stage a surprise attack. Another difference was that the Indigenous partisans were less numerous on this front, at times nearly absent.[50] And finally, the transportation of munitions and provisions was more straightforward than in the Great Lakes region,

being entrusted here to purveyors and their employees. The militiamen were primarily occupied with military duties, a distinction they
themselves made by describing departures to Carillon as "marching
into battle" (*marcher au feu*).[51]

The camps at this location, whether composed of regulars or other
soldiers, were widely dispersed. The 2,000 militiamen living there
seasonally at the behest of the general staff occupied three outposts.
The closest, at La Chute, was four kilometres from the fort. The men
divided their time among construction work (land clearing, building
fascines and ramparts of felled trees, etc.), watch, and patrols.[52] They
were essentially the sentinels of the army.

Totally different were the conditions at Beauport, near Quebec,
where some 13,000 combatants, half of them militiamen, were gathered from June to September 1759.[53] The camp stretched out behind
the entrenched banks, covering prairies and tilled land over a distance
of ten kilometres between the Saint-Charles and Montmorency rivers. In the centre were houses whose windows had been transformed
into embrasures for musketry and artillery; along with the redoubts,
these formed an unbroken row around which the various contingents
were ranged.[54] The militiamen were certainly less isolated and felt less
vulnerable than in camps stuck in the middle of the woods, where
the enemy could attack from any angle at any time. At Beauport,
there was no need to protect the rearguard or participate in unending
reconnaissance missions: The men were free to move about within the
surrounding agricultural lands. As a result, there was an increase in
both desertion and marauding; having worked feverishly to entrench
and fortify the site in early summer, the troops subsequently became
rather idle, with the exception of the Indigenous partisans and others
stationed near the Montmorency River. Regaining immemorial habits denied them by the North American context until then, they stole
from chicken coops, stables, fruit trees, and vegetable gardens. In the
large, formerly prosperous parishes of Beauport and Charlesbourg,
few properties were spared, and nearly everyone – soldiers, militiamen, and Indigenous allies – took part.[55]

The colony's officers were silent on the deplorable sanitary conditions in the militia camps. The sudden influx of men had taken them
unawares. While the conduct of the regulars was entrusted to their
sergeants and corporals, the militiamen did not enjoy such supervision.[56] They were left to their own devices to house, dress, and feed
themselves as best they could. Historians owe their knowledge of the

scene to the accounts of army officers shocked by the casual abandon they witnessed, and what they observed at Carillon applied equally well to strongholds in the Great Lakes region, Fort Duquesne in particular, where crowding inevitably exacerbated the filthy condition of the site. The branch-and-bark shacks in which militiamen huddled offered them little protection from the elements, nor did they encourage cleanliness. As we have seen, tents were reserved for the regulars, and blankets too were absent from the basic kit. Militiamen slept fully dressed for months at a time, exposed to the cold nights and the autumn chill.[57] At Beauport in 1759, tarps were handed out for use as tents, since the bare ground offered nothing with which to build a shelter. The lightest drizzle turned the grounds into mud pits. The water is up to our knees, wrote one regular in late June, and we have had to move our tents three times.[58] After wearing out the breeches, vest, and shoes with which they had left home, recruits had to make do with the items supplied by the intendancy – in general just a shirt and a breech-cloth. They are all in shirtsleeves, wrote an officer in regard to the Fort Lévis garrison (present-day Ogdensburg, NY) in August 1760, with kerchiefs on their heads and "bare-bottomed like the Canadians generally are."[59] Scruffy and filthy, the militiamen had never been taught to cook the provisions they were given as the soldiers had; they had no notion of pooling rations among the men in each tent and slow-cooking them in a single pot. They ate catch as catch can, wrote another observer, often subsisting on nearly raw meat and lard.[60] Finally, it appears that beer made from molasses, hemlock, or fir – the only available remedy for scurvy – was not as well distributed in the militia camps as it was among the regulars.[61]

The connection between these unsanitary conditions and the diseases running rampant among the recruits, the youngest and most inexperienced of them especially, was plain for all to see. "I fear that the disease affecting most of the militiamen arises from their casual attitude toward cleanliness and neatness," wrote Governor Vaudreuil.[62] The French officers saw things differently. Instead of blaming the victims, they accused the colonial officers of incompetence, criticized the organization of the militia, and proposed reforms that had no chance of being implemented. In August 1756, there were 600 sick men at Carillon, nearly all of them militiamen, and the commandant expected many of the 400 who were hospitalized to die.[63] Material conditions, and hence sanitary conditions, did not improve over time; in some places, shortages or poor-quality provisions exacerbated morbidity.[64]

The situation remained the same in late 1759: the militiamen were ill-attired, ill-fed, and more disease-prone than the soldiers.[65] All the main forts had a hospital and at least one surgeon, and the army at Carillon also had field hospitals. Where their condition allowed, sick men were evacuated to Fort Saint-Frédéric and on to Montreal. Only those "too severely weakened to travel" were kept in the tents and inside Fort Carillon.[66] The risk of contamination was dire. Anyone admitted to hospital with incipient scurvy or a minor wound stood a good chance of dying from an infection.

The forts could not do without a chaplain, if only to minister to the sick. As the commandant of Presqu'Île explained in connection with the proposed relocation of Father Luc: "He is extremely necessary here, this post being the repository of all the sick; furthermore, being deprived of a missionary would render this fort much more hateful to me."[67] The Récollets, dedicated military chaplains since the royal edict of 1692, ministered to soldiers and militiamen at the outposts and in the army.[68] Unlike missionaries to the Indigenous people, who accompanied them to war and blessed the troops before battle, these men generally remained in the rear. Before becoming chaplains, most of these begging monks had practised their ministry in the parishes of the colony, either as alternate celebrants or as temporary ones in côtes lacking a resident priest, where their simplicity and disinterestedness had been appreciated.[69] This prior experience certainly facilitated their work with the militiamen. Through them, the Church's lesson of deference and resignation was extended into the camps. It is unfortunate that the archives of this community have disappeared, depriving us of sermons, correspondence, and other valuable accounts of military life.

When the October cold set in and all danger of an enemy attack subsided, the camps withdrew toward the forts. The remaining militiamen, a few hundred at most, were housed in the huts. They chopped firewood and did other tasks that would detain them until winter. For these jobs, they earned certificates convertible into cash upon return to the colony. These tardy benefits aside, the Carillon militiamen ordinarily had no wages to spend with the king's storekeepers or with the sutlers who followed the army.[70] In contrast, those who served in the Great Lakes region were regular customers of the fort store both out of necessity, since the men assigned to the work and the transports were not equipped by the intendancy, and out of habit, since the flow of alcohol and tobacco at the remote posts was copious. It was said that storekeepers took a profit on sales and that they enticed soldiers and militiamen to spend money by extending advances against wages or by discounting their certificates.[71] According to the commandant of Niagara, these practices created shortages of goods when the time came to fit out partisans and encouraged militiamen to squander their meagre wages.[72] In such a context, it must have been the rare young man who managed to salt away any earnings for his future settlement.[73]

Mercenary enterprises such as those of the buccaneers and other turn-of-the-century partisans had ceased to exist, but looting retained powerful symbolic value far in excess of its real value. A sizeable prize added luster to a victory, and this fact explains the exaggerations to be found even in the official correspondence.[74] As soon as the fighting ended, the winning side proceeded to loot what it could find – from the fort, in the case of the sieges of Oswego and Fort George, or from corpses on the battlefield. According to regulations, all artillery, powder, munitions, provisions, and other items useful to the army, in addition to the commandant's cash on hand, belonged to the king. The remaining items were, in principle, to be divided among the combatants by rank and merit, with priority given, for example, to the soldiers who had dug the trench.[75] Was this order always strictly obeyed in Europe at the time, and was the free-for-all a phenomenon peculiar to North America, as the army officers implied?[76] There is cause to doubt. Be that as it may, they had to give way, for it was nearly impossible to prevent the Amerindians from grabbing what they wanted or to hold off any regulars who might try to claim their share in the melee. Since these customs were not limited to the Canadian militia but extended to soldiers and even to paid troops in the British colonies, it cannot be said whether the unpaid nature of military service had any bearing on the situation.[77]

Prizes were the combatants' obligatory reward. The sacking of stores held few surprises, and since the troops came in after the allies were done, they must have had to content themselves with whatever was left at the forts on Lake Ontario and Lake George, celebrating their spoils with rounds of aqua-vitae. Battles like those of Monongahela and Carillon, which happened on French territory and left hundreds of enemy corpses on the field, offered better opportunities for those not repulsed by the sight of bodies disemboweled, scalped, and disfigured beyond recognition. Soldiers collected muskets, bayonets, pistols, medals, shoes, still usable headdresses or clothing, and the baggage left behind by Braddock's particularly well-equipped officers.[78] The looters easily found buyers, either in the camp itself or back in the colony.[79] As a general rule, looting close to home yielded profits, while prizes captured in enemy territory normally had to be left behind and destroyed, for soldiers who weighed themselves down for the return voyage risked being overtaken.

Such scenes of wheeling and dealing and barbarity at the ends of battles are briefly mentioned in my sources but impossible to verify. More banal scenes consistent with the image of military ethics, such as assistance and transportation for the wounded or funeral honours in the camps, are never mentioned in the military journals.[80]

3. THE MILITIA AND THE REGULARS

Relations between the militia and the regulars cannot be described without first discussing the internecine squabbles that take up so much room in the documentation and the historiography. It was a secret to no one in the colony that generals Vaudreuil and Montcalm were bitter enemies and that discord reigned between the colonial regulars and the French army officers.[81] How did this situation affect the militiamen? Were they content to observe and comment on their leaders' quarrels, or did they take sides, coming to the governor's defence as a group and protesting his alleged mistreatment at the hands of the French officers? This is the thesis of Guy Fréchette and several other historians in his wake, who saw in these disputes much more than rivalries between two corps, two strategic conceptions, but a conflict pervading the whole society and pitting Canadians against Frenchmen, the colony against the metropole by which it was oppressed.[82] However, this argument rests on a slim and highly debatable corpus of documents. As discussed earlier, historians know nothing about how the militiamen felt. Should we accept the sentiments ascribed to them by the governor? This is the crux of the matter.

Early in his career as a naval officer, Pierre de Rigaud de Vaudreuil had resolved to succeed his father to the governorship of New France. Honourable service records and powerful backing at court gave him hope of being speedily appointed, but two other candidates – La Jonquière in 1746 and Duquesne in 1752 – beat him out. When he finally obtained the coveted position in 1755, Vaudreuil was a man in his declining years, one whom waiting had perhaps turned bitter and distrusting. He could not accept that the reinforcements sent to

Canada that year were to be commanded by a high-ranking army officer.[83] Although he nominally wielded supreme authority over all the troops and had the last word in matters of strategy, the new arrangement forced him to listen to contrary opinions, and he found this vexing. When the new commandant, Jean-Armand Dieskau, fell into enemy hands shortly after arriving and his troops beat a retreat, the governor set about trying to turn these unfortunate events to his advantage. "There is no need for a general at the head of these battalions," he explained to the minister, stressing the danger of entrusting troops to someone who did not know the lay of the land and who, like Dieskau, did as he pleased. To show that this was not a mere power struggle, he added in closing: "I must not hide from you, Monseigneur, that the Canadians and the Natives would not march with as much confidence under the orders of a commander of the French troops as they do under the officers of this colony."[84] But it was to no avail. Ignoring these objections, Versailles put another major-general at the head of the battalions and went as far as to propose giving him command of the colonial forces, militia and naval regulars alike.[85] The governor's riposte came in two letters. The first explained that the heavily burdened militia had to be spared and that he alone, thanks to his intimate knowledge of parish resources, could do the job fairly.[86] But more forceful arguments would be needed to persuade the minister to abandon his plan. Vaudreuil's denunciation of the ill-treatment inflicted on the militiamen by Montcalm, the new commandant, and his officers fell at just the right moment. In a letter of 23 October 1756, he gave an emotional description of these brutalities: a leader in the grip of mood swings; a group of officers who, following his example, always had a stick or sword in hand to strike the poor Canadians; French troops who took it easy and lived well while the Canadians were assigned the hardest campaigns and given the spoiled food; and one shocking image, of militiamen barefoot in the glacial water of the rapids, carrying French officers on their shoulders and pelted with blows at the slightest misstep. "They told me of their unhappiness," added the governor, "and nothing less than their blind submission to my every command has been necessary, on many occasions and principally at Oswego, for many of them to show their respect." He had also, he claimed, been obliged to defuse the anger of the Indigenous allies, who had the same reasons for rejecting Montcalm's command.[87] The minister took these charges seriously and gave Vaudreuil control over all the colonial forces.[88] Two years later, in the aftermath of the Battle of Carillon, when the animosity between the two commandants reached a paroxysm, the governor again brought up Montcalm's excesses, the cruelty of the French officers, and the sufferings of the Canadians, who were subjected to the most demeaning labour and positioned at the riskiest sites yet accepted this treatment without grumbling.[89] "Allow me to be so immodest as to claim," he wrote, "that I alone enjoy the Canadians' trust and respect."[90] In short, Vaudreuil drew on his relations with the militia and the Indigenous people for strategic support in the conflict of authority pitting him against Montcalm. If he could demonstrate that the militia represented a military force superior to that of the army and that this force was entirely, exclusively devoted to him, he bolstered his position. It should be noted that none of the memorialists of the day echoed his remarks.

But it is primarily problems of verisimilitude that cause me to doubt the governor's account. Brutality was commonplace, and some of his accusations may have had a basis in actual incidents. But his generalization was unwarranted, for until 1759 the militiamen served under the command of the colonial regular officers and had little or no contact with the army officers. Whether on the march, in the camps, or in battle orders, the separation between the newly arrived battalions and the "colonial troops" – a frequent conflation of militia and regulars – was largely preserved. The two corps came together in certain small detachments, but the army officers had no authority over the "Canadians" in these instances and were not free to mistreat them. Only Montcalm, who had general command of the army, and his staff held any sway over the militias, whether directly or through the colonial officers. Did they expose the militias to undue danger? Apparently not, as indicated by the toll of dead and wounded during the engagements. Were the corvées imposed at Carillon arduous? No doubt, but no more so than those in which the colonists had long become accustomed to participating. Add to this that Montcalm and his officers had no control over the distribution of provisions, which was a matter for the storekeepers and other intendancy employees. In short, the known military context belies a putative clash between Canadians and Frenchmen in the roles of victims and victimizers.

As does the sociocultural context. Why would the militiamen, who did not ordinarily (unlike the regulars) let themselves be beaten or whipped even when clearly in the wrong, suddenly tolerate undeserved blows without complaining?[91] Because he asked them to, wrote the governor. But if so, what could explain his powerful influence over them, their "blind submission" to him? Historians have taken this relationship as a given. They have evoked the prestige attaching to Vaudreuil's name and personal attributes and put special emphasis on his Canadian birth, a flag that he flew on any number of occasions. The combination of these things is said to have made him a natural leader. It took a man of the colony to win the confidence of the colonists and the Indigenous people, he tells us. Yet the history of the colony offers nothing to support this argument.[92] What ordinarily matters are not the commander's origins but his military prowess. In armies everywhere, soldiers readily become committed to their commander – especially if he leads them to victory. Why would Canadian militiamen act differently, and why would they show such devotion to a general who stayed behind and did not share the dangers?[93]

And would they have had more fellow feeling with the officers who commanded them in the war, whom personal interests had pushed into Vaudreuil's camp? For a second clash was taking place in the shadow of the generals: between the army officers and the colonial regular officers, with the latter, as the persons responsible for local military organization, bearing the brunt of the former's criticism and mockery. The most frequent reproaches directed at these officers were neglect of their duties, a mercantile mindset, and abandonment of partisan warfare, in that order.[94] Of these, the remarks on the officers' inability to preserve order and discipline among the troops point to a genuine weakness that had been noted by many others. The attack on mercantile practices was an amalgam of stubborn prejudices against the commercial nobility and judicious observations on the dishonest behaviour of certain colonial officers that wound up dragging all the others through the mud.[95] Equally insulting were references to degeneracy, to the loss of ancestral warlike virtues. This assumed that these officers had a special role to play as leaders of the Indigenous allies and that any who failed to play it were cowards. The riposte was sharp – no doubt as arrogant as the criticism – for the colonial corps, which had enjoyed unchallenged authority until that point, was not prepared to rethink its customs and competencies.[96] But it was not unanimous. While the majority formed a common front in support of the governor, others proved less susceptible and carried on cordial relations with the new arrivals. In doing so, they earned the wrath of Vaudreuil, who demanded unblinking loyalty.[97]

In the army, the antagonism took the form of sharp words and petty rivalries, such as quarrels over precedence. While these did not necessarily hinder operations, they did on occasion poison the atmosphere.[98] The militiamen were witnesses, but I doubt that they ascribed much importance to such incidents. They had no positions to protect. Moreover, as we have seen, their unstable and impersonal relations with the colonial officers had done nothing to build esprit de corps.[99] Historians are too apt to forget that the peasants who made up the bulk of the militia, on the one hand, and the regular officers (irrespective of background), on the other, belonged to two different worlds, each with its own priorities. Jealousies and power struggles in the upper echelons were not likely to monopolize the energies of the rank and file, especially not in such difficult times. In 1755, the new fort erected on Pointe de Carillon at the top of Lake George was named after Vaudreuil, but the toponym prevailed over the official designation.[100] Might this not be interpreted as a sign of indifference?

The militiamen had closer relations with the regular troops than with their officers, yet these have received little attention. The ad hoc companies or brigades formed for the medium- and large-scale military expeditions of the Seven Years' War, as well as the small reconnaissance parties, brought militiamen and soldiers together in varying proportions.[101] The practice of having them serve side by side was so widespread that chroniclers came to confound the two groups. One officer spoke of his "men," while army officers routinely conflated militiamen and regulars under the term *troupes de la colonie*.[102] There had been a time when naval soldiers had grown old in the colony and forged bonds with the population, but this, after 1750, was no longer the case. Three successive troop increases had remade the corps almost entirely: its 2,000 to 2,500 new arrivals were as much strangers as the army troops were. Yet there is no indication that this was a source of friction, for the mixed units worked fairly well. The incorporation of the militia into the regulars in 1759 would take the amalgam further, extending it to all the regulars.

The French army officers routinely acknowledged the military potential of the Canadian militias while deploring the systemic deficiencies, the weaknesses of command, that prevented them from giving their all.[103] Further to these observations, Montcalm proposed a four-point reform in 1758: replace mass recruitment with a selection of the best subjects and incorporate a portion of these into the troops in order to instill military discipline in them; pay them wages and, as

applicable, a disability pension; provide good muskets, suitable clothing, and tents and make the men responsible for their equipment, with
corporal punishment if necessary; enhance the status and authority
of militia officers who marched with their company.[104] The moment
was not conducive to such reforms; all that survived of this ambitious
program was the idea of incorporating the militiamen into the army
and naval troops for the duration of a campaign. Vaudreuil surely
had good reasons to accept an arrangement so contrary to his sentiments. These reasons are not known, no more than the operation of
a plan that can barely be glimpsed in the sources.[105] The regulation
of 1 June 1759, marking the entry into force of this plan, does not
specify, for example, how many militiamen were incorporated into
the battalions of the Beauport army and marched with them on the
Plains of Abraham on the morning of 13 September. The question is
of some importance, since observers attributed the rout of the French
troops to the presence of too many militiamen amid the soldiers. The
historian cannot take a position.[106] The incorporation was not limited
to this example; it extended to the naval companies present at the
siege of Quebec, which also received their contingent of militiamen, as
well as to the army at Carillon, as attested by an adjutant at the start
of the 1759 campaign.[107] The procedure was still in use the following
year for the Sainte-Foy army, the troops on Île-aux-Noix, and those
commanded by François-Charles de Bourlamaque at Sorel. It had the
advantage of simplifying the problem of recruitment, since habitants
were presumed to depart with the troops quartered in their parish
and continue to serve with them until the end of the campaign "so
that they would be with soldiers they know," as the governor put it.[108]

Although this information is much too vague, it is enough to indicate that the final two years of war saw the creation of new relations
between a portion of the militiamen and the army troops, as well as fos-
tering closer ties with the naval troops. The men went to war together,
shared the same camps, and obeyed the same officers. Relations were
close, but also ambivalent. Soldiers from France ate the habitants'
bread, took up space in their homes, and created an occasional distur-
bance in the parishes. But they were also comrades in arms.

4. MARCHING INTO BATTLE

Observers concurred in acknowledging two attributes of Canadian
peasants that predisposed them to be good soldiers: endurance and

docility.[109] They had learned to obey, and to suffer without complaining, in the harsh school of pioneer agriculture and the corvée system. It remained for them to gain the military experience that most of them lacked when the first shots were fired on the colony's frontiers. The few hundred militiamen who had taken part in the campaigns of 1745–48 accounted for only a small minority. The thousands recruited each year between the wars had learned to carry bundles, to build dugout canoes and forts, but not to fight. Too young to have fought in the previous war, the majority of the recruits of 1755 were taking up arms for the first time. It was only then, when mobilization reached the higher age brackets, when men did multi-year tours of duty, that the experience became generalized. Little by little, the militia became war-hardened, and it was no accident that its best performance came during the last two campaigns.

Pace historians who seem to believe that the Canadians' military prowess was hard-wired into their genes, contemporary military commentators knew that it resulted from experience acquired on the ground.[110] "I knew the weakness of my detachment," wrote one officer in 1749, "two-thirds being young men who had never gone out, who would have taken flight at the sight of ten made-up Natives."[111] But even a majority of experienced fusiliers does not guarantee good performance by a militia, which remains a vague, unstable formation, more fragile than a structured military corps. Context accounts for as much as experience. Writing in 1759, the commandant of the Lake Champlain army cogently explained it thus: "[The governor] sees the Canadians at Quebec, and similarly the Natives, as brave, full of good will, but he should not make the same judgment of those who are here. Superiority or equality in numbers offers assurance. Marked inferiority in numbers robs men of their courage, and he who would be brave at Quebec with ten thousand others would be a coward here, for he would see an enemy who is four or five times stronger than us."[112] Quality of command is another relevant factor. The naval regulars had good officers capable of leading their men, but the continual reappearance of the same names in the military journals leaves the impression that they were few in number. A study of officer careers remains to be done, but the most important variable for an assessment of military experience is, of course, the nature of the operations in which the militiamen participated. I have divided them into three categories: raids or parties, scouting missions, and major engagements.[113]

a) Raids and parties

As in the past, Canada's favoured strategy included a large number of raids on British settlements, with the goal of forcing the enemy onto the defensive and fragmenting his forces. As in the past, the members of these parties were Indigenous people, accompanied at times by officers, cadets, or other volunteers from the colony. These small parties were not an object of discord between Vaudreuil and Montcalm. As long as the strategy worked, the army officers never questioned its merits; their journals take regular note of these movements with evident satisfaction. Barbarity was condemned as a matter of humanitarian principle but encouraged for military reasons.[114] The Indigenous allies of the Ohio country "are working wonders," wrote Louis-Antoine de Bougainville, and Montcalm spoke of his own "punctilious accounting of the small detachments of Natives who make war as they please and find it no more unnatural to take a prisoner or a scalp than to ... lie in wait for game."[115] The partisan war took place to the south of Lake Ontario and Lake Erie, from New York to the Carolinas, mobilizing residents of the Ohio Valley, such as the Delawares and the Shawnees, along with other allies from the Great Lakes region such as the Mississauguas, Ottawas, Hurons, Ojibwas, and certain Iroquois groups. Outfitted at Fort Duquesne and other posts, the partisans fell upon the unprotected borders of Maryland, Pennsylvania, and Virginia starting in the spring of 1755. A year and a half later, 3,000 victims were reported killed or captured, along with massive destruction of agricultural settlements.[116] The attacks continued with the same intensity in 1757. That summer reportedly witnessed more than 300 parties on the borders of the British colonies, adding up to 2,000 warriors at a minimum.[117] They were less numerous in 1758, a decline presented by historians as the result of a political reversal: abandonment of the traditional offensive tactics championed by Vaudreuil in favour of retreat and European tactics under Montcalm's growing influence.[118] In reality, the French generals' preferences had nothing to do with it. For one thing, the numbers of partisans had been affected by a severe outbreak of smallpox,[119] and for another, the French were steadily losing their allies in Ohio. The British had retaken the offensive: militarily, with the advance of Forbes's army, and diplomatically, through the peace talks begun in earnest in June 1758, concluding in October with the Treaty of Easton that marked the end of the French-Indigenous alliance.[120]

The militia had an insignificant role to play in this partisan war. The sources do not allow for an analysis of troop movements in 1755–59 like the one I produced for 1745–48, but several clues suggest a rather similar composition: small bands of ten to thirty men on average, most entirely comprised of Amerindians. In perhaps 20 per cent of cases, they were accompanied by naval regular officers and cadets, more rarely by a few "Canadians" or soldiers.[121] The colony had not yet given up on the large mixed parties that had made its reputation, in which militiamen were found in larger numbers. There were 300 of these men in the detachment that intercepted Washington at Fort Necessity in 1754, 162 in the one that destroyed Fort Bull in March 1756, and more than 200 in another that blocked Fort Ligonier in October 1758.[122] These were said to be "men of good will" because they joined the parties of their own accord, the leaders having no interest in dragging unwilling militiamen on long, arduous expeditions into enemy territory. But they had initially been conscripted for military duty, unlike the volunteers of old who had enlisted on their own initiative.[123] It has been observed that the large parties of this period were directed at military targets, in contrast to those of previous wars. But the attack on German Flatts (present-day Herkimer, NY), a prosperous Palatine settlement in the province of New York, on the night of 13 November 1757 was a significant exception. Commanded by Ensign François-Marie Picoté de Belestre, the detachment was composed of a majority of domiciliés, many officers and cadets, and thirty militiamen "who departed their parish without a commander," as the author of the corresponding campaign journal specified in regard to this unusual move. The partisans killed fifty and took more than 150 prisoners, mostly women and children. They burned and destroyed the sixty houses, their outbuildings, and their herds and carried off a considerable quantity of booty, all in the purest colonial tradition.[124]

It may be noted in passing that the official correspondence continued, more than ever, to minimize the Amerindians' role. When reporting the destruction of the Palatine settlement, Governor Vaurdreuil weighed his words. Twice he mentioned the "intrepidity" of the officers, cadets, soldiers, and Canadians "along with the cries of our Natives," as if the warriors who made up 75 per cent of the troops were merely noisy hangers-on.[125] The tirelessly repeated phrase "our parties of Canadians and Natives" creates the false impression that the first were always there leading the operations.

b) Scouting missions

Parties were also sent into the Lake Champlain region but more rarely or, rather, differently. An example will serve to elucidate the distinction and the conflict inherent in scouting missions (*découvertes*). In early April 1757, sixty domiciliés camped at Carillon were offered to go with two officers to scout out the movements of the enemy army around forts George and Lydius (Edward). They refused, preferring to conduct a raid on a village near Boston. They returned three weeks later with five prisoners from whom no useful information could be extracted.[126] While traditional parties were autonomous enterprises bound for remote locations, scouting missions took place in the shadow of the army, for which they provided a shield. Reconnoitering the enemy's positions, intercepting his mail, destroying his convoys, carrying away his soldiers to extract information from them, protecting the fort and its advance posts from intruders: These were the various missions of the scouts. The support of the Amerindians – skilled trackers who could navigate through the woods – was indispensable if these manoeuvres were to be conducted successfully,[127] but those who agreed to take part in them were never enough to please the officers.[128] When they went to war, the domiciliés liked to take as much time as necessary, choose targets and prisoners in accordance with their priorities, and avoid exposing themselves to mortal danger. The relatively dangerous scouting missions between the two armies camped at either end of Lake George – always hasty, tirelessly repeated – left little latitude, hence the shortage of guides and their frequent ill will.[129] Less often, scouting missions launched from other posts also caused problems. It was even said that partisans at Fort Duquesne were accustomed to being paid to scout.[130]

In traditional mixed parties, the number of Indigenous allies had generally equalled or exceeded those of other participants. In reconnaissance missions around Carillon, the contrary was the case: militiamen and soldiers significantly outnumbered Amerindians. These missions were often rather large detachments of 300 or even 500 men at the outset, which could be subdivided along the way. The command structure – one officer for every fifty men or more – seems scanty. Thus, the expeditions were short, and encounters with enemy scouts frequent and deadly.[131] Unlike other parties for which volunteers were recruited, militiamen usually had to be ordered to join scouting missions, since there were never enough "men of good will." Any recruits who were ready to hand were taken; depending on the circumstances and their prior experience, they might be bold and valiant or slow and fearful. The campaign journals take note of these missions and their outcomes without dwelling on the quality of the detachments.[132] Several officers no doubt believed, as did Lapause and Bourlamaque, that the army would be better served, the forts better defended, by a corps specializing in petty warfare or by companies of hunters made up of the best subjects serving on a voluntary, long-term basis, similar to the way the rangers operated with respect to the Anglo-American army.[133] Pending reforms that failed to materialize, the scouts' performance remained uneven.

Nor were patrols in the advance camps any sinecure. Enemy partisans were always prowling around, and it took little – a shadow at the edge of the woods, the crack of a branch – for the watchman to believe he was surrounded. False alarms and mad stampedes were frequent.[134] Our history books only remember the big battles, but there were few of these, lasting just a few hours, and they did not involve all the militiamen. Meanwhile, all of them participated – day after day, night after night – in patrols and scouting missions. These represented the quotidian face of war, the workaday fear, a shared experience that perhaps left the most vivid memories.

c) Large engagements

In this section, I discuss a dozen engagements that had an impact on public opinion and the course of the war.[135] The number of combatants ranged from 1,000 to 8,000: few in comparison to the great European battles but many as a proportion of the forces available to the colony. These engagements have been described by battle historians innumerable times and rigorously analyzed in certain cases, always with the goal of attempting to descry the strategy and tactics that made the difference between victory and defeat.[136] From this perspective, the conduct of the militia, which ordinarily accounted for at least 40 per cent of troop numbers, takes on great importance, yet the analysis rarely goes beyond the battle in question. Any change in the composition or conduct of the corps between the beginning and the end of the war goes unnoticed. This is how the innovative character of the Montreal battalion, which suddenly appeared in 1759, has been able to elude specialists. For it was not a fortuitous gathering of voyageurs but a reorganization of the urban militias. It consisted of some 500 men commanded by their own officers, who were to distinguish themselves several times during the final two campaigns.[137] It was perhaps the result of a local decision rather than a staff order, an initiative that may be situated within the urban military tradition.[138] Before 1715, as we have seen, the majority of the young men volunteering for privateering expeditions on land and sea came from Quebec and Montreal. After the loss of Port-Royal, Plaisance, and Hudson Bay and the end of the maritime campaigns, Quebec seems to have lost the taste for warfare, which remained very much alive in Montreal. The lower-ranking militia officers and volunteers who had taken part in expeditions since 1745 were in large part traders, merchants' sons, notaries, or artisans of Montreal origin.[139] Business relations and alliances between these social categories and the military nobility clearly had something to do with these townspeople's predisposition for war. It seems that during the year 1758, they decided to put an end to the dispersal of urban and suburban militiamen, select good subjects from among fur trade personnel, train and drill their men, and go to war with them.[140] At that critical moment, when the regular officers were no longer equal to the task, the authorities could only rejoice at such an initiative and regret that the rest of the colony could not do likewise for lack of militia officers ready to take charge.

This leads to the first of several general observations about the conduct of the militiamen in detachments and during battles. The inadequacy of militia command, discussed in the previous chapter, remained a major problem to the end. "The more officers there are, the more the troops are reassured," noted one chronicler, who denounced "the unfortunate but long-standing custom in Canada of placing two or three hundred men under a single officer instead of assigning several officers to them."[141] The number that sufficed to accompany Amerindians, who had their own commanders and discipline, was inadequate to lead a large colonial force filled with mediocre men. The one commanded by Luc de La Corne on 5 July 1759 consisted of 1,180 men and only twenty-one officers, or one officer for every fifty men, a ratio four times higher than was typical of the regulars. One witness reported that as they approached Fort Oswego, the Canadians marching on the left "had a vision and cried out: 'Run away! We are surrounded!'"[142] The defeat sustained on the night of 12–13 July offers another example of an improvised expedition that ended badly. In besieged Quebec, 1,500 men, including

1,000 militiamen, had been gathered for an expedition aiming to destroy the enemy batteries that, from the heights of Lévis across the river, were preparing to bombard the city. The troops disembarked and commenced to march in disorderly fashion. Halfway there, they believed they were surrounded by the British and began firing on each other; then, succumbing to a mad stampede, they fled toward their boats. The competence of the commander, who tried in vain to rally them, was not in doubt. Nor was the initial good will of the participants, all volunteers; however, many of them had no experience, and nothing had been done to remedy this. If divided into small, well-commanded companies, the troops might, despite their weakness, have followed their marching orders and perhaps supported, by their mere presence, the minority capable of going into action.[143]

The second observation has to do with the dependence of the large expeditions on the Amerindians, who always formed the advance guard. Thanks to their remarkable talents as scouts, the troops could advance with the assurance that they were not encircled, that no enemy detachment was lying in wait. Without this shield, they fell prey to fear and unpleasant surprises. The militia's initial retreat from Braddock's oncoming army on 9 July 1755 can be attributed to the momentary disappearance of the Indigenous vanguard.[144] When in action, the colonists tended to imitate their allies' movements, which created no difficulties as long as the latter stuck to the plan. But when the allies' tactics changed abruptly – if they decided, for example, to begin firing sooner or beat a retreat – the militia were caught off guard, became unsure of their next move, and succumbed to confusion. Accounts of the militiamen's conduct in the affair of 8 September 1755 at Lake George are contradictory, but it is clear that they followed the Amerindians' lead throughout the day.[145]

Toward the end of the war, there was a discernible effort to shake off this dependency. On 14 September 1758, the troops at Fort Duquesne set off to repulse Major James Grant's forces without waiting for the allies, and the French had already won by the time the latter joined.[146] The success of 31 July 1759 at Montmorency redounded first and foremost to the Montreal militia, with the Indigenous partisans playing a supporting role – not the reverse. The latter were perhaps present on 13 September among the snipers on the Plains of Abraham who prevented the Scottish soldiers from pursuing the routed army into the city, but they did not have the initiative. Nor was there any Indigenous cover at the battle of 28 April 1760, where the enemy once again had to be confronted on an exposed battlefield.[147]

On this score, how appropriate are rote comparisons of European tactics with those borrowed from the Amerindians? Before it became a military concept specific to local cultures, the refusal to advance under enemy fire – flight toward the nearest tree – partook of a universal principle: the instinct for self-preservation. The purpose of drills was precisely to snuff out this impulse in soldiers, to make them momentarily lose their fear of death.[148] The militia were not so well drilled and had more difficulty suppressing such reactions when the enemy came into view. Instead of pressing forward and waiting to be in firing range before letting off a shot, they stopped and fired at once. When the adversary responded to this ineffective shot with a well-targeted volley that hollowed out the ranks of the militia, flight was the next resort. This was the pattern observed on the Monongahela River in 1755 and at Oswego on 6 July 1759, and it provoked the stampede away from James Wolfe's army on 13 September. The Battle of Carillon on 8 July 1758, with a frontal assault and bayonet charges, was not the kind that militiamen were ready to face, but a musket aimed at those attempting to flee left them no choice, and for seven hours they supported the battalions as best they could.[149] The militiamen who went to retake Quebec in the spring of 1760 knew in advance that they would be fighting on exposed ground. Of the 2,551 militiamen counted in Lévis's army, 1,200 (47 per cent) "did not follow their corps," wrote the garrison adjutant, and 20 per cent were assigned to the rear. The remaining men on the battlefield numbered 843, or a third of the initial group of recruits, who conducted themselves as disciplined soldiers and fought determinedly without cover.[150]

5. CASUALTIES

How many militiamen died in the war and its aftermath? The question seems straightforward, yet historians and demographers have not addressed it. Historians make occasional mention of military casualties, as a footnote to an account of a given engagement, but not globally, as a problem to be solved. The stereotype of the militiamen that pervades the historiography – a practised shooter hiding behind a tree – is not conducive to this line of thinking.[151] Nor have demographers taken any greater interest in the hypothesis that the mid-eighteenth-century wars may have eaten into a whole generation of Canadians. They do note the epidemics, the peaks of mortality between 1755 and 1760, but make no allowance for substantial unrecorded casualties; instead, the tendency has been to raise previous population estimates. In recent work, the 60,000 colonists of the end of the French regime have grown to 70,000 or more, as if there were no way the high natural growth rate observed at the turn of the century could have sagged.[152] A study of parish registers would clearly be insufficient to count deaths dispersed in space and time, but the possibility that adult male mortality was under-recorded might surely be noted in passing. Perhaps traces of the phenomenon could even be discovered in marriage trends or – who knows? – an overabundance of incomplete records in the computer database.[153] Even with serious caveats, a comparison of male with female population growth from one census to the next might yield interesting results; certainly, the contemporary accounts gathered here suggest that such research should be undertaken.[154] For while it is true that the demographic effects of the war and its attendant shortages and epidemics eventually faded, this mortality had an immediate impact on the population's behaviour and state of mind.

Like all soldiers of the era, militiamen mainly died of disease. Research on seventeenth-century European armies has shown that combat casualties accounted for only a quarter of deaths – even just 10 per cent, in some estimates – and this rule of thumb surely applies to the armies serving in North America as well.[155] Needless to say, the Canadian militia was just as vulnerable to disease as the regulars – more vulnerable, according to some accounts. There is no need to reiterate the deplorable sanitary conditions described in the previous chapter and elsewhere. Ill-dressed, ill-housed, ill-fed, many recruits collapsed under the immense fatigue brought on by these colonial campaigns, a phenomenon worth emphasizing even more than I have already done. In addition to the weight of the equipment carried along impracticable trails and the work done around the camps and forts, there was also artillery that had to be carried before and after a siege or other manoeuvre. Men did the work of horses or oxen, always in short supply on the frontiers. Weakened, wracked by scurvy, they were inordinately likely to suffer an accident which, even if benign, might set in motion a chain of events leading to death. Deaths multiplied when a contagious disease struck, whether it was smallpox or another hemmorhagic fever. A small fraction of these deaths might be traced in the records of certain forts, but this source is very incomplete and not especially helpful, for the most important thing is missing: accurate records of the militiamen attached to any given post.[156]

Based on the nominal rolls of 2,681 Massachusetts militiamen serving in the Lake Champlain army between July and October 1756, Fred Anderson derived a mortality rate of 5.74 per cent. Adding the sick and wounded, the casualty rate rises to 28.30 per cent, meaning that barely three months after arrival at the camp, more than a quarter of this contingent had been sidelined before ever fighting a battle.[157] Does this example offer any lessons for the Canadian context? Perhaps: there are commonalities, such as the youth and inexperience of the majority, the hard labour to which they were subjected, and the unsanitary conditions prevailing in the camps.[158] There are no accurate mortality figures for the 600 militiamen sent to Acadia in June 1746 but enough references to death and illness during the campaign, and to hospitalizations on returning from it, to conclude that the figures are on the same order of magnitude. The causes are clear: poor management of provisions, lack of adequate winter clothing, forced marches, and contagious fever to culminate the ordeal. The Battle of Grand-Pré, in which 130 British soldiers and only three Frenchmen died, according to official statistics, cost the colony much dearer in terms of human lives and destroyed health.[159] Although it was not, strictly speaking, a military manoeuvre, the campaign of 1753 in the Ohio region must also be mentioned. Of the 2,000 men – 1,700 militiamen and 300 soldiers – mobilized to carry materials and build new forts, no fewer than 400 lost their lives, for a mortality rate of 20 per cent.[160] Disorganized handling of provisions was at the root of the catastrophe, and the inhuman efforts demanded of those already stricken with scurvy did the rest. One officer left behind a gripping description of men collapsing under their loads, lying down to cry during portages, and, when evening came, being "as if dead, lacking the strength to eat." While all claimed to be sick, only those with a high fever or spitting blood were sent back to the colony to die, generally, unless they succumbed on the way home.[161] After this miserable experience, denounced by public opinion, the officers seem to have learned how to manage the provisions and men who were now going to the Ohio country every spring; at least, the silence of the sources suggests as much.[162] The morbidity rate surely remained high, but within acceptable bounds. Soon, scurvy and exhaustion were joined by other problems. Smallpox entered the colony in the autumn of 1755 and lingered in the camps for much of the war. It produced many casualties, among the Indigenous people especially, and also among the rural recruits, who were less immune than the soldiers and city residents.[163] In vague terms, and with no figures to support the assertion, the army officers often decried the diseases of sanitary or epidemic origin that were hollowing out the ranks of the militiamen in the Lake Champlain army.[164] They considered the situation alarming, although whether it was or not is impossible to say.

Pierre Sigouin, a labourer from Quebec, declared before a Montreal notary that he and his brother having been ordered to go to the Ohio country, "the said Joseph Sigouin *dit* Godon, his brother, last spring in 1759, was stricken with a scurvy-like disease, which caused him to suffer from trembling fevers" and that he "had been sent along with forty men to scout around the fort, where they found British soldiers with whom they engaged in a battle that lasted two to three hours, in which Godon took a bullet to the thigh, of which injury he died, after eight days, in the presence of the said Pierre Sigouin."[165] All is exemplary in this account, including the fact that the death was not recorded. Yet many militiamen killed or wounded by gunfire – the majority perhaps – met this fate under similar circumstances in the hundreds of small, incessant troop movements taking place around the camps, in which weakened, ill-trained men exposed themselves to mortal danger. The scattered references to these comings and goings, and to casualties if any, that may be found in Vaudreuil's correspondence and a few officers' journals give no indication of the true numbers. More is known about the number of victims of large and medium-scale engagements, for which there exists an official report and other, more or less concordant personal versions that report the forces on the battlefield and the numbers of dead, wounded, and prisoners from each corps.[166] Even taking account of the general staff's tendency to underestimate its own casualties and exaggerate the adversary's, these figures can serve as orders of magnitude. Four especially murderous battles stand out from a larger group in which French casualties were generally quite limited. The battle of 8 September 1755 at Lake George killed twenty-seven and injured thirty-five among the 600 militiamen present, or 10 per cent of the troops. For the 250 militiamen involved in the battle of 8 July 1758 at Carillon, casualties amounted to only 5 per cent. In both cases, these men were fighting on the flanks of the army, and the number of victims was much higher for the regulars who led the manoeuvres.[167] On 13 September 1759 and 28 April 1760, this gap disappears, since the militia found itself in the thick of battle. Let us begin with the last battle of Quebec, for which reliable statistics exist: the forty-five killed and 170 wounded amount to a full fourth of the 843 militiamen who saw action here.[168] Was the battle of the previous 13 September on the Plains of Abraham equally deadly? The answer is not in the archives – the confusion reigning on the ground prevented the officers from gathering data on troop numbers and casualties.[169] Yet a series of comparisons can serve to propound some hypotheses. Montcalm was said to have had some 4,500 men under his command. The five (very incomplete) army battalions accounted for at most 1,900 soldiers, the naval regulars a maximum of 500. This means that at least 2,100 militiamen took part in this battle and maybe as many as 2,500. So it is not impossible that 500 or 600 of them were killed, wounded, or taken prisoner in the course of such a violent engagement.[170] Many more militiamen died by gunfire during the disastrous campaigns of 1759 and 1760 in the sieges of forts Niagara and Lévis (the Battle of the Thousand Islands); for example, at the Battle of Neuville or in the Belle-Famille ambush, which alone produced 400 or 500 casualties, nearly all militia members.[171]

In sum, while disease was, on the whole, deadlier than battle, the number of those who fell under enemy fire, who died in British prisons, or who were crippled for life is non-negligible. Parishes kept their own records of men who died in the war from all causes. According to figures gathered by the provost court judge from militia captains in the government of Quebec, 150 militiamen died at Carillon in the summer of 1758, not a mere thirty-eight, the number that was published.[172] Canada did receive immigrants during the last two decades of the regime, but what mattered to public opinion was not so much this influx as the empty spaces left by the war: rightly or wrongly, the people believed that the population had stagnated since 1745.[173] The disorder surrounding militia movements and the lack of accounting at the end of campaigns prevented families from jumping to the worst conclusions when they were without news of a son or a husband. The silence might go on, but hope was stubborn. The widow Brisson wrote that she was still hoping to see her son, who had been gone a long time and was reportedly being held prisoner in New England. Capitalizing on her good relations with a British captive who had returned to his Massachusetts village, she begged him to look for the young man, "and if you should find him, to take good care of him."[174] In 1762, two years after the end of the war, a woman of Saint-François in the Côte-du-Sud kept a piece of cake for reassurance as to the fate of her vanished husband. If the cake spoiled, she would know he was dead.[175]

It was said that many militiamen were taken on board British ships in 1759, and as long as the war went on, families clung to the belief that the young men they awaited were detained somewhere in Great Britain. In 1762, they requested Governor Murray's help in getting them released. A list of 128 "prisoners of war" from Quebec (fifty) and nineteen rural parishes in that government (seventy-eight) accompanied the petition.[176] The name of an English city appearing after that of twenty-four Quebecers suggests that the families had received proof of incarceration in those cases. For the others, there was none, and only the place of disappearance is listed: for thirty-one men, various sites along the St Lawrence during the siege of Quebec; for thirty-four, the battle of 13 September; and for the rest, elsewhere at the colony's forts. Joseph Dutau of Berthier-en-Bas had not been seen since the battle of Lake George in 1755.[177] The little parish of Château-Richer in the Côte-de-Beaupré supplied twenty-nine names, all lost during the siege, which must be added to the known deaths and losses of the previous campaigns. In 1750, 133 militiamen were counted there, but twelve years later there were only 108 men left in the same age bracket.[178] It seems unavoidable to connect this population decline with military casualties. While it is true that Château-Richer was hit harder than the other parishes, none was spared during all those years of war, and the colony was still grieving long after the battles ended.

"It is surely time for historians to distance themselves from overly idealized accounts and to incorporate the unending physical and moral 'fatigue' engendered by the war, which has been dutifully muted in their words," suggests Arlette Farge in a beautifully written piece that, in its own way, lets the documentation speak for itself.[179] But how is one to follow the advice, other than to discuss the military event in one's own words? "I will spare you the details of the battle we fought on the 8th of this month with the English," wrote one militiaman in July 1758 from Carillon. "We've never seen the like of it. Baptiste will tell you."[180] Lacking the accounts of Baptiste, Nicolas, Pierre, and all the others, nothing enables us to penetrate the mixture of intoxication and anguish, bravery and terror pervading the battlefield, nor the confusion and despondency that followed a violent engagement, even a victorious one. The only letter found in the archives expresses the assurance and optimism that generally prevail before a battle. The author, a naval regular who took a wife in Montreal, wrote to her from the Beauport camp on 21 June 1759. His mental state must have coincided with that of the militiamen camped alongside him. The first British ships had just entered the channel at Cap Tourmente and were sailing along the south shore of Île d'Orléans, and the army believed an attack to be imminent.

My dear Amy and daughter,
This is the sixth letter I have sent you without receiving any of yours, which causes me much sorrow. I hope your health is as good as mine, since I am very well, apart from the provisions we are lacking. We are reduced to a pound and a quarter of bread and a half pound of lard. We have already decamped three times and I lost my bag in the scuffling. However, I was given a white shirt that a German had, and my haversack was recovered, so I lost my blanket, three shirts, a thing or two more. Your foster father can tell you, as can Jolibois, who lost some things too. I've been plying my trade and managed to shave the whole troop, which might earn me something. I know you must be sad, but you could scarcely be sadder than I am. We are camped in water up to the knee, on rich, ever-muddy ground, where we must stay until the enemy arrives. We are a league from Beauport, awaiting the English. The certain news I have from our major, whom I am accommodating, is that fourteen ships have made the crossing. We took twenty-eight prisoners, eight in one case and then another twenty. He reports that thirty thousand men are coming. I can assure you that we fear them not, God willing. We do not know the number of their ships. So don't trouble yourself with what the town news-sheets tell you: what I'm telling you is the truth. Goodbye, my dear Amy. I embrace you with all my heart. May God's blessings be upon you. I pray every day for you and for my dear children, whom you will embrace for me. I am, until the pleasure of seeing you again, your faithful husband, Miller.[181]

This cheery optimism would not survive the events to follow, and at the same time the militiamen's docility – still their primary characteristic – would fade.

The Invasion

It was with astonishment, at first mixed with incredulity, that the colony learned that the British fleet had passed the mouth of the river and then watched it calmly sailing up the St Lawrence toward Quebec. Yet there had been warning signs. The fall of Louisbourg in July 1758, and especially the destruction of the sedentary fisheries off the Gaspé Peninsula that September, had left hardly any doubt about Great Britain's intentions. Yet the colonial government seemingly did not believe the danger on this front to be imminent. Letters sent to the minister the previous winter had dwelled endlessly on the harassment operations and scouting missions on the Ohio and Lake Champlain frontiers, as if positions had not changed since the year before.[1] In a summary of the military operation plan published 1 April 1759, the defence of Quebec was far from a priority, and the idea of blocking the river, or at least slowing down the ships, was not even glancingly mentioned. "I presume the enemy is not undertaking to come to Quebec," wrote Vaudreuil, and in any event, there would be time to bring over some of the troops massed at Carillon.[2] On this subject, moreover, the governor's opinion had long been firm, and suggestions to place cannons at points where the ships would have to approach land, such as at Cap Tourmente or in the strait between Île d'Orléans and Île Madame, were brushed aside.[3] A final attempt by Montcalm to prepare for invasion by leaving as many men as possible in the government of Quebec and drawing up a detailed operation plan was also ignored.[4]

In this final campaign that was to decide its fate, Canada was very much the dupe of its past successes, notes military historian C.P. Stacey in recalling Phips's defeat at Quebec in 1690 and the shipwrecking of Walker's fleet at the mouth of the St Lawrence in 1711.[5] There had been much talk in those days of protection by the Virgin, but half a century later, the enduring memory of those events had the general effect of entrenching prejudices: The Canadian troops were invincible, the British troops worthless, and the colony's natural barriers insurmountable. The military officers had always had a very high opinion of their own capabilities and consequently of the men they commanded. Recall the pages of rapturous prose written by Bacqueville de la Potherie about the Nine Years' War, the chimerical plans to subdue Boston and New York, or the smug remarks reported in the journal of Swedish botanist Pehr Kalm after the War of the Austrian Succession.[6] This self-assurance relied in large part on the successes of the Indigenous allies, for which the colony often readily took the credit, and on the catalogue of blunders committed by the British colonial troops over the years. "Nothing equals the bravery of the Canadians, and the contempt they have for the English of this new world," wrote Financial Commissary of Wars André Doreil shortly after arriving in the colony in 1755.[7] The jeering of British prisoners of war during the celebrations that marked the Oswego victory shows that the people shared these prejudices.[8] Looking back, Captain Pierre Pouchot reserved a harsher judgment for the boastfulness of the officers, "who had always imagined that one Canadian could send ten Englishmen fleeing, a prejudice entrenched by unexpected successes over the years."[9] In the moment, it was too convenient and tempting to believe the accounts of prisoners and deserters describing the adversary's problems: colonists who refused to enlist, revolts reaching the boiling point, and other reassuring but false news.[10]

And arrogance begat negligence. The colonial general staff did not feel the need, for example, to verify the depth soundings taken by sailors in the river over the years, since it was convinced that the enemy's ships of the line would never dare enter it. Winter was another insurmountable obstacle – for foreigners, of course. It was thought that the cold and the snow would not prevent the colonists from marching. Although relatively rare and conducted by elite partisans against ill-defended towns, winter campaigns captured the imagination and created this illusion. Michel-Jean-Hughes Péan, captain and adjutant in the colonial regulars, entrusted with representing Vaudreuil's views on the 1759 campaign to the minister, was still in France when rumours of the landing reached him. His first reaction was disbelief, although if it had indeed happened, then the Canadians would opt for the tactic of burning and abandoning Quebec, carrying the provisions and munitions into the woods, and making camp there until winter. And then, if the British were still there – another prospect he though unlikely – "we will set them afire and cut their throats in the season of ice and snow."[11] These remarks to Bordeaux merchant Abraham Gradis reiterated a scenario going around in Quebec as early as 1745, which the governor of the day had considered utterly unrealistic.[12] They are more than surprising coming from an influential military officer.

This certainty on the part of the officers had won over other segments of society. The lieutenant-general of the provost court believed, despite prisoners' depositions, that the British would not come in the spring "due to the risks posed by the river."[13] "My idea," explained the merchant and storekeeper Guillaume Estèbe, "is not that they will never undertake to come up river with a fleet, but that they will block it in such fashion as to intercept any relief that might be offered you."[14] This mindset held sway at the other end of the social ladder too. The officer in charge of mobilizing peasants in the Côte-du-Sud had a hard time convincing them that the enemy was at their door. They still believed, even after the unpleasant surprise, that their leaders would somehow, by the grace of God and with the help of the allies, ward off the attack, that, as one of the navigators impressed into guiding the fleet bragged, Canada would be "the grave of the whole army," "the walls of Quebec ornamented with British scalps."[15] Others thought the colony was riding for a fall: one anonymous Quebecer in the employ of the intendancy began his siege journal by noting, with mordant irony, the government's lack of foresight and the officers' inertia during the initial encounters with the enemy.[16] Before long, with bombs raining down, the city would be condemning the strategy of its generals in chorus, but dissidents were apparently still in the minority as of May 1759.

This chapter begins by discussing the rural areas of the colony, where the majority of the population lived. How did they factor into the French generals' strategy and that of their adversaries? Reliant on urban and military sources, anchored in the siege of Quebec and the other decisive events surrounding the defeat, historical accounts have generally paid little attention to what was happening in the rural parishes. The facts concerning them are sprinkled throughout analyses of the large operations as just so many anecdotes. These motley bits of information about evacuations, fires, desertions, or oaths give no indication of the severity of the problems confronted by the rural population, the militia in particular, between June 1759 and September 1760. I have no new facts to present, but by offering an orderly presentation of known ones, I shall attempt in the rest of this chapter to home in on the dilemma of either resisting or collaborating with the enemy – the reasons to either fight or give in to the immense fatigue of a never-ending war.

I. THE COLONIAL PLAN

The first plan for evacuating the downriver parishes at the approach of an enemy fleet had been drawn up by the elder Vaudreuil at the turn of the century. It answered to two imperatives: assembling the able-bodied men at Quebec and protecting the women and children. The two were inseparable, since the militiamen would refuse to defend the capital if it meant leaving their families exposed to an enemy landing and the tortures that would inevitably ensue. And to weaken the enemy by depriving him of fresh meat, the cattle would also be evacuated. The invasions apprehended in 1709 and 1711 never occurred, so the plan was not put into effect.[17] During the War of the Austrian Succession, when the fall of Louisbourg aroused new fears of an attack by sea, the habitants of parishes downriver from Quebec received orders to build cabins in the woods and remove their families and livestock to them as soon as word of arriving ships was received. The militiamen on Île-aux-Coudres and environs would then attempt to barricade the river with makeshift fire ships and rafts, while those on the Côte-du-Sud would fend off any attempted enemy landing. And if the enemy continued upriver despite these efforts, everyone would go to Quebec with weapons and stocks of provisions to participate in the defence of the city alongside the combined forces of the colony.[18] Deaf to the colonial sirens' song, Governor Beauharnois took the rumours of invasion seriously, and his timely directives set the plan's application in motion.[19] But the homes were never evacuated, for the enemy again failed to materialize.

In 1759, he was at the gates. On 21 May, the vanguard – ten Royal Navy ships and several transports – sat in the St Lawrence off Rimouski. These ships put in on Île-aux-Coudres on the 28th and reached Île d'Orléans on 8 June. The fleet proper, composed of forty-nine ships of the line and about 150 smaller vessels, followed. Reported at Bic on 18 June, it stood off Kamouraska on the 22nd, dropped anchor on Île-aux-Coudres the next day, and, on 27 June, Wolfe and his army landed at Saint-Laurent on Île d'Orléans.[20] The spectacle of hundreds of sails suddenly rising above the horizon sowed panic along the route of the fleet, hastening the habitants' decision to take flight.

It was far from a straightforward affair to move 3,000 families and their livestock.[21] Several factors delayed and complicated the evacuation, beginning with the scarcity of salt and wheat, which meant that the population could not put by provisions in anticipation of departure. They could not salt meat or fish, for there was no salt to be had in the colony, nor any wheat in the government of Quebec in the spring of 1759. From one requisition to the next, the city had exhausted the reserves of the Côte-du-Sud. On the north shore, three battalions – stationed at Beauport, in the Côte-de-Beaupré, and on Île d'Orléans – had had to be withdrawn in late April, for the habitants could no longer feed them.[22] The absence of a contingent of men at evacuation time was another cause of difficulty, since it meant that they could not assist their families. A thousand militiamen from the government had left for Carillon in early May, and 500 were already serving at the rapids south of Montreal, Lake Ontario, and beyond.[23] These 1,500 absent men, equally divided among the parishes as per custom, accounted for 20 per cent of the 7,500 militiamen enumerated that year.[24]

The governor's directives – tardy, chaotic, to some extent impracticable – were another significant source of disorder. Written in Montreal on 4 May and directed at militia captains downriver, they were transmitted with agonizing slowness. At the remotest locations, such as Rivière-Ouelle, they arrived shortly before the British did.[25] The lead time was longer elsewhere, but since the peasants did not hasten to obey, all were equally caught off guard. When the time for departure came, they had yet to put their belongings in safekeeping or to build cabins in the woods to house their families. To secure a commitment from them to interrupt their planting and make these preparations would have taken more time and a more positive attitude than that of Vaudreuil, who all but implied that the measures ordered were superfluous. He did not believe that a sea offensive was imminent, as he wrote in a letter, but that "it is always prudent to plan for the most unexpected events."[26] The follow-up to the 4 May directives posed other problems. Rather than hew to the arrangements used by his predecessors, the governor grafted an army resupply operation onto the parish evacuation, making the ordeal even more painful (e.g., on the south shore). The plan was that as soon as the enemy was reported, the women, children, sick, and livestock would be sent to Pointe-Lévy across from Quebec, while all men capable of bearing arms would join Gaspard-Joseph Chaussegros de Léry, the commanding officer in the region, in fending off an attempted British landing.[27]

Taking advantage of the initial fright, the officer succeeded in persuading the families at Portage and Kamouraska to leave as of 22 May, but the other parishes did not follow. On foot or by cart, the road to Lévis was long – about 200 kilometres for these people – and strewn with obstacles, including three wide, deep, unbridged rivers. No one knew what awaited the refugees at journey's end.[28] To believe that these peasants would willingly abandon their women and children to such an uncertain fate would be to betray a profound ignorance of who they were. Léry and Joseph-Michel Legardeur de Croisille et de Montesson, the two officers delegated by Vaudreuil, lacked the means to coerce them and were indeed the first to realize that men would be needed to lead the families and livestock to their destination.[29] After ten days of protests and hesitations, the governor had to give up his plan and order the families to hide in the woods behind their respective parishes. They would keep their livestock, except for the cattle that the militiamen took to Pointe-Lévy when they went to join the army: a difficult task to reconcile with their coast guard duties, be it noted.[30] In short, between the arrival of Philip Durell's vanguard in May and that of Charles Saunders's fleet three weeks later, confusion reigned, as is fairly well documented in Vaudreuil's near-daily letters to Léry and the latter's journal.[31] One after the other, the parishes demanded powder and bullets to defend themselves; the militiamen assembled at Rivière-Ouelle deserted to help their families move;[32] Léry had no provisions to give them and, most important, did not know what the governor expected of him. On numerous occasions, he wrote, "I begged him for more decisive orders, in less general terms, than in his previous letters ... as to how I was to manoeuvre when the rest of the enemy ships arrived."[33] Explanation came there none. On 22 June, the fleet was in sight. The officer shut his journal and left without waiting for the cowherds. We find him seven days later on the cliffs of Beaumont across from Quebec, with habitants from that parish and a few Indigenous people, trying in vain to repulse the first landing by the British in the Côte-du-Sud.[34] Most of the militiamen had presumably joined the army already, and the livestock were sent back to the prairies to graze, since the passage was now blocked.

The movements of the parishes on the islands and the north shore are not as well documented, but there too, livestock requisitions were given higher priority than family safety. The small populations of Île-aux-Coudres and Île d'Orléans – 500 families divided into five parishes – were abruptly evacuated in the last week of May.[35] Given how badly the situation on the south shore was bungled, historians should have no trouble believing a witness who wrote that nothing had been planned to facilitate this migration – neither boats, provisions, nor places of refuge – and that some people perished in the mad scramble.[36] The refugees were not permitted to stop in inhabited areas. Moreover, the four parishes in the Côte-de-Beaupré had also received evacuation orders, while others were planned for Beauport. The plan was similar to the one Vaudreuil had sought to impose on the Côte-du-Sud. Instead of making off into the woods, the families would camp fairly far inland, from Lake St Charles near Lorette to the environs of the Jacques-Cartier River, where they would place their livestock at the army's disposal.[37] Distances being shorter than on the south shore, the enemy's arrival further off, and the men more available to help their families, at least some part of this plan was successfully put into action. In addition, a number of refugees from Île d'Orléans, Beaupré, and Beauport appear in the registers of the parishes situated upstream of Quebec. Charlesbourg and Ancienne-Lorette head the list of host sites, followed by Saint-Augustin, Pointe-aux-Trembles (Neuville), and Cap-Santé. The city residents had to evacuate twice, before the siege and when bombardment began; they formed the main category of outsiders in these parishes and were generally housed in habitants' homes. Peasants, by contrast, moved into huts on the edge of the occupied territory.[38]

The bishop asked the priests to withdraw into the forest with their parishioners, suggesting that they were not scattered behind their homes but gathered at a single site or in a few collective camps.[39] To be sure, one can scarcely imagine how a woman alone with her children could have survived in an isolated cabin. The camps downriver from Quebec had to be far enough removed from cleared land for people to build fires and hunt without alerting the enemy yet close enough to come in and collect forage and livestock as needed or legumes and wheat later in the season. These furtive comings and goings left traces in the reports of British soldiers who chanced upon groups of peasants – old people, women, and children for the most part – pursued them, and often took them prisoner.[40] To live in the woods this way for months was a hard experience. Taking advantage of their credit or relations, a minority of families succeeded in avoiding it and moving into more comfortable quarters elsewhere in the colony. The others had no alternative.

How long did their exodus last? Once the initial panic was over, were the habitants tempted to regain their homes? In the vicinity of Quebec, near the theatres of war, the question did not arise, but what about outlying parishes such as Sainte-Anne and Saint-Roch in the Côte-du-Sud, where the first British incursion did not occur until 15 August? There too the invading army found only long-abandoned houses with signs of occasional visits.[41] I had at first thought that the parish registers, the records of baptisms in particular, would make it possible to identify patterns of absence.[42] The results were disappointing, with only ten parishes out of a total of twenty-seven offering a clear image. The records are interrupted in May or June and only resume in late autumn.[43] In five other parishes, the registers, which the priests probably took with them, have disappeared.[44] That leaves thirteen parishes in which certain changes can be detected but are hard to interpret. How can it be told whether baptisms or burials recorded during the siege of Quebec took place outside the parish if nothing indicates this and if birth and death dates are lacking as well? A few acts are annotated, as in the case of some burials on 9 September at Baie-Saint-Paul: "Several other children who died while we were refugees in the woods." Or again, "All died during the time when the enemy was in the land and were, for this reason, buried in unsanctified ground about a month and a half ago," found in the register of Sainte-Anne-de-la-Côte-du-Sud on the occasion of their exhumation the following 23 November. But vague explanations of this sort are the exceptions. Still, the ambiguity of the source is insufficient to reject the hypothesis that the majority of the 3,000 peasant families from the downriver parishes lived upwards of four months in the forest.[45]

Vaudreuil had stressed the difficulties of navigation and the action of the fire rafts in blocking the invader, and when these defences fell, there was no fallback plan to protect these parishes. A few

small detachments were sent hither and yon to fend off the landings in June, but these derisory efforts were uncoordinated and
ill-commanded and were abandoned in short order. The army did not
want to divide its forces; its efforts were limited to encouraging the
Indigenous allies to harass the British camps. All summer long, these
parishes were left defenceless, giving the enemy free rein to move in
and familiarize himself with the territory. The upriver parishes were
better defended. On the night of 18 July, under fire from the urban
batteries, British ships traversed the narrow, supposedly impassable
strait facing Quebec and dropped anchor upriver. In addition to directly threatening the fortified site, this manoeuvre jeopardized the
Beauport army's communication and supply line. A contingent of
600 to 1,000 men, including 100 cavalry, was dispatched to the site.
It succeeded in fending off two landings at Pointe-aux-Trembles but
reached Deschambault too late to prevent the destruction of the military stores and proved incapable of stopping the landings on the
south shore at Saint-Antoine and Saint-Nicolas.[46] What was lacking
was not will but the ability to be everywhere at once with limited
numbers of not especially mobile troops. Now in control of the river,
the British could cross from shore to shore at will while the French
were trapped on land.[47]

Safeguarding the parishes thus became part of the system of defence
organized by François de Lévis after the fall of Quebec. To preserve
those that now formed the eastern frontier of the colony, he established a fort at the mouth of the Jacques-Cartier River, with advance
posts up to Saint-Augustin and Ancienne-Lorette. This strategy served
to prevent the British from expanding the occupied zone, as they
tried several times to do.[48] Nor was there any question of giving up
the contest, as unequal as it was, when the enemy fleet began sailing toward Montreal in July 1760. The territory had to be defended
tooth and nail by soldiers and habitants or by the latter alone when
the troops were unable to assist them. To this end, the French relied
on bombarding the ships where the channel brought them near the
shore; trying to make the British army land on the north shore and
fight the French troops, who were advantageously positioned there;
and heading off the ships by blocking the entrance to the Richelieu.
Each of these plans failed, and the British tactics ultimately prevailed.
The troops stood powerless along the banks as the enemy fleet sailed
by, while the midriver and upriver parishes gave in to fear and surrendered, one after the other, most of them without a shot fired. On

2 September, after having retreated as far as La Prairie, Lévis tried to regroup and attack William Haviland's army at Chambly, but the defection of the domiciliés forced him to give up this plan. The next day, the French troops withdrew to await the enemy at the gates of Montreal, abandoning the countryside to its fate.

2. RESISTANCE IN THE PARISHES

In the French archives of the final campaigns, the colonists are most often painted as deserters in a hurry to make peace with the enemy. So the sources will have it, for officers did not comment on the conduct of their men when they obeyed orders or on activities taking place in the parishes while they were absent. Following their own logic, the British sources convey the contrary impression: that the Canadians persisted in taking up arms and joining the army in spite of the threat. The contrast between the two images suggests that historians should tread carefully and, above all, avoid generalizations.

The summer of 1759 was a period of active resistance. Alone or with Indigenous support, the downriver habitants fired on enemy soldiers when they approached their settlements and at times conducted raids in the vicinity of the camps; it was even reported that women angered by British acts of violence joined in.[49] Several letters from Vaudreuil to the priests and militia officers of four rural parishes, which somehow fell into British hands and thereby survived to the present day, illuminate these operations from within.[50] A small sample of a large body of correspondence carried on by the governor with the local authorities, they afford a plausible approximation of what was happening throughout the colony. The correspondents report enemy movements and call for guns, munitions, provisions and, most of all, the return of the parish men from Beauport for purposes of self-defence. The governor has little but encouragement to offer them. Arms and munitions are meted out stingily and, with one exception, he refuses to diminish his army. "There is every reason to believe that the English will not stay long in the colony. As soon as the fleet departs, I will send all your parishioners home," he wrote to the priest of Saint-Charles parish on 28 August.[51] Apparently, the majority of the habitants trusted him and shared his optimism, since despite the futility of their acts of resistance and the misfortunes that these brought upon them, they did not disarm.

The fall of Quebec fractured this consensus: The British conquest of the whole colony went from unthinkable to either possible,

probable, or inexorable, depending on who was opining. For lack
of witnesses in the occupied parishes, there is no way to describe
divisions among neighbours or relatives, inevitable clashes between
those who abided by their oath of neutrality to avoid the worst and
those who kept up the fight by refusing to serve the enemy, secretly
supporting the colonial detachments, or participating in the defence
of Quebec in April 1760. It cannot be ruled out that violence played
a part in settling such disputes, as shown by accusations of treachery
and by denunciations or attacks against habitants who resupplied
the British garrison.[52]

3. THE BRITISH STRATEGY

When he set foot on Canadian soil, the British general put out a call
for demobilization of the "hard-working colonists and peasants."[53]
Notices posted on church doors in deserted parishes had few readers,
but the message steadily made its way into places of refuge by word
of mouth and, with greater difficulty, into the camps at Beauport,
Carillon, and other sites where the general staff tried to control the
spread of the information. Wolfe's objective was to dismantle the
French forces by depriving them of the militiamen who made up
60 per cent of their numbers and provided a large proportion of
services. He began by abolishing the habitants' military status by the
expedient of deleting the word "militia" from what he wrote. The
on-the-ground consequences of this gambit are clear: militiamen
captured during and after the siege would not be protected by international rules applicable to prisoners of war.[54] The declaration of
27 June was addressed to the "Canadians," those peaceful peasants
who had been forced to take up arms because of a dispute "concerning the two crowns only" – a cause that was not theirs. Now they
were free to choose between France, "which oppressed them" and
left them to their fate, and England, "which extended a powerful,
uplifting hand." They had only to return to their homes and swear
neutrality. If they did not, they would bear the terrible brunt of the
soldiers' furor and excesses. Note that the line of demarcation here
is between the people and their officers and governors, regardless of
origin, not between colonists and Frenchmen. Knowing how heavily
an army could weigh on a civilian population and the material difficulties of the colony, the British trained their bellows on the embers
of discontent, seeking to foment a popular revolt. Wolfe's message

and its successors paint a picture of contrasts between France and Great Britain, setting the weakness, cruelty, and harshness of the first against the power, humanity, and generosity of the second: pitting despotism against liberty under a just and equitable government.[55] But if Canadians were subjugated by their leaders, what freedom of choice did they have? The habitants quickly grasped the advantage they could derive from this contradiction, as attested by the depositions of three men in the Côte-du-Sud who were caught with weapons in hand on several occasions. The parish would have surrendered, said one, were it not for the priest's orders and the fear of the Indians instilled in them by the authorities. The two others proffered the same excuse, claiming that they were merely trying to protect themselves against the Indians, whom Vaudreuil and Montcalm would set upon them at the slightest sign of desertion.[56] But in any case, the proclamation was without effect. The Canadians were still with the army as of late July, and snipers were still attacking enemy patrols in the countryside. Wolfe had never imagined, in any case, that a lofty speech would be enough to make the population switch allegiances; the invitation served as a pretext, a preamble to more persuasive measures. To study the behaviour of the British army in the occupied territory, I shall distinguish between two periods: the first marked by an escalation of indiscriminate brutality throughout the colony; the second, beginning with the conquest of Quebec on 18 September, in which the victor exhibited prudence and meted out punishment more selectively.

For most of the siege, the enemy troops were divided into three camps – Île d'Orléans, Pointe-Lévy, and Montmorency – from which various sorties were made into the côtes. Upon landing, Wolfe gave the rangers the task of gathering the livestock for the subsistence of his 8,500-man army.[57] Other raids to supply Admiral Saunders's sailors (more than 13,000 of them) were launched in various directions, particularly around Île-aux-Coudres, which served as a naval base of sorts. The detachments periodically returned to the military's stores with hundreds of horned animals, sheep, and pigs left behind by the habitants when they evacuated. Later in the season, they also brought back peas and other legumes. In addition to these authorized levies, the soldiers and sailors violated orders by looting whenever they had an opportunity.[58] The owners' absence meant that the marauders were at leisure to empty back yards and gardens, loot houses, and, with a little luck, make off with other items poorly hidden around the settlements.[59] As General Murray acknowledged in the aftermath of the siege, they had clearly been given free rein: "The plundering kind of war, which has been carried out on this last campaign, had so debauched the soldier, that there was no putting a stop to these [disorders] without very severe punishment."[60]

The enemy soldiers' incursions into the parishes were punctuated by skirmishes with peasants and Indigenous partisans, who either fired on the intruders from hiding places at the edge of the woods or were hunted down before they could shoot. These clashes produced casualties on both sides: British officers' journals report findings of scalped and mutilated corpses along roadsides. Both fascinated and shocked by the ambient barbarity, they held to their received ideas. They believed, for example, that the Canadians were in the habit of disfiguring enemy corpses in Amerindian fashion and decided that it was fair play to repay them in kind, even if the practice revolted them.[61] A digression is necessary here in regard to the rangers, who played a crucial role in sacking and subduing the countryside and must not be confused with the militias and other provincial units. The latter did not participate in the siege of Quebec. The rangers of Wolfe's army were hardened volunteers, New England natives for the most part but recruited directly by Great Britain and maintained at its expense. The six companies were commanded by Major George Scott, a friend of Robert Monckton's who had served in North America since 1753 and could boast of having destroyed several Acadian villages.[62]

At the end of July, before sending his light infantry to attack the parishes, Wolfe told the men that scalping was strictly prohibited unless the enemies were Indigenous or Canadians wearing Indigenous disguise.[63] One might infer from the order that the rangers had indulged in the practice rather freely to that point, but the hypothesis is not verifiable.[64] What can be known is whether the custom of disguising oneself as an Indigenous person was widespread among Canadian militiamen, as the British officers believed. It was not. Not a single reference to the practice is to be found anywhere in the archives, from the beginning of the colony to the end. And if that evidence is insufficient, how to explain the silence of the French army officers, who were quick to observe and criticize local customs, on such a peculiar practice? "It is the custom among the British partisans to wear their hair as the Natives do," wrote one, implying that this custom was not to be found among the Canadians.[65] With so many Indigenous partisans in its camp, the French colony had no need of this stratagem to frighten its enemies. When the colonists disguised themselves as Indigenous people, it was not for purposes of war but to do bad deeds – to steal and loot without being recognized, to put the law off the scent.[66] During the siege of Quebec, the British were harassed by real Indigenous people. Very numerous near Montmorency and between the Etchemin and Chaudière rivers on the south shore, they posed a constant threat at the edges of the camps and to any patrols straying from them. The Canadian holdouts were neither as numerous nor as dangerous. Those who fired their guns from the woods or were caught trying to harvest crops or claim their animals were, in many cases, men who had been found unfit to serve because of age or poor health. It is hard to imagine them in body paint disfiguring an enemy corpse. But by maintaining the fiction, by declaring that the thirty residents of Beaupré who were killed and scalped on 23 August had been dressed as Indians like so many others, the headhunters ensured their own impunity.[67]

After a month of looting and small skirmishes, relations between the occupying army and the countryside deteriorated. This second phase began with a hostage-taking incident near Pointe-Lévy, the location of the batteries that had, since 12 July, been pounding the city with bombs and cannonballs. On the 25th of the month, two detachments commanded by Major John Dalling and Colonel Malcolm Fraser departed, one for Saint-Henri, the other toward Beaumont, with orders to capture the habitants. Dalling brought back 300 prisoners. After two attempts, Fraser returned on the 27th with what was said to be a large number of families.[68] The prisoners, perhaps 500 in total – mainly women, children, old people, and invalids – were put on ships while waiting for their compatriots, relatives, and friends to decide their fate.[69] For these were the terms of the notices that could be found on the church doors in the prisoners' home parishes:

> His Excellency, annoyed at the little attention paid by the habitants of Canada to his notice of the 27th of last month, is resolved not to listen to the humane sentiments that inclined him to succour people blinded by their own misery. The Canadians have shown themselves by their conduct to be unworthy of the advantageous offers he made to them. He has thus given orders to the commander of his light troops, and to the other officers,

to move into the land, there to seize inhabitants and livestock, and to destroy and overturn whatever they see fit. Furthermore, angered at being forced to go to the barbarous extremes for which the Canadians and the Indians their allies have set the example, he intends to wait until 10th August to decide the fate of the prisoners, against whom he shall take reprisals; unless, during this interval, the Canadians should come and submit to the terms of the first notice, and by their submission awaken his clemency and incline him to kindness.[70]

Although the population did not respond to the ultimatum, the prisoners were probably released fairly quickly, as the silence of the sources suggests. Any other solution – a much-feared deportation, for example – would have caused some commotion. Wolfe ultimately opted for physical destruction on a large scale, a more classic, less cumbersome method of intimidation. During a period of six weeks, some thirty parishes and their adjacent strongholds were systematically ravaged and burned. On 6 August, ranger captain Joseph Goreham set sail for Île-aux-Coudres and Baie-Saint-Paul with orders to burn all human habitation beyond the capes all the way to La Malbaie. The punitive expedition extended to Sainte-Anne and Saint-Roch across the river, where the officer collected livestock.[71] Starting in mid-August, the Côte-de-Beaupré, Île d'Orléans, and several parishes in the Côte-du-Sud similarly went up in flames. Night after night, from the cliffs of Quebec and the heights of Beauport, the city and the army watched the spectacle in horror.[72] Further away, over the horizon, Saint-Nicolas and Saint-Antoine had already been ravaged, and in the week after 8 September, fires were lit from one end of the Côte-du-Sud to the other.[73] This was not the ordinary sort of damage done in haste by troops on the march, or the depredation of an occupying army, but a planned operation, carefully and methodically executed by large detachments. Some 500 regulars and rangers spent a week following Captain Alexander Montgomery from Saint-Joachim to Ange-Gardien, torches and axes in hand.[74] The 800 men commanded by George Scott landed at Kamouraska in the early morning hours of 9 September and began a slow march to Cap Saint-Ignace, six parishes upstream, burning everything they encountered along the way, moving inland as necessary. At the end of each day, Scott took methodical note of the numbers of miles travelled and buildings burned.[75] The report by Goreham, who had orders to also destroy the part of the Côte-du-Sud from Saint-Thomas to Beaumont, is not extant.[76]

These expeditions took a heavy toll. On the two islands and on either shore of the river, wooden barns and houses were burned to the ground. Of the stone houses, with their thatched or wooden roofs, all that remained were blackened walls. Only the churches, where the enemy troops could take shelter or seek cover, were spared. Carts and implements were destroyed, fruit trees chopped down, and hundreds of acres of ripe wheat burned.[77] After the intendant's requisitions in early summer and two months of looting by Wolfe's army, the habitants had no livestock left. Moreover, these parishes, which derived much of their subsistence from the river, had lost all their boats along with the fisheries that had occupied the river bank.[78] "If we can't beat them, we shall ruin their country," wrote a British officer in early August.[79] A month later, the deed was done.

The enemy's brutal tactics bore fruit, in particular the treatment reserved for militiamen in battle. It was said that no quarter was given: that the habitants could not, like the soldiers, lower their weapons and become prisoners but were savagely exterminated. Whether or not these generalizations are well-founded is of little import, since the population believed them and acted accordingly.[80] The attitude of the Quebec militia after the defeat of 13 September offers a good example. After two months of bombardment, the city had been reduced to ashes, rubble, and gutted houses. With a mediocre garrison and an inadequate supply of munitions and provisions, it could not bear up under a siege without the support of the army with which it had always maintained close ties. But on the morning of 14 September, the people woke up to find the tents of Beauport empty, the army having fled during the night, leaving them alone to face the British troops camped at the walls and the fleet lying offshore.[81] The townspeople gathered at the office of the civil and criminal lieutenant of the provost court, instated as mayor for the occasion, to deliver a petition to Jean-Baptiste-Nicolas-Roch de Ramezay, the person responsible for the defence of the upper town, in which they hid neither their anger at the general staff nor their terror. The city had been abandoned and all hope was gone, they wrote: "an honourable surrender" would have to be negotiated immediately. Any delay would only increase the enemy's savagery.[82] To a military man, the word "honourable" referred to the honours of war; to the townspeople, it meant saving their lives and keeping their property. Most of the twenty-two merchants who signed this petition were militia officers, and it was in this capacity that they responded to Ramezay on the evening of the 17th when he tried to mobilize his troops to repulse an apprehended landing. He recounted that an adjutant had told him that none of the militiamen wanted to fight. At the same time, the militia officers came to tell him that they were totally unprepared for an attack: "that they were going to return their weapons to the store so that the enemy, on entering the city, would find them unarmed and would not run through them with his sword; that they no longer regarded themselves as soldiers but as townspeople."[83]

Driven by the same sentiments, the urban militia began deserting the city on the 14th to join the army or hunker down in the country, with the flow of exiles increasing night by night. It was not so much the dangers of the siege that drove these artisans and shopkeepers to abandon their families and flee – they had, after all, survived sixty-three days of bombardment – as it was the fear of being taken prisoner. The desertion continued until two days after capitulation; that is, for as long as they lacked the assurance that the victors would not take reprisals against combatants.[84]

Brigadier General George Townshend committed to this in articles 3 and 5 of the capitulation, signed 18 September, but it was not until the 20th, apparently, that these provisions were officially made known to the population, to the beat of a customary drum. The next day, an initial ceremony took place at which the residents of the city and its outskirts laid down their arms and swore oaths of allegiance.[85] To the country people, Monckton sent the following message:

[They] may return to their parishes and take possession of their lands, homes, and belongings, harvest their crops, enjoy their religion without let or hindrance on the part of the English, who are not come to ruin the Canadians, but to give them a taste of the sweetness of just and righteous government, provided that they, for their part, hand over their arms, swear an oath of allegiance, and stay tranquilly in their homes.[86]

"But what property are our habitants to occupy, after the ravages he ordered his men to commit?" exclaimed Jérôme de Foligné, a naval officer who had been assigned to the urban batteries during the siege. He continued:

Only today did we see our poor wives come out of the woods, trailing behind them their little children covered in fly bites, naked, crying with hunger. What a knife blow to women who do not know if they have husbands or where they are, and what assistance they will be able to give their poor children, with the arrival of the season in which they were hard pressed to guarantee it even when they were living comfortably in their homes. The sieges of Jerusalem and Samaria offered no more dreadful spectacle.[87]

Foligné kept a journal whose sober, concise tone stands in marked contrast to this emotional passage. Apart from a letter from the bishop describing the misery of the colony, and in particular that of the refugees from the downriver parishes who wandered the colony in search of relief, his compassionate account is the only one to have survived.[88] Nothing is known about how this population survived the winter.

Much, in contrast, is known about the problems experienced by the British army in the aftermath of its victory. After clearing the streets of rubble and repairing and requisitioning whatever houses were still livable for its 6,000 soldiers, it had to bring in firewood quickly while protecting itself against the French troops stationed on the Jacques-Cartier River. Brigadier Murray, who had become governor of Quebec, tried to extend the zone under his control out to Pointe-aux-Trembles and Saint-Antoine on either side of the river so as to create a vast demilitarized zone upstream of the capital. But the vanguard of Lévis's army stood in the way, and he had to make do with a narrower occupied area around Beauport, Charlesbourg, and Sainte-Foy.[89] Since there was nothing to be derived from the devastated countryside downstream, Murray was counting on these three parishes to provide for the needs of the garrison. He ordered an inventory of their resources and demanded regular cart trips, earthmoving parties, and requisitions of animals, forage crops, provisions, snowshoes, blankets, and so forth.[90] Where it had only recently been tolerated if not encouraged, looting by individual soldiers was now severely punished, and these levies took place in orderly fashion.[91] Isolated and vulnerable, under siege from both winter and the enemy, its circumspect policy is understandable, especially as regards loyalty: the British army needed the habitants' collaboration. Officers visited the parishes collecting weapons and oaths of neutrality. At ceremonies attended by one or more companies, the militiamen stated their names, raised their right hands, and repeated that they:

> Do severally swear, in the presence of Almighty God, that we will not take up arms against George the Second, King of Great Britain &c. &c. or against his troops or subjects; nor give any intelligence to his enemies, directly or indirectly: So Help me GOD.[92]

While the habitants readily submitted to this procedure, few, it seems, felt bound by their oath beyond strict neutrality. Contrary to the British general's expectations, they did not report small movements of colonial partisans who came to seize livestock or harass soldiers on the outskirts of their parishes. When, in February 1760, the habitants of the seigneury of Lévis concealed the presence of a detachment of 400 men, Murray could no longer turn a blind eye and ordered the burning of some fifteen houses near La Chaudière as punishment for this "perfidy."[93] The real test came at the end of April and, to all appearances, the oaths had not really taken hold. How were the British to treat habitants who, answering the call of Vaudreuil and Lévis, had gone to work in the trenches and returned home after the siege was lifted?[94] To punish them all would be to destroy the rural areas around Quebec and thus to weaken the garrison's already precarious position. Murray ruled it out. The peasants, who had been deceived by ruses and stratagems – read the placard of 20 May – were entitled to his clemency. Their sin was great, but punishment was suspended, for the king of England "did not wish to reign over an unpeopled province": let them show themselves worthy of such generosity by staying in their homes and providing no aid to the enemy.[95] Three exemplary punishments, whose symbolism certainly did not escape contemporaries, backed up these exhortations: A parish priest, a seigneur, and the captain of a Saint-Charles militia company were convicted of having induced the habitants to join the French army.[96] The priest, apparently of Charlesbourg parish, was imprisoned; the seigneur of Beauport was dispossessed of all his lands and property; and the militia captain was hanged.[97]

Perhaps 3,000 to 4,000 people had remained in the city or returned to it after capitulation and shared their homes with the British soldiers. On 21 April 1760, a few days before Lévis's army arrived at Quebec, Murray ordered the residents to gather their things and leave. They were not authorized to return before the fall.[98] The measure was not punitive but preventive, for these people had had no opportunity to betray their oath. While the initial evacuation in anticipation of a siege had not in itself been an act of mistrust, its extension had no other justification. On the point of leaving Quebec with his best troops, Murray did not think the weak garrison left behind would be sufficient to keep the population quiet. Other precautions were taken to defend the rearguard in the weeks leading up to departure, including disarming and taking oaths from the residents of Saint-Nicolas, just downriver from La Chaudière.[99]

On 13 July, thirty-two ships, nine floating batteries, and several barges departed for Montreal where the three armies – Haviland's from Lake Champlain, Jeffery Amherst's from Lake Ontario, and Murray's from Quebec – were to meet. Cautiously, the fleet advanced.[100] Wanting to go easy on his rather small contingent, Murray avoided skirmishes by keeping as far as possible from the French troops and artillery massed on the north shore, instead spending time on the now-defenceless south shore, where he proceeded to subdue the parishes. The placard used during this campaign was shorter and more direct than the previous ones: Colonists caught bearing arms would pay with their lives, and the homes and lands of absentees would be burned and ravaged.[101] Between the arrival of the detachment in charge of reconnoitering the area and spreading this message and the execution of the threat, the habitants – those who had taken flight at the sight of the ships and those who were with the army – generally had two days to return to their homes. In the interval, soldiers were permitted to loot abandoned properties. The habitants did not hesitate for long. One by one, the ten parishes spread out between Saint-Antoine and Île Saint-Ignace laid down their arms; some did so spontaneously, so great was their fear.

The fleet drew fire as it sailed by Jacques-Cartier, Deschambault, Batiscan, Trois-Rivières, and Sorel and returned it with cannonballs, but it did not stop. To give his soldiers a chance to stretch their legs after a month of navigation, Murray let them off on islands – first Saint-Ignace and then Sainte-Thérèse – where he was sure the French would not venture. Always prudent, he waited for Bourlamaque's army to vacate Sorel before sending Major Scott and his rangers to burn part of this parish that had been guilty of resistance. On 30 August, it was Varennes's turn to chase off a British reconnaissance party, and the next day no fewer than three battles took place between local militias and the detachment sent by Murray to defeat them. The day produced casualties and some twenty prisoners, whom the general pardoned and sent back to the parish. Between the threat of capital punishment as a method of intimidation and the cold execution of prisoners of war lay a gulf that Murray did not want to cross, hence this magnanimity and the acknowledgment *in extremis* of the militia's military status by virtue of its incorporation into the regulars. According to the new placard published during those days, militiamen caught bearing arms would be transported to Europe with the other soldiers.[102] But the new wording was superfluous: In the grip of panic, the habitants were demobilizing even faster than anticipated.

Varennes laid down its arms on 1 September, and the neighbouring parishes followed suit, with Murray's army bearing down on them and Haviland's coming up from Lake Champlain to take the countryside from behind. After occupying Saint-Jean and Chambly, Haviland sent his rangers to take the hinterlands. Robert Rogers claimed that his men were well received, by the women in particular; this can be doubted given the disposition of this corps and what was happening along the river, at Varennes and elsewhere, where looting, burning, and rape were part and parcel of the occupation.[103] Despite this brutality, contradicting Murray's promises, the habitants apparently preferred to surrender to the British soldiers rather than confront the Iroquois of Amherst's army, who were rumoured to be coming to attack the parishes.[104] From his headquarters at Longueuil, Murray negotiated a peace settlement with the domiciliés on 5 September, sending detachments across the river to collect weapons and administer oaths to the militia. By the time the capitulation was signed, nearly the whole colony had been disarmed.

4. CONFUSION AMONG THE RECRUITS

Let us take another look at the events of 1759 and 1760, this time focusing on the experience of the militia. Their first appearance finds them with the troops, trying to block the invaders' path. The extant data are insufficient to gauge the size of this force as a proportion of the male population with any accuracy. According to the colonial census taken in early 1759, there were 15,229 men of arms-bearing age. But the document itself has not survived, and the memorialists who knew of it believed that it had overstated the available forces.[105] According to my own calculations and those of the leading historians of the period, 10,000–11,000 militiamen took part in the campaigns of 1759. For a population of at most 70,000 weakened by years of war and scarcity, this was an impressive contribution.[106] Recruitment took place without apparent coercion and even with a degree of excitement. "Never was an order received with so much joy and carried out with such exactness," wrote a witness about the 6,000 men who came to defend Quebec.[107] Recruitment outside the occupied territory was still considerable in 1760, but the men's heart was no longer in it and new enlistment methods had to be employed.

Not only was mobilization more intense than in the past, but it also took new forms. The custom of proceeding by successive drafts, and of spreading them out over several parishes so that only a small number of men were taken from each, no longer made sense in a context of all-out war. To expedite the task and lighten the regular officers' burden, entire rural militia companies now moved as units led by their own officers. These officers were mainly lieutenants and ensigns, who were younger and stronger than the militia captains and less necessary to local administration. The best of them were employed as non-commissioned officers for the rest of the campaign. Some militiamen joined the army on their own, but if possible they marched with the soldiers housed in the same parishes, with whom they were *ipso facto* integrated, and were commanded by the same officers.[108] However, since the army was housed in the côtes while the naval companies were clustered in the cities and on the west end of Montreal Island,[109] the army officers had command over the rural militias. This procedure stemmed from the regulation of June 1759, although it was not applied uniformly before 1760. Much stricter than the old system, it excluded special favours and explains why recruitment stayed strong that year despite the general aversion to leaving the parish.

With the regulars, the militiamen were called on to defend the colony's borders: remote in early 1759 but steadily moving closer to the settlements. Not a single defensive operation in those two years ended in anything other than retreat or surrender. This series of setbacks sapped morale. As we have seen, it had begun in 1758 with the fall of Fort Frontenac and the evacuation of Fort Duquesne, but this was not enough to make the colony abandon its old positions. Pushed back to Fort Machault, François-Marie Le Marchand de Lignery, commander of the Ohio forces, received major reinforcements in the spring of 1759 with orders to harass the enemy and retake the lost ground. But on 24 July, as they hastened to Fort Niagara to relieve the troops under siege from the British army, his troops were decimated at the Belle-Famille ambush.[110] Niagara surrendered the next day after a twenty-day siege.[111] The decision by the Six Nations (Iroquois League) to break the old treaty and rally to the British, coupled with the defection of the allied nations, played a decisive role in these events and took the colony by surprise.[112] At Lake Champlain, the retreats were strategic. Facing an army nearly three times as large, Fort Carillon was evacuated on 26 July under cover of night and then burned to the ground. Three days later, Bourlamaque blew up Fort Saint-Frédéric and moved his troops onto Île-aux-Noix at the mouth of the Richelieu.[113] Although consistent with Vaudreuil's plan, this retreat was nonetheless traumatic for its participants, who had to destroy the forts they had built and long defended. Then came the shockwaves set off by the 13 September defeat on the Plains of Abraham, Montcalm's death, the routing of the Beauport army, and the capital's subsequent surrender. The 1760 campaign opened with the 28 April victory at the walls of Quebec: an unconsummated success wiped out in mid-May by the arrival of British ships, forcing the French to lift the siege and destroy their own fleet as the British gave chase.[114] At the end of August, the two forts recently built to guard the western and southern frontiers surrendered almost simultaneously after more than a week of continual bombardment. Fort Lévis at the head of the St Lawrence River rapids capitulated, while Bougainville's army managed to leave Île-aux-Noix under cover of night.[115] The other forces – Dumas's north of the river, Bourlamaque's to the south, and La Corne's at the foot of the rapids – disintegrated without managing to slow the march of the invaders.

The combatants can be presumed to have had a rather hazy image of the military situation. Nevertheless, it must have been enriched by details, sensations, and curious events in which lived experience intermingled with reports of what was happening elsewhere, conveyed by rumours and officers' speeches.[116] Remoteness and slow mail allowed for the spread of sensational rumours, such as the alleged assassination of Louis XV and the captivity of the Queen of Hungary, announced by an Iroquois at the Niagara garrison in May 1757.[117] News at first arrived piecemeal, wrote an officer, with truth generally preceded by falsehood.[118] It was up to the local commandant to filter the intelligence and present military events, whether

European or colonial, in a favourable light so as to preserve troop morale. As Montcalm explained about a pastoral letter deemed too explicit: "It is no good telling simple habitants that the English have at least six times as many troops as we do, and that they can invade Canada from all sides."[119] This principle had hitherto been observed, but in the final campaigns, the officers could no longer stem the tide of negative information about the ongoing operations, the alarming news from the parishes. In vain, the officers at Carillon withheld the news of Quebec's surrender for a few days, no doubt in the hope of a miraculous refutation.[120] As much as Vaudreuil might dream of punishing messengers whose tongues wagged too freely, the troops got wind of everything – true and false rumours, reasons for holding the line or giving up.[121] At times, rumours took the form of a wild expectancy, as at Jacques-Cartier in March 1760. The news that Murray's army had been annihilated by disease was received with joy by the troops and with skepticism by Dumas, their commandant: "I think it politic to credit this news," he wrote to Vaudreuil, "so I am doing my best to do so, but between you and me, Sir, I must say that we should be on guard against the exaggerated reports of a people blinded by its hardships and desires."[122] More often a cause of despair than rejoicing, rumours drowned out the voices of the officers, who tried against all odds to reassure and retain their men.

Militiamen began deserting the Beauport and Île-aux-Noix camps in August 1759. The phenomenon gathered speed, and by 1760 it was out of control. Bands, whole companies left the army, joined by their officers in some cases. Until then, desertion had been a matter of individuals or small groups and limited to the regulars. It was an endemic scourge on the frontiers, where soldiers could escape their pursuers by covering the short distance to the enemy camps; even the most rebellious of militiamen were not tempted to follow. Much as they might have liked to go home, the distance between the outposts and the colony, plus the dangers and difficulties of travel, kept them from doing so. The few who attempted it were quickly captured and punished by being sent to a fort in the Great Lakes region for a long stay. The wave of desertion reported in late summer 1759 was thus a new phenomenon, and it was due to several factors. On the one hand, reasons for leaving the army – fatigue, fear, discouragement, desire to protect one's harvest and family – multiplied; on the other, flight was now facilitated by proximity to one's home parish. Militiamen in the government of Quebec who were assigned to the defence of Lake Champlain learned that the British were ravaging their homes and began deserting after the retreat from Carillon upon reaching Île-aux-Noix.[123]

The general staff found itself at a loss as to how to curtail this peculiar form of desertion. According to the ordinances, soldiers who abandoned their corps without permission risked the death penalty, but since they were rarely caught, at least in this colony, executions were sporadic and mainly served exemplary purposes.[124] If meted out to deserting militiamen, wrote one officer, such punishment would have resulted in a slaughter, since they were both numerous and easy to find in their respective parishes.[125] Thus, the capital punishment measure decreed in 1760 would go unenforced. The governor had to give in to Lévis's arguments, but in his mind and in actual fact – he remained the final judge – it had only been a means of intimidation.[126] As Bourlamaque argued several times, particularly at the end of August when trying in vain to curtail the mass desertion of militiamen and of soldiers married in the colony, the threat would have no effect unless backed up by exemplary punishment. With not one deserter having been executed, he wrote, "a mockery has been made of the proclamation I made."[127] Indeed, it was not without a degree of irony that the habitants greeted the threats brandished by the despairing officers. "The people of Ste. Croix refuse guard duty," wrote Dumas on 27 June 1760. "I threatened to order their homes burned. They answered that it was as well to be burned by us as by the enemy, and that he would burn everything without fail if we were to retreat. This is all very embarrassing."[128] And what punishment might be reserved for militia officers who deserted with their men, to the great consternation of Lévis, Dumas, and the other officers, instead of putting a stop to the stampede? Divided from the soldiers by birth or social pretentions and by custom, the regular officers sided with the hierarchy and against the mutineers. But a captain at Batiscan named Villeneuve, in refusing to hand over seven militiamen of the parish wanted for desertion, acted neither as a military officer nor as a government representative but as the leader of the local peasantry.[129]

The numbers of militiamen willingly fighting on the frontiers with the troops plummeted after the fall of Quebec. The considerations mentioned earlier in regard to wheat and cattle apply equally well to military service.[130] While the habitants had never acquired the habit of individually or collectively resisting orders, they departed for the front with feet dragging, under the close watch of the army, and deserted at the first opportunity. Militiamen "of good will," those who fought alongside the soldiers of their own accord, were a minority. In the spring of 1760, they accounted for a third of the recruits; by August, as the three British armies were converging on Montreal, only a handful of stalwarts remained.[131] A man named Bray from Les Cèdres was one of them. On 15 August, when his son returned home after deserting from Fort Lévis, just upriver from the parish, he returned the young man to his post "to do his duty," as Commandant Pouchot wrote, moved by this story – and even more so by the fact that the son was killed a few days later during the siege.[132]

12

Tangible and Intangible Issues

To this point, my emphasis has been on describing the conditions under which militiamen were recruited and served, as well as their attitudes insofar as the documentation provides any insight into them. I have deliberately put off until the end the question that arises throughout this study: Why did the habitants accept this military role? Why did they fight? For beyond occasional attempts to dodge recruitment or dangerous jobs, beyond cases of insubordination, muttering, and seditious remarks, the militia – the rural militia in particular – behaved with great docility on the whole.

Of course, there was hardly any choice: The coercive nature of the enterprise, the presence of troops to bolster the officers' authority, and the justified fear of punishment should not be underestimated. But it still deserves acknowledging that the habitants served for sixteen years without generally having to be coerced at gunpoint, that some of them volunteered, and that on some occasions they showed much good will.

The question is not one that has concerned Canadian historians of the period, who have accepted the militia's role in the war as a fact needing no explanation.[1] It was an instinct of sorts: for some a patriotic one, for others a matter of pure belligerence, for a few perhaps both at once, depending on the circumstances. What have clearly been lacking are efforts to escape the rut of popular psychology and to situate the problem in its context – the social relations of the day – even if this does not lead to an immediate solution.

Resistance is favoured terrain for those who interrogate history. Any protest movement, by revealing the latent tensions in a society, lays bare the texture of that society, the logic driving these phenomena. Obedience has attracted less attention and is difficult to decode. I, for one, do not believe it to be the negative image of resistance, with one reflecting will and conscience, the other passivity and mindlessness.

The militia's acquiescence was not a reflex inscribed within a tradition of cheerful submission to the tutelary authorities. The peasants were capable of putting up various forms of passive resistance to the demands of those who dominated them; they were undeterred by legal clashes over tithes, seigneurial rights, or corvées, for example.[2] Yet this much more onerous human levy for military purposes appears to have aroused much less opposition – either that, or little means were found to express it.

The habitants went to war because they were forced to and at the same time found enough grounds for doing so that the duty appeared acceptable. These justifications differed in importance and exerted greater or lesser influence depending on the individual and the year. In this chapter, I present various factors that could have influenced the habitants' behaviour to varying degrees, as well as others that do not appear to pertain. Succinctly put, it is an inventory of probable and improbable motivations. Among the latter is the prospect of material gain that the militiamen might have associated with the looting of enemy villages and forts. This motive does not appear to have been decisive: no more, for that matter, than the information, or rather disinformation, put about by the authorities. If not, then was their compliance driven by loyalty to the king or by a nascent feeling of Canadian identity? Without dismissing patriotism outright, of which loyalty to the king would have been a form, there are reasons to downplay its influence. What remained was fear. The fear of reprisals by the British, whom the French colonies had attacked periodically over three-quarters of a century, undoubtedly weighed into the militias' decision to march. However, the fear of a vengeful God, present in religious discourse as of February 1759, surely had the effect of discouraging them. But until that time, the clergy played its role of bolstering royal authority.

1. MATERIAL INCENTIVES: PROFITS AND PRIZES

Pecuniary gain is the primary factor that attracts men to armies: a recruitment bonus and an annual salary, with the possibility of a raise for those who attain non-commissioned officer status. Such

considerations induced the young men of Massachusetts to enlist in
the militia for one or more campaigns. It offered them six months or
more of guaranteed wages equivalent to those of a labourer, as well
as a bonus and the prospect of promotion. Under these conditions,
military service was just another way of saving up a nest egg in
the years before marriage.[3] Sons of Canadian habitants had similar
motivations for seeking temporary jobs off the family farm, as farm-
workers or as canoeists for fur traders, or again as sailors and fishermen in the employ of Quebec merchants. The war disrupted these
ordinary mechanisms whereby young people achieved independence
and made provision for the future, but it did not substitute any other
source of income. In chapter 3, I discussed the meagre, always uncertain pay offered to certain categories of recruits, particularly in the
Great Lakes region. The mass of militiamen who followed the army
received nothing at all, apart from rations and a mediocre kit. Promotions through the ranks of the militia, which were not necessarily
tied to active duty, had no monetary value.

That left looting, which, in the North American wars, was not
just tolerated but encouraged.[4] Was this compensation sizeable
enough that money lust can be considered to have been a significant
inducement to fight? There had been a time when the colony's wars
were semi-private affairs offering handsome profits to expeditionary
corps. For the clearest example, the men who accompanied Iberville
to Newfoundland and Hudson Bay in the late seventeenth century
did not come home empty-handed. Similar motivations probably
inhabited the hundred "volunteers" who went off with Paul Marin
to conquer Acadia in 1745. The detachment, bolstered by 500–600
Amerindians, boarded two enemy ships in Port-Royal harbour, and
a prisoner described what ensued. The men encircled the prizes
piled up on the bank and lots were drawn. Later, the Amerindians
would return this property to the Acadians. There was also a long
discussion between the commandant and the Amerindians on how
to divide up the prisoners.[5] The two ships – making up the lion's
share of the prize – were brought back to Quebec and sold for the
king at a profit, helping to offset the costs of the campaign.[6] This
account shows that things had changed since the time of the great
adventurers. Henceforth, the administration bore the entire cost of
the operations, and officers were accountable for items of any value
seized from the enemy.[7] In the wake of sieges and other fighting, the
Amerindians demanded and obtained prisoners in addition to those

whom they brought back from their own expeditions. The treasurer paid them 123 livres a head when they decided to hand these captives over to the king, and more could presumably be earned by selling them as servants to the officers and townspeople of Quebec and Montreal.[8] Other prisoners, regulars in particular, were sent straight to prison. So while the allies were able to keep prisoners in exchange for a ransom, the other combatants did not have this opportunity.

As to scalps, those brought back by the Amerindians fetched thirty-one livres each, sometimes a bit more in the Great Lakes region. As with prisoners, these bounties were not offered to combatants of European origin; for this period at least, store accounts and the colony's expense slips (*bordereaux*) offer no reason to doubt this.[9] If militiamen did practise scalping, as one author asserts, the act would have been gratuitous, but there is no serious testimony to this effect.[10]

All that remained was looting plain and simple, and the militia, like the soldiers for that matter, indulged in the practice when the opportunity arose. But there was little to take from frontier villages and forts, and the Amerindians, generally more numerous on these expeditions, helped themselves first. The need for a rapid retreat, so that the enemy had no time to send reinforcements in pursuit of the attackers, forbade the men from weighing themselves down with booty. There was more destruction and waste than profit in the attacks by Léry on Fort Bull and by Picoté de Belestre on the Palatine village, which figure among the four or five largest free-for-alls of the final war.[11] When the army was strong enough to protect the rear, it could loot at will, as it did after the capture of forts Ontario, George, and Oswego in August 1756 or that of Fort William Henry the next summer.[12] Instead of organizing a fair distribution of the loot as was the practice in the British army, the officers let the troops fight it out.[13] There is no way of knowing what each of the 1,500 militiamen present at Oswego and the 3,000 present at William Henry was able to take home. A good musket, shoes, or a coat for the nimblest; provisions; rum to celebrate the victory ... No one scrupled at removing the clothes from a corpse, as long as he did not expose himself to enemy fire.

All things considered, the lure of loot helped the officers recruit small groups of volunteers for a few bold enterprises, but it is not certain that the take met their expectations. For the mass of militiamen, such windfalls were too few, and not profitable enough to make up for the time spent, to break even.

The real spoils of war went to those who did not fight in it. This is obviously true for the purveyors, the big contractors and their subcontractors. But the profits were spread around more broadly, in the cities especially. In the early days, country people got their share as well. The preparations surrounding the Acadian campaigns of 1744 and 1746 added up to a small fortune for the parishes of the Côte-du-Sud, downriver from Quebec, through which the convoys passed.[14] These spinoffs probably compensated in part for the ill effects of the mobilization. A habitant who could rent horses and a cart to the king, or who could fetch a higher price for his wheat, perhaps resigned himself more readily to watching his sons depart – as long as they returned, as long as good money was paid for the services, as long as the harvest was abundant: in a word, as long as everything went well. But it all went sour: service turned into corvées, sales into requisitions, money into worthless paper. Under the circumstances, the word compensation inaccurately describes what the rural families who bore the brunt of this huge mobilization got out of it. Regardless of the angle from which the question is addressed, the prospect of material gain had little to do with the good will of the militia.[15]

The reasons why the habitants willingly did military duty must therefore have been different. Let us begin with the ones put forward by the military authorities.

2. INFORMATION

The manipulation of news was one of the means used by the government to keep up public morale and stimulate the militiamen's good will. They and the regulars were always the first to be informed, at the reviews and the assemblies held in the camps. It was crucial to give them the impression that the administration was keeping them abreast of the news; that nothing could be hidden from the colony's faithful defenders; and that any message from the king or his ministers was addressed specifically to them and should be the object of their greatest concern. Couriers were dispatched to meet detachments announcing the arrival of a ship and whatever news it might carry. The apparent excitement with which this news was conveyed counted for as much as its content in cementing the union between governors and governed and their shared attachment to the royal personage. These speeches have left no traces in the archives. The absence of a printing press, and hence official gazettes and placards, means that historians would have no inkling of what the public was told were it not for the surviving series of highly politicized pastoral letters.[16] There was surely some distance, in tone at least, between what was read to the faithful from on high and what the army officers said, for not many members of the general staff could rival the bishop for rhetoric. But they shared the same goals and agreed on what ought to be published.

The war of 1744–49 was presented to the colonists, essentially from a European standpoint, as a just war undertaken to support "an Emperor whose estates are cruelly ravaged," "the restoration of a prince despoiled of his estates." The five *Te Deums* punctuating this period made much of the victories in Europe. They told of the victories at Nice, Montalbano, Villafranca (Villefranche-sur-Mer), and Metz; Fontenoy and its aftermath, with the fall of Tournai, Bruges, Oudenaarde, and the ports at Ostend and Nieuwpoort; and the other memorable conquests in Flanders and Italy, the list of which was accompanied by very specific details: length of siege, enemy numbers, etc.[17] The letter from the king describing the siege of Tournai, read out with the pastoral letter of 17 July 1746, rounds out the list of these political lectures. Besides a brief allusion to the arrival of a naval escort to "shelter us from the ambitious designs of our neighbours" and another to the threat "looming over a considerable location in this diocese," which the bishop chose to leave unnamed, the people learned nothing through official channels of what was happening on their doorstep, nothing about the fall of Louisbourg, the rumblings of revolt among the nations of the Great Lakes region, or the failure of the Duc d'Anville's enterprise.

From 1755 to late 1758, the pastoral letters continued to observe the same discretion and to evince the same enthusiasm for feats of military prowess, but the angle of view had moved from Europe to North America. The bishop briefly mentioned the French victories in the Mediterranean, the successes against Prussia and Hanover, and it was via a letter from the king that the faithful learned the details of the Fall of Minorca. By contrast, victories in the colony were now amply discussed, with plenty of figures provided. Everyone was to know the extraordinary attributes of a general capable of planning such bold actions and of the officers who carried them out, not to mention the bravery of the soldiers and militiamen. These descriptions, at times remarkably precise (one includes the diameter of the mortars), should not be regarded as mere flights of oratory. The pastoral letters in fact superimposed an official, definitive version on other, probably less high-flown versions of popular origin. It was important always to minimize French losses with respect to the enemy's or to assert the auspicious long-term consequences of an expedition ridiculed by wags.[18] Seven *Te Deums* were sung in the churches of the colony during this period, six to celebrate local successes and one at the behest of the king in celebration of the Minorca victory and in gratitude that the assassination attempt against him had come to nothing.[19] While military setbacks – in Acadia in 1755 and at Louisbourg, Gaspé, and forts Frontenac and Duquesne in 1758 – were minimized, the authorities quickly perceived the hay that could be made out of the deportation of the Acadians.

In 1759, the episcopal discourse changed radically. No longer patterned on the government's line, the last pastoral letters unabashedly turned their back on politics. The hour of atonement and truth had come. The bishop "should have gone into fewer details about the danger in which the colony finds itself," wrote Montcalm.[20] Through thick and thin, the military authorities had continued to hide the colony's defeats and to offer the people, the troops first and foremost, reasons to hold out. At the Carillon camp in September 1759, the news of Quebec's capitulation "was kept secret for several days."[21] In early June 1760, Vaudreuil unhesitatingly reported to the militiamen that the French advantage over Prussia and England had now been cemented, that the adversary hunkered down at Quebec could no longer expect relief, and that the colony had ample supplies of provisions, munitions, and artillery to fend him off if he dared come out. "As you see, Sir, the colony is reaching the end of its ordeal."[22] And in order for these encouraging remarks to have the intended effect, it was necessary, as he wrote to one officer, to punish couriers and other persons who spoke indiscreetly, for it was important that all the news "be an impenetrable secret," at least until it reached him.[23]

But in reality, all these precautions were a pitiful dam trying to contain a flood of information washing over the colony. News from abroad came in from everywhere at once, brought by ship's crews and fishermen, recruits and engagés, Indigenous allies who continually crossed borders, Acadian refugees, deserters and British prisoners walking around freely in the colony, soldiers and militiamen returning from outposts or from prisons in New York and Boston.

The news was muddled and distorted, telling of the pretender to the English and Scottish thrones who haunted Britain; the adventures of the Queen of Hungary; the assassination of the king of France, reported by an Iroquois; shipwrecks, privateers, revolutions about to erupt in Pennsylvania or New England; and on and on.[24] Assemblies of troops and militiamen aided the spread of this disparate and bizarre information, which was then taken over by public opinion and turned into a popular version of current affairs. Nothing that happened in the colony eluded public curiosity; the government might rail against "the multitude of letters coming by the post, full of false news," but it could not prevent the people from discussing alleged Indigenous conspiracies or the officers' treachery or brutality.[25] "Rumours," writes Jean Delumeau, "are born into a context of pervasive worry; they are a by-product of the mental preparation done by people who perceive themselves to be facing a convergence of multiple threats or hardships with cumulative effects." At times, they take the form of mad expectancy; most often, they embody an expectation of disaster.[26] Indeed, the bad news – the real news – spread like a powder train and hit harder. "Extraordinary ferment" was roiling the various contingents of militiamen in 1759 and 1760. Before hardship can be accepted, it must be explained, and given the circumstances, it did not take much imagination to believe in a conspiracy.[27]

The obfuscations and lies of the general staff could not keep tongues from wagging; indeed, it may be supposed that, quite the contrary, they awakened the distrust and rancour of the people, who had every reason to believe that they were being duped – tricked into fighting a war they could not win.

3. LOYALTY AND IDENTITY[28]

Yet I do not think that the colonists were insensitive to patriotic exhortations or that the evocation of French victories and the sacred ties binding them to the king left them indifferent. But neither do I believe in the existence of a shared colonial identity transcending social divides and pitting the Canadians against the French. The question of Canadian loyalty is not straightforward. Often ignored by historians of the French regime, it makes a sudden appearance in narratives of the events immediately preceding the Conquest. The militias' abdication, in the throes of defeat and terror, takes on a political meaning for some commentators, looking to them as the logical culmination of a long-standing divide between colony and metropole. By dint of stressing the specificity of colonial society, these historians are led to conclude that it had a clear awareness of that specificity. It is a big logical leap, but since the problem is never posed explicitly, the interpretation seems unassailable. The fog enveloping this question has to do with two factors. On the one hand, it never appears in the writings of contemporary observers, and since these writings have always been the primary source for New France's political history, that history is condemned to miss what those observers left out, either because they did not know it or because they chose to keep it quiet. On the other hand, the idea of a cultural and emotional break from France, and that of an embryonic nation developing in the mid-eighteenth century, are the foundations of nationalist history in Quebec. Like the American historians of yesteryear – who projected the shadow of the Revolution on the period leading up to it, reading portents of 1776 into everything they studied – French-Canadian historiography looked to the French regime for the roots of the particularisms it valued, when in fact these phenomena derived from later developments. Furthermore, the notion that the Canadians became disaffected with France early on has the advantage of softening the blow of the Conquest, and this might partly explain the favour in which this interpretation is held by English-speaking historians.

In the following example, is Canadian identity really at issue, or is it something else? In the spring and summer of 1747, the governor employed militiamen from the Quebec region to stand guard at a makeshift camp where hundreds of British prisoners were detained. A prisoner reported that "several peasants did not scruple to let us know that they would rally to the British cause in the event of an offensive against the colony, rather than lose their property, since they have lost interest in old France."[29] Such an attitude seems plausible and jibes with my understanding of country wisdom. Together with the defeatism of the Quebec townspeople in September 1759 and the mass desertions of September 1759 to September 1760, it gives a glimpse of a people looking out exclusively for their material interests. Read through the nationalist gauze in which history has wrapped these events, however, it confirms the idea of a total, decades-old divide between Canadians and French, colony and metropole.

But this historiography is mistaken. To put things in their place, it is first necessary to dispense with the hazy, artificial notion lying behind the word "Canadian." Ethnic characterizations, always pernicious, are particularly inappropriate in the case of such a small, underdeveloped colonial society. It need hardly be said that no common cause existed in the colony that might have made different interest groups coalesce into a larger collective awareness. Other colonial populations, later in the century, secured popular assent for a realistic economic agenda and a degree of administrative autonomy and on this basis succeeded in taking their distance from the metropole. Canadian society was just an assemblage of factions, individual interests existing as a function of their positioning within the French empire. One's birthplace, whether in Canada or elsewhere, counted for much less than the place one occupied in the metropole's commercial, governmental, and religious networks. Local control, vexations, and favouritism divided people instead of uniting them, and their only counterweight was protection and backing solicited from across the Atlantic. For the upper crust of this society, the presence of France was palpable. As people whose interests were inseparable from their sentiments, they could not perceive themselves as anything but Frenchmen, loyal subjects of the king. And their attachment to the land where they had made their careers and raised their families did not vitiate this allegiance: on the contrary, it strengthened it.

At first sight, the lower classes had less robust reasons for loyalty to France and the king. Like everywhere else, the world of the peasant was confined: family, property, and parish formed its primary boundaries; material security was a matter of labour and patient planning. From nothing, nothing would come. If rural society tended to turn in on itself this way, it was simultaneously solicited and invaded by experiences and institutions of external origin, and these too were incorporated into its worldview. Why should these influences have reached Quebec and stopped there? How could the habitants have recognized the legitimacy of officers who spoke and acted for the monarchy if they considered it a foreign entity? Because it was a symbolic relationship, distance was more or less immaterial, and there is no reason that the Canadian peasant would not have shared a political faith in the king's benevolence with his Auvergnat counterpart. In one instance, the habitants of Pointe-à-la-Caille, embroiled in a dispute with their seigneur, appealed to Versailles after exhausting their legal remedies in the colony, and it was only natural for them to go over the heads of the colonial judges and administration in this way.[30] Such spontaneous trust was cultivated by the speeches of the priests and administrators and by the urban celebrations that commemorated each happy event in the royal family, reports of which also reached the countryside. Even in the backwoods, St Louis was feasted noisily and sumptuously.[31] A provider in time of need, a defender in time of war, the image of the king offered for public consumption was the same in the colony as in the realm and elicited the same sentiments. France was also a place of origin, one whose memory had been passed down from generation to generation in the stories and songs woven around its history and geography. As collected in twentieth-century Quebec, this folk-loric corpus remains astonishing in its breadth and richness.[32] All by itself, it would suffice to refute the argument of an early break with, and loss of, the original culture. Even though the rural population was reproducing itself without outside assistance by the start of the eighteenth century, the continued integration of small numbers of immigrants into the côtes kept them open to outside influences. The parishes, nearly all of them strung out along the same highway, were stopping points where strangers, bearers of news, kept curiosity about Old France alive. Cultural transformations always proceed slowly, and the lifestyle of the majority of habitants was not such as to favour their acceleration.

Without question, the rural areas of Canada had peculiarities that distinguished them from their counterparts elsewhere in the realm. In Quebec historiography, however, all such disparities are brought down to a simple dichotomous model: on the Canadian side, freedom of action, relative comfort, absence of privileges and taxes, social harmony; on the French side, servitude, abject poverty, oppressive privileges and taxes. Given these circumstances, we are told, the colonists must surely have appreciated their situation and shown indifference or even hostility toward all things French. It is beyond the scope of this book to review each of the propositions from which this model is built; let us say that on the whole, they do not stand up to scrutiny. But even if they did have some basis, it still could not be confidently asserted that this was the habitants' view of the matter. How did they perceive these differences and resemblances? What was their point of reference? Can we even be sure that their worldview was influenced by these sorts of comparisons? All these questions are destined to remain unanswered. We must accept this and above all refrain from taking our own deductions for emanations from the mind of the people.

In the case of the militiamen, three specific questions, linked to feelings of identity and loyalty, must be asked: How did they perceive their relations with the colonial command structure? What was their attitude vis-à-vis the French battalions? And how did they conceive of the enemy? The first question can be answered with some assurance on the basis of what is known about the structure of Canadian society and the procedures of government and impressment. It was a hierarchical society in which military officers held the highest rank, peasants the lowest. War accentuated these social divides by transforming hitherto distant, perhaps even non-existent interactions into hierarchies of direct subordination. The obligations represented by requisitions and recruitment combined to create a feeling of mistrust vis-à-vis all forms of command, and the abuses and scandals swirling around the administration of provisions by the intendancy were bound to spill over onto the military government as a whole, widening the gap even further. We do not know the habitants' feelings toward their governments prior to this time – perhaps a mixture of fear and respect. But there is no doubt that fear now took over, and respect for the intendant and his circle evaporated. Whatever the various affinities that ran deep within society, the peasants did not benefit from them – they were simply the ones forced to hand over their food.

As a result, it is my belief that relations between governors and governed in New France were at their lowest ebb in 1759–60. It beggars belief that the habitants, even as they rejected the intendant and the officers responsible for the requisitions and distributions, somehow retained boundless admiration for Vaudreuil, their general, the first governor of the colony to be born in Canada. Did this appointment raise the spirits of officers who were waiting to be shown more favour? Did it hold out the hope of faster promotions? Without a doubt. Did the population as a whole feel a little proud that the king had bestowed this honour on a man of the colony? Perhaps. But that the habitants valued the man's birthplace so much as to confound their interests with the governor's seems impossible.

"I flatter myself that I have won the hearts, the confidence, and the sensibilities of the colonists," wrote Vaudreuil.[33] Why should he have taken this for granted? Presence and bravery are the primary leadership qualities that command soldiers' respect, and Vaudreuil was a general who had never been to war, whom the minister even forbade from going to the forts.[34] If, instead of taking Vaudreuil at his word, we inquire as to the reasons why the militiamen might have wanted to serve under him, there are none. Being a Canadian did not by itself earn him the militia's confidence.[35] Indeed, not a single officer from the colony distinguished himself in this war without heroes. Montcalm? At least it can be said that he was present. The militiamen obeyed their officers, but there is no indication that their obedience was diminished in any way when, on occasion, they were commanded by a French army officer.

We do not know if the susceptibilities that divided the officers of one corps from the other translated into acts and words in the presence of their men, nor how the pitched battle between Vaudreuil and Montcalm was perceived among the rank and file. These personal rivalries surely did not escape public notice, but neither were they very likely to retain people's attention what with the problems of the moment. There is no reason why the habitants should have taken sides in these quarrels, although what they knew of them may have sapped their confidence in the hierarchy. That said, the militiamen surely had no way to get a clear view of what was happening on the ground, hence no basis on which to criticize orders. Reflection would come in hindsight. The chaos characterizing the command structure under which the militias served was bound to provoke feelings of insecurity, and this state of confusion gave way to defeatism when the enemy won the day.[36]

As to the militias' attitude toward the French battalions, there are no specific indications in the archives. The militiamen were certainly directly affected by the presence of the French troops, who represented both a reassuring military force and an onerous burden for their families. Until 1755, only the cities had been called on to billet soldiers. This imposition came down on the countryside for the first time at a juncture when the peasants were also squeezed by recruitment and requisitions. According to a few brief, rare accounts by officers, the peasants and their guests got along well together, and this version garners support from a number of marriages between soldiers and colonial women. But these loves did not necessarily sprout up out of a medium of perfect harmony. In fact, nothing at all is known about how these arrangements worked, since habitants' grievances were routed to the commissaries or subdelegates, whose offices left no archives.[37] Even supposing that the soldiers were

angels, the obligation to share cramped quarters for six months or
more, and to feed these guests in the final two winters, added up to a
considerable burden that not everyone accepted out of the goodness
of his or her heart.[38] This burden must have been particularly odious
to militiamen forced to serve in the garrisons all winter long while
soldiers occupied their homes.

4. FEAR OF REPRISALS

There are even fewer accounts that can give us some idea of how
the population felt about the enemy. This silence is perhaps indic-
ative of a rather ambiguous stance that cannot readily be squared
with reflexive anglophobia. I will set aside the position of certain
Montreal merchant-outfitters who were probably torn between
their good business relations with Albany merchants and their loyalty to the French cause, especially given that they bore much of the
brunt of the military government's decisions in the final years. But
their position remains a matter of conjecture, and one should avoid
projecting the highly favourable opinions expressed about the new
regime after 1760 onto the years preceding the Conquest.[39] What
must be discerned are the sentiments of the public, which would
have been shared by the majority of militiamen. A large number of
former British subjects had settled in the colony since the beginning
of the war. Arriving largely as deserters, they had become artisans
or labourers in the cities and villages and in some cases colonists
in the côtes. They testified in various criminal trials as either defendants or witnesses, and the impression one derives from their depositions, and those of their neighbours and acquaintances, is that of an
overall integration into the community. Their ethnic status does not
appear to have aroused any particular antagonism.[40]

I also read the accounts published by prisoners who were taken to
Canada by their Indigenous captors and came into contact with habitants while there. This research proved disappointing. These works
conform to the rules of a literary genre in which pride of place is
given to white–Indigenous relations and a spiritual lesson is derived
from the hardships imposed by providence. This being the motive,
time spent working in colonists' homes or occasional encounters
with them are of too little importance to merit the author's comment.[41] There is, moreover, a large measure of fabulation in some
of these accounts. When they turn their attention to public attitudes

and behaviours toward outsiders, we learn little from the rather ordinary behaviour they describe. According to several mutually consistent accounts by British prisoners held at Quebec from 1745 to 1747, the population was generally indifferent, but when the prisoners were gathered on the square after their prison burned down, the crowd turned hostile, holding them responsible for the disaster.[42] Another captive, describing the festivities at Montreal after the capture of Oswego, writes of how some people made mocking remarks about an enemy so easily defeated.

On both sides, the colonial authorities did their best to inflame public opinion. The authorities of Canada emphasized the odious yoke weighing upon the British colonists, squeezed by taxation, impressed into the militia under threat of beatings.[43] Until 1756, no more specific arguments were available to whip up hatred. The official discourse on the British side, backed up by newspaper propaganda, was more substantial and may well have been more effective. Apart from political considerations and the climate of holy war against Papism, the authorities strove to fan the flames of vengeance, stirring up the crowds by evoking the massacres and depredations perpetrated against the British settlements since 1745 and by reviving those of the previous century. Yet, according to Fred Anderson, it should not be blindly assumed that this official discourse reflected the sentiments of the American colonists, that the soldiers who came from their ranks were motivated by vengeance.[44]

While it is true that atrocities were a common denominator in this century-old conflict, they were highly unequally divided between the two camps. In the past, Canada had suffered much less from terrorism, and the recrudescence of hostilities left its countryside practically untouched for quite some time, while the adversary's frontier villages were laid waste. How was this reality perceived by the population?

With distance and with documents in hand, it is easy for the historian to assert, for example, that Canada conducted an offensive war from 1744 to 1748 and that the few Mohawk and Flemish incursions onto its territory were trifles. But the habitants had no reason to believe they were safe, and the war manoeuvres of this period surely looked to them like defensive measures directed at an enemy ready to attack them at any time.[45] The notion of reprisals was certainly not extraneous to this fear. All the militiamen had watched prisoners marching by, trailing children behind them, and the habitants of the cities and riverside parishes were accustomed to the spectacle of men parading through town brandishing scalps hung on hooks. Vengeance, "an eye for an eye," is not an abstract notion but a form of conduct perfectly familiar to the popular mentality. Serious conflicts were resolved in precisely this way. The habitants, as both participants and witnesses, found themselves embroiled in a very serious conflict that could easily go badly for them without warning.[46] Strictly speaking, the placards posted by the enemy in the parishes of Île d'Orléans and other Quebec locales in 1759, evoking acts of barbarity committed by the Canadians and their allies, would appear to have missed their mark, but even though these habitants had probably never taken part in such expeditions, their conscience was not clear, and the veiled threat did not escape them.[47] The idea that it was now their turn to be massacred, that their families would not escape the typical fate of the losers, heightened the panic felt in Montreal and its rural parishes the following year. The Amerindians were rumoured to be advancing with Amherst's army, the old allies to have joined the British. People believed this because this change of colours made perfect logical sense.[48]

If, as I believe, the people were convinced that their very existence was in peril and that the enemy would not hesitate to take revenge for the tortures inflicted by Canada, then haven't we found the primary motive for their acquiescence to military service? The deportation of the Acadians confirmed their worst apprehensions. As the accounts of the tragedy, spread by the victims themselves, made their way through the colony, that which had been no more than a threat now became a reality, a certainty. The feared outcome now had two faces: The losers would be massacred or deported – probably some of both, so no one would escape. Such an eventuality can do more to galvanize energies than any number of speeches and sermons. As for the invaders, their first task was to defuse this fear, and they were wise to do so.[49] Once the habitants came to believe that their fate could be avoided, their resolve faltered.

5. THE RELIGIOUS DIMENSION

The Catholic Church in Canada played an important role in the course of this war as auxiliary to the military government and as interpreter of the divine will. The pastoral letters offer insight into this contribution, for even though there are no extant series of sermons, one can assume that parish priests on the whole followed their bishop's instructions and modelled their sermons on his writings.

The first intervention by the Church was to help with militia recruitment. The pastoral letter of 20 June 1745 is essentially a call for mobilization and for submission to military command. The enemy represented heresy: churches had been profaned, priests proscribed, the people deprived of the sacraments. "To die in the defence of one's religion is the effect of grace; it is to die, in some sense, as a martyr, and when one is driven by this divine motive, one finds in death the principle of eternal life."[50] Nothing was beyond the reach of a people protected by the God of armies. The second intervention of this type, in July 1753, was aimed at quieting the unrest stirred up by the mass recruitment of militiamen as labourers for the Ohio country. "You should ... rejoice at the sight of your relatives busy with procuring the increase and the safety of the colony. With you, we ask for their prompt return, but ask without grumbling, ask submissively: This is how it will be obtained, with a good outcome for them and with glory for the nation." The pastoral letter of 15 February 1756 (quoted on p. 253) takes the form of a bona fide police ordinance, using a description of the Acadians' hardships to arouse the zeal of the recruits and excoriate those who attempted to outwit the recruiters.[51]

Since 1755, the priests had been asked not to leave their parishes; the biannual retreats were cancelled, for "although the people must perceive that the raising of the militia was essential in the present position ... I think a few rumours could be stirred up that the presence of a priest could quell."[52] The government was increasingly relying on the parish priests to support the militia captains' authority in matters of recruitment, as they had always done for other matters. This close collaboration would continue until the invasion of the colony. At that point, according to Marcel Trudel, the priests of the occupied parishes generally followed the directives of the bishop, who recommended submission and neutrality,[53] and this despite the governor's imperious orders.[54] Only a few took up arms or encouraged their parishioners to resist. But until then, the clergy was unstinting in its support for the military enterprises. The Récollets, who traditionally served as chaplains at the posts, took charge of ministering to the soldiers and militiamen; no detachment of any size was without a clergyman to give absolution just before battle and to administer the sacraments to the sick and the injured.[55]

Public prayers were added to the regular ecclesiastical schedule in the form of special orations, antiphonies, litanies, novenas, benedictions of the holy sacrament, and processions held with great solemnity in the cities. In the countryside, these prayers were incorporated into Sunday mass and vespers, since work, distances, and the burdens of ministry ruled out weekday ceremonies. The faithful were also exhorted to pray as a family and to ensure that each household was represented in church every day. The population responded with enthusiasm, the churches bustled, and this public fervour grew as the situation deteriorated.

More than these practices and exhortations, all rather mundane under the circumstances, what is notable is how the message coming from the church changed over time.[56] From 1744 to 1758, the directives were simple and encouraging: It sufficed to obey, pray, and have confidence. God could only be found in the camp of the just, and he would not let heresy win the day. The faithful were exhorted to bow down and give gratitude to the God of armies. The population was eager to hear this message and greeted the military successes as so many miracles confirming the Almighty's favour. Rumour had it in the colony that the Virgin had appeared above the French army during the Battle of the Monongahela, protecting her people by redirecting the enemy's bullets toward herself.[57] The bishop did not go as far as mentioning this extraordinary apparition, but the pastoral letter of 9 August 1755 does contain allusions to a "nearly miraculous" victory coinciding with the octave of the Visitation, manifestly proving that the Virgin had heard the colony's prayers.[58]

For the first time, the pastoral letter of January 1758 speaks of the war as a calamity and intimates to the habitants that they may bear some responsibility for this state of affairs: "God did not promise to listen with favour to the sinner's prayer."[59] But the lecture was directed at a limited audience: essentially that of any peasants who might be grumbling about the ordinances and refusing to hand over their wheat to the purveyors. They were advised to regain a proper attitude, humbly accept the privations, and keep their hopes up.

So far, nothing in this preaching had prepared the population for a close encounter with a vengeful God. In accordance with official policy, the bishop had avoided alarming the faithful, asking for their untroubled trust in the goodness of providence. Outside of the vague stirrings of popular resistance to the mobilization and the requisitions, sin was singularly absent from these sermons. Starting in

February 1759, sin became their exclusive subject. With no segue, the habitants learned that they had brought God's wrath down upon them and were enjoined to repent. Their crimes were more frightful than the miseries of war: profane entertainment, games of chance, impure attire, theft and plunder, drunkenness, licentiousness, failure to sanctify the Sabbath and the holidays, even irreligion, not to mention profaning the government and scheming to avoid carrying out its orders. God had judged them, and they must now pray for the sinners' repentance. Perhaps, by doing so, they might stay his hand? But the tone was not optimistic. This explanatory schema belongs to the oldest Judeo-Christian tradition (which did not, moreover, invent it). Since time immemorial, the church has blamed the masses in efforts to make them learn a lesson from collective hardships – major epidemics in particular.[60] The striking thing here is the brusqueness of the text and the defeatism it evinces in a military context.[61] At the very moment when the colony was gearing up for its bloodiest battle, the gaze of the faithful was turned away from the enemy without and toward the enemy within – certainly a blunder from a political standpoint. For most of the "crimes" denounced are not of the sort that a population reduced to living on crumbs and subjected to the harsh exigencies of military service could have afforded. These pastoral letters confirmed for rural residents what they already knew: that neither the sacrifices nor the responsibility for the hardships were being borne equally. But the condemnation jarred them too – for who has never grumbled or cheated? – and the malaise it engendered led more readily to the confessional than the army.

There is no way of knowing whether all the parish priests were just as harsh and pessimistic, but the acts of public penitence ordered after the publication of the last pastoral letters extended the reach of the bishop's rhetoric.[62] Among other events, there were public processions bereft of the holy sacrament in which the participants chanted litanies and the Miserere, at the end of which the priest offered a public apology on behalf of the sinners. The colonial population was religious and attached to its priests,[63] but this does not necessarily mean that the preaching of the Church had an immediately demoralizing impact, which is belied in any case by the general good will shown at the start of the siege of Quebec. Still, these damning words certainly did nothing to bring the habitants closer to the authorities or the militiamen to their officers and may have made them more fatalistically accepting of setbacks. As if to prove the bishop right, the heavens sent repeated omens, starting with the defeat of 13 September, which was treated as a trial by ordeal. A nun at the Hôpital Général de Quebec, surely no more credulous than the average habitant, saw all sorts of evil omens "controlled by a power we cannot oppose," such as the terrible storm in the hours preceding the attempt to retake Quebec on 28 April 1760.[64]

On the night of 18 May 1760, after waiting in vain for relief from French ships, Lévis ordered the burning of his beached ships at Neuville, where he had retreated with his army, to keep them from falling into enemy hands. After witnessing this operation, the militia-men left the camp "and no orders would keep them from going."[65] The historiography tells us that "abandonment by France" overcame the resistance of the last holdouts. Was it not, in fact, God who had just abandoned them for good?

Conclusion

Sylvie Dépatie and Catherine Desbarats

How can intentions be reconstructed from disparate elements? What is the proper interpretation of missing pieces if surviving vestiges are not to be given too much attention? This is, after all, the specialty of the historian, and yet, when this book reached the editing stage, we found our hesitations taking up more room.

Louise Dechêne did not live long enough to write the conclusion to this book. The little we found consisted of some notes dictated a few days before her death and three sheets attached with a paper clip, written in 1996 or shortly afterwards.[1] The message of these two documents is consistent, and we shall come to it in a moment. But so as not to give all the importance to what was found, it should be noted that her handwritten notes specify that "[the conclusion] applies to the whole period of the regime, from 1660 to 1760, and not to the specific problems of the Seven Years' War, which will all be discussed in chapter 11, 'The Invasion.'"[2] We feel certain that if she had been able to write this conclusion herself, she would have addressed the points we will stress here with her characteristic combination of stylistic concision and nuance.

But these two documents – the handwritten pages and the dictation – are all we have. Furthermore, the circumstances surrounding the latter strongly suggest, in our view, that their content reflects what Louise Dechêne, at the end of her endeavour, considered most important.

This conclusion takes us straight into the heart of her historiographic project. It is here that she situates her novel account of the origins with respect to a potent historical tradition, while simultaneously delving into the origins of that traditional version, with its obsessions and blind spots; her intent was to navigate between the history of the French regime as she saw it and an analysis of how others have presented it. The starting point was the Seven Years' War, but from there the author widened her lens to encompass the regime as a whole. She wanted to make three main points, forming as many angles. The first angle involved contesting the historiographic postulate of a Canadian identity distinct from that of France, linked to the notion of the colony's abandonment by the metropole. The second, had she been able to articulate it fully, would consist of a different version of the abandonment experienced by the colonists: abandonment by God. Dechêne's plan was to address, from a novel perspective, the religious dimension of Canadian identity and its consequences for historical memory. The third angle, tying back to chapter 1, would have involved revisiting the myths about pre-Conquest Canadians that still inhabit the public mind in Quebec. It would have contrasted these myths with the author's reinterpretation based on a nuanced approach to the dynamics of that society.

The first question, then, is: Were the French perceived as an enemy in Canada? This question derives its pertinence from a historiography that has continually focused on the putative early emergence of a Canadian sense of nationality under the French regime.[3] It is said that the Canadians were confronting two enemies – the British and the French – in 1755 but that the break with France had long been in the offing, that the war only made it more visible, and that the opposition between Montcalm and Vaudreuil personified it. Since the late seventeenth century, the people had been developing their own way of life. Abundant land, participation in the fur trade, relative economic prosperity, and, for some historians, the influence of Indigenous lifeways had contributed to the emergence of a distinct society. The populace, deprived of contact with the metropole, is said to have felt Canadian while the elite remained French, as attested by the many who returned to France after 1760.[4] On this view, the people had in some sense already rejected a France that was in the process of abandoning them.

Dechêne contests this vision in three ways. First, she emphasizes its anachronistic character: The principle of nationality is a later notion that would not fully emerge until the nineteenth century. More narrowly, in relation to the French/Canadian divide supposedly revealed by the Seven Years' War, she points out that the ethnonyms appearing to distinguish French from Canadians in the troops must not be taken at face value. She also notes that the adversarial relationship allegedly obtaining between the two groups on the ground squares with neither the military nor the sociocultural context. Since the officers and the peasants making up the bulk of the militia "belonged to two different worlds," it is implausible that these peasants would have taken sides in power struggles playing out higher up in the hierarchy.[5] She proceeds to refute the idea of a break between the colonists and the metropole more generally. The colonists were devoted to the king and hence to France;[6] symbols can cross oceans, as she shows in her analysis of that era's pastoral letters in chapter 12.[7] A sentence she dictated offers an image: "Quebec was no farther away than Saint-Malo; Quebec did not see the king less often than Saint-Malo did." What is more, the colony had just taken in, since 1750, its second-largest contingent of French immigrants. Nor are there any contemporary accounts attesting to the idea that the colonists rejected France. The habitants were no doubt discouraged, their hopes betrayed, but not to the point of questioning their identity. Canadians *and* Frenchmen, they knew that France did not begin and end with incompetent generals and corrupt administrators. The idea of abandonment by France that later found a home in the historiography is very much contemporaneous with the Seven Years' War but does not originate with the Canadian colonists: It makes its appearance in placards published by the British generals, who were trying to pry the militiamen away from the French army.[8]

The colony unquestionably felt abandoned, continues Dechêne, coming to her second point, but by God more than by France. This religious dimension – people's conceptions of their relationship to the divine – is another component of the colonial identity that historians have neglected, even obscured. It was an important factor in the colonial wars, of which Dechêne decided to begin her study by adopting a longer-term perspective. In chapter 2, she discusses invocations of divine intervention, which were customary for the both the Church and the colonists. In the discourse of the clergymen, the colony's wars had always been holy, whether the enemy was (in their eyes) a barbarian or a heretic. The colonists, religious and devoted to their parish priests, were comforted in the belief that providence was on their side. A succession of British setbacks and defeats kept this assurance alive until the eve of the decisive invasion. Yet the colonists' inner religious world remains hard to discern, for popular accounts become increasingly rare in the sources, which take a turn toward the secular in the late seventeenth century. So the author's method, reiterated in her succinct notes, relies largely, for the eighteenth century, on an analysis of the bishops' pastoral letters. Dechêne draws particular attention, in both text and conclusion, to one of these letters, dated 20 June 1745. It shows that the mid-eighteenth century wars were still regarded as holy and that the bishop was still preaching to the colonists a message of political and military submission. Nevertheless, the hierarchy of values remains clear. In the midst of the War of the Austrian Succession, Bishop Pontbriand offered the faithful a gauge of the spiritual and military might of their intentions: to fight, or die, for one's "interests," or even for love of king and country, was to be pitifully armed. In contrast, nothing was impossible for a people driven by the fear of a heretical enemy, whose religious fervour caused the effective grace of the "God of armies" to smile upon them.[9] But the winds of providence turned during the Seven Years' War and with them the discourse of the Church, which now diverged from that of the government in highlighting all the calamities that were threatening to encourage desertion. Once a protector, God had abruptly become an avenger, showing the sinful colonists his wrath by abandoning them to their fate at the hands of a heretical power.

Not much survives to indicate the impact of these pastoral letters on the colonists, and Dechêne, at the end of chapter 12, remains cautious on this score. As to her handwritten notes for the conclusion, they devote more space to new historiographic blind spots and memory lapses, for in her view the Church – the guardian of Quebec's historical memory and the ideology that shapes it – obliterated the war, quite simply consigned it to oblivion so as not to reopen the wound. The folklorists (who later took over from the clergy as guardians of Quebec's historical memory) were more interested in "stories of werewolves and flying canoes" than in painful war memories. And the historians, she writes, completed the task of destroying this living memory and replacing it with a history of their own creation.

For her third point, Dechêne emphasizes the contrast between her interpretation and the "myths of yesterday and today." These enduring myths give pride of place to a stock portrait of sorts, a psychology of the Canadian "people." Among the Canadians' flaws are said to be a spirit of "independence" if not insubordination, of capriciousness; among their innate talents are warfare and the ability to conduct all manner of "raids" (*courses*). And this pronoun "their" corresponds to a conception of the Canadians as an undifferentiated mass. To this, Dechêne counterposes a portrait of a subjugated but non-military population that is highly stratified. With limited experience of war and its exigencies, this population would be caught off guard when war broke out for real – when the final sixteen years of war began in 1744. It was then that participation in the militia became something more than a "pleasant varnish."

Dechêne's primary basis for this interpretation is her analysis of context, since direct testimony is scarce. The result, she conjectures, "has the merit of offering an image of the Canadian combatant that accords with the scholarly literature on agriculture, the family, and trade." With this reference to the social referents of her thought, we come full circle to *Habitants and Merchants*. But the historian does not stop there: She gives the outline of the conclusion one last enigmatic twist by writing of the "founding *event*, the defeat." Readers might wonder for a moment if they are reading Guy Frégault, in whose work the effects of the Conquest are always palpable, yet Dechêne's lapidary phrase resists such facile interpretation. There are enough clues elsewhere in the book to suggest that this is in fact an allusion to the notion that the coalescence of a Quebec national identity would not occur until after the Conquest. That was when, for the first time, the French Canadian collectivity was compelled to define itself in contradistinction to the conqueror.[10] However, the last two sentences of the outline suggest a bitterer interpretation of the event in question. They evoke a tradition of obedience dating back to the French regime and continuing under the new one: a tradition of which the British and the Catholic Church would take advantage. Nor would they be the last beneficiaries, she suggests in closing: "Be careful! Submissiveness can be internalized."

Introduction

Catherine Desbarats

Louise Dechêne left a nearly completed manuscript version, in the form of tables, of each of the three appendices presented in this section. These are chronological lists of military movements compiled from her reading notes, whose initial purpose was to guide her analysis. They are a help to the reader as well, offering an overview of the era's war parties along with details of the makeup of each expedition.[1] We transcribed them, taking account insofar as possible of additions and comments that the author intended to incorporate at a later date. No attempt was made, however, to take inventory of any expeditions or military engagements beyond the capitulation of Montreal. That is where Louise Dechêne's work ends, even though the empty spaces in her handwritten table range up to 1765. In a few specific cases, it was possible to fill in certain gaps from the suggestions given in the notes accompanying the handwritten tables. Furthermore, the data contained in the tables were verified only where the author indicated that additional research was in order. In general, then, this data has not been checked. On another note, the original tables did not provide source citations for the descriptions of the war parties. Specialists will find most of these sources in the notes accompanying chapters 4, 8, and 11 in particular.

There is nothing straightforward or transparent about the preparation of such lists, with identification of the military and in some cases ethnic status of the participants, so it is important to reiterate here the clarifications provided by the author in those passages of the text that explicitly refer to the appendices. In each case, it is the sources that are at issue, for they are, among other things, pervaded by a social vision that routinely obscures the presence of peasants and Indigenous people. She writes in chapter 4:

The list of military movements presented in the appendices to this book reflects the bias of my sources, which boil down to the governors' and intendants' correspondence augmented by the occasional first-hand account. In their reports to Versailles, the administrators emphasized those engagements in which regular officers and other people of rank were involved. The most inconsequential engagement merited a detailed account as long as Sieur So-and-So had been there and not disgraced himself. Meanwhile, a clash involving only peasants, so many of which occurred in the colony in the early 1690s, got no more than a vague mention in passing: "The enemy made numerous incursions into our côtes." The bias is even more blatant with regard to the majority of detachments of Indigenous people, whether domiciliés or allies, who were not accompanied by officers; all these merited no more than "Our Natives continued to harass the [enemy] settlements."[2]

The counts of troop numbers found in first-hand accounts or official correspondence vary in terms of not only quality but also precision. In some instances, the tables can provide no more than an order of magnitude for all groups represented in the war parties, instead of the detailed breakdown that the author would have preferred in order to properly contextualize the role of the militias. Where the sources permit, the tables do allow for a distinction between colonial (naval) regulars, army regulars, volunteers, militiamen, Indigenous allies from the Great Lakes region, and Indigenous people living in the St Lawrence Valley, mostly designated throughout the text by the term domiciliés, which was used by people of European origin at that time.

These breakdowns were subjected to a rigorous critique by the author, who reminds us that even where the sources provided detailed figures, their authors sometimes manipulated them to support an argument, blame somebody else in the event of defeat or failure to act, or, on the contrary, throw somebody's bravery into relief.[3] She adds that care must be taken to "avoid taking ethnonyms at face value" and, in particular, not to confuse them anachronistically with ethnic identities where – to cite just one potential source of confusion – they in fact designate social categories. It is this patient decoding of seventeenth- and eighteenth-century language and its social context that lends the author's appendices all their subtlety and complexity.

The tables reflect not only the limitations of the sources and the historian's critical judgment (as well as her questions and uncertainties) but also choices of a different nature. Appendix A, covering the period from 1666 to 1740, does not, for example, make any claims to being exhaustive, an impossibility anyway given the biases just discussed. It also reflects a more specific selectivity, for the tables do not contain the sum total of war parties documented for New France but "only those to which Canada contributed, plus those that were part of a single strategy and had direct and immediate repercussions for the colony's security."[4] Expeditions to Acadia, Newfoundland, Hudson Bay, or Louisiana are not systematically included.

On a final note, it is worth mentioning that even stricter criteria applied to the compilation of Appendices B1 and B2, covering the periods 1740–48 and 1749–60. It made little sense to include the hundreds of parties reported by the Montreal storekeeper during the War of the Austrian Succession, especially for the year 1746, or by the fort commandants during the Seven Years' War, since it would have been impossible to produce a satisfactory analysis of them on the basis of a solid comprehension of the role and identity of the various Indigenous groups involved.[5] Quoting the author again:

So as not to overwhelm the reader, I proceeded in the traditional way, listing only the most decisive episodes, the ones that made noise in their day, as well as those in which the militia played a part, even if this means that the prominent Indigenous presence on all battlefronts is regretfully minimized. In the majority of cases, several convergent sources served to establish the numbers of participants in each category. Where they differ, the choices of other historians are considered.[6]

Legend of Appendices

REGULARS: Members of the colonial (naval) regulars, starting with those who made up the Carignan-Salières regiment, plus French army regulars who arrived during the Seven Years' War.

VOLUNTEERS AND MILITIAMEN: The distinction here is between men who received pay for their service and men who served without pay.

DOMICILIÉS: Christianized Indigenous people living in villages in the St Lawrence Valley in proximity to French settlements.

ALLIES: Indigenous people from the Great Lakes region, mainly, but also Atlantic coast Mi'kmaq in some cases.

C: Combat with the enemy.
X: Presence attested but number unknown.
?: Sources imprecise or contradictory on this point.

Military Movements (1666–1740)

Year	Duration or date	Place	Commander and other officers	Total number	Regulars
1666	January–March	Mohawk villages	Courcelle	600	400
	July–August	Mohawk villages	Sorel	280	150
	September–November	Mohawk villages	Tracy, Courcelle	1,300	600
1671		Lake Ontario	Courcelle	56	
1673	June–July	Cataraqui	Frontenac, 5 ex-officers	400	
1674		Pentagouet and Jemseg (Acadia)	Joybert (at Jemseg)	10	9
1676–1678		Acadia			
1684	June–September	Seneca villages	La Barre, Dugué	1,190	142
1686	March–October	Hudson Bay (James Bay)	Troyes, 3 Le Moyne brothers, Robutel	105	31
1687	May–August	Seneca villages	Denonville, Callière, Vaudreuil	2,580	843
	August–November	Ottawa River, Montreal Island, Chambly and environs			
1688	March–April	Upper St Lawrence			
	summer–fall	Richelieu River and environs of Montreal			
	spring–fall	New England (Connecticut River)			
	September	Oswego		100	
	various times	Great Lakes region			
	April	Pentagouet			
	July	Chedabucto and Canso			
	summer	Casco Bay			

Volunteers	Militia	Domiciliés	Allies	C	
	200	30			The party gets lost and is decimated by exposure and hunger.
	50	80			Expedition cancelled along the way.
	600?	100			Destruction of 4 deserted villages and crops.
56					Encounter between Iroquois and governor with a group of nobles.
	400				Construction of Fort Frontenac.
					Fortified trading post at Jemseg captured by English pirates.
					Abenakis rise up against the English.
	670	265	113		La Barre negotiates; no action.
70				X	Capture of forts Rupert, Moose, and Albany and a large prize.
180 voyageurs	804	353	400	X	Brief combat; enemy retreat; destruction of four villages and crops.
				X	Scattered Iroquois attacks.
				X	A convoy of voyageurs (50) and soldiers (30) falls into an ambush.
				X	Scattered attacks.
		X		X	Denonville sends domiciliés in parties to attack English settlements.
			100	X	Huron attack on Iroquois embassy.
			X	X	Various engagements between allies and Iroquois.
				X	Pillage of trading post by Edmund Andros, governor of New England.
				X	Capture of settlements and ships by English pirates.
			X	X	Abenaki attacks on English settlements (capture of several forts and 200 people killed).

Year	Duration or date	Place	Commander and other officers	Total number	Regulars
1689	spring–summer	government of Montreal			
	5 August	Lachine			
	5–6 August	Fort Rolland	Vaudreuil (after Subercase)	500	mainly
	5–6 August	Fort Rémy	Rabeyre, Longueuil and 3 other officers	80	50
	Fall	Pointe-aux-Trembles	Colombet (?)		
	16 October	Lake of Two Mountains	Manthet and Dulhut	28	
	13 November	Lachenaie			
	13 November	Lachenaie			
	June	Dover (New England)			
	15 August	Pemaquid			
1690	18 February	Corlaer (Schenectady), New England)	Manthet, Sainte-Hélène, and 7 other officers and volunteers; Togouiroui (Mohawk chief)	210	←
	January–27 March	Salmon Falls (New England)	J.-B.Hertel, 3 of his sons, other relatives	52	
	January–29 May, June	Casco, Fort Loyal, 3 other small posts	Portneuf, joined by Hertel and Saint-Castin	~300?	
	spring–summer	Bécancour, Sorel, Pointe-aux-Trembles, etc.			
1690 (or 1691?)	2 June	Ottawa River "Les Chats"	Louvigny	203	30 (escort
1690	29 August–2 September	La Prairie	Frontenac, Callière	1,200	X

Volunteers	Militia	Domiciliés	Allies	C	
				X	Scattered attacks throughout the territory.
				X	Parish sacked by Iroquois.
	X				The troops stay in the fort without attacking the enemy.
		30		X	Detachment decimated within sight of Vaudreuil's party.
	X			X	Attack repelled by habitants.
28				X	Three French canoes defeat a party of 22 Iroquois.
				X	Attack causing many casualties.
		X			The domiciliés fail to catch the enemy.
			X	X	Village captured by Penobscot Abenakis.
			100	X	Abenaki campaign against Pemaquid, accompanied by missionary Louis-Pierre Thury. Siege and surrender of English fort.
→ 114		96 (80 Ir., 16 Alg.)		X	Party from Montreal, village captured: numerous victims, large prize. Pursued on return by Iroquois.
24		25 (from Saint-François)		X	Party from Trois-Rivières; takes 3 small posts. Pursuit and battle. Proceeds to join Portneuf at Casco. Village razed.
50		60	?	X	Party from Quebec. Later reinforced by 36 men from Hertel's party and Saint-Castin's (Penobscot) warriors. Settlement razed, many killed or taken prisoner.
				X	Scattered attacks in the governments of Montreal and Trois-Rivières.
143 voyageurs		30		X	En route to Michilimackinac, they defeat an Iroquois party.
	X	350	510		An Indigenous force of 500 fur traders from the Great Lakes region joins the army assembled in anticipation of an invasion. Deciding it is a false alarm, the party breaks camp after five days.

Year	Duration or date	Place	Commander and other officers	Total number	Regulars
1690	4 September	La Prairie (La Fourche)			
	May	Pentagouet and Port-Royal; Chedabucto and Isle Percée			
	16–25 October	Quebec (under siege)		3,000	X
	20 October	St Charles River	Longueuil, Sainte-Hélène	200	
	21 October	St Charles River	Ignace Juchereau Duchesnay, commander of Beauport militia		
1691	January–December	New England			
	January–December				
	May–November	government of Montreal			
	6–7 June	Îles Bouchard	Vaudreuil, Mine, Bienville, etc., Catalogne	120	50
	10–11 August	La Prairie	Callière	800	450
	10–11 August	near Chambly	Valrennes, Leber, Duchesne	160	X
	December	Lake Champlain			
	June	Wells (New England)			
1692	January	York (New England)	Madokawando	150	
	June	Cocheco and Wells (New England)	Saint-Castin, Portneuf, La Broquerie (killed)	440	

Volunteers	Militia	Domiciliés	Allies	C	
				X	Harvesters ambushed by a detachment of Mohawks and Iroquois commanded by John Schuyler.
				X	Phips's fleet captures Pentagouet. Port-Royal surrenders, is sacked.
	X from the whole colony	X			Colonial forces assembled at Quebec. Enemy landing. Bombardment of the town.
	200			X	The French prevent a detachment of 1,400 men from crossing the river.
	X			X	The Beauport, Beaupré, and Île d'Orléans militias fall into an ambush and repulse the enemy.
		X		X	Several parties of domiciliés, some including volunteers (cadets, officers), harass New England settlements.
			X	X	Allies from the Great Lakes region also very active.
				X	Scattered attacks on the territory by 900 Iroquois.
	70			X	The party attacks 50 sleeping Iroquois; indiscipline allows the enemy to react and kill some Frenchmen.
	150	X	X Ottawa traders	X	During the night, a detachment commanded by Schuyler attacks and is repulsed by the soldiers (the militia had abandoned the position).
	X			X	Violent fighting between Schuyler's party and Valrennes's detachment.
		X		X	Amerindians from Sault pursue and defeat a party of Iroquois and release captives from their village.
			X	X	Abenakis fail to take the village; sacking of surrounding area.
			150	X	Abenakis, accompanied by Thury, take village.
40 Canadians			400	X	Failure: the detachment is repulsed in both places. Pillaging in the area.

Year	Duration or date	Place	Commander and other officers	Total number	Regulars
1692		Abenaki villages			
	various times				
	various times				
	various times	governments of Montreal and Trois-Rivières			
	February–March	Lake Saint-Francis (Tonihata Island)	Orvilliers, Beaucours, other officers	325	X
	June	Long Sault	Saint-Michel		
	July	Long Sault	Vaudreuil	500	X
1693	January–March	Seneca villages	Manthet, Courtemanche, etc. (30 officers)	625	100
	spring	Lake of Two Mountains	Lavaltrie fils		
	various times	Orange (Albany) and Boston			
	June	Fort Albany (James Bay)			
	August	Plaisance (Placentia)			
	August	Île Perrot	Callière	800	X
1694	various times				
	June–July	Oyster River (Durham, NH)	Claude-Sébastien de Villieu, possibly accompanied by a few Frenchmen	215	
	July–September	Groton, MA; Boston coast	Taxous (Abenaki chef), Madokawando	200	
1694	August–September	York Factory (Hudson Bay)	Iberville, Serigny, etc.	—	crews

Volunteers	Militia	Domiciliés	Allies	C	
				X	Attacked by Bostonians.
		X		X	Harassment of enemy settlements.
			over 800 men		Manoeuvres by Ottawas and Hurons against Iroquois in the Great Lakes region.
				X	Scattered attacks on Saint-Lambert, La Montagne, Lachenaie, Verchères, etc.
	X	205		X	En route for Cataraqui, they defeat an Iroquois party hunting in the area.
				X	Saint-Michel, escorting voyageurs, is attacked and a massacre ensues.
	100	X	X	X	Pursuit and defeat of 150 Iroquois who had attacked voyageurs and habitants of Lachenaie.
	310	200		X	Three villages destroyed, 310 prisoners. Pursued, the party suffered casualties on the return journey.
				X	An escort accompanying voyageurs bound for the Great Lakes region is attacked and decimated on the return journey.
		X	X	X	Numerous parties of domiciliés and Abenakis harass the enemy.
				?	The English retake control of James Bay.
					Attack, repulsed, by about 20 ships under Rear-Admiral Wheler's command.
	X	X			Troops assembled to block an enemy landing and protect harvesters.
		X		X	Five parties harass Iroquois (winter) and other actions.
			215	X	Two posts and 60 houses destroyed. Other posts hold out and the attackers lift the siege. Pillaging in the countryside.
			200	X	Destruction continues along the coast.
100				X	Capture of English fort by Iberville's 2 ships.

Year	Duration or date	Place	Commander and other officers	Total number	Regulars
1695	October	York Factory (Hudson Bay)			
	summer	Cataraqui	30 officers	700	300
	various times	government of Montreal			
		Maine coast			
1696	January–March	Onondagua villages		300	X
	June–August	Onondagua and Oneida villages	Frontenac, Callière, Vaudreuil; Ramezay commanding the militias	2,150	800
	various times				
	15 August	Pemaquid (Kennebec River)	Iberville, Villieu, Saint-Castin, Montigny	—	25
	September	Beaubassin, Nashwaak (present-day Fredericton, NB)			
	November	St John's (Newfoundland)	Brouillan, Iberville, Muy, etc.	224	100
1696–1697	December–March	Conception Bay and Trinity Bay (Newfoundland)	Iberville, Montigny, about 10 officers and gentlemen	120	50
1697	12 September	York Factory (Hudson Bay)	Iberville	?	crews
	spring–October	Boston coast			
	June–September	initiative against Boston and New York	Nesmond, commander of the squadron, joins the army troops	1,500	X
	summer	Iroquois territory			
1697–1698					

Volunteers	Militia	Domiciliés	Allies	C	
				?	The English (William Allen) retake the fort.
	160	200			Expedition to re-establish Fort Frontenac.
					Resumption of Iroquois attacks after lull of 1693–94.
					Coast abandoned by English colonists.
	X	X			The party turns around at Cataraqui because of supply problems and bogging down in the snow.
50	800	500			Villages and crops devastated.
		X		X	Several small parties harass the Iroquois.
→ X and Iberville's crews			230	X	Capitulation of English fort after short siege by Iberville's 2 ships and land troops.
				X	English attack: Beaubassin destroyed; Nashwaak holds out (Benjamin Church).
124			3 Mi'k maq		They lay siege to St John's, resulting in English surrender (Avalon Peninsula Campaign).
30 Can., 27 men from France				X	Canadians ravage the coasts and destroy 27 fishing posts.
30				X	Iberville retakes York Factory after a naval victory.
			X	X	Abenaki parties on the Boston coast.
	X	X	X		An army of soldiers, militiamen, and domiciliés, accompanied by allies from Acadia, waits all summer; enterprise cancelled on 8 September.
			X		Numerous parties of Ottawas and other allies against the Iroquois.
					20 September: Peace of Ryswick; February 1698: announcement of the Peace at Quebec via Albany

Year	Duration or date	Place	Commander and other officers	Total number	Regulars
1698		Maine coast			
1698– 1699		Great Lakes region			
1703	spring–fall	Connecticut River (New England)	La Durantaye, etc.		
	July–October	New England coasts from Wells to Falmouth	Leneuf de Beaubassin, Rouville, etc. Nescambiouit, Wenemouet (Abenaki chiefs)	400	5
	fall	Pentagouet			
1704	February–March	Deerfield (Connecticut Valley)	Rouville, 4 of his brothers, etc.	250	←
	spring–summer	Pascommuck (Connecticut Valley)	Montigny		
	July	Les Mines, Beaubassin, Port-Royal			
	July	New England	Beaucourt and many officers	800	←
	summer	Bonavista (Newfoundland)	La Grange	144	
1705	January	Newfoundland	Subercase, Beaucourt, 12 other officers of Canada	450	X
	March–June	Newfoundland	Montigny, 5 other officers and chaplains	72	←
	winter	Norridgewock (Kennebec Valley)			
1706	various times	New England			
1707	June and August	Port-Royal			
	summer	Quebec		2,000?	700

Volunteers	Militia	Domiciliés	Allies	C	
					Abenakis continue the war.
					The allies harass the Five Nations.
		X			Parties of domiciliés, some mixed with Frenchmen.
50		100	250	X	Party from Canada reinforced by Abenakis destroys several English settlements along 50 miles of coastline.
				X	Destruction of village by the English, who carry on their attacks against the Abenaki in 1704, taking many prisoners.
→ 48		200		X	Destruction and massacre.
5			X	X	Montigny leads Abenakis in harassing English at various sites.
				X	English fleet destroys Les Mines and Beaubassin; Port-Royal holds out.
→ 120		680		X	Party routed before achieving its goals (many recent Abenaki domiciliés).
120	X		X Mi'k maq	X	Two French privateers attack the coast and burn barques.
X	X		X	X	Capture of two English settlements but forced to lift siege of St John's after taking heavy casualties.
→ 37		30		X	Sacking of Conception and Trinity bays as far as Bonavista.
				X	Abenaki village destroyed by the English.
		X	X	X	Parties of domiciliés and allies sent to attack New England.
60 Canadians				X	Port-Royal twice succeeds in repelling attackers (fleet/1,000 men).
	X	X			Start of general mobilization with announcement of enemy fleet's arrival; militias assembled at Quebec (false alert): used for corvées.

Year	Duration or date	Place	Commander and other officers	Total number	Regulars
1708	1 January–April	St John's (Newfoundland)	Saint-Ovide and Costebelle, Denys de La Ronde with La Chesnaye, Argenteuil and his brother	170	X
	July	toward New England (via Lake Champlain)	La Perrière	200	←
	26 July (departure from Montreal)	Haverhill (Merrimack River, via Saint-François River)	Deschaillons, Rouville, 12 other young officers	160	←
	summer–fall	New England			
1709	April	Fort Albany (Hudson Bay)	Manthet, Robutel, La Noue, Martigny, Croisille, etc.	100	
	spring				
	June	Deerfield (Connecticut Valley)	?	180	
	28 July–beginning of August	Lake Champlain (near Wood Creek)	Ramezay, Rouville, and other officers (12)	1,500	100
	August–September	Quebec		1,500?	X
	16 September– 15 October	Chambly	La Chassaigne	1,600	300
1710	13 October	Port-Royal			
1710– 1711		Newfoundland			
1711	September– October	Quebec	Vaudreuil	2,300	300

Volunteers	Militia	Domiciliés	Allies	C	
X			X	X	Capture and destruction of St John's. The detachment has support from La Ronde's frigate.
→ ?		(200)			A party of Iroquois domiciliés from Sault and La Montagne, who were to have taken part in the same campaign, defect.
→ 100 "selected Canadians and soldiers"		60 Abenakis and Nepissings		X	Destruction of the village. Fighting on the homeward journey (via the Saint-François River).
		X	X	X	Several small parties of 200–300 allies step up attacks.
90				X	Privateer fitted out to recapture the fort. Failure, several dead on French side.
				X	Rumours of invasion. Several scouting parties sent to New England.
40		140			Village alerted and prepares to defend itself; party beats a retreat.
50	600	750			Army supposed to go destroy English army's stores on the frontier is discovered by the enemy; panic and retreat.
	X	X			Troops begin to assemble at Quebec with announcement of approaching enemy fleet; false alarm.
	800	500			Troops assembled in case of invasion via Lake Champlain but sent home for want of provisions.
				X	Besieged by an army of 1,900 men, Port-Royal surrenders.
X				X	Reciprocal attacks on fishing parties; presence of Canadian volunteers.
	1,400	400	X		Entirety of the colony's forces assemble to meet the enemy fleet (Walker); his ships wrecked at the mouth of the river.

Year	Duration or date	Place	Commander and other officers	Total number	Regulars
1711	October	vicinity of Orange	Rouville	200	
	October	Chambly	Vaudreuil, Ramezay	nearly 3,000	300
1711–1712		Port-Royal			
1712	spring–summer	New England		350	
	spring–summer	vicinity of Port-Royal and New England coast			
	May	Detroit	Dubuisson, commandant of Fort Pontchartrain; Vincennes commanding the pursuit	900	
1715	August	Fox territory (Wisconsin)	Lignery (commandant at Michilimackinac)		
	November	Fox territory (Wisconsin)	Viennay Pachot (cadet), Bisaillon (interpreter)	100	
1716	summer	Fox village	Louvigny	800	
1727	July	Oswego			

Volunteers	Militia	Domiciliés	Allies	C	
X		X			Vicinity of Orange, to observe Nicholson's movements; small detached parties take prisoners.
	1,500	500	400		Army gathered to await Nicholson's via Lake Champlain; upon learning of Walker's shipwreck, Nicholson withdraws.
			X	X	Movements of Amerindians and Acadians to root out the British.
		X			Troops (300–400 plus Amerindians) harass the Boston coast.
			X Abenakis		Others harass from their side.
A few accompany Vincennes			900		An army of Ottawas, Hurons, and men of other nations commanded by Dubuisson lays siege to the fortified village where the Foxes and Mascoutens have taken refuge. After 19 days, the targets of the siege escape but are caught and massacred (over 1,000 victims).
Over 200 (voyageurs)			X		Planned for 1,100 men, the expedition is aborted. Neither the allies from the south nor the French and allies assembled at Michilimackinac go to Fox territory.
			Hurons and Illinis		They defeat a party of Mascoutens and Kickapoos and are then surprised by a troop of Foxes but manage to get away.
400 voyageurs			400		The Foxes surrender after 3-day siege and agree to defray the costs of the expedition borne by the voyageurs and their purveyors.
	2,000				Mass mobilization following the construction of Fort Oswego by the British; 500 militiamen are dispatched from Quebec to Montreal before the operation is cancelled.

Year	Duration or date	Place	Commander and other officers	Total number	Regulars
1728	5 June–late September	Fox territory	Lignery; Vaudreuil de Cavagnial, an officer in the colonial regulars, is involved	1,650	
1730	April	Fox territory	Paul Marin accompanies the party	600	
	August–September	Illinois (near Prairie du Rocher)	Saint-Ange, commandant at Fort de Chartres; Coulon de Villiers, commandant at Fort Saint-Joseph; Noyelles, commandant at Fort Miami; Simon Réaume, voyageur	1,428	←
1732	February	Fox territory	Paul-Joseph Lemoyne de Longueuil; a Sulpician	118	
1733	September	Sauk territory (Fox neighbours)	Coulon de Villiers, 3 of his sons, his son-in-law Regnard Dupuis, Repentigny, etc.	370	←
1735	Winter	Baie-des-Puants (Green Bay, WI; Sauk territory)	Noyelles, 6 officers, cadets; Croisille, Chabert (killed), La Pérade, Saint-Ours, Joncaire Jr (killed)	247, not counting allies and French at posts	56
1736	?	Chickasaws	d'Artaguette, commandant of Illinois district (killed), Vincennes, Ailleboust, Saint-Ange, Dutisné, Drouet	? army of over 400	

Volunteers	Militia	Domiciliés	Allies	C
50	400	800	400	The Foxes flee before the army's arrival; four villages are burned with their crops. Amerindians and militias refuse to pursue enemy; lack of provisions and equipment.
50			550	At allies' request, Marin and some Frenchmen stationed at the posts go off in pursuit of Foxes but in vain.
128 (100 Frenchmen from Fort de Chartres, 28 voyageurs)			1,300	Fleeing their enemies, the Foxes are intercepted in Illinois by 4 detachments of allies (largely Illinis) and Frenchmen; they escape after a 23-day siege but are caught and massacred (nearly 1,000 victims).
		48	70	Lake Iroquois and Detroit Hurons wage war on the Foxes. The commandant at Detroit urges them to kill the prisoners.
(garrison) 60 (voyageurs)			300	Siege of Sauk fort where Foxes have taken refuge goes awry; detachment decimated, its commandant and several officers killed.
22 "guides" and voyageurs		159	X	Party departs Montreal in October with order to exterminate the last Foxes; reinforced by Detroit Hurons, etc. Famished and disorganized, it is forced to lift the siege of the fort and retreat, a resounding failure.
	140 (Illinis)	many domiciliés	X	From Canada, a party of domiciliés and young officers and cadets joins an Illini detachment to march against the Chickasaws with Bienville's army arriving from New Orleans. Before the two corps can be merged, d'Artaguette's is encircled and pursued by the enemy; 40 Frenchmen, including 7 officers, are killed, and Bienville is forced to retreat.

Year	Duration or date	Place	Commander and other officers	Total number	Regulars
1737	April–September	Chickasaw territory			
1739–1740	November, February–March	Fort de l'Assomption	Lemoyne de Longueuil, commandant; 11 officers, 25 cadets; Léry (journal) and Céloron, commandant at Michilimackinac; Sabrevois	596	39

Note: Figures given with arrows indicate the combined total for the categories in question.

Volunteers	Militia	Domiciliés	Allies	C	
		X	X		Several parties of domiciliés and allies attack Chickasaws and return with scalps and prisoners.
80 from Great Lakes region	45	320 (168 from Sault)	76		Canadian detachment joins Bienville's army (1,300) in November 1739. Skirmishes around Fort Assomption. At the army's approach in February, the Chickasaws surrender and Bienville accepts. (The army has not fought because of major logistical problems.)

Military Movements (1744–48)

Year	Duration or date	Place	Commander and other officers	Total number	Regulars
1744	May	Canso	Joseph Du Pont Duvivier (war declared 8 March; news reaches Louisbourg 3 May, Quebec in June)	374	X and sailors
	August–September	Annapolis	Joseph Du Pont Duvivier	350	50
1745	January–August	Annapolis	Paul Marin, 12 officers and cadets	180	
	11 May–27 June	Louisbourg			
	July	Île Saint-Jean			
	summer	Quebec		3,000?	
	29 November–	Saratoga (NY)	Paul Marin, 12 officers and cadets	500	
1746	January	Saint-Frédéric	26 officers	256	
	January–December	New England and New York			
	September–October	Chebucto	Duc d'Anville, squadron commander		
	4 June–	Acadia	Ramezay 50 officers and cadets	680	
	September–November	Annapolis	Ramezay with officers and cadets	1,200?	

Volunteers	Militia	Domiciliés	Allies	C
				Captures post (New England fishing hub) with detachment from Île Royale and some sailors.
			300 Mi'k maq, Abenakis	Four-week siege, no assault, awaiting French squadron that only arrives after the party's departure, in October.
100		80? 400		Lifts siege to provide relief at Louisbourg; returns to Quebec at news of surrender.
				Siege and surrender; Bostonians (4,000 men) occupy fort.
				Occupation by Bostonians.
	X (mainly)	X	X	Capture of Louisbourg raises alarm; militias from three governments and domiciliés spend the summer at Quebec; 1,310 men work on fortifications.
?	200	300		Destruction of village; Marin brings back 100 prisoners.
5	205	120		Frontier surveillance; invasion apprehended.
				Sixty-nine small parties of domiciliés and allies fitted out at Montreal.
				Squadron of 7,000 men arrives to retake Louisbourg, Acadia, and Placentia, encounters many problems; returns to France having done nothing.
	600			Embarkation of whole group (including officers).
600		300	300? Mi'k maq	Lifts siege at news of squadron's departure; the domiciliés and half the Canadians return to Canada. The others winter at Beaubassin.

Year	Duration or date	Place	Commander and other officers	Total number	Regulars
1746	July–August	Saint-Frédéric	Muy, 15 officers and cadets	455	
	August–September	Fort Massachusetts	Rigaud, 17 officers and cadets	900	
	July	Montreal			
	October–November	near Saratoga	Dubreuil, La Corne, 2 cadets, 1 militia officer	56	
1746		Fort Lajoie	Croisille de Montesson		
1746–1747	November–December April–June	government of Montreal			
1747	February	Grand-Pré (Les Mines)	Coulon de Villiers, 16 officers and cadets?	286	
	April	near Chateauguay	Coulon de Villiers, 8 cadets	109	
	May	Lake St Francis	Legardeur de Saint-Pierre, 15 officers and cadets	116	
	June	Montreal Island	Chevalier de La Corne, Saint-Pierre, etc.	200	
	August	near La Prairie	Chevalier de La Corne, etc.	100	
	March–May	near Haverhill (March)	Boucher de Niverville, 3 cadets	91	
	March–April	near Saratoga	Horlin	60	

Volunteers	Militia	Domiciliés	Allies	C
	33	400		Exploration around the fort. They work on blocking the Chicot River while waiting for Rigaud.
		400		Having departed Montreal with 700 men, he merges Muy's troops with his own. The fort (22-man garrison) surrenders after a 24-hour siege. Adjacent countryside sacked.
				New mass mobilization announced in case of attack on Fort Saint-Frédéric.
		50		They return with 6 prisoners, 10 scalps.
			210 Mi'k maq	They attack Fort Lajoie, killing 40–50 men and cattle.
				About 8 attacks by parties of Mohawks and "Flemish" between November 1746 and late 1747, along with a few false alarms.
10 Acadians	200		60	Surprise attack by detachment of 500 on New Englanders, night of 11 February; they surrender the next day.
	100			Pursuit of Mohawk parties.
	100			Pursuit of Mohawk parties.
	200			They divide into two detachments to pursue a party of 40 Mohawks and Flemish.
	100			Pursuit of Mohawks.
6		81 Abenakis and Sault Amerindians		They burn 40 leagues of country, 5 forts, 3 temples, 110 abandoned houses, kill 600 sheep, etc., and bring back 2 scalps.
30		30		Two consecutive parties commanded by Horlin; second returns with 3 prisoners and 12 scalps.

Year	Duration or date	Place	Commander and other officers	Total number	Regulars
1747	May	Fort Massachusetts	Coulon de Villiers, Céloron, 7 cadets	101	
	June	Saratoga (Fort Clinton)	La Corne Saint-Luc (and other officers and cadets)	230	
	8 June–23 July	Saratoga	Rigaud, 19 officers and cadets, 12 militia officers	1,250?	
	July	near Schenectady (against Mohawks)	Chevalier de La Corne, 8 cadets, Dubreuil, La Corne Saint-Luc, Jumonville, 2 militia officers, 3 interpreters	346	
	October– November	Schenectady and Connecticut River	Léry	80	
	November	near Orange	Noyelles	70	
	December	Saratoga	Coulon de Villiers, Jumonville	70	
1748	various times	New England and New York			
	May–June	?	Jumonville, Ensign Hertel and Épervanches, cadets	70	
	June–July	Norfield	Duplessis Faber, Ensign Simblin, Laplante	About 70	
	June	Beaubassin	Marin, Ensign Bailleul, another ensign	140	
	17 July– 27 August	near Fort Massachusetts	Chevalier de Niverville, Hertel de Beaubassin, several cadets	126	
	Return 10 May	near Albany	Hertel de Beaubassin	15	

Volunteers	Militia	Domiciliés	Allies	C	
12		80			They attack the rebuilt British fort but are repelled.
20			200		They chase the British out of the fort, taking 40 prisoners and 28 scalps (party detached from Rigaud's army).
voyageurs	700		500		After three days of inactivity in front of the fort, the detachment gives up and returns to Montreal.
22		85	223		In the field, they divide into small parties, returning with 6 prisoners, 2 scalps.
X		X mainly			I.e., 2 consecutive parties, one of which adopts a new target and returns with one prisoner.
X		X mainly			They return with 2 scalps.
X		X mainly			They find the fort abandoned.
					Numerous parties of domiciliés and allies fitted out at Montreal (accurate count lacking).
7		60			They return with 5 scalps (Hertel and domiciliés are killed).
15		50			Merger of three separate parties; they bring back a few scalps.
	40	100			They set sail for Acadia with orders to harass the British. Disease, followed by cessation of hostilities, prevent them from taking action.
?	46	80			Party attacks isolated individuals, returning with 5 scalps (excuse: disease).
3		11			They burn 30 houses, one mill, 3 small deserted posts.

Military Movements (1749–60)

Year	Duration or date	Place	Commander and other officers	Total number	Army regulars
1749	13 June–10 November	Ohio	Céloron de Blainville, 8 officers and cadets	255	
	winter	Saint John River and Isthmus of Chignecto	Boishébert	180	
	September	Canso			
1749–1750	November–May	Isthmus of Chignecto	Chevalier de La Corne	100?	
1750	summer	Saint John River and Isthmus of Chignecto	Léry Jr	50	
	October	Fort Lawrence			
1750–1751	various times	Acadia			
1751	summer	Isthmus of Chignecto	Legardeur de Montesson	250	
1752	June	Pickawillany (Ohio)	Mouet de Langlade, cadet	300	
1753	January–December	Lake Erie, Ohio	Paul Marin, followed, in October, by Jacques Legardeur de Saint-Pierre	2,600	
1754	April	Lake Erie, Ohio	Claude-Pierre Pécaudy de Contrecœur	1,100	

Naval regulars	Militia	Volunteers	Domiciliés	Allies	
20	180		46		Tour of the region to reaffirm French protectorate and incite Amerindians to chase out British traders.
	180				Arriving overland, the detachment is to fortify the site and force the Acadians to emigrate.
					Mi'kmaq declare war on British, sack post at Canso, continue their harassment.
X	X		X		Landing at Baie Verte, La Corne organizes Acadian militia companies. In May, he orders British landed at Beaubassin to withdraw. Returning in September, they erect Fort Lawrence on ruins of village.
20	30				Joins La Corne with a mission to map and fortify the region.
					Assassination of Captain How.
					British seize 3 French boats at Baie Verte and mouth of Saint John River. Sacking of British ship by Mi'kmaq.
	150		100		Arrives to assist parties harassing British; domiciliés cut short their sojourn; Canadians employed in building forts Beauséjour and Gaspareaux.
			60?	240	Party largely composed of Ottawas and Ojibwas pursues British settled there and destroys Miami village.
300	2,100		200		Army of labourers recruited to build 3 forts south of Lake Erie: 400-man vanguard departs in January, the rest in the spring. Fatigue and disease claim many victims.
	1,100				New detachment of labourers.

Year	Duration or date	Place	Commander and other officers	Total number	Army regulars
1755	17 April	Monongahela River (Ohio)	Contrecœur	600	
	28 May	Ohio	Joseph Coulon de Villiers de Jumonville plus 1 officer, 2 cadets	32	
	3 July	Fort Necessity (Ohio)	Louis Coulon de Villiers, Le Mercier, several cadets	615	
	16 June	Fort Beauséjour	Vergor Duchambon	450	
	17 June	Fort Gaspareaux	Villeray	25	
	9 July	Monongahela River	Beaujeu, commander, Dumas, second-in-command, plus 11 officers and 22 cadets	868	
	8 September	Lake George	Dieskau, commander, Montreuil, second-in-command	1,500	210
1756	27 March	Fort Bull (near Oswego)	Léry, commander, plus 15 officers and 3 cadets	393	51
	May–July	Niaouré (Sacket's Harbor, near Oswego)	Louis Coulon de Villiers, commander	660	

Naval regulars	Militia	Volunteers	Domiciliés	Allies	
	600				Contrecœur orders Ward and 41-man garrison to leave fort under construction, naming it Fort Duquesne.
	28				Bearing an ultimatum for the British to leave the valley, Jumonville is surprised by Washington's party of 159 and killed with 9 of his men.
200	300		100	11	Villiers, on his way to intercept a 300-man Virginian detachment, attacks fort where it has taken refuge. After an intense 9-hour gunfight, Washington surrenders with honours of war.
150	350 Acadians				Attacked by Colonel Monckton's 2,000-man force, the fort surrenders after a 4-day siege.
25					The fort, a warehouse on Baie Verte, surrenders without resistance.
72	146		230	407	Departing Fort Duquesne to intercept Braddock's army (1,450 men), the force, composed largely of Amerindians, inflicts heavy losses on the enemy, forcing it to withdraw.
12	600		678		After defeating an initial 1,000-man detachment, the force attacks William Johnson's army, which had been threatening Fort Saint-Frédéric, but gives up after a 4-hour firefight; two other violent clashes take place. Despite the setbacks, the threat to Saint-Frédéric is eliminated.
27	162	9	128		Attack on wagon train, capture of Fort Bull after an intense attack; destruction of warehouses.
	500		100	60	Detachment prepares army's camp on the bay, spies on and harasses British. On 3 July, with 60 members of the Wild Rice group, he wages an intense battle on the Onondaga River and takes 40 prisoners.

Year	Duration or date	Place	Commander and other officers	Total number	Army regulars
1756	2 August	Fort Granville (Pennsylvania)	François Coulon de Villiers, Jacobs (Delaware chief)	55	
	14 August	Oswego (forts George, Oswego, and Ontario)	Montcalm; Rigaud, commander of the colonial militias and soldiers: Rigaud's detachment is vanguard of army	3,047	1,100
	8 September	Delaware village of Attigué (Kittanning), near Fort Duquesne	Normandville, commander; Delaware chief Jacobs, other officers	?	
1757	23 February–22 March	Fort William Henry	Rigaud (Paulhaies, Dumas, and Longueuil, etc.)	1,535	300
	30 June	Wood Creek	not given		
	24 July	near Fort Edward	Marin, lieutenant (Rochebeaucourt)	480	←
	24 July	Lake George (Sabbath Day Point)	Corbière, lieutenant (Langlade, Hertel de Saint-François)	550	
	9 August	Fort William Henry	Montcalm	7,954	2,759
	June	Fort Cumberland	Picoté de Belestre (commander), his nephew Saussaye, Saint-Ours	84	

Naval Regulars	Militia	Volunteers	Domiciliés	Allies	
	23			32	Arriving from Fort Duquesne, partisans burn fort and force small garrison to surrender, returning with 27 prisoners.
137	1,500		234	36	Army lays siege to Fort Ontario; enemy (1,244 men) escapes, taking refuge at Fort George. The British commander is killed early in attack on this latter fort, the garrison surrenders, and the men are taken prisoner.
	X			X	Troop of 300 men arriving from Pennsylvania attacks village, but arrival of Normandville's party forces them to withdraw. Jacobs is killed in this battle.
250	600	35	350		After a fruitless ultimatum, the detachment makes do with burning boats and warehouses around the fort; returns without doing battle.
	10		25	200	On reconnaissance, they are ambushed by 55 rangers commanded by Putnam. Several Amerindians and 1 Canadian killed.
→	80?			400	Returns with 1 prisoner and several scalps after an attack on labourers near the fort and an intense gunfight with garrison that came to their aid.
	50			500	They return with over 150 prisoners after attacking Colonel Parker's forces at the tip of Lake George.
524		2,946	690	1,035	Enemy garrison (2,400 men) capitulates after 6-day siege with honours of war. It is attacked the next day by Amerindian allies on its march to Fort Edward.
				78	Abandoned by the Amerindians, they fall into an ambush on returning from Fort Cumberland; 6 dead.

Year	Duration or date	Place	Commander and other officers	Total number	Army regulars
1757	12 November	German Flatts (New York) (Palatine village)	Picoté de Belestre (7 other officers and 12 cadets)	265	
1758	6 July	near Carillon	Langis and Trépezec (Béarn régiment)	300	150
	8 July	heights of Carillon	Montcalm	3,526	3,111
	26 July	Louisbourg	Drucourt (only 6 French ships due to blockade of French coast)		3,500 soldiers
	28 August	Fort Frontenac	Payen de Noyan	100	←
	4 September	Gaspé			
	14 September	Fort Duquesne	Le Marchand de Lignery	1,500	
	12 October	Fort Loyalhanna (Pennsylvania)	Captain Aubry	550	

Naval egulars	Militia	Volunteers	Domiciliés	Allies	
15		30	200		The party leaves the colony on 4 October, travels up the Mohawk River, attacks and sacks the village on the night of 12 November. It returns with considerable booty and over 150 prisoners.
	130		?		Abandoned by his Amerindian guides, Trépezec is lost and comes upon an enemy column commanded by General Howe. Howe is killed along with Trépezec and 4 other officers; 150 soldiers and Canadians are killed or captured.
150	250		15		French army blocks Abercromby's army (15,000 men) as it advances toward Carillon. The 7-hour battle takes a heavy toll on both camps.
3,000 sailors	X				The enemy (15,000 men, 17 ships, etc.) lands at Gabarus Bay on 8 June. Fort surrenders 26 July after 7-week siege; habitants taken to France.
100					Bradstreet's 3,600-man army lands on the 24th and sets up batteries almost unopposed; fort surrenders after 2-day siege. Large loss of provisions, artillery, and barques from Lake Ontario.
					Settlement undefended; General Wolfe ravages the post and the whole coastline, from Mont-Louis to Pabos (present-day Chandler, QC), 4–18 September. Of 100 residents, 47 are captured and sent to France; the others flee.
	950			550	Allies surprise 800-man detachment commanded by Major Grant near the fort; garrison, assembled by Lignery, routs it.
	450			100	Formed at Fort Duquesne, the party successfully attacks an enemy detachment and blocks the fort for two days before withdrawing.

Year	Duration or date	Place	Commander and other officers	Total number	Army regulars
1758	23 November	Fort Duquesne	Lignery	300	
1759	4 July	Oswego	La Corne Saint-Luc (21 officers)	1,190	
	12 July	Pointe Lévy	Jean-Daniel Dumas, adjutant general of the colonial regulars	1,560	60
	24 July	near Niagara Belle-Famille	Le Marchand de Lignery	700	
	26 July	Niagara	Pouchot	486	149
	26 and 31 July	forts Carillon and Saint-Frédéric	Bourlamaque	3,100	1,500
	31 July	Montmorency	Lévis commands the left flank of the camp		
	9 August– 17 September	parishes up and down river from Quebec			

Naval regulars	Militia	Volunteers	Domiciliés	Allies	
	300				Lignery sends most of garrison home for lack of provisions. With the approach of Forbes's army of 7,000, he evacuates and blows up the fort, retreating to Fort Machault.
261	820		75	34	Having failed to surprise the enemy, the detachment beats a retreat after a gunfight.
100	1,200		200		At the request of Quebec townspeople, a detachment is sent to destroy the batteries on the heights of Lévis that are preparing to bombard the city. On the way, while the Amerindian advance guard scouts ahead, the party thinks it is surrounded, fires on its own men, gives in to panic, and scrambles for the boats.
	700			X	Coming from Fort Machault to relieve Niagara, the party (including a detachment of Illinis and a majority of Canadian militiamen) falls into an ambush and only 150 manage to escape.
204	133			X	Besieged since 6 July by John Prideaux's 2,500-man army, the fort surrenders 20 days later.
500	1,200				With the advance of Amherst's army, the French evacuate and destroy the two forts, then retrench on Île-aux-Noix.
	Montreal battalion			X	Wolfe attacks the retrenchments west of Montmorency Falls. He is pushed back by storms and sniper fire from Montreal militiamen and Amerindians posted on the heights. (Reinforcements from the army's centre and right flank do not contribute.) For Parkman, one of the great battles of the era.
					Burning and destruction of 30 parishes of the government of Quebec.

Year	Duration or date	Place	Commander and other officers	Total number	Army regulars
1759	13 September	walls of Quebec	Montcalm	4,500	? 1,500
	5–6 October	Saint-François (Odanak)			
	11 October	Île-aux-Noix	Bourlamaque	3,023	1,376
1760	February–March	Pointe Lévis	Saint-Martin and ?	X	?
	28 April	Sainte-Foy	Lévis	4,028	2,062 145 offic = 2,207
	28 April–16 May	siege of Quebec	Lévis	6,000	2,900
	18 May	St Lawrence River at Neuville	Vauquelin commanding the *Atalante*	170	
	25 August	Fort Lévis (Île-de-la-Galette?)	Pouchot	277	
	27–8 August	Île-aux-Noix	Bougainville	1,453	775
	8 September	Montreal	Lévis	2,782	2,132 (Lévis)

Naval regulars	Militia	Volunteers	Domiciliés	Allies	
	3,000		X	X	With an army much reduced since the start of the siege, Montcalm faces Wolfe's 4,441-man army and is defeated with the first salvo. Snipers positioned on the flanks hinder the pursuit.
					140 Rangers commanded by Rogers raze the Abenaki village.
417	1,230				
	X				Detachments confront British troops twice around Lévis church. (They capture the church, but the British drive them out. They then attack the garrison left behind by the British.)
898 + o officers = 978	843				The troop advances toward Quebec. The British make a sortie on the 27th and are repelled. They make a second one on the 28th. After a long, hard battle, the French hold their ground.
660	1,840	200	270		They are augmented by militiamen from the government of Quebec used as labourers for digging the trenches. The French artillery opens fire on the 11th, lifting the siege on the 16th after the arrival of the British ships.
o sailors	60				Small fleet supporting Lévis's army pursued by British frigates; several ships run aground, including the *Atalante* after a pitched battle.
	277				Amherst's army (11,000) destroys French warships and lays siege to the fort, which surrenders after a week of intense fire.
	678				After an eight-day siege and uninterrupted bombardment, the weak garrison leaves by night, managing to reach Saint-Jean.
650 (Bernier)					Surrounded by three armies arriving from Quebec, Lake Champlain, and Oswego, Montreal surrenders.

Notes

ABBREVIATIONS

AC   Archives des Colonies: Centre des archives d'outre-mer,
            Archives nationales de France. The series concerning
            the North American colonies under the Ancien Régime
            are, for the most part, available on microfilm at
            Library and Archives Canada and the Centre
            d'archives de Montréal of the Bibliothèque et
            Archives nationales du Québec.

AG   Archives de la Guerre, Bibliothèque du service
            historique de l'armée de terre (France).

ARC   Annual Reports – Public Archives of Canada.

BAnQ-Montréal   Bibliothèque et Archives nationales du Québec, Centre
            d'archives du Vieux-Montréal.

BAnQ-Québec Bibliothèque et Archives nationales du Québec, Centre
            d'archives de Québec.

BRH   *Bulletin des recherches historiques.*

DCB   *Dictionary of Canadian Biography.* Toronto: University
            of Toronto Press, 1966–.

DOLQ   Lemire, Maurice. *Dictionnaire des œuvres littéraires du
            Québec.* Vol. 1, *Des origines à 1900.* Montreal: Fides,
            [1978] 1980.

LAC   Library and Archives Canada, Ottawa.

MCQ   Musée de la civilisation, Quebec.

RAPQ   *Rapport de l'archiviste de la Province de Québec.*

FOREWORD TO THE FRENCH EDITION

I wish to thank Aline Charles, Catherine Desbarats, and especially Sylvie Dépatie for their comments and suggestions on the manuscript, as well as Hélène Paré for her references, corrections, transcriptions, and, most of all, her patience.

1   Paris: Plon, 1974. The thesis bears the same title and was submitted to the Université de Paris-X (Nanterre) in December 1973. For the English translation, see the bibliography of this book.

2   Dechêne, *Power and Subsistence*.

3   *Habitants and Merchants*: ten pages out of nearly 600; *Power and Subsistence*: just three out of nearly 300.

4   On the bellicose character of "traditional" history, see Wien, "En attendant Frégault." Dechêne's work falls within the "war and society" tendency, a field harbouring a great variety of approaches but increasingly insistent upon experience and representations. On the beginnings and progress of this research, see Jones, "New Military History," and Black, "Warfare, State and Society." Keegan, *The Face of Battle*, an important milestone in the study of the experience of war, looms over certain chapters of this book. In 2000, Dechêne reacted to Krusenstjern and Medick, *Zwischen Alltag und Katastrophe*, a book about the social experience of the Thirty Years' War.

5   "The history of the colonial administration – not according to the edicts and ordinances, of course, but as regards its practices – is of additional interest in that it casts a sidelight on the Ancien Régime's perception of its own institutions," she wrote in 1977; Dechêne, "Coup d'oeil," note 53. Desbarats, "La Question de l'État," has some enlightening remarks on the insight into the Ancien Régime as a whole that is to be derived from colonial history.

6   See, e.g., Hamelin, *Économie et société*, influenced by the decolonization of that author's day, or the numerous historians in the nationalist tradition beginning with Garneau, *Histoire du Canada*. Garneau's view (2: 399) is that, for lack of strong commercial opportunities, the Canadians were a "hunting and warring people." See Tocqueville to Abbé Lesueur, 7 September 1831, in Hébert, *L'Amérique française*, 101: "[The Canadians] are warriors par excellence and love excitement more than money."

7   Lambton, *Report*, 7. Cf. Bougainville's remark that Canadians and the French were "of a different, even an enemy nation": Bougainville to his brother, 7 November 1756, in Bougainville, *Écrits*, 392–4; also Horguelin, "Le XVIIIe siècle."

8 These consist essentially of the two plates prepared for the *Historical Atlas of Canada* (Harris, ed., *From the Beginning*), two related articles about Quebec, and a paper on Lower Canadian agriculture in the early nineteenth century. See the bibliography in Dépatie et al., eds, *Vingt ans après*, 296–7.

9 Dechêne, *Power and Subsistence*, 150.

10 Pontchartrain to Vauban, 21 January 1699, in Vauban, *La Correspondence*, 30–6 (note on p. 32), cited *infra*, p. 9.

11 Dechêne, "Les Entreprises."

12 On the historiography up to 1960, see the critical work of Blain in "Économie et société" and "L'Historiographie."

13 Taken from an interview hosted by François Ricard as part of the series *Écrire l'histoire au Québec*, produced by André Major and broadcast on Radio-Canada in July 1981. Transcript, Radio-Canada Archives, Montreal (hereinafter, Dechêne, "Écrire l'histoire"), 7. Cf. Dépatie, "¿El ser más independiente?"

14 In the historian's mind, the two were closely connected. She argued that the historiography up to 1960 did no more than season the discourses found in the sources with various sauces. Given this observation, there was no point in stressing the various schools of thought: She had to take issue with them all. She reserved individual treatment for the most recent works, sometimes in scathing footnotes. A passage deleted from the introduction to this book reads as follows: "the stereotypical image [of the Canadians] just evoked is not a creation of historians, who have merely compiled the remarks of contemporaries, sorted them, and strung them together as their talents and prejudices would permit. I will therefore not undertake to analyze and refute the historiography."

15 Dechêne, *Habitants and Merchants*, xvii.

16 Cf. Wien, "Introduction: Habitants, marchands et historiens," in Dépatie et al., eds, *Vingt ans après*, 3–27.

17 Dechêne, *Habitants and Merchants*, 280. In the typescript of the thesis, the sentence ends with "inflected by the administration's interference": Dechêne, "Habitants et marchands," 2: 571.

18 Dechêne, *Habitants and Merchants*, 280.

19 Ibid. The reference to public economy clearly indicates her awareness of the stimulating paper by Bosher, "Government and Private Interests."

20 Dechêne, "Coup d'oeil sur l'historiographie," 48.

21 Ibid., 53.

22 Orange "Canada"-brand notebook, Dechêne papers (hereinafter, Dechêne, "Problèmes"). The notebook has writing on fifteen or so

pages and is undated, but the works cited on the last pages date from 1977 or 1978.

23 Ibid., [2] (my pagination). Author's emphasis in this citation and the following ones.

24 The historian refers to Marx's preface to *Contribution to the Critique of Political Economy.*

25 Poulantzas, *Political Power and Social Classes.*

26 Dechêne, "Problèmes," [2].

27 Ibid., [3].

28 Ibid., [6].

29 Ibid., [3].

30 Ibid., [5].

31 Dechêne, *Habitants and Merchants,* 196. On this structural nostalgia, see Wien, "Introduction: Habitants, marchands et historiens," in Dépatie et al., eds, *Vingt ans après,* 12–16.

32 Dechêne "Coup d'oeil sur l'historiographie," 53–4.

33 Dechêne, "Écrire l'histoire," 12. See also the introduction to *Habitants and Merchants,* xv.

34 "Ordre public et organisation militaire au Canada à la fin du régime français," grant proposal by L. Dechêne to SSHRC, 1984.

35 André Corboz offers a good description of this sort of trajectory, more representative of the actual path followed by researchers than the nice linear fictions we make up for our grant proposals. See his celebration of the sinuous paths taken by humanities researchers, characterized by "the work of coming up with hypotheses, making one's way painstakingly through the maze, doubting oneself, taking detours, doubling back, making productive mistakes, following the path that diverges, even reaching impasses": Corboz, "La recherche," note 25. Thanks to Catherine Desbarats for pointing me toward this paper.

36 Dechêne, "Problèmes," [9–11] and detached sheet found between pages [11] and [12]: an outline for McGill University course numbered History 643D, September 1977, listing the following as some of the "Problems in [Quebec and Canadian] rural history" to be discussed: "mediations between rural society and the state; the role of certain intermediaries (militia captains, parish priests, seigneurs, local bourgeoisie) ... the measure of participation in local decisions; conflict or passivity."

37 Notable among numerous contributions is Bouchard, *La Nation québécoise.*

38 Dechêne, *Power and Subsistence,* 5.

39 On this subject, see Colin M. Coates's study on M. de Verchères in Coates and Morgan, *Heroines and History*, 17–40; Gervais and Lusignan, "De Jeanne d'Arc à Madeleine de Verchères."

40 Here and in subsequent citations to *People, State, and War* in the front matter, the number in parentheses indicates the page number in the body of the text.

41 See the appendices for a list of troop movements, which is discussed at the beginning of ch. 4.

42 Useful in this connection is Sulte, *Histoire de la milice*, 59: "The few companies sent to us from France, from 1684 to circa 1740, were to some extent mere auxiliaries of our militia, for the latter had, with manifest preponderance, taken on the task of defending Canada." See also Eccles, *The Canadian Frontier*.

43 Cf. Eccles, *The Government of New France*; Zoltvany, *The Government of New France*; Standen, "Politics." On the nominations and the elbowing match surrounding them in a colony where offices could not be purchased, see Moogk, *La Nouvelle France*, 184, 189–91.

44 Title of ch. 6.

45 On the legend that gives an entirely different meaning to this murder case, see Jean-Claude Dupont, "Jacquin, dit Philibert, Nicolas," DCB, 3: 328–9.

46 Stanley, *New France*.

47 The citation repeats the provisional title of ch. 8, whose final title is "Sixteen Years of War (1744–60)."

48 The author was devoting close study here to Anderson, *A People's Army*, which makes skillful use of the wealth of sources from Massachusetts, including militiamen's diaries.

49 See, e.g., Casgrain, *Guerre du Canada*; Eccles, "The French Forces."

50 L. Dechêne, undated card, "L'effort final." There are striking parallels between this discussion, on the ground and subsequently among historians, and the one taking place in the Anglo-American sphere. Shy, *Toward Lexington*; Leach, *Roots of Conflict*; Higginbotham, "The Early American Way"; Anderson, *Crucible*; Brumwell, *Redcoats*; Chet, *Conquering the American Wilderness*.

51 This is apparently also true of ch. 1.

52 References in Stacey, *Quebec*. In a hurry to get to the battles of the Plains of Abraham and Sainte-Foy, military history tends to give short shrift to the rural invasion of the summer of 1759. As to the systematic destruction wrought during the month of August, even French-language historians devote very little space to it. Ferland, *Cours d'histoire*, 575, 584–6; Casgrain, *Guerre du Canada*, 192–5; Stacey, *Quebec*, 103–8,

193–4; Frégault, *Canada*, 251–2. A useful local history: Deschênes, *L'Année des Anglais*. On Stacey, see *infra*, note 62.

53 Notes dictated on 28 June 2000.

54 Steele (*Betrayals*, 113, 132) emphasizes this aspect of the Canadians' motivation.

55 Holy war was of course quite prominent among many Anglo-American provincials' motives for fighting. On the sermons, see Hatch, "The Origins"; on their reception by the Massachusetts militiamen, see Anderson, *A People's Army*, 196–223.

56 After the Conquest, Murray (*Report*, 5–30) and Brooke (*History of Emily Montague*) took up, to a degree, where the British military propagandists had left off.

57 "Conclusion générale de l'étude."

58 Cf. Frégault, *Canada*. The thesis according to which the Canadians faced two adversaries (the British and the French) is taken to extremes in LaPierre, *The Battle for Canada*.

59 It might even be hypothesized that this loyalty *manifests itself* under certain conditions as a prickly form of particularism. According to V.H. Breen, the awakening of the independence movement in the Thirteen Colonies in the 1760s reflected the rise, in Great Britain, of a nationalist sentiment *excluding* the Anglo-Americans, who had always thought of themselves as British. While the resemblances between the two colonial situations should not be exaggerated, Breen's argument suggests that manifestations of Canadian particularism in the face of criticism from the mother country should be read not as a sign of colonial disaffection but as a demand for recognition of French identity. It would be stimulating to reread the sources in order to ascertain whether French soldiers, who typically served as witnesses to the existence of Canadian nationalist sentiment, also incited its first stirrings by refusing to regard their Canadian counterparts as fully French. Breen, "Ideology and Nationalism"; cf. Greene, "Search for Identity."

60 The author's sensibility here is close to that of Arlette Farge, e.g., in "De la guerre."

61 Historians interested in the Anglo-American victims have understandably laid more stress on this violence: Demos, *The Unredeemed Captive*; Haefeli and Sweeney, *Captors and Captives*. See also Steele, *Betrayals*, an analysis of the Fort William Henry "massacre" (1757) and a meditation on the category of "savagery" and its subsequent enactment.

62 One of the few authors to devote a few pages to the devastation of the countryside in August 1759, Stacey is palpably ill at ease but nonetheless

concludes that the Canadians would not have hesitated to do likewise on the outskirts of the Anglo-American towns: "War in the eighteenth century was a nasty business ... and no one knew it better than the people of Canada." Stacey, *Quebec*, 103–8, citation 108.

63 See Wien, "Vie et transfiguration."

64 John Mitchell, *The Contest*, 137–8.

65 In a revealing chain of events, Wolfe invoked the rumour that the Indigenous people were on the point of subjecting three British grenadiers to ritual torture when he threatened to raze the Canadian countryside: "If this be true, the Country shall be but one universal blaze." Wolfe to Monckton, 25 July 1759, Monckton Documents, Northcliffe Collection, vol. 22, quoted in Way, "The Cutting Edge," quote on p. 135.

66 It remains that the Canadian militiamen are not always so clearly differentiated, in British or Anglo-American discourse on the enemy, from the men who fought alongside them. These accounts are replete with striking images of Frenchmen as devil worshippers – a typical trope of nascent English or British nationalism – and "savages," "French and Indians." At least at first sight, these portrayals are vastly more frequent than those of mere "Canadians." See Hatch, "The Origins"; Way, "The Cutting Edge." On nationalisms, see Kidd, *British Identities*, adding nuance to Colley, *Britons*, and Bell, *The Cult of the Nation*. Older English-language historiography follows this same pattern; e.g., Leach, *Arms for Empire*. Much more clarity is to be found in Anderson, *Crucible*.

67 See Pritchard, *In Search of Empire*.

68 Ibid.

FOREWORD TO THE ENGLISH EDITION

My thanks to Aline Charles, Sylvie Dépatie, and Catherine Desbarats, who were kind enough to comment on one version or another of this text. All responsibility for errors or omissions remains with me.

1 Church, "Review," 761; Dechêne, *Power and Subsistence*.

2 Dechêne, *Le Peuple, l'État et la guerre.*

3 "This is obviously a long-term endeavour and I am perseverant," wrote Dechêne – more prophetically, presumably, than she might have wished – in the 1976 sabbatical leave application that officially launched the enterprise. The project initially concerned the Seven Years' War alone. Louise Dechêne, Canada Council Leave Application, 30 September 1976, p. 3b. Université de Montréal, Division de la gestion des documents et des

archives, E 0016, fonds du Département d'histoire, dossiers "carrière des professeurs."

4 Desbarats and Greer, "The Seven Years' War," 160. This 2007 article, which summarized *Le Peuple* and situated it in the *longue durée* of the historiography of New France, was part of the advance billing the study received from several of those who had revised or reviewed the manuscript. Historical geographer Cole Harris dedicated his survey of early Canadian history to Louise Dechêne and took into account her interpretation of state power: Harris, *The Reluctant Land*, 83, 87–8, 90. The following cited the forthcoming book: Horguelin, "Le XVIIIᵉ siècle des canadiens," 211; Desbarats, "La Question de l'État," 196; Ruggiu, "La Noblesse du Canada," 72, n. 22, and 74, n. 46.

5 This is true of all three of her monographs: Desbarats, "Foreword," x. The other monograph is Dechêne, *Habitants and Merchants*.

6 "It is because there [is] a contest that there is something to narrativize," wrote Hayden White a third of a century ago: White, *The Content of the Form*, 19.

7 See this historian's enormously influential 1971 article: W.J. Eccles, "The Social, Economic, and Political Significance."

8 Quotation: Dull, *The French Navy*, xii. Dechêne continued the systematic comparison between colony and metropole that she had begun in *Habitants and Merchants* and sketched out even earlier. See, for example, her 1970 review of W.J. Eccles's *The Canadian Frontier*. Taking issue with Eccles's contention that "enlightened legislators" (Dechêne's ironic expression) had endowed the colony with institutions that were remarkably well-adapted to colonial conditions, she continued: "To convince, the argument should take into account the evolution of the same institutions in [France] and measure the discrepancies." Dechêne, "Compte rendu," 322.

9 Reviews and comments: Bariteau, "Compte rendu"; Bernier, "Travail de Louise Dechêne"; Delâge, "Les Premières Nations," 45–52; Tremblay, "Questions de méthode," 258–60; Blais and Saint-Pierre, "*Le Peuple*"; Dickinson, "Compte rendu"; Gagnon, "Compte rendu." The *Revue d'histoire de l'Amérique française*, the French-language journal of record in the field, did not publish a review of the work.

10 For example, there has been no equivalent for New France of Jill Lepore's or Peter Silver's innovative work on war and culture in the British colonies: Lepore, *The Name of War*; Silver, *Our Savage Neighbours*. In addition to much traditional military history, some of it reissued, the anniversary did prompt the publication of new perspectives on the global

character of the Seven Years' War. On such international aspects (including Indigenous nations), see, for example: Baugh, *The Global Seven Years' War*; Dziembowski, *La Guerre de Sept Ans*; Danley and Speelman, eds, *The Seven Years' War*; Delâge, "Les Premières Nations"; Beaulieu, "'Under His Majesty's Protection.'" Souvenirs of the 200th anniversary (1959): Stacey, *Québec, 1759*; Frégault, *Canada*. For surveys of some of the work marking the 250th anniversary, see Wien, "Note de lecture," and Wien, "La Conquête racontée en 2009."

11 Canadian Historical Association, "CHA Prizes," https://cha-shc.ca/english/ what-we-do/prizes/the-cha-best-scholarly-book-in-canadian-history-prize. htm. Page consulted 31 July 2020. The Institut d'histoire de l'Amérique française awarded *Le Peuple* the Prix Lionel-Groulx for 2009.

12 Delâge, "Les Premières Nations," 50.

13 Greer, "National, Transnational, and Hypernational Historiographies," 709 and 709, n. 22.

14 The expression is Gilles Havard's: *Histoire des coureurs de bois*, 181.

15 Already noted in Nicolai, "A Different Kind of Courage" (1989), such hybridity is very much in evidence in more recent studies: Nerich, *La Petite guerre*; Balvay, *L'Épée et la plume*, 150–9; Mourin, *Porter la guerre*; Fonck, "'Joindre au système tactique d'Europe'"; Noël, *Montcalm*; Panissié, "La Petite guerre"; Thévenin, "*Changer le système*." See also Rice, "War and Politics," on the overlap between European and Indigenous ways of war.

16 Dechêne pointed to the brutality of certain joint Canadian/Indigenous border raids (pp. 96–9), attributing it in part to *French* traditions, but carefully circumscribed colonists' adoption of Indigenous practices of war. More recent work has turned up additional evidence of such participation. See, above all, Havard, *Empire et métissages* (1st ed.), 173–7, 737–47. On colonists' involvement in scalping: ibid., 742, where it is presented as an "occasional" practice, a more cautious judgment than Jean-François Lozier's description of recourse to the practice "without scruples": Lozier, "Lever des chevelures," 526.

17 J.-F. Lozier similarly notes some metropolitan officers' instrumental attitudes toward scalping: Lozier, "Lever des chevelures," 535.

18 Principally Crouch, *Nobility Lost*. Osman, "Pride, Prejudice" treats the same themes more schematically. Both argue that metropolitan officers' disenchantment with colonial ways of war decisively undermined their resolve to defend the colony during the war's last phase – and in Crouch's case, that it contributed to the decision not to seek the return of New France during the peace negotiations. For different interpretations of the

diplomacy, see Ruggiu, "Une relation tombée dans l'oubli?"; Dewar,
"Canada or Guadeloupe?" Among the officers, Bougainville has attracted
the most attention recently; he emerges as a more complex figure than pre-
viously suspected: Richard, "Bougainville à la lumière de ses lectures";
Veyssière, "Louis-Antoine de Bougainville au Canada"; Crouch, *Nobility
Lost*, 178–90. Another example: Passerat de La Chapelle, in Gagné,
Inconquis. Pichichero, *Military Enlightenment*, 45–8, 148, signals certain
French officers' ethnographic interest in Indigenous peoples.

19 Pichichero, *Military Enlightenment*. Historians of war in Europe have
increasingly explored the limits of eighteenth-century "civilized" warfare
("guerre en dentelles"). For a summary of these studies, see Thévenin,
"*Changer le système*," 154–60. A revealing case study for early in the
century: Vo-Ha, "Le Sort des vaincus." On the horror of warfare on both
sides of the Atlantic: Plank, *Atlantic Wars*, 152–76. All this points to the
selective amnesia of a Montcalm denouncing the "savagery" of war in
North America. The discussion on the evolution of tactics, intermittently
Atlantic in scope, bears revisiting: Paret, "Colonial Experience"; Picaud-
Monnerat, *La Petite guerre*; Drévillon, "Les Lumières," 385.

20 Fonck, "Joindre au système," 171–2; Ward, "Crossing the Line?"
On mobilization: Chartrand, "La Milice canadienne."

21 Plank, *Rebellion and Savagery*, 171–4.

22 Drévillon, "Les Lumières," 404.

23 Appropriately, the book's very first pages present unwilling recruits whom
the intrepid, cross-dressing Anne Edmond, a sort of anti–Madeleine de
Verchères, attempts to save from the dangers of military service far from
home. Dechêne summarily debunks Verchères's claim to heroism
(p. 91–2). In *Women at War*, Gina Martino usefully proposes a broader
approach to women's "war-making" in New England and New France.
Yet in focusing on various forms of female participation in the French
colony's successive war efforts, she inadvertently reinforces the militaristic
stereotype Dechêne calls into question. Leslie Choquette takes inventory
of colonists' fears, relativizing the importance of war among the causes:
Choquette, "From Sea Monsters and Savages." On resilient Canadian
families during the Seven Years' War: Mathieu and Imbeault, *La Guerre
des canadiens*. Dechêne's re-evaluation of the militia's contribution to
colonial defence has been generally accepted; perhaps it has helped the
colony's uniformed defenders to emerge from the militia's shadow. In any
case, by 2008, the heroic militiaman was clearly coming to the end of his
run, as evinced by the appearance earlier in the decade of work skeptical
of received ideas on the Canadian militia's role. Cassel, "The Militia

Legend"; Lozier, "Les Officiers de milice canadiens." A sign of general acknowledgment of Dechêne's revisionist perspective: senior military historian René Chartrand's 2009 article relativizing colonists' military importance and referring the reader to *Le Peuple* "on all questions relative to the militia." Chartrand, "La Gouvernance militaire," 130, n. 9. For a sample of Chartrand's earlier views on the militia, see his "Death Walks on Snowshoes." A holdout: Lépine, "Les Stratégies militaires." Recent work on non-professional combatants has focused on *coureurs de bois*: Havard, *Histoire des coureurs de bois*, 175–82; Mourin, "Le Nerf de la guerre." On the regular troops, see Cassel, "The Troupes de la Marine" (1989), a pioneering study; Fournier, ed., *Combattre pour la France*, a collective volume containing both chapters (including Lessard, "Les Soldats," on the *colonial* regulars) and capsule biographies of nearly 7,500 members of the French battalions sent to protect Canada and Louisbourg during the regime's final war; Lesueur, *Les Troupes coloniales*; Lesueur, "Les Mutations"; Fournier, ed., *Les Officiers des troupes*. Databases: http://www.ccbn-nbc.gc.ca/fr/histoire-patrimoine/batailles-1759-1760/soldats/; http://sgq.qc.ca/bases/marine.php. More generally, historians have tended to revise upward their evaluation of the French monarchy's efforts to defend the colony in the Seven Years' War. Witness, for example, Jonathan Dull's observation: "France made great, perhaps excessive efforts to save Canada, *including* becoming involved in a European war." Dull, *The French Navy*, xii. A notable early correction on the French effort to defend its colony is J.S. Pritchard's study of shipping patterns, making much of the intense supply ship traffic between metropole and colony during the last two wars: Pritchard, "The Pattern," 196–200.

24 The term is Allan Greer's: *Property*, 357.

25 Introducing "negotiated empires": Greene, "Transatlantic Colonization." See notably Havard, *Empire et métissages* (1st ed.), 336–46, 777; Dubé, "S'approprier l'Atlantique"; Weyhing, "Le Sueur in the Sioux Country"; Weyhing, "'Gascon Exaggerations'"; Rushforth, "Insinuating Empire." To varying degrees, the above authors take issue with those who present the French empire's reliance on insubordinate "rogues" as a sign of dysfunction: Dawdy, *Building the Devil's Empire*; Pritchard, *In Search of Empire*; Banks, *Chasing Empire*; Hinderaker, *Elusive Empires*. Accomodation: Beik, "The Absolutism of Louis XIV." Adding colonial elites to the equation: Greer, *Property*; Houllemare, "Procedures."

26 See notably Brett Rushforth's spectacular example of two successive colonial governors, slaveowners themselves, who were discreetly complicit in the subversion through trade in Indigenous slaves of royal policy on

western expansion, by Indigenous allies and a network of colonial officers, traders, merchants, and slaveholders. Rushforth, *Bonds*, 197–221.

27 Havard, *Histoire des coureurs de bois*, 183–91; Horguelin, "Le XVIIIᵉ siècle"; Belmessous, "Être français en Nouvelle-France"; Coates, "Problems of Precedence"; Vidal, ed., *Français?*; Englebert and Wegmann, eds, *French Connections*. On other empires, see for example: Breen, "Ideology and Nationalism"; Greene, "Colonial History"; McConville, *The King's Three Faces*; Cañeque, *The King's Living Image*; Adelman, "An Age of Imperial Revolutions." In elite circles, Frenchness came to be reinforced by racialism: Aubert, "'The Blood of France'"; Belmessous, "Assimilation and Racialism."

28 Jesuits: Greer, *Mohawk Saint*; True, *Masters and Students*; Sayre, "*Michipichik* and the Walrus." Domiciliés and slaves: Grabowski, "Les Amérindiens domiciliés"; Grabowski, "French Criminal Justice"; Greer, *Mohawk Saint*; Lozier, *Flesh Reborn*; Beaugrand-Champagne, *Le Procès de Marie-Josèphe Angélique*; Rushforth, *Bonds of Alliance*; Deslandres, "Femmes devant le tribunal du roi"; Deslandres, "Voix des esclaves autochtones."

29 Greenblatt, "Cultural Mobility," 2–3.

30 Contact zone: Pratt, *Imperial Eyes*, 1–12.

31 "Forward-looking" history: Cooper, *Colonialism in Question*, 19.

32 Recent perspectives: Rushforth, *Bonds of Alliance*; Greer, *Property*; Havard, "Les Pays d'en haut."

COMPILING AND EDITING THE TEXT

1 We wish to thank the following archivists who helped us with this work: Denise Beaugrand-Champagne, Centre d'archives de Montréal, BAnQ; Pierre-Louis Lapointe, Centre d'archives de Québec, BAnQ; Anne Laplante, Centre de référence de la Nouvelle-France, Musée de la civilisation, Québec; Marc Lacasse, Archives de l'Univers culturel de Saint-Sulpice, Montreal, as well as Jean-François Palomino, Direction de la recherche et de l'édition, BAnQ, who identified the drawings (views of Quebec and Fort Chambly) used for the cover illustration of the French edition.

INTRODUCTION

1 The explanation given was that the heavy snow pack made walking too hard. The army numbered 2,150 men when it left Montreal on 4 July. The number of militiamen is not specified, but it is known that two of the four

militia battalions came from the eastern end of the colony, so 400 men at a minimum may be assumed. *RAPQ* (1928–29): 308–18, Frontenac to the minister, 25 October 1696, and 320–2, Frontenac and Champigny to the minister, 26 October 1696. For the configuration and command of the militia, see Bacqueville de La Potherie, *Histoire*, 3: 270–82.

2 The preceding and following details come from examinations of the accused and depositions by the witnesses dated 14–16 June 1696: BAnQ-Québec, TP1–S777–D2. The documents were published in Pierre-Georges Roy, "Un procès criminel au dix-septième siècle: Anne Edmond accusée de s'être travestie en homme et d'avoir répandu de fausses nouvelles," *BRH* 10 (1904): 193–211, 229–43. I have attempted here to preserve the text of the testimony without necessarily quoting it directly.

3 In general, trials before the intendant left few traces – a judgment at best – while the great majority of those presided over by his subdelegates left no trace at all. It was purely by accident that the charges laid against Anne Edmond were found amid the archives of the Conseil Supérieur.

4 *RAPQ* (1926–27): 37, Frontenac to Colbert, 13 November 1673. Since he did not really believe the rumour, the governor carried on with his plan, but the false news did oblige him to take certain precautions.

5 The party consisted of 625 men, including 310 militiamen. After destroying three villages and taking many prisoners (women and children), it was attacked on the return journey and struggled to reach the colony. For details, see the biographies of Nicolas d'Ailleboust de Manthet and Augustin Legardeur de Courtemanche, who commanded the expedition: Jean Blain, "Ailleboust de Manthet, Nicolas d'," *DCB*, 2: 13–14; Nora T. Corley, "Le Gardeur de Courtemanche, Augustin," *DCB*, 2: 398–400.

6 The information is from Tanguay, *Dictionnaire généalogique*, 1: 224, 257; Roy, "Les Terres de l'Île d'Orléans: Les terres de Sainte-Famille," in *RAPQ* (1949–51): 201, and Roy and Roy, eds, *Inventaire*, which contains several land transactions involving the Gaulins. Ordained as a priest in 1697, Antoine would spend his life among the Abenakis and the Mi'kmaq of Acadia and Île Royale, where he earned the reputation of a militarily and politically engaged missionary: David Lee, "Gaulin, Antoine," *DCB*, 2: 246–7. Two other Gaulin sons died in 1687 at the ages of 21 and 24, no doubt carried off by the epidemic then sweeping through the colony, but the fact that one of them died at Montreal may not be unrelated to the military campaign of that year. If so, that could explain the determination of the two younger boys to stay home.

7 The version used here is that of Anne, which, despite a few contradictions, is more coherent than that of her brother, who denied all knowledge of the

facts and swore that he wanted nothing better than to go to war. It seems obvious that Anne was a clever girl who had more of what it took to play the role of a mysterious stranger than the four boys.

8 See Frégault, *Iberville*, 192–209, for the movements of 1696. Iberville (with the help of the Iroquois) had come to the relief of Villebon on the Saint John River and captured the English fort of Pemaquid during the summer, then went over to Newfoundland to pillage the English fisheries during the winter.

9 See Roy, "Le Flibustier Baptiste," on the prizes taken by Baptiste and Guyon in 1695. Claude Guyon, Joseph's uncle, was a habitant of Sainte-Famille, and the Gaulins were vaguely related to the Guyons through their mother, Marie Rocheron. This is a good source of information.

10 AC, F3, 7: 54v, "Relation de ce qui s'est passé en Canada...," 4 November 1693; Frégault, *Iberville*, 161–2.

11 The affair was deemed serious enough to merit a brief mention in the official account of the year 1696: AC, CI IA, 14: 35–64, "Relation de ce qui s'est passé..."

12 Bacqueville de la Potherie, *Histoire*, 3: 269–70. The memory of the affair was still alive two years later when the author arrived in the colony. He inserted it to break the monotony of battle stories.

13 Iberville was accompanied by French and Canadian sailors, young merchant adventurers in the service of the Compagnie du Nord.

14 Dechêne, *Habitants and Merchants* (published in its original French edition in 1974) hardly mentions war, even though it was omnipresent on the Island of Montreal.

CHAPTER ONE

1 Pontchartrain to Vauban, Versailles, 21 January 1699, in Vauban, *La Correspondence*, 32. Pontchartrain (1674–1747) was to hold the position of secretary of state for the navy from September 1699 to 1715. Vauban's plan is set out in "Moyen de rétablir nos colonies d'Amérique et de les accroître en peu de temps" [1699], in *Les Oisivetés*, 539–73. He proposed sending 50,000 soldiers along with contingents of war brides; after five years, some 10,000 had settled, enough to revive the settlement plan.

2 The possibility that there was a colonial audience for works on New France at the time of their publication was not even envisaged by Maurice Lemire (*La Vie littéraire*, 1: xii and ch. 1). These books, he claimed, were written by Frenchmen for Frenchmen and would not reach a Canadian audience until the nineteenth century. I shall return to the author's

assumption that there was a cultural conflict between French and Canadians, with which I disagree: see *infra*, 196 and note 16.

3 Duchet, *Anthropologie et histoire*, 125–36.

4 Pierre de Troyes kept a journal of his Hudson Bay campaign (April–September 1686) and a Quebec canon transcribed verbatim a passage from this journal in a handwritten memorial on miracles dating from 1687: Troyes, *Journal de l'expédition*, 88–9; MCQ, Fonds d'archives du Séminaire de Québec, "Miracles opérés à la bonne Sainte-Anne," MS 297. Accounts of the siege of Quebec in 1690 circulated locally, being plagiarized from author to author: Myrand, ed., *Sir William Phips*.

5 Map legend by Desceliers (1546–50): La Roncière, *Jacques Cartier*, 194–5. Roberval was authorized to draft men from prisons to fill out his crews: Lacoursière, "La tentative."

6 Le Blant and Baudry, eds, *Nouveaux documents*, 26.

7 Ibid., 27. On these various episodes, see Trudel, *Les Vaines Tentatives*.

8 Dollier de Casson, *Histoire du Montréal*, 201–2.

9 Lebrun, "Les soulèvements populaires," cited in Frostin, "Du peuplement pénal," 72.

10 See Frostin, "Du peuplement pénal"; also Farge, *Dire et mal dire*, 167–71; Revel, *Logiques de la foule*, 98–111; Giraud, *Histoire de la Louisiane française*, 1: 152–4, 3: 252–4.

11 See Gutton, "La Déportation." Charles de Biencourt and Isaac de Razilly were among those who called for vagrants to be impressed into their enterprises. See, e.g., the charter of the Compagnie de Morbihan (1626): Trudel, *Les Événements*, 1–6.

12 Archives du séminaire de Saint-Sulpice, fonds Faillon, cahier X (136), f. 61–2: letter from Voyer d'Argenson (unidentified recipient), 14 October 1658. The policy was much clearer in England: As of 1615, sentences could be commuted to "parts abroad," and relegation became an important phenomenon after the Restoration. Davies, *The North Atlantic World*, 91–3.

13 Chevalier de Baugy to his brother, Quebec, 27 October and 22 November 1682, in Baugy, *Journal*, 151, 153–4.

14 AC, CIIA, 6: 184–84v, de Meulles to the minister, 4 November 1683.

15 [Raudot], *Relation par lettres*, 4. Despite a printing permit dated 25 August 1725, the work would go unpublished. Raudot was co-intendant of Canada with his father from 1705 to 1711.

16 La Tour, *Mémoires*, 56–7. The work was written before 1755. The turpitude of the first immigrants was stressed in order to throw the merits of the holy bishop into relief. "God blessed his care" in sending the Carignan

regiment, "whose officers were men of honour and merit, the soldiers quite good men" (p. 57).

17 See, e.g., Aleyrac, *Aventures militaires*, 25–34.

18 Lahontan, "Nouveaux voyages," in *Œuvres complètes*, 1: 265–7.

19 Challes, *Journal*, 217, 522–8. The work was first published at Rouen in 1721, shortly after the death of the author, who was a naval scrivener after having made several sojourns in Acadia with Clerbaud Bergier's Compagnie de la pêche sédentaire. See the preface by Frédéric Deloffre, whose writing did much to publicize the works of Challes, considered today one of the era's most interesting writers.

20 Lesage, *The Adventures*. See also Chinard, *L'Amérique*, 271–312. It was only in the eighteenth century that Canada began to receive prisoners regularly. C. Le Beau's romanticized memoir, *Avantures*, describes one of these experiences of relegation.

21 Thwaites, ed., *The Jesuit Relations*; see the relations of 1634 (6: 98–106), 1635 (7: 254–6), and 1637 (11: 74–8); Morin, *Histoire*, 36–8, 49–55; Dollier de Casson, *Histoire du Montréal, passim*, e.g., 48–66, 78.

22 Charlevoix, *History*, 2: 99. This passage rounds out a description of the "edifying conduct of the inhabitants of Quebec" in 1638. Charlevoix lived in Canada from 1705 to 1708, at which time the pioneers of heroic days would have been over 100 years old.

23 Bacqueville de La Potherie, *Histoire*, 1: 368. Partly written in Canada, the work was submitted for publication in 1702, but Jérôme de Pontchartrain, to whom the author was related, had its printing delayed until after the war. A first edition is said to have appeared in 1716, while the one known to us is from 1722; it was republished in its entirety in 1997 by Éd. du Rocher (n.p.). See also the biographical article by Léon Pouliot, "Le Roy dit Bacqueville de La Potherie, Claude-Charles," *DCB*, 2: 439–41, and Marie-Aimée Cliche, "*Histoire de l'Amérique septentrionale*, de Claude-Charles Le Roy, dit Bacqueville de La Potherie," *DOLQ*, 322–5.

24 AC, F3, 24: 88, "Description du Fleuve St. Louis au Mississipi et de la Riviere de la Mobile par M. de Rémonville," 1715. Rémonville was an old friend of La Salle's, according to Giraud, *Histoire de la Louisiane française*, 1: 14.

25 Even Charlevoix, who readily forgot what he had just written as he jumped from source to source, ascribed the numerousness of the nobility in Canada to the men of the Carignan regiment: *History*, 3: 111; *idem*, *Journal*, 401–2. His remarks are reproduced nearly verbatim by Nicolas-Gaspard Boucault, special lieutenant of the provost court of Quebec, in "État présent du Canada," *RAPQ* (1920–21): 16. The regiment sent to

Canada in 1665 to subdue the Iroquois left some 400 soldiers and about twenty officers in the colony – a very small proportion of total seventeenth-century immigration and no more than 20 per cent of the nobles who settled there. See Gadoury, *La Noblesse*, 33 and Appendix 2, 166–70.

26 Boucher, *Histoire véritable*, particularly the foreword and pp. 155–6.

27 Le Clercq, *First Establishment*, 2: 16.

28 Dollier de Casson, *Histoire du Montréal*, 235.

29 Thwaites, ed., *The Jesuit Relations*, 12: 159. Similarly, Maisonneuve covered his men while they retreated, and he stayed alone, brandishing two pistols, to face the enemy army. Dollier de Casson, *Histoire du Montréal*, 94–6.

30 Hertel's conduct during his captivity is described in Charlevoix, *History*, 3: 43, Brigeac's in Dollier de Casson, *Histoire du Montréal*, 233–5.

31 Charlevoix, *History*, 2: 251.

32 Dollier de Casson is particularly hard on the Hurons, whom he calls "basilisks": *Histoire du Montréal*, 112–13. A passage in which Lejeune indulges in sarcasm is quoted in Pioffet, "L'arc et l'épée," 45.

33 [Raudot], *Relation par lettres*, 5–8. Unlike the other authors, Raudot believed that Frenchmen accustomed to the terrain were as competent as Canadians.

34 Franquet, *Voyages*, 193.

35 Charlevoix, *Journal*, 403; Kalm, *Voyage*, 422, and similar remarks at pp. 413, 450, and 552.

36 Franquet, *Voyages*, 193.

37 [Raudot], *Relation par lettres*, 5; Charlevoix, *Journal*, 402; Bacqueville de La Potherie, *Histoire*, 1: 167–70.

38 "That climate being suited to the production of warlike men": Vauban, *La Correspondence*, 28.

39 Bacqueville de La Potherie, *Histoire*, 1: 51. The only image of the colonists left us by the French regime, this woodcut is often reproduced as an illustration of the militiaman or the *coureur de bois*. Contrary to what some have written, there is nothing typically "Canadian" about this costume: Landry, ed., *Pour le Christ*.

40 Exquemelin, *Bucaniers of America*. See, on this subject, Chinard, *L'Amérique*, 245–79, a chapter in which the author draws parallels between Exquemelin's adventures and those of Beauchêne, the Canadian adventurer dreamed up by Lesage. The woodcut is reproduced in Cardini, *La Culture*. Exquemelin's book first appeared in a 1678 Dutch edition published in Amsterdam.

41 Bacqueville de La Potherie, *Histoire*, preface to vol. 3.

42 Ibid., 1: 366.

43 Ibid., 1: 167. Frontenac's correspondence contains no such statement.

44 See Léon Pouliot, "Le Roy de la Potherie, *dit* Bacqueville de la Potherie (La Poterie), Claude-Charles," in DCB, 2: 439–41, and Marie-Aimée Cliche, "*Histoire de l'Amérique septentrionale*, de Claude-Charles Le Roy, dit Bacqueville de La Potherie," DOLQ, 322–5. I am using the name that appears on the title page of the book. The full name is Claude-Charles Le Roy de Bacqueville de La Potherie (not "dit Bacqueville" as the two biographers indicate). See Le Blant, *Histoire*, 65–76, for the family histories. Even though the *Nouveau d'Hozier* (Bibliothèque nationale, Paris) dates the author's birth to 1663 in Paris, I think it is better to trust the author himself, who has no reason to lie about his colonial background. Moreover, the *Nouveau d'Hozier*'s information does not accord with the history of the family as retraced by Le Blant.

45 Kalm, *Voyage*, 422–3. On the passages concerning the degeneracy of the Americans (comparative longevity of humans and animals, etc.) in the 1761 French edition, see Echeverria, *Mirage*, 8–9. Apparently, Kalm had been thinking along these lines before the publication, in 1749, of the first volumes of Buffon's *Histoire naturelle*.

46 The authenticity of this memoir was a matter of dispute among early twentieth-century scholars, as discussed by René Baudry in his biographical article on a man named Robert Chevalier, who was said to have had such adventures: "Chevalier, dit Beauchêne, Robert," DCB, 2: 148–9. In my view, all indications are that these adventures were imaginary and that this is precisely what makes them interesting. Note that among other sources, Lesage made copious use of Bacqueville de La Potherie's work and even had that author make a cameo in one of the book's last episodes. The novel did not enjoy much success. See Laufer, *Lesage*, 389–94.

47 Moniker adopted by buccaneers; see Deschamps, *Pirates et flibustiers*, 39–63. Exquemelin, *Bucaniers of America*, and Labat, *Nouveau voyage*, popularized these themes. "We are all equals," said the buccaneers to Beauchêne to induce him to go to sea with them (p. 56). See *supra*, note 20.

48 References to Indigenous people's unconditional devotion to the heroes of the novel are frequent. On the death of Miss Du Clos, eight Huron women immolate themselves to accompany in the afterlife the woman whom their village has chosen as sovereign.

49 Challes, *Mémoires*, 274–5. Challes (or Challe) made several voyages in Acadia in 1683 and 1688 as a partner in the Compagnie de la pêche

sédentaire (Acadia). A portion of his memoirs, written ca. 1714–16, deals with his colonial experiences. The author mixes realistic description with flights of imagination.

50 Ibid., 84, on the Canadians' ability to survive by hunting or cannibalism, like their enemies. For an example of this fascination, see the letter of 24 August 1757 from Lieutenant Méritens de Prodals to his brother, stating that he fed the soldiers of his regiment on the corpses of Englishmen after the capture of Fort William Henry: Douville, ed., "Le Canada en 1756–1758." See Slotkin, *Regeneration*. In Great Britain, writes Slotkin (124–5), cannibalism was spontaneously associated with America as if the practice were common even among the colonists. For their part, the British colonists believed the practice to be widespread among the French, and Slotkin seems to accept their testimony.

51 Charlevoix, *History* (see *supra*, note 22). The *History* presents two portraits of men of war: one corresponding to the pioneer days, which largely hews to the Jesuit *Relations*, the main source for the initial chapters, and the one at issue here, impressionistically built up from one event to the next starting in the tenth book (1670–84). But the author rarely interrupts the narrative to describe the protagonists; these character sketches of the inhabitants of the colony are found in Charlevoix, *Journal*, mainly in the third, fourth, and tenth letters. For our purposes, this last (401–5) is the most important.

52 See Le Bras, "Les Relations." I make no bones about asserting that the portrait given in Charlevoix, *Journal* (401–5) is that of the military nobility. Of a total of thirty-nine lines, half relate to the material difficulties of gentlemen, to questions of salaries and loss of privileges (*dérogeance*). The rest is less clear, but the allusions to aptitudes for command certainly do not apply to peasants. Likewise the end, where the author suggests exporting these brave soldiers for service to the state, can only concern officers.

53 Charlevoix, *Journal*, 404.

54 Ibid., 405.

55 Ibid., 404.

56 Charlevoix, *History*, begins with two questions (1: 12): "Who has arrested the progress of the gospel among the Indians, and whence comes it that the most ancient of our colonies, which should naturally be the most populous, is still the weakest of all?" Charlevoix does not answer these questions explicitly. He alludes a few times to discord among administrators and to Versailles's slowness in sending relief, but these remarks occupy little space compared to the multiple accusations against the *coureurs de bois*, alleged to be the real parties responsible for the colony's

economic and moral failure. According to Maurice Lemire (*La Vie littéraire*, 59), Charlevoix attributed the failure to the trading companies and, beyond them, to greedy, short-sighted French administrators. This is to commandeer the Jesuit's endorsement for the thesis, developed by nineteenth- and twentieth-century Quebec historians, of the bad mother country that snuffed out the colonists' economic initiatives. See also Blain, "Économie et société," 5–6. Charlevoix was the first to write about this conundrum of failure, but his answers were not the same.

57 Pierre Berthiaume uses the terms "patchwork" and "amalgam" to describe the *Journal*, and the same may be said of the *History*: Berthiaume, "Introduction," in Charlevoix, *Journal*, 43, 53.

58 Quoted in Jacob, "Homme économique," 39. The first part of this thesis, summarizing the evolution of the concept of work, is very useful.

59 *RAPQ* (1930–31): 42, Colbert to Intendant Jean Talon, 5 January 1666.

60 Denunciations of the *coureurs de bois* were particularly virulent between 1675 and 1713: Charlevoix, *History*, 3: 194–5, 3: 310, 5: 288. Quarrels between governors and intendants continually raised the tone in efforts to blame each other for the disorder. In the eighteenth century, unlicensed fur traders ceased to monopolize the attention of the administrators and memorialists. To understand Charlevoix's remarks, they must be situated in the context of the previous century. Just one author explicitly acknowledged that the voyages into the Great Lakes region were not idle wanderings, and that was Lahontan. "Their work is inconceivable," he wrote: "Nouveaux voyages," in *Oeuvres*, 1: 323.

61 AC, CIIA, 67: 80, 95–107, "Détail de toute la colonie de l'intendant Hocquart [1737], à propos de l'oisiveté à laquelle la longueur de l'hiver donne occasion." Diéreville, *Relation*, 72:

> "Idleness suits them, they enjoy rest,
> The land relieves them of a thousand vexations,
> For they bear no burden of taxation,
> And by excess of leisure are they blest."

One finds similar remarks about the Canadians elsewhere, although not as poetically expressed.

62 [Raudot], *Relation par lettres*, 4.

63 AC, CIIA, 5: 51, Duchesneau to the minister, 10 November 1679; CIIA, 17: 73v, Champigny to the minister, 20 October 1699; *RAPQ* (1942–43): 416, summary of a letter from Mrs Vaudreuil to the minister, 1709; *RAPQ* (1946–47): 409, "Mémoire de Madame de Vaudreuil au ministre (1710)." On the issue of horses, which directly concerns the militiamen's conduct, see pp. 134–5.

64 Kalm, *Voyage*; see 183, 198, 315, 380, and 440–2 for remarks about the women. Moreover, the peasants were spared his criticisms: He described them as simply attired and hard-working.

65 Saint-Vallier, *État présent de l'Église*, 256–7.

66 Allusions to the laziness of the peasants, the women in particular, are fairly frequent in the correspondence of the Seven Years' War officers. One might add, to avoid accusations of bias, that these texts also contain compliments about society women, their sharp-wittedness, grace, and seductiveness, but that these in no way alter the generally misogynistic tone of the discourse.

67 Jesuits, Canada, *Lettres édifiantes*, 4: 321–2, letter from father Gabriel Marest, Caskaskias, 9 November 1712; also published in Thwaites, ed., *The Jesuit Relations*, 66: 218–54 (quote on 218–20). The list of vices that follows is long.

68 The weight of conventional wisdom can cloud one's judgment. This is true of Claude-Thomas Dupuy, who, during his first year as intendant of Quebec, had trouble collecting tax arrears and curtailing a smuggling ring with Albany. It was enough for him to ask the minister to renew the "French race" since that of the colony had become ungovernable, or, in his words, "prouder and more Canadian the more it departs from its essence." The assumption was that tax collection and smuggling posed no problems elsewhere. AC, C11A, 49: 292v–93, Dupuy to the minister, 20 October 1727.

69 See Jouanna, *Ordre social*, 60 et seq. in particular; also *idem*, *Le Devoir de révolte*; Elias, *La Société de cour*.

70 AC, C11A, 8: 143v–44, Denonville to the minister, 10 November 1686. On the issue of the delinquency of nobles in the 1670s and 1680s, see Dechêne, *Habitants and Merchants*, 217–19. From the 1690s on, references to the scandalous conduct of the nobility become scarce.

71 AC, C11A, 26: 167–8, Raudot Sr to the minister, 10 November 1707. These remarks are reproduced in his son's memoirs.

72 Charlevoix, *Journal*, 404. See the observations of Lescarbot, Denys, Leclercq, Lamothe Cadillac, and Raudot on the support given by Indigenous children to parents in their old age, cited by Ouellet and Beaulieu: Lahontan, *Oeuvres*, 1: 675n574. See also Lemieux, *Les Petits Innocents*, ch. 5, for other observations derived from the *Relations* and from Lafitau (p. 153). Moreover, Charlevoix contradicts himself on this point later in the *Journal*. Of four passages concerning parent–child relationships in Indigenous society, two describe families with no cohesion, parents treated with indignity (Charlevoix, *Journal*, 563–4, 629–30); two

others mention deference and respect and the fact that, despite their free approach to education, parents were able to instill certain principles of honour in their children (ibid., 627, 654–5). According to an editor's footnote, this latter passage mimics one from Lafitau.

73 Kalm, *Voyage*, 316, 323, and also 223, on being repeatedly invited to the governor's mansion. See also the pastoral letter of 22 October 1686 in which Bishop Saint-Vallier (*État présent de l'Église*, 183 et seq.) berates women "who exhibit the luxury and the criminal fashions of the century" and urges them to be "attired in a manner suited to the profession of Christianity, one that does not exceed their condition."

74 Roche, *La Culture des apparences*. The work demonstrates the acceleration of clothing consumption during the eighteenth century, marked by a unification of costume. See, in particular, p. 481 for a 1768 text describing the attire of men and women in Montpellier.

75 Lahontan, "Nouveaux voyages," in *Oeuvres*, 1: 283. See other descriptions in Bacqueville de La Potherie, *Histoire*, 1: 367, and Le Beau, *Avantures*, 1: 65.

76 Letter 9 of "Nouveaux voyages" presents a precise and relatively accurate description of the structure of trade in which merchants are clearly distinguished from *coureurs*. Lahontan, "Nouveaux voyages," in *Oeuvres*, 1: 321–3.

77 Charlevoix, *History*, 5: 265.

78 Charlevoix, *Journal*, 403; *idem*, *History*, 5: 286–7.

79 Charlevoix, *Journal*, 235.

80 Charlevoix, *History*, 5: 47–8. These reflections follow the account of military events in Acadia, Newfoundland, and Hudson Bay ca. 1696–97.

81 Charlevoix, *History*, 4: 138. My view is that the ideological system that guided Charlevoix consisted of affirming military power as the right arm of the priests in the immutable order of society. "Forced, in his latter days, to leave the army, he entered the magistracy," he wrote of Olivier Morel de la Durantaye (ibid.), the implication being that this was an instance of moral decline.

82 Charlevoix did not feel the need to stress their loyalty, since loyalty to king and Church were inseparable in his mind. And vice versa: Bad Christians could only have been turncoats siding with the English.

83 On Charlevoix's popularity, see Ouellet, "Jésuites et philosophes," 141–3 in particular.

84 *RAPQ* (1928–29): 225, "Journal d'une campagne au Canada à bord de *La Sauvage* (mars-juillet 1756), par Louis-Guillaume de Parscau Du Plessix, enseigne de vaisseau."

85 Duchet, *Anthropologie et histoire*, 77, on Voltaire, and 81–95 and 101–2 for the relationships of other authors to Charlevoix's work; *idem*, "L'histoire des Deux Indes"; *idem*, "Bougainville, Raynal, Diderot." Pierre Berthiaume, in his introduction to the *Journal* (63), briefly discusses Charlevoix's influence on Abbé Prévost. A biographical article by David M. Hayne, "Charlevoix, Pierre-François-Xavier de," DCB, 3: 111–18, and another, by Marie-Aimée Cliche, "*Histoire et description générale de la Nouvelle-France,* du père François-Xavier de Charlevoix," DOLQ, 366–73, touch on the popularity of the *History* in its day.

86 The method consisting in comparison of Charlevoix's text with the work of Quebec historians is particularly sterile and often circular, since the historians called as witnesses to Charlevoix's veracity often do no more than repeat his assertions. See, e.g., the reference to Gustave Lanctôt in Charlevoix, *Journal*, 402n26.

87 Mirabeau, *L'Ami des hommes*, part 3, 326.

88 Hilliard d'Auberteuil, *Considérations*, 2: 148.

89 *Editors' note*: In the manuscript, the author left the following remarks in the margin to this paragraph: "rewrite/look for other points of view/ counterweights." It seemed to us that these words constituted an invitation to pursue this line of thinking and that the remainder of the chapter and its footnotes constitute a first attempt to do precisely that.

90 Greene, *The Intellectual Construction*, is undoubtedly the best recent introduction to this literature. See also, among older works, Slotkin, *Regeneration*. There was no lack of pejorative remarks by foreigners. An English visitor from New England wrote in 1699 that continued cohabitation with the "Indians" had made the colonists "lazy and [they] work their women to death while they themselves eat, drink, sleep and smoke their lives away." Edward Ward, *A Trip to New England* (London: n.p., 1699), quoted in Slotkin, *Regeneration*, 192. The passage might as well have been taken from Raudot's memoirs or a letter from a French army officer during the Seven Years' War. There is an important nuance, however: Such remarks are counterbalanced by a great many words of praise. Generally speaking, while English authors tended to emphasize the colonists' Americanness, North American ones sought to bridge the cultural gap between themselves and England, to identify with the metropolitan model. There is no indication that the Canadians behaved any differently. This question of identity and allegiance is taken up again in chapter 12, section 3, of this book.

91 Boucher, *Histoire véritable*, 1–169; Denys, *Description*.

92 Denys, *Description*, 457.

93 On Boucher, see the articles by Albert Tessier ("Introduction historique," xxxiv–lxiii), Léon Pouliot ("Pierre Boucher et les Jésuites," 212–25), Séraphin Marion ("Pierre Boucher, écrivain," 236–47), and Jacques Rousseau ("Pierre Boucher, naturaliste et géographe," 262–401) accompanying the text in Boucher, *Histoire véritable*; see also Raymond Douville, "Boucher, Pierre," DCB, 2: 86–91, and Léopold Leblanc, "*Histoire véritable et naturelle des moeurs et productions du pays de la Nouvelle-France, vulgairement dite le Canada*, de Pierre Boucher," DOLQ, 374–7. On Denys, see William F. Ganong, introduction to Denys, *The Description*, as well as George MacBeath, "Nicolas Denys," DCB, 1: 264–7, and Christian Morissonneau, "*Description géographique et historique des côtes de l'Amérique septentrionale*, de Nicolas Denys," DOLQ, 178–9. Denys was from a noted Tours family of engineers, sailors, and merchants. A native of Mortagne in the province of Perche, Boucher went to Canada with his family as a youth. His father was a tenant farmer with the Jesuits, and the son was clearly their student, first in Quebec and later in Huronia. And the Jesuits were good teachers. The two authors adhered to the custom, established since the Renaissance, according to which the voyageur's simple style was a gage of authenticity, whence their apologies to readers for an absence of rhetoric. On this literary convention, see Greenblatt, *Marvelous Possessions*, 147–8. Neither Boucher nor Denys was a man of letters, but that did not harm their writing; on the contrary, they wrote better than the majority of authors of accounts of New France. But their biographers regarded their apologies with an uncritical eye, repeating that they had enjoyed little schooling and wrote awkwardly. Finally, Boucher was not a "servant" of the Jesuits, much less a lay missionary (*donné*), as Maurice Lemire asserts (*La Vie littéraire*, 52). "He writes from a Canadian point of view," adds Lemire, and yet Boucher, unlike so many other chroniclers, did not distinguish Frenchmen from Canadians.

94 Boucher's military activities are reported in the Jesuit *Relations*, not the *Histoire véritable*.

95 Boucher coldly envisions the extermination of the Iroquois, as Léopold Leblanc notes, and there is undoubtedly a desire for appropriation in his description of Iroquois territory as a land of admirable beauty and sweetness: Leblanc, "*Histoire véritable et naturelle des moeurs et productions du pays de la Nouvelle-France, vulgairement dite le Canada*, de Pierre Boucher," DOLQ, 376. Boucher was to be ennobled for his services, and his sons, turning their backs on the enterprises that had earned them this promotion, would secure officer's commissions and join the military nobility of the colony.

96 Remarks reported in Kalm, *Voyage*, 422.

97 According to statistics on pelt and fur imports to Britain and France. See Wien, "Castor, peaux et pelleteries." During Charlevoix's first stay in Quebec (1705–09), the fur trade was at a standstill in the wake of a crisis of overproduction on the European market, so the Jesuit remained under the impression that French trade had failed to recover. The fact that he made no inquiries and spoke so casually shows how little emphasis he placed on economic development.

98 Trigger, *Natives and Newcomers*. The chapter titled "Who Founded New France?" raises the issue of the representativeness of the sources.

99 Perrot, *Mémoires*. The son of a low-ranking Burgundy court officer, he began trading in the Great Lakes region in his early twenties, acquiring a great deal of influence over the remote nations. The administration acknowledged his abilities and retained his services as an interpreter and a diplomatic officer in the 1670s and 1680s. His marriage well below his station certainly harmed his career, and he was unsuccessful in business. Bacqueville de La Potherie claimed to have obtained the information about the nations directly from Perrot, but he was clearly looking at a memorial that Perrot would have written between 1697, when he retired, and 1701. Furthermore, it is my belief that the last part of this memorial, starting at chapter 24, was written later. The tone changes abruptly. Perrot, misused by the administration, has become embittered. Charlevoix, who had borrowed much from Perrot, gave him his due, writing that he had "some education" and had "take[n] service among the Jesuits": *History*, 3: 165. After Charlevoix, Perrot was repeatedly described as a Jesuit servant or lay missionary, but this would have to be verified: Claude Perrault et al., "Perrot, Nicolas," DCB, 2: 540–3. Perrot deserves better than his treatment by Marie-Aimée Cliche, who presents him as an "all but uneducated man": "*Mémoires sur les moeurs, coutumes et religion des sauvages de l'Amérique septentrionale*, de Nicolas Perrot," DOLQ, 485–7.

100 There were surely some priests who rejected war, but Canada's clergy were on the whole quick to support all military enterprises. Moreover, regardless of their personal opinions, missionaries were often obliged to follow the government's directives for strategic reasons.

CHAPTER TWO

1 The Iroquois may not have been the fearsome, invincible power depicted by historians of old, yet despite their demographic losses and internal divisions, they could readily deal with the French, whose might was

minuscule in comparison. See Jennings, *The Ambiguous Iroquois Empire*, ch. 6; Trigger, *Natives and Newcomers*.

2 Eccles, "The Social, Economic, and Political Significance," 114; *idem*, *France in America*, 60. We return to this interpretation.

3 See, e.g., Abbé Baudoin's journal of the Newfoundland campaign of 1696–97 in Williams, ed., *Father Baudoin's War*, 179.

4 Bloch, *Apologie pour l'histoire*, 5.

5 Corvisier, "Guerre et mentalités," 226.

6 Trudel, *Les Événements*, 40.

7 Ibid., 122.

8 Ibid., ch. 4, *passim*. Faillon, *Histoire de la colonie*, 2: 27–8.

9 Just before being broken up in 1653, the flying column was increased to seventy men. Archives du séminaire de Saint-Sulpice, fonds Faillon, cahier X (110), f. 28, "État des charges de la Communauté de la Nouvelle-France." (*Editors' note*: We were unable to find this part of cahier X). Trudel, *Les Événements*, 192–3, 221.

10 Trudel, *Les Événements*, 199n30, 200n35. The documents signed before Quebec notaries explain to some extent why what should have been a military relief action degenerated into a fur traders' journey. If there were abuses during the summer of 1649, they can be laid at the door of these inexperienced, poorly commanded men, not the Jesuits and their lay missionaries. Trigger, *The Children of Aataentsic*, 775–6, 785.

11 The first group stayed in Huronia only briefly in the summer of 1649. The 1650 contingent turned around after encountering the Jesuits and the Huron refugees. It might be assumed that a corps of volunteers sent to relieve a colony at war would be commanded by an experienced man, one of the colony's military leaders, and if that had happened, his name could not have failed to appear in the *Relations* or the *Journal des Jésuites*. That no such information is to be found illustrates the slapdash character of the expedition.

12 *RAPQ* (1924–25): 378–9, "Ordonnance du gouverneur de Lauzon qui porte que le sieur Pierre Boucher continuera sa charge de capitaine du bourg des Trois-Rivières," 23 August 1653.

13 Trudel, *Les Événements*, 265.

14 Ibid., 221; see also *idem*, *La Société*, 264–9, 53–4, 64–5. Of 579 indenture contracts located by the author, apparently only twelve related to soldiers, but his analysis obscures the specific details. It is no easier to make use of the ill-defined job categories: the category of "military trades" includes 171 individuals.

15 Dollier de Casson, *Histoire du Montréal*, 53, 204, 210. Marcel Trudel notes the presence of four Knights of Malta among the commanding officers: *Les Événements*, 142–3.

16 Having failed to grasp the fluidity of titles, Trudel sees examples of "social mixing" everywhere. Most of these are figures who elude the rigid and quite inadequate categories in which the author places them: *La Société*, *passim*.

17 Bercé, "Guerre et État"; Meyer, "De la guerre." See also Contamine, ed., *Histoire militaire*, ch. 14 by André Corvisier.

18 Thwaites, ed., *The Jesuit Relations*, 9: 141.

19 Trudel, *Les Événements*, 144. The attack took place at the entrance to Lake St-Pierre. The French did not succeed in recovering the furs.

20 See the chronology of the principal internal and external conflicts in Mandrou, *La France*, 32–41; see also Porchnev, *Les Soulèvements populaires*, 475–9, on the suppression of the Nu-Pieds revolt.

21 See Jacquart, *La Crise rurale*, ch. 16, for a detailed account of how the Fronde unfolded; also Lebrun, *Les Hommes et la mort*, particularly 324–8. The information on the immigrants' provincial origins is taken from Trudel, *La Société*, 24–8.

22 Corvisier, "Guerre et mentalités"; Bercé, *Fête et révolte*, 105–11; Lavallée, "Vivre en doulce France," in Landry, ed., *Pour le Christ*, 15–49.

23 *RAPQ* (1924–25): 378–80, ordinances by Governor de Lauson of 23 August and 18 October 1653. On the town of Trois-Rivières and the Amerindian mission, see Trudel, *La Société*, 172–4, 377–80.

24 Order by Governor Louis d'Ailleboust to Pierre Boucher, captain of the town of Trois-Rivières, 6 June 1651, cited in Lanctôt, "Les troupes," 44.

25 Faillon, *Histoire de la colonie*, 2: 145–6, according to Laverdière and Casgrain, eds, *Le Journal des Jésuites*. Fifteen Frenchmen were killed, including Governor Guillaume Guillemot, and seven men, including two Amerindians, were taken prisoner.

26 Faillon, *Histoire de la colonie*, 2: 160–6. The siege was lifted through the intervention of the Huron allies, who negotiated a prisoner exchange.

27 Trudel, *Les Événements*, 221. It should be noted in passing that the historian was led astray by a misprint in the *Relation* for 1652–53: There cannot have been a parade of "400 well-armed musketeers" in Quebec in 1653, since that number exceeds the population of men able to bear arms. The correct number is forty. Trudel, *La Société*, 267.

28 Archives du séminaire de Saint-Sulpice, fonds Faillon, cahier X (126), f. 44, Voyer d'Argenson to unidentified recipient, 5 September 1658.

29 Morin, *Histoire simple*, 66–7. On 27 January 1663, the governor of
    Montreal called for volunteers in squads of seven to serve under him in
    fending off an anticipated all-out attack that never materialized. The
    ordinance, followed by the names of those who answered the call, has sur-
    vived. Historians have incorrectly regarded it as the founding document of
    the Montreal militia or even the colonial militia. This is to confuse militia
    duty with volunteering and to underestimate the initiative of the
    Montrealers, who surely did not wait until 1663 to make arrangements
    for their own protection. I myself repeated this mistake: Dechêne,
    Habitants and Merchants, 201.

30 "Ordonnance de M. de Maisonneuve pour la sûreté des colons et du pays,
    18 mars 1658," in Faillon, *Histoire de la colonie*, 2: 383–5. See also RAPQ
    (1924–25): 390, order by Governor Lauson to all Frenchmen to "carry at
    all times, along with their weapons, enough powder and lead to fire six
    shots." Quebec, 14 November 1654, published at Trois-Rivières on
    22 November 1654.

31 These thirty-six Montreal inventories were drawn up between 1651 and
    1664. The inventory of arms appearing on them is a minimum, since they
    do not take account of any that the family might have hidden or any that
    disappeared when men died in battle. In all cases, these were the
    deceased's personal weapons and not those intended for the fur trade.

32 In the early years of the century, in the era of Marc Lescarbot for example,
    there were matchlock arquebuses in the colony. Marcel Trudel (*La Société*,
    270) mentions a wheellock arquebus at Quebec in 1639. By 1651, only
    flintlock muskets were to be found in Montreal. I read with interest the
    thesis by Brian Given, *A Most Pernicious Thing*. It is indeed possible that
    historians have exaggerated the role of firearms in the Indigenous wars of
    the period. The importance of knives among both Montrealers and
    Iroquois lends weight to the argument. But as ineffective as guns were, the
    Iroquois used them and not bows against the French, contradicting
    Given's argument.

33 Moreover, the inventories mention swords lacking hilts, bayonets, and
    knives that some slipped into baldrics in imitation of a sword.

34 Trudel, *Les Événements*, 203, and *La Société*, 266–8. Quebec, with the
    natural protection offered by its promontory and port, was relatively
    privileged.

35 Le Blant, ed., "Le livre de raison." The officer spent four years in Canada.

36 Draft submitted by Champlain to Richelieu in 1633 after a skirmish
    between his soldiers and a small Iroquois party at Sainte-Croix, upriver
    from Quebec. Cited in Faillon, *Histoire de la colonie*, 1: 355. The Jesuits

were those who most readily envisaged the extermination of the Iroquois: Pioffet, *La Tentation*, 120–1.

37 Trudel, *Les Événements*, 348–52. There were other little-known (or unknown) plans around this time, such as the idea, evoked in 1650 by d'Ailleboust, the Conseil de Quebec, and the Jesuit missionary and explorer Gabriel Druillettes, of a military alliance with New England against the Iroquois and the Dutch: ibid., 205–6.

38 Laverdière and Casgrain, eds, *Le Journal des Jésuites*. The river sorties took place in 1637, 1652, 1658, 1660, and 1661. A similar case is that of a 1641 negotiation offshore of Trois-Rivières that turned violent. Dollier de Casson (*Histoire du Montréal*, 94–6) recounts a 1644 offensive by Maisonneuve that ended in defeat. Adam Dollard des Ormeaux and his companions met the enemy in 1660, and it is reported that thirty Quebec residents went on a raid in 1662 without encountering their adversary. It is quite possible that certain sorties eluded the chroniclers, but battles were faithfully reported. Only four ensued from a French offensive; more often, it was the French who came under siege. On two occasions (Fort Richelieu in 1642 and Fort des Trois-Rivières in 1653), Iroquois parties attacked their forts and were repelled.

39 As André Vachon notes in "Dollard des Ormeaux, Adam," DCB, 1: 274–83.

40 Dickinson, "La Guerre iroquoise." I have compared the figures from Table 1 (p. 36) of this paper with the following population estimates provided by Marcel Trudel (*La Société*, 92): thirty-two out of 600 for the period 1642–49, 108 out of 1,500 for 1650–59, and 150 out of 3,000 for 1660–66. Dickinson's analysis cannot change the conventional image of this war, but it does shed considerable light on the actions of the Iroquois.

41 Charbonneau et al., *Naissance d'une population*, 139–41 and Figure 22; also Dechêne, *Habitants and Merchants*, 59–61.

42 The example that naturally comes to mind is that of the Thirty Years' War. See Roupnel, *La Ville et la campagne*, 1–25. The internal civil wars were no less cruel. The Treaty of the Pyrenees (1659) is often regarded as marking the end of total war, the shift to regular warfare. Meyer, "De la guerre." American historians have been the most apt to make such comparisons; among others, Richter, "War and Culture," 528; Ferling, *A Wilderness of Miseries*.

43 On the religious aspect of torture in Indigenous culture, see Trigger, *The Children of Aataentsic*, 73–5, 145; Richter, "War and Culture," 533.

44 Faillon, *Histoire de la colonie*, 2: 158–9, on the peace treaty signed with the Onondagas and the Oneidas in June 1653 and the Mohawk attack three weeks later.

45 Thwaites, ed., *The Jesuit Relations*, 45: 154, 46: 88, relation of Jérôme Lalemant for 1659–60.

46 Steele, *Guerillas and Grenadiers*, 17. Eccles, *France in America*, 60, also situates the learning of petty warfare in this period.

47 As Marcel Trudel notes, Frenchmen who lived among the Indigenous people in the early decades did so in an official capacity, to encourage their hosts to bring furs down into the St Lawrence Valley. Their activities had nothing to do with the *course des bois* conducted in the private interests of the merchant and his supplier in violation of official policy: *Les Événements*, 223–4. Specialists of the period often overlook this distinction.

48 The Jesuits would have lost no relevant opportunity to denounce them, as they did later in other missions, and as the Récollet Gabriel Sagard had done before them in regard to those "brutal, unbelieving, carnal" Frenchmen who kept company with the Hurons. Ouellet and Warwick, eds, *Le Grand Voyage*, 213.

49 One example of such caution: Thirty young Frenchman fitted out for the fur trade and two Jesuits joined a convoy of Ottawas who left Quebec in August 1656 to return to their territory. When they heard that the Mohawks had been reported on the St Lawrence, they abandoned the convoy, which continued on its journey and was massacred. Faillon, *Histoire de la colonie*, 2: 255–6.

50 Trigger, *The Children of Aataentsic*, 305–19, 339, 484–5.

51 Frenchmen who came to the colony in the first third of the seventeenth century generally returned to the mother country. Only two or three of these armed traders (*commis-soldats*) settled in the colony.

52 Trigger, *The Children of Aataentsic*, 552–3, 617.

53 Adams, ed., *Explorations*, 36. Raised from an early age to handle weapons, young Amerindians did not join war parties until completing the rites of puberty. Even then, novice warriors were entrusted with auxiliary tasks until they were deemed fit for battle. Richter, "War and Culture."

54 Other sections of Radisson's account have been disputed, but no one, to my knowledge, has devoted serious consideration to the years of captivity. See Grace Lee Nute, "Radisson, Pierre-Esprit," DCB, 2: 558–63; *idem, Caesars of the Wilderness*.

55 The most negative discourse was unquestionably that of Dollier de Casson (*Histoire du Montréal, passim*), who incessantly complained of the cowardice and cunning of the Hurons and other allies.

56 RAPQ (1930–31): 7, memorandum from king to Talon, 27 March 1665.

57 The commandants left no accounts of these three campaigns. The slim, contradictory information comes mainly from the Jesuits. Jean Talon also noted these campaigns in his letter to Colbert of 13 November 1666: AC, CIIA, 2: 217v, 226–26v. For a good discussion of the sources and an account of the expeditions, see Verney, *The Good Regiment*, chs. 3, 5. See also *infra*, Appendix A.

58 Francis Jennings (*The Ambiguous Iroquois Empire*, ch. 6) stresses the weakness of the Five Nations, decimated by epidemics and wars.

59 *RAPQ* (1930–31): 7, memorandum from king to Talon, 27 March 1665.

60 Thwaites, ed., *The Jesuit Relations*, 50: 140 and 180, relation for 1666, cited in Verney, *The Good Regiment*, 42–3. The author, like other historians, unquestioningly accepts these figures. He even imagines that the "Canadians," driven by a desire for vengeance, petitioned the authorities for the right to go along with the army, an absurd hypothesis. Dollier de Casson (*Histoire du Montréal*, 254–5) also provides figures but for the Montrealers only (seventy for Courcelle's campaign and 110 for Tracy's).

61 I.e., 600 out of 1,380 men. See the tables in Charbonneau and Légaré, "La population du Canada."

62 The number of male immigrants in the 1660s was around 1,075, according to demographers who generally only counted "pioneers"; H. Charbonneau and N. Robert, "French Origins of the Canadian Population, 1608–1759," in Harris, ed., *From the Beginning*, pl. 45. Real immigration was much higher. It is still premature to speak of "Canadians" as many historians do, since the large majority of combatants at this time had been born in France. No Montreal-born boys had reached the age of military service by 1666.

63 Dollier de Casson, *Histoire du Montréal*, 254–5. The Sulpician had little but disdain for the military prowess of the other colonists.

64 René-Louis Chartier de Lotbinière, "Vers burlesques."

65 Marie de l'Incarnation, *Lettres*, 2: 332–3, letter to her son, 12 November 1666.

66 See *infra*, ch. 12, section 5, "The Religious Dimension."

67 Le Blant, ed., "Le Livre de raison," 112.

68 Dollier de Casson, *Histoire du Montréal*, 267.

69 It is easily demonstrated that the figure of 400, or four-fifths of the total, is too high. Such a massacre, leaving only 100 survivors (forty colonists and sixty soldiers), does not square with the comments, and we know that there were still 1,200 soldiers that fall. Jack Verney (*The Good Regiment*, ch. 3) errs on this point and a number of others in regard to this

campaign. Contrary to what he contends on the basis of a misreading of the Chartier poem, the soldiers did in fact set off on snowshoes; the problem was that they did not know how to use them. There were also dogs to pull the sleighs.

70 Deeming the number insufficient, the king ordered six infantry companies to be raised for New France in 1669, and these were demobilized in similar fashion: AC, B, 1: 108, and CI IA, 3: 43–5, "Mémoire instructif de ce qui a été fait pour le Canada ... de Colbert du Terron," 22 June 1669.

71 Roy, ed., Édits, ordonnances, 2: 29–33, "Projet de règlements qui semble [sic] être utiles en Canada, proposés à MM. de Tracy et de Courcelle par M. Talon."

72 See Beaune, Naissance, ch. 2, "Saint Clovis." Talon had served as commissary at Le Quesnoy and was a talented courtier; I am led to believe that the references are borrowed from Colbert or the king, who was mindful of colonial affairs during this period.

73 The seigneuries close to towns and markets, which selected new censitaires according to their own criteria, had all been granted by the Compagnie des Cent-Associés. The more distant ones received by the Carignan officers were less attractive. Certain officers nonetheless tried to attract the soldiers of their company to their fiefs, an example being that of the settlement of soldiers of the Compagnie de La Fouille at the mouth of the Rivière-du-Loup: Lesage, Manereuil.

74 There were exceptions, but this was the general trend. Allan Greer (Peasant, Lord and Merchant, 9–10) stated the problem of deferred rents clearly in the case of Pierre de Saint-Ours, from an old family of the Dauphiné region, a captain in the Carignan regiment who received a seigneury.

75 In this era, the dispersal of rural habitation was most visible in the vicinity of Quebec. More exposed to attacks, Montreal long retained a form of grouped habitat, but as soon as the danger subsided, the colonists hastened, as elsewhere, to occupy more remote plots of land. See Dechêne, Habitants and Merchants, 144–7.

76 AC, CI IA, 3: 22–25v, king to Courcelle, Paris, 3 April 1669.

77 See the regulations of 1651 and 1653 for the defence of Trois-Rivières, supra, 39.

78 Historians such as Gustave Lanctôt ("Les Troupes," 40) who date the foundation of the militia back to Pierre Boucher or to an ad hoc ordinance of 1660 by Maisonneuve are mistaken. The colony's entrance into the royal domain marked a new start, and nothing remained of the old forms of service.

79 The instructions to Jean-Charles de Baas, governor of the French Antilles, date from 16 September 1668. Pluchon, *Histoire de la colonisation française,* 629–30.

80 Debien, *Esprit colon,* 30–1; Tarrade, *Le Commerce colonial,* vol. 1, ch. 2: an excellent summary, especially of the dual (public and secret) character of colonial legislation; Petit, *Dissertations.*

81 AC, B, 39: 235v, Conseil de la Marine to Intendant Bégon ..., 1717. Any number of examples could be given. On 5 June 1672, the king wrote two letters to the governor, the first forbidding any unmarried Frenchmen who had not formally settled in Canada from moving back to France, the second keeping the order secret so as not to frighten Frenchmen wanting to settle in the colony: *RAPQ* (1926–27): 8. On another occasion, the intendant explained that he had to take jurisdiction over a merchant's trial away from the ordinary court and hear the case himself because "the order by the king that will have him convicted" had not been registered with the Conseil: AC, F3, 9: 82, Raudot to [Ramezay], 16 September 1707.

82 BAnQ-Québec, TP1–S37–D16, decree of the Conseil Supérieur forcing the habitants to arm themselves, 14 January 1686; *RAPQ* (1947–48): 291–2, memorandum from Vaudreuil to the Duc d'Orléans, 1716. There were, he wrote, 4,484 habitants able to bear arms, ranging in age from fourteen to sixty; AC, G1, vols. 460–1, *passim,* Recensements du Canada.

83 AC, C11A, 95: 351, «Modèle de la façon dont il faudrait dresser des rôles des compagnies de milice pour être en règle, par Joseph Fleury Deschambault," 1750. The roll was amended each year by deleting the names of the dead and adding those of boys who had turned fifteen.

84 AC, F3, 10: 305, memorandum from the king to Beauharnois and Dupuy, 14 May 1726. The recommendation was regularly repeated.

85 *RAPQ* (1947–48): 278, Vaudreuil and Bégon to the minister, 20 September 1714. The letter clearly summarizes the structure of the militia. This issue is revisited in detail in ch. 5.

86 Arms are the only part of the service that is well documented, since they directly affected public finances. The intendant had to sell or lend muskets to those who lacked them and make other arrangements giving rise to various ordinances. See Roy, *Ordonnances, commissions,* 2: 80–2, 119–21, 163.

87 "His Majesty willing that in the case of any disobedience, wrongs or crimes that may be committed by militia officers or soldiers ... they shall be judged by council of war and sentenced as prescribed by the regulations." Royal ordinance, 3 August 1707, quoted in Petit, *Dissertations,*

286. The same rule applied in Canada, in practice, but was never published there. As we shall see, the militia also acted as a rural police force under the authority of the intendant. It was not, of course, subordinated to military justice when exercising these civilian powers.

88 Contamine, ed., *Histoire militaire*, 308; Zeller, *Les Institutions*, 312–14; Gallet, "En Bretagne." In this province, the *ban* and the *arrière-ban* seem to have been conflated with the *garde-côtes*. Marion, *Dictionnaire*, 379; Zeller, *Les Institutions*, 333–4; Gallet, "En Bretagne."

89 Contamine, ed., *Histoire militaire*, 309; Zeller, *Les Institutions*, 47–54; Descimon, "Milice bourgeoise"; Dolan, "Liturgies urbaines."

90 Marion, *Dictionnaire*, 379; Zeller, *Les Institutions*, 333–4; Gallet, "En Bretagne."

91 Marion, *Dictionnaire*, 377–9; Corvisier, *L'Armée française*, 1: 197–258; Contamine, ed., *Histoire militaire*, 397–8; Delmas, ed., *Histoire militaire*, 2: 18–20; Bodin, "Un exemple de recrutement"; Godard, *Les Pouvoirs des intendants*, 514–16.

92 Example cited in Mousnier, *Les Institutions*, 2: 560–4. See also Habault, *La Corvée*, 10–14, on the subject of the military corvées.

93 The Antillean colonists adopted the uniform of the *garde-côtes*, and it was correspondingly their wish that military service be limited to defence of the territory. Frostin, *Les Révoltes*, 294 et seq.

94 Keegan, *A History of Warfare*, 231–2; Cardini, *La Culture*, 89 et seq.

95 Cited in Chagniot, *Histoire de la France militaire*, 110–11.

96 The idea was taken up again by Vauban in "Moyen de rétablir nos colonies d'Amérique (1699)," in *Les Oisivetés*, 539–73; also, ca. 1750, by naval engineer Louis Franquet (*Voyages*, 192–200).

97 I am using Furetière, *Le Dictionnaire*, and Rey, ed., *Dictionnaire*.

98 Marie de l'Incarnation, *Lettres*, 324, letter to her son, 16 October 1666. René-Louis Chartier de Lotbinière ("Vers burlesques," 277) also used the word *milice* to refer to the whole army. See also Daniel, *Histoire de la milice*, in fact a history of the royal armies.

99 It was a call for volunteers. The words *milice* and *Sainte-Famille* are not in the text. See *supra*, note 29. More recently, Marcel Trudel (*Histoire de la Nouvelle-France, passim*), who always tends to substitute his own vocabulary for that of contemporaneous texts, also abuses the word *milice*.

100 Under the Ancien Régime, the word *milice* had yet to acquire the policing connotation it has today.

CHAPTER THREE

1 See, e.g., Frégault, *La Civilisation*. The other period was 1667–87. In both cases, the peace was partial, limited to the St Lawrence Valley, and did not interrupt wars among Indigenous groups or between them and the French elsewhere.

2 Dechêne, *Habitants and Merchants*, 152–6. The phenomenon is observable in the oldest seigneuries, such as those surrounding Quebec. Yet recent studies have focused on seigneuries that were unpopulated until the late seventeenth century. For example, Louis Lavallée analyzes the pattern of concessions in the case of the Laprairie seigneury but not the clearing and farming of the land: Lavallée, *La Prairie*.

3 See Mathieu, *La Nouvelle-France*, and the section on New France in Hamelin, ed., *Histoire du Québec*. Also, Mathieu and Courville, eds, *Peuplement colonisateur*. From one publication to the next, Mathieu repeats two false ideas: that agriculture grew at a sluggish pace in the seventeenth century because of the attractions of the fur trade and that the latter underwent a long-term crisis in the eighteenth century that drove labour into agriculture for want of better opportunities.

4 The administrators had their gaze riveted on the Island of Montreal and the upstream regions where numerous active fur traders competed to purchase shipments of pelts. Historians who generalize from this situation forget that two-thirds of the colonial population lived at least 300 kilometres away. This distribution persisted until the early eighteenth century. LAC, G1, vols. 460–1, censuses of Canada, *passim*.

5 White, *The Middle Ground*. See, in particular, ch. 1, "Refugees: A World Made of Fragments."

6 Instances include the encounters between the French and the Sioux as recounted by Radisson, Perrot, Hennepin, Le Sueur, etc. in White, "Encounters with Spirits."

7 Roy, ed., *Édits, ordonnances*, 1: 86, royal edict, 15 April 1676.

8 AC, B, 7: 32–5, Colbert to Duchesneau, 15 April 1676, and king to Frontenac, 7: 29–31. See also Pontchartrain to Frontenac, 21 May 1698, reiterating these arguments: RAPQ (1928–29): 360–1.

9 On the regulations governing public markets, see the summary in Dechêne, *Power and Subsistence*, ch. 2.

10 Roy, ed., *Édits, ordonnances*, vols. 1–3, *passim*; Roy, ed., *Ordonnances, commissions, passim*. One cannot be more precise in the case of local regulations that were never registered and have in part been lost.

11 AC, CIIA, 5: 38–42, Duchesneau to the minister, 10 November 1679; 5: 161–81, letter from Duchesneau, 13 November 1680; 5: 296–8, 320–23, letter from Duchesneau, 13 November 1681. The tone of these letters is nothing short of hysterical.

12 Frontenac, who bore much of the responsibility for the quarrels and panics, was recalled at the same time as the intendant. The head count of 1681 and its accompanying agricultural statistics belie the alarmist reports. Growth was steady, which would not have been the case if a third of the colony's men had deserted, as Eccles (*France in America*, 90n59) rightly notes.

13 The emergence of the phenomenon can be dated by the earliest appearance of the phrase *coureur de bois* in two ordinances and a letter from Frontenac dated 1672: Roy, ed., *Ordonnances, commissions*, 1: 107, ordinance by Talon, 5 June 1672, and 1: 111, ordinance by Frontenac, 27 September 1672. As early as 1670, Talon was denouncing the volunteers or vagrants, i.e., former engagés who wandered the colony instead of marrying and settling on the land; Jean-Baptiste Patoulet, his secretary, echoed his remarks. AC, CIIA, 3: 100, memorandum from Talon to the king; 3: 274–9, memorandum from Patoulet to Colbert; 3: 201, [Sulpician priest Gabriel Thubières de Levy de Queylus], "Description du Canada ..." 1671. For an analysis of the westward movement, see Dechêne, *Habitants and Merchants*, 95.

14 AC, B, 1: 105–8, ordinances concerning wages for companies and arrangements with their captains, 22–25 March 1669. A sixth company went to Acadia.

15 Courcelle's correspondence has disappeared, but echoes have come down to us through that of the intendant. The latter, who was not on good terms with the governor, weakly supported the troop demands and reported that Courcelle was very angry when the companies were disbanded in 1671. *RAPQ* (1930–31): 119–21, "Mémoire de Talon sur le Canada," 10 October 1670; 146–7, Colbert to Talon, 11 February 1671; 166, Talon to Colbert, 11 November 1671.

16 *RAPQ* (1926–27): Frontenac's correspondence with the court; see, in particular, 15, Frontenac to the minister, 2 November 1672; 43, Frontenac to the minister, 13 November 1673; 99, king to Frontenac, 25 April 1679; 128, Frontenac to the king, 2 November 1681. Frontenac's letters of 1675–79 are lost but can be partly reconstructed from those of the court.

17 Dubé, ed., *La Nouvelle-France*, 47, La Barre to the king, 4 October 1682; 73, La Barre to the king, 30 May 1683; 104, 107, La Barre to the minister, 4 November 1683.

18 *RAPQ* (1930–31): 63, Talon, "Mémoire," 1667.

19 In the summer of 1673, the Dutch met with no resistance in retaking New Amsterdam, Orange, and the whole of the colony captured by the English in 1664. Rumour had it that they were planning to attack Boston and Quebec. In February 1674, Holland and England signed a separate peace, and New York returned to English rule. All this news, arriving distorted and with much delay, aroused fears in Canada. *RAPQ* (1926–27): 45, 52, Frontenac to Colbert, 13 November 1673 and 16 February 1674.

20 Two years earlier, in 1671, Courcelle had gone to Lake Ontario with a small contingent of fifty-six volunteers in arms – former officers and other gentlemen with a few merchants – in a show of force against the Iroquois. Faillon, *Histoire de la colonie*, 3: 332–6.

21 The same small core of former officers and other gentlemen volunteers from the 1671 expedition led the habitants recruited in the parishes: AC, C I I A, 4: 12–15, account of Frontenac's voyage to Lake Ontario; *RAPQ* (1926–27): 36–41, Frontenac to the minister, 13 November 1673.

22 See Cassel, "The Troupes de la Marine," Appendix B.

23 AC, B, 11: 49v, cited in Desbarats, "Colonial Government Finances," 37n25.

24 *RAPQ* (1927–28), 7, instructions for Frontenac, 7 June 1689.

25 Desbarats, "Colonial Government Finances," 23–45.

26 Exceptional sources are available for 1684 and 1687: two rolls of militia companies about to go to war. AC, C I I A, 6: 297–8, army review conducted at Fort Cataraqui, 14 August 1684; Baugy, *Journal*, 82 et seq., "Liste générale des officiers, soldats, habitans, sauvages, canots et bateaux qui sont avec Monsieur le Marquis pour son expédition," as per the review conducted at Cataraqui in 1687. For an overview of troop numbers, see *infra*, Appendix A.

27 The official correspondence makes sporadic mention of militia roles that have not survived. These might be estimates derived from the censuses rather than actual head counts of the companies. There does exist such a count for 1687, parish by parish, of militiamen ages twenty to fifty that is reproduced in Lahontan's papers. But these figures are discrepant with those taken from the censuses and the army rolls and thus were unusable for my purposes. Lahontan, *Oeuvres*, 2: 1,086–8.

28 The militia companies of 1684 were organized on a territorial basis and identified as such. See pp. 80–1 and note 112 of this chapter, as well as ch. 9, section 2, "Raising the Militia."

29 Roy, ed., *Ordonnances, commissions*, 2: 69, ordinance of 13 August 1684, reiterating (with modifications) the terms of the ordinance of 10 July

(lost). See also Dubé, ed., *La Nouvelle-France*, 213, de Meulles to La Barre, Montreal, 14 August 1684.

30 BAnQ-Montréal, CN601–S99, minutes of notary F. Coron, 27 June and 25 July 1728, by the militia captain of Île Jésus on behalf and with the consent of the habitants, undertakings by two men to do the work of Noël Chaplo and Joseph Sire, drafted for the Fox War, at seventy livres for a period of three months. Thanks to Sylvie Dépatie for providing these documents.

31 Roy, ed., *Ordonnances, commissions*, 2: 11, ordinance by La Barre, 24 October 1682; 80–2, ordinance by Jacques de Meulles, 10 October 1684; 119–21, ordinance by de Meulles, 24 August 1685. Dubé, ed., *La Nouvelle-France*, 80–3, king to La Barre, 5 August 1683; AC, CIIA, 6: 167–70 and 401, de Meulles to the minister, 2 June 1683 and 12 November 1684.

32 BAnQ-Québec, TP1–S37–D16, Conseil Supérieur decree of 14 January 1686 requiring habitants to have muskets for themselves, their sons, and their servants once they reached the age of fourteen and forbidding creditors from seizing weapons. AC, CIIA, 8: 63, Denonville to the minister, 12 June 1686; 8: 238–51, Champigny to the minister, 16 November 1686; 9: 6v, Denonville and Champigny to the minister, 6 November 1687.

33 Prior to 1663, financing sources for the colony were largely private. It appears that the military expenses of 1665–68 were applied to the account of the Département de la Guerre. The 1684 expenses took the naval administration by surprise. See Desbarats, "Colonial Government Finances," 36–45.

34 AC, CIIA, 6: 400–12v, de Meulles to Seignelay, 12 November 1684; B, 11: 25 et seq., letter to Seignelay, 10 March 1685. The annual charges of the colony borne by the holder of the Domaine d'Occident trading concession amounted to 36,000 livres.

35 AC, CIIA, 6: 388–91v, de Meulles to the minister, 10 October 1684. The intendant claimed that the lack of provisions invoked by the governor to explain the failure of the expedition was a false pretext. By his accounting, he had supplied all the necessary provisions and, for the most part, the militiamen had brought their own. In these circumstances, he may have exaggerated the proportion of the latter. Ibid., f. 394–5, de Meulles to the king, 12 November 1684. He suggested a second, three-month-long campaign to "purge the land of the Iroquois"; the men would bring their own provisions.

36 AC, CIIA, 10: 121, Champigny to the minister, 8 August 1688.

37 BAnQ-Québec, CN301–S238, minutes of notary G. Rageot, contract between François Hazeur, acting for Simone Soumande, and Marin

Richard *dit* Lavallée, 5 July 1684. Marin Richard *dit* Lavallée, a Normandy native who married in Quebec in 1669, appears to have come with the Carignan regiment; his marriage is reported in Tanguay, *Dictionnaire généalogique*, 1: 516.

38 BAnQ-Montréal, CN601–S280, minutes of notary C. Maugue, undertaking by Antoine Delmay to go to war in place of François Blau for thirty livres and his equipment, 6 July 1684; identical contract between Pierre Le Jamble and Abel Sagot *dit* Laforge, 24 July 1684.

39 Annales des Ursulines de Quebec for 1696, quoted in Gourdeau, *Les Délices*, 112n153.

40 The two ordinances mentioned in the correspondence of de Meulles in 1684 and of Denonville in 1687 have not survived. AC, CI1A, 6: 382–85v, de Meulles to the minister, 12 July 1684; 9: 20–21v, Denonville to the minister, 8 June 1687.

41 AC, F3, 6: 288, "Mandement fait par les sieurs de Bernières, doyen de la cathédrale, et Louis Ango de Maizerets, vicaire-général de Québec, pour faire des prières et des processions à la prospérité des armes des Français dans la guerre déclarée aux Iroquois," 24 April 1687.

42 See *supra*, note 37.

43 See *infra*, Appendix A. In 1684, the militia accounted for nearly 60 per cent of troop numbers, but in the following campaigns the proportion was closer to 30 per cent. On the subject of the domiciliés, see *infra*, ch. 5, section 1.

44 Dubé, ed., *La Nouvelle-France*, 235, memorandum from La Barre to the minister, 1 October 1684, in regard to the shortage of canoeists; AC, CI1A, 9: 68–68v, Denonville to the minister, 25 August 1687: he had never seen the like in terms of pain and fatigue; 9: 6v, Denonville and Champigny to the minister, 6 November 1687, on the loss of muskets, canoes, etc. in the rapids. "It had to be seen to be believed."

45 Dubé, ed., *La Nouvelle-France*, 271, La Barre to the minister, 14 November 1684, in regard to freight costs; AC, CI1A, 9: 168–73, "Mémoire des choses absolument nécessaires pour l'entreprise de guerre...," in which the journey from Montreal to Cataraqui accounted for 39 per cent of projected expenses; 9: 32–8, Champigny to the minister, 16 July 1687: The intendant counted 100 men paddling the convoys; 10: 130–9, statement of war-related expenses for 1688, 1 November 1688.

46 Lahontan provides a good description of the trip up the St Lawrence and its terrors. The author took part in the expeditions of 1684 and 1687 and observed the militiamen's clumsy attempts to navigate the rapids; his

account accords with the governor's remarks: Lahontan, "Nouveaux voyages," in *Oeuvres*, 1: 294–9.

47 Catalogne, "Recueil," 172–4; Lahontan, "Nouveaux voyages," in *Oeuvres*, 1: 298–312.

48 Catalogne, "Recueil," 125.

49 Lahontan, "Nouveaux voyages," in *Oeuvres*, 1: 351; AC, CIIA, 9: 115, Denonville, "Mémoire du voyage"; Baugy, *Journal*, 99–100. This excludes the wounded, who numbered twenty or thirty according to the sources.

50 Baugy, *Journal*, 190–206, marching orders relating to the expedition described at pp. 54–125.

51 Lahontan, "Nouveaux voyages," in *Oeuvres*, 1: 344–57 and untitled woodcut, 350. See also Catalogne, "Recueil," 184–94; Saint-Vallier, *État présent de l'Église*, 257–64; Bacqueville de La Potherie, *Histoire*, 2: 207–8. Neither Bacqueville nor Saint-Vallier was there; they repeated the version going around in the colony. One spoke of "disorder among the troops and the militia," the other of "irregular movements." Denonville, for his part, said nothing about the conduct of the militia but took the opportunity to complain to the minister that inexperienced soldiers had been sent. AC, CIIA, 9: 61–78, 177–9, Denonville to the minister, 25 August and 7 November 1687; 9: 104–20, report of the campaign. Belmont, who accompanied the warriors on La Montagne's mission, also left a brief description of the 1687 campaign in which he contrasts the bravery of the Christianized Indigenous people with the cowardice of the "pagan" allies – an interpretation at odds with that of other accounts: Belmont, *Histoire du Canada*, 19–27.

52 See Contamine, ed., *Histoire militaire*, e.g., ch. 14 by André Corvisier, 401–2, on the birth of the modern army; Foucault, *Discipline and Punish*, 162–9, on seventeenth-century military manuals; Keegan, *The Face of Battle*, 173–8.

53 Dubé, ed., *La Nouvelle-France*, 46–7, La Barre to the king, 4 October 1682; 107, La Barre to the minister, 4 November 1683; 255, La Barre to the king, 13 November 1684.

54 AC, CIIA, 8: 31–33v, Denonville to the minister, 8 May 1686.

55 Bacqueville de La Potherie, *Histoire*, 3: 253. The author comments on a plan for another winter campaign in 1696, which was abandoned. See also Charlevoix, *History*, 5: 9–11.

56 See Eccles, *Frontenac*, 252–4 for a summary of this campaign. The domiciliés were accused of not having killed the old people, who managed to

flee and alert the warriors and the people of Albany: Catalogne, "Recueil," 227–8.

57 See the introduction to this book.

58 AC, CIIA, 14: 35–64, "Relation de ce qui s'est passé," 1695–96; *RAPQ* (1928–29): 307–18, Frontenac to the king and the minister, 25 October 1696. Charlevoix (*History*, 5: 12–22) gives precise details on the composition of the army.

59 Eccles, *The Canadian Frontier*, 125; *idem*, *France in America*, 99–104. The accounts leave the impression that the Iroquois were overpowered by the military superiority of the Canadian militia. Other historians interpret the Iroquois's position with more subtlety; see Richter, *The Ordeal of the Longhouse*.

60 Miquelon, *New France*, 21–2; Eid, "The Ojibwa-Iroquois War." Drawing primarily on Ojibwa oral tradition, Peter S. Schmalz, in *The Ojibwa of Southern Ontario*, shows that the gradual decline of Iroquois hegemony over the Great Lakes region resulted, first and foremost, from the war waged by the Ojibwas from 1650 to 1700; see also Havard, *La Grande Paix*, 101–6.

61 See, e.g., Diamond, "An Experiment in 'Feudalism.'"

62 For opinions on the character and utility of the French nobility, see Jouanna, *Le Devoir de révolte*; *idem*, "Le thème de l'utilité publique.

63 AC, CIIA, 3: 178–9, Talon to Colbert, 2 November 1671.

64 AC, CIIA, 5: 50 et seq., Duchesneau to Colbert, 10 November 1679. The correspondence of his successor Jacques de Meulles and that of Governor Denonville dwell at length on the debasement of the nobility. Lorraine Gadoury (*La Noblesse*, ch. 2 and Appendices 1–2), touches on these problems, offering a list of nobles who settled in Canada with their dates of arrival. For other examples of poor and unruly nobles, see Meyer, *La Noblesse bretonne*, ch. 3.

65 The reformed officers of the Carignan regiment received a small annuity: Dubé, ed., *La Nouvelle-France*, 256–7, La Barre to the minister, 13 November 1684. Ennobled men such as Lemoyne and Boucher did not have these problems. Originally merchants, they also had better situated, already inhabited seigneuries and were on a solid economic footing.

66 AC, CIIA, 6: 411, de Meulles to the minister, 12 November 1684; 7: 147, de Meulles to the minister, thanking him, 28 September 1685. The three *garde-marine* companies at Brest, Rochefort, and Toulon were founded in 1670 for the purposes of naval officer training. Young officers in training served as soldiers while pursuing their studies.

67 AC, C I I A, 7: 93v, Denonville to the minister, 13 November 1685; 8: 143–4, Denonville to the minister, 8 May 1686. See also a letter from Vicar-General Saint-Vallier to Seignelay that likewise takes up the idea of having a small corps of young Canadian gentlemen in order to instill discipline in them: C I I A, 10: 116–17v [1685]; 8: 44v, excerpts from minister's replies to letters from Canada, 20 May 1686.

68 AC, C I I A, 10: 277–78v, Chevalier de Callière to the minister [1690]; see also 9: 12, Denonville and Champigny to the minister, 6 November 1687; 9: 197, Champigny to the minister, 5 November 1687; 10: 17, excerpt of replies to letters from Canada, 8 March 1688. Gédéon de Catalogne ("Recueil," 204–5) reported that the "musketeers" company was guilty of uncooperativeness and insubordination. Yet the idea persisted. One regular officer opined that the king ought, in wartime, to maintain one or more companies of "natives," officers and soldiers, to encourage emulation: Duplessy Faber to Vauban, Quebec, 16 September 1698, in Vauban, *La Correspondence*, 16.

69 Selesky, *War and Society*.

70 There is an obvious contradiction between the awarding of commissions to colonial nobles and the intent to send the troops home to France as soon as possible.

71 AC, B, 12: 27–40, memorandum from the king to Denonville, 31 May 1686; C I I A, 8: 140, Denonville to the minister, 20 November 1686; 9: 9, Champigny to the minister, 6 November 1687; 10: 229, Champigny to the minister, 6 July 1689 (on the settlement of soldiers).

72 AC, C I I A, 10: 261, Callières to the minister, January 1689: Of the thirty-five companies that should have comprised 1,750 men, only 1,300 remained. AC, B, 15: 78v, order from the king reducing the number of infantry companies garrisoned in Canada from thirty-five to twenty-eight, 24 May 1689.

73 See, e.g., AC, C I I A, 11: 102–3, 223–4, "États des emplois vacants auxquels Frontenac a pourvu ... " in 1690 and 1691.

74 *RAPQ* (1927–28): 120, Frontenac to the minister, 15 September 1692.

75 *RAPQ* (1928–29): 355–60 (in particular 356 and 360), memorandum from the king to Frontenac and Champigny, 21 May 1698; AC, B, 20: 71v–81, same memorandum; 82, royal ordinance allowing soldiers garrisoned in Canada to settle there by granting them one year's salary, 21 May 1698.

76 AC, C I I A, 16: 107, Champigny to the minister, 15 October 1698; 17: 95–7, "Mémoire sur la réforme des troupes au Canada et en Acadie," 1700; 18: 3–21, Callières and Champigny to the minister, 18 October 1700.

77 AC, CIIA, 39: 232–32v, "Mémoire sur les petites enseignes en Canada,"
    1718; 42: 182–9, Vaudreuil to Conseil de la Marine, 10 November 1720;
    44: 151–55v, Vaudreuil to Conseil de la Marine, 6 October 1721; B, 45:
    767v, Conseil de la Marine to Vaudreuil and Bégon in regard to the royal
    ordinance providing for one second ensign per company, 20 May 1722.

78 Cassel, "The Troupes de la Marine," ch. 2, table 2. The figures are grouped
    by five-year periods. An annual statistic would yield more precise results.

79 Corvisier, L'Armée française, 1: 171, 364–5, 480–3.

80 Since the minister did not object to the cadets receiving a loan, provisions,
    and clothing as the soldiers did, it may be surmised that the practice was
    not specifically Canadian and applied to all naval infantry companies.

81 AC, CIIA, 35: 232–4, naval commissary Clairambault to the minister,
    31 October 1715. A few cadets came from France on the minister's recom-
    mendation, but the majority were of local origin. Cadets were being inte-
    grated into the troops by 1685; see Donald Chaput, "Renaud Dubuisson,
    Jacques-Charles," DCB, 2: 587–8 for the case of Renaud Dubuisson.

82 Varachaud, Vergé-Franceschi, and Zysberg, "Qui étaient les capitaines?"
    The 54 per cent breaks down into 24 per cent ennobled commoners and
    30 per cent nobles who retained that status. From 1700 on, the group
    slowly dwindled, and the old nobles became relatively more numerous.

83 There are no extant lists, but such a sizeable group would suggest the
    presence of several cadets of bourgeois background. Service in the troops
    is mentioned only when the candidate was recommended for a commis-
    sion. There is no way of knowing how many did not succeed and returned
    to civilian life. Jay Cassel identified thirty-three Canadian officers who
    began life as commoners in the officer corps between 1683 and 1760. But
    he counts as commoners members of the Le Moyne, Boucher, and Denys
    families who were ennobled in the 1660s. Only five true commoners
    (Bourdon, Hertel, Testard, Robutel, and Migeon) received their commis-
    sions during the Nine Years' War, two more (Charly and Raimbault) dur-
    ing the War of the Austrian Succession – in sum, a very small number.
    Furthermore, and contrary to Cassel, not all the officers who came from
    France were nobles: Cassel, "The Troupes de la Marine," 79.

84 AC, CIIA, 49: 43–4, Beauharnois and Dupuy to the minister, 20 October
    1727.

85 One troop list from 1748 shows sixty-six soldier-cadets rather than
    twenty-eight, an exceptional situation caused by the need to fill the ranks,
    at their lowest during the war just ended: AC, CIIA, 91: 229v.

86 Cadets à l'aiguillette were so called because of the decorations they wore
    on their uniforms. AC, CIIA, 56: 112–13, minister to Beauharnois and

Hocquart, 15 May 1731, in regard to a just-issued ordinance establishing one gentleman cadet per company; 59: 163–206 and 61: 80–1, Beauharnois and Hocquart to the minister, 14 October 1733 and 7 October 1734, in regard to selection criteria for junior cadets. Years of service were only recorded starting from appointment to gentleman cadet, so two years were necessary to obtain credit for one. See Fauteux, *Les Chevaliers*, 34–5, for the case of Joseph-Alphonse Duplessis Faber, who was denied the cross of the order of Saint-Louis in 1764 because his eight years as a junior cadet from 1737 to 1745 did not count.

87 AC, CIIA, 67: 180–4, and 69: 40v, Beauharnois and Hocquart to the minister, 16 October 1737 and 5 October 1738. See also *RAPQ* (1923–24): 55, Bougainville, "Mémoire sur l'état de la Nouvelle-France," 1757.

88 Participation in raids and privateering by volunteers of all social backgrounds is discussed in ch. 4.

89 AC, CIIA, 66: 145–7, summary of October 1735 letters from Beauharnois and Hocquart about these young volunteers who sought to be admitted as cadets.

90 After 1700, the size of the twenty-eight companies, which had been set at 840 men, fluctuated between 600 and 700. I have used 750 in my calculations so as not to exaggerate the trend. For comparison, this ratio was on the order of one officer for fifteen soldiers in the eighteenth-century French army. Corvisier, *Armées et sociétés*, 115.

91 For changes in the number of families or lines of nobility, I am relying on lists provided by Lorraine Gadoury (*La Noblesse*, 155 and Appendix 2). She estimates the demographic weight of the colonial nobility at 2.5 per cent before 1685, 3.5 per cent from 1690 to 1709, and 1.1 per cent from 1755 to 1759.

92 Le Jeune, *Dictionnaire général du Canada*, 2: 716–18. *RAPQ* (1927–28): 67, memorandum from Frontenac to the minister, 15 October 1691, in regard to Tilly's sons. The elder, Pierre-Noël, obtained an ensign's commission in 1688 and his father's seat on the Conseil the following year. Yet he carried on his military career, rising very slowly through the ranks and ultimately selling his councillorship in 1695: Robert Lahaise, "Legardeur de Tilly, Pierre-Noël," *DCB*, 2: 402–3. Cadets in France began their careers with the rank of *garde-marine* (at Rochefort). The younger son, Daniel, died at twenty-two at Hudson Bay, too early to know whether he could have obtained a ship's officer commission.

93 Chagniot, "Guerre et société," 252. Jay Cassel ("The Troupes de la Marine," 80–1) writes that oldest sons accounted for 16 per cent of persons entering the officer corps prior to 1700, 55 per cent from 1701 to 1720, 40 per cent

from 1720 to 1740, and 16 per cent from 1740 to 1760. These calculations would have to be redone on a solider demographic basis.

94 Gadoury, *La Noblesse*, concerns only the demographic behaviour of the group taken as a whole.

95 Constant, *Nobles et paysans* (quoted in Contamine, ed., *Histoire militaire*, 372, and Chagniot, "Guerre et société," 253) found that nobles from the Beauce region were relatively unlikely to pursue military careers but that their participation increased markedly during wartime.

96 Since the officers were continually demanding gratifications and pensions, historians have tended to take pity on them. See, e.g., Eccles, "The Social, Economic, and Political Significance," 115–16. In fact, their wages were far from negligible, and the fact that they did not have to purchase their commissions also deserves consideration. This is not to speak of the fur trade profits associated with command of posts in the Great Lakes region, since only a minority had access to them. According to Jay Cassel ("The Troupes de la Marine," 155 et seq., 160 in particular), less than 19 per cent of the corps was assigned to these posts, and a small proportion engaged in trade.

97 AC, CIIA, 67: 95–107, [Hocquart], "Détail de toute la colonie," [1737].

98 See, e.g. AC, CIIA, 54: 416, "Liste des jeunes gens de famille qui demandent de l'emploi à la Louisiane," 10 October 1731; 91: 218–19, La Galissonnière to the minister, 21 October 1748; 93: 96–7, list of officers of Canada seeking a transfer to the West Indies, 20 September 1749. Rather oddly, Cassel's study ("The Troupes de la Marine," *passim*) ignores these movements and presents the colonial regulars as "the troops of Canada": a separate corps cut off from France and the other colonies.

99 *RAPQ* (1930–31): 63, Talon, "Mémoire," 1667.

100 Vauban, *La Correspondence*, 16–19, Duplessy Faber to Vauban, Quebec, 16 September 1698.

101 Ibid., *passim*, p. 19 in particular; see also pp. 21–2, Duplessy Faber to Vauban, 1 October 1698.

102 The son of one of the king's *maîtres d'hôtel*, Duplessy Faber wedded the daughter of a merchant of Champlain, near Trois-Rivières, shortly after his arrival – a mediocre marriage that did nothing for his career. He was also reproached for misbehaviour. Thanks to the protection of Vauban and Pontchartrain, his eldest son obtained the rank of ensign in the regulars at age eleven, no doubt in compensation for his father's stalled career. See C.J. Russ, "Lefebvre Duplessis Faber (Fabert), François," *DCB*, 3: 401–3; also AC CIIA, 17: 331–8, Duplessy Faber to the minister, 7 October 1698.

103 The comparison with the Carignan officers is somewhat strained, since they were paid to give up their commissions while officers in the colonial regulars who settled in the colony kept their jobs. They did not see the matter so objectively, however.

104 These are partial observations based on biographical articles in the *Dictionary of Canadian Biography*. A systematic analysis of careers can be performed on the basis of the officers' list provided in Cassel, "The Troupes de la Marine," Appendix H, and Lorraine Gadoury's lists.

105 Among the twelve "principal families" identified by Bougainville in 1757, four descended from the first colonists, three from Carignan officers, and five from naval regular officers. But to foreigners they made up a single bloc welded together by marriage: *RAPQ* (1923–24): 62, memorandum from Bougainville, 1757.

106 Charlevoix (*History*, 5: 20–2) took malicious pleasure in relating these remarks against Frontenac, whom he disliked, even while pretending not to believe them.

107 *RAPQ* (1922–23): 73–8, "Addition au mémoire fait en 1715, intitulé mémoire sur l'état présent du Canada (25 janvier 1719)," by François-Madeleine-Fortuné Ruette d'Auteuil. The son of one of the king's *maîtres d'hôtel* who journeyed to Canada in 1648, he succeeded his father to the position of attorney general in 1679. His quarrels with the royal administrators and the Pontchartrains led to his dismissal in 1707. An ardent advocate for colonial interests, he deserves better than the mean-spirited biography by Marine Leland, "Ruette d'Auteuil de Monceaux, François-Madeleine-Fortuné," *DCB*, 2: 611–14.

108 We return in chapter 9 (*supra*, 227–9) to the divide between the societies of Canada and the West Indies. Among economic and social factors, the fact that Canada was not taxed for the maintenance of the troops certainly made the colony more tolerant.

109 Eccles, "The Social, Economic, and Political Significance," 116. Based on one or two examples of upward mobility in the early years of the colony, Eccles presents the officer corps as a locus of steady integration of talented commoners into the nobility; he even employs the phrase "military caste system." My interpretation is much closer to that of Dale Miquelon ("A Supplement to Europe"), for whom the corps was essentially composed of nobles and served to reinforce the specificity of that social category.

110 Versailles denied the letters of nobility claimed by the brave but poor François Hertel for many years, whereas those who acceded to that status through trade obtained them without fuss.

111 The Parchemin notarial database offers the possibility of searching on all acts in which either party is identified as a militia officer.

112 AC, CIIA, 6: 297–8; Baugy, *Journal*, 82 et seq. In 1684, the companies were identified by a geographic name such as "Beauport militias." But in 1687, each bore the name of its captain. The territorial structure clearly remained the same.

113 AC, B, 11: 19v–20, royal ordinance in regard to deserters, 10 April 1684, which mentions the composition of the councils of war that heard these trials.

114 Roy, ed., *Ordonnances, commissions*, 1: 143–5, commission from Frontenac to Legardeur de Tilly, 15 May 1673.

115 Jean-Jacques Lefebvre, "Le Moyne de Longueuil et de Châteauguay, Charles," *DCB*, 1: 474–6. The son of a Dieppe innkeeper who came to Canada at age fifteen in the wake of his uncle, a surgeon, Le Moyne took advantage of the Jesuits' favour, and a long stay in their mission, to affirm his talents. The fortune that allowed his sons to complete their education in France played an important role in the family's spectacular rise.

116 Roy, ed., *Ordonnances, commissions*, 2: 67, ordinance by La Barre to Migeon, 16 June 1684; Jean-Jacques Lefebvre, "Migeon de Branssat, Jean-Baptiste," *DCB*, 1: 519–20.

117 The militia review of 1696 has not survived. Only the names of the four battalions (Quebec, Beaupré, Trois-Rivières, and Montreal) and their commandants are known. The first three battalions were commanded by regular officers: Bacqueville de La Potherie, *Histoire*, 3: 271, and Charlevoix, *History*, 5: 12–13. Lemoyne died in 1685, and it is not known who replaced him at the head of the urban militias before the arrival of Fleury Deschambault.

118 *RAPQ* (1926–27): 47, Frontenac to the minister, 13 November 1673.

119 Clearly, not every militia officer stated his title in notarial acts, but the correlation between the number of individuals who did and the actual number of militia officers is undeniable.

120 Besides being very incomplete, the list of militia officers published by Claude de Bonnault (*RAPQ* [1949–51]): 261–527, "Le Canada militaire: état provisoire des officiers de milice de 1641 à 1760") conflates parish officers with Carignan or naval officers who commanded the habitants during wartime. Ouellet, "Officiers de milice," inevitably distorts the reality by basing its analysis of militia officers under the French regime on this misleading source.

121 *RAPQ* (1967): 230, "Registre des recettes et dépenses de l'église Sainte-Anne du Petit-Cap (1659–1700)." In 1696, Noël Gaignon, a

thirty-six-year-old householder, had been a militia captain in the Côte-de-Beaupré for several years: Tanguay, *Dictionnaire généalogique*, 1: 247.

122 AC, CIIA, 26: 150–75, Raudot to the minister, 10 November 1707.

123 The workings of the militia in the mid-eighteenth century are discussed in ch. 6.

124 Frostin, "Les enfants perdus," 320; Pluchon, *Histoire de la colonisation française*, 617 et seq.

125 Steele, "Governors or Generals."

126 *Editors' note*: In an earlier version of this chapter, the author closed on the following note: "In entrusting command of the regulars to the local nobility, the administration introduced a confusion between French and colonial interests, between military men and civilians." She deleted this sentence and wrote the following note: "Rework and clarify the ending: make the segue from militia to society."

CHAPTER FOUR

1 Catalogne, "Recueil," 191. The officer did not neglect to mention (ibid., 203) that the destruction of Lachine in 1689 confirmed Ataria's prediction.

2 See Steele, *Warpaths*, 137–50.

3 See *infra*, Appendix A.

4 It is not uncommon to find figures being manipulated to shore up an argument. Intendant de Meulles wrote that 800–900 habitants had gone to Lake Ontario with La Barre in 1684 (and not the 670 present at the review) in order to add weight to his denunciation of the general's inaction. AC, CIIA, 6: 394–5, de Meulles to the king, 12 November 1684.

5 See, e.g., the parish registers of Lachine and Pointe-aux-Trembles: BAnQ-Montréal, CE601–S8 and S5.

6 See 1685 map titled "Villemarie dans l'isle de Montréal," in Robert, *Atlas historique de Montréal*, 39.

7 Faillon, *Histoire de la colonie*, vol. 3, ch. 9.

8 BAnQ-Montréal, CN601–S17, minutes of notary B. Basset, 27 March 1685, inventory of estate of the late Charles Le Moyne.

9 Poirier, "The Fortifications of Montréal," 29–62. Joachim Leber, a habitant of La Prairie who was a prisoner at Albany in 1692, claimed that Montreal possessed fifty-six cannon, possibly an exaggeration: Bayard and Lodowick, *Journal*. See pp. 35–6 for Leber's testimony before Benjamin Fletcher at Albany, 4 October 1692.

10 BAnQ-Montréal, CN601–S2, minutes of notary A. Adhémar, assignment of a lot to Pierre Roy for construction of the village of La Prairie Saint-Lambert, 25 February 1690; TL4–S11–D1, Registres de procès-verbaux d'audiences, 1693–98, f. 551v–54v, lawsuit by Pierre Perthuy, merchant, against the habitants of Pointe-aux-Trembles, 26 March 1697. They were accused of ruining his land and enjoined to return 1,500 cords of wood to him. The trial had been ongoing for two years. See excerpt of ordinance by Callière and Gaillard of 29 November 1689 cited during the proceeding (the original is lost).

11 AC, CIIA, 11: 273–77v, [Champigny], "Remarques ... pour la conservation de la Nouvelle-France," 1691.

12 AC, CIIA, 13: 303, Frontenac and Champigny to the minister, 10 November 1695. BAnQ-Montréal, CN601–S2, minutes of notary A. Adhémar, 7 April 1693, inventory of estate of Cartier *dit* Larose: The house and shed owned by the widow at Pointe-aux-Trembles fort are described as having no value.

13 AC, CIIA, 9: 73v, Denonville to the minister, Ville-Marie, 25 August 1687. Since his orders of 13 June 1687 had not been obeyed, the governor issued a second ordinance on 1 September, with punishments for offenders. By 1688, most parishes had a fort and a garrison, but the habitants were slow in moving into them. Roy, ed., *Ordonnances, commissions*, 2: 163–4, 166–8, ordinances of 13 June and 1 September 1687.

14 This governor misunderstood the logic of dispersed habitat, which was the norm in North America. He believed that its sole purpose was so that the habitants could secretly engage in illicit activities and all manner of vices. See AC, CIIA, 7: 92, 178–86v, letter and memorandum from the governor, 12–13 November 1685; 9: 127v, "Mémoire de l'estat présent des affaires de Canada," 27 October 1687.

15 Despite the presence of garrisoned forts Rémy, Rolland, and Cuillerier in the parish of Kahnawake across the river, the enemy managed to move into the countryside during the night.

16 Catalogne, "Recueil," 194. The author, the officer to whom the supervision of work on the rural forts had been entrusted, counted twenty-nine forts (not including Chambly) in the government of Montreal, two of which were built of stone: the one at Kahnawake, completed in 1692, and the one at Longueuil, erected at the seigneur's behest and expense. "[His] fort, his house, and all the outbuildings giving us ... an impression of a fortified French castle": AC, CIIA, 16: 14v, Frontenac and Champigny to the minister, 15 October 1698. The king was impressed and raised the seigneury to the rank of a barony: Céline Dupré, "Le Moyne de Longueuil, Charles,"

DCB, 2: 418–20. There were perhaps four or five more forts in the vicinity of Trois-Rivières.

17 Roy, *Ordonnances, commissions*, 2: 166–8, ordinance by Denonville of 1 September 1687; Catalogne, "Recueil," 208.

18 AC, C11A, 12: 87v, Champigny to the minister, 3 November 1692.

19 Charles de Monseignat, "Relation de ce qui s'est passé de plus remarquable en Canada depuis le départ des vaisseaux, au mois de novembre, 1689 jusqu'au mois de novembre, 1690," *Collection de manuscrits*, 1: 482–531, p. 501 in particular; Catalogne, "Recueil," 231–2, on one of these failed pursuits at Trois-Rivières, which caused the death of the captives.

20 Catalogne, "Recueil," *passim*, 233 in particular. There is a degree of chronological disorder in this chronicle that is easy for a researcher conversant with the period to correct.

21 Faillon, *Histoire de la colonie*, 2: 5–6: attack on Fort Richelieu in August 1642. On the military tactics of the Iroquois and their ability to adapt to new ballistic devices, see Otterbein, "Why the Iroquois Won."

22 André Vachon, "Jarret de Verchères, Marie-Madeleine," *DCB*, 3: 331–7. Vachon contrasts the various sources, among them the passages taken from Bacqueville de La Potherie, *Histoire*, 1: 324–8 and 3: 152–4, in which these events are discussed. Twenty years later, Madeleine wrote a second, even more detailed and dramatic version of her feat in which Vachon detects several implausible particulars. Yet he unblinkingly accepts the 1699 version, without situating it in its military context or wondering about the silence of the other sources. My summary relies on the first version but omits certain even more improbable details, such as the hand-kerchief that the heroine supposedly had time to untie while running away from the warrior who was chasing her. The two texts were published as an appendix to Gervais and Lusignan, "De Jeanne d'Arc à Madeleine de Verchères." It may be added that Charlevoix (*Journal*, 1: 312, letter 7, March 1721, and note 30) repeated the account found in Bacqueville de la Potherie. *Editors' note*: See also Coates and Morgan, *Heroines and History*.

23 The battle at Lake Champlain, between warriors from Sault-Saint-Louis and Mohawks who had set upon them and fled with a number of prisoners, took place in 1691: Charlevoix, *History*, 4: 216–17.

24 AC, C11A, 12: 182–205v, "Relation de ce qui s'est passé en Canada depuis le mois de September 1692 jusqu'au départ des vaisseaux en 1693" (p. 364 in the transcriptions). Catalogne, "Recueil," a detailed journal of military events, does not mention Verchères.

25 Intendant Champigny, who relayed Madeleine de Verchères's letter to the Comtesse de Maurepas in 1699, attested to the veracity of the account. Is this enough to reject to my critique?

26 Landry and Lessard, "Les causes de décès." The recent "downward revisions" mentioned by the authors are merely hypotheses reflecting the ideology of the moment.

27 Dickinson, "La Guerre iroquoise."

28 The small number of parishes and the small population in the government of Montreal are two factors that would facilitate such research.

29 BAnQ-Montréal, CN601–S280 and S3 3 1, minutes of notaries C. Maugue, 22 September 1691, and J.-B. Pottier, 6 March 1697.

30 BAnQ-Montréal, CN601–S2 and S260, minutes of following notaries: A. Adhémar, 15 June 1693, inventory of estate of Jean Lelat and petition by Louis Lemaistre; A. Adhémar, 6 October 1693, petition by guardian of Faye children and inventory; M. Lepailleur, 19 January 1716, statement concerning the Éthier family; other acts cited in Lavallée, *La Prairie*.

31 Vaughan and Clark, eds, *Puritans*, 9.

32 Demos, *The Unredeemed Captive*, 22–3, analysis of Deerfield victims based on lists compiled by contemporaries; Vaughan and Richter, "Crossing the Cultural Divide"; Nash, "Captives among the Abenakis."

33 Note, for example, the presence of women, apparently many of them, among the captives. Although they left no accounts of captivity, shouldn't their lived experience be noted? It would afford an opportunity to incorporate the particular experience of women into the study of a little-understood phenomenon, that of captivity and its consequences. On New England women who were taken captive, see Ulrich, *Good Wives*.

34 For example, when journeying to Michilimackinac in 1690, Louis de La Porte de Louvigny, the new commandant of this post, and his detachment overcame an Iroquois party, killing more than thirty and taking four prisoners, including two men. One was given to the Ottawas, who burned him at the stake, while the other was taken to the governor, who offered him to Oureouharé, a pro-French Iroquois chief: Charlevoix, *History*, 2: 56–7. See also AC, C I I A, 61: 339, de Beaucourt, "Extrait de ce qui s'est passé dans le gouvernement de Montréal," 1734: the Indigenous people of the two missions, wrote the governor, had asked him for the Fox prisoners so that they could feast on them. We return to the question of prisoners. The only cases of concern to us here are those in which the captives were taken by the French acting alone.

35 Lahontan, "Nouveaux voyages," in *Oeuvres*, 1: 481–4. For another example of torture and public execution at Quebec, see Thwaites, ed., *The Jesuit Relations*, 46: 84–8, relation of J. Lalemant for the year 1659–60.

36 The one brought to Montreal was spared because of his young age. See Catalogne, "Recueil," 231, for what took place in 1689 at the Lake of Two Mountains, which the author erroneously dates to 1692, and 220–1 for the events at Repentigny (Îles Bouchard). A party of seventy Canadians commanded by Vaudreuil surprised a group of forty Iroquois sleeping in a cabin but made so much noise that the enemy had time to mount a fierce defence.

37 Cited in Myrand, ed., *Sir William Phips*, 65–74.

38 Juchereau de la Ferté and Regnard Duplessis, *Les Annales*, 363–72.

39 *RAPQ* (1927–28): 39, Frontenac to the minister, 12 November 1690; AC, CIIA, 27: 9v, Ramezay to the minister, 12 November 1707.

40 Keegan, *The Face of Battle*, 197. The same attitudes as during the Seven Years' War – collective excitement followed by stupour and prostration after the engagement – are found here: *infra*, ch. 11, section 3.

41 See the various accounts gathered in Myrand, ed., *Sir William Phips*, in particular those of Sylvanus Davis, a war prisoner; the Jesuit Germain de Couvert; Gédéon de Catalogne; and Charles de Monseignat, the governor's secretary. While the colony assuredly defended itself well, it is clear that Phips's failure had more to do with the lateness of the season, disease, and an accumulation of blunders, which the French implicitly recognized in attributing their victory to the Virgin Mary.

42 *RAPQ* (1942–43): 426–32, Vaudreuil to the minister, 14 November 1709. In this letter, the governor described his efforts to impose his plan but said nothing of its results. It was not until two years later that he admitted having failed in 1709 in the case of Île d'Orléans: *RAPQ* (1946–47): 434–5, Vaudreuil to the minister, 25 October 1711. It is not known whether the evacuation order was delivered to the peasants in the government of Montreal. Be that as it may, the plan came to nothing in the western part of the colony. Note that in 1707, with the first alarm under his government, Vaudreuil had no specific plan for the defence of Quebec. His evacuation plan must have come into being after that date.

43 *RAPQ* (1946–47): 432–5, Vaudreuil to the minister, 25 October 1711. That year, Vaudreuil made two tours of the côtes of the government of Quebec, the first in the early spring, the second in September. Two officers, one on the south shore and the other on the north shore, were put in charge of assembling the habitants after they had put their families and

property out of harm's way, taking them to Quebec, and fending off
enemy landings along the way. For a brief but excellent summary of the
issues and the main military events that occurred between 1702 and 1712,
see Miquelon, *New France*, ch. 3.

44 Catalogne, "Recueil," 223–5; AC, F3, 6: 397 et seq., "Relation ... jusqu'au
15 octobre 1691"; John H.G. Pell, "Schuyler, Peter," DCB, 2:
628–30; William J. Eccles, "Clément du Vuault (Vault) de Valrennes,
Philippe," DCB, 2: 154–5. Belmont (*Histoire de l'eau-de-vie*, 18) blamed
the routing of the militia on the previous day's libations; given his crusade
against aqua-vitae, however, the Sulpician was not an objective witness.
Note that a few Englishmen were mixed in with the Iroquois party that
attacked harvesters at La Prairie in 1690.

45 Overconfidence, cockiness, a tendency to consider the British colonists
rebellious, ungovernable, incapable of concerted action: These were the
sentiments of the governors, intendants, and senior officers. How widespread were they among the population? That is another question that I
will try to answer, in ch. 12 of this study.

46 These remarks are directed at francophone historians, who do not profit,
in my view, from substituting words belonging to other contexts for the
vocabulary of the era. The problem is different for anglophone historians,
who have to translate, and my English is not good enough to assess the
quality of these translations. On European experiences and publications
concerning petty warfare during the eighteenth century, see, e.g., Russell,
"Redcoats in the Wilderness." Charlevoix used the phrase *petite guerre*
several times.

47 The word *parti* is the root of the word *partisan*, which also appears in the
official correspondence and in Bacqueville, but less frequently than *parti*.
Bacqueville de La Potherie, *Histoire*, 3: 256 ("our partisans"); RAPQ
(1946–47): 428, Vaudreuil to the minister, 25 October 1711, which
describes two officers as "good partisans."

48 Melvoin, *New England Outpost*, 191, 223.

49 Founded in 1682 by Canadian and French merchants, the Compagnie du
Nord claimed trading posts for which the English had been vying since
1670. In 1684, the French were chased out of the Bourbon (York) and
Sainte-Thérèse (New Severn) posts on the west coast of Hudson Bay.
Having failed to obtain a ship with which to harass the "English pirates
and French renegades," it organized this overland expedition to James Bay.
In 1693, the English company returned to the head of the bay, but in
1696, the French retook York and held it until the Treaty of Utrecht. AC,
C11A, 7: 261–3, petition from the Compagnie du Nord to the minister,

Quebec, 10 November 1685. There are two accounts of this campaign: Troyes, *Journal de l'expédition*, and Catalogne, "Recueil," 174–82.

50 Saint-Vallier, *État présent de l'Église*, 223–4.

51 See *supra*, 47–8.

52 The officers who commanded these parties left no recounting of them. See the account in AC, CIIA, 11: 5–40, Charles de Monseignat, "Relation de ce qui s'est passé de plus remarquable en Canada depuis le ... mois de novembre 1689 jusqu'au mois de novembre 1690," 1690; also, the good summary in Eccles, *Frontenac*, 224–8, based on French and English sources. Eccles numbers Portneuf's forces at 400–500 men. These figures, undoubtedly from English observers, are inflated: They would mean that the Abenakis supplied a contingent of 400 men, yet their detachments rarely attained such a large size and such a troop movement would have been noted in the Acadian sources. A more likely estimate would put the number of Frenchmen at about sixty and the number of Abenakis at 200–250.

53 See Appendix A for a list of the well-known and lesser-known expeditions on which this analysis is based.

54 *RAPQ* (1927–28): 50–6, two memoranda from the king, 7 April 1691; AC, CIIA, 11: 281–89v, Champigny to the minister, 12 October 1691, in regard to forty habitants who went to Acadia with Villebon; 13: 104–09v, Callière to the minister, 19 October 1694; see also Frégault, *Iberville*, 181, 218–19, on these conflicts.

55 With a population roughly equal to that of Canada, Connecticut enlisted one-seventh of its militiamen in the "dragoons" in 1690 (after the attack on Schenectady). The majority, but not all, served voluntarily. Selesky, *War and Society*, 36–66. The proportion is obviously much higher in warring societies where war and hunting are the men's main activities. Clearly, what those who assume that almost all the Canadians were ready for war are positing is that the colony, through interbreeding or otherwise, knew almost nothing about the division of labour and the diversification of production. Dickason, *Canada's First Nations*; Morton, *A Military History*; Jennings, *The Ambiguous Iroquois Empire*; Vaughan and Clark, *Puritans*, *passim*.

56 Far from being a training ground for soldiers, the fur trade would serve as a refuge for those who fled conscription during the Seven Years' War. See *infra*, 217–18.

57 *Collection de manuscrits*, 2: 189–90, Champigny to the minister, 6 November 1695; *RAPQ* (1927–28): 30, Frontenac to the minister, 30 April 1690.

58 Far from having a deterrent effect, the attacks drove the English colonies to unite and organize various offensives against New France. On another note, it is easy to show that the Amerindians were good strategists, capable of striking hard without the French. See, e.g., the Abenakis' campaign against Pemaquid in August 1689, described by Father Thury in *Collection de manuscrits*, 1: 477–81, "Relation du combat de Cannibas, par Monsieur Thury, missionnaire."

59 The proportion of Frenchmen in the Haverhill party was 60 per cent as opposed to the anticipated 30 per cent because some of the Amerindians defected.

60 *RAPQ* (1928–29): 287, Frontenac and Champigny to the minister, 10 November 1695.

61 The Amerindians did not take part in the fighting, but Troyes's party would not have reached James Bay without the aid of the guides, provisions, canoes, and other services supplied by Indigenous bands throughout the voyage. See *supra*, note 49. Circumstances prevented Iberville from taking the party of Mi'kmaq awaiting him at La Hève to Newfoundland, and the three Amerindians who embarked on Cape Breton seem to have stayed at Plaisance. According to the account of the Sulpician Jean Baudoin, who left a very detailed journal of this campaign, Iberville left the thirty Mi'kmaq who had accompanied him to Pemaquid in Cape Breton; moreover, this meticulous account mentions no Amerindians alongside the 124 Frenchmen; Jean Baudoin, "Journal du voyage que j'ay fait avec M. D'Iberville, Capitaine de Frégate, de France en l'acadie et de l'acadie en l'isle de terre-neuve," reproduced in Williams, ed., *Father Baudoin's War*. The idea that the chronicler kept quiet about their presence to throw French bravery into relief is ridiculous: ibid., 103–6.

62 *RAPQ* (1939–40): 443–4, Vaudreuil and Raudot to the minister, 13 November 1708. The Jesuits, in their *Relations*, Gabriel Sagard, and every author from Pierre Boucher to Charlevoix, including Lahontan, Nicolas Perrot, and Lafitau, were struck by this cultural trait.

63 *Collection de manuscrits*, 2: 135–43, "Relation du voyage faict par le sieur de Villieu, cappitaine d'un destachement de la marine, a la teste des Sauvages Abenakis, Kanibats et Malecoites de l'Acadie pour faire la guerre aux Anglois de Baston: au printems de l'an 1694." On the issue of command and the importance of carefully choosing officers for parties going to war with the Amerindians, see White, *The Middle Ground*, 177–85.

64 On this issue, see Cardini, *La Culture*, 388–90.

65 Troyes, *Journal de l'expédition*, 27–8, 31, 34. An expedition to Hudson Bay two years earlier had failed in large part because of weak command.

See [Raudot], *Relation par lettres*, xxxiii–lxiii, "Journal du P. Silvy depuis Bell'Isle jusqu'à Port Nelson."

66 On the origin and fate of the volunteers, see *infra*, 123 et seq.

67 The phrase *maistre de la guerre d'hyver* is reported by Baudoin in Williams, ed., *Father Baudoin's War*, 176, 178.

68 *RAPQ* (1939–40): 458, Vaudreuil and Raudot to the minister, 14 November 1708. On the finesse required of officers who led Indigenous troops but did not command them, see White, *The Middle Ground*, 174 et seq.

69 Charlevoix, *History*, 5: 205–8. Vaudreuil's letter (see note 68) mentions numerous requests for promotion concerning some of the fourteen officers and cadets of the party. According to other sources, the number of victims was smaller. Raymond Douville, "Hertel de Rouville, Jean-Baptiste," *DCB*, 2: 295–7; Demos, *The Unredeemed Captive*, 87.

70 The contrast between terrifying descriptions of Iroquois acts at Lachine, or Natchez acts at Fort Rosalie, and accounts of French acts is evident in Charlevoix, *History*, Bacqueville de La Potherie, *Histoire*, and the official correspondence in general.

71 See, e.g., the writings of Cotton Mather, presented in Vaughan and Clark, *Puritans*, 135–44; also, Penhallow, *The History*.

72 See, among others, Ferling, *A Wilderness of Miseries*; Higginbotham, "The Early American Way."

73 Jaenen, *Friend and Foe*, ch. 4, "Barbarism and Cruelty"; see also *idem*, "Inhuman Barbarism."

74 In early documents, the words *tête* and *chevelure* are used more or less interchangeably. The French word *scalp*, which has the advantage of possessing a verb form, is attested in the writings of the Comte de Volney (1757–1820), who was conversant with American authors. See Axtell and Sturtevant, "The Unkindest Cut."

75 Axtell, "Scalping"; Abler, "Scalping."

76 See the above-cited papers by Axtell and Abler (note 75); Steele, *Betrayals*, 84–8; Jaenen, *Friend and Foe*, 127.

77 As do Alden T. Vaughan and Daniel K. Richter in "Crossing the Cultural Divide," quoted in Nash, "Two Stories," 41. See "Récit des affaires du Canada" [1688], in *Collection de manuscrits*, 1: 444, on scalps brought back by Abenaki warriors from English settlements.

78 *Collection de manuscrits*, 1: 435–6, report by Menneval, 10 September 1688; AC, C I I A, 11: 185–94, memorandum from Denonville to Seignelay, 1690; *RAPQ* (1927–28): 33, memorandum from the king to Frontenac and Champigny, 14 July 1690.

79 *RAPQ* (1927–28): 125, Frontenac and Champigny to the minister,
   11 November 1692; AC, CIIA, 12: 56, Champigny to the minister, 21
   September 1692. A passage in Catalogne, "Recueil" (213–14) indicates
   that the first bounties were offered toward the end of 1690 or the
   beginning of 1691.

80 *RAPQ* (1927–28): 143–4, memorandum from the king [1693], who proposed to offer six livres per prisoner and three "per person killed"; ibid.,
   174, Frontenac and Champigny to the minister, 4 November 1693: The
   allies would not join a war party for so little, they wrote; AC, B, 17:
   66–84, 173–87, memoranda from the king to Frontenac and Champigny,
   May 1694 and 14 June 1695. In their last attempt, the governor and the
   intendant specified that the reward "is not given at all when there are large
   parties of Frenchmen and Natives mixed together": *RAPQ* (1927–28): 202,
   Frontenac and Champigny to the minister, 9 November 1694.

81 *Collection de manuscrits*, 2: 456–9, "Paroles des Abenakis à Monsieur le
   marquis de Vaudreuil" and latter's response, Quebec, 14 September 1706.

82 Desbarats, "The Cost."

83 AC, CIIA, 75: 329–34, Hocquart to the minister, 3 October 1741.

84 AC, CIIA, 88: 204v, or 117: 150–51v, statement of payments ordered at
   Montreal, 1 September 1746–31 August 1747.

85 AC, CIIA, 85: 101–69, "Extrait en forme de journal ... des mouvements de
   guerre ... depuis le 1 décembre 1745." See the entry for 26 September 1746.

86 AC, CIIA, 85: 284 et seq., statement of supplies made by Michel Gamelin.
   Dickason (*Louisbourg and the Indians*, 98–100) asserts without proof
   that payment for scalps was a common practice in Île Royale. It would
   seem at first sight that here too purchases of individual scalps were
   uncommon, but this would have to be verified.

87 See AC, CIIA, 86: 302–07v, and 87: 02–14 bis, memoranda from war
   parties fitted out in Montreal in 1745, 1746, and 1747; 86: 178–236, 117:
   168–320, for the complementary series of expenditures made in the king's
   stores in Montreal during the same years. In some cases, the clerk indicates the number of scalps, but quite often he stops at noting "revenue
   with scalps."

88 Bond Jr, ed., "The Captivity of Charles Stuart," 81; Sullivan, ed., *The
   Papers*, 2: 717–19, examination of a French soldier, 27 June 1757. Based
   on this latter testimony, Steele (*Betrayals*, 84) concludes that Bourlamaque,
   commander of the Lake Champlain army in 1757, had just eliminated
   payments for scalps brought by Canadians. This unlikely interpretation
   (for the French officer had no authority over colonial finances) accords

with the author's general thesis in which the Canadians' greed and sordid practices are contrasted with the noble sentiments and sense of honour prevalent among the Frenchmen and the Amerindians.

89 Day, "Roger's Raid," 7. Around 600 scalps, wrote Roger. Bounties paid during the war may have had another purpose: gaining assurance that deserters would not reveal French troop positions. This was Lévis's intent when, in 1756, he sent a detachment of Amerindians and Canadians in pursuit of three colonial regulars who had deserted; he promised the Amerindians 300 livres per deserter brought back alive or 150 livres per scalp. Casgrain, ed., *Collection*, 2: 29–30, Lévis to Vaudreuil, Carillon, 24 July 1756, and 8: 18, Vaudreuil's reply, 7 August 1756.

90 Drake, *A Particular History*, 89. Terrorized British colonists often made poor witnesses; still, they must be given the benefit of the doubt when their accounts are plausible, as is the case here. *Editors' note*: The author revisits this subject in ch. 12, p. 310 and note 12.

91 Passage from the Jesuit relation for the year 1644, quoted in Faillon, *Histoire de la colonie*, 2: 34. See also Heidenreich, *Huronia*, 268. The governor needed these captives for purposes of trade and to negotiate a truce with the Iroquois. Despite the pressures, the Hurons went away with their prisoners.

92 See Slotkin, *Regeneration*, ch. 4. Not all the accounts of captivity fit this model. Mid-eighteenth-century accounts tend to be less laden with spiritual allusions: Bumsted, "Carried to Canada"; also, Gray, "Captives in Canada."

93 Vaughan and Clark, eds, *Puritans*, 17–18.

94 Ibid., 1; Vaughan and Richter, "Crossing the Cultural Divide," 77; Austen, "Captured," 35.

95 Contamine, ed., *Histoire militaire*, 368–9. See also Redlich, *De Praeda Militari*, 27–37.

96 On prisoner exchanges and the price of prisoners, see Vattel, *The Law of Nations*.

97 Coleman, *New England Captives*, is still the standard work. Some 600 captives from New England are estimated to have been taken to New France between 1689 and 1713. Of the hundred or so buyers identified from the list of captives given in Fournier, *De la Nouvelle-Angleterre*, which is derived from the parish registers, all or nearly all belonged to the upper crust of society. If the operation had truly been lucrative, other social strata would have been represented.

98 See Demos, *The Unredeemed Captive*, 83–4, and the account of Elizabeth Hanson in Vaughan and Clark, *Puritans*, 229–44.

99 The arrangements made by Governor Costebelle in 1709 to house and feed the St John's, Newfoundland, garrison by sending several hundred prisoners to Quebec were an example of this. "This shipment remains an encumbrance upon the colony," wrote Vaudreuil and Raudot to the minister on 14 November 1709: *RAPQ* (1942–43): 423. The new Quebec prison housed a large number during the War of the Austrian Succession, but there was a return to makeshift arrangements after its destruction by fire in April 1747 (see *infra*, 320–1 and note 46).

100 Richter, "War and Culture"; Clastres, "Malheur du guerrier sauvage."

101 See the account of Hannah Swarton, captured on this occasion, in Vaughan and Clark, *Puritans*, 147–57; Eccles (*Frontenac*, 227) offers a good summary of this affair, drawing on the account of fort commandant Silvanus Davis, whom Frontenac ransomed from the Abenakis.

102 Frégault, *Iberville*, 192–209; Williams, ed., *Father Baudoin's War*, 174: "The Natives did not want us to demand the surrender of the fort, for they wanted revenge," wrote their chaplain. "Extract from the Narrative by M. de Gouttin of the Taking of the Fort of Pimiquid, 22nd August, 1696," *ARC* (1912), Appendix F, 73–4.

103 Steele, *Betrayals*. A notable earlier incident was the capture of Fort Massachusetts in 1746 by a majority-French detachment of 900 men commanded by Rigaud. Fearful of imposing his will, he reneged on his promise and abandoned some of the prisoners to the Amerindians: Norton, *Narrative*. Also relevant here is the destruction of the Palatine village of German Flatts: Casgrain, ed., *Collection*, 11: 127–42, "Journal de la campagne de M. de Bellestre en octobre et novembre 1757." The Fox War provides other examples.

104 Historians have often played down the cultural differences by contrasting Indigenous warfare with equally violent European practices, examples of which are readily found. But irrespective of practices, the rules grounded in these cultures were totally different, and that is what matters.

105 The "humanitarian tendencies" descried by Marcel Giraud ("Tendances humanitaires") in Jérôme de Pontchartrain's correspondence are conspicuous for their absence from his correspondence with New France.

106 *Collection de manuscrits*, 2: 499–500, summary of a letter from Subercase to Pontchartrain, 25 and 30 December 1708, with two marginal notes, one by Chevry and one anonymous. Chevry was a principal in the Compagnie de pêche sédentaire de l'Acadie, founded in 1682, whose establishments were destroyed by the English in 1688.

107 There is no reference to the Haverhill affair in the letters of 1709. Meanwhile, Vaudreuil provided a less disturbing account; the number of victims, always exaggerated by rumours, was much smaller.

108 See Miquelon, *New France*, 38–42; Zoltvany, *Philippe de Rigaud de Vaudreuil*, 59–80.

109 AC, CIIA, 12: 182–205v, "Relation de ce qui s'est passé en Canada depuis le mois de septembre 1692 jusqu'au départ des vaisseaux en 1693"; Green, "A New People," 141–2.

110 *Collection de manuscrits*, 2: 191–3, Frontenac to Stroughton, governor of New England, 1695, in regard to prisoner exchanges; see also Coleman, *New England Captives*, ch. 4; Demos, *The Unredeemed Captive*, 80–4, on the correspondence between Vaudreuil and Dudley. Following the example of contemporaries, historians have tended to hold both parties accountable, to record the very real violence committed by the English, against the populations of Acadia in particular. Since my point has to do with the capacity of the French for self-criticism, these considerations are not relevant.

111 *Note reintroduced by the editors*. In *Histoire de la France coloniale*, Jean Meyer writes that by 1715 Canada was "beyond France's military control." Yet it suffices to peruse series B of the colonial archives to discover that Versailles always encouraged partisan war and that Canada acted in accordance with its instructions. In contrast to Meyer's discussion of the Seven Years' War, the desirability of partisan war was not a matter of dispute between European officers and Canadian militiamen driven by "anti-English xenophobia" whipped up by "unending discord" and "bolstered by religious opposition." Meyer et al., *Histoire de la France coloniale*, 153.

112 Haefeli and Sweeney, "Revisiting *The Redeemed Captive*." This was the explanation offered by a Jesuit at this mission to John Williams. *Editors' note*: See also Haefeli and Sweeney, *Captors and Captives*.

113 See the accounts of Quentin Stockwell, Hannah Swarton, John Gyles, and John Williams in Vaughan and Clark, eds, *Puritans*, as well as p. 21 of the introduction; for the subsequent period, see Pote, *The Journal*.

114 See *supra*, 102–3.

115 Pote, *The Journal*, 76–8. William Pote was one of three prisoners; the two others were Indigenous. Thanks to intervention by Marin, the commander of the detachment, Pote escaped the treatment meted out to prisoners and the governor took him out of the Hurons' hands, over their protests. This sailor, a native of Falmouth on the Maine coast at Casco Bay, was a keen observer. See Gray, "Captives in Canada," 47–60. In other descriptions, the warriors saluted with a volley of gunshots, to which the fort responded

with three cannon shots: *RAPQ* (1923–24): 208, journal of Bougainville, arrival of forty Menominees at Montreal, 11 July 1756.

116 The widely used vernacular phrase *cri de mort* no doubt comes from these recurring experiences. Shortly after his arrival in Canada, Montcalm had learned to count these cries: "I see two barques of Natives coming toward us. They are making the death cry. I have counted them, and they tell us that they have killed or taken prisoner eleven Englishmen." *Collection de manuscrits*, 4: 46, Montcalm to the minister of war, Montreal, 19 June 1756.

117 Mandrou, *Louis XIV*, 263, 283, 484–9, on the actions of the royal armies in the Palatinate and foreign reactions. But as Ladurie (*L'Ancien Régime*, 292 et seq., 313 et seq.) rightly notes, France had no monopoly on intolerance and military destruction.

118 Historians have been too invested in linking the colonial wars to trade issues and have readily overlooked this political and religious dimension as a result. The news of the "glorious revolution" reaching New France in the spring of 1689 captured the public imagination and reinforced any prejudices that the authorities and the officer corps might entertain in regard to the neighbouring "republics."

119 AC, CIIA, 22: 77–8, Ramezay, governor of Montreal, to the minister, 14 November 1704; *RAPQ* (1938–39): 56, Vaudreuil and Beauharnois to the minister, 17 November 1704.

120 Catalogne, "Recueil," 260–4; AC, CIIA, 30: 135–6, excerpt from a letter from Vaudreuil to Ramezay, commander of this expedition, 11 August 1709, and 30: 346–51, Ramezay to the minister, 4 November 1709; *RAPQ* (1946–47): 417–18, minister to Vaudreuil, 7 July 1711. The merchant Trottier Desruisseaux did prison time for having loudly announced the presence of an advance guard of the British army that was actually only a small detachment.

121 See Casgrain, ed., *Collection*, 7: 233–4, journal of Montcalm, 18 July 1757, on the panic of 1709.

122 Miquelon, *New France*, 168; Audet, *Les Premiers Établissements*, 76; Edmunds and Peyser, *The Fox Wars*, 79.

123 See *supra*, 68–9.

124 AC, F3, 11: 152–55v, Le Marchand de Lignery, commander of the expedition, to Governor Beauharnois, 30 August 1728; AC, CIIA, 50: 87–89v, Beauharnois to the minister, 1 October 1728; CIIA, 50: 257–69v, Clairambault to the minister, 8 November 1728; CIIA, 50: 284–86v, expense statement; Audet, *Les Premiers Établissements*, ch. 16; Edmunds and Peyser, *The Fox Wars*, 108–16; Yves F. Zoltvany, "Le Marchand de

Lignery, Constant," *DCB*, 2: 404–5. Eighteenth-century opinion was less indulgent: a failure was a failure. The French conduct of the Chickasaw campaign of 1736 had been "shameful," wrote Luc-François Nau, a missionary of Sault-Saint-Louis: Thwaites, ed., *The Jesuit Relations*, 69: 40–8.

125 *RAPQ* (1922–23): 156–90, journal of Léry, February-May 1740, journal of Bienville, New Orleans, 15 June 1740, and letters from Beauharnois and Hocquart, 1739–40 and 1742. On the Chickasaw campaigns of 1736 and 1739–40, see Woods, *French-Indian Relations*. For the Iroquois campaigns of 1666, 1684, 1687, 1693, and 1696, see *supra*, chs. 2–3.

126 *RAPQ* (1928–29): 307–8, Frontenac to the king, 25 October 1696; *RAPQ* (1938–39): 56, Vaudreuil and Beauharnois to the king, 17 November 1704.

127 *RAPQ* (1947–48): 289–90, Conseil de la Marine to Vaudreuil and Bégon, 3 November 1715. Although strict at the outset, observance of these directives would subsequently lapse, but the long-winded letters of the previous century were now firmly in the past. Grandiloquence, too, went out of fashion. The lyrical flights of Vaudreuil the younger during the Seven Years' War were anachronistic. See *infra*, 195.

128 See, e.g., AC, C11A, 13: 283–95v, Frontenac to the minister, 4 November 1695; *RAPQ* (1939–40): 421, minister to Vaudreuil, 6 June 1708, in regard to Ramezay's urging that a major offensive be launched: "It would greatly please His Majesty."

129 These accusations are summarized in Charlevoix, *History*, 5: 20–1.

130 AC, B, 48: 891, minister to Vaudreuil, 5 May 1725; 43: 607, Compagnie des Indes to Beauharnois, 5 November 1726.

131 Miquelon, *New France*, 188. The author compares and contrasts the campaigns against the Chickasaws and the expeditions of 1704 and 1715 with those of the British in 1711.

132 For example, in 1727, the intendant had to requisition 334 canoes to take 2,000 militiamen to Montreal in anticipation of an expedition against Oswego that was then countermanded. The excursion cost 30,000 livres. Dubé, *Claude-Thomas Dupuy*, 203–5.

133 *RAPQ* (1947–48): 241, memorandum from the king to Vaudreuil and Bégon, 19 March 1714; 248, minister to Vaudreuil, 19 March 1714; 273–4 and 279–81, Vaudreuil to the minister, 20 September 1714; 297–8, memorandum from the king to Vaudreuil and Bégon, 15 June 1716. The system was used in 1715 and 1716. There were surely many subsequent private arrangements of this kind, but the idea of privatizing the entirety of an expedition was abandoned.

134 E.g., the licences or permits granted to Bouat, to Catignon and Guillet, and to Paul Dumouchel, BAnQ-Montréal, CN601–S2, minutes of notary A. Adhémar, 30 April (two acts) and 12 July 1715; also, the permit granted by Vaudreuil to Quéret for trade on the Ouabache (Wabash) River, coupled with an obligation to send his men to war before continuing on his journey: ARC (1905), 1: lxix, Quebec, 3 August 1714.

135 Among merchants who put their diplomatic talents to work for the military command were Nicolas Perrot, Daniel Greysolon Dulhut, and Simon Réaume, whose conduct during the Fox War was meritorious. For an example of voyageurs shying away from combat, see AC, CI IA, 67: 172–5, "Relation du sieur de Saint-Pierre, commandant au poste des Sioux," 1737: To the commandant who wanted to continue manning the post despite the hostility of the Sioux, the twenty or so voyageurs replied "that they preferred to sacrifice their property, not their lives," and opted for evacuation.

CHAPTER FIVE

1 Eccles, "The French Forces," DCB, 3: xviii–xix. In this passage, the author summarizes the military organization of the preceding years. See also *idem, France in America*, 102–3.

2 See, e.g., RAPQ (1938–39): 80, 84, Vaudreuil, Beauharnois, and Raudot to the minister, 19 October 1705. The administrators supported the founding of the Sulpician mission on Île-aux-Tourtres (or Tourtes), which would cover the upriver portion of the colony, and they were relying on recent Abenaki immigration to protect the downriver portion. See, in this regard, Dumont-Johnson, *Apôtres ou agitateurs*.

3 The history of diplomatic and military relations between France and its Indigenous allies, and their long-range transformations, remains to be written. Eccles ("Sovereignty Association, 1500–1783," in *Essays on New France*, 156–81) outlines some of the problems. For a good discussion of the issues and of Versailles's early eighteenth-century blundering, see Miquelon, *New France*, ch. 3.

4 White, *The Middle Ground*, 142. White's metaphor has the military alliance holding sway in the east and, in the west, the intertribal peace of the calumets, with Onontio in the role of the great mediator.

5 For the period 1744–48, there are extant accounting documents covering the entirety of Amerindian military movements. These documents confirm the discrepancy between the small number of parties mentioned in the correspondence and the large number on the ground. See *infra*, 198.

6 See Delâge, "Les Iroquois chrétiens."

7 AC, CIIA, 81: 397–97v, memoranda of expenses incurred by the Sault-Saint-Louis missionaries for the king's service in 1744.

8 My data is from Dickinson and Grabowski, "Les Populations amérindiennes."

9 Ibid., 55–7. As the authors note, the ratio was normally smaller (one-seventh to one-sixth) because the men had to provide for their families' subsistence and safety. The domiciliés did not have these responsibilities, since the government provided for them, and could therefore send all their men to war.

10 AC, CIIA, 66: 236–56, census of Indigenous nations [1736].

11 Thus there were no Amerindians in the party of 120 men that destroyed the English settlements of Newfoundland in the winter of 1697. See *supra*, ch. 4, note 61.

12 See, e.g., the admiralty's judgment in regard to a prize taken by thirty-seven Mi'kmaq and three Frenchmen at their own initiative, mentioned in a letter from the minister to Intendant Bégon, 3 July 1713: *BRH* 34 (1928): 172.

13 Circa 1700, the population of the Great Lakes basin and the territory ranging southward to Kaskaskia was probably in the neighbourhood of 50,000–60,000. Historians such as Richard White are not forthcoming with figures, and for good reason: The continual migration taking place in that era renders all the data uncertain.

14 In addition to taking part in several expeditions or large gatherings of troops, the visitors also joined war parties during their stay in the colony.

15 Richter, "War and Culture"; Green, "A New People." By virtue of attempting to prove that the Sault Iroquois were not the Frenchmen's playthings (a straw man in any case), Green is led to present them, improbably, as an essentially peaceable community.

16 Clastres, "Archéologie de la violence."

17 See White, *The Middle Ground*, ch. 1.

18 See *supra*, ch. 1.

19 Franquet, *Voyages*, 193; AC, CIIA, 11: 291, Champigny to the minister, 12 November 1691.

20 Jean Baudoin, who accompanied Iberville during the sacking of Newfoundland in 1697, makes the same mistake. Although the detachment consisted of fifty soldiers out of a total of 120 men, in writing of the "Canadians" he alludes to their natural attributes and their pioneering experiences against the Iroquois. His assumptions blind him to the diversity of the corps. Williams, ed., *Father Baudoin's War*, 173–91.

21 In Eccles's reading (*France in America*, 103, 123), the troops were essentially a labour pool but were useless as soldiers. He adds the cartoonish portrait of the soldier standing on a habitant's doorstep, waving goodbye to the father and sons as they go off to war before moving in and snuggling up by the fire with the women of the household.

22 Proulx, "Soldat à Québec"; Sévigny, "Le soldat"; *idem*, "'S'habituer dans le pays'"; Lachance, "La désertion"; Chartrand, *Le Patrimoine militaire*; *idem*, "Une place de guerre."

23 Cassel, "The Troupes de la Marine," e.g., 135.

24 Of particular interest are the annual chronicles in the C11A series titled "Relation de ce qui s'est passé ... "; Catalogne, "Recueil," despite its muddled chronology, also offers a good account of movements.

25 Frontenac claimed to have lost 500 soldiers in 1690 and 1691, but doubt was cast on the figure the following year: AC, C11A, 11: 239v–40, Frontenac to the minister, 20 October 1691; *RAPQ* (1927–28): 76, memorandum from Frontenac to the minister, 17 February 1692, and 105, Frontenac and Champigny to the minister, 15 September 1692. But what is certain is that troop numbers were visibly eroding and that military mortality had something to do with it.

26 AC, C11A, 15: 83, Champigny to the minister, 13 October 1697.

27 Seventeenth-century soldiers included a number of sons of good families, such as Lahontan, Étienne de Véniard de Bourgmond, or Gédéon de Catalogne (a Huguenot when he arrived), to mention three known cases of men who obtained commissions.

28 Stereotyped phrases used by contemporary chroniclers, such as "our Canadians," should not be taken at face value, for officers arriving from France were just as brave as colonial officers. Examples include Philippe Clément du Vuault de Valrennes, Pierre de Troyes, and Claude Sébastien de Villieu.

29 According to figures presented by Jay Cassel ("The Troupes de la Marine," 83).

30 With the help of Tanguay, *Dictionnaire généalogique*, and the *Dictionary of Canadian Biography*, I managed to identify 162 volunteers for the period 1686–1712. This identification is complete for volunteers from the upper social stratum, summary for the majority who came from the lower classes, but sufficient to ascertain the parish of origin and approximate age when the sources provide full names.

31 No one could recruit soldiers or sailors in the colony without permission. Notwithstanding the private character of several military enterprises, the administration had a lock on recruitment.

32 AC, C11A, 12: 359v, excerpt from applications, 1693; Nive Voisine, "Robutel de La Noue, Zacharie," *DCB*, 2: 607; Louise Dechêne, "Testard de Montigny, Jacques," *DCB*, 2: 653–5.

33 AC, C11A, 11: 5–40, "Relation de ce qui s'est passé" for November 1689–November 1690; André Vachon, "Genaple de Bellefonds, François," *DCB*, 2: 250–2. After the attack on Salmon Falls, one of the five Genaple sons travelled with the Abenakis on several expeditions and eventually died alongside them; two other sons of François Genaple served with Iberville.

34 AC, C13C, vol. 2, list of Canadians slated to embark on the *Renommée* at Rochefort, 5 August–1 September 1699. The ratio here is 21 per cent (fourteen out of sixty-seven) as compared with 1 per cent (twenty-four groups of brothers out of 5,000 enlisted men) in the Vivarais infantry regiment analyzed in Corvisier, *L'Armée française*, 1: 356.

35 *RAPQ* (1939–40): 462, Vaudreuil and Raudot to the minister, 14 November 1708; AC, C11A, 71: 32–3, Beauharnois to the minister, 10 June 1739. There were "eight older boys" in this family. Four obtained positions in the colonial regulars, while the three who died in 1739 served as volunteers.

36 The Lemoyne, Leber, and Messier families, who emigrated from Normandy to Montreal in the 1650s in the wake of Charles's success, formed a veritable clan comprising simple habitants, merchants, and officers of the king, within which services and protection were exchanged.

37 AC, C11A, 8: 272–5, statement of expenses made by the Compagnie du Nord, 1686; Troyes, *Journal de l'expédition, passim*. There were at least twelve experienced navigators: ibid., 113–15, letter from Father Antoine Silvy, 30 July 1686.

38 Williams, ed., *Father Baudoin's War*, 176, 178. The other half of the booty from St John's went to the governor of Plaisance and his men. Those who came from Canada were also entitled to a share as the campaign went on.

39 See, e.g., BAnQ-Québec, TL5–D269, papers relating to buccaneering by John Outlaw, 1696–98; TL5–D217, proceedings relating to a prize taken by Denys de Bonaventure, 25–28 July 1691; BAnQ-Montréal, CN601–S2, minutes of notary A. Adhémar, 29 July 1695, agreement between Joseph Guyon and his crew. The same rules were followed as in the other admiralties of the realm: Wismes, ed., *Jean Bart*, 27–41.

40 Carbonear was a Newfoundland fishing port; Cartagena, a rich city of Hispanic America on the Caribbean, was raided in 1697 by Bernard Desjean, Baron de Pointis, and sacked by buccaneers commanded by Jean-Baptiste du Casse, yielding a great quantity of booty: Symcox, *The Crisis*, 218–19. Another example: the huge prize, in the form of over 6,000

slaves, captured by Iberville and his fleet of eleven ships from the island of Nevis in 1706: *BRH* 31 (1925): 385–9.

41 BAnQ-Montréal, CN601–S17, minutes of notary B. Basset, 12 May 1688.

42 AC, F3, 9: 387–8, decree of the Conseil de la Marine in the matter of the English forts at St John's, referred to the Conseil Supérieur, 18 June 1716. The Canadians who arrived on the *Vénus* and took part in this expedition are not included in these agreements.

43 BAnQ-Montréal, CN601–S3 and S260, minutes of notaries J.-B. Adhémar, 13 September 1715, and M. Lepailleur, 17 September 1715. The ransom, in the form of bills of exchange drawn on Boston, was paid. The dispute between Montigny and Schuyler, who acted as intermediary, concerned the method of payment. In his campaign journal, Montigny describes the capture of Bonavista without mentioning this ransom: *RAPQ* (1922–23): 293–8, "Journal du Sr de Montigny ... jusqu'au 13e mars 1705."

44 Greer, "Mutiny at Louisbourg, December 1744," in Krause, Corbin, and O'Shea, eds, *Aspects of Louisbourg*, 70–109.

45 *RAPQ* (1939–40): 414, minister to Vaudreuil, 6 June 1708; *RAPQ* (1946–47): 371–2, minister to Vaudreuil, 10 May 1710.

46 BAnQ-Montréal, CN601–S280, minutes of notary C. Maugue, division among the Descarri sons, 14 May 1690; Charlevoix, *History*, 4: 122–7; Eccles, *Frontenac*, 225. Another example: After the Deerfield attack in 1704, the partisans were pursued and forced to abandon their booty: Demos, *The Unredeemed Captive*, 20.

47 Selesky, *War and Society*, 38–40.

48 For example, AC, CI1A, 12: 273v–74, Champigny to the minister, 4 November 1693. The intendant attempted to justify salaries that the minister found too high.

49 *RAPQ* (1927–28): 123–9, Frontenac and Champigny to the minister, 11 November 1692.

50 Bromley, "The French Privateering War," 216, 225; Pritchard, "Ships, Men and Commerce," chs. 5–6, *passim*; Rameau de Saint-Père, *Une colonie féodale*, 311–14. For the period 1702–13, Bromley identifies seven prizes brought back to Quebec, eighteen to Acadia, and sixty-three to Plaisance: Miquelon, *New France*, 48. Note that privateers were authorized to bring prizes in to the closest port.

51 Indeed, the words *flibuste* and *flibustier* (buccaneer) recur more frequently than *corsaire* (privateer) in notarial acts, partnerships, charter parties, undertakings, and so on. The renowned privateer of Acadia, Pierre Maisonnat (Baptiste), was said to be able to board his target ships from a dugout canoe: Roy, "Le flibustier Baptiste," *BRH* 5 (1899): 8–17.

52 Cloutier, "La peinture votive."

53 Among the merchants, Riverin, Gaillard, Fromage, Peire, Gauld, Pacaud, Pauperet, Perthuis, La Garde, and Léger de Lagrange; among the officers and magistrates, Dupont de Neuville, Regnard Duplessis, Chartier de Lotbinière, Renaud d'Avène Des Méloizes, etc. Even in the absence of admiralty archives, it would be possible to study these activities using the notarial acts, provided that the survey is extended to Acadia and Newfoundland.

54 Meyer, "La course"; Swanson, "American Privateering." According to Meyer, a privateer's crew was seven to twelve times larger than usual, since men were needed to bring back the prizes. An identical ratio of around one man per ton can be observed for the *Frontenac* in 1696, captained by naturalized Englishman John Outlaw, and for the frigate *Nostre-Dame-de-Victoire* in 1707, captained by Alexandre Leneuf de la Vallière de Beaubassin: *RAPQ* (1922–23): 348–55; BAnQ-Québec, TL5–D269.

55 Pierre-Georges Roy, "Un corsaire canadien: Jean Léger de La Grange," *BRH* 24 (1918): 33–48, 65–76, 97–104 provides the relevant documents.

56 This opinion was held, for example, by a former attorney general of Quebec, François-Madeleine Fortuné Ruette d'Auteuil, whose sons were active in privateering: *RAPQ* (1922–23): 58–69, memorandum to the Duc d'Orléans, 12 December 1715.

57 See *supra*, 14 and 22 and notes 20 and 46.

58 BAnQ-Québec, CN301–S58, minutes of notary L. Chambalon, donations of 3 January 1693, 7 May 1693, and 18 May 1694, and discharge of 12 October 1697 due to donor's death. Dain was, like a good many "Canadian" partisans, an immigrant.

59 Frégault, *Iberville*, 174; the incident occurred in 1693.

60 Remarks made in 1696 by Anne Edmond, whose case is discussed in the introduction to this book, 3 et seq.

61 *RAPQ* (1930–31): 48–9, Talon to Tracy and Courcelle, 1 September 1666. The same idea is found in a memorandum from the Chevalier d'Aux [1692] suggesting the conquest of New England and New York: *BRH* 38 (1932): 550–2.

62 *RAPQ* (1930–31): 61, Talon to Colbert, 13 November 1666; *Collection de manuscrits*, 1: 285–7, Duchesneau to Colbert, 13 November 1681; also note a suggestion made by Frontenac, 13 November 1673, in *RAPQ* (1926–27): 46.

63 AC, CIIA, 10: 260–4, draft by Louis-Hector de Callière, governor of Montreal, January 1689; 10: 271–4, 275–6, memoranda from Callière to

the minister [1689]; 11: 185–94, memorandum from Denonville, January
[1690]; *RAPQ* (1927–28): 12–16, "Mémoire pour servir d'instruction à
M. le comte de Frontenac sur l'entreprise de la Nouvelle York," 7 June
1689. Frontenac, who had just been appointed to a second mandate as
governor, replacing Denonville, was to command the operation.

64 *Collection de manuscrits*, 1: 449, minister to Denonville, 1 May 1689;
ibid., 463–4, ordinance from the king to Denonville and Champigny in
regard to the declaration of war against England, Marly, 26 June 1689.
On the rebellions against the representatives of James II in New York and
Boston that March, see Steele, "Governors or Generals?" The news of
these events spread rapidly and with growing excitement in Canada.
Lahontan, returning from the Great Lakes region, learned it from Jacques
Lemoyne de Sainte-Hélène, whom he met on the Ottawa River in early
summer: Lahontan, "Nouveaux voyages," in *Oeuvres*, 1: 438. See also
Eccles, *Frontenac*, 200–2, on Versailles's hesitations and Denonville's
initial plan.

65 See, e.g., *Collection de manuscrits*, 1: 270–2, memorandum from
Duchesneau in regard to New England, 14 November 1679; AC, CIIA, 11:
252–60, Champigny to the minister, 10 May 1691; BRH 38 (1932): 550–2,
memorandum from the Chevalier d'Aux. "The populace rules that land,"
wrote Janclot, a regular officer: Myrand, ed., *Sir William Phips*, 62.

66 *RAPQ* (1927–28): 17, Frontenac to the minister, 15 November 1689.

67 *RAPQ* (1927–28): 43, Frontenac to the minister, 12 November 1690: Since
this plan could only be put into effect from the sea, "I think it impossible,
as I had the honour to tell you when leaving Paris, to [include the
Canadian troops]"; see also AC, CIIA, 13: 53–63v, 283–95v, 322, 329v,
Frontenac to the minister, 25 October 1694 and 2 and 4 November 1695.

68 *Collection de manuscrits*, 2: 225–6, "Projet d'une entreprise sur Boston et
la Nouvelle Angleterre par M. de Villebon [governor of Acadia]," Port-
Royal, 26 July 1696; ibid., 253–8, "Projet d'entreprise sur Boston et
Manhatte par M. de Lagny," Paris, 20 January 1697. The latter specified
that the plan had been devised by Iberville during his voyage to Pemaquid.
Lagny, in charge of Canadian affairs for the naval ministry, was a share-
holder in the Compagnie du Nord, whence his close ties to Iberville. Their
correspondence has not survived.

69 *Collection de manuscrits*, 2: 263–8, instructions from Nesmond, 21 April
1697; ibid., 268–73, memorandum in regard to the Boston entreprise,
Versailles, 21 April 1697; see also, in regard to booty, the memorandum
from Villebon cited in the preceding note. It is possible that private
interests contributed to Nesmond's expedition.

70 In a report of 15 October 1697, Frontenac clearly indicated to the minister that the plan, which had not been submitted to him, was inept: *RAPQ* (1928–29): 339–42.

71 AC, CIIA, 19: 241–52, Memorandum from Iberville in regard to Boston and its dependencies [1701]; *Collection de manuscrits*, 2: 342–51 and 397–9, a second memorandum from Iberville erroneously attributed to Saint-Castin. Iberville wrote these memoranda in France between two voyages to Mississippi ca. 1701–02. His plan called for the participation of the Abenakis of Acadia. He believed that the lure of booty would mobilize the Canadians but that an order from the king would be necessary "to force those who might not participate of their own accord." It is the only realistic passage in the plan.

72 Charlevoix, *History*, 4: 24–47, 4: 277–8, and 5: 68. The plans were good – indeed, "infallible" in the case of the 1689 plan, whose failure was ascribed to France's indifference. Guy Frégault ("L'Empire britannique" and *Iberville*, 363–70) is notable among historians who share this interpretation.

73 In 1775, Benedict Arnold's revolutionary army of about 1,100 men followed the Kennebec-Chaudière route in mounting an attack on Quebec. It lost over a third of its numbers on the six-week journey and was only able to recover thanks to the welcome offered by Canadian peasants.

74 Excluding the plan for the conquest of Boston datelined Louisbourg, 19 November 1744, published in *Collection de manuscrits*, 3: 211–15.

75 AC, CIIA, 28: 131–31v or *RAPQ* (1939–40): 436, Vaudreuil to the minister, 5 November 1708, in response to the minister's letter of 6 June 1708, *RAPQ* (1939–40): 418; AC, CIIA, 27: 9v, Ramezay to the minister, 12 November 1707. See also Miquelon, *New France*, 38, on Ramezay's plans and on Vaudreuil's prudence after acceding to the position of governor-general.

76 See *supra*, ch. 4, section 3, "Major Enterprises"; *RAPQ* (1942–43): 431, Vaudreuil to the minister, 14 November 1709.

77 AC, CIIA, 17: 53–8, Champigny to the minister, 26 May 1699. According to the intendant, Callière, the governor of Montreal, had encouraged this trade.

78 *RAPQ* (1946–47): 409, "Mémoire de Madame de Vaudreuil au ministre" (1710). The letter was written in France in early 1710, and the comment was quoted in the king's memorandum of 10 May (ibid., 375).

79 *RAPQ* (1947–48): 139, 207, memoranda from the king to Vaudreuil and

Bégon, 15 June 1712 and 25 June 1713. Raudot published two ordinances on the subject for the government of Montreal. The one dated 13 June 1709 brings up an impending shortage of cattle and sheep; another one, not extant, blames the peasants for having traded their snowshoes for sleighs. *RAPQ* (1946–47): 388, Vaudreuil and Raudot to the minister, 2 November 1710, in regard to the two ordinances; BAnQ-Québec, E1–S1–P547 and P724, intendants' ordinances, 13 June 1709 and 7 July 1710.

80 Dechêne, *Habitants and Merchants*, 70; Dépatie, "L'Évolution," 236; Wien, "Accumulation," 136. These observations are derived from several hundred after-death inventories of peasants, a more reliable source than the censuses, which also indicate an average of fewer than two horses per household.

81 AC, CIIA, 56: 124–6, Maurepas to Beauharnois and Hocquart, 29 May 1731; AC, B, 49: 609 et seq., memorandum from the king serving as an instruction to Dupuy, 1 May 1726, which put the matter back on the agenda.

82 See the correspondence between Hocquart and the Court on this subject: AC, CIIA, 53: 113–27, 17 October 1730; B, 55: 537, 29 May 1731; CIIA, 54: 54–7 and 70–76v, 4 October 1731; B, 57: 652v, 22 April 1732; CIIA, 57: 40v, 1 October 1732; B, 60: 537, 27 April 1734; B, 74: 93, king's memorandum of 30 April 1742.

83 AC, CIIA, 61: 303–13v, Beauharnois to the minister, 10 October 1734; see also 50: 87–89v, Beauharnois to the minister, 1 October 1728, and 69: 237v, Hocquart to the minister, 30 September 1739.

84 *RAPQ* (1946–47): 443, Vaudreuil and Raudot to the minister, 7 November 1711. See also *RAPQ* (1947–48): 170, Vaudreuil to the minister, 6 November 1712, and 278, Vaudreuil and Bégon to the minister, 20 September 1714, as well as AC, CIIA, 35: 15–52v, Ramezay and Bégon to the minister, 7 November 1715. Starting in 1707, Raudot began making recommendations in favour of the militia officers; he suggested that "to keep the habitants of these côtes in a sort of dependency at all times, the militia captains living there be given the rank of sergeant in the regular troops, with a salary of one hundred livres, to carry out the orders of the governors and intendants, and that it be ordered that the intendants appoint them in conjunction with the governors": AC, CIIA, 26: 175, Raudot to the minister, 10 November 1707.

85 See *infra*, ch. 9, section 1.

CHAPTER SIX

1 Eccles, *The Government of New France*, 71–82. The other specialists of the French regime are less categorical, but none to date has challenged this interpretation. The critique voiced by liberal historians of old – F.-X. Garneau, Francis Parkman, Raymond DuBois Cahall, or Gustave Lanctôt – has been swept into the dustbin, and what has taken its place is the idealized image of public life in New France typical of clerico-nationalist historiography. Among recent eulogists is André Vachon, who writes in "The Administration of New France" (*DCB*, 2: xv–xxiv) of the "elegant simplicity," the "state of perfection," of the colony's administrative structures. In focusing on inconsistencies and conflicts, Christophe Horguelin's *La Prétendue République* affords a less sanitized (and no doubt more realistic) image of governmental structures in the decades following the mid-seventeenth century.

2 Tocqueville, *The Old Régime*, 253–4.

3 I am thinking in particular of the edicts governing marriage and of Colbert's plan to deprive girls of their inheritance in order to favour the earlier settlement of boys; or again, of Talon's suggestion of a regulation forcing Indigenous women to breastfeed for shorter periods so that they would have more children. This administrative fever did not last long. In the seventeenth century, the word *peuplade* was commonly used to mean "settlement"; or, as Furetière (*Le Dictionnaire*) defined it, "inundation by people looking for land to live on."

4 Frostin, *Les Révoltes*; Debien, *Esprit colon*; Pluchon, *Histoire de la colonisation française*, ch. 8, "Idéologies et institutions."

5 *RAPQ* (1926–27): 25, Colbert to Frontenac, 13 June 1673, in regard to abolition of the syndics.

6 See Furet, "Tocqueville."

7 AC, CIIA, 6: 240–1, "Difficultés qu'il plaira à Monsieur le marquis de Seignelay de décider sur les fonctions des gouverneur et intendant de Canada: réponses du Roy du 10 avril 1684; décisions." Versailles favoured the colonial courts and sought to rein in the ambitions of its commissioners. The latter would continue to undermine local jurisdiction, and the Pontchartrains would do nothing to stop them.

8 The resignation of the Conseil Supérieur is discussed in an old but still useful work, Cahall, *The Sovereign Council*. Historians have toiled in the judicial archives since then, but institutional history has been largely ignored. The problems I bring up here go unmentioned in the syntheses by William J. Eccles and André Vachon.

9 As Alain Guéry ("The State," 23) observes, the venality of offices was not without its advantages.

10 Remarks by Madame de Sévigné, quoted in Bordes, *L'Administration provinciale*, 27.

11 Pierre Pluchon (*Histoire de la colonisation française*, 605–10) reaches the same conclusion in regard to the West Indies. In doing so, he contradicts Jean Meyer (*Histoire de la France coloniale*, 156), who sees the power of the colonial governors as ebbing – an untrue statement for the Canadian context at least. My observations relate to the period of royal government, 1663–1760. Comparison with previous governments, from the time of the trading companies when settlement of the colony had barely begun and the Jesuits made the rules, is of no use.

12 The collaboration was interrupted during the brief tenure (1726–28) of Claude-Thomas Dupuy (the only one of ten Quebec intendants to have followed the career path of a provincial intendant), who clashed frontally and clumsily with the governor. There followed a rocambolesque quarrel that clearly illustrated the weakness of the civilian authorities, as Colin Coates ("Authority and Illegitimacy") has correctly noted. But Coates misses the fact that it simultaneously illustrated the solidity of the military authorities, making his conclusions on the weakness of "colonial absolutism" highly tentative at best.

13 Corvisier, *L'Armée française*, 1: 88–92.

14 AC, C11A, 9: 110, memorandum from Denonville on the expedition against the Iroquois, October 1687.

15 This is the interpretation of William J. Eccles. Note that Eccles, in "The Social, Economic, and Political Significance," emphasized the colony's military character and the consequences of this orientation for its sociocultural and economic development. However, he fails to account for the time dimension and the implications for the workings of institutions, the matters of interest here.

16 Martel, *Mémoire*, 59.

17 The community of Montreal possessed a cemetery, a shed in which to hold its meetings, and rights to the commons: Faillon, *Histoire de la colonie*, 2: 198–201. According to Faillon, the creation of a town council (*corps de ville*), as provided by the Ville-Marie charter, dates from 1644. The minutes of assemblies predating 1656 have not survived. See Dechêne, *Habitants and Merchants*, 207–8.

18 Trudel, *Les Événements*, 187–94. This study meticulously describes the contents of the documents but does not go beyond the meagre sources of the period. That which is not documented does not exist for the historian, resulting in a shallow history that asks no questions.

19 *RAPQ* (1926–27): 25: "and it will even be necessary, with a little time, and once the colony is yet stronger than it is now, to gradually abolish the syndic," wrote Colbert to Frontenac. The syndics of Quebec and Trois-Rivières were apparently eliminated shortly afterwards. The Montreal assembly of habitants was abolished in 1677 following a petition remonstrating against the military corvées that it had entrusted to its syndic: Dechêne, *Habitants and Merchants*, 208.

20 AC, CIIA, 7: 240–7, preamble to a petition from the habitants of the Lower Town of Quebec to Seignelay [1685]. I reiterate here the conclusions derived from my analysis of the Montreal assemblies and the events leading to their disappearance: Dechêne, *Habitants and Merchants*, 207–9.

21 There were royal judges in Quebec and Trois-Rivières and seigneurial judges in Montreal until 1693, when the bailiwick (*baillage*) came under royal jurisdiction. The royal judges had at first believed they were authorized to rule on rural cases as well – involving cabarets, for example – until the intendancy clearly asserted its exclusive authority over rural policing.

22 AC, CIIA, 85: 274, Monrepos to the minister [1746].

23 This was the case of Pierre André de Leigne, lieutenant-general of the provost court of Quebec from 1717 to 1744 and subdelegate to Bégon and Hocquart, who approved of the enforcement of these regulations: AC, CIIA, 45: 401–04v, André de Leigne to the minister, 6 October 1723, and 45: 244–45v, Bégon to the minister, 26 October 1723, as well as Jean-Claude Dubé, "André de Leigne, Pierre," *DCB*, 3: 15–16. For a list of subdelegates at Quebec and a critique of their role, see *RAPQ* (1922–23): 55, "Mémoire au ministre de Pontchartrain sur la mauvaise administration de la justice au Canada (1715)," by former attorney general Ruette d'Auteuil. From 1716 to 1730, Pierre Raimbaut, attorney general and later lieutenant-general at Montreal, acted as subdelegate simultaneously with naval commissary François Clairambault, who was often absent.

24 On the intendancy's taking of control over grain policing, see Dechêne, *Power and Subsistence*.

25 AC, CIIA, 81: 334v, Hocquart to the minister, 10 October 1744.

26 Roy, ed., *Édits, ordonnances*, 1: 97–8, edict creating an office of the provost of the marshalcy in Canada, 9 May 1677. On the origin and functions of the marshalcy in France, see Castan, *Justice et répression en Languedoc*, ch. 5; Emsley, "La maréchaussée"; Martin, "La maréchaussée au XVIIIe siècle."

27 *RAPQ* (1946–47): 443, Vaudreuil and Raudot to the minister, 7 November 1711; AC, CIIA, 49: 404–05v, Dupuy to the minister, 25 October 1727,

and 56: 159–63, provost of the marshalcy to the minister, 19 October 1728 and 14 October 1731.

28 AC, CIIA, 89: 230–3, provost of the marshalcy to the minister, 8 November 1747. The marshalcy left no archives, but the pursuit reports (*procès-verbaux de recherche*) show that the soldiers and rural militias were largely responsible for conducting these pursuits. André Lachance (*La Justice criminelle*, 29–30) concludes – too quickly, in my view – that the corps did not function as a court. If not, then why did it have a clerk? And why did the provost deplore the absence of a prosecutor? See also the biographies of provosts Paul and Charles-Paul Denys de Saint-Simon: A.J.E. Lunn, "Denys de Saint-Simon, Paul," DCB, 2: 186; André Lachance, "Denys de Saint-Simon, Charles-Paul," DCB, 3: 192–3.

29 The troops comprised twenty-eight companies of thirty men, nineteen of them stationed at Montreal, seven at Quebec, and two at Trois-Rivières. They were perpetually incomplete, so the number of soldiers in Montreal actually fluctuated around 500; in the colony, it amounted to about 840. The numbers doubled in 1750, and the distribution among the three cities changed as well.

30 AC, F3, 7: 748–64, "Règlement du roi pour la conduite, police et discipline des companies que Sa Majesté entretient dans le Canada," 30 May 1695.

31 AC, CIIA, 27: 46–54v, draft regulation to prevent imprisonment without a decree by attorney general Ruette d'Auteuil, 15 April 1707; 17: 63–71v, Callière, governor of Montreal, to the minister, 16 October 1700; 41: 342–4, attorney general Collet to the minister in regard to the same abuses, 10 March 1720; BAnQ-Montréal, TL4–S35, register of ordinances, 1743–56, f. 106, ordinance by Bigot, 8 February 1751, forbidding the Montreal jailer from receiving any habitant arrested by the regular officers.

32 The harassment was reported by the naval commissary in 1697 and persisted until 1721. The judge and the merchants finally won, and the market stayed in the centre of town. See, e.g., AC, CIIA, 15: 162–7 and 44: 222–22v; also, Poirier, "The Fortifications of Montréal," 54–6. The trial pitting the lieutenant-general against the surgeon Sylvain and the Montreal military officer corps concerning a refusal to lend assistance is a good illustration of the arrogance in question: BAnQ-Montréal, TL4–S1–D4907, December 1742–April 1743.

33 See, e.g., AC, CIIA, 67: 308–12v, Hocquart to the minister, 7 October 1737.

34 This observation transpires from the testimony delivered in criminal trials before ordinary judges: The regulars acted as the police in the modern sense of the term.

35 BAnQ-Québec, TP1–S777–D40, f. 271–2, cited in Dechêne, *Power and Subsistence*, 142.

36 The archives of the intendancy, so well endowed in France, are quite disappointing on this side of the Atlantic. The series of ordinances only begins in 1705 (a few scattered earlier ordinances remain, but most have been lost), and these documents rarely contain more than the text of the judgment or regulation. Most of the supporting documentation, complaints, investigations, testimony, and so forth are lacking, and all indications are that the intendants saw no interest in keeping them. They sometimes intervened in urban policing, especially in Quebec, but most often left these matters to the subdelegates. These latter, except when acting as interim intendants, as in 1736–37 and 1749, left no traces of their activities. "Neither the intendant nor his subdelegates ... keep records of most of their regulations," wrote Ruette d'Auteuil: RAPQ (1922–23): 55. The few scattered ordinances of Honoré Michel de Villebois, naval commissary and subdelegate in Montreal, tracked down in the judicial archives, offer no evidence of his assiduous administration over a period of seventeen years; see AC, F3, 78: 35–8, Michel to the minister, New Orleans, 15 September 1749, in regard to this experience and his collaboration with the military command. The interventions of the military, like those of the marshalcy for that matter, have left no traces.

37 A word or two in the official correspondence, phrases inserted here and there in a legal document, reveal the existence of these undocumented disruptions.

38 In various publications, André Lachance contends that authority was very weak in the colonial towns, coercive power nearly non-existent. He forgets the role of the troops in assisting the judicial system and as a police force. Lachance, "Le contrôle social; *idem*, "La régulation des conduites dans la ville canadienne au XVIIIe siècle (1700–1760)," in Lebrun and Séguin, eds, *Sociétés villageoises*, 327–36.

39 RAPQ (1947–48): 242, memorandum from the king to Vaudreuil and Bégon, 19 March 1714; *idem*, 278, Vaudreuil and Bégon to the minister, 20 September 1714, giving notice of an "excerpt of the inspections of the militia officers of this colony, company by company"; AC, C11A, 49: 142, Beauharnois to the minister, 25 September 1727, and 64: 252–5, Governor of Montreal de Beaucour to the minister, 2 October 1735, in regard to a census of the militias of his government.

40 Corvisier, *Armées et sociétés*, 41. On the Quebec artillery unit, see AC, C11A, 45: 142–3, 50: 168–68v, and 51: 139. Louis and Charles Levrard,

father and son, were master gunners at Quebec and Montreal ca.
1725–50.

41 AC, CIIA, 95: 66–66v, La Jonquière and Bigot to the minister, 13 October
1750; Cassel, "The Troupes de la Marine," 62–3. According to the militia
roll of 1750, the Quebec company consisted of 140 gunners, the Montreal
company fifty-eight.

42 AC, CIIA, 100: 178 et seq., artillery officer Le Mercier to the minister,
20 October 1755, and "Mémoire sur l'artillerie du Canada," [1756].

43 There was generally one ensign, one lieutenant, one senior captain, and
one junior captain per company. I was able to identify most of the
Montreal captains who served after 1710, while the Quebec captains were
harder. Almost all the subordinate officers proved elusive because they
rarely stated their titles in notarial acts. On the social background of
urban militia officers, see *supra*, 81–3.

44 José Igartua, "Guy, Pierre," *DCB*, 3: 291–2; Dechêne, *Power and
Subsistence*, 111; Lanctôt, "Les troupes," 46–7.

45 The colonels of Montreal were, in chronological order: J.-A. Fleury
Deschambaut (ca. 1690–1715), F.-M. Bouat (1725–26), J.-B. Charly *dit*
Saint-Ange (1726–28), É. Volant (1728–35), J.-B. Neveu (1735–54), and
René de Couagne (1751–60). For Quebec: R.-L. Chartier de Lotbinière
(1690–1709), Jean Crespin (1710–34), J. Fleury de La Gorgendière
(1734–55), and J.-J. Riverin Sr (1755–56). The case of Trois-Rivières is
peculiar, since the colonel in the 1740s and 1750s was Louis-Joseph
Godefroy de Tonnancourt, merchant, king's attorney, and member of the
colonial nobility. His father, René Godefroy, may have been a militia
colonel before his death in 1738.

46 Massicotte, *Répertoire*, 123, permission to resign granted by the governor
of Montreal to Louis Charly Saint-Ange, 11 July 1752. Only forty-seven
years old, the son of a former militia colonel, he made this request at a
time when his responsibilities as a captain were becoming more burdensome and keeping him from looking after his business dealings.

47 The incident took place at the start of the War of the Austrian Succession:
letter from the governor-general to militia captain De Couagne, Quebec,
12 August 1746, quoted in Lanctôt, "Les troupes," 47.

48 MCQ, Collection du Séminaire de Québec, fonds Viger-Verreau 47, no. 1.8,
1 March 1750: town major's commission in the Rivière-du-Loup militia
awarded to Lamirande, with order to the colonel of Trois-Rivières to
receive him; see also the junior captain's commission given to Pierre Guy,
1 August 1738, in Lanctôt, "Les troupes," 47.

49 In 1741, 70 per cent of Montreal heads of households were homeowners: Dechêne, "La croissance de Montréal," 169. There is no reason to believe the situation was much different in Quebec, as Yvon Desloges (*A Tenant's Town*) maintains without offering a satisfactory demonstration.

50 They preferred to serve as volunteers or not at all. During the Seven Years' War, they founded their own "gentleman's company," which drew jeers from the French army officers. See *infra*, 216–17.

51 Myrand, ed., *Sir William Phips*, 91–3, testimony of Sylvanus Davis: Sixty merchants and artisans kept watch every night at Quebec from July to October 1690 after the departure of the troops; AC, CIIA, 12: 87v, Champigny to the minister, 10 November 1692: The habitants of Montreal kept watch after the assignment of the troops to the nearby forts.

52 AC, CIIA, 78: 317, "Mémoire (de Beaucours) concernant les défenses du gouvernement de Montréal," [1 November] 1744; 79: 211–12, Beauharnois to the minister, 31 October 1743; also 61: 343, Dubois Berthelot de Beaucours in regard to the state of the troops in Montreal, 1734; Poirier, "The Fortifications of Montréal," 67–73.

53 AC, CIIA, 77: 135–36v and 79: 140–1, Beauharnois to the minister, 26 September 1742 and 19 September 1743. The procedure was so unusual that it created a conflict of authority between the governor and the intendant. One need only read the police regulations and the testimony in assault cases to learn that the militia was not the primary arm of law enforcement in the city, as René Chartrand ("Une place de guerre," 215) contends.

54 BAnQ-Québec, TL5–D183, criminal trial in the provost court of Jean Gauthier *dit* Larouche, edge-tool maker, on a petition from Joseph Petit Bruneau and Simon Jarent, brother and brother-in-law of the victim, 25 November–10 December 1686; AC, CIIA, 9: 218–21v, decree of the Conseil Supérieur, 26 February 1687, reducing the damages awarded at trial level to nearly nothing.

55 The receptions accorded to the following figures are described in the works indicated: Frontenac (1689), in Lahontan, "Nouveaux voyages," letters 17–18, in *Oeuvres*, 1: 446 et seq.; Saint-Vallier (1713), in Saint-Félix, *Monseigneur de Saint-Vallier*, 225–6, 231; Bishop Dosquet, in Navières, "Un voyage à la Nouvelle-France," 29; Governor La Galissonnière (19 September 1747), in AC, CIIA, 88: 36–8; Intendant Bigot (Montreal, February 1749), in *RAPQ* (1934–35): 33–5, "La correspondence de Madame Bégon (1748–1753)."

56 Moreau de Saint-Méry, *Description topographique*. See the description of the *milices du Cap*, 1: 484–7. On the significance of the uniform, see Roche, *La Culture des apparences*, ch. 9.

57 The mythology around the Canadian militias has led artists and historians to imagine how the uniforms might have looked. See, e.g., Henri Beau's illustrations as reproduced in Miquelon, *New France*, or Francis Back's drawings in Landry, ed., *Pour le Christ*, 159. "The militias wore gray with red linings and decorations," writes Gérard Filteau (*Par la bouche*, 105).

58 AC, CIIA, 89: 138–41v, draft regulation by Hocquart, 1747. The policing responsibilities of the seigneurial courts had formerly been more extensive. For example, the power to issue cabaret permits had been taken away from them by a decree of the Conseil d'État dated 22 May 1724, confirmed by Bégon's ordinance of 18 January 1725: AC, F3, 10: 271–72v, 282.

59 Provisional commissions of subdelegates were, at least in part, recorded with the intendants' ordinances: BAnQ-Québec, E1–S1, *passim*.

60 I counted the ordinances for each year from 1705 (when the series begins) to 1760 and analyzed their contents for 1720–22, 1740–42, and 1750–52. The number of matters of all sorts handled by the intendant varies from year to year, ranging from about fifty to 150, and private law disputes account for half of them. Thus it seems that Hocquart exaggerated when he claimed to devote two days a week to disputes involving habitants in the government of Quebec: AC, B, 76: 28, minister to Hocquart, 15 April 1743. As to the 2,000 judgments that Raudot, a particularly busy intendant, boasted of having rendered fourteen months after arriving in the colony, it seems certain that his secretary mistakenly added a zero to the number, which should read 200, thus corresponding to the 170 or so ordinances recorded during this period: AC, CIIA, 24: 331–52, Raudot to the minister, 2 November 1706. After 1744, the intendants were taken up with military matters and had less time to dedicate to rural policing and legal proceedings, and the number of ordinances plummeted.

61 An ordinance by Raudot dated 25 June 1710 is revealing. It provides for remuneration for militia captains in return for "enforcing our ordinances, which we are almost always obliged to route through them." The practice was still perceived as a stopgap. Roy, ed., *Édits, ordonnances*, 2: 275.

62 See Table 6.1.

63 The Parchemin notarial database, held by Bibliothèque et Archives nationales du Québec, is tremendously helpful. It is regrettable, however, that the managers of the project took such liberties with the titles of the acts when they were computerized. Some of the names are unrecognizable, and *dit* is replaced by *de* or a hyphen, creating confusion as to social class background. The word *habitant*, which would have served to identify farmers, was deleted along with many other keywords relating to profession and residence.

64 See the source list at the bottom of Table 6.2.

65 See Table 6.1.

66 Lefebvre, "Les Officiers de milice"; Lavallée, *La Prairie*, 42–3, 241–2.

67 AC, CIIA, 54: 136–67v, 57: 5–42, 59: 71–95v, and 65: 28–53,
    Beauharnois and Hocquart to the minister, 12 October 1731, 1 October
    1732, 1 October 1733, and 12 October 1736; also, 67: 95–107,
    [Hocquart, 1737], "Détail de toute la colonie."

68 *RAPQ* (1946–47): 385, Vaudreuil to the minister, 25 October 1710. For a
    very late example of a recommendation, see the letter of 24 November
    1780 from the parish priest of Saint-Gervais (then commonly known as
    Nouvelle-Cadie) recommending J.-B. Perrault, "who comes from a long
    line of militia captains" and was said to be the most capable of holding
    the position. Surely many such letters, dating from the turn of the century,
    have been lost. Archives de l'Université de Montréal, Baby Collection,
    B2598. Thanks to Thomas Wien for this reference.

69 This analysis includes only persons included in the 1721 survey.

70 This is the interpretation of Benjamin Sulte and Lionel Groulx, summar-
    ized with force and conviction by Claude de Bonnault in the introduction
    to "Le Canada militaire: État provisoire des officiers de milice de 1641 à
    1760," *RAPQ* (1949–51): 263–5.

71 Ouellet, "Officiers de milice." The author bases his demonstration on the
    list of militia officers published by Bonnault (see preceding note), which,
    among other mistakes, conflates militia officers with regular officers. The
    paper is a muddle, mixing up periods and confusing urban with rural
    militias. The main argument – that townspeople monopolized positions in
    the militia in hopes of being ennobled and receiving the cross of the order
    of Saint-Louis – is surprising given that not one militia officer was
    ennobled in the eighteenth century and that this military reward was
    reserved for regular officers.

72 Calculated on a total of 180 individuals. See Table 6.2.

73 Dechêne, "The Seigneuries," in Harris, ed., *From the Beginning*, pl. 51.
    In the Trois-Rivières region, seigneuries such as Maskinongé or
    Lussaudière, though granted to nobles, soon fell into the hands of
    commoners.

74 *RAPQ* (1947–48): 146, minister to Vaudreuil, 25 June 1712; ibid., 170–1,
    Vaudreuil to the minister, 6 November 1712. Governor of Trois-Rivières
    François de Galiffet drew the minister's attention to these disputes. See
    also AC, CIIA, 33: 122–36, Bégon to the minister, 12 November 1712.

75 Although the majority of the seigneuries and more than half the land area
    belonged to the church and the military nobility, the government also

comprised a few landowners of local and commoner background who held commissions in the militia. Three cases have been identified: René Messier, co-seigneur of Varennes, and Jacques Brunet, son of a co-seigneur of Île du Pas, were militia captains in the period 1710–29; in the 1740s, the captain of Terrebonne was the brother of Louis Lepage de Saint-Claire, the local seigneur.

76 The sample is derived from the following sources: BAnQ-Montréal, TL4–S1–D4984 and D5578, proceedings against deserters, 28 January 1743, 13 February and 20 September 1751; AC, CIIA, 76: 265–70 and 91: 162–71, other proceedings, 1741 and 1748. The pursuit reports list the parishes visited and the captains' names; see also Grenier, ed., *Papiers Contrecoeur*, 329–33, for a list of militia captains in 1755 (Ohio campaign).

77 Jean Boucher de Montbrun was an exception to the rule. A merchant in the 1720s living on his land in the seigneury of Boucherville, he stated his title of militia commander or colonel in the Côte-du-Sud each time he went before a notary. Most of his brothers had commissions in the troops. I have not found any other such cases.

78 The calculation is based on fifty militia captains and fifty-two lieutenants or ensigns who appeared in the 1721 survey of parish boundaries. See Table 6.2.

79 Lefebvre, "Les Officiers de milice."

80 BAnQ-Québec, TL5, and BAnQ-Montréal, TL4–S1, *passim*. Witnesses were required to state their name, title, profession, domicile, and age, all of which could easily be verified.

81 BAnQ-Montréal, CN601–S95, minutes of notary F. Comparet, statement of Guillaume Bômer in regard to reading of the ordinances, 29 December 1750, followed by a petition by Bazinet, who stated that he was unable to sign his name.

82 See the source list at the bottom of Table 6.2. Of fifty-five captains, thirty-six signed, along with thirty-six out of sixty-one lieutenants and ensigns, for an overall proportion of 62 per cent. The proportion would have been much lower twenty years later, since schools were still lacking in most of the parishes and illiteracy grew as the population did.

83 AC, CIIA, 6: 190–1, de Meulles to the minister, 4 November 1683, and 7: 178–86v, memorandum from Denonville, 12 November 1685.

84 The description applies to the fifty rural parishes founded before 1700, except for certain ecclesiastical seigneuries, such as the Island of Montreal, where the seigneurs played a more active role in the early years. But on the whole, the habitants took their own measures, for these chapels did not cost much and the desire to have their own place of worship was very

strong. Lavallée, *La Prairie*, 113–14 et seq., contrasts the building of the first churches with that of the stone church. In my work on the Island of Montreal (Dechêne, *Habitants and Merchants*, 266–7), I mistakenly conflated the two stages.

85 See, e.g., BAnQ-Montréal, TL2, Registre des audiences, lawsuits filed by the church wardens of Pointe-aux-Trembles and Lachine, 22 July and 11 October 1681. One defendant argued that his promise had been merely conditional, the other that he had not attended the assembly. "[A]ccustomed to making many promises and keeping none," wrote a parish priest in regard to his parishioners: petition from Louis-Michel de Vilermaula to the intendant, 7 October 1707, Archives du séminaire de Saint-Sulpice, fonds Faillon, cahier DD (319).

86 Roy, ed., *Édits, ordonnances*, 2: 270, ordinance by Intendant Raudot for the presbytery of La Durantaye, 5 February 1709; ibid., 435, 443, 295, and 474, ordinances and judgments by Intendant Bégon for the Boucherville church (9 September 1713), the Kamouraska presbytery (30 September 1715), and the churches of La Chenaye and Repentigny (16 April 1722 and 2 March 1723); ibid., 507, ordinance by Intendant Hocquart for the Deschambault presbytery, 14 March 1730, etc.

87 BAnQ-Montréal, TL2, Bailliage de Montréal, Registre des audiences, ordinance by d'Ailleboust, 15 April 1668; Archives du séminaire de Saint-Sulpice, fonds Faillon, cahier GG (1st series) (337), petition against Louis Fortier, 9 December 1681.

88 Archives du séminaire de Saint-Sulpice, M1584, no. 34, petition by the seigneurs further to an initial assembly, followed by an ordinance by Duchesneau ratifying the decisions, 3 July 1680; microfilm 4, no. 38, minutes of assemblies of 16 and 23 March 1681. In the country, contributions varied between three livres for "the poor" – about half the taxpayers – and six to eight livres for the "better off."

89 BAnQ-Québec, E1–S1/6, cahier 9, ordinance by Bégon, 17 January 1723, and other documents relating to the construction of the La Prairie bridges.

90 Sanfaçon, "La construction," 23. See also Pozzo-Laurent, "Le Réseau routier."

91 Habault, *La Corvée*; Letaconnoux, *Le Régime de la corvée*.

92 Harris, *The Seigneurial System*, 81. These narrow domains often stretched all the way to the back of the seigneury.

93 Since these customs were not codified in regulations, they are hard to discern. Historians have been at leisure to depict the seigneur as captive to the road crews under the orders of the militia captain, and that is undoubtedly the image that inspired Sanfaçon, since nothing in the

ordinances or the assembly minutes indicates that seigneurs contributed monetarily or otherwise to the corvées, as he asserts. Cugnet, *Traité général de la police*, contends that seigneurs were exempt from these obligations under the French regime, and the fight waged by *censitaires* in the latter half of the eighteenth century for the abolition of seigneurial privileges as regards the roads would seem to corroborate his position. For a good summary of the issue, see Robichaud, "Le Pouvoir," 13–21.

94 Roy, ed., *Édits, ordonnances*, 2: 430–1, ordinance by Raudot, 18 June 1709. Road building without the seigneur's assistance was all the harder in that the Rivière-Ouelle seigneury was still sparsely populated. The intendant authorized the habitants to sue their seigneur, a regular officer, for the cost of the work they did in his stead. See Robichaud, "Le Pouvoir," 18, 63.

95 *Censitaires* might resist by withholding payment of duties or by taking their wheat to a different mill, for example. There were instances when they united and took the seigneur to court, as at Rivière-du-Sud in 1742 and 1743 (BAnQ-Québec, TL5–D1287 and D1343), but these were exceptional. Most often, the seigneurs were the plaintiffs.

96 BAnQ-Québec, TL5–D2606, petition by the notary appointed by the roads superintendent to make payment on the Charlesbourg road, to force the habitants to pay for it, 13 August 1706; TL5–D2651, list of habitants of Pointe-à-la-Caille for payment to the roads superintendent, two days at ten livres per day, 11 June 1736.

97 BAnQ-Québec, TP1–S777–D10, petition by the parish priest of Saint-Pierre and Saint-Thomas-de-la-Rivière-du-Sud and the parish priest of Saint-François-Xavier and Sainte-Geneviève-de-Batiscan complaining of the poor condition of the roads. The militia captain was summoned to appear before the Conseil Supérieur, 16 October 1719. See also an ambiguous ordinance by Dupuy making the militia captain responsible for accidents attributable to his refusal to carry out orders: BAnQ-Québec, E1–S1–P1900. For the various responsibilities relating to the roads, see Sanfaçon, "La construction," and the reports of the road superintendents, BAnQ-Québec, E2, *passim*.

98 Jacques Mathieu, "Les réunions de terres au domaine du seigneur, 1730–1759," in Lebrun and Séguin, eds, *Sociétés villageoises*, 79–89.

99 AC, F3, 10: 282v, ordinance by Bégon, 18 January 1725, in regard to cabaret policing in the côtes, and 12, ordinances by subdelegate of Montreal Honoré Michel de Villebois, 26 February 1738 and 30 July 1742; BAnQ-Québec, E1–S1–P3955, ordinance by subdelegate of Montreal Jean-Victor Varin de la Marre, 19 August 1749;

BAnQ-Montréal, CN601–S95, minutes of notary F. Comparet, 30 March 1749, statement by Joseph Bazinet, militia captain of Saint-Léonard, in favour of two cabaret owners of the parish.

100 Roy, ed., *Ordonnances, commissions*, 2: 326–7, ordinance by Vaudreuil, 12 December 1704; BAnQ-Montréal, REE, Beauharnois and Michel, 19 June 1744 [*editors' note*: this document not found]); BAnQ-Québec, E1–S1–P1867, ordinance by Dupuy, 4 June 1727.

101 Frostin, "Du peuplement pénal"; Malchelosse, "Faux sauniers." The bulk of penal immigration occurred between 1723 and 1743. Quantification is difficult, particularly for soldier-prisoners in the 1720s. Malchelosse counted 648 salt smugglers sent to the colony between 1730 and 1743. They were authorized to settle there after completing their years of service.

102 BAnQ-Québec, E1–S1/13, cahier 24, ordinance by the governor and the intendant, 10 May 1736; BAnQ-Montréal, Archives judiciaires, pièces détachées, decree by the king, 14 February 1742 [*editors' note*: this document not found].

103 BAnQ-Québec, E1–S1–P2211, ordinance of 1 September 1730.

104 BAnQ-Québec, E1–S1–P3334, ordinance of 16 June 1741.

105 AC, C11A, 76: 265–8, pursuit report by Sieur Moineau, sergeant of the regulars, 4 March 1741; 76: 260–1, 269–70, Beauharnois to Governor of Montreal Dubois Berthelot de Beaucours concerning these incidents and the conduct of the militia officers, February–March and March–April 1741. Beauharnois suspected the churchmen, the Récollets and Louis Lepage, parish priest and seigneur of Terrebonne, of having abetted the soldiers' desertion and encouraged the militia officers' disobedience: One of the two captains accused was Lepage's brother, and the other was Parent, captain of Île Jésus. It is unknown whether they succeeded in exonerating themselves and getting their jobs back. The threat of revocation of commissions appears in several ordinances, but I did not find any other such examples.

106 BAnQ-Montréal, TL4–S1–D4984, pièces détachées, pursuit report and council of war against Louis Plichon, 31 August–19 September 1743. Plichon, who suffered from an unspecified "disability," was absolved of the crime of desertion and authorized to resume his service.

107 BAnQ-Québec, E1–S1/15, cahier 30, ordinances of 28, 29, and 30 August and 18 October 1742 (other numbers for the three August ordinances are E1–S1–P3432, P3433, and P3434); AC, C11A, 77: 135–36v, Beauharnois to the minister, 27 October 1742.

108 BAnQ-Montréal, Registres et carnets, 1738–1762, report of capture of accused banknote counterfeiter Nicolas Desse, 14 March 1756.

109 Without indicating the bias of the source, André Lachance
(*Les Marginaux*, 163–5) concludes, perhaps too quickly, that the people
adopted the attitude of the authorities.

110 AC, CIIA, 65: 127–31v, Beauharnois to the minister, 13 October 1736.
To exonerate the regular officers, whom the minister held responsible for several recent desertions, the governor accused the militia officers of complicity,
but there is no illustrative example to be found in trials of deserters.

111 The court officers counted on the colonial regulars in the cities and their
environs and on the militias in the more remote parishes. See, e.g.,
proceedings concerning contempt of court (*rebellion à justice*) dated
21 September 1745 and 22 January 1750, BAnQ-Montréal, TL4–S1–
D5177 and D5480.

112 BAnQ-Québec, EI–SI–P1615, P4354, P2970, and P4109, ordinances of
10 June 1724, 16 August 1735, 25 January 1738, and 12 October 1752;
TL5–D1668, inventory containing a statement of expenses by the officer of
the provost court, 16 March 1752.

113 BAnQ-Montréal, TL4–S1–D5270, criminal trial of Josèphe Estier, 29
October 1746–21 January 1747. She was convicted in absentia, having
apparently fled the colony with her lover. Her twelve-year-old son,
suspected of complicity, was released.

114 BAnQ-Québec, TL5–D1830 and D1851, criminal trials of René Lusignan,
surgeon, and Joseph Ouellet, blacksmith, his accomplice, February-April
1756. He was sentenced to death in absentia.

115 BAnQ-Québec, EI–SI–P4072, ordinance of 26 January 1752 to the
habitants of Berthier to enlarge the fort and add bastions.

116 BAnQ-Québec, EI–SI–P2990, ordinance of 21 July 1730.

117 These details are from Franquet, *Voyages*, 129–47. The dignitaries' sleighs
carried two passengers each, and I am assuming that the servants' sleighs
carried four. Officers and their wives each had their own domestic servant,
sometimes two, and the intendant brought along his domestic staff.
In summer, the travellers went by barque with stopovers in habitants'
homes for the noonday and evening meals. Franquet mentions prison
terms for militia officers who were remiss in these duties, but this may
have been an exaggeration intended to impress itself on the mind of
Governor Duquesne, who was hated by all the officers for his harsh
treatment of them.

118 *RAPQ* (1925–26), facsimile inserted between pp. 96 and 97, "Commission
de capitaine de milice pour Pierre Dupré," 27 February 1717. These parishes, still very sparsely populated, had until then been incorporated into
the militias of the seigneury of Beaupré.

119 The issue of military training is revisited in chapter 7. There is much discussion in the official correspondence of what should be done to arm the habitants, with no mention of militia officers' responsibility. The military formulation of commissions corresponds, however, to the image Versailles had formed. It was an affirmation of the governor's preponderant authority over the militia and has survived for that reason.

120 AC, CIIA, 26: 150–75, Raudot to the minister, 10 November 1707. A sergeant in the colonial regulars earned about 240 livres a year after food, clothing, and other expenses.

121 Roy, ed., *Édits, ordonnances*, 2: 275, 365, 542, ordinances of 25 June 1710, 19 April 1734, and 17 January 1737; ibid., 1: 352–4, regulation by the king concerning honours in the churches of New France, 27 April 1716. Under the laws of the realm, naval officers had no rank in the colony's churches (governors and king's lieutenants did but in the capacity of administrators). The precedence given to militia officers in rural churches and processions represented an implicit indication that they were not soldiers.

122 AC, CIIA, 76: 73–8, and 78: 35–8, excerpts from the records of the king's stores in Quebec for 1741 and 1742.

123 Sons on the family land, servants, rents, or pension are some of the possibilities that might be revealed by studying these rural communities.

124 Appeals to the captain in crisis situations are well documented in the judicial archives. In contrast, arbitration (not ordered by the intendant) left no direct traces, although it can be traced indirectly in these same archives or simply by default, as Jean-François Leclerc attempted to do in "Justice et infra-justice."

125 In the seventeenth century, when the militia had yet to become a law enforcement body, few were the rural parish officers who mentioned their titles in notarial acts: only twenty (fifty-five mentions) between 1676 and 1699, according to the Parchemin notarial database. My observations for the period 1710–29 are based on 110 rural officers (some 330 mentions of titles).

126 BAnQ-Montréal, CN601–S368, minutes of notary N. Senet, after-death inventory of Jacques Richaume, 19 June 1713. The captain's commission of 30 July 1706, signed by Vaudreuil, appears in the inventory of papers of the succession. The notarial acts involving Richaume between 1706 and 1713, and his heirs subsequently, do not mention his title.

127 See Wien, "Les conflits sociaux."

128 Apparently, militia captains in the West Indies had broader powers that represented the source of an "incontestable local autonomy," wrote Jean

Meyer (*Histoire de la France coloniale*, 156), erroneously claiming that their counterparts in Canada played the same role. Kenneth J. Banks ("Communications and Imperial Absolutism," 104–6) makes the same mistake, believing that Canadian captains, like those of Martinique, had decision-making powers in connection with the publication of royal orders.

129 BAnQ-Montréal, TL4-S1-D2775, trial of Pierre Paris, 12 July 1722; see also Archives du séminaire de Saint-Sulpice, fonds Faillon, cahier HH (128). Paris was imprisoned by Governor Vaudreuil in connection with a complaint by Captain Henri Jules Le Fournier Duvivier, settled in Canada since 1687. Duvivier had not followed custom.

130 Bercé, *Révoltes*; on the incorporation of small communities into the structure of government, see Levi, *Le Pouvoir au village*, ch. 4 in particular.

131 This idea is found in most of the syntheses and essays on New France published in Quebec, but no demonstration is ever provided, so intuitive does it seem. See, e.g., Mathieu and Courville, eds, *Peuplement colonisateur*; Mathieu, *La Nouvelle-France*.

132 Lavallée, *La Prairie*, 159–81. The author correctly poses the problem of representation by the *senior pars*. In La Prairie, about 10 per cent of heads of households regularly participated in assemblies. I obviously reject the surprising idea (introduced in the conclusion, p. 181) according to which the Canadian rural community was free of constraints, whether imposed by the war or by the seigneurs and the state.

133 This fact would not have excluded collective action but would have made it more difficult, since the government always regarded it as subversive. Consider, for example, the determination of the habitants of Saint-Thomas to sue their seigneur for better flour mills (Wien, "Les conflits sociaux").

134 Le Goff, *Vannes and Its Region*, 205–6. The reminder precedes an excellent analysis of social relations based on villagers' accounts.

135 This is the exemplary approach adopted in Sabean, *Power*. The author seeks to grasp the interface between individual and community by means of a very close reading of certain incidents.

CHAPTER SEVEN

1 An "autonomous" rural settlement, both economically and socially, with the seigneurs and the government exerting no control over the countryside. This is the argument of Mathieu and Courville, eds, *Peuplement colonisateur*. It should be added that the caricature of the

French peasant worn down by hard labour and taxation that is found in Canadian works also needs to be revised in light of the work on rural history done in the past thirty years.

2 See, e.g., *RAPQ* (1947–48): 179, 182, Vaudreuil and Bégon to the minister, 12 November 1712.

3 This is a summary of the arguments making the rounds in Quebec in the early and middle eighteenth century and in Montreal in the 1710s and 1720s. A denunciation of this putatively seditious discourse is found in AC, CIIA, 47: 149–54, Vaudreuil to the minister, 18 May 1725, or 85: 208 et seq., Beauharnois to the minister, 10 October 1746.

4 AC, F3, 7: 748–64, "Règlement du Roy pour la conduite, police et discipline des compagnies que Sa Majesté entretient dans le Canada," 30 May 1695. Colonists also built more remote forts; this construction work took the form of military expeditions. For a description of the construction of Fort Niagara, see Baugy, *Journal*, 117–19.

5 Charbonneau, Desloges, and Lafrance, *Québec, the Fortified City*. See ch. 1 for a good history of the project, from which I borrowed some of the details that follow.

6 AC, CIIA, 11: 252–60, Champigny to the minister, 10 May 1691. The tax of 1690 had been set at 4,000 livres Canadian currency, or 3,000 French livres. In 1693, it appears that some 1,600 livres was collected.

7 Except for 1690 when this was clearly a fixed tax payable in cash. See *supra*, note 6.

8 See Louvigny, commandant at Quebec in the governor's absence, to the minister, 21 October 1706, AC, CIIA, 25: 18–23, and especially the tax roll ordered at Montreal in 1714 by the intendant, who wanted to replicate the system in use in Quebec.

9 AC, CIIA, 27: 22–6, Jacques Levasseur de Néré to the minister, 12 November 1707; letter from Louvigny, 1706 (see preceding note). The townspeople and the religious communities raised objections to lending their teams. The engineer took particular issue with urban militia officers and law officers who sought exemptions for themselves or who came to direct the earthmovers: They delayed the work rather than advancing it, he wrote.

10 *RAPQ* (1939–40): 448, Vaudreuil and Raudot to the minister, 14 November 1708: "yet there are a few people here who, because they have done well for themselves, and wish to do even better, think everyone must be rich," they wrote, suggesting that the well-off also favoured another form of taxation.

11 Callière ordered the habitants of the city and its environs to prepare the stakes during the winter of 1685, and this palisade began to be erected the

following summer. The work was still ongoing in 1687. The palisade was subsequently completed and enlarged: Lahontan, "Nouveaux voyages," in *Oeuvres*, 1: 313; Baugy, *Journal*, 57. The contributions left traces in proceeding minutes and after-death inventories: BAnQ-Montréal, CN601–S280 and S368, minutes of notary C. Maugue, 6 April 1691, inventory of J. Bauvais, and minutes of notary N. Senet, 9 July 1714, inventory of Jacques Millet. The contributions were sizeable, thirty to fifty stakes at a time, but staggered over time.

12 Converted into money according to the equivalences used by the administration, the tax ranged from two to seventy-five livres, with the data tightly clustered around the mean: LAC, MG17–A7–2, 1, 2: 487 et seq. I used this source to sketch the socioeconomic profile of the people living on the Island of Montreal: Dechêne, *Habitants and Merchants*, 212–14 and graph 24, p. 322.

13 *RAPQ* (1947–48): 182, 284–5, Vaudreuil and Bégon to the minister, 12 November 1712 and 20 September 1714; AC, C11A, 34: 330–52v, ordinance by Bégon, 6 November 1714, followed by minutes of parish assemblies and tax rolls (16 December 1714–25 March 1715); AC, C11A, 35: 93v, Ramezay to the minister, 28 October 1715.

14 Roy, ed., *Édits, ordonnances*, 1: 355–6, "Arrêt au sujet des Fortifications de Montréal," 5 May 1716. The tax unit was Notre-Dame parish: i.e., the city and its outskirts. The tax only applied to property owners and was levied on the value of the property. See ordinance of 23 December 1729: BAnQ-Québec, E1–S1–P2037.

15 The governor was in France in 1715–16, so his discussions with the ministry are, to a large extent, missing from the correspondence. The deliberations of the Conseil de la Marine in 1716 reveal in retrospect that the initiative to levy a monetary tax came from Canada. Roy, ed., *Inventaire*, 1: 5–6; AC, C11A, 36: 231–41.

16 It was a *taxe de répartition*, meaning a tax whose total amount is determined in advance. See, in this regard, Hincker, *Les Français devant l'impôt*, 20–2, 34–6, and, in this chapter, p. 173 and note 23.

17 See the decree of 1716 and AC, F3, 11: 235–7, 257–9, and 261–2: memorandum giving instructions for the tax levy, 23 December 1729; minutes of the assembly of 27 February 1730; remonstrances of the assembly members for the city and the communities of Montreal, 4 March 1730. Also, LAC, MG17–A7–2, 1, 2: 487–8, procurator of Saint-Sulpice de Paris to M. Chaumaux, 19 March 1717.

18 See the sources given *supra*, note 13, for the explanations given in the correspondence of the governor and the intendant for 1714 and the

townspeople's undertakings to build their own wall in the 1714–15 tax roll; Roy, ed., *Inventaire*, 1: 30, memorandum from Léry, 10 August 1717; LAC, MG17–A7–2, 1, vol. 2, *passim*, correspondence between the Sulpician seminaries of Paris and Montreal. The Sulpicians had no leverage, for the king could quite simply eliminate or reduce his subsidy to their mission in order to collect their share of the tax.

19 LAC, MG17–A7–2, 1, 6: 742–6, memorandum concerning the Montreal fortifications from Montreal masons Jourdain and Deguire to the governor of Montreal, followed by a letter from the governor-general to the governor of Montreal and by the comments of a Sulpician priest, 1729–30. The submissions were reviewed in Quebec, and the contract had been awarded to a Quebec resident since 1717. To elude charges of favoritism, the governor-general claimed that Montreal labourers were incompetent. See AC, G3, 2040, *passim*, for the contract awards and other documents about the fortifications.

20 AC, CIIA, 42: 51, Vaudreuil and Bégon to the minister, 26 October 1720.

21 Roy, ed., *Inventaire*, vol. 1, *passim*; *idem*, *Édits, ordonnances*, 1: 462–3, Conseil d'État decree, 24 March 1722, granting a postponement after the fire; BAnQ-Québec, E1–S1–P2037 and P2078, ordinances by Beauharnois and Hocquart, 23 December 1729 and 15 March 1730; AC, G1, 460, nominal roll of taxpayers who did not pay their contributions, 1732–41. Arrears were small, less than 2 per cent of tax due during those years, and mainly concerned vagrants or people who had left the city.

22 Roy, ed., *Édits, ordonnances*, 1: 355–6, 567–8, decree concerning the Montreal fortifications, 5 May 1716, and declaration by the king, 1 May 1743. According to the decree of 1716, the city was to pay 4,000 livres and the seminary 2,000 until the end of the work, for a total of 162,000 livres over twenty-seven years (1716–43), less 115,524, leaving 46,476 of arrears. According to the declaration of 1 May 1743, the city still owed 329,617 livres on a total expenditure of 445,141 livres. The king forgave half of this fictitious debt, resulting in a balance of 164,808 livres, or four times more.

23 From three to six livres for artisans and no more than twenty-five or thirty livres for well-off merchants at mid-century. AC, G1, 460, outstanding accounts; AC, G1, 460, outstanding accounts; BAnQ-Québec, E1–S1–P4112, ordinance of 15 December 1752, establishing the contribution of homeowning officers at nine livres in the case of a captain, fifteen in the case of a major, and "no more than twenty-one" for the king's lieutenant.

24 Ozouf, "L'opinion publique."

25 AC, CIIA, 85: 208 et seq., Beauharnois to the minister, 10 October 1746.

26 Roy, ed., *Inventaire*, 2: 68–9, Léry to the minister, 9 November 1745.

27 AC, F3, 13: 225–8, minutes of the assembly of 12 August 1745; CIIA, 83: 182, Hocquart to the minister, 24 September 1745; 86: 283–86v, Desauniers to the minister, 11 November 1746.

28 AC, B, 83: 259v, 261, minister to Hocquart and to Beauharnois and Hocquart, 7 March 1746. His insistence on the presence of the "principal habitants of Quebec" is surely what led to the increase of their deputation.

29 The staff officers at Montreal and Trois-Rivières had sent their notice in writing in 1746, hence the period of sixteen days between the arrival of the minister's letter and the first assembly of 26 July. Varin de la Marre, controller of the Navy, and Rigaud, town major of Trois-Rivières, who had supported the construction the previous year, sent a negative reply in 1746, no doubt so as not to displease the minister. All the others voted as before.

30 AC, CIIA, 85: 208 et seq., Beauharnois to the minister, 10 October 1746.

31 AC, CIIA, 86: 246, François-Étienne Cugnet, director of the Domaine d'Occident, to the minister, 31 October 1746.

32 AC, CIIA, 85: 323–30v, Hocquart to the minister, 1 October 1746.

33 They were Riverain Sr, Riverain Jr, J.-A. Bedout, and J.-F. Roussel. Colonel Joseph Fleury de la Gorgendière and officers Étienne Charest and Pierre Trottier Desauniers voted with the military men. Joseph Perthuis abstained. These captains and subordinate officers attended the assembly in an individual capacity, as merchants. The militia as a corps was not consulted.

34 Roy, ed., *Édits, ordonnances*, 1: 589, 591–4, Conseil d'État decree, 23 January 1747, and king's edict, February 1748. All told, the new taxes yielded some 80,000 livres per annum.

35 Some nuance is needed. Once the Quebec labourer had provided his five days of labour, he could work for wages if the demand for manpower exceeded what the corvée members could offer. In sum, in both cities, corvée members (and soldiers) competed with wage workers.

36 LAC, MG18-G6, 2: 309–10, "Mémoire de l'estat présent de la Nouvelle-France, laissé par le Sr de Champigny à M. de Beauharnois intendant pour Sa Majesté audit pays," 1 October 1702.

37 *RAPQ* (1938–39): 133, memorandum from the king to Vaudreuil and Raudot, 9 June 1706, and 151, latter's response, 3 November 1706; *RAPQ* (1939–40): 362–3, memorandum from the king to Vaudreuil and Raudot, 30 June 1707, and 395–6, reply of Vaudreuil and Raudot, 15 November 1707. Champigny, who had become an advisor to the minister on Canadian affairs, could have urged him to repeat these directives.

38 AC, CIIA, 25: 18–23, Louvigny to the minister, 21 October 1706.

39 I am assuming that remote parishes such as La Pocatière, Kamouraska, and Baie-Saint-Paul, which were sparsely populated and not easily reached, were exempted from corvées.

40 *Collection de manuscrits*, 2: 131–3, Champigny to the minister, 4 November 1693; RAPQ (1939–40): 395–6, Vaudreuil and Raudot to the minister, 15 November 1707.

41 BAnQ-Québec, TP1–S777. The trial of Chauveau was heard by Lieutenant-General René-Louis Chartier de Lotbinière, acting as subdelegate to the intendant. All that remains is the prisoner's petition of 13 July 1695 and the testimony of the people who were at the supper. History does not record why Jean-Baptiste Bécart de Fonville hit the boy.

42 BAnQ-Québec, E1–S1–P591, ordinance by Raudot, 16 November 1709. The text mentions an allocation "among the various côtes," indicating that the city was excluded.

43 Ibid., and RAPQ (1947–48): 284–5, Vaudreuil and Bégon to the minister, 20 September 1714: "Sr Rocbert storekeeper at Montreal, who received the money from the corvées for Fort Chambly, shall be in charge of it [Montreal]." The tax rolls for Chambly have not survived.

44 See *supra*, 172 et seq. and notes 12–13. For the purposes of this contribution, the price of a man-day of labour was set at two livres (when in reality it was worth thirty sols) and that of a team-day at five livres.

45 On Bégon's policies, official wheat pricing and requisitions, and rural unrest, particularly in the government of Quebec in 1714 and 1715, see Dechêne, *Power and Subsistence*, 87–8, 128–36.

46 AC, CIIA, 35: 93v–94, Ramezay, interim governor of the colony, to the minister, 28 October 1715. "The corvées were under discussion," he wrote in regard to the Pointe-aux-Trembles assembly, whose chief concern was the terms of trade.

47 LAC, MG17–A7–2, 1, 2: 406, M. Magnien, P.S.S., to M. Chaumaux, P.S.S., 19 March 1717; RAPQ (1947–48): 303, memorandum from the king to Vaudreuil and Bégon, 15 June 1716; Roy, ed., *Inventaire*, 1: 20–1, Vaudreuil to Conseil de la Marine, 14 October 1716.

48 On non-convertibility, see the letter from Ramezay, *supra*, note 46. Once the city had begun paying a money tax, the paltry flow of deniers from the côtes was no longer necessary. This meant that country folk now had no choice but to provide their labour and teams for the corvées or find a replacement if they could not personally take part. I have found only one specific reference to peasants serving as carters: Roy, ed., *Inventaire*, 1:

258–60, Léry to the minister, 20 October 1732. Apparently, their contribution was limited to this work.

49 AC, CIIA, 38: 121–4, Vaudreuil to Conseil de la Marine, 17 October 1717. It is the only contemporary account of the event that I know of. The detail of the tie comes from a letter from Hocquart of 30 September 1733: AC, CIIA, 60: 3–19; see also Zoltvany, *Philippe de Rigaud de Vaudreuil*, 156–7. About ten people identified as ringleaders were imprisoned for a few months.

50 In 1745, the militias of the three governments, assembled at Quebec to fend off an invasion, spent the summer working on the fortifications: Roy, ed., *Inventaire*, 2: 68–9, Léry to the minister, 9 November 1745. There is no subsequent mention of corvées in the engineer's correspondence or in that of the intendant, which nonetheless devotes considerable space to the work. The habitants of the côtes were required to bring their dumping carts into the city to help with carrying earth but were paid on the same basis as city carters: ibid., 82–4, Bigot to the minister, 3 November 1748.

51 See *supra*, ch. 1, on representations of the colonists.

52 AC, CIIA, 35: 94v, Ramezay to the minister, 28 October 1715.

53 The issue of military brigades under the French regime is addressed in Desloges, "La corvée militaire," as well as Charbonneau, Desloges, and Lafrance, "Manpower," in *Québec, the Fortified City*, 248 et seq. The author asserts that since fortification work was remunerated in France, it must also have been in Canada and that the word *corvée*, as used by the colonial administrators, actually denoted paid employment. In support of this curious argument, the author resorts to a second postulate: namely, that the same system was typical in Quebec from 1690 to 1760, as well as in Montreal to some extent. On this basis, he feels justified in scrambling citations without regard for time and place, using allusions to paid work from 1748, for example, as proof that the work had also been remunerated sixty years earlier. Nor is Charbonneau, Lafrance, and Poirier, "The Fortifications of Montréal," especially useful for my purposes, despite the elegant presentation and the solidity of the architectural information. That paper contains a number of errors and inaccuracies in regard to the work schedule, a confusion between plans and accomplishments. Montreal labourers, who paid the tax in cash like other city dwellers, were not required to participate in the corvées, and this well-regulated tax, based as it was on tax rolls, cannot be called "arbitrary."

54 These exactions left traces in the intendant's accounts; see AC, CIIA, 73: 90v, "Bordereau de la dépense faite ... pour la construction et de la flûte du roi le *Canada*," 1740, and 92: 199–201v and 226, "Bordereau de la

dépense faite ... pour la construction et armement des vaisseaux du roi," 1747 and 1748. For the locations of the numerous small private work sites around Quebec, see Brisson, *Les 100 premières années*.

55 Franquet, *Voyages*, 113; AC, CIIA, 93: 275 et seq., Bigot to the minister, 7 October 1749, in regard to a plan to relieve these habitants, which was then abandoned as too costly.

56 See *infra*, 246 et seq., and Dechêne, *Power and Subsistence*, 88. This latter work presents details on the origin and operation of the requisitions.

57 For a useful summary of these procedures, to my knowledge the only one, see Cassel, "The Troupes de la Marine," 391–403. For a brief overview of housing problems on the Island of Montreal in the seventeenth century, see also Dechêne, *Habitants and Merchants*, 200.

58 Corvisier, *L'Armée française*, 1: 94–8, 2: 848–9; Marion, *Dictionnaire*, 339–40, which quotes a 1684 memorandum from future controller-general Nicolas Desmaretz: "The accommodation of the troops is much more onerous than the *taille*."

59 Four companies augmented the Carignan companies for a total of 1,300 men. I am using the number of households counted in the 1666 census as an order of magnitude to estimate the number of houses the previous year.

60 BRH 32 (1926): 265–79, bailiff's ordinance, 28 November 1673, and minutes of the December assembly.

61 BRH 32 (1926): 265–79, "Rolle des habitans de l'isle de Montréal"; see also BAnQ-Montréal, TL2, bailiff's ordinances, 10 November 1672 and 31 December 1686; Roy, ed., *Ordonnances, commissions*, 1: 147–8, regulation for the guard house of the Montreal garrison, 28 November 1673, 222–3, ordinance by Duchesneau, 25 October 1677; BAnQ-Montréal, CN601–S280, minutes of notary C. Maugue, 6 April 1691. In 1677, the guard house was moved to another house, this one rented by the king, and the habitants continued to contribute to maintenance and heating.

62 Lahontan, "Nouveaux voyages," in *Oeuvres*, 1: 262–4; Catalogne, "Recueil," 172–3, on the stationing of three companies that arrived in 1683 at Beauport, Beaupré, and Île d'Orléans; for the distribution of the companies in the western côtes of the colony (Montreal Island, Boucherville, Laprairie, etc.), see Roy, ed., *Ordonnances, commissions*, 2: 96–7, 104–6, 126–9, ordinances by de Meulles, 28 April and 15 May 1685, and by Denonville, 5–6 October 1685. On the provisions supplied by the rural hosts, see AC, CIIA, 11: 41–79v. "Relation de ce qui s'est passé ... depuis le départ de la frégate ... le 27 novembre 1690 jusqu'au départ de 91," and 11: 252–60v, 290, Champigny to the minister, 10 May

and 12 November 1691; LAC, MG18–G6, 2: 263, Champigny, "Mémoire de l'estat présent de la Nouvelle France," 1 October 1702. In 1688, there were in principle 1,750 men or thirty-five companies of fifty men, and the following year the numbers were reduced to 1,400 men or twenty-eight companies. The numbers on the ground never attained these levels.

63 *RAPQ* (1928–29): 288–9, Frontenac and Champigny to the minister, 10 November 1695.

64 It was hard to assemble soldiers for exercises and to deliver rations to them when they were dispersed in the côtes, and since most of the officers and perhaps half of the noncoms lived in the city with their families, the troops had to be housed there too, inasmuch as possible.

65 These figures are those of the nominal censuses of Quebec. For Montreal, only an approximation can be ventured. See Louise Dechêne, "The Town of Québec, 18th Century," in Harris, ed., *From the Beginning*, pl. 50; *idem*, "La croissance de Montréal."

66 There is a reference to billeting of officers in BAnQ-Québec, TP1–S28–P514, ordinance concerning petition by Jean Maheu, 23 July 1667; more-over, Captain Tapie apparently bore the costs of his room and board: Le Blant, ed., "Le livre de raison," 116.

67 *RAPQ* (1928–29): 288, Frontenac and Champigny to the minister, 10 November 1695; BAnQ-Québec, TP1–S28–P8991, decision on petition by four Quebec hoteliers "housing officers of war," 3 August 1711.

68 *BRH* 32 (1926): 265–79; i.e., eighteen individuals and communities missing from the tax roll.

69 BAnQ-Québec, E1–S1–P63, P670, P835, P1217, and P3137, intendants' ordinances and commissions of 4 February 1706, 11 May 1710, 11 March 1713, 23 September 1720, and 16 June 1739; AC, C11A, 71: 137–37v, Hocquart to the minister, 28 September 1739, in regard to an exemption granted to the surgeon Jordain Lajus.

70 LAC, MG17, A7–2, 1: 584–5, correspondence of procurator of seminary, April 1719.

71 AC, C11A, 95: 332, La Jonquière to the minister, 1 November 1750. The governor supported the petition by the militia captains of Quebec to keep their exemption.

72 AC, C11A, 96: 60–2, Bigot to the minister, 22 October 1750. Note that in contrast to what this intendant wrote, it was not the police magistrates who abused the exemptions, since they had no decision-making power in this regard, but his predecessors.

73 BAnQ-Montréal, TL4–S1–D4709, 24 May 1740. The billet is signed by Mailhiot, special lieutenant of the jurisdiction, and bears the soldier's

surname, Printemps, at the bottom. Lanctôt, "Les troupes," 51–2, 59–60, regulation issued by the king, 30 May 1695, and ordinance issued by La Jonquière to put an end to housing-related disputes, 9 September 1750.

74 The list was compiled from the names of witnesses and defendants in criminal trials and councils of war for desertion between 1739 and 1759. The clerk notes the soldier's domicile, the host's name, and generally his profession. The sample comprises forty-seven noncoms and 109 soldiers, all of them colonial regulars. The billeters consist of seventy-one artisans, twenty-one innkeepers and cabaret owners, twenty merchants and voyageurs, six labourers and carters, five noncoms and domiciled soldiers, one notary, and thirty-two persons of unknown profession, including several widows. Cadets (not included in the sample) avoided the soldier's pallet by living with relatives. Finally, note that all the billeters lived in either the city or its outskirts.

75 Roy, ed., *Inventaire*, 1: 94–5, Léry to Conseil de la Marine, 30 September 1723. This letter concerns Quebec, where the profile of billeters was certainly the same as in Montreal. Since there were half as many soldiers and twice as many billets available, it is hard to see why judges would place soldiers with the poorest citizens.

76 BANQ-Québec, TL5–D1795, criminal trial of Benoît LeRoy *dit* Lyonnais, drummer of Dumas's company, which was garrisoned at Trois-Rivières, November 1755.

77 BANQ-Québec, TL5–D1237, criminal trial of Pierre L'Enclus *dit* Lapierre, 17 May 1738–8 April 1740.

78 I have previously, in *Habitants and Merchants* (p. 200), emphasized the onerousness of this tax, albeit nuancing as I do here. Cassel ("The Troupes de la Marine," 395n7) prefers to categorize me among those who believed that the relationship was generally tranquil, which is inaccurate.

79 AC, C11A, 92: 316–23, letter and petition by Legardeur de Repentigny, Fort Saint-Frédéric, 1 September 1748; 92: 388–89v, bishop to the minister, 6 September 1748; 91: 3–4v, La Galissonière and Hocquart to the minister, 17 August 1748; 91: 218–19, La Galissonière to the minister, 21 October 1748; B, 89: 32–32v, letters of pardon, April 1749; C11A, 93: 195v–96v, La Jonquière to the minister, 11 October 1749. There is only one version of the facts: the murderer's, carefully written and abiding by all the rules of the genre. On this subject, see Davis, *Fiction in the Archives*; Céline Cyr, "Legardeur de Repentigny, Pierre-Jean-Baptiste-François-Xavier," DCB, 4: 484–5. Jean-Claude Dupont, "Jacquin, dit Philibert, Nicolas," DCB, 3: 328–9, mentions an account favourable to the victim by the merchants Havy and Lefebvre. La Galissonière had decided

to keep the officer in Canada in spite of everything, but the new governor, La Jonquière, deemed it more prudent for him to be sent away in the interests of public order. Repentigny, a member of one of the colony's oldest families, returned to Canada in 1757 and pursued his military career in France after 1760. The drama gave birth to the legend of the "golden dog," but the social dimension was lost as history was transformed into legend.

80 *RAPQ* (1947–48): 243, memorandum from the king to Vaudreuil and Bégon, 19 March 1714; 278, Vaudreuil and Bégon to the minister, 20 September 1714; 307, minister to Vaudreuil and Bégon, 16 June 1716; 322, Vaudreuil and Bégon to Conseil de la Marine, 14 October 1716; AC, CIIA, 45: 366–7v, Léry to Conseil, 30 September 1723; 46: 19–21, Vaudreuil and Bégon to Conseil, 2 November 1724.

81 AC, CIIA, 48: 60–68v, Beauharnois and Dupuy to the minister, 20 October 1726; 49: 15–17v, Beauharnois and Dupuy to the minister, 20 October 1727; 50: 468–73, Maurepas to Beauharnois and Dupuy, 14 May 1728; 50: 156–58v, Beauharnois to the minister, 30 December 1727; 50: 17–22, Beauharnois and Clairambault to the minister, 1 October 1728.

82 See letter of 20 October 1726 in preceding note.

83 According to a list of troops from 1748, the seven companies stationed at Quebec comprised 169 soldiers and noncoms. Subtracting forty-five married men and twenty-one cadets, the number of those billeted is reduced to 103: AC, CIIA, 91: 229, "État des effectifs militaires du gouvernement de Québec," 1748. The decline was not due to the war but to a chronic deficit. In 1744, the census counted 1,055 households in Quebec.

84 AC, CIIA, 91: 6–7v, La Galissonière and Bigot to the minister, 3 September 1748; 92: 230–30v, Bigot to the minister, 8 November 1748, with attachment of excerpts from the inspection of the eight companies of Île Royale serving in Canada and the twenty-eight companies of the colony; see also AC, B, 85: 206, royal ordinance, 3 April 1747; CIIA, 95: 84v–85, La Jonquière and Bigot, 16 and 18 October 1750; 95: 335–37v, La Jonquière, 1 November 1750.

85 They were already billeted there in 1702: see *supra*, note 62. Cassel, "The Troupes de la Marine," 397, reports that the building was rebuilt in 1723.

86 Just prior to this reform, troop numbers had fallen below 400, if married men and cadets are subtracted from the 1748 roll: see *supra*, note 83. When the number of companies dropped from nineteen very incomplete ones to thirteen with fifty men each, Montrealers had to billet more soldiers but fewer officers. It was also planned to barrack the Montreal

garrison at some point: AC, B, 89: 37, minister to La Jonquière and Bigot, 28 February 1749.

87 AC, F3, 14: 6, "Première représentation des bourgeois et négociants de la ville de Québec," 30 April 1750, with twenty-four signatures; 14: 7–10v, "Seconde représentation des bourgeois, négociants et habitants de Québec," 2 May 1750, with forty signatures, and ordinances issued by Bigot, 1 and 4 May 1750; BAnQ-Québec, E1–S1–P3979, ordinance of 1 May 1750, and E1–S1–P3972, P3975, P3987, and P4196, other ordinances concerning collection of amounts owing, 15 and 20 April 1750 and 15 May 1755.

88 AC, C11A, 92: 124–5, "Avis sur le contenu de la lettre de M. [Bigot]," 26 October 1748; B, 89: 35, minister to La Jonquière and Bigot, 30 April 1749; F3, 14: 40, decree of June 1753. The tax was set at 13,350 livres per annum. It covered utensils and heating for the Royale and Dauphine barracks, the new barracks added in 1753, and the guard house for the Saint-Jean and Saint-Louis gates, where soldiers were also housed: Gilles Proulx, "Soldat à Québec," 550.

89 Séminaire de Québec, Ms, 139, "Rolle de l'imposition pour l'entretien des casernes pour l'année 1755." The total of 1,003 appears in the document. I have not verified it.

90 The Conseil d'État decree is explicit: Quebec residents were henceforth "dispensed" from billeting: AC, F3, 14: 40.

91 BAnQ-Montréal, TL4–S35, Register of ordinances 1743–56, ordinances issued by the lieutenant-general of police, 22 June, 18 October, and 22 November 1755; for more details on military housing from 1755 to 1760, see *infra*, 247–58.

92 *RAPQ* (1947–48): 284, Vaudreuil and Bégon to the minister, 20 September 1714.

93 Hincker, *Les Français devant l'impôt*, 34; Villain, *Le Recouvrement*, 244; Chaunu, "L'État," ch. 3.

94 AC, C11A, 59: 71–95v, Beauharnois and Hocquart to the minister, 1 October 1733.

95 The West Indian planters had been paying a head tax (in pounds of sugar) since 1671. The colony of Saint-Domingue, established on the territory ceded by Spain to France in 1697, still had only indirect taxes like Canada did. Between the loss of the 25 per cent tax on beaver pelts in the early eighteenth century and the increase of customs duties in the 1740s, the revenues of the Domaine d'Occident collected in Canada were reduced to very little: Desbarats, "Colonial Government Finances," ch. 2.

96 *RAPQ* (1947–48): 212, 242, memoranda from the king to Vaudreuil and Bégon, 25 June 1713 and 19 March 1714.

97 Frostin, *Les Révoltes*, 159–63; May, *Histoire économique de la Martinique*, 280 et seq.; Pluchon, *Histoire de la colonisation française*, 638–42.

98 *RAPQ* (1947–48): 281–2, Vaudreuil and Bégon to the minister, 20 September 1714.

99 AC, CIIA, 59: 71–95v, Beauharnois and Hocquart to the minister, 1 October 1733; see also B, 59: 205–9, minister to Beauharnois and Hocquart, 24 April 1733; 61: 185–90, 6 May 1734; CIIA, 60: 3–19, Hocquart to the minister, 30 September 1733.

100 AC, B, 93: 17, minister to La Jonquière and Bigot, 25 June 1751; F3, 14: 49, minister to Duquesne and Bigot, 30 May 1754. The repeated requests give a sense of the contents of Quebec's replies, some of which have not survived.

101 Marion, *Les Impôts directs*, 1 et seq. The royal *taille* was definitively instated by an ordinance of 1439 that simultaneously abolished the feudal militias and transferred defence of the realm to the king's army. Subjects were required to contribute to its maintenance.

102 Corvisier, *L'Armée française*, 1: 216, 2: 942.

103 Debien, *Esprit colon*, 20–1.

104 As early as 1684, Seignelay reportedly wanted to convert the 25 per cent tax on beaver pelts and the 10 per cent tax on moose hides into a head tax or other duty "less onerous to trade": king to La Barre, 10 April 1684, in Dubé, ed., *La Nouvelle-France*, 156–7.

105 On the controversies, the attempts to reform the *taille*, the inception of the head tax in 1695, the *dixième* in 1710, and the *vingtième* in 1749, see Hincker, *Les Français devant l'impôt*; Villain, *Le Recouvrement*; Marion, *Les Impôts directs*; and Touzery, *L'Invention de l'impôt*.

106 AC, CIIA, 59: 71–95v, Beauharnois and Hocquart to the minister, 1 October 1733, plan for *taille* proportional to sown area, payable in wheat and collected by the parish syndic; 66: 171–202, [Antoine-Denis Raudot, former intendant in Canada], "Mémoire sur le Domaine d'Occident en Canada," 1736: a good plan, he said, and unlike Hocquart recommended that it be put into effect immediately; F3, 14: 49–49v, Rouillé to Duquesne and Bigot, 30 May 1754. Duquesne and Bigot indicated their preference for a fixed amount in the form of a head tax to be levied "in part on the three cities, with the remainder to be divided among the rural habitants by taxing each parish as a function of the number and wealth of its

habitants." See also CIIA, 99: 529–33v, for an outline of another planned head tax.

107 Maurepas argued for this formula, instead of a discretionary assessment, as a form of compensation. Despite what had happened in the Indies, he believed that the intendant would be able to control the assemblies: AC, CIIA, Maurepas to Beauharnois and Hocquart, 24 April 1733.

108 Frostin, *Les Révoltes*, chs. 3–4. In 1720s Montreal, it sufficed that assessors demanded accounts before trying to collect arrears for Bégon to abandon this idea and look for other sources of financing: AC, CIIA, 42: 51–60v, Vaudreuil and Bégon to the minister, 26 October 1720. In general, the administrators did anything they could to avoid confrontation.

109 AC, F3, 14: 49v, Rouillé to Duquesne and Bigot, 30 May 1754; MCQ, fond d'archives du Séminaire de Québec, 5, no. 53, "Mémoire pour engager la Cour à exempter le Séminaire de Québec à la capitation," 12 October 1754; AC, CIIA, 22: 137–41, "Premier mémoire sur les impôts que le Roy veut imposer sur le Canada" [1755]. Another copy of this anonymous memorandum is found in the archives of the Séminaire de Saint-Sulpice in Paris (bound ms. 1200, document 37), leading one to believe that the author was a Séminaire de Montréal priest.

110 *RAPQ* (1936–37): 400, Abbé de l'Isle-Dieu to Bishop Pontbriand, Paris, 25 March 1755.

111 The taxes created in the eighteenth century did not, in principle, allow for any exemptions. In France, the tradition was such that exemptions subsisted, which would not have been the case in the colony, where the head tax was supposed to be universal.

112 Desbarats, "France in North America," 20. On the taxes collected on the fur trade, see Wien, "Selling Beaver Skins."

113 See, e.g., Hincker, *Les Français devant l'impôt*, 42, for an example taken from Pierre Goubert. These are difficult comparisons because the levies in France varied and because the cost of living and the general agricultural conditions were very different in the colony.

114 Or an edict issued by Turgot, cited in Letaconnoux, *Le Régime de la corvée*, 57.

CHAPTER EIGHT

1 Anderson, *A People's Army*.

2 I have identified the proportion of male witnesses (civilians only) who signed their names in the colonial courts from 1740 to 1760. The source is just as reliable, if not more so, than the parish registers and has the

advantage of clearly identifying the profession. Among peasants (346 cases in total), the proportion is 16 per cent (only 12 per cent in the western part of the colony, where rural schools were even scarcer than in the vicinity of Quebec). In Quebec and Montreal (523 cases in total), the proportion is around 60 per cent, with considerable variations among occupational categories: a higher stratum of large merchants, employees, etc., all of whom were literate; a middle stratum of small merchants and tradesmen (the majority of the workforce), 60 per cent of whom were literate, and a lower stratum of labourers, sailors, carters, and servants, of whom only 15 per cent were able to sign their names.

3 *RAPQ* (1927–28): 355–429, "Journal de Joseph-Gaspard Chaussegros de Léry, lieutenant des troupes, 1754–1755," in which the author makes allusion to this regular correspondence.

4 Grenier, ed., *Papiers Contrecoeur*, 226, Duquesne to Contrecoeur, commander of the Ohio Valley forces, 25 July 1754.

5 AC, CIIA, 104: 344–5, Kerdisien Trénais to the minister, 22 September 1759. Inspections were not conducted at the forts, wrote the intendant: *Mémoire pour Monsieur Bigot*, Archives de la Bastille, Imp. 50746.

6 Grenier, ed., *Papiers Contrecoeur*; Roy, ed., *Inventaire*; *RAPQ* (1926–27 and 1927–28). See also the Baby Collection (Archives de l'Université de Montréal) and the Northcliffe Collection (Library and Archives Canada).

7 A few journals and reports by colonial regular officers were gathered by French army officers and appear in their collections (Charly, Coulon de Villiers, Jacau de Fiedmont, Léry, etc.).

8 AC, CIIA, 102–4, and F3, 14–15. These contain several documents that eluded the general correspondence. Also found here are reports on artillery, a few requests for pardons from officers, but nothing approaching the earlier diversity. The intendant's letters were perhaps removed by the Châtelet lawyers, which would explain their scarcity.

9 AC, CIIA, 103: 218–19, Vaudreuil to the minister, 6 October 1758. He had just learned that in spite of his instructions, two artillery officers had dared to send memoranda on the defence of the St Lawrence directly to the minister.

10 *Editors' note*: AC, CIIA, vols. 102–5, *passim*.

11 Twenty or so authors for over 300 officers from France, not counting all the soldiers and noncoms, whose correspondence and other writings have disappeared forever.

12 Casgrain, ed., *Collection*, 1: 37; William J. Eccles, "Lévis, François (François-Gaston) de, duc de Lévis," *DCB*, 4: 515–21. In addition to the papers he himself collected on the Canada campaign, Lévis inherited

Montcalm's, hence the importance of the collection offered (in the form of collated copies) to the province of Quebec by the family and published in twelve volumes between 1889 and 1895, edited by Casgrain, who also authored the introduction to the first volume.

13 A hypothesis worth considering for the following texts: Aleyrac, *Aventures militaires*; Gabriel, *Le Maréchal de camp Desandrouins*; RAPQ (1931–32): 1–125, (1932–33): 305–91, and (1933–34): 65–231, Lapause papers; Malartic, *Journal*; Pouchot, *Mémoires*.

14 However, a few passages concerning family matters were considered too intimate and cut from the publication: Comte de Nicolay to Abbé Casgrain, 8 August 1888, in Casgrain, ed., *Collection*, 6: 7–8.

15 Identical passages in the journals of Montcalm and Bougainville may be attributable to the latter, although the former cannot be ruled out. Montcalm's journal stops in late June 1759 with the arrival of a new secretary who wrote his own account. On this subject, see the foreword by Abbé Casgrain, in Casgrain, ed., *Collection*, 7: 7–16, and the introduction by Amédée Gosselin to "Journal de M. de Bougainville," in RAPQ (1923–24): 202–3.

16 Lemire, ed., *La Vie littéraire*, 61–71. The author of the section presents all sorts of inaccurate information on the purpose of the military campaign journals, the status of the officers in France, and the contents of the texts he comments on without having read them – not even the preface to Casgrain, ed., *Collection*, which would have enlightened him on the origin of the documents; see also Marie-Aimée Cliche, "Journal du marquis de Montcalm durant ses campagnes en Canada, de 1756 à 1759," DOLQ, 423–4, and William J. Eccles, "Montcalm, Louis-Joseph de, marquis de Montcalm," DCB, 3: 495–507; this latter article is a damning indictment of the French battalions and their commander.

17 See the titles cited in the preceding note as an indication of a general pattern.

18 Childs, *Armies and Warfare*, 116 et seq.; Chagniot, *Histoire de la France militaire*, 66 et seq.; Russell, "Redcoats in the Wilderness"; Nicolai, "A Different Kind of Courage." This last is useful for its tactical conceptions, but its description of the Canadian militia – landless habitants surviving on hunting and trapping – is straight out of the author's imagination.

19 Gabriel, *Le Maréchal de camp Desandrouins*, 207.

20 Casgrain, ed., *Collection*, 2: 38–41, Lévis to Bigot, 2 August 1756. Albeit little inclined to comment, he could not help noting that most of the militiamen were children incapable of bearing up under fatigue.

21 See *infra*, Appendix B, and also my presentation of the sources of Appendix A at the beginning of ch. 4.

22 This ambiguity explains the error that slipped into plate 42 of Harris, ed., *From the Beginning*, in regard to the Battle of Fort Necessity in July 1754. About 300 militiamen are included in the "500 Frenchmen." The texts are often more explicit, mentioning 200 "French soldiers and habitants."

23 Casgrain, ed., *Collection*, 7: 90, 228, journal of Montcalm, July 1756 and 11 July 1757.

24 I return in ch. 10 to ethnonyms as they relate to the identity question. Gervais Carpin (*Histoire d'un mot*, 131–8) notes the use of "Frenchmen" as a generic term in the late seventeenth century, a usage still found fifty years later, despite the dissemination of the word "Canadian."

25 AC, B, 78: 73 et seq., minister to Beauharnois, 30 April 1744.

26 AC, C11A, 82: 159–64, Hocquart to the minister, 29 October 1744.

27 Swanson, "American Privateering." Swanson counts forty-eight prizes around Cape Breton and Newfoundland in 1744, a record without precedent to that time or afterwards, the West Indies remaining the hub of privateering. Until the capitulation in June 1745, the merchants and sailors of Louisbourg, too, fitted themselves out for privateering, with some success: Moore, *Louisbourg Portraits*, 189–98.

28 AC, C11A, 82: 338–43, October 1744, petition by merchants of Canada.

29 AC, C11A, 81: 141–54, Beauharnois to the minister, 8 October 1744.

30 Pritchard, *Anatomy of a Naval Disaster*; Rawlyk, *Nova Scotia's Massachusetts*.

31 On the naval disasters, see Lacour-Gayet, *La Marine militaire*; Pritchard, *Anatomy of a Naval Disaster* and *Louis XV's Navy*.

32 Pote, *The Journal*, 1–51; AC, C11A, 83: 173–81, "Extrait de ce qui s'est passé de plus intéressant ...," 26 August 1745; 84: 103–07v, Hocquart to the minister, 2 November 1745; Rawlyk, *Nova Scotia's Massachusetts*, 181 et seq.; *Collection de manuscrits*, 3: 243, Du Chambon to the minister, Rochefort, 2 September 1745.

33 AC, B, 83: 246, minister's order of 24 January 1746 determining the number of troops.

34 AC, C11A, 87: 314–63, "Journal de la campagne du détachement de Canada en Acadie en 1746 et 1747, par le lieutenant Liénard de Beaujeu"; 117: 79v, for the composition of the detachment; 85: 106 et seq., "Extrait en forme de journal ... " (1746); 87: 27, "Extrait en forme de journal ... " (1747); Moore, *Louisbourg Portraits*, 196; Rawlyk, *Nova Scotia's Massachusetts*, 188–9; Stanley, *New France*, 20–5.

35 AC, CIIA, 87: 29–97, "Extrait en forme de journal ... " (1747); Pritchard, *Anatomy of a Naval Disaster*, 228–9, on the spread of typhus among the Mi'kmaq by the Duc d'Anville's men. The men in good health returned to Canada on foot, getting there faster than those who waited for the boats.

36 AC, CIIA, 83: 96–100v, Beauharnois to the minister, 15 October 1745.

37 AC, CIIA, 115: 150–228, statement of revenues and expenses for 1745, containing information on these work sites and other defensive measures.

38 AC, F3, 11: 229–38, campaign journal of Rigaud in 1746. For French troop numbers, see *infra*, Appendix B.

39 AC, CIIA, 89: 168–71v, Rigaud to the minister, 4 October 1747.

40 See *supra*, ch. 4, section 4.

41 Groups that did garrison duty and patrolled around the forts, those who gave chase to enemy soldiers making incursions into the colony, and, of course, those who joined Rigaud's armies in 1746 and 1747 are thus excluded.

42 Warriors came and went, often joining more than one raid a year, and so the number of distinct individuals counted as returnees may be smaller. The sources used are: AC, CIIA, 85: 101–69, "Extrait en forme de journal ... " December 1745–4 November 1746; 86: 302–07v, "Extrait des différents mouvements qui se sont faits à Montréal," December 1745–31 August 1746; 86: 178–236, expenditures made at the king's stores in Montreal, 1 September–31 December 1746.

43 AC, CIIA, 87: 02–14 bis, memorandum from parties fitted out at Montreal, 22 September 1746–1 August 1747; 87: 22–97v, "Journal (de La Galissonière et Hocquart) concernant 'ce qui s'est passé d'intéressant dans la colonie ... '" November 1746–7 October 1747; 87: 175–225, "Journal (de La Galissonière et Hocquart) concernant ce qui s'est passé d'intéressant dans la colonie ... " November 1747–October 1748; 117: 168–320, excerpt of expenditures at the king's stores in Montreal to fit out the war parties, 1 January–31 August 1747. Attacks on the British settlements continued until August 1748, but the sources no longer provide exact numbers of Indigenous warriors or colonists.

44 Dickinson and Grabowski, "Les Populations amérindiennes," 60–1.

45 Several groups of domiciliés went with the militiamen to do garrison duty at the following forts: Saint-Frédéric, Soulange, Châteauguay, Sainte-Thérèse, and La Prairie; however, immobility weighed on them, and they did not await orders before departing. The Nipissings of the Lake of Two Mountains were recruited for garrison duty at Niagara in 1744: Chagny, *Un défenseur*, 63–4.

46 AC, CIIA, 88: 18–19v, Hocquart to the minister, 24 September 1747; see the analysis in Desbarats, "The Cost."

47 AC, CIIA, 87: 16–21, Dubois Berthelot de Beaucours, "Mémoire de Canada de 1747"; Joncaire, ambassador to the Iroquois territory, reported that a secret accord had been signed between the Iroquois domiciliés and the Six Nations: 87: 32, "Extrait en forme de journal ... "; Archives de l'Université de Montréal, Baby Collection, P58/U, 2512 (and microfiche 4404), Céloron de Blainville [to Guy, merchant], Fort Saint-Frédéric, 4 October 1747, in regard to the antagonism of "all our nations, both domiciled or in the Great Lakes region."

48 There were seven attacks on the settlements and one on Saint-Frédéric between November 1746 and June 1747: AC, CIIA, 85: 101–69, 87: 22–97v. Since their adoption of Christianity and their settlement among the French, the Sault Iroquois had always avoided making war on their Six Nations brethren. On the administration's suspicious attitude, see Demos, *The Unredeemed Captive*, 136–7. *Editors' note*: See also Parmenter, "At the Wood's Edge."

49 Selesky, *War and Society*, 75.

50 AC, CIIA, 84: 142–4, 151–3, accounts of Acadian campaigns.

51 *RAPQ* (1934–35): 72, "La correspondence de Mme Bégon, 1748–1753," 4 June 1749. As a point of departure for an analysis of large merchants during this period, see Bosher, *Men and Ships*.

52 AC, B, 89: 203, minister to La Galissonière, 2 January 1749.

53 AC, CIIA, 97: 34–34v, La Jonquière's order to the Acadians to join the militia or be considered rebels, 12 April 1751.

54 Griffiths, *The Contexts of Acadian History*, 82–3. See also Reid, "Acadia or Nova Scotia"; Dumont-Johnson, *Apôtres ou agitateurs*.

55 AC, CIIA, 96: 137–38v, Bigot to the minister, 6 November 1750; see also 87: 373–4, 375–75v, two petitions to La Jonquière, dated December 1749, and 87: 388–99v, Le Guerne, missionary, to financial commissary of Louisbourg, 10 March 1756, in regard to a request to go to Canada that Vaudreuil had denied.

56 These were the detachments commanded by Boishébert that arrived during the winter of 1749 and was quartered on the Saint John River; the one commanded by Chevalier de La Corne, which landed on the Isthmus of Chignecto in the fall and was joined by Léry's detachment in 1750, and the one commanded by Joseph-Michel Legardeur de Croisille et de Montesson that arrived in 1751 and was to contribute to the construction of Fort Beauséjour. See AC, CIIA, 93: 130 et seq., 87: 376–86, and Roy, ed., *Inventaire*, 2: 112–20.

57 The Acadians at Fort Beauséjour did not make a spontaneous choice to join the French camp. Most were refugees from the Beaubassin region, who had numbered 2,500 souls in 1748 before the destruction of the village and the erection of Fort Lawrence in September 1750. See AC, CIIA, 87: 363–4, description of Acadia, 1748.

58 Griffiths, *The Contexts of Acadian History*, 86–127; Jean Daigle and Robert Leblanc, "Acadian Deportation and Return," in Harris, ed., *From the Beginning*, pl. 30; Frégault, *Canada*, ch. 6.

59 According to Richard White, the shortage of goods, which is well documented, was made up by the merchants to distract from their greed. The alliance would then have existed in spite of the merchants rather than thanks to them. His analysis of political relations between the Ohio "rebels" and the governors as a sequence of abrupt changes is equally unsatisfactory: *The Middle Ground*, ch. 5, pp. 199–200 in particular.

60 AC, CIIA, 87: 22–97v, "Journal (de La Galissonière et Hocquart) concernant 'ce qui s'est passé d'intéressant dans la colonie ... '" November 1746–October 1747; 87: 175–225, "Journal (de La Galissonière et Hocquart) concernant ce qui s'est passé d'intéressant dans la colonie ... " November 1747–October 1748.

61 AC, F3, 11: 318 et seq., campaign journal of M. de Céloron (1749); Thwaites, ed., *The Jesuit Relations*, 69: 150–98, "Relation du voyage de la Belle rivière fait en 1749, sous les ordres de M. de Céloron, par le P. Bonnecamps."

62 Governor-general from September 1747 to September 1749, La Galissonière lost no time in expounding on his conception of the colonial system and the essentially military role that must be assigned to Canada. His views concurred with those of Maurepas. On returning to France, he served as an advisor to Rouillé, the new secretary of state for the navy. He was thus the driving force behind the aggressive policy of expansionism carried out between the wars. See, in particular, AC, CIIA, 96: 248–70, "Mémoire de La Galissonière (et Silhouette) sur les 'colonies de la France dans l'Amérique septentrionale,'" December 1750, and 91: 116–23, La Galissonière to Maurepas, 1 September 1748.

63 During the summer of 1753, Niverville forced the British to abandon Venango, where Fort Machault would then be built; in December, Washington arrived at Fort Le Boeuf with an ultimatum from his government; in April 1754, the Virginians deserted their fort and Fort Duquesne was built in its place. See Stanley, *New France*, 43–52, and Eccles, *The Canadian Frontier*, 160 et seq., for a more detailed account.

64 *Editors' note*: See Bell, *The Cult of the Nation*, in particular ch. 3, "English Barbarians, French Martyrs," which discusses the murder of Jumonville.

65 See Eccles, "The Fur Trade and Eighteenth-Century Imperialism," in *Essays on New France*, 79–95, on the conflict between politics and the fur traders' interests; also, Dechêne, *Power and Subsistence*, 114–21, on military pressures on the wheat and flour trade.

66 See, e.g., Miquelon, "Havy and Lefebvre," for the reactions of merchants Havy and Lefebvre to the war.

67 Baby Collection, microfiche 4417, d'Ailleboust de Cerry to his brother, an officer on Île Saint-Jean, Quebec, 14 May 1753.

68 Raymond, *On the Eve of Conquest*, 146. The author uses the courtier Surlaville to reach the minister's ear.

69 Grenier, *Papiers Contrecoeur*, 87–8, Duquesne to Legardeur de Saint-Pierre, 25 December 1753; Archives de la Bastille, 12145: 15, excerpt of a letter from Captain Péan to Duquesne, 1 July 1753.

70 O'Callaghan, ed., *Documents*, 6: 825–6, M. Smith to governor of Massachusetts, Cape Cod, 24 December 1753. Smith had just run away from Canada.

71 General Braddock crossed the Atlantic with two regiments, adding to the three stationed at Halifax since 1749. The regiments consisted of ten companies of 100 men: Stacey, "The British Forces." France sent six battalions (3,600 men), for a total of some 6,000 men when added to the colonial regulars stationed in Canada and Île Royale.

72 For the government of Quebec specifically, see Casgrain, ed., *Collection*, 7: 63, journal of Montcalm, 13 May 1756.

73 Steele, *Warpaths*, ch. 9; Stanley, *New France*, chs. 7–9; Kopperman, *Braddock*; MacLeod, *The Canadian Iroquois*, chs. 3–4.

74 Stacey, "The British Forces"; Rogers, *Journals*. There were a few Amerindians among the rangers. Wolfe's army at Quebec comprised six ranger companies commanded by Joseph Gorham.

75 Gruber, "The Anglo-American Military Tradition."

CHAPTER NINE

1 Marion, Dictionnaire, article on the word *milice*; Corvisier, L'Armée française, 1: 197 et seq. For an example in the generality of Bordeaux, see Lhéritier, L'Intendant Tourny, 1: 338–42.

2 See *supra*, 145 and Table 6.2; I have identified seven high-ranking officers or members of the general staff for 1721. There would be many more after

that. The possibility of entrusting certain tasks to these officers (exercises, supervision of captains in choice of recruits, accompaniment, etc.) is never discussed.

3 See *supra*, 51–2, "The enabling text of the militia," on the non-existence of a regulation for the militia.

4 This issue is briefly addressed in ch. 5, 135–6 and note 84. *RAPQ* (1946–47): 443, Vaudreuil and Raudot to the minister, 7 November 1711; *RAPQ* (1947–48): 170, Vaudreuil to the minister, 6 November 1712, and 222, minister to Vaudreuil, 4 July 1713; see also AC, CIIA, 32: 115–16v, Louvigny to the minister, 31 October 1711.

5 Responsible for troop detail and discipline, the military commandant was the ideal officer to look after the instruction of the militias. Yet this position was eliminated after the death of Charles-Henri d'Aloigny in 1714, perhaps contributing to the momentary abandonment of the plan. The job of garrison adjutant, too, was eliminated in 1743. Only the fort commandants remained.

6 AC, CIIA, 54: 70–76v et 136–67v, Beauharnois and Hocquart to the minister, 4 and 12 October 1731, first in a series of references to visits by assistant town majors to the côtes. Officers' names and payments are noted in the statements of expenses under the heading *Courses et voyages*. See CIIA, 113: 474–82 for the year 1732, or 114–15, *passim*, for the years 1737–45.

7 AC, CIIA, 81: 151–51v, Beauharnois to the minister, 8 October 1744, and 83: 23, Beauharnois and Hocquart to the minister, September-November 1745; Archives de la Bastille, 12145, defence of Péan, July 1762, in which Péan describes his duties vis-à-vis the militias in 1747 when he was assistant town major at Quebec: drawing up the rolls and initiating them to "war exercises."

8 Pote, *The Journal*, 124; "The Journal of a Captive."

9 In 1721, there were five ex-soldiers among militia officers in the vicinity of Montreal and four among the militia sergeants. The proportion probably did not increase, since demobilizations became increasingly rare. See *supra*, 253 et seq., for the profile of the militia officers. Youths in this region were more familiar with canoes and with transportation of trade goods, but this does not lead to an automatic conclusion that they were naturally fit for war. Accounts claiming the superiority of the Montreal militias came later. See the accounts of Governor Duquesne on the "rather well-drilled" youths from the Quebec region and youths from the Montreal area, described as "the best" in AC, CIIA, 98: 83v, Duquesne to the minister, 3

November 1752, and 99: 240, Duquesne to the minister, 29 September 1754.

10 BAnQ-Québec, TL5–D4083, petition of 13 May 1755 in regard to a scuffle that broke out at the door of the Saint-Vallier church one Sunday "after the exercise."

11 Grenier, ed., *Papiers Contrecoeur*, 256, Duquesne to Contrecoeur, 17 September 1754; Archives de la Bastille, 12145, memorandum from Péan, 6 December 1750; *BRH* 58 (1952): 200, order issued by the governor de Montreal to F.-X. de Saint-Ours, assistant town major, 13 September 1748.

12 Grenier, ed., *Papiers Contrecoeur*, 329–43.

13 In both cases, this was a pattern, not a rule. There were a few large companies in the west as well as parishes such as Saint-Thomas in the east that divided their men into several small companies.

14 See the mobilization orders and the numerous criticisms of the system, in particular those of Governor Vaudreuil who, on arriving in 1755, complained of the recruiters' incessant travels and the costs they engendered. He implicitly ascribed this disorder to his predecessor, yet this had always been the officers' practice. What is more, Vaudreuil would do nothing to change it: AC, CIIA, 100: 90–91v, Vaudreuil to the minister, 18 October 1755.

15 Grenier, ed., *Papiers Contrecoeur*, 87, Duquesne to Contrecoeur, 24 December 1753.

16 As with the army, the militia companies designated under their captains' names serve to identify the conscripts on the rolls.

17 AC, B, 83: 272–72v, king's memorandum serving as an instruction to Governor La Jonquière, 1 April 1746. The letters of service were added to the earlier directives.

18 See Table 6.1. The city of Trois-Rivières and its rural surroundings, conflated in the 1744 census, are not included in the calculations that follow.

19 *RAPQ* (1939–40): 1–154, "Le Recensement de Québec en 1744"; see also Gauvreau, *Québec*, Table B.1, 210.

20 Mathieu, *La Construction navale*, 55, 95–101.

21 *RAPQ* (1934–35): 71, Élisabeth Bégon to her son-in-law, Montreal, 1 June 1749.

22 The officers' servants were among those exempted, their hosts too in some cases. See Casgrain, ed., *Collection*, 10: 55, Péan to Lévis, 26 July 1756.

23 AC, CIIA, 82: 159–64, Hocquart to the minister, 29 October 1744, and 117: 75, war preparations, 1746.

24 AC, CI IA, 86: 178–236 and 302–07v for the details of the war parties, 1746, in which a distinction is made between "volunteers" and "habitants" in one or more detachments. Volunteers are in some cases mentioned by name.

25 That is, "make certain there is no habitant, servant or labourer who is not included in the [militia] companies, and that if there are gentlemen who do not wish to take officer positions, [the governor] make them serve as soldiers." As to the repetition of the directives, see, e.g., AC, B, 83: 272, 86: 318–19v, 89: 49–53v, 95: 212–17, and 101: 126–30v, king's memoranda running from 1746 to 1755.

26 Volunteers enjoyed the same privileges as militia officers who joined detachments. See *infra*, ch. 9, section 4, "Status of militia officers."

27 BAnQ-Montréal, CN601–S308, minutes of notary Panet, 24 April 1756, act in which René Gauthier of Varennes, a reformed captain in the colonial regulars, identifies himself as "captain of the company of gentlemen of the government of this city." There is no prior reference.

28 Casgrain, ed., *Collection*, 11: 71–86, two accounts of the winter 1757 expedition against Fort George, commanded by François-Pierre de Rigaud de Vaudreuil. His brother-in-law Dufy Desauniers commanded the company of nobles: ibid., 7: 158–9, journal of Montcalm, 21–25 February 1757. On Île-aux-Noix, see ibid., 5: 27, Bourlamaque to Vaudreuil, 10 August 1759.

29 Casgrain, ed., *Collection*, 5: 139–42, Montcalm to Bourlamaque, 20 February 1757; other disparaging remarks on this company of gentlemen are found in ibid., 5: 27 and 11: 81. See also Aleyrac, *Aventures militaires*, 131–2. This last volume contains a diatribe against the company of gentlemen volunteers, whom the author (or the editor who reorganized his memoirs) confounds with the elite troops consisting of the 300 volunteers commanded by Coulon de Villiers at the vanguard of the army in the attack on Fort George in August 1757.

30 Courville, *Mémoires*, 155. In another passage, Courville offers erroneous details about the town militias, which are repeated verbatim by the anonymous author who plagiarized his memoirs: ibid., 29, and RAPQ (1924–25): 103, anon., "Mémoire du Canada."

31 Lavallée, *La Prairie*, 227–8.

32 See the chart by Gratien Allaire titled "Origin of Engagés, 1700–1764," in Conrad E. Heidenreich, Françoise Noël, and Gratien Allaire, "French Interior Settlements, 1750s," pl. 41 of Harris, ed., *From the Beginning*; the chart shows the social background of the engagés at different dates, including 1755.

33 Ibid.; charts derived from licences and notarial acts. Note, however, that the value of fur exports did not increase. Might the rise in numbers of engagés be due to changes in categories of furs or to an expansion of trading areas? To answer this, an analysis of destinations would be necessary. See Wien, "Castor, peaux et pelleteries."

34 BAnQ-Montréal, CN601–S372, minutes of notary F. Simonnet, contracts of engagement for the La Baie post by Rigaud and his partners, 1755–59, *passim*; Kellogg, *The French Regime in Wisconsin*, 382–3.

35 See the table indicating the destinations of engagés on different dates in Conrad E. Heidenreich, Françoise Noël, and Gratien Allaire, "French Interior Settlements, 1750s," pl. 41 of Harris, ed., *From the Beginning*; see also "The Fur Trade, ca. 1755," a map of the northern and southern trade networks, in Conrad E. Heidenreich and Françoise Noël, "France Secures the Interior, 1740–1755," pl. 40 of Harris, ed., *From the Beginning*.

36 The transportation of munitions and provisions from Lachine to Lake Ontario had been contracted out since the 1720s, perhaps earlier. The arrangement was known as the *canots du Cent* in reference to the price of the contract, ranging from four to five livres per hundredweight: BAnQ-Québec, CN301–S189, minutes of notary J.-C. Louet, 4 May 1724, and other contracts in AC, G3: 2040, *passim*. Similar contracts were signed for transportation to Lake Champlain.

37 BAnQ-Montréal, CN601–S202, minutes of notary G. Hodiesne, 5 and 12 July 1758. Berthelet was represented by his wife because of an illness at age forty-two. Cousineau, twenty-nine, was still unmarried. The two contracts use the same boilerplate.

38 BAnQ-Montréal, TL4–S1–D6141, criminal trial of Pierre Gouëtte *dit* Lalime, 26 February–2 June 1757; ibid., TL4–S1–D6225, court martial of Pierre Richard, accused of desertion, 19 July 1758; BAnQ-Québec, TL5–D1874, TP1–S777–D180, and TP1–S28–P17369, other documents relating to trial of Gouëtte, 20 July–16 August 1757.

39 AC, C11A, 95: 343 and 350–1, petition from Joseph Fleury Deschambault to the minister, 1750, accompanied by a "model" roll with explanations.

40 AC, C11A, 100: 90–91v and 126–27v, Vaudreuil to the minister, 18 and 30 October 1755; 100: 46, petition by Joseph Fleury Deschambault, 1755.

41 Casgrain, ed., *Collection*, vol. 7, journal of Montcalm, 1758. *Editors' note*: Exact reference not found.

42 *RAPQ* (1931–32): 10, 74–5, Chevalier de Lapause, "Mémoire et observations sur mon voyage au Canada." His accusations targeted the mobilization and grain requisition procedures, which likewise reeked of favouritism.

43 See *supra*, ch. 6, section 3, on the power of militia captains.

44 Grenier, *Papiers Contrecoeur*, 311–20, 329–43. They were boys from the governments of Trois-Rivières and Montreal. From the name and place of residence, I traced only forty-three out of 248 individuals in Tanguay, *Dictionnaire généalogique*, these being the ones who had a patronymic or given name rare enough to avoid confusion with similarly named people.

45 Faribault-Beauregard, ed., *La Population des forts français*.

46 *RAPQ* (1920–21): 248–96, "Registre mortuaire (extraits) de l'hôpital-général de Québec pour 1759 et 1760." Most died of injuries sustained on 13 September 1759 and 28 April 1760, but the list includes others besides militiamen. I identified eighteen older married men in this ill-defined group.

47 See *supra*, 74, on the reform of 1699. In 1750, the troops were increased to thirty companies of fifty men; in 1756, the thirty companies were increased to sixty-five men; the last reform, in 1757, called for forty companies of sixty-five men, or 2,600 in total. But numbers on the ground were always well below these levels. See Cassel, "The Troupes de la Marine," Appendix B.

48 Only two new infantry companies were added in 1750, plus one company of gunners followed by a second in 1757. Ten more infantry companies were added on this latter date for a total of forty companies of sixty-five men. A large proportion of these troops never reached the colony. Most of the officers for the new companies were recruited in France. See AC, B, vols. 91–3 and 103–5, *passim*.

49 There is, for example, the case of Hertel de Rouville, who began serving as a cadet in 1722 and was still a second ensign twenty-seven years later, or the rather similar case of Denys de la Ronde, or that of Lusignan, who had taken part in every campaign since he was fifteen years of age and, at fifty-three, was still awaiting his captain's commission: AC, CIIA, 87: 181–82v, and 93: 220, 231. As Cassel notes ("The Troupes de la Marine," 105–15), the government let officers grow old without promotion to avoid having to pay pensions.

50 AC, CIIA, 91: 229–29v, status of troops [1748]; the mean and the median are both fifty-one.

51 *ARC* (1886), clxxxii–clxxxiv.

52 AG, section ancienne, series X, service records for various officers who fought in the Canadian war. The calculation of ages is based on a total of seventy-eight captains and twenty-three lieutenants.

53 AC, CIIA, 101: 292–3, Le Mercier, captain in the colonial regulars, to the minister, 30 October 1756.

54 AC, CIIA, 78: 320, Dubois Berthelot de Beaucours to the minister,
6 September 1742; see also CIIA, 80: 290–3, Dubois Berthelot de
Beaucours to the minister, 12 June 1743. The Montreal officers whom he
asked to put in a token appearance did not recognize his authority and
complained to Quebec.

55 Cited in Cassel, "The Troupes de la Marine," 132.

56 Aleyrac, *Aventures militaires*, 32; Lapause, "Dissertation sur le gouvernement," in *RAPQ* (1933–34): 208 (no date); Pouchot, *Mémoires*, 1: 32–3.

57 The mediocrity of the recruits, the indiscipline of the troops, and the
utility of the barracks are subjects that came up regularly in the official
correspondence. Beauharnois came to the defence of his officers on several
occasions when the minister blamed them for desertion, among other
problems.

58 See Cassel, "The Troupes de la Marine," 160–3, on careers in the Great
Lakes region; also *supra*, 181 et seq., on the winter quartering of soldiers
in the cities.

59 AC, CIIA, 75: 189–91v, Beauharnois to the minister, 1 October 1741; 99:
131, Duquesne to the minister, 31 October 1753, in regard to the rank of
major being awarded by seniority and not merit.

60 Duquesne, governor since 1752, was replaced by Vaudreuil in 1755. AC,
CIIA, 98: 82 and 99: 95–100, 128–136v, Duquesne to the minister, 3
November 1752, 26 and 31 October 1753; also AC, B, 99: 204, minister
to Duquesne, 31 May 1754.

61 This was true of officers from France and even of several others, such as
the Le Moyne sons, who were born in Canada and sent to France to finish
their education.

62 AC, CIIA, 83: 182–8, Hocquart to the minister, 24 September 1745.
Governor Beauharnois had a career as a naval officer behind him but was
too old at seventy-four to lead his troops.

63 AC, CIIA, 118: 159–63v, La Galissonière to the minister, 15 September
1748.

64 Étienne Taillemite, "Dumas, Jean-Daniel," *DCB*, 4: 261–2. Dumas was the
commandant at Fort Duquesne in 1755–56. He was named adjutant general of the colonial regulars in 1759. After the defeat of 13 September, he
took command of the troops and militias upriver from Quebec until the
capitulation of 1760. Note that at least twenty Frenchmen were integrated
into the officer corps in the first half of the eighteenth century, almost all
as cadets or ensigns and hence possessing no prior experience.

65 See, e.g., *RAPQ* (1933–34): 161–2, "Mémoire et réflexions politiques et
militaires sur la guerre du Canada depuis 1746 jusqu'à 1760," by Lapause.

The soldiers had once made up a good corps, but the officers had become incapable of making war Amerindian style: "the colonists have neglected this war ... and that, I say, has caused them to degenerate."

66 The governor encouraged the practice, arguing that it served to train good officers: AC, CIIA, 69: 145–6, Beauharnois to the minister, 18 October 1737.

67 AC, CIIA, 100: 248–9, Contrecoeur, commandant at Fort Duquesne, to the minister, 20 July 1755.

68 William J. Eccles, "Coulon de Villiers, Louis" (1710–57), "Coulon de Villiers, Nicolas-Antoine" (1708–50), and "Coulon de Villiers de Jumonville, Joseph" (1718–54), DCB, 3: 158–61. François and Pierre also served in the troops. The sixth died with his father in the Siege of the Foxes.

69 Archives de l'Université de Montréal, Baby Collection, P58/U, 2507 (and microfiches 4402–3), Pierre-Joseph Céloron de Blainville to Guy, a Montreal merchant, 1 June 1747; William J. Eccles, "Céloron de Blainville, Pierre-Joseph," DCB, 3: 106–8. Four sons had careers in the troops while a fifth served as a naval administrator.

70 The social backdrop is not at issue. Langlade, for example, descended from an officer of the Carignan regiment. But as one generation succeeded another, bad marriages hindered advancement, and the fur trade became a living and a lifestyle alike. Marin, like his father and brothers, began as a merchant and saw his military career develop very slowly. These are fascinating careers, exceptional cases, yet often depicted by historians as typical.

71 AC, CIIA, 87: 19v, Dubois Berthelot de Beaucours, "Mémoire de Canada, 1747."

72 See ch. 3, section 3.

73 I used the expense slips and the accounts of the king's stores, where the war parties were fitted out, to supplement the expedition narratives. Mentions are more numerous because the same individuals are mentioned more than once. I identified forty-five names and six other anonymous officers. See Table 6.1.

74 Archives de l'Université de Montréal, Baby Collection, P58/P2, 48–9 (and microfiches 2573–4), militia rolls for Fort Frontenac and others, Lachine, 28 August–27 October 1756; Grenier, ed., *Papiers Contrecoeur*, 229–45, 278–80, 284–304, 311–20, 329–45, lists of soldiers and militia-men employed at Fort Duquesne, 1754–55.

75 Aleyrac, *Aventures militaires*, 33.

76 There are at most a dozen or so officers from the rural parishes on my lists, including Dazé, the son of a well-to-do peasant on Île Jésus; Messier,

the owner of a fief at Varennes; and Mercure, from Cap Santé, a protégé of the Vaudreuils. Few peasants, apparently.

77 The lack of given names means that the identification cannot be precise, but the patronymics of the colony's leading merchants are in evidence: Hervieux Jr, Noreau Jr, de Couagne Jr, Blondeau, La Comble, La Coste Jr, Trottier Desauniers, Trottier des Rivières, Le Moine Despins, Douaire, Pierre Guy, etc. The preponderance of city dwellers is confirmed by Vaudreuil, who praised the officers of Quebec and Montreal for their zeal at the battle of 8 September 1755: AC, C11A, 100: 90–91v, Vaudreuil to the minister, 18 October 1755.

78 See *supra*, ch. 3. Recall that in the seventeenth century, a few individuals who had at first served as volunteers obtained officer's commissions. Although rare, these examples held out hope. Fifty years later, these avenues had long since been closed off.

79 Casgrain, ed., *Collection*, 7: 158–9, journal of Montcalm, 21–25 February 1757; AC, C11A, 115: 254–76v, "État de la dépense faite à Montréal pour et à l'occasion du parti de Français et de Sauvages, commandé par Rigaud de Vaudreuil, pour aller sur les côtes de la Nouvelle-Angleterre, parti de Montréal le 3 août 1746," Montreal, 30 September 1746; ibid., 117: 79–81v, list of regular and militia officers, cadets, and volunteers returning from Acadia, 1747; also of note are the ten militia officers in Rigaud's detachment of 1747: ibid., 117: 20–31, "État de la dépense qui a été faite à Montréal, à Chambly et au fort Saint-Frédéric pour ... un parti de guerre" commanded by Rigaud, departed 8 June 1747, Montreal, 14 August 1747. The following details on equipment and gratifications come from these two statements of account.

80 Jacqueline Roy, "Trottier Dufy Desauniers, Thomas-Ignace," DCB, 4: 802–3. Dufy's self-regard went so far that he stabbed to death a drunken soldier who had insulted him. His captain's commission in the Montreal militias postdates 1750. There are a number of inaccuracies in the service record that he sent to the minister of the navy in 1764 to obtain the cross of the order of Saint-Louis.

81 Casgrain, ed., *Collection*, 5: 108, Bourlamaque to Lévis, Saint-Ours, 25 August 1760. Custom had it that militia officers escaped ordinary corporal punishment such as caning. I have not found any specific information about the gorget. See also ibid., 8: 160–1, Vaudreuil to Lévis, 24 April 1760, on rural militia companies led by their officers that joined Lévis's army.

82 In the French West Indies, Virginia, or Connecticut, to cite a few examples. See Titus, *The Old Dominion*, 121; Selesky, *War and Society*, 205.

83 Pluchon, *Histoire de la colonisation française*, 629–36; Petit, *Dissertations*, 282–90. The royal ordinance of 1705 defining the status of the West Indian militias was complemented and amended by other regulations in 1707, 1727, and 1732. On this last date, the regiments created in 1705 were abolished and the militias resumed the form of *compagnies franches*. Captains with royal warrants could sit on councils of war.

84 The letters from the ministry merely allude to the Saint-Domingue model without offering further details. The details provided here are reported by Bougainville, who had news of the reform during his trip to Versailles in the winter of 1758–59: *RAPQ* (1923–24): 55, "Mémoire sur l'état de la Nouvelle-France (1757)."

85 AC, B, 83: 272–72v, 86: 318–19v, 89: 49–53v, and 93: 29, minister to La Jonquière, 1 April 1746, 1 April 1747, 30 April 1749, and 27 August 1751; 95: 212–17, instructions to Duquesne, 15 May 1752; 101: 123–25v, 103: 148–49v, 105: 13 and 34, 107: 15, and 111: 9, minister to Vaudreuil, 22 March 1755, 31 March 1756, 16 April and 19 October 1757, 10 February 1758, 22 February 1760; CIIA, 100: 90–91v, 102: 137–8, 103: 232–4, 104: 109–10, and 105: 92–93v, Vaudreuil to the minister, 18 October 1755, 29 October 1757, 26 October 1758, 3 November 1759, and 26 June 1760. The file is voluminous, clearly, and yet to my knowledge no historian has mentioned this initiative and its failure, perhaps so as not to tarnish the image of the militia in a putatively harmonious, egalitarian society. Vaudreuil's changing stance is tortuous. In 1755, he asked for blank commissions from the king to be completed with the names of militia officers who had distinguished themselves in the battle of 8 September but did not send a list of candidates when asked. In 1759, he decided not to award such commissions prior to the implementation of the reform. Moreover, although pressed in 1756 to announce the imminent reform to the colony, he would not do so until two years later.

86 AC, CIIA, 100: 46, petition from Joseph Fleury Deschambault to the minister.

87 See *supra*, notes 39–40.

88 See the ministerial correspondence for these years, particularly AC, B, 105: 34.

89 A few younger captains, active ca. 1755 – Joseph Perthuis and Étienne Charest of Quebec, Simon Réaume, Dufy Desauniers, and Le Pellé de Mézières of Montreal – were identified. The profile of the urban militia captains in 1750 is discussed *supra*, 145.

90 Two former Canadian militia officers requested and obtained the cross of the order of Saint-Louis fifteen years after the defeat: Étienne Charest, who was then living in France, and Dufy Desauniers, who, having decided in the interim to stay in the colony, was forced to decline the honour: Roland-J. Auger, "Charest, Étienne," DCB, 4: 152–3, and Jacqueline Roy, "Trottier Dufy Desauniers, Thomas-Ignace," DCB, 4: 802–3. Bonnault's view of the reform as a fait accompli led him into several errors of interpretation: "Le Canada militaire: état provisoire des officiers de milice de 1641 à 1760," RAPQ (1949–51): 265. Note, too, that the conservatism of the colonial general staff had been evident since the turn of the century. "It is best to leave things as they are," wrote Vaudreuil in response to the court's suggestion that the militias be formed into regiments: RAPQ (1947–48): 242, memorandum from the king to Vaudreuil and Bégon, 19 March 1714, and 278, Vaudreuil and Bégon to the minister, 20 September 1714.

91 AC, CIIA, 100: 41–3, Duquesne to the minister, 6 July 1755. For the other details, see Archives de l'Université de Montréal, Baby Collection, P58/P2, 28 (and microfiche 2569), order to La Naudière to escort the militias, 5 June 1747; AC, CIIA, 117: 168–320, fees paid to officers escorting the militias, 1747; Archives de la Bastille, 12145, memorandum from Péan in regard to an inspection at Lachine in April 1753; RAPQ (1927–28): 355–6, "Journal de Joseph-Gaspard Chaussegros de Léry, lieutenant des troupes, 1754–1755," April 1754.

92 RAPQ (1926–27): 373, Léry, "Journal de la campagne d'hiver du 13 février au 9 avril 1756 ... " 24 February 1756; Casgrain, ed., Collection, 11: 53–64, journal of the same campaign kept by Charly; ibid., 127–42, anon., "Journal de la campagne de M. de Bellestre en octobre et novembre 1757."

93 AC, CIIA, 115: 254–76v, expenses for the party led by Rigaud that departed Montreal on 3 August 1746, Montreal, 30 September 1746. The domiciliés, under the command of Captain de Muy, took the lead and do not appear to have taken part in the feast at Chambly.

94 AC, CIIA, 84: 103–07v, Hocquart to the minister, 2 November 1745, in regard to the tafia (rum) necessary for the troop assemblies. There are no other references.

95 See Grenier, ed., Papiers Contrecoeur, passim, and RAPQ (1927–28), Léry, "Journal de la campagne d'hiver ... 1754," passim.

96 RAPQ (1931–32): 25, journal of Lapause, captain of the Guyenne regiment acting as assistant town major, August 1756. While disorder was normal, the destitution of the contingent was not, leading to the surmise that there had been no inspection at Lachine prior to departure. The officers of the

French regiment were stunned by a procedure to which the colonial officers had become accustomed.

97 Keegan, *The Face of Battle*, 72–3, 114. In the British colonies, militias were grouped into local companies for the duration of their contract and led by their own officers; see Anderson, *A People's Army*, 44–8; Selesky, *War and Society*, ch. 5 in particular; Titus, *The Old Dominion*, 132 et seq. Keegan stresses "small-unit cohesion" as the main factor in the effectiveness of the provincial troops in 1758.

98 Corvisier, *L'Armée française*, 1: 121.

99 Some examples are given *infra*, 272 et seq. Good officers were the difference between a crowd and an army: Keegan, *The Face of Battle*, 173–4.

100 AC, F3, 7: 748–64, "Règlement du Roy pour la conduite, police et discipline des compagnies que Sa Majesté entretient dans le Canada," 30 May 1695. Note the resemblance between this dual system and the decision, in 1720, to stop using corvées for the construction of the Quebec enceinte: *supra*, 171–3.

101 AC, CIIA, vol. 119, *passim*, miscellaneous expenses for 1749–50; see other sources in the following notes.

102 AC, CIIA, 119: 224 et seq., certificates issued to Louis Saint-Jean and François Lebeau of Longue-Pointe, signed by the commandant and storekeeper of Detroit, 28–29 September 1749.

103 AC, CIIA, 116: 91–140, expense statement for 1748. Merchants offered 200 livres on average, more for front and rear canoeists.

104 See *supra*, 217–18.

105 Grenier, ed., *Papiers Contrecoeur*, 22–3, Varin to Contrecoeur, 6 March 1753; Archives de la Bastille, 12145: 7–55, defence of Péan; see also *RAPQ* (1924–25): 124, anon., "Mémoire du Canada," on these payments.

106 AC, CIIA, 119: 102–12, 121, 125–7, certificates issued by the Comte de Raymond, commandant at Fort Miami, to various "militiamen-soldiers" who escorted the sick or went for provisions from the Weas, in 1749–50. The fee paid for a journey was thirty-five livres.

107 AC, CIIA, 115: 150–228, expense statement for 1745, payment for work done on the Saint-Jean road from 10 May to 31 July 1745; Kalm, *Voyage*, 171, in regard to the work on this same road in 1748–49, for which, according to the author, labourers were paid thirty sols per day; AC, CIIA, 117: 75–7, payments in 1746 for construction, watch, and handling of fire ships on Île-aux-Coudres; 88: 199–207, expenses to organize signaling between the Côte-du-Sud and Gaspé. In both cases, wages were thirty sols per day.

108 For similar work in the Lake Champlain camps during the Seven Years' War, Massachusetts militias earned one shilling per day or the equivalent at the exchange rate then current. Anderson, *A People's Army*, 81.

109 Grenier, ed., *Papiers Contrecoeur*, 229–45, 284–304. There were some soldiers among the workers at Fort Duquesne, and the foremen were sergeants of the troops. The work took place from 13 August to 27 November 1754 and from 24 March to 27 August 1755: Archives de la Ville de Montréal, fonds BM7, Gagnon Collection, 31: 40121, certificate issued by the commandant and storekeeper of Fort Duquesne to Louis Fortin, 20 September 1758; Durham and Johnstone, *Lady Durham's Journal*, 95–6. This officer of the colonial regulars specified that the intendant paid twenty sols per day for work on the entrenchments. Montcalm's journal indicates thirty sols as the wages paid for this same work, but the source is less reliable.

110 Casgrain, ed., *Collection*, 4: 174: "the battalion commanders ... shall also ensure that the said militiamen are paid for their labour," reads Vaudreuil's regulation of 1 June 1759 for the incorporation of the militias.

111 AC, C11A, 83: 111–13 and 85: 202–3, Beauharnois to the minister, 1 November 1745 and 1 October 1746; 88: 192, Hocquart to the minister, 31 October 1747.

112 AC, F3, 7: 748–64, regulation for the conduct of the *compagnies franches* maintained in Canada, 30 May 1695; AC, B, 76: 74–5, ordinance concerning the keeping of arms, 1 May 1743.

113 AC, C11A, 100: 178 et seq., François-Marc-Antoine Le Mercier, colonial artillery officer, to the minister, 20 October 1755; see also Cassel, "The Troupes de la Marine," 316–23. Appreciated by the Amerindians for the same reasons, hunting muskets were known as "fur trader's muskets" (*fusil de traite*) because of their use in that pursuit.

114 AC, C11A, 85: 27–9, Beauharnois and Hocquart to the minister, 26 September 1746.

115 *RAPQ* (1931–32): 74–5, Lapause, "Mémoire et observations," October 1757; *RAPQ* (1923–24): 29–31, Bougainville, memorandum on the militias, January 1759; see also the remarks of Le Mercier quoted *supra*, note 112.

116 Pouchot, *Mémoires*, 2: 107, 132 et seq.; Casgrain, ed., *Collection*, 2: 288–90, circular from Lévis to battalion commanders, 16 April 1760.

117 AC, C11A, 115: 254–76v, expenses for the party led by Rigaud that departed Montreal on 3 August 1746, Montreal, 30 September 1746; 117: 20–31, expenses for a party commanded by Rigaud that departed 8 June 1747, Montreal, 14 August 1747.

118 AC, CIIA, 84: 103–07, Hocquart to the minister, 2 November 1745, in
regard to expenses for Marin's detachment in Acadia; 119: 02–02v, Bigot
to the minister, 31 October 1749, in regard to goods sent to Acadia for the
detachments of Boishébert and La Corne; *RAPQ* (1923–24): 251, journal
of Bougainville, February 1757, description of equipment of detachment
commanded by Rigaud.

119 *RAPQ* (1923–24): 251, journal of Bougainville, February 1757; see also
description of winter equipment in *Mémoire pour Messire François Bigot*,
39–40.

120 "A Faithful Narrative of the Many Dangers and Sufferings as Well as
Wonderful Deliverance of Robert Eastburn during his Late Captivity
among the Indians, Written by Himself," in Drake, ed., *Tragedies of the
Wilderness*, 269.

121 Casgrain, ed., *Collection*, 7: 317, journal of Montcalm, 13 November
1757, and journal of Bougainville, cited *supra*, 165–6.

122 See *supra*, ch. 6, note 57.

123 AC, CIIA, 102: 233–34v, excerpt from Bigot's letters, 15 January
1757. Tents do not appear on the list of supplies for the colonial
regulars before 1751 (the end of the series): Cassel, "The Troupes de
la Marine," 404. But the officers had them, as shown by the statements
of account.

124 See *supra*, note 118; Grenier, ed., *Papiers Contrecoeur*, 91, Duquesne to
Contrecoeur, 25 December 1753.

125 "The Marquis de Vaudreuil, it is said, never gave them to the garrisons in
Canada," reported Montcalm in regard to the equipment demanded by the
Quebec militias in July 1759: Casgrain, ed., *Collection*, 7: 566, journal of
Montcalm, 5 July 1759.

126 *RAPQ* (1931–32): 25, journal of Lapause, August 1756. Other observations
on clothing and sanitary conditions are found in the journals of the French
army officers: *supra*, note 56.

127 AC, CIIA, 104: 478 et seq., anonymous memorandum denouncing the
abuses, among other things: "Some soldiers have been outfitted four times
during a single campaign, and have resold the surplus." Since control over
the militias was more lax than over the troops, such fraud cannot be
ruled out.

128 We return to the decreases in military rations beginning in 1757 and the
other new conditions imposed on the militia due to flour and meat shortages in the colony.

129 See *supra*, 115–16.

130 See Keegan, *A History of Warfare*, 301. Experience has shown, writes the historian, that soldiers cannot carry more than seventy pounds and that equipment accounts for about half of this load – a proportion that never varied from the Roman army to the First World War. At three pounds per day, the provisions carried on a man's back would thus last for about eleven days.

131 *RAPQ* (1927–28): 365, journal of Léry, June 1754.

132 Casgrain, ed., *Collection*, 11: 127–42, "Journal de la campagne de M. de Bellestre en octobre et novembre 1757."

133 Casgrain, ed., *Collection*, 11: 53–64, "Journal de la campagne de M. Léry," attributed to Charly, February–April 1756; *RAPQ* (1926–27): 377, 390–1, Léry, "Journal de la campagne d'hiver ... 1756," March 1756.

134 These details are recorded in the accounts of the king's stores and on the expense statements, cited previously. For rentals of horses between La Prairie and Sainte-Thérèse-sur-le-Richelieu in 1745–47, see AC, CIIA, 115: 150–228 and 117: 150–1.

135 Even officers travelling overland to Hudson Bay in the late seventeenth century had valets to carry their packs, but this is almost never mentioned in the texts. In 1758, Léry and the Chevalier de Longueuil each travelled with a black slave: Roy, ed., *Inventaire*, 3: 13, journal of a voyage to the five Iroquois nations, July–August 1758. See also ibid., 20, journal of a voyage from Quebec to Carillon, September–October 1758.

136 Archives de la Bastille, 12145: 47v–48, defence of Péan; see also *supra*, 17, remarks reported in 1749 by the Swedish traveller Pehr Kalm.

137 Casgrain, ed., *Collection*, 7: 156–8, journal of Montcalm. He describes the preparations at Saint-Jean, including carriages, equipment, and a profusion of poultry. For another example of a generously outfitted expedition, see AC, CIIA, 115: 254–76v, expenses for the party led by Rigaud that departed Montreal on 3 August 1746 (Montreal, 30 September 1746).

138 See preceding note. This transpires from some of the testimony produced at trial in the "Canada Affair" of 1763.

139 AC, F3, 14: 23, ordinance by La Jonquière, 16 September 1751.

140 BANQ-Montréal, TL4-S1-D5681, criminal trial of Joseph Favre *dit* Lafeuillade, a soldier accused of having killed Pierre Labelle, a militiaman-soldier at Fort Ouiatenon, heard on a petition by commandant de Ligneris, 16 March 1752, followed by a motion from the king's attorney in Montreal and the opinion of the assessors, 1 February 1753. A second council of war concluded that the death was accidental, and the soldier was acquitted. Was this also an attempt to shield a sensitive case from public scrutiny?

141 AC, CIIA, 99: 81–82v, Bigot to the minister, 28 August 1753.

142 Courville, *Mémoires*, 168.

143 AC, CIIA, 99: 95–97v, Duquesne to the minister, 26 October 1753.

144 Contributing to this severity were the war and the recrudescence of deser-
     tion following the troop increase of 1750. The temptation to desert was
     stronger among the new recruits, who fled to the British in the hope of
     regaining their country. They were rarely caught. See, e.g., the prosecutions
     and sentences in BAnQ-Montréal, TL4–S1–D5667, trials of four soldiers at
     the Sandoské garrison, 10 January–1 February 1752, and TL4–S1–D5875,
     trial of Leroy *dit* Beausoleil, arrested near Niagara, 24 April–14 June
     1754; also, BAnQ-Québec, TP1–S777–D167, trial of eight Alsatians garri-
     soned at Fort Frontenac, who were hanged in Montreal on
     13 September 1757. See also Corvisier, *L'Armée française*, 2: 694–5, and
     Vigié, "Justice et criminalité."

145 BAnQ-Montréal, TL4–S1–D6070, trial of soldier Dubosc, 3–4 February
     1756; "M. Jean-Félix Récher," 304–5.

146 AC, F3, 14: 23, ordinance by La Jonquière, 16 September 1751.

147 Archives de la Bastille, 12145: 22, Péan to the governor, Niagara, July 1753.

148 Grenier, ed., *Papiers Contrecoeur*, 39, Duquesne to Marin, 13 May 1753.

149 Ibid., 278–80, 311–20, rolls of Belle-Rivière detachments, 3 March and
     19 April 1755. The men were Gabriel Masse (Quebec), Pierre Dupré
     (Saint-Ours), Jean-Baptiste Ménard (Longue-Pointe), and Charles Grenier
     (Rivière-des-Prairies), for a total of four out of some 250 conscripts.

150 In December 1758, three Canadians charged with theft were caned at Fort
     de La Présentation before being sent to Montreal for further punishment –
     exceptionally harsh treatment, according to Montcalm's journal: Casgrain,
     ed., *Collection*, 7: 491, 16 December 1758.

151 AC, CIIA, 99: 81, Bigot to the minister, 28 August 1753; 99: 242,
     Duquesne to the minister, 29 September 1754; F3, 14: 51, minister
     to Duquesne, 31 May 1754; B, 101: 72, order to Daubigny, ship's com-
     mander, to deliver the two Canadians to the governor of Île Royale.

152 That is to say, what explained the militiamen's delinquent behaviour in such
     cases was not the poor conditions under which they served but rather a con-
     cern for the families they had had to leave behind in the confusion of defeat.

153 Macarty to Vaudreuil, 18 March 1752, and Vaudreuil to Macarty, 28 April
     1752, in Pease and Jenison, eds, *Illinois*, 506–36, 615–26. Vaudreuil, then
     governor of Louisiana, commended the commandant for his prudence.

154 The incident is reported by Montcalm, who approved of Vaudreuil's leni-
     ency in the presence of apparently extenuating circumstances. Having

asked to go to war with Rigaud's detachment, in February 1757, the sixteen prisoners were freed and the collective fine set at 6,000 livres was lowered to 3,000. Casgrain, ed., *Collection*, 7: 113 and 155, journal of Montcalm, late August 1756 and 21 February 1757.

155 Contrary to what Montcalm wrote, there was no mutiny at Fort Duquesne before the evacuation: Casgrain, ed., *Collection*, 5: 279–81, Montcalm to Bourlamaque, 27 November 1758. See AC, F3, 15: 225–30, excerpts of letters from Le Marchand de Lignery, commandant at Fort Duquesne, to Vaudreuil, October–November 1758.

156 See, e.g., AC, C11A, 98: 320–1, "Rôle des officiers d'épée et de plume, officiers mariniers et soldats invalides établis en Canada, auxquels on a payé leur demi-solde pour l'année 1751." The soldier's pension ranged from six to twelve livres per month. The fund was financed by amounts withheld from wages and by various taxes, including the four sols per livre collected on military supply contracts.

157 AC, C11A, 85: 97–97v, Beauharnois and Hocquart to the minister, 2 November 1746. For other denied requests, see 87: 163–4, La Galissonière and Hocquart to the minister, in favour of six wounded men, 2 November 1747; 66: 64–64v, "Liste des invalides morts en 1735" and "Invalides proposés en remplacement" for 1736 and 1737, [1736]; 66: 77–77v, Beauharnois and Hocquart to the minister, 16 October 1736, in favour of Jacques Réel, a habitant wounded in the Fox War.

158 AC, C11A, 87: 65, "Extrait en forme de journal de ce qui s'est passé d'intéressant dans la colonie," November 1746–October 1747; 117: 79v–81v, war expenses for the year 1747.

159 AC, C11A, 99: 25, revenues and expenses for parties to the Great Lakes region for the year 1752; see also 116: 144–54, for the years 1748–49.

160 AC, C11A, 100: 24–34, Duquesne to the minister, 12 July 1755, followed by statement of revenues and expenses for the posts. Women and orphans of dead militiamen (number not given) and eighteen wounded men shared 3,344 livres with fire and hurricane victims.

161 The incident was reported by Montcalm and confirmed by Vaudreuil himself, who explained to the minister the circular and the search he had ordered in the parishes before giving out the king's money. He had 6,000 livres in total with which to reward the regular officers and the militiamen. I assume that the latter would have been entitled to 1,000 livres: AC, C11A, 102: 137–41v, Vaudreuil to the minister, 29 October 1757, and Casgrain, ed., *Collection*, 6: 97–100, Montcalm to Lévis, Quebec, 16 December 1757.

CHAPTER TEN

1 Courville, *Mémoires*, offers a good illustration of the conspiracy theory.

2 Dechêne, *Power and Subsistence*, in particular ch. 1, "Grain Demand: An Overview," ch. 6, "Shortages and Controls, 1690–1744," and ch. 8, "Grain during Wartime."

3 I use the heading "number of families" to estimate the number of farmers. This presupposes that all heads of rural households had land – not an unreasonable assumption for this era.

4 See Wien, "Les travaux pressants."

5 In the absence of a census (the last dates from 1739), the phenomenon is not measurable with any precision. The seigneurs continued to grant land, but it lay uncultivated.

6 To encourage the habitants to thresh early and to compensate them for the losses thus incurred, the intendant paid more for wheat in early autumn 1756: BAnQ-Québec, E1–S1–P439, ordinance of 20 November 1756.

7 BAnQ-Québec, E1–S1/26, cahier 42 (12 June 1755–26 February 1760), ordinance by the intendant of 8 October 1755 placing seals on bolters in the Côte-du-Sud, downriver from Quebec, and ordinance of 24 December 1757 extending the measure to the rest of the colony. The milling ban was a radical measure to reduce peasants' consumption.

8 Requisitions had been used in former times of scarcity to bring the wheat out of the barns, but where once they had been sporadic, in the last decade of the regime they became regular. The series of ordinances setting the official price of wheat is incomplete for this period, and instructions by the intendant to various individuals responsible for "seizing the wheat" in the côtes have not survived, but indirect accounts surrounding the procedure are explicit and numerous. See, e.g., AC, C11A, 104: 5–6, excerpts from Bigot's dispatches of 1758 and the other accounts cited in *Power and Subsistence*. Some historians, it seems, have failed to read and/or understand them; André Côté (*Joseph-Michel Cadet*, 121–2), for example, asserts that freedom of trade was always respected in the colony.

9 *RAPQ* (1931–32): 74, "Mémoire et observations sur mon voyage au Canada" by Lapause, observation by a French officer.

10 For the importance of the local economy, see Dechêne, *Power and Subsistence*, ch. 2.

11 As long as the troops were camped in frontier country, deep in the woods, the absence of roads and the lack of forage limited the use of oxen and horses as beasts of burden and mounts.

12 *BRH* 32 (1926): 691, orders issued by Vaudreuil to La Naudière, 23 July
   and 13 August 1759, and ordinance of 13 August issued by Vaudreuil and
   Bigot warning any habitants who might be tempted to hide their animals
   that these could be confiscated without payment.   .

13 *ARC* (1905), vol. 1, 4th part, 20–36, Captain Dumas to Vaudreuil from
   Jacques-Cartier, 28 March–late June 1760.

14 *RAPQ* (1931–32): 104, journal of Lapause, October–November 1759; also
   Casgrain, ed., *Collection*, 5: 112, Bourlamaque to Lévis, 27 August 1760.

15 On the organization of winter quarters for the colonial regulars since the
   turn of the century, see *supra*, 181 et seq.

16 See Table 10.1. The notes to this table contain references to troop movements and numbers.

17 That is, the côtes connected to the Notre-Dame-de-Montréal parish;
   see Dechêne, "La croissance de Montréal."

18 Casgrain, ed., *Collection*, 6: 51–3, 54–7, 68–71, Montcalm to Lévis, 9 and
   14 September and 24 October 1757; ibid., 2: 171–3, Lévis to the minister
   of war, 8 October 1757.

19 Ibid., 10: 79, Péan to Lévis, 26 October 1757.

20 See AC, C11A, 142–44v, examples of payments distributed in the parishes
   in conjunction with the war.

21 For the contract between the king and the purveyor, see Frégault, *François
   Bigot*, 2: 186 et seq. The amount of twelve sols was paid for a ration delivered to the countryside before markup: Casgrain, ed., *Collection*, 7: 428,
   journal of Montcalm, 5 August 1758, and 6: 56 and 74, Montcalm to
   Lévis, 14 September and 2 November 1757; *RAPQ* (1924–25): 191, anon.,
   "Mémoire du Canada"; Archives de l'Université de Montréal, Baby
   Collection, P58/P2, 53 (and microfiche 2574), order to board a soldier for
   fifteen livres per month, 1 June 1758. Note too that the parishes collectively supplied an additional forty pounds of flour per month to the officer
   billeted there, apparently without charge.

22 Casgrain, ed., *Collection*, 7: 428, journal of Montcalm, 5 August 1758.

23 Durham and Johnstone, *Lady Durham's Journal*, 155–6.

24 AC, F3, 15: 341v, Bigot to the minister, 15 October 1759; see also "Le
   siège de Québec en 1759 par un militaire de l'armée française," in Hébert,
   ed., *Le Siège*, 65–7, 101. Some 20,000 minots were found, thanks in part
   to payment, to ordinary pressure no doubt, or perhaps even to the desire
   to help the army at this crucial moment – who knows?

25 Courville, *Mémoires*, 181.

26 Dechêne, *Power and Subsistence*, 128–40.

27 See *supra*, 200 et seq.

28 *Mémoire pour Messire François Bigot*, 132–4: "he sent garrisons to several habitants to take from them the quantity of wheat for which they had been taxed." BAnQ-Québec, E1–S1/24, cahier 40, E1–S1/25, cahier 41, and E1–S1/26, cahier 42, intendant's ordinances, 1752–60, *passim*; Casgrain, ed., *Collection*, 7: 327–30, journal of Montcalm, late December 1757 and 21 January 1758; Têtu and Gagnon, eds, *Mandements*, 2: 130–1. The archives of the intendancy (apart from the ordinances) have not survived, so we do not know whether prosecution of offenders was common and whether punishment was strictly enforced.

29 Durham and Johnstone, *Lady Durham's Journal*, 156.

30 See, in particular, Jaenen, *The Role of the Church*; Crowley, "The Inroads of Secularization." The paper also deals with Canada. Deslandres, "Le christianisme," concurs with this interpretation but without offering any further basis for it.

31 Cliche, *Les pratiques de dévotion*; Caulier, "Bâtir l'Amérique des dévots"; Greer, "L'Habitant."

32 According to the list produced by Marcel Trudel (*L'Église canadienne*, 1: 91–112) of parishes and their priests in 1760; see also MCQ, Fonds d'archives du Séminaire de Québec, "Projet d'un mémoire de l'évêque en faveur des curés," ca. 1756, polygraphie 7, no. 23. There were 107 parishes by my count, ninety of them with resident priests. Lay clergy were still scarce, but the bishop could rely on the Récollets to replace an absent priest or to serve more remote parishes with missions.

33 *RAPQ* (1936–37): 400, Abbé de l'Isle-Dieu to Pontbriand, Paris, 25 March 1755, quoted in Lacelle, "Monseigneur Henry-Marie Dubreil," 41–2.

34 On the radical change in the bishop's message in 1759, see *infra*, 313.

35 Têtu and Gagnon, eds, *Mandements*, 2: 28, circular to the parish priests in regard to the wheat tax during the shortage, 20 March 1743.

36 Lacelle, "Monseigneur Henry-Marie Dubreil," 278, circular to the parish priests of the diocese, [summer] 1755.

37 Têtu and Gagnon, eds, *Mandements*, 2: 102, pastoral letter giving thanks to God for the dauphin's recovery, 12 July 1753.

38 Ibid., 108, pastoral letter calling for public prayer in response to the Acadians' hardships, 15 February 1756.

39 Ibid., 126, pastoral letter calling for public prayer, 20 January 1758.

40 Letter published in Roy, *Histoire*, 2: 259–60. In this text, the verb *espérer* has the older meaning of "to expect," which had survived in western France. *Ennuyé* can mean either "exhausted" or "troubled," and I am inclined to believe that the first is correct. Rey, ed. *Dictionnaire*.

41 Casgrain, ed., *Collection*, 7: 202, journal of Montcalm, 15 May 1757.
42 Tanguay, *Dictionnaire généalogique*, 3: 184–5 and 4: 444–5: Louis-Marie, baptized at Lévis in 1721, married in 1750 to Marie-Josèphe Couture. According to Tanguay's data, the couple was reunited after the war.
43 Anderson, *A People's Army*, ch. 3.
44 These were the forts along the Richelieu and Lake Champlain and the ones lying to the south of the Great Lakes, from Fort Frontenac to Fort Miami. The composite description relies on several sources, including Grenier, ed., *Papiers Contrecoeur*, and the Lapause papers, in *RAPQ* (1931–32): 1–225.
45 Wives did not accompany their husbands during the war and were by all accounts few in number among the servants. See, e.g., BAnQ-Montréal, CN601–S308, minutes of notary P. Panet, undertaking by a widow and her son to the storekeeper of Fort Frontenac, 5 April 1756.
46 Malartic (*Journal*, 19–20) describes the teals, plovers, ducks, and other species sold by the Iroquois at Fort Frontenac in 1755; according to Montcalm, equally good business was done at Niagara in 1756: Casgrain, ed., *Collection*, 7: 169, 5 March 1757.
47 White, *The Middle Ground*, 240–5.
48 "Further examination of Michael La Chauvignerie Junior ... 26 October 1757," in Stevens and Kent, eds, *Wilderness Chronicles*, 115. The interpreter would not have used the English word "labourers" if the prisoner were speaking of the militia.
49 Pouchot, *Mémoires*, 1: 169–70; see also the partial descriptions in "Life and Travels of Col. James Smith," in Peckham, ed., *Narratives*, 71–124; *idem*, "Thomas Gist's Indian Captivity"; *idem*, "The Captivity of Charles Stuart."
50 The numbers varied greatly, up to 2,000 in August 1757 at the siege of Fort George, but the officers ordinarily complained of being short-handed.
51 Casgrain, ed., *Collection*, 7: 421, journal of Montcalm, 31 July 1758.
52 The numbers fluctuated greatly as a result of incessant troop movements, rarely dipping below 1,000 and reaching 3,000 in the summer of 1757. For the layout of the camps, see in particular Casgrain, ed., *Collection*, vol. 1, "Journal des campagnes du chevalier de Lévis en Canada de 1756 à 1760," and the journals of Lapause; also, the map titled "Sketch of the Country Round Tyconderoga," reproduced in Parkman, *Montcalm and Wolfe*, vi.
53 There are no precise figures; 13,000, without the Indigenous allies, is likely the highest number, occurring at the outset of the siege. The size of the Beauport army subsequently dropped to 6,000.

54 Knox, *Journal*, 1: 394, 455. For a more picturesque description highlighting uniforms and flags, including those erroneously attributed to the militia, see Filteau, *Par la bouche*, 104–7.

55 Casgrain, ed., *Collection*, 9: 56–7, Bigot to Lévis, 8 September 1759. According to the intendant, the decrease in the military ration was what had touched off the looting. Several chroniclers attribute the misdeeds to the Amerindians, others to the "troops," without further qualification. See, e.g., AC, CIIA, 104: 257, anon., "Journal tenu." For Frégault (*François Bigot*, 2: 260–1), only army soldiers took part in the looting. He regards it as an episode in the ethnic conflict between Frenchmen and Canadians. In fact, it was a clash between civilians and soldiers, and the whole army – militiamen included – took part in looting the parishes.

56 According to the army officers, the colonial soldiers' camps were more squalid than their own; see Aleyrac, *Aventures militaires*, 132.

57 On the clothing handed out to militiamen who went to war, see *supra*, 235 et seq. Blankets, greatcoats, and other warm clothing were for the minority who participated in winter campaigns.

58 The letter is reproduced in full *infra*, 280.

59 Pouchot, *Mémoires*, 2: 261.

60 *RAPQ* (1923–24): 29, Bougainville, memorandum on the militias, January 1759; Aleyrac, *Aventures militaires*, 43.

61 Malartic, *Journal*, 112.

62 Casgrain, ed., *Collection*, 8: 18, Vaudreuil to Lévis, 7 August 1756.

63 Ibid., 2: 32, 38–42, 45–6, etc., Lévis to Vaudreuil and Bigot, August 1756.

64 *Collection de manuscrits*, 4: 164–8, Montcalm to the minister of war, 20 July 1758. All the data I have obtained concerns Carillon, but the situation was probably worse in the Great Lakes and Ohio camps.

65 Casgrain, ed., *Collection*, 10: 190, Captain Beauclair to Lévis, Fort Lévis, 23 October 1759; 5: 17, Bourlamaque to Lévis, Île-aux-Noix, 6–7 August 1759; 5: 41, Bourlamaque to Vaudreuil, Île-aux-Noix, 5 September 1759.

66 *RAPQ* (1944–45): 67, Doreil to the minister, 29 October 1755, on the mobile hospitals; Casgrain, ed., *Collection*, 6: 19, Montcalm, "Instructions pour M. le chevalier de Lévis," July 1756.

67 Benoît to Contrecoeur, 1755, cited in Michel Paquin, "Callet (Collet), Luc," *DCB*, 3: 100–1.

68 The Carillon army had at least two chaplains. Five were assigned to the Beauport army: AC, CIIA, 104: 270, Foligné, "Journal mémoratif de ce qui s'est passé de plus remarquable pendant qu'a duré le siège de la ville de Québec ... " 6 June 1759.

69 See the following biographies of Récollets (Franciscans): Michel Paquin, "Callet (Collet), Luc," "Constantin, Justinien," "Foucault, Simon," and "Rouillard, Ambroise," DCB, 3: 100–1, 143–4, 242–4, 618; Fidèle Thériault, "Carpentier, Bonaventure," DCB, 4: 145–6; Jean-Guy Pelletier, "Crespel, Emmanuel," DCB, 4: 196–7.

70 See AC, CI IA, 103: 380–3, Vaudreuil to Montcalm, 21 July 1758, in regard to the colonial sutlers who followed the army.

71 AC, CI IA, 105: 296–301v, Michel de Couagne to Choiseul, La Rochelle, 22 August 1761, in regard to embezzlement of funds at the forts and the custom of selling aqua-vitae to labourers, soldiers, and militiamen.

72 Pouchot, Mémoires, 1: 59–65.

73 In contrast to the militias of New England, who were relatively well paid and could not collect their wages until the end of their contract, hence forced to build up savings: Anderson, A People's Army, 38.

74 RAPQ (1924–25): 113 and 123, anon., "Mémoire du Canada"; AC, F3, 15: 86–86v, Vaudreuil to the minister, 12 February 1758, in regard to looting of the Palatine village. A single Indigenous warrior brought back 30,000 livres in gold, he wrote. The troop had carried off more than 100,000 livres in cash, plus porcelain, silver, and other valuables.

75 Casgrain, ed., Collection, 7: 102–3, 190, 292, journal of Montcalm, in regard to the money found at Oswego (August 1756), which was remitted to the intendant, and to the looting of Fort George (August 1757); see also RAPQ (1923–24): 301–2, journal of Bougainville, 1757.

76 AG, A1, 3417, no. 210, Montcalm to the minister, 28 August 1756; RAPQ (1931–32): 34, Lapause in regard to the unruliness observed at the looting of Oswego.

77 Anderson, A People's Army, 155–60; Steele, Warpaths, 53–6.

78 It was mainly the Amerindians who made off with the spoils from Braddock's army, slaughtered horses, and poured flour and powder on the ground. This victory was theirs. See "Life and Travels of Col. James Smith," in Peckham, ed., Narratives, 71 et seq.; Peckham, ed., "Thomas Gist's Indian Captivity"; Pouchot, Mémoires, 1: 43; RAPQ (1932–33): 309–10, anon., "Relation de l'affaire de la Belle Rivière," 9 July 1755. On the booty brought back after the Battle of Carillon, see Malartic, Journal, 191.

79 The Amerindians too looted for resale or trade. The phrase "big junk shop" (grande brocanterie) employed by Montcalm seems appropriate: Casgrain, ed., Collection, 7: 420–1, journal, 28 July 1758. After the Battle of Beauport, the intendant purchased the weapons and tools that the

combatants had collected on the bank: orders of the day, 2 August 1759, cited in Knox, *An Historical Journal*, 2: 5 (in note).

80 This is an allusion to the men wounded on 13 September 1759 whom the people under siege tried to recover is found in AC, CIIA, 104: 390, Foligné, "Journal mémoratif." On the 14th, they asked for a cease-fire so that they could collect their dead. The British replied that they were already buried: Knox, *An Historical Journal*, 2: 114. See also "Relation du siège de Québec par une religieuse de l'Hôpital Général," in Hébert, *Le Siège*, 27–8, for a description of the battlefield after the battle of 28 April 1760.

81 The words "our generals" were readily pronounced in the colony, even though Montcalm did not accede to the rank of lieutenant-general until 1759.

82 Frégault, *Canada, passim*, in particular 243–58; Eccles, *France in America*, 209–11, and also two articles by the same author, "The French Forces," *DCB*, 3: xv–xxiv, and "Rigaud de Vaudreuil de Cavagnial, Pierre de, marquis de Vaudreuil," *DCB*, 4: 716–30. These articles contain an acerbic critique of the French battalions that is not found in the historian's previous publications. See also Meyer et al., *Histoire de la France coloniale*, 110 et seq., and LaPierre, *The Battle for Canada*, 45–54.

83 He was born at Quebec in 1698, the fourth son of Philippe de Rigaud de Vaudreuil, the governor of New France from 1703 to 1725. See the flattering portraits given in Frégault, *Le Grand Marquis*, and William J. Eccles, "Rigaud de Vaudreuil de Cavagnial, Pierre de, marquis de Vaudreuil," *DCB*, 4: 716–30.

84 Casgrain, ed., *Extrait*, 107, Vaudreuil to the minister, 30 October 1755.

85 AC, B, 103: 12–14, minister to Vaudreuil, 15 March 1756, followed by the king's order indicating that he was free to relay it to Montcalm or not.

86 AC, CIIA, 101: 3–4, Vaudreuil to the minister, 16 [June] 1756.

87 AG, A1, 3457, no. 163, copy of Vaudreuil's letter to the minister of the navy, 23 October 1756.

88 Moras severely reprimanded Montcalm without revealing to him the source of the accusations. They were false, replied Montcalm, who, irony of ironies, was counting on the governor and the intendant to remove the stain from his reputation: AC, B, 105: 25–6, Moras to Montcalm, 27 May 1757, and latter's reply, 19 February 1758, in AG, A1, 3498, no. 14.

89 AC, F3, 15: 129–36, Vaudreuil to the minister, 4 August 1758; AC, CIIA, 103: 302, Vaudreuil to the minister, 4 November 1758.

90 AC, CIIA, 102: 185–6, Vaudreuil to the minister (1757).

91 See *supra*, ch. 9, section 7, on the relatively moderate punishments meted out to militiamen by colonial officers.

92 Before Vaudreuil, all governors-general had been born in France. In contrast, several Canadians figured among the local governors and other staff officers. Contemporaries held the outcome of operations, whether military or diplomatic, to be a function of the commanders' experience and not their origins.

93 Vaudreuil was the only governor of New France who lacked military experience; his participation in the campaign of 1728 against the Foxes was no substitute.

94 The criticisms are ranked according to the space they occupy in the documentation as a whole, including correspondence, memorials, and campaign journals. For a brief overview of the army officers' assumptions and frustrated expectations, see *supra*, ch. 8, section 1.

95 The same scorn was heaped upon officers who robbed the public treasury, those who had interests in the fur trade, and, by association, the majority who did not.

96 The colonial officers did not allude to these quarrels in their writings, but their supposed arrogance and aggressiveness often come up in those of their detractors.

97 AC, C I I A, 103: 299–300, 318–20, Vaudreuil to the minister, 4 and 20 November 1758, in regard to naval artillery officers who were beyond his control and to colonial youth who obtained army commissions. Note too that the esteem in which Montcalm and his officers held several colonial officers contradicts the lapidary generalizations contained in their writings.

98 Since Vaudreuil required the parties to be commanded by his officers, some army officers declined to participate, particularly those whose rank was at least equal to that of the commander. Also of note are the jealousies surrounding the recall of Pouchot, the commandant at Niagara.

99 See *supra*, ch. 9, section 5, on the weaknesses of militia leadership.

100 Têtu and Gagnon, eds, *Mandements*, 2: 131, pastoral letter of 15 July 1758 ordering a *Te Deum* for "the victory won on the 8th of this month near Fort Vaudreuil." The bishop, a loyal partisan of the governor, seems to have been the only one to remember that Fort Carillon (built by Chartier de Lotbinière, a nephew) was supposed to be called Vaudreuil.

101 "The Canadians are, in one camp, mingled in each company with the colonial troops": Aleyrac, *Aventures militaires*, 33. At the siege of Oswego, there were fifty militiamen and fifteen soldiers; in the expedition of

February 1757, thirty-three and seventeen, respectively, and so on, not counting cadets and noncoms.

102 *RAPQ* (1928–29): 5–86, *passim*, Nicolas Renaud d'Avène Des Méloizes, "Journal militaire tenu par Nicolas Renaud d'Avène Des Méloizes, Ch^er, seigneur de Neuville au Canada," 19 July–30 October 1756 and 8 May–21 November 1759; or *RAPQ* 1933–34): 67–231, Lapause, "Relation de la campagne de Canada jusqu'au 20 août 1757," *passim* (e.g., 194).

103 There was some griping about the behaviour of the militiamen themselves, but the bulk of the criticism was directed at the colonial general staff, which had responsibility for recruitment and command.

104 Casgrain, ed., *Collection*, 4: 45–51, "Réflexions générales sur les mesures à prendre pour la défense de cette colonie," 10 September 1758, and 7: 444, journal of Montcalm, [September 1758]; AC, CI IA, 103: 460–61v, "Inconvénients dans la constitution des milices" [1758].

105 Casgrain, ed., *Collection*, 4: 171–4, "Règlement pour l'incorporation des Canadiens dans les bataillons des troupes de terre," signed by Vaudreuil, Quebec, 1 June 1759. This is the main source addressing the discipline problems, but it leaves the essential aspects murky.

106 For the criticisms, see Pouchot, *Mémoires*, 2: 132 et seq., and AC, CI IA, 104: 200. As to numbers, there are only two widely differing references, with Montcalm mentioning 300 militiamen per battalion and Malartic 108: Casgrain, ed., *Collection*, 7: 566; Malartic, *Journal*, 240.

107 *RAPQ* (1928–29): 29, Nicolas Renaud d'Avène Des Méloizes, "Journal militaire..." late October 1756; *RAPQ* (1931–32): 91, journal of Lapause, who writes in regard to the Beauport army: "in these governments, all the colonial regular officers and soldiers native to these departments were incorporated."

108 Casgrain, ed., *Collection*, 4: 171–4, regulation of 1 June 1759; 2: 283–90, Lévis to battalion commanders, March–April 1760; 5: 88 and 95, Bourlamaque to Lévis, August 1760. The distribution of housing in 1759–60 corresponds to the distribution of militias between the colonial regulars and the various battalions; see Table 10. 1.

109 Brave, docile, submissive, and easy to lead, wrote one officer in a burst of enthusiasm. "They are patient in their suffering, as nimble as the Natives, of strong temperament, and indefatigable during campaigns. It is one of the best militias in the world." Durham and Johnstone, *Lady Durham's Journal*, 176.

110 See *supra*, 17 et seq., as well as Eccles, "The French Forces," xviii; see also Nicolai, "A Different Kind of Courage," 70, on military customs handed down from generation to generation.

111 AC, F3, 13: 318–47, Céloron de Blainville, journal of his campaign at Belle-Rivière, 1749.

112 Casgrain, ed., *Collection*, 5: 23, Bourlamaque to Rigaud de Vaudreuil, Île-aux-Noix, 8 August 1759.

113 Excluded are certain defensive manoeuvres of 1759 and 1760, sieges, and abandonment of posts, which are discussed in the next chapter.

114 A number of noble statements of principle regretting the violence of Indigenous-style warfare are found in the writings of the army officers. Quoted outside the military context, they readily give the impression that their authors firmly opposed this kind of warfare. They must be read in their entirety to see that this was not at all the case.

115 *RAPQ* (1923–24): 313, journal of Bougainville, October 1757; Casgrain, ed., *Collection*, 7: 191, journal of Montcalm, May 1757.

116 Jennings, *Empire of Fortune*, 189–98; Steele, *Warpaths*, 197.

117 Casgrain, ed., *Collection*, 11: 107, journal of Pouchot, commandant at Niagara, 20 July 1757.

118 This is the interpretation found in Eccles, *France in America*, 199–206, and Mathieu, *La Nouvelle-France*, 225.

119 MacLeod, "Microbes and Muskets."

120 White, *The Middle Ground*, 250–5; Titus, *The Old Dominion*, 121–5.

121 Among other sources, I am relying here on the journal of Pouchot, commandant at Niagara in 1756 and 1757, in Casgrain, ed., *Collection*, 11: 87–116, and on his *Mémoires*, vol. 1, *passim*. The commandants at Fort Duquesne left behind no journals, but information on the parties is found in Vaudreuil's correspondence with the minister and in the journals of Montcalm and Lévis, which also relate what was happening in places other than Carillon. On the parties of the War of the Austrian Succession, see *supra*, 204.

122 See Appendix B. Also, Grenier, ed., *Papiers Contrecoeur*, 196–202, "Journal de la campagne de M. de Villiers au fort Nécessité"; *RAPQ* (1926–27): 372–94, Léry, "Journal de la campagne d'hiver du 13 février au neuf avril 1756"; Casgrain, ed., *Collection*, 11: 53–64, "Journal de la campagne de M. de Léry," attributed to Charly, February–April 1756; Pouchot, *Mémoires*, 1: 170–3.

123 Because they were commanded to join the army, these men appear in the "militia" column of Appendix A rather than in the "volunteers" column, which is reserved for those who left home voluntarily.

124 Casgrain, ed., *Collection*, 11: 127–42, "Journal de la campagne de M. de Bellestre en octobre et novembre 1757."

125 AC, F3, 15: 86–86v, Vaudreuil to the minister, 12 February 1758.

126 Casgrain, ed., *Collection*, 7: 198, journal of Montcalm, 6 May 1757; for another example of embezzlement, see *RAPQ* (1928–29): 33, Nicolas Renaud d'Avène Des Méloizes, "Journal militaire..." 9 June 1759.

127 Without Indigenous guides, even experienced colonial officers got lost in the woods. See, e.g., the misadventures of Jean-Baptiste Levrault de Langis's detachment: Casgrain, ed., *Collection*, 7: 390, 393, journal of Montcalm, 5–6 July 1758. Léry, who was to take 100 men to Lake Champlain scouting for enemy barges, delayed his departure, "convinced that ... Natives were necessary to the endeavour": *RAPQ* (1928–29): 229–34 et seq., "Journal," Carillon, September 1756.

128 The shortage of Indigenous scouts at Carillon was endemic, except in the weeks leading up to the siege of Fort George – July and early August 1757 – when 1,000 warriors from the Great Lakes region were camped near the fort. Montcalm could then "inundate the road to Lydius [Fort Edward] and the surrounding woods with small parties": Casgrain, ed., *Collection*, 7: 283, journal of Montcalm, 5 August 1757.

129 MacLeod, *The Canadian Iroquois*, essentially concerns the role of the Iroquois domiciliés in the major operations of the Seven Years' War. It neglects the small troop movements and, consequently, the problems specific to reconnaissance.

130 Casgrain, ed., *Collection*, 5: 279–81, Montcalm to Bourlamaque, 27 November 1758.

131 According to the accounts found in the journals of Lévis, Bougainville, Montcalm, Malartic, Lapause, Renaud d'Avène Des Méloizes, and Léry. The incessant comings and goings are hard to follow, and my attempts at quantification proved fruitless.

132 One might cite the criticisms of a military engineer who, when a clash occurred between the parties of Marin and Rogers (Carillon, August 1758), accused the Canadians of cowardice, but such criticism was exceptional: Gabriel, *Le Maréchal de camp Desandrouins*, 202–3.

133 *RAPQ* (1931–32): 67–9, plan by Lapause to "restore partisan war" by creating companies of partisans composed of a majority of militiamen (1757); AC, C11A, 105: 361–70, "Mémoire de François-Charles de Bourlamaque sur le Canada," [1762].

134 *RAPQ* (1923–24): 349, journal of Bougainville, 28 July 1758, on the spread of panic in the militia camps in 1756 and 1758.

135 For data on these engagements, see Appendix B.

136 The best work of this kind is Stacey, *Quebec*.

137 I base this statement on the fact that the battalion is named in the tables of military forces alongside the various army and navy battalions. Among the many references to the troop movements of 1759 and 1760, see, most importantly, the journal of Lévis, in Casgrain, ed., *Collection*, vol. 1, *passim*, and that of Lapause, in particular RAPQ (1933–34): 143, on the battalion's role on 28 April 1760.

138 An order by Vaudreuil would have left traces, drawn commentary. The military archives' silence indicates that this was a civilian initiative.

139 See *supra*, 225 et seq.; also 123 et seq., on the origins of volunteers before 1715.

140 Simon Réaume, the commander of the Montreal battalion who was killed at the battle of 28 April 1760, is surely the same Réaume listed as a militia captain in 1750. Most of the other captains were too old and had presumably given up their place. Of the fifteen other militia officers killed or wounded at Sainte-Foy, the majority appear to have been townspeople, but the lists are very imprecise.

141 "Le siège de Québec," in Hébert, *Le Siège*, 59.

142 Casgrain, ed., *Collection*, 11: 215–18, "Relation de la campagne de M. Le chevalier de La Corne à Chouaguen, en 1759."

143 Among the many accounts of this affair, see RAPQ (1920–21): 170–1, anon., "Journal du siège de Québec du 10 mai au 18 septembre 1759." The detachment included 200 Abenakis who were off on reconnaissance at the time of the rout, 160 soldiers, and some 300 militiamen from the Beauport camp. The others were inexperienced Quebecers (older artisans and employees, plus thirty-five schoolchildren).

144 AG, A1, 3405, no. 106, "Relation depuis le départ des troupes ... "; Grenier, ed., *Papiers Contrecoeur*, 390 et seq.; Kopperman, *Braddock*, *passim*; MacLeod, *The Canadian Iroquois*, ch. 3. The militiamen rallied after this retreat, yet they were few in number and credit for the victory certainly rested with the Indigenous participants.

145 AC, F3, 14: 183–8, "Relation de l'action qui s'est passée le 8 septembre au lac St-Sacrement"; AG, A1, 3417, 8 and 11, Chevalier de Montreuil to the minister, 18 September and 10 October 1755; RAPQ (1931–32): 19–22, journal of Lapause; Steele, *Betrayals*, 44–56; MacLeod, *The Canadian Iroquois*, 70–7; Stanley, *New France*, 102.

146 Casgrain, ed., *Collection*, 7: 473–5, "Extrait d'une lettre de M. Du Vernys, officier d'artillerie," 16 September 1758.

147 See Stacey, *Quebec*, 174–8, for a summary of these actions.

148 See Keegan, *The Face of Battle*, ch. 5; Corvisier, "La Mort du soldat."

149 *RAPQ* (1944–45): 136–40, Doreil to the minister, 28 July 1758; *RAPQ* (1923–24): 340, journal of Bougainville, 10 July 1758; AG, A1, 3499, no. 60, Relation.

150 Casgrain, ed., *Collection*, 1: 255–7, 269–71; *RAPQ* (1933–34): 141–7, journal of Lapause, who fulfilled the duties of major. See also AC, C11A, 105: 23 et seq., and Casgrain, ed., *Collection*, 4: 304 et seq.

151 See, e.g., Eccles, *France in America*; Stacey, *Quebec*; Mathieu, *La Nouvelle-France*; Lacoursière, *Histoire populaire du Québec*; and Trudel, *Le Régime militaire*. "Wars in New France were never as deadly as in France," writes André Lachance (*Vivre, aimer et mourir*, 189). He forgets an important dimension: Only a tiny proportion of Frenchmen took part in the war, as soldiers or militiamen, whereas all Canadians were mobilized. To my knowledge, only Christopher Moore ("Colonization and Conflict," 188) poses the question of loss of life during the Seven Years' War, conjecturing a proportion of 10 per cent for the whole population.

152 Henripin, *La Population canadienne*, 12–17; Henripin and Péron, "La transition démographique"; Hubert Charbonneau and R. Cole Harris, "Resettling the St. Lawrence Valley," in Harris, ed., *From the Beginning*, pl. 46; Hubert Charbonneau et al., "La population française de la vallée du Saint-Laurent avant 1760," in Courville, *Atlas historique du Québec*, 31–45; Landry and Lessard, "Les causes de décès."

153 Programme de recherche en démographie historique (https://www.prdh-igd.com/), computerized record of the population of Quebec in the seventeenth and eighteenth centuries, directed by Bertrand Desjardins, assisted by Denis Duval. Montreal, Department of Demography, Université de Montréal, and Gaëtan Morin, c 1999–.

154 I refer here to the census of 1739 and the militia census of 1750, on the one hand, and the census of rural parishes of the government of Quebec of 1762, on the other. For lack of time and resources, I had to abandon this research.

155 The proportion increased with the Napoleonic Wars, but it was not until 1914 that the ratio was reversed. Alain Guéry, "Les comptes"; Corvisier, "La Mort du soldat"; Cornette, *Le Roi de guerre*, 288–90; Parker, *The Military Revolution*, 53–5; Keegan, *A History of Warfare*, 360–1.

156 *Editors' note*: The records in question, among other items, were not found.

157 Anderson, *A People's Army*, 98–9.

158 Ibid., chs. 2–3. In contrast to the Canadian militiamen, however, the New Englanders rarely went on reconnaissance.

159 One would also have to account for Amerindian losses, which are even more poorly known. For a succinct account of this campaign and the

sources relating to it, see *supra*, 200–1 and notes 34–35. See also Rousseau, *L'Oeuvre de chère*, 39.

160 These rounded figures are approximate, of course, but close enough to the reality, since the accounts agree and the general staff did not contradict them.

161 Archives de la Bastille, 12145: 12–35, defence of Péan, July 1762; see also Grenier, ed., *Papiers Contrecoeur, passim,* and *supra*, 258.

162 See, e.g., *RAPQ* (1927–28): 355–429, journal of Léry, 1754.

163 MacLeod, "Microbes and Muskets." A third of the warriors at Sault-Saint-Louis died during the first wave of the epidemic in 1755–56. The presence at Fort Duquesne of a cemetery for smallpox victims as of 1756 shows that the epidemic spread quickly: record of burial of Thomas Proulx of Saint-Thomas, age twenty-one, 5 December 1756; Faribault-Beauregard, ed., *La Population des forts français.*

164 See *supra*, 258–9; also, *Collection de manuscrits*, 4: 164–8, Montcalm to the minister of war, 20 July 1758.

165 BAnQ-Montréal, CN601–S202, minutes of notary G. Hodiesne, 30 January 1760. The deposition was made at the request of Marie-Françoise Arbour, widow of Joseph Sigouin, who wanted to remarry.

166 The custom was that only officers were named in these casualty lists, a distinction that extended to militia officers.

167 Only 250 militiamen took part in the Battle of Carillon, and their losses were conflated with those of the 150 colonial soldiers who fought alongside them: AG, 3499, no 60. On the events of 8 September 1755, see Steele, *Betrayals*, 44–56, and the other references in note 145, *supra*.

168 See *supra*, 274 and note 150. A comparison of the figures given by Lapause and Lévis, to ascertain the number of combatants in each corps, makes it possible to estimate the numbers of casualties.

169 The disparate figures that I found have no basis in fact. There is no official report in the Archives de la Guerre.

170 Stacey (*Quebec*, ch. 8) estimates that the French had some 4,500 combatants on 13 September 1759, the same number as the British. It is known that the five battalions comprised only 1,900 soldiers at the start of the siege: Casgrain, ed., *Collection*, 6: 169, Montcalm to Lévis, 1 July 1759. (The correct figure is the one found in the manuscript, not the erroneous one introduced by the editor.) A minority of militiamen incorporated into the army were with them at the centre, with the majority grouped on either side.

171 Pouchot, *Mémoires*, 2: 110–11, 273–82; Casgrain, ed., *Collection*, 11: 263–71, "Extrait du journal de M. Vauquelin, commandant la frégate

l'*Atalante*, dans le fleuve Saint-Laurent, en 1760." He took sixty militiamen on board to fill out his crew, and they were involved in the battle of 16–17 May, which produced forty-three casualties. There are no accurate figures on the Belle-Famille incident of 24 July 1759. The detachment comprised Illinois warriors, soldiers, and a majority of militiamen mobilized in the spring to fortify the rapids, who then left to join Le Marchand de Lignery at Fort Machault. There were reportedly 500 killed and 100 taken prisoner. Pouchot, *Mémoires*, 2: 3 et seq.; Chagny, *Un défenseur*, 506; Casgrain, ed., *Collection*, 5, 306–8, Montcalm to Bourlamaque, 31 March 1759, on the number of soldiers and militiamen in the Great Lakes region for the 1759 campaign.

172 AG, A1, 3499, no. 30, Daine to minister of war, 13 August 1758.

173 AG, A1, 3417, no. 182, Duchat, captain of Languedoc regiment, to his brother, writing from Carillon, 15 July 1756.

174 Hastings, *A Narrative*, 142–3: the widow Brisson to Mrs Johnson, writing from Quebec, 15 September 1757. The son, Jacques, who would have been eighteen in 1757, probably died: Tanguay, *Dictionnaire généalogique*, 2: 293.

175 Cliche, *Les Pratiques de dévotion*, 68. The parish priest regarded it as a dangerous superstition. Arlette Farge (*Les Fatigues*, 30–1) tells of how a Parisian mother used the same secret to learn her son's fate during the War of the Austrian Succession.

176 LAC, Great Britain, Colonial Office, 42, 24: 52–7v, "list of Canadians who are prisoners of war in Great Britain or Ireland or supposed to be so," Quebec, 8 September 1762. The document is in English. Murray interceded on behalf of the prisoners in his cover letter to the secretary of state but believed that there were fewer of them. See also LAC, MG18–M, series 1, vol. 33, letters from the nuns of the Hôtel-Dieu de Québec to General Murray, September–October 1759, calling for the return of relatives presumed to be held prisoner.

177 In contrast to the practice for country residents, the place and date of disappearance were not recorded for most townspeople. As a side note, the likelihood of finding the prisoners alive after three years of captivity was small, given the high death rate in British prisons.

178 AC, C11A, 95: 346, "Récapitulation des milices du gouvernement général de Canada pour l'année 1750"; *RAPQ* (1925–26): 127–9, "Le Recensement du Gouvernement de Québec en 1762." Included are all men aged fifteen or over, counting servants. The Acadian "refugees" and three "foreigners" are excluded.

179 Farge, *Les Fatigues*, 100.

180 *BRH* 31 (1925): 300, Lebert-Laforce to his in-laws, Carillon, 28 July 1758.
    He referred her to Baptiste, who was returning to Kamouraska on leave
    due to injury or illness.

181 [BAnQ-Montréal], Archives judiciaires, pièces détachées, box 1759–60.
    There is a postscript concerning the rental of a small house, serving as a
    power of attorney for Marie-Joseph Miller to sign a lease at Montreal
    before notary Danré de Blanzy, 9 July 1759. The original of this letter is
    said to have been stolen by a collector and replaced by a copy, whose
    spelling is reproduced although the punctuation is restored to its original
    state. Mathieu Valentin Jacques Miller, born at Paris in 1732, married at
    Montreal on 8 January 1757, a soldier in Boucherville's company in 1759,
    appears to have died in the war. *Editors' note*: This document not found at
    BAnQ-Montréal, since it was a copy and not the original, as the author
    states in her note.

CHAPTER ELEVEN

1 AC, CI IA, 104: 8–18v, Vaudreuil to the minister, January 1759, *passim*.
2 Ibid., 47–52v, "Précis du plan des opérations générales de la campagne de
    1759," 1 April 1759.
3 Casgrain, ed., *Collection*, 7: 307, 313, journal of Montcalm, October
    1757; 6: 67, Montcalm to Lévis, 14 October 1757, in regard to a tour of
    the Côte-de-Beaupré and Cap Tourmente with Pellegrin, port captain, an
    artillery officer, etc., and his report on the measures to be taken for the
    defence of Quebec, which Vaudreuil rejected; 4: 64–74, "Côtes du Sud du
    fleuve Saint-Laurent," anonymous memorandum, 1758; AC, CI IA, 103:
    468–74, memorandum by Bougainville, 29 December 1758.
4 Casgrain, ed., *Collection*, 4: 144–52, Montcalm's comments and
    Vaudreuil's replies in the margin of the latter's plan for the next campaign,
    20–21 March 1759.
5 Stacey, *Quebec*, 50.
6 See *supra*, ch. 1, *passim*, and ch. 5, section 2. Self-glorifying remarks and
    expressions of vanity abound in the official correspondence.
7 *RAPQ* (1944–45): 33, Doreil to the minister, 19 August 1755; see also AG,
    A1, 3417, no. 182, account of Duchat, captain in the Languedoc battalion.
8 "A Faithful Narrative of the Many Dangers and Sufferings as Well as
    Wonderful Delivrance of Robert Eastburn during his Late Captivity
    among the Indians," in Drake, ed., *Tragedies of the Wilderness*, 277.
9 Pouchot, *Mémoires*, 1: 28 et seq. The remark particularly targeted officers
    Péan and Le Mercier, the governor's councillors. Note that these army

officers were, albeit less chauvinistic than those of the colony, just as susceptible to underestimating the Anglo-American forces. Anglophilia had yet to affect the French army.

10 Casgrain, ed., *Collection*, 10: 86–7, Péan to Lévis, Chambly, 13 July 1758, in regard to famine and imminent civil war in Boston. This is the same officer cited below.

11 *RAPQ* (1944–45): 296–7, Abraham Gradis to Moïse Gradis, Bagnères, 26 July 1759. After his mission to Versailles, Péan repaired to this resort town for hydrotherapy, and it was here that Gradis met him.

12 AC, CIIA, 85: 208–15v, Beauharnois to the minister, 10 October 1746. On the debate surrounding the Quebec fortifications just after the fall of Louisbourg in 1745, see *supra*, ch. 7, section 1.

13 AG, AI, 3499, no. 197, Daine, lieutenant général for civil and criminal cases before the provost court of Quebec, to the minister of war, 3 November 1758.

14 *RAPQ* (1970): 71–2, Estèbe to Quebec merchant Jacques Perrault, Bordeaux, 30 January 1759. He left Quebec in the fall.

15 Knox, *An Historical Journal*, 1: 371–3. The British admiral took French skippers on board to help his crew negotiate difficult passages. On reactions in the Côte-du-Sud, see Roy, ed., *Inventaire*, 3: 26 et seq., "Journal de M. de Léry," May–June 1759.

16 *RAPQ* (1920–21): 140–241, anon., "Journal du siège de Québec du 10 mai au 18 septembre 1759." The manuscript was found in the Bibliothèque Saint-Sulpice in Montreal, proving (in conjunction with the personal references in the text itself) that the author, an employee of the king's stores, was indeed from the colony and that "Frenchmen" were not the only ones criticizing the government.

17 As we have seen, the habitants initially rejected this plan, preferring to stay home and defend their families and property; *supra*, 95.

18 AC, CIIA, 81: 141–54v, Beauharnois to the minister, 8 October 1744; 83: 3–36, Beauharnois and Hocquart to the minister, September–October 1745; 85: 101–72v, *passim*, "Extrait en forme de journal de ce qui s'est passé ..." December 1745–November 1746. See also Roy, ed., *Inventaire*, 2: 53–63, "Dispositions pour la défence de Québec et du pays remise à monsieur le marquis de Beauharnois ... au commencement de l'année 1745, par monsieur de Léry, premier ingénieur," and "Dispositions de la manoeuvre que feront les brulots," also given to Beauharnois.

19 The orders to build fire ships, fire rafts, and cabins in the woods went out in early April 1746. Note also the distribution of munitions and provisions

in the parishes and the efforts expended to perfect the watch system (sources mentioned in preceding note).

20 See Stacey, *Quebec*, ch. 3, for a detailed analysis of these movements.

21 A very approximate figure, since there was no census between 1739 and 1762. I assume 14,000 habitants from Lévis and downriver on the south shore and from Beauport on the north, which would make 2,800 families at five individuals per family.

22 Casgrain, ed., *Collection*, 1: 175–6, journal of Lévis, [May] 1759.

23 The sending of 1,000–1,200 militiamen from the government of Quebec to Carillon was part of Vaudreuil's plan: AC, CIIA, 104: 47–52v; see also *RAPQ* (1928–29): 29–30, Nicolas Renaud d'Avène Des Méloizes, "Journal militaire tenu par Nicolas Renaud d'Avène Des Méloizes, Ch^{er}, seigneur de Neuville au Canada," 19 July–30 October 1756 and 8 May–21 November 1759, on the various troop and militia movements south and west of Montreal; also Stacey, *Quebec*, 58–9.

24 *RAPQ* (1924–25): 147, anon., "Mémoire du Canada."

25 AC, CIIA, 104: 79–83, Vaudreuil to the minister, 8 May 1759, concerning the orders to the downriver parishes; Roy, ed., *Inventaire*, 3: 26–39, journal of Léry, May–June 1759. He arrived in Rivière-Ouelle on 21 May at the same time as the governor's letter.

26 MCQ, Fonds d'archives du Séminaire de Québec, "Lettre de Vaudreuil à un capitaine de milice," 4 May 1759, polygraphie 18, no. 64. The orders have not survived, but they are well summarized in Léry's instructions, also dated 4 May: LAC, MG18–M (Northcliffe Collection), series 1, 24: 195–6.

27 "You must see that, in the evacuation, there are none but women, children and the sick who follow the animals": LAC, MG18–M, series 1, 24: 200, Vaudreuil to Montesson, 31 May 1759, and the corresponding orders, 24: 195–6.

28 Roy, ed., *Inventaire*, 3: 26–39, journal of Léry, May–June 1759. Quebec sent six boats for the crossing of the Ouelle, with the Rivière-du-Sud and the Boyer still to come.

29 Ibid., 3: 28, 23 May 1759. Montesson commanded the operations between Sainte-Anne and Lévis, Léry those of the downriver parishes, Rivière-Ouelle, Kamouraska, and Le Portage. Both were captains in the colonial regulars.

30 Ibid., 3: 32, 1 June 1759; LAC, MG18–M, series 1, 24: 210, Vaudreuil to Léry, 31 May 1759.

31 After the landing at Beaumont on 29 June, Léry's papers – his journal and the letters he'd received from Vaudreuil – fell into the hands of the British, who preserved them.

32 Roy, ed., *Inventaire*, 3: 33–4, journal of Léry, 3, 6, and 10 June 1759. The men were finally authorized to go tend to their families, and 110 Montreal militiamen came to guard the côte in their stead.

33 Ibid., 3: 35–6, 15 June 1759. Vaudreuil was incapable of working out the details of an operation, as the army officers repeatedly noted. In this source, one of his own officers could not contain his exasperation. Gaston Deschênes (*L'Année des Anglais*) offers an interpretation of the facts based on that of Vaudreuil, not taking issue with the latter's orders, but ascribing the difficulties to insouciance and restiveness on the part of the habitants, depicted by the governor and the author as capricious children.

34 Deschênes, *L'Année des Anglais*, 54. See also Knox, *An Historical Journal*, 1: 386–90.

35 On the forced evacuation of Île-aux-Coudres by Charles-François Tarieu de La Naudière and a detachment of 300 men, see "Le siège de Québec," in Hébert, *Le Siège*, 55–7.

36 On the wrongs done by Saint-Vincent, the officer responsible for the evacuation of Île d'Orléans, three witnesses concur: "Le siège de Québec," in Hébert, ed., *Le Siège*, 55–6; RAPQ (1920–21): 147–8, anon., "Journal du siège de Québec," 8–11 June 1759; Panet, *Journal*, 5.

37 Archives de l'Université de Montréal, Baby Collection, P58/P2, 57 (and microfiche 2575), order issued by Vaudreuil to La Naudière to lead the families and animals of the Côte-de-Beaupré to Lake St Charles, 1 June 1759; P58/K, 27–8 (and microfiche 2387), ordinance issued by Vaudreuil and Bigot to the habitants of the downstream parishes to bring their cattle to the military warehouses of La Canardière and the Jacques-Cartier River, published 7 and 15 June.

38 At Quebec, the evacuation of "extra mouths to feed" was recommended but not required. It was mostly the better-off citizens who were able to put their families out of harm's way. Outsiders appear in the registers as parents at their child's baptism or among the deceased. For more details on the source, see *infra*, note 42.

39 Têtu and Gagnon, eds, *Mandements*, 2: 137–41, circular from the bishop dated 5 June and another letter from the vicar-general to the clergy of the imperiled parishes, n.d. (illegibly dated in this edition, it was written ca. 18–22 June).

40 Knox, *An Historical Journal, passim*; Fraser, *Extract* (copy in the McCord Museum of Canadian History, Montreal, M. 22060).

41 LAC, MG18–M, series 1, vol. 21, Goreham to Wolfe, 19 August 1759.

42 Charbonneau and Légaré, eds, *Répertoire*, vols. 32–35. Viewing the transcriptions as opposed to the originals deprived me of information on the

appearance of the documents (condition of registers, detached sheets, etc.) that could have been useful but would not have solved the other problems. Interruptions are harder to detect in the sparsely populated parishes – the majority – where notarial records are often sporadic. The series of baptisms is the most complete. Note too that peasants did not marry in the summer, so the lack of marriages between May and October 1759 is not significant.

43 Kamouraska, Rivière-Ouelle, Islet Bonsecours, Pointe-Lévy, Île-aux-Coudres, and the five Île d'Orléans parishes.

44 Sainte-Anne de la Côte-du-Sud, Saint-Thomas, Beaumont, Saint-Joachim, and Château-Richer. The priests received orders to take church belongings with them when retreating: see *supra*, note 42. "The registers for 21 January 1759 to 8 September 1759 were carried off by the English, who took them in the woods," wrote the priest of Saint-Thomas (22 September).

45 This number does not include those of the Saint-Nicolas, Saint-Antoine, and Sainte-Croix parishes upriver from Quebec, which did not receive evacuation orders. When the British landed there in mid-August, the habitants fled into the forest.

46 See Stacey, *Quebec*, ch. 4–5, *passim*. At first made up of 600 militiamen, soldiers, and Amerindians, the detachment was increased to 1,000 men on 6 August, and Bougainville took over command from Dumas.

47 My interpretation coincides with that of Stacey and diverges from that of Eccles ("The Battle of Quebec: a Reappraisal," in *Essays on New France*, 125–33), who believed that the French had no reason for pessimism as to the outcome of the campaign and the Battle of Quebec.

48 *RAPQ* (1938–39): 1–9, journal of Fournerie de Vezon, "Événements de la guerre du Canada depuis le 13 septembre 1759 jusqu'au 14 juillet 1760"; Casgrain, ed., *Collection*, 1: 220 et seq., journal of Lévis, September–October 1759; Knox, *An Historical Journal*, vol. 2, *passim*; AC, F3, 16: 12–19, Vaudreuil to the minister, 15 April 1760.

49 AC, F3, 15: 280, Vaudreuil to the minister, 5 October 1759, on the subject of such women, although this is not confirmed by other sources. See Knox, *An Historical Journal, passim*; *RAPQ* (1920–21): 191, anon., "Journal du siège du 10 mai au 18 septembre 1759," 19 August, on prisoners taken by habitants. Wolfe wrote to Holderness on 9 September 1759, "Old people of seventy years and boys of fifteen fire at our detachments from the edge of the woods, killing or wounding our men": cited in Frégault, *Canada*, 245.

50 LAC, MG18–M, series 1, vol. 28, Vaudreuil to the militia captain and priest of Baie Saint-Paul, 18 and 23 July and 1 August 1759; to the priest of

Saint-Joachim, 20 August; to M. de la Haussaye, militia officer and priest of Saint-Michel, 27 August; to the priest of Saint-Charles, 28 August. The correspondence was continual, almost daily in some cases.

51 Only the Côte-de-Beaupré received reinforcements: Casgrain, ed., *Collection*, 8: 71–2, Vaudreuil to Lévis, 28 July 1759; Vaudreuil to parish priest Portneuf [?], cited in the preceding note.

52 ARC (1905), vol. 1, 4th part, 12–48, correspondence between Dumas and Vaudreuil, 6 March–27 June 1760, *passim*; Knox, *An Historical Journal*, 2: 272.

53 Casgrain, ed., *Collection*, 4: 273–6, copy of placard by James Wolfe posted on the door of Saint-Laurent church on Île d'Orléans, 27 June 1759. The British handed out copies wherever they set foot. It was the first in a series of at least eight placards directed at the general public that were posted between July 1759 and August 1760.

54 During the seventeenth- and eighteenth-century wars, Europeans engaged in prisoner exchanges according to rules of reciprocity between soldiers and officers. The practice existed in North America, and until 1759 the militiamen of New France, like those of the British colonies, were considered prisoners of war and exchanged, albeit at a lesser value than regulars. See AC, CIIA, 103: 91–2, 95–9, correspondence between Vaudreuil and Abercrombie, 24 April and 4 June 1758, in regard to the exchange of Jacques Corriveau, militia captain; see also RAPQ (1933–34): 104, journal of Lapause, 25 July 1759, on Vaudreuil's protestations when Murray denied prisoner of war status to militiamen captured in the Côte-de-Beaupré.

55 See Casgrain, ed., *Collection*, 4: 273 et seq. for the other placards, in particular pp. 280–2 for the one dated 14 November 1759.

56 Knox, *An Historical Journal*, 1: 431, 433, 441. It need hardly be mentioned that the excuse of Amerindians threatening reprisals was a complete and utter fiction.

57 Ibid., 1: 379, order of 28 June 1759.

58 Ibid., 1: 400, order of 5 July 1759 in which Wolfe reminded his soldiers to bring animals, etc., taken during the campaigns to the army's storehouses and refrain from destroying houses and churches unless he ordered them to do so.

59 Ibid., 1: 385, 441 (in note); Serjeant-major of Gen. Hopson's grenadiers, *A Journal of the Expedition up the River St. Lawrence*.

60 Ibid., 2: 273 (in note), excerpt from journal of Murray, 13 November 1759.

61 Fraser, *Extract*, entry for 1 July 1759.

62 Stacey, *Quebec*, 23–6; *idem*, "Scott, George," DCB, 3: 637–8. Each company normally comprised 100 men, so there would have been 600 rangers in Wolfe's army. On the founding of this corps, see *supra*, 209. On the ranger corps in general, see Jennings, *Empire of Fortune*, 199.

63 Order from Montmorency dated 27 July, cited in Knox, *An Historical Journal*, 1: 438. Whether it was a new regulation or a reminder is not known.

64 It is impossible to quantify the skirmishes and the number of casualties. The officers reported only a few. Knox (*An Historical Journal*, 1: 385) mentions a fight between rangers and colonial regulars at Beaumont on 30 June, at the end of which seven French soldiers were killed and scalped.

65 Pouchot, *Mémoires*, 1: 89.

66 The references are in the archives of criminal cases. See, e.g., Dechêne, *Habitants and Merchants*, 217, for the case of young nobles in Montreal (ca. 1683) who disguised themselves as Indians to rob passersby.

67 Knox, *An Historical Journal*, 2: 42–5; "Journal de l'expédition sur le fleuve Saint-Laurent par un militaire de l'armée de Wolfe," in Hébert, *Le Siège*, 42; Fraser, *Extract*, entry for 23 August. This operation was not commanded by an officer of the rangers but by Captain Montgomery of the 43rd regiment.

68 Knox, *An Historical Journal*, 1: 439–41, on the movements of Dalling and Fraser, who, in addition to prisoners, brought back many animals. The order was from Brigadier Monckton, commandant at Pointe-Lévy, acting for General Wolfe, as shown by the phrasing of the placard that followed.

69 See Knox, *An Historical Journal*, 1: 441, remark by Le Mercier during a ceasefire on the cost of feeding the prisoners on the boats.

70 AC, CIIA, 104: 309–10v. This is the Saint-Henri copy, the only one found. See "Le siège de Québec," in Hébert, ed., *Le Siège*, 101.

71 LAC, MG18–M, series 1, vol. 21, report of Captain Joseph Goreham to Wolfe, August 1759. With 300 men, he destroyed all the houses up to La Malbaie between 8 and 15 August.

72 "Le siège de Québec," in Hébert, ed., *Le Siège*, 112; AC, CIIA, 104: 193, anon., "Journal tenu à l'armée." To be visible from Quebec, the fires on the south shore must have been near Saint-Michel and Beaumont. No details of these latter operations, or of those carried out on Île d'Orléans, are known.

73 Knox, *An Historical Journal*, 2: 14–15 (in note); Serjeant-major of Gen. Hopson's grenadiers, *A Journal of the Expedition up the River St. Lawrence*. Murray's brigade was responsible for the fires and destruction upriver from Pointe-Lévy.

74 Fraser, *Extract*, entries for 23 August to 1 September. Montgomery went to Saint-Joachim on 17 August with a small detachment that was subsequently reinforced twice.

75 LAC, MG18–M, series 1, vol. 21. Since the number of houses or households in these parishes in 1759 is unknown, it is pointless to dwell on Scott's figures. He notes 998 "good buildings" [houses or barns?] destroyed.

76 Deschênes, *L'Année des Anglais*, 66–84. The author ventures some interesting but nonetheless unverifiable hypotheses. Recall that some of these parishes had already been burned in August. *Editors' note*: In the foreword to the second edition of the book (Quebec: Septentrion, 2001, ix–x), Deschênes adduces a source according to which young women from Sainte-Anne-de-la-Pocatière disguised themselves as men to fire on British soldiers who were burning habitants' barns.

77 Montgomery had been unable to burn the unripe wheat in the Côte-de-Beaupré, and the habitants came to harvest it in early September, protected by French troops, after the British army's departure. Serjeant-major of Gen. Hopson's grenadiers, *A Journal of the Expedition up the River St. Lawrence*, 23 August 1759; "Le siège de Québec," in Hébert, ed., *Le Siège*, 115; Knox, *An Historical Journal*, 2: 136.

78 AC, C11A 104: 366–70v, bishop of Quebec to the minister, 9 November 1759, and his "Description imparfaite de la misère du Canada" of 5 November 1759; Récher, *Journal*.

79 Letter of 10 August 1759, cited in Frégault, *Canada*, 245.

80 The few cases reported in British officers' journals are certainly not a complete account of the tortures inflicted on militiamen captured with weapons in hand, but it is impossible to ascertain the number of such reprisals.

81 AC, C11A, 104: 318–27, memorandum from Jean-Baptiste-Nicolas-Roch de Ramezay, "hereinafter king's lieutenant, commandant at Quebec, on the surrender of this city," n.d. [1759–60]. It was Ramezay who specified that the city took some time to realize that the tents were empty.

82 AC, C11A, 104: 331v–33, petition from the townspeople and citizens of Quebec and the hawkers (*marchands forains*), n.d. [14 September], with twenty-two signatures; see also AC, A1, 3540, nos. 101–2, Daine, lieutenant-general of the provost court for civil and criminal cases, to the minister of war, 9 October and 22 September 1759.

83 AC, C11A, 104: 318–27, memorandum from Ramezay.

84 There were about 1,500 combatants in the city, a third of them militiamen. On the morale of this garrison, see the memorandum from Ramezay

cited in the preceding note; Casgrain, ed., *Collection*, 10: 111–14, de Bernetz to Lévis, 18 and 20 September 1759, and AC, CIIA, 104: 390–93v, Foligné, "Journal mémoratif de ce qui s'est passé de plus remarquable pendant qu'a duré le siège de la ville de Québec."

85 AC, CIIA, 104: 390–93v, Foligné, "Journal mémoratif," cited in preceding note; RAPQ (1931–32): 101–2, Lapause papers, for a copy of the articles of capitulation.

86 ARC (1918), Appendix B, 1, proclamation of 22 September 1759.

87 AC, CIIA, 104: 393v, Foligné, "Journal mémoratif," cited *supra*, note 84.

88 AC, CIIA 104: 366–70v, bishop of Quebec to the minister, 9 November 1759, and his "Description imparfaite de la misère du Canada" of 5 November 1759.

89 The capitulation of Quebec concerned the city only, so the delimitation of the boundary between the two armies depended on the balance of forces. On troop movements and clashes that fall and winter, see RAPQ (1938–39): 1–9, journal of Fournerie de Vezon; Casgrain, ed., *Collection*, 1: 220 et seq., journal of Lévis, September–October 1759; Knox, *An Historical Journal*, 2: 336 (in note), letter from Murray of 24 December 1759, stating that the occupation did not go beyond the Cap Rouge and Chaudière rivers.

90 Casgrain, ed., *Collection*, 4: 278–80, orders to the priest and militia officers of Sainte-Foy, 14 and 21 October 1759; AC, F3, 16: 17v, Vaudreuil to the minister, 26 March 1760.

91 Knox, *An Historical Journal*, 2: 134, 137, 159. See also ARC (1912), Appendix 1, 84–7, inventory of General Murray's correspondence, 1759–60.

92 Knox, *An Historical Journal*, 2: 475, which also contains a description of the ceremony held at Saint-Antoine in July 1760. The French text recited by the habitants has not survived.

93 ARC (1918), Appendix B, 7, placard by Murray, 26 February 1760. For the troop movements, see Casgrain, ed., *Collection*, 1: 226–42, journal of Lévis, October 1759–March 1760. Some houses in Sainte-Foy were burned down as well.

94 The letters from Vaudreuil to the militia officers and parish priests of the government of Quebec and Lévis's orders at the outset of the siege, on 28 April, obviously influenced the habitants. See Knox, *An Historical Journal*, 2: 429, which notes the return of a large number of Canadians to the northern and southern parishes on 16–17 May and mentions a letter from Lévis begging Murray not to punish these men because they had been forced to come to the siege and had not taken part in the fighting.

95 AC, CIIA, 105: 64–64v, manifesto issued by General Murray, 20 May 1760; another copy dated 22 May is found in ARC (1918), Appendix B, 9–10.

96 The exemplary value of the three convictions described here has eluded historians, in particular Marcel Trudel (*Le Régime militaire*, 27), who suggested that Duchesnay was not the seigneur of Beauport, but his son, a young man of twenty who was an ensign in the colonial regulars. This makes no sense since, as an officer, he could not have taken an oath of neutrality, and moreover he owned nothing.

97 Knox, *An Historical Journal*, 2: 453–7. The sentence of 30 May 1760 was enforced immediately. "It is reported that ... the captain at Saint-Charles was hanged," wrote Dumas to Vaudreuil on 31 May: ARC (1905), vol. 1, 4th part, 29. The presence of Lévis's order of 28 April to this same Captain Nadeau of Saint-Charles in the Archives de la Guerre (AG, 3574, no. 31) remains unexplained. The seizure of the property of Antoine Juchereau Duchesnay (1704–72) probably took place in early June, simultaneous with the priest's arrest. On 2 July 1760, Murray made a gift of it to two of his officers: Archives de l'Université de Montréal, Baby Collection, P58/P2, 64 (and microfiche 2576). Later, these arrangements were cancelled. Duchesnay regained his seigneury, the priest his freedom.

98 Knox, *An Historical Journal*, 2: 374. The order is dated 21 April and these people had three days to prepare for departure. On 2 July, they were authorized to make a brief trip to the city to collect any remaining belongings: 2: 463 and 3: 307, journal of Murray.

99 Ibid., 3: 307, journal of Murray.

100 At first Murray had only 2,800 soldiers. Along the way he received reinforcements from Louisbourg, about 1,000 men. See Frégault, *Canada*, 281 et seq.

101 Casgrain, ed., *Collection*, 4: 284–5, placard by Murray [initial date 13 June], 23 July 1760. The following information is mostly taken from the journals of Knox and Murray and from the correspondence between Bourlamaque and Lévis (Casgrain, ed., *Collection*, vol. 5) as well as the latter's journal (ibid., vol. 1).

102 Knox, *An Historical Journal*, 2: 512–14. This new placard mentioned by the British officer has not survived.

103 AC, F3, 16: 111–14, 121–6, Bigot and Vaudreuil to the minister, 2 and 10 September 1760; journal of Major Robert Rogers, commander of the rangers, cited in Stanley, *New France*, 254–5.

104 A false rumour that was not dispelled for several days. See Knox, *An Historical Journal*, 2: 514–15; MacLeod, *The Canadian Iroquois*, 173–6.

105 *RAPQ* (1924–25): 147, anon., "Mémoire du Canada"; Casgrain, ed.,
     Collection, 5: 286, 289, Montcalm to Bourlamaque, 7 and 11 March
     1759.
106 See Stacey, *Quebec*, 59, and Stanley, *New France*, 294n19. The estimate
     is based on all accounts of the operations. If it is assumed (and this is
     probable) that 15,229 includes all men ages fifteen to sixty, the 11,000
     participants would amount to 72 per cent of the total. Recall that the
     colony's last census dated back to 1739. For there to be a population of
     70,000 twenty years later, the pace of growth could not have flagged
     during the war. I think it did and that this generally accepted figure is
     too high.
107 AC, CIIA, 104: 268, Foligné, "Journal mémoratif," cited *supra*, note 84.
     There are no reliable estimates of the numbers of militiamen at Beauport,
     given the confusion with the colonial regulars. The figures presented here
     are those of Montcalm: Casgrain, ed., *Collection*, 6: 166–72, Montcalm to
     Lévis, 1 and 3 July 1759.
108 Casgrain, ed., *Collection*, 4: 171–4, regulation issued by Vaudreuil, 1 June
     1759; 2: 283–90, 348–50, circulars from Lévis to army commanders,
     25 and 29 March, 16 April, and 14 June 1760; 8: 160–1, Vaudreuil to
     Lévis, 24 April 1760. See also *supra*, ch. 10, section 3, "The Militia and
     the regulars."
109 See *supra*, Table 10.1 for the distribution of soldiers' housing.
110 See *supra*, ch. 10, 278 and note 171.
111 Pouchot, *Mémoires*, 1: 40–111. The garrison consisted of 486 men,
     including 133 militiamen.
112 Steele, *Warpaths*, 216–17; Stanley, *New France*, 215–19; Casgrain, ed.,
     Collection, 1: 188–92, journal of Lévis, [July] 1759.
113 Casgrain, ed., *Collection*, 5: 13–81, Bourlamaque to Vaudreuil, Rigaud,
     and Lévis, 7 August–18 November 1759; Stanley, *New France*, 234 et seq.
114 Stanley, *New France*, ch. 17; Casgrain, ed., *Collection*, 11: 263–71,
     "Extrait du journal de M. Vauquelin, commandant la frégate l'*Atalante*,
     dans le fleuve saint-Laurent, en 1760." The king's two ships and the other
     ships carrying the army's supplies sank at Neuville and were burned, the
     Atalante after a violent battle. The crew of 170 men included sixty
     militiamen.
115 Stanley, *New France*, ch. 17, 254 in particular.
116 This is mentioned in Anderson, *A People's Army* (153–5), based on the
     correspondence and journals of New England militiamen who served on
     Lake Champlain.
117 Pouchot, *Mémoires*, 1: 92–3, entry for 6 May 1757.

118 *RAPQ* (1928–29): 8 et seq., Nicolas Renaud d'Avène Des Méloizes, "Journal militaire ..." Carillon, August 1756.
119 Casgrain, ed., *Collection*, 7: 511, journal of Montcalm, 1 May 1759.
120 *RAPQ* (1928–29): 76–8, Nicolas Renaud d'Avène Des Méloizes, "Journal militaire ..." September 1759.
121 ARC (1905), vol. 1, 4th part, 39, Vaudreuil to Dumas, 1 June 1760.
122 Ibid., 25, Dumas to Vaudreuil, 12 April 1760.
123 Casgrain, ed., *Collection*, 5: 32, Bourlamaque to Lévis, Île-aux-Noix, 13 August 1759. Around 1,000 militiamen, arriving from the government of Quebec in early spring, served in Bourlamaque's army. At Beauport, it was the militiamen of the government of Montreal, worried about their crops and fearing an attack via Lake Ontario, who deserted the army in large numbers: AC, C I I A, 104: 286–7, Foligné, "Journal mémoratif," cited *supra*, note 84.
124 Lachance, "La désertion."
125 Casgrain, ed., *Collection*, 5: 109, Bourlamaque to Lévis, Saint-Ours, 26 August 1760.
126 Casgrain, ed., *Collection*, 2: 323–6, Lévis to Vaudreuil, 25 May 1760; AC, F3, 16: 115, Vaudreuil to the minister, 29 August 1760. The regular officers were authorized to announce the proclamation but not to enforce the sentence without the approval of Vaudreuil, whose indulgence was well known.
127 Bourlamaque began calling for this proclamation in August 1759 when he was the commander on Île-aux-Noix; in 1760, he often revisited the subject in his correspondence with Lévis: Casgrain, ed., *Collection*, 5: 32, 13 August 1759, and 87 et seq., p. 91 in particular, August 1760.
128 ARC (1905), vol. 1, 4th part, 36, Dumas to Vaudreuil, Jacques-Cartier, 27 June 1760. Sitting at the edge of the occupied zone, Sainte-Croix was particularly vulnerable, and its militia refused to leave the parish to follow the army. Other officers used the threat of fire, which had served the British so well, but there is no evidence that they made good on it, as Frégault asserts: Casgrain, ed., *Collection*, 5: 103, Bellot to Bourlamaque, Sorel, 22 August 1760; Frégault, *Canada*, 286.
129 Casgrain, ed., *Collection*, 2: 323–6, Lévis to Vaudreuil, 25 May 1760; ARC (1905), vol. 1, 4th part, 27–8, Dumas to Vaudreuil, Jacques-Cartier, 18 April 1760, in regard to Captain Villeneuve and Jean Trépanier, assistant town major of Batiscan, who had deserted with the other habitants of that parish. In citing this anecdote out of its military context, Colin Coates (*The Metamorphoses*, 89) gives it a meaning it does not possess.
130 See *supra*, 250.

131 According to the assessment of Dumas, who had no powers of coercion and had to rely on good will: ARC (1905), vol. 1, 4th part, 21, Dumas to Vaudreuil, 28 March 1760. See also *supra*, 274, for the proportion of militiamen in Lévis's army who participated in the battle of 28 April.

132 Pouchot, *Mémoires*, 2: 261 et seq. The siege caused sixty casualties on the French side. Pouchot lauded his garrison, with its sixty militiamen, for standing firm.

CHAPTER TWELVE

Editors' note: As Thomas Wien explains in the foreword (p. xxvii), this chapter is the one that came to us in its least finished form. It consisted of an introduction plus four parts with no predetermined order and a section that we moved to chapter 11. In addition, several notes in the margin of the text suggested the need for nuance or highlighted areas of uncertainty. Many of the references were incomplete or lacking. Finally, in some instances, the order in which the arguments were presented did not conform to the stated outline and there was more than one version of certain passages. The editing entailed deletion of incomplete argumentative passages, completion of telegraphically written sentences, addition of logical transitions where needed, and some reconfiguration to restore the coherence that the author would have given to the text if she had revised it. Sylvie Dépatie took charge of this work. As a result, readers may find that the chapter does not always reflect the style of the author; we have not indicated all the changes made to the text, although a good many are mentioned in the notes.

1 *Editors' note*: An attitude clearly evinced in Eccles, "The Social, Economic and Political Significance." Eccles contends, in part, that given the frequency of armed conflict, the military mentality was a characteristic feature of the colony. He posits a process of percolation of the mindset of the military officers down into the lower strata of society, without posing the problem of social relations. Other historians subscribe to this point of view: see Steele, *Warpaths*, 73, 75 (where the author contrasts the Canadian militiamen's obedience with the Virginians' resistance), 77; *idem*, *Betrayals*, 47. Eccles (*The Canadian Frontier*, 102), after having compared the levels of development of cultural institutions in Canada and the American colonies, writes: "In short New France was the Sparta, not the Athens of North America."

2 *Editors' note*: See, among others, Greer, "L'Habitant"; Wien, "Les conflits sociaux." Dickinson (*Justice*, 121–3) mentions more than 150 cases

relating to seigneurial rights under the jurisdiction of the provost court of Quebec alone.

3   Anderson, *A People's Army*, 38–9. At the end of each campaign, militiamen received a substantial sum composed of their accrued wages and an enrolment bonus equaling a month's pay or at times more. The author values these benefits at fifteen livres on average, or about what a Canadian peasant determined not to march would pay to be replaced. See *supra*, 65 and note 38.

4   *Editors' note*: In the margin next to the title of this section, Dechêne wrote: "rewrite and link to the 'volunteers.' See Greer's articles on the mutiny. People volunteered for the booty. True of soldiers and also, no doubt, militiamen." The author refers here to volunteers engaged in specific military operations, such as the March 1744 attack on the British post at Canso under the authority of the governor of Louisbourg, involving eighty colonial regulars and thirty-seven "Swiss" soldiers from the Karrer regiment, who volunteered in exchange for a promised share of the loot. Greer, "Mutiny at Louisbourg, December 1744" and "Another Soldiers' Revolt in Isle Royale, June 1750," in Krause, Corbin, and O'Shea, eds, *Aspects of Louisbourg*, 70–109 and 110–14, respectively. On looting, see also *supra*, 260.

5   See Pote, *The Journal*, 1 et seq.

6   See the various accounts in AC, C I IA, 83: 3 et seq., 156 et seq., and 173–81, as well as 84: 103–07v.

7   They did not always do so honestly, however. Pouchot reported that officers and employees at Fort Frontenac kept for themselves a portion of the Oswego loot belonging to the king: Pouchot, *Mémoires*, 68.

8   AC, C I IA, 115: 150–228, statement for 1745; 116: 91–140, statement for 1748.

9   See AC, C I IA, 116: 91–140, statement for 1748, where a line item reads "ransom of English prisoners and scalps"; AC, C I IA, 85: 284 et seq., statement of supplies to the Ouiatenons for 1743–46. The bounty had not increased since the seventeenth century. On this subject, see BRH 21 (1915): 187–9. The British colonies, with smaller numbers of Indigenous troops, had to offer these bounties to the colonists: Axtell and Sturtevant, "The Unkindest Cut."

10 Morton, *A Military History*, 5. The author no doubt relied on the account of an American colonist according to whom Raimbault, a cadet in the colonial regulars, while leading a party of Abenakis on the Boston coast, had scalped one man himself. See Drake, ed., *Tragedies of the Wilderness*, 89. To my knowledge, there is nothing else. Moreover, if the militia had

scalped the dead, the French army officers would certainly have reported it, since these practices scandalized them and they were not in the habit of sparing the reputation of the colonial troops. On this issue, see *supra*, 106–7. *Editors' note*: A more recent contribution by Jean-François Lozier ("Lever des chevelures," 526) reiterates Morton's position.

11 Léry's troops, composed of seventy-six soldiers, 110 Amerindians, and 166 carefully chosen militiamen, committed a massacre: RAPQ (1926–27): 372 et seq., journal of Léry, February 1756. As to the Palatine village, fifteen soldiers, 300 Canadian volunteers, and 200 Amerindians took part in its destruction and that of its inhabitants: journal of Picoté de Belestre, October–November 1757, in Casgrain, ed., *Collection*, 11: 127–42, and journal of Montcalm, 7: 305; AG, A1, 3498, no. 85, letter from Daine, 19 May 1758, on exaggerated reports of the quantity of booty; AC, C11A, 104: 127–33, letter from Vaudreuil, 28 November 1759, on waste, "fearing being pursued."

12 AG, A1, 3417, no. 208, Montcalm to the minister, 28 August 1756; journal of Montcalm, Casgrain, ed., *Collection*, 7: 292. See also Pouchot, *Mémoires*, 38, on the Monongahela victory in July 1755: "all the belongings of the officers, who were well equipped, to which the Natives and Canadians helped themselves."

13 Lapause described the confusion at Oswego, where the whole army, soldiers included, took part in the looting: RAPQ (1931–32): 33–4. On the British side, by contrast, after the taking of Fort Frontenac, the considerable booty was brought to Fort Bull and shared out among the 2,700 men involved in the action, each receiving a value of thirteen £: Anderson, *A People's Army*, 158–9. But order did not always reign, and Anderson describes the looting of corpses on the battlefield as an ordinary practice.

14 See AC, C11A, 84: 142–44v, for payments to the habitants of the Lévis and Rivière-du-Loup parishes; or C11A, 71: 146 et seq., for similar payments in the vicinity of Montreal on the departure of a war party to fight the Chickasaws in 1739. *Editors' note*: On this issue, see *supra*, 250.

15 *Editors' note*: The author wrote in the margin next to this sentence: "[Their motivations] were not unrelated to their unwillingness to march." This remark clearly alludes to the indifference shown by the authorities, when raising militias, toward the demands of agricultural labour. See *supra*, 220–1, 250, 272–3, 305–6.

16 Têtu and Gagnon, eds, *Mandements*, 2: 34–146 for Pontbriand's pastoral letters from 1744 to 1760. Lacelle, in *Monseigneur Henry-Marie Dubreuil de Pontbriand*, found several unpublished pastoral letters and circulars and reproduced them in an appendix; these include the circulars of

14 May 1746, 14 July 1753, and summer 1755 as well as the pastoral letters of 9 August 1755, 1756 (to the domiciliés), [October] 1756, 21 February 1757, and 31 May 1759. In total, the analysis that follows uses twenty-three pastoral letters and eight circulars to the parish priests concerning these pastoral letters and to various measures to be taken in regard to the war.

17 See Gilot, "Le souvenir." The author counted twenty-three *Te Deums* in France from 1744 to the signing of the peace accord in 1749. Since news only reached the colony once a year, the victories and the celebrations were telescoped.

18 The bishop was particularly devoted to the interests of the Vaudreuil family, and there is no other explanation for the *Te Deum* ordered in celebration of the sacking of boats and sheds by a big detachment commanded by the governor's brother, for an operation so obscure and undistinguished did not deserve mention among the great victories. See Montcalm's criticism. *Editors' note*: Exact reference not found.

19 The *Te Deums* were sung to the noise of cannon fire from the city and the ships in the port. These were days of rejoicing. See AC, CIIA, 85: 206, letter from Beauharnois, 7 October 1746.

20 Casgrain, ed., *Collection*, 7: 510, journal of Montcalm, on the pastoral letter of 18 April 1759 that spoke openly of the danger.

21 *RAPQ* (1928–29): 78, Nicolas Renaud d'Avène Des Méloizes, "Journal militaire tenu par Nicolas Renaud d'Avène Des Méloizes, Ch[er], seigneur de Neuville au Canada," 19 July–30 October 1756 and 8 May–21 November 1759.

22 AC, CIIA, 87: 363–7, circular from Vaudreuil to the militia captains dated 30 May 1760 and distributed that week; the fact is reported with great irony by an anonymous contemporary chronicler, in *RAPQ* (1924–25): 175.

23 *ARC*, (1905), vol. 1, 4th part, 39, Vaudreuil to Dumas, 1 June 1760; Vaudreuil to Dumas, 3 June, in regard to the above-cited circular.

24 Casgrain, ed., *Collection*, 10: 87, Péan to Lévis, 13 July 1758, in regard to the famished, rebellious colonists of New England who sought French protection, according to three Acadians who had escaped from Boston. Pouchot, *Mémoires*, 55, on the rumour that Louis XV had been assassinated: "On 6 May [1757], an Iroquois Native and an Englishmen living among them came to Niagara. They told M. Pouchot that the king of France had been killed and that the king of Prussia had taken the queen of Hungary, although no ship had yet arrived from France. [Pouchot] found this news so extraordinary that he felt duty-bound to inform M. de

Vaudreuil. It was verified that the king had been wounded and that the queen of Poland had been arrested by the king of Prussia."

25 Grenier, ed., *Papiers Contrecoeur*, 226, Duquesne to Contrecoeur, 25 July 1754.

26 Delumeau, *La Peur en Occident*, 174–6.

27 *RAPQ* (1924–25): 168, anonymous memorandum on the reaction to the news of Quebec's capitulation in September 1759.

28 *Editors' note*: On the question of identity, see Horguelin, "Le XVIIIe siècle."

29 Pote, *The Journal*, 158. Passage reproduced nearly verbatim in another (anonymous) prisoner's diary: "The Journal of a Captive," 87. There is no way of knowing whether the reported remarks are true or false.

30 *Editors' note*: The incident is related in Wien, "Les Conflits sociaux."

31 Thwaites, ed., *The Jesuit Relations*, 69: 150–98, "Account of the Voyage on the Beautiful River Made in 1749, under the Direction of Monsieur de Celoron, by Father Bonnecamps": "In the evening [of 25 August], there was a bonfire to celebrate the feast of St. Louis. All the detachment was under arms; they fired three volleys of musketry, preceded by several cries of *Vive le Roy!*" (quote on 181). Macarty to Vaudreuil, 2 September 1752, in Pease and Jenison, eds, *Illinois*, 702, stating that they had celebrated the feast of St Louis by drinking the health of the king; ibid., 722, Guyenne to Vaudreuil, 10 September 1752, bonfire in celebration of the birth of the Duke of Burgundy.

32 *Editors' note*: The author was obviously thinking of Marius Barbeau, who, from 1916 to 1969, collected more than 900 songs, and Luc Lacourcière, who, in 1944, founded the Archives de folklore et d'ethnologie at Université Laval: Centre Marius-Barbeau, "À la mémoire de Marius Barbeau (1883–1969)," online at https://www.cdmb.ca/MariusBarbeau.html; Denis Lessard, "Un chercheur aux cent préfaces, Luc Lacourcière," *Bulletin Mnemo*, online at http://mnemo.qc.ca/bulletin-mnemo/article/un-chercheur-aux-cent-prefaces-luc (both viewed August 2020).

33 AC, CIIA, 102: 185–6, letter to the minister, [1757].

34 Letter of 3 February 1759, B109, cited in Stacey, *Québec*, 40; see Casgrain, ed., *Collection*, 3: 162, letter to Montcalm, 10 February 1759.

35 On Vaudreuil's mean-spirited, pompous character, the best summary is that of Stacey, *Québec*, ch. 1, "Dramatis Personae," *passim*. "'My firmness penetrated each and every heart,' he said aloud. 'We will be buried under the ruins of Canada, our native land, before we surrender to the English'": AC, F, 315: 265–70, letter from Vaudreuil, 28 May 1759.

36 See Anderson, *A People's Army*, on morale in New England: on the absence of heroes in the militiamen's eyes, 23; on the lack of criticism immediately after the defeat, 153–5.

37 *Editors' note*: Traces of tension between habitants and soldiers are detectable in a few sources, generally cited in the context of a critique of Montcalm's actions; see, e.g., Frégault, *François Bigot*, 2: 261; *idem*, *Canada*, 256; Ferland, *Cours d'histoire*, 588-9. One would have to go back to the documents in series C11A (Archives des Colonies) on which these two authors rely and peruse them carefully. This is our interpretation of Dechêne's inscription "check this" found in the margin.

38 See Casgrain, ed., *Collection*, 5: 246, 250, and elsewhere, Montcalm to Bourlamaque, on conflicts between officers and militia captains.

39 Brunet, *Les Canadiens après la conquête*, 27–8; Dechêne, *Power and Subsistence*, 148–9, letter from merchant Jacques Hervieux, 25 September 1761.

40 They were mainly Irishmen: BAnQ-Montréal, TL4–D5542, D6091, and D6194, and BAnQ-Québec, TL5–D1794, trials held between 1750 and 1758.

41 I refer to the accounts of Titus King, Stephen Coffen, Robert Eastburn, Peter Williamson, and, among the less credible witnesses, Jemima Howe and Thomas Brown. See King, "Narrative," and Drake, ed., *Tragedies of the Wilderness*, for the accounts of Eastburn, Williamson, and Howe. There is little discussion of the residents of the côtes and the cities, but the captives make fairly frequent mention of their encounters with officers at the posts, priests who try to convert them, and townspeople who ransom them from the Amerindians for use as servants. But it is hard to draw conclusions from this assemblage of anecdotes, which reveal a motley set of attitudes.

42 Pote, *The Journal*; "The Journal of a Captive," 54–6, 93, entry for 28 April 1747.

43 Casgrain, ed., *Collection*, 7: 254, 530, journal of Montcalm; AG, A1, 3417, no. 182, account of Duchat, captain of Languedoc, 15 July 1756. (*Editors' note*: The author specifies that she noted other references on the abuses of the colonial governments, but we were unable to find these references.) The Church's arguments are presented below.

44 *Editors' note*: Exact reference not found.

45 See *supra*, ch. 6.

46 Rural notary Louis Aumasson de Courville (*Mémoires*, 128–9) argued that the British had grounds for complaining about how the Canadians and their allies operated. Yet it is hard to know whether this remark was

written in 1759 or added later. On learning of the massacre of British prisoners after the conquest of Fort George, a Montreal merchant reportedly declared that Canada had brought holy vengeance down upon its head: "Captain Jonathan Carver, Narrative of his Capture," in Drake, ed., *Tragedies of the Wilderness*, 172–8.

47 AC, C I IA, 104: 309–10v, 296–96v, placards of 27 June and 25 July 1759, published at Saint-Laurent on Île d'Orléans and at Saint-Henri.

48 AG, A1, 3574, no. 102, 348, Malartic quoting a letter from Benoît-François Bernier, financial commissary of wars, 12 September 1760; *RAPQ* (1924–25): 178, "Mémoire du Canada."

49 There is a letter dated August 1759 from Wolfe to the parish priest of L'Ange-Gardien, dismissing the prospect of deportation. See *RAPQ* (1933–34): 119, Lapause papers.

50 I combed through the notaries' books in search of militiamen's wills that might indicate, even in the form of boilerplate text, the reception accorded these sermons. Unfortunately, such wills are much too rare for any pattern to be discerned. A royal surveyor stated before setting out "that the circumstances of the war in which we find ourselves must expose us to death in the cause of the Catholic, apostolic, Roman religion and the glory of God"; others set off simply "to go to war against the enemies of the state." But these scattered examples are not representative. My search produced only four wills in the minutes of Panet and Hodiesne (1759) and Simonnet (1756). I abandoned this tack. BANQ-Montréal, CN601–S308, minutes of notary P. Panet, 30 June 1759, will of Louis Lefebvre, merchant voyageur, and 25 February 1761 (date of filing; this undated will would appear to be from 1759), Jean-Baptiste Chevrefils Belisle, royal surveyor; CN601–S202, minutes of notary G. Hodiesne, 20 May 1759, will of Michel Demers, cooper; CN601–S372, minutes of notary F. Simonnet, 23 July 1756, will of Pierre-Amable Gadoua, militia officer.

51 Têtu and Gagnon, eds, *Mandements*, 2: 105–10, pastoral letter of 15 February 1756.

52 Circular to parish priests, summer 1755, in Lacelle, *Monseigneur Henry-Marie Dubreuil de Pontbriand*, 278.

53 Trudel, *L'Église canadienne*.

54 MCQ, Fonds d'archives du Séminaire de Québec, "Lettre de Vaudreuil à un capitaine de milice," polygraphie 18, no. 64, 4 May 1759; AC, F3, 16: 42, circular from Rigaud de Vaudreuil to the parish priests of the government of Quebec, 16 April 1760; Têtu and Gagnon, eds, *Mandements*, 2: 137–40, circular from the bishop to the parish priests, 5 June 1759.

55 Pouchot, *Mémoires*, 127, [12 July 1759]; Grenier, *Papiers Contrecoeur*, 198, in regard to ceremonies at Fort Duquesne.

56 The analysis that follows is derived from the whole series of war-related pastoral letters of this period, these being the twenty-one published in Têtu and Gagnon, eds, *Mandements*, and five more reproduced in Lacelle, *Monseigneur Henry-Marie Dubreuil de Pontbriand*.

57 The apparition is said to have been reported by an enemy prisoner, and Mother Duplessis mentions it in her correspondence. Cited in Frégault, *Canada*, 15–16. See also [Regnard Duplessis], "Lettres," 57.

58 Lacelle, *Monseigneur Henry-Marie Dubreuil de Pontbriand*, 275–7, pastoral letter ordering a *Te Deum* for the victory of 9 July in the Ohio country.

59 Têtu and Gagnon, eds, *Mandements*, 2: 126, pastoral letter by the bishop, 20 January 1758.

60 Delumeau, *La Peur en Occident*, 136–42.

61 Jean-Guy Lavallée ("Dubreil de Pontbriand, Henri-Marie," DCB, 3: 206–13) draws on the bishop's correspondence in contending that he had ceased early on to believe in the possibility of French victory and was solely devoted to saving his church. This may well be true, but it is not an all-purpose explanation. He knew he was suffering from a serious illness and indeed died in June 1760. There is also his history of obsequiousness vis-à-vis the governor.

62 Lacelle (*Monseigneur Henry-Marie Dubreuil de Pontbriand*, 63–4) found only one gloss of these pastoral letters, for the Notre-Dame-de-Montréal parish, which was served by the Sulpicians. It is known too that they often remonstrated in their sermons against feasts, games, and other entertainments of polite society, particularly by the civilian and military officers, deeming such activities "unmeet" in a time of poverty. Clearly, the bishop's indignation hit its target more directly in this garrison town than in the remote countryside.

63 In my view, recent theses on the decline of religious fervour and the rise of immorality among the eighteenth-century colonials are baseless. Of course, by stringing together all the sins denounced by priests over a period of years, any people in any historical era can be painted as depraved and irreligious, since denouncing sin is what sermons are designed to do. Parishioners' squabbles with their priests in connection with the building of churches and rectories evidence a desire for autonomy in the temporal affairs of the parish, not any sort of disaffection with the spiritual realm. See Dechêne, *Habitants and Merchants*, and Greer, "L'Habitant." For the contention that religious sentiment was declining, see Jaenen, *The Role of the Church*.

64 "Relation du siège de Québec," in Hébert, ed., *Le Siège*, 26.
65 *RAPQ* (1924–25): 173–4, anon., "Mémoire du Canada."

CONCLUSION

1 A portion of these notes was written on the back of a sheet of McGill University letterhead bearing the 175th anniversary logo (1821–1996).
2 Word underlined in the manuscript.
3 On the development of this idea in Quebec historiography and the underlying argumentation, see Horguelin, "Le XVIIIe siècle," which lays out a dissident position.
4 This discourse on early "Canadianization" and on a distinction between the people and the elites in this respect has a long history. It first appeared in the nineteenth-century writings of French-Canadian historians (e.g., Casgrain, *Guerre du Canada*) and has continued to this day (e.g., Mathieu, *La Nouvelle-France*, which does not, however, discuss the impact of this phenomenon on how the "Canadians" experienced the Conquest). This discourse is omnipresent in the work of Guy Frégault (e.g., *Canada*). The same idea has been taken up by English-Canadian historians; see, e.g., Eccles, *The Canadian Frontier*. Belmessous, "Être français en Nouvelle-France," illustrates the persistence of this idea of a latent opposition between Frenchmen and Canadians that suddenly burst into view during the Seven Years' War.
5 See *supra*, 198–9 and 261 et seq.
6 This idea of devotion to the king is evoked by Colin M. Coates ("La mise en scène," 116), who contends that in spite of the conflicts among the colonial leaders, "at no time did the colonists of New France ever reject the legitimacy of royal power."
7 See *supra*, ch. 12, section 2, "Information." Kenneth J. Banks (*Chasing Empire*) gives examples of public rejoicing in Canada in relation to the royal family and France's military destiny.
8 This fact is attested by the analysis in Horguelin, "Le XVIIIe siècle."
9 Henri-Marie Dubreil de Pontbriand, "Mandement sur les prières publiques," Quebec, 20 June 1745, in Têtu and Gagnon, eds, *Mandements*, 2: 44.
10 Fernand Dumont (*Genèse de la société québécoise*, 84 et seq.) also expresses this idea. More recently, it was taken up and convincingly argued in Horguelin, "Le XVIIIe siècle."

APPENDICES

1 Jay Cassel ("The Troupes de la Marine," Appendix D) presents the results of a similar effort, albeit a less complete one that is in some respects less reliable as regards counts of militiamen, volunteers, and Indigenous allies. Plates 42 and 44 of Harris, ed., *From the Beginning*, do this work for the Seven Years' War. Appendix E of Haefeli and Sweeney, *Captors and Captives*, based on particularly intensive research into Anglo-American sources, presents a more complete list of raids against New England for the period 1703–12 (thirty for 1704 alone, for example) but only distinguishes between "French" and "Indian" partisans. In most cases, the sources are silent as to the number of men who took part in these attacks.

2 See *supra*, 86.

3 See *supra*, ch. 4, note 4.

4 Ibid.

5 See *supra*, 198.

6 Ibid.

Bibliography

Abler, Thomas S. "Scalping, Torture, Cannibalism and Rape:
  An Ethnohistorical Analysis of Conflicting Cultural Values in War."
  Anthropologica 34 (1992): 6–9.
Adams, Arthur V., ed. *The Explorations of Pierre Esprit Radisson.*
  Minneapolis: Ross and Haines, 1961.
Adelman, Jeremy. "An Age of Imperial Revolutions." *American Historical
  Review* 113(2): 319–40 (2008).
Aleyrac, Jean-Baptiste d'. *Aventures militaires au XVIIIe siècle d'après les
  mémoires de Jean-Baptiste d'Aleyrac.* Edited by Charles Coste. Paris:
  Berger-Levrault, 1935.
Anderson, Fred. *Crucible of War: The Seven Years' War and the Fate of
  Empire in British North America, 1754–1766.* New York: Knopf, 2000.
– *A People's Army: Massachusetts Soldiers and Society in the Seven Years'
  War.* Chapel Hill: University of North Carolina Press, 1984.
Aubert, Guillaume. "'The Blood of France': Race and Purity of Blood in
  the French Atlantic World." *William & Mary Quarterly* 61(3): 439–78
  (2004).
Audet, F. Émile. *Les Premiers établissements français au pays des Illinois:
  la guerre des Renards.* Paris: F. Sorlot, 1938.
Austen, Barbara E. "Captured ... Never Came Back: Social Networks
  among New England Female Captives in Canada, 1689–1763." In Peter
  Benes, ed., *New England/New France 1600–1850,* 28–38. Boston:
  Boston University, 1992.
Axtell, James. "Scalping: The Ethnohistory of a Moral Question." In James
  Axtell, ed., *The European and the Indian: Essays in the Ethnohistory of
  Colonial North America,* 207–41. New York: Oxford University Press,
  1981.

Axtell, James, and W.C. Sturtevant. "The Unkindest Cut, or, Who Invented Scalping." *William and Mary Quarterly* (3rd series) 37(3): 451–72 (July 1980).

Bacqueville de La Potherie, Claude-Charles Le Roy. *Histoire de l'Amérique septentrionale*. 4 vols. Paris: Nion et Didot, 1722.

Balvay, Arnaud. *L'Épée et la plume: Amérindiens et soldats des troupes de la marine en Louisiane et au Pays d'en haut (1683–1763)*. Quebec: Presses de l'Université Laval, 2006.

Banks, Kenneth J. "Communications and Imperial Absolutism in Three French Colonial Towns, 1713–1763." PhD diss., Queen's University, 1995, 104–6. *Editors' note*: This thesis was published under the title *Chasing Empire across the Sea: Communications and the State in the French Atlantic, 1713–1763*. Montreal and Kingston: McGill-Queen's University Press, 2002.

Bariteau, Claude. "Compte rendu de Louise Dechêne, *Le Peuple, l'État, et la guerre*." *Anthropologie et sociétés* 32(3): 265–7 (2008).

Baugh, Daniel. *The Global Seven Years' War, 1754–1763*. London: Routledge, 2011.

Baugy, Chevalier de. *Journal d'une expédition contre les Iroquois en 1687 rédigé par le chevalier de Baugy, aide de camp de M. le marquis de Denonville*. Edited by Ernest Serrigny. Paris: Ernest Leroux, 1883.

Bayard, Nicholas, and Charles Lodowick. *Journal of the Late Actions of the French at Canada by Nicholas Bayard and Lieut. Col. Charles Lodowick*. New York: Reprinted for Joseph Sabin, 1868.

Beaugrand-Champagne, Denyse. *Le Procès de Marie-Josèphe Angélique*. Outremont, QC: Libre Expression, 2004.

Beaulieu, Alain. "'Under His Majesty's Protection': The Meaning of the Conquest for the Aboriginal Peoples of Canada." In Frans De Bruyn and Shaun Regan, eds, *The Culture of the Seven Years' War: Empire, Identity, and the Arts in the Eighteenth-Century Atlantic World*, 91–115. Toronto: University of Toronto Press, 2014.

Beaune, Colette. *Naissance de la nation France*. Paris: Gallimard, 1985.

Beik, William. "The Absolutism of Louis XIV as Social Collaboration." *Past & Present* 188(1): 195–224 (2005).

Bell, David A. *The Cult of the Nation in France: Inventing Nationalism, 1680–1800*. Cambridge, MA: Harvard University Press, 2001.

Belmessous, Saliha. "Assimilation and Racialism in Seventeenth and Eighteenth-Century French Colonial Policy." *American Historical Review* 110(2): 322–49 (2005).

- "Être français en Nouvelle-France: identité française et identité coloniale aux dix-septième et dix-huitième siècles." *French Historical Studies* 27(3): 507–40 (Summer 2004).

Belmont, François Vachon de. *Histoire de l'eau-de-vie en Canada d'après un manuscrit récemment obtenu de France.* N.p., 1840.

- *Histoire du Canada.* Quebec: Imprimerie de William Cowan et Fils, 1840.

Bercé, Yves-Marie. *Fête et révolte: des mentalités populaires du XVIe au XVIIIe siècle.* Paris: Hachette, 1976.

- "Guerre et état." *XVIIe siècle,* no. 148 (July-September 1985): 257–66.

- *Révoltes et révolutions dans l'Europe moderne, XVIe–XVIIIe siècles.* Paris: Presses universitaires de France, 1980.

Bernier, Serge. "Le Travail de Louise Dechêne intitulé *Le Peuple, l'État, et la guerre.*" *Bulletin d'histoire politique* 18(1): 137–42 (2009).

Black, Jeremy. "Warfare, State and Society in Europe, 1510–1914." *European History Quarterly* 30(4): 587–94 (2000).

Blain, Jean. "Économie et société en Nouvelle-France: le cheminement historiographique dans la première moitié du XXe siècle." *RHAF* 26(1): 3–31 (1972).

- "L'historiographie des années 1950–1960." *RHAF* 28(2): 163–86 (1974).

Blais, Christian, and Jocelyn Saint-Pierre. "*Le Peuple, l'État et la guerre au Canada sous le Régime français.* Montréal, Boréal, 2008: l'État sous le Régime français selon Louise Dechêne." *Bulletin d'histoire politique* 18(1): 263–73 (2009).

Bloch, Marc. *Apologie pour l'histoire ou métier d'historien.* Paris: Armand Colin, 1961.

Bodin, Michel. "Un exemple de recrutement de la milice provinciale: Tours au XVIIIe siècle." *Revue historique des armées,* no. 4 (1980): 3–22.

Bond Jr, Beverley W., ed. "The Captivity of Charles Stuart, 1755–1757." *Mississippi Valley Historical Review* 13 (June 1926): 58–81.

Bordes, Maurice. *L'Administration provinciale et municipale en France au XVIIIe siècle.* Paris: Société d'édition d'enseignement supérieur, 1972.

Bosher, J.F. "Government and Private Interests in New France." *Canadian Public Administration* 10(2): 244–57 (1967).

- *Men and Ships in the Canada Trade, 1660–1760: A Biographical Dictionary.* Ottawa: Minister of Supply and Services, 1992.

Bouchard, Gérard. *La Nation québécoise au futur et au passé.* Montreal: VLB, 1999.

Boucher, Pierre. *Histoire véritable et naturelle des moeurs et productions du pays de la Nouvelle France vulgairement dite le Canada.* Paris: Florentin Lambert, 1664. Reprint, Boucherville: Société historique de Boucherville, 1964.

Bougainville. *Écrits sur le Canada.* Compiled by R. Lamontagne. Sillery: Éditions du Pélican, 1993.

Breen, V.H. "Ideology and Nationalism on the Eve of the American Revolution: Revisions *Once More* in Need of Revising." *Journal of American History,* no. 84 (1997): 13–39.

Brisson, Réal N. *Les 100 premières années de la charpenterie navale à Québec, 1663–1763.* Quebec: Institut québécois de recherche sur la culture, 1983.

Bromley, John S. "The French Privateering War, 1702–1713." In Henry E. Bell and Richard L. Ollard, eds, *Historical Essays, 1600–1750: Presented to David Ogg,* 203–31. London: Adam & Charles Black, 1963.

Brooke, Frances. *The History of Emily Montague.* Dublin: G. Faulkner, 1769.

Brumwell, Stephen. *Redcoats: The British Soldier and War in the Americas, 1755–1763.* Cambridge: Cambridge University Press, 2002.

Brunet, Michel. *Les Canadiens après la conquête, 1759–1775.* Montreal: Fides, 1969.

Bumsted, J.M. "Carried to Canada: Perceptions of the French in British Colonial Captivity Narratives, 1690–1760." *American Review of Canadian Studies* 13(1): 79–86 (1983).

Cahall, Raymond DuBois. *The Sovereign Council of New France: A Study in Canadian Constitutional History.* New York: Longmans, Green, 1915.

Cañeque, Alejandro. *The King's Living Image: The Culture and Politics of Viceregal Power in Colonial Mexico.* London and New York: Routledge, 2004.

Cardini, Franco. *La Culture de la guerre.* Paris: Gallimard, 1992.

Carpin, Gervais. *Histoire d'un mot: l'ethnonyme "canadien" de 1535 à 1691.* Sillery: Septentrion, 1995.

Casgrain, H.-R., ed. *Collection des manuscrits du maréchal de Lévis.* 12 vols. Montreal: Beauchemin, 1889–95.

– *Extraits des archives des ministères de la marine et de la guerre à Paris.* Quebec: n.p., 1890.

– *Guerre du Canada, 1756–1760: Montcalm et Lévis.* Vol. 2. Quebec: Demers et Frère, 1891.

Cassel, Jay. "The Militia Legend: Canadians at War 1665–1760." In Yves Tremblay, ed., *Canadian Military History since the 17th Century, Proceedings of the Canadian Military History Conference, 5–9 May 2000*, 59–67. Ottawa: National Defence, 2001.

– "The Troupes de la Marine: Men and Material, 1683–1760." PhD diss., University of Toronto, 1987.

Castan, Nicole. *Justice et répression en Languedoc à l'époque des Lumières*. Paris: Flammarion, 1980.

Catalogne, Gédéon de. "Recueil de ce qui s'est passé au Canada au sujet de la guerre, tant des anglais que des Iroquois, depuis l'année 1682." In Robert Le Blant, ed., *Histoire de la Nouvelle France*, vol. 1, *Les Sources narratives du début du XVIIIe siècle et le recueil de Gédéon de Catalogne*, 170–272. Dax: P. Pradeu, 1940.

Caulier, Brigitte. "Bâtir l'Amérique des dévots: les confréries de dévotion montréalaises depuis le Régime français." *RHAF* 46(1): 45–66 (Summer 1992).

Chagniot, Jean. "Guerre et société au XVIIe siècle." *XVIIe siècle*, no. 148 (July-September 1985): 249–56.

– *Histoire de la France militaire*. Vol. 2, *De 1715 à 1871*. Edited by Jean Delmas. Paris: Presses universitaires de France, 1992.

Chagny, André. *Un défenseur de la "Nouvelle-France": François Picquet, "le Canadien" (1708–1781); contribution à l'histoire du Canada pendant les vingt-cinq dernières années de la domination française*. Montreal: Beauchemin, 1913.

Challes, Robert. *Journal d'un voyage aux Indes orientales (1690–1691)*. Edited with an introduction and notes by Frédéric Deloffre and Melâhat Menemencioglu. Paris: Mercure de France, [1721] 1979.

– *Mémoires de Robert Challes, écrivain du roi: un colonial au temps de Colbert*. Edited by A. Augustin-Thierry. Paris: Plon, 1931.

Charbonneau, André, Yvon Desloges, and Marc Lafrance. *Québec, the Fortified City: From the 17th to the 19th Century*. Ottawa: Parks Canada, 1982.

Charbonneau, André, Marc Lafrance, and Monique Poirer. "The Fortifications of Montréal." In Phyllis Lambert and Alan Stewart, eds, *Opening the Gates of Eighteenth-Century Montréal*, 19–30. Montreal: Canadian Centre for Architecture, 1992.

Charbonneau, Hubert, et al. *Naissance d'une population: les Français établis au Canada au XVIIe siècle*. Paris: Institut national d'études démographiques, Presses universitaires de France; Montreal, Presses de l'Université de Montréal, 1987.

Charbonneau, Hubert, and Jacques Légaré. "La Population du Canada aux recensements de 1666 et 1667." *Population* 22(6): 1031–54 (November-December 1967).

– eds. *Répertoire des actes de baptême, mariage, sépulture et des recensements du Québec ancien.* 47 vols. Montreal: Presses de l'Université de Montréal, 1986.

Charlevoix, Pierre-François-Xavier de. *History and General Description of New France.* 6 vols. Translated by John Gilmary Shea. New York: Francis P. Harper, 1900.

– *Journal d'un voyage fait par ordre du Roi dans l'Amérique septentrionale.* Edited by Pierre Berthiaume. 2 vols. Montreal: Presses de l'Université de Montréal, 1994.

Chartrand, René. "Death Walks on Snowshoes." *Horizon Canada* 1: 260–4 (1987).

– "La Gouvernance militaire en Nouvelle-France." *Bulletin d'histoire politique* 18(1): 125–36 (2009).

– "La Milice canadienne et la guerre de Sept Ans." In Bertrand Fonck and Veyssière, eds, *La Guerre de Sept Ans en Nouvelle-France,* 291–300. Quebec: Septentrion, 2012.

– *Le Patrimoine militaire canadien: d'hier à aujourd'hui.* Vol. 1, *Début à 1754.* Montreal: Art Global, 1993.

– "Une place de guerre." In Yves Landry, ed., *Pour le Christ et le roi: la vie au temps des premiers montréalais,* 210–15. Montreal: Libre Expression/Art Global, 1992.

Chaunu, Pierre. "L'État." In Fernand Braudel and Ernest Labrousse, eds, *Histoire économique et sociale de la France.* Vol. 1, *1450–1660.* Paris: Presses universitaires de France, 1977.

Chet, Guy. *Conquering the American Wilderness: The Triumph of European Warfare in the Colonial Northeast.* Amherst and Boston: University of Massachusetts Press, 2003.

Childs, John. *Armies and Warfare in Europe, 1648–1789.* New York: Halmer and Meier, 1982.

Chinard, Gilbert. *L'Amérique et le rêve exotique dans la littérature française au XVIIe et au XVIIIe siècle.* Paris: Droz, 1934.

Choquette, Leslie. "From Sea Monsters and Savages to Sorcerers and Satan: A History of Fear in New France." In Lauric Henneton and L.H. Roper, eds, *Fear and the Shaping of Early American Societies,* 38–59. Leyden: Brill, 2016.

Church, Christopher M. "Review of Louise Dechêne, *Power and Subsistence: The Political Economy of Grain in New France.*" *Agricultural History* 93(4): 759–61 (2019).

Clastres, Pierre. "Archéologie de la violence: la guerre dans les sociétés primitives." In *Recherches d'anthropologie politique*, 171–207. Paris: Seuil, 1980.

– "Malheur du guerrier sauvage." In *Recherches d'anthropologie politique.* Paris: Seuil, 1980.

Cliche, Marie-Aimée. *Les Pratiques de dévotion en Nouvelle-France: comportements populaires et encadrement ecclésial dans le gouvernement de Québec.* Quebec: Presses de l'Université Laval, 1987.

Cloutier, Nicole. "La Peinture votive à Sainte-Anne-de-Beaupré." In Benoît Lacroix and Jean Simard, eds, *Religion populaire, religion de clercs?* 156–7. Quebec: Institut québécois de recherche sur la culture, 1984.

Coates, Colin M. "Authority and Illegitimacy in New France: The Burial of Bishop Saint-Vallier and Madeleine de Verchères vs the Priest of Batiscan." *Social History* 22(43): 65–90 (May 1989).

– *The Metamorphoses of Landscape and Community in Early Quebec.* Montreal and Kingston: McGill-Queen's University Press, 2000.

– "La Mise en scène du pouvoir: la préséance en Nouvelle-France." *Bulletin d'histoire politique* 14(1): 109–18 (Autumn 2005).

– "Problems of Precedence in Louis XIV's New France." In Colin M. Coates, ed., *Majesty in Canada: Essays on the Role of Royalty*, 181–95. Toronto: Dundurn Group, 2006.

Coates, Colin M., and Cecilia Morgan. *Heroines and History: Representations of Madeleine de Verchères and Laura Secord.* Toronto: University of Toronto Press, 2002.

Coleman, Emma Lewis. *New England Captives Carried to Canada, 1677–1760.* 2 vols. Portland, ME: Southworth Press, 1925.

Collection de manuscrits contenant lettres, mémoires et autres documents historiques relatifs à la Nouvelle-France. 4 vols. Quebec: A. Coté et Cie, 1883–85.

Colley, Linda. *Britons: Forging the Nation, 1707–1837.* New Haven: Yale University Press, 1992.

Constant, Jean-Marie. *Nobles et paysans en Beauce aux XVIe et XVIIe siècles.* Lille: Service de reproduction des thèses, 1981.

Contamine, Philippe, ed. *Histoire militaire de la France.* Vol. 1, *Des origines à 1715.* Paris: Presses universitaires de France, 1992.

Cooper, Frederick. *Colonialism in Question: Theory, Knowledge, History.* Berkeley: University of California Press, 2005.

Corboz, André. "La Recherche: trois apologues." In *Le Territoire comme palimpseste et autres essais*, 21–30. Besançon: Éditions de l'Imprimeur, 2001.

Cornette, Joël. *Le Roi de guerre: essai sur la souveraineté dans la France du Grand Siècle.* Paris: Éditions Payot et Rivages, 1993.

Corvisier, André. *Armées et sociétés en Europe de 1494 à 1789.* Paris: Presses universitaires de France, 1976.

– *L'Armée française de la fin du XVIIe siècle au ministère de Choiseul: le soldat.* 2 vols. Paris: Presses universitaires de France, 1964.

– "Guerre et mentalités au XVIIe siècle." *XVIIe siècle*, no. 148 (July-September 1985): 219–32.

– "La Mort du soldat depuis la fin du Moyen Âge." *Revue historique* 254(1): 3–30 (1975).

Côté, André. *Joseph-Michel Cadet, 1719–1781: négociant et munition-naire du roi en Nouvelle-France.* Quebec: Septentrion, 1998.

Courville, Louis Aumasson de. *Mémoires sur le Canada, depuis 1749 jusqu'à 1760.* Quebec: Société littéraire et historique de Québec (Quebec: T. Cary), 1838.

Courville, Serge, ed. *Atlas historique du Québec: population et territoire.* Quebec: Presses de l'Université Laval, 1996.

Crouch, Christian Ayne. *Nobility Lost: French and Canadian Martial Cultures, Indians and the End of New France.* Ithaca, NY: Cornell University Press, 2014.

Crowley, Terry. "The Inroads of Secularization in Eighteenth-Century New France: Church and People at Louisbourg." In *Canadian Catholic Historical Association, Historical Studies* 51 (1984): 5–27.

Cugnet, François Joseph. *Traité de la police: qui a toujours été suivie en Canada, aujourd'hui province de Québec, depuis son établissement jusqu'à la conquête, tiré des diférens reglemens, jugemens et ordon-nances d'intendans, à qui par leurs commissions, cette partie du gouvernement était totalement atribuée, à l'exclusion de tous autres juges, qui n'en pouvaient connaître qu'en qualité de leurs subdélégués: traité qui pourrait être de quelqu' utilité aux grand voyers, et aux juges de police en cette province.* Quebec: Chez Guillaume Brown, [1775].

Daniel, Gabriel. *Histoire de la milice française.* Paris, 1721.

Danley, Mark H., and Patrick J. Speelman, eds. *The Seven Years' War as a Global Conflict: Essays and Interpretations.* Leiden: Brill, 2012.

Davies, K.G. *The North Atlantic World in the Seventeenth Century.* Minneapolis: University of Minnesota Press, 1974.

Davis, Natalie Zemon. *Fiction in the Archives: Pardon Tales and Their Tellers in Sixteenth-Century France.* Stanford, CA: Stanford University Press, 1987.

Dawdy, Shannon Lee. *Building the Devil's Empire: French Colonial New Orleans.* Chicago: University of Chicago Press, 2008.

Day, Gordon M. "Roger's Raid in Indian Tradition." *Historical New Hampshire* 17 (June 1962): 3–17.

Debien, Gabriel. *Esprit colon et esprit d'autonomie à Saint-Domingue au XVIIIe siècle.* Paris: Larose, 1954.

Dechêne, Louise. "Compte rendu de W.J. Eccles, *The Canadian Frontier, 1534–1760.*" *Canadian Historical Review* 51(3): 321–3 (1970).

– "Coup d'oeil sur l'historiographie de la Nouvelle-France." *Canadian Studies* 3 (1977): 45–58.

– "La Croissance de Montréal au XVIIIe siècle." RHAF 27(2): 163–79 (September 1973).

– "Les Entreprises de William Price, 1810–1850." *Histoire sociale/Social History* 1(1): 16–52 (May 1968).

– *Habitants and Merchants in Seventeenth-century Montreal.* Translated by Liana Vardi. Montreal: McGill-Queen's University Press, 1992.

– "Habitants et marchands de Montréal au XVIIe siècle." PhD diss., Paris X-Nanterre, 1973.

– *Le Peuple, l'État, et la guerre sous le Régime français.* Montreal: Boréal, 2008.

– *Power and Subsistence: The Political Economy of Grain in New France.* Translated by Peter Feldstein. Montreal and Kingston: McGill-Queen's University Press, 2018.

Delâge, Denys. "Les Iroquois chrétiens des réductions, 1667–1770." *Recherches amérindiennes au Québec* 21(1–2): 59–70 and 21(3): 39–50 (1991).

– "Les Premières Nations et la Guerre de la Conquête (1754–1765)." *Cahiers des Dix* 63: 1–67 (2009).

Delmas, Jean, ed. *Histoire militaire de la France.* Vol. 2, *De 1715 à 1871.* Paris: Presses universitaires de France, 1992.

Delumeau, Jean. *La Peur en Occident (XIVe–XVIIIe siècles): une cité assiégée.* Paris: Fayard, 1978.

Demos, John. *The Unredeemed Captive: A Family Story from Early America.* New York: Alfred A. Knopf, 1994.

Denys, Nicolas. *The Description and Natural History of the Coasts of North America (Acadia)*. Edited and translated by William F. Ganong. Toronto: Champlain Society, [1672] 1908.

Dépatie, Sylvie. "L'Évolution d'une société rurale: l'île Jésus au XVIIIe siècle." PhD diss., McGill University, 1988.

– "¿El ser más independiente del mundo? La construcción del arquetipo del *habitant* canadiense." In C. Poupeney Hart and A. Chacón Gutiérrez, eds, *El discurso colonial: construcción de una diferencia americana*, 189–221. Heredia (Costa Rica): EUNA, 2002.

Dépatie, Sylvie, et al., eds. *Vingt ans après*, Habitants et marchands: *Lectures de l'histoire des XVIIe et XVIIIe siècles canadiens*. Montreal and Kingston: McGill-Queen's University Press, 1998.

Desbarats, Catherine M. "Colonial Government Finances in New France, 1700–1750." PhD diss., McGill University, 1993.

– "The Cost of Early Canada's Native Alliances: Reality and Scarcity's Rhetoric." *William and Mary Quarterly* (3rd series) 52(4): 609–30 (October 1995).

– "Foreword to the English Edition." In Louise Dechêne, *Power and Subsistence: The Political Economy of Grain in New France*, trans. Peter Feldstein, ix–xxi. Montreal and Kingston: McGill-Queen's University Press, 2018.

– "France in North America: The Net Burden of Empire during the First Half of the Eighteenth Century." *French History* 11(1): 1–28 (1997).

– "La Question de l'État en Nouvelle-France." In Philippe Joutard and Thomas Wien, eds, *Mémoires de Nouvelle-France: Actes du Colloque de la Commission franco-québécoise sur les lieux de mémoire communs (Poitiers-La Rochelle, septembre 2001)*, 187–98. Rennes and Quebec: Presses universitaires de Rennes and Éditions du Septentrion, 2005.

Desbarats, Catherine M., and Allan Greer. "The Seven Years' War in Canadian History and Memory." In Warren Hofstra, ed., *Cultures in Conflict: The Seven Years' War in North America*, 145–78. Lanham, MD: Rowman and Littlefield, 2007.

Deschamps, Hubert. *Pirates et flibustiers*. Paris: Presses universitaires de France, 1962.

Deschênes, Gaston. *L'Année des Anglais: la Côte-du-Sud à l'heure de la conquête*. Sillery: Septentrion, 1988.

Descimon, Robert. "Milice bourgeoise et identité citadine à Paris au temps de la Ligue." *Annales: Économies, Sociétés, Civilisations*, no. 4 (July–August 1993): 885–906.

Deslandres, Dominique. "Le Christianisme dans les Amériques." In Marc
Venard, ed., *Histoire du Christianisme IX: l'Âge de raison, 1620–1750,*
615–736. Paris-Tournai: Desclée-Fayard, 1997.

– "Femmes devant le tribunal du roi: la culture judiciaire des appelantes
dans les archives de la juridiction royale de Montréal (1693–1760)."
Cahiers des Dix 71: 35–63 (2017).

– "Voix des esclaves autochtones et des esclavagistes: un cas d'histoire
intersectionnelle dans les archives judiciaires de la juridiction de
Montréal." *Cahiers des Dix* 72: 145–75 (2018).

Desloges, Yvon. "La Corvée militaire à Québec au XVIIIe siècle." *Social
History* 15(30): 333–56 (November 1982).

– *A Tenant's Town: Québec in the 18th Century.* Ottawa: Canadian Parks
Service, 1991.

Dewar, Helen. "Canada or Guadeloupe? French and British Perceptions of
Empire, 1760–1763." *Canadian Historical Review* 91(4): 637–60
(2010).

Diamond, Sigmund. "An Experiment in 'Feudalism': French Canada in the
XVIIth Century." *William and Mary Quarterly* (3rd series) 18(1): 3–34
(January 1961).

Dickason, Olive. *Canada's First Nations: A History of Founding Peoples
from Earliest Times.* Toronto: McClelland and Stewart, 1992.

– *Louisbourg and the Indians: A Study in Imperial Race Relations,
1713–1760.* Ottawa: Parks Canada, 1976.

Dickinson, John A. "Compte rendu de Louise Dechêne, *Le Peuple, l'État,
et la guerre.*" *Recherches sociographiques* 50(2): 427–9 (2009).

– "La Guerre iroquoise et la mortalité en Nouvelle-France, 1608–1666."
RHAF 36(1): 31–54 (June 1982).

– *Justice et justiciables: la procédure civile à la Prévôté de Québec,
1667–1759.* Quebec: Presses de l'Université Laval, 1982.

Dickinson, John A., and Jan Grabowski. "Les Populations amérindiennes
de la vallée laurentienne, 1608–1765." *Annales de démographie historique* 1993, 51–65.

Diéreville. *Relation du voyage du Port Royal de l'Acadie, ou de la
Nouvelle France. Dans laquelle on voit un détail des divers mouve-
mens de la mer dans une traversée de long cours; la description du
païs, les occupations des François qui y sont établis, les maniéres des
différentes nations sauvages, leurs superstitions, & leurs chasses; avec
une dissertation exacte sur le castor.* Rouen: Chez Jean Baptiste
Besogne, 1708.

Dolan, Claire. "Liturgies urbaines et rapports sociaux en France au XVIe siècle: fascination militaire, quartiers et corporations de métier." *Journal of the Canadian Historical Association* 5(1): 87–109 (1994).

Dollier de Casson, François. *Histoire du Montréal.* Edited by Marcel Trudel and Marie Baboyant. Montreal: Hurtubise, 1992.

Douville, Raymond, ed. "Le Canada en 1756–1758 vu par un officier du régiment de La Sarre." *Cahiers des Dix*, no. 24 (1959): 113–32.

Drake, Samuel G. *A Particular History of the Five Years French and Indian War: In New England and Parts Adjacent, from its Declaration by the King of France, March 15, 1744, to the Treaty with the Eastern Indians, Oct. 16, 1749, Sometimes Called Governor Shirley's War; with a Memoir of Major-General Shirley, Accompanied by His Portrait and Other Engravings.* Albany, NY: J. Munsell, 1870.

– ed. *Tragedies of the Wilderness; or, True and Authentic Narratives of Captives, Who Have Been Carried Away by the Indians from the Various Frontier Settlements of the United States, from the Earliest to the Present Time.* Boston: Antiquarian Bookstore and Institute, 1844.

Drévillon, Hervé. "Les Lumières et les ombres de la guerre (1715–1789)." In Hervé Drévillon and Olivier Wieviorka, eds, *Histoire militaire de la France*, vol. 1: *des Mérovingiens au Second Empire*, 381–414. Paris: Perrin, 2018.

Dubé, Alexandre. "S'approprier l'Atlantique: quelques réflexions autour de *Chasing Empire across the Sea*, de Kenneth Banks." *French Colonial History* 6:3–44 (2005).

Dubé, Jean-Claude. *Claude-Thomas Dupuy, intendant de la Nouvelle-France, 1678–1738.* Montreal: Fides, 1969.

Dubé, Pauline, ed. *La Nouvelle-France sous Joseph-Antoine Le Febvre de La Barre, 1682–1685: lettres, mémoires, instructions et ordinances.* Quebec: Septentrion, 1993.

Duchet, Michèle. *Anthropologie et histoire au siècle des lumières: Buffon, Voltaire, Rousseau, Helvetius, Diderot.* Paris: Maspero, 1971.

– "Bougainville, Raynal, Diderot et les Sauvages du Canada: une source ignorée de l'"Histoire des Deux Indes,'" *Revue d'histoire littéraire de France* no. 63 (April–June 1963): 228–36.

– "L'Histoire des Deux Indes,' une histoire philosophique et politique." In *L'Histoire au dix-huitième siècle, Colloque d'Aix-en-Provence, 1er, 2 et 3 mai 1975*, 79–100. Aix-en-Provence: Edisud, 1980.

Dull, Jonathan R. *The French Navy and the Seven Years' War.* Lincoln: University of Nebraska Press, 2005.

Dumont, Fernand. *Genèse de la société québécoise*. Montreal: Boréal, 1993.

Dumont-Johnson, Micheline. *Apôtres ou agitateurs: la France missionnaire en Acadie*. Montreal: Boréal Express, 1970.

Durham, John George Lambton, Lord. *Report on the Affairs of British North America from the Earl of Durham, Her Majesty's High Commissioner* ... Montreal, [1839].

Durham, Louisa Elizabeth Grey Lambton, Countess of, and James Johnstone, chevalier de Johnstone. *Lady Durham's Journal and Mémoires de M. le chev. de Johnstone*. Quebec: Telegraph Printing, 1915.

Dziembowski, Edmond. *La Guerre de Sept Ans, 1756–1763*. Quebec: Septentrion, 2015.

Eccles, William J. *The Canadian Frontier, 1534–1760*. Albuquerque: University of New Mexico Press, 1969.

– *Essays on New France*. Toronto: Oxford University Press, 1987.

– *France in America*. Markham, ON: Fitzhenry and Whiteside, [1972] 1990.

– "The French Forces in North America during the Seven Years' Wars." In Ramsay Cook, ed., *Dictionary of Canadian Biography*, 3: xv–xxiv. Toronto: University of Toronto Press, 1974.

– *Frontenac, the Courtier Governor*. Toronto: McClelland and Stewart, 1959.

– *The Government of New France*. Ottawa: Canadian Historical Association, 1965.

– "The Social, Economic and Political Significance of the Military Establishment in New France." *Canadian Historical Review* 52(1): 1–22 (1971).

Echeverria, Durand. *Mirage in the West: A History of the French Image of American Society to 1815*. New York: Octagon Books, 1966.

Edmunds, R. David, and Joseph L. Peyser. *The Fox Wars: The Mesquakie Challenge to New France*. Norman: University of Oklahoma Press, 1993.

Eid, Leroy V. "The Ojibwa-Iroquois War: The War the Five Nations Did Not Win." *Ethnohistory* 26(4): 297–324 (1979).

Elias, Norbert. *The Court Society*. New York: Pantheon Books, 1983.

Emsley, Clive. "La Maréchaussée à la fin de l'Ancien Régime: note sur la composition d'un corps." *Revue d'histoire moderne et contemporaine* 32: 622–44 (October–December 1986).

Englebert, Robert, and Andrew N. Wegmann, eds. *French Connections: Cultural Mobility in North America and the Atlantic World, 1600–1975*. Baton Rouge: Louisiana State University Press, 2020.

Exquemelin, Alexandre-Olivier. *Bucaniers of America, or, A True Account of the Most Remarkable Assaults Committed of Late Years upon the Coasts of the West-Indies, by the Bucaniers of Jamaica and Tortuga, Both English and French: Wherein Are Contained More Especially the Unparallel'd Exploits of Sir Henry Morgan, Our English Jamaican Hero, Who Sack'd Puerto Velo, Burnt Panama, &c*. London: Printed for William Crooke, 1684.

Faillon, Étienne-Michel. *Histoire de la colonie française en Canada*. 3 vols. Montreal: Bibliothèque paroissiale, 1865–66.

Farge, Arlette. "De la guerre." In Arlette Farge, ed., *Des lieux pour l'histoire*, 46–66. Paris: Seuil, 1997.

– *Dire et mal dire: l'opinion publique au XVIIIe siècle*. Paris: Seuil, 1992.

– *Les Fatigues de la guerre: XVIIIe siècle, Watteau*. Paris: Gallimard, 1996.

Faribault-Beauregard, Marthe, ed. *La Population des forts français d'Amérique, XVIIIe siècle: répertoire des baptêmes, mariages et sépultures célébrés dans les forts et les établissements français en Amérique du Nord au XVIIIe siècle*. 2 vols. Montreal: Éd. Bergeron, 1982–84.

Fauteux, Ægidius. *Les Chevaliers de Saint-Louis en Canada*. Montreal: Éditions des Dix, 1940.

Ferland, J.-B.-A. *Cours d'histoire du Canada*. Part 2. Quebec: Augustin Côté, 1865.

Ferling, John E. *A Wilderness of Miseries: War and Warriors in Early America*. Westport, CT: Greenwood Press, 1980.

Filteau, Gérard. *Par la bouche de mes canons! La Ville de Québec face à l'ennemi*. Quebec: Septentrion, 1990.

Fonck, Bertrand. "'Joindre au système tactique d'Europe l'usage à faire des sauvages': le commandement de l'armée française en Nouvelle-France." In Bertrand Fonck and Laurent Veyssière, eds, *La Guerre de Sept Ans en Nouvelle-France*, 155–72. Quebec: Septentrion, 2012.

Foucault, Michel. *Discipline and Punish: The Birth of the Prison*. Translated by Alan Sheridan. New York: Vintage Books, 1979.

Fournier, Marcel, ed. *Combattre pour la France en Amérique: les soldats de la guerre de Sept Ans en Nouvelle-France, 1755–1760*. Montreal: Société généalogique canadienne-française, 2009.

— *De la Nouvelle-Angleterre à la Nouvelle-France: l'histoire des captives anglo-Américains au Canada entre 1675 et 1760*. Montreal: Société généalogique canadienne-française, 1992.

– *Les Officiers des troupes de la Marine au Canada, 1683–1760*. Quebec: Septentrion, 2017.

Franquet, [Louis]. *Voyages et mémoires sur le Canada*. Montreal: Élysée, 1974.

Fraser, Malcolm. *Extract from a Manuscript Journal, Relating to the Operation before Quebec in 1759, Kept by Colonel Malcolm Fraser, Then Lieutenant of the 78th (Fraser Highlanders), and Serving in That Campaign*. Quebec: Literary and Historical Society of Quebec, 1868.

Frégault, Guy. *Canada: The War of the Conquest*. Translated by Margaret M. Cameron. Toronto: Oxford University Press, 1969.

– *La Civilisation de la Nouvelle-France, 1713–1744*. Ottawa: Fides, [1944] 1969.

– "L'Empire britannique et la conquête du Canada (1700–1713)." *RHAF* 10(2): 153–7 (September 1956).

– *François Bigot, administrateur français*. 2 vols. Montreal: Guérin, [1948] 1994.

– *Le Grand Marquis: Pierre Rigaud de Vaudreuil et la Louisiane*. Montreal: Fides, 1952.

– *Iberville le conquérant*. Montreal: Guérin, [1944] 1996.

Frostin, Charles. "Du peuplement pénal de l'Amérique française: hésitations et contradictions du pouvoir royal en matière de déportation." *Annales de Bretagne* 85(1): 67–94 (1978).

– "Les 'Enfants perdus de l'État' ou la condition militaire à Saint-Domingue au XVIIIe siècle." *Annales de Bretagne et des pays de l'Ouest* 80(2): 317–43 (1973).

– *Les Révoltes blanches à Saint-Domingue aux XVIIe et XVIIIe siècles*. Paris: L'École, 1975.

Furet, François. "Tocqueville et le problème de la Révolution française." In *Penser la Révolution française*, 209–56. Paris: Gallimard, 1978.

Furetière, Antoine. *Le Dictionnaire universel d'Antoine Furetière*. 3 vols. Paris: SNL-Le Robert, 1978. Reprint of the 1690 edition, published by A. and R. Leers, The Hague.

Gabriel, Charles Nicolas. *Le Maréchal de camp Desandrouins 1729–1792: guerre du Canada, 1756–1760; guerre de l'indépendance américaine, 1780–1782*. Verdun: Renvé-Lallemant, 1887.

Gadoury, Lorraine. *La Noblesse de Nouvelle-France: familles et alliances*. Montreal: HMH, 1991.

Gagné, Joseph. *Inconquis: deux retraites françaises vers la Louisiane après 1760*. Quebec: Septentrion, 2016.

Gagnon, Jean-Pierre. "Compte rendu de Louise Dechêne, *Le Peuple, l'État, et la guerre.*" *Bulletin d'histoire politique* 18(2): 281–6 (2010).

Gallet, Jean. "En Bretagne, seigneurs et pouvoir militaire du XVIe au XVIIIe siècle." *Revue historique des armées* 158: 3–13 (March 1985).

Ganong, William F., ed. *The Description and Natural History of the Coasts of North America (Acadia).* Toronto: Champlain Society, 1908.

Garneau, François-Xavier. *Histoire du Canada: depuis sa découverte jusqu'à nos jours.* 3 vols. Quebec: Imprimerie de N. Aubin, 1845.

Gauvreau, Danielle. *Québec: une ville et sa population au temps de la Nouvelle-France.* Sillery: Presses de l'Université du Québec, 1991.

Gervais, Diane, and Serge Lusignan. "De Jeanne d'Arc à Madeleine de Verchères: la femme guerrière dans la société d'Ancien Régime." *RHAF* 53(2): 171–205 (Fall 1999).

Gilot, Michel. "Le Souvenir d'une belle bataille." In *L'Histoire au dix-huitième siècle, Colloque d'Aix-en-Provence, 1er, 2 et 3 mai 1975,* 307–28. Aix-en-Provence: Edisud, 1980.

Giraud, Marcel. "Tendances humanitaires à la fin du règne de Louis XIV." *Revue historique* 209 (1953): 217–37.

– *Histoire de la Louisiane française.* Vol. 1, *Le Règne de Louis XIV (1698–1715).* Paris: Presses universitaires de France, 1953.

– *Histoire de la Louisiane française.* Vol. 3, *L'Époque de John Law (1717–1720).* Paris: Presses universitaires de France, 1966.

Given, Brian J. *A Most Pernicious Thing: Gun Trading and Native Warfare in the Early Contact Period.* Ottawa: Carleton University Press, 1994.

Godard, Charles. *Les Pouvoirs des intendants sous Louis XIV: particulièrement dans les pays d'élections, de 1661 à 1715.* Paris: 1901. Reprint, Geneva: Slatkine-Megariotis, 1974.

Gourdeau, Claire. *Les Délices de nos coeurs: Marie de l'Incarnation et ses pensionnaires amérindiennes, 1639–1672.* Quebec: Septentrion/Celat, 1994.

Grabowski, Jan. "Les Amérindiens domiciliés et la 'contrebande' des fourrures en Nouvelle-France." *Recherches amérindiennes au Québec* 24(3): 45–52 (1994).

– "French Criminal Justice and Indians in Montreal, 1670–1760." *Ethnohistory* 43(3): 405–29 (1996).

Gray, Colleen. "Captives in Canada, 1744–1763." MA thesis, McGill University, 1993.

Green, Gretchen Lynn. "A New People in an Age of War: The Kahnawake Iroquois, 1667–1760." PhD diss., College of William and Mary, 1991.

Greenblatt, Stephen. *Marvelous Possessions: The Wonder of the New World*. Chicago: University of Chicago Press, 1991.

– "Cultural Mobility: An Introduction." In *Cultural Mobility: A Manifesto*, 1–23. New York: Cambridge University Press, 2009.

Greene, Jack P. "Colonial History and National History: Reflections on a Continuing Problem." *William and Mary Quarterly* 64(2): 235–50 (2007).

– *The Intellectual Construction of America: Exceptionalism and Identity from 1492 to 1800*. Chapel Hill: University of North Carolina Press, 1993.

– "Search for Identity: An Interpretation of the Meaning of Selected Patterns of Social Response in Eighteenth-Century America." In *Imperatives, Behaviors, and Identities: Essays in Early American Cultural History*, 143–173. Charlottesville: University Press of Virginia, 1992.

– "Transatlantic Colonization and the Redefinition of Empire in the Early Modern Period: The British-American Experience." In Christine Daniels and Michael V. Kennedy, eds, *Negotiated Empires: Centers and Peripheries in the Americas, 1500–1820*, 267–82. New York: Routledge, 2002.

Greer, Allan. "L'Habitant, la paroisse rurale et la politique locale au XVIIIe siècle: quelques cas dans la vallée du Richelieu." *Société canadienne d'histoire de l'Église catholique, Sessions d'études* 47 (1980): 19–33.

– *Mohawk Saint: Catherine Tekakwitha and the Jesuits*. Oxford: Oxford University Press, 2006.

– "National, Transnational, and Hypernational Historiographies: New France Meets Early American History." *Canadian Historical Review* 91(4): 695–724 (2010).

– *Peasant, Lord and Merchant: Rural Society in Three Quebec Parishes, 1740–1840*. Toronto: University of Toronto Press, 1985.

– *Property and Dispossession: Natives, Empires and Land in Early Modern North America*. Cambridge: Cambridge University Press, 2018.

Grenier, Fernand, ed. *Papiers Contrecoeur et autres documents concernant le conflit anglo-français sur l'Ohio de 1745 à 1756*. Quebec: Presses de l'Université Laval, 1952.

Griffiths, Naomi E.S. *The Contexts of Acadian History, 1686–1784*. Montreal and Kingston: McGill-Queen's University Press, 1992.

Gruber, Ira D. "The Anglo-American Military Tradition and the War for American Independence." In Kenneth J. Hagen and William B. Roberts, eds, *Against All Enemies: Interpretations of American Military History from Colonial Times to the Present*, 21–47. Westport, CT: Greenwood Press, 1986.

Guéry, Alain. "Les Comptes de la mort vague après la guerre: pertes de guerre et conjoncture du phénomène guerre." *Histoire et mesure* 6(3–4): 289–312 (1991).

– "The State: The Tool of the Common Good." In Pierre Nora, ed., *Rethinking France: Les Lieux de Mémoire*, vol. 1, *The State*, trans. Mary Trouille, 1–52. Chicago: University of Chicago Press, 2001.

Gutton, Jean-Pierre. "La Déportation des pauvres aux colonies." In *La Société et les pauvres: l'exemple de la généralité de Lyon, 1534–1789*, 289–93. Paris: Les Belles Lettres, 1971.

Habault, Gabriel. *La Corvée royale au XVIIIe siècle*. Paris: Larose, 1903.

Haefeli, Evan, and Kevin Sweeney. *Captors and Captives: The 1704 French and Indian Raid on Deerfield*. Amherst: University of Massachusetts Press, 2003.

– "Revisiting *The Redeemed Captive*: New Perspectives in the 1704 Attack on Deerfield." *William and Mary Quarterly* (3rd series) 52(1): 22–3 (January 1995).

Hamelin, Jean. *Économie et société en Nouvelle-France*. Quebec: Presses de l'Université Laval, 1960.

– ed. *Histoire du Québec*. Montreal: Éditions France-Amérique, 1977.

Harris, Cole, ed. *From the Beginning to 1800*. Vol. 1 of *Historical Atlas of Canada*, edited by Geoffrey J. Matthews. Toronto: University of Toronto Press, 1987.

– *The Reluctant Land: Society, Space, and Environment in Canada before Confederation*. Vancouver: UBC Press, 2008.

– *The Seigneurial System in Early Canada: A Geographical Study*. Madison: University of Wisconsin Press, 1966.

Hastings, Susanna Willard Johnson. *A Narrative of the Captivity of Mrs. Johnson: Containing an Account of Her Sufferings, during Four Years, with the Indians and French*. 2nd ed. Windsor, VT: Printed by Alden Spooner, 1807.

Hatch, Nathan O. "The Origins of Civil Millennialism in America: New England Clergymen, War with France, and the Revolution." *William and Mary Quarterly* (3rd series) 31(3): 407–30 (July 1974).

Havard, Gilles. *Empire et métissages: Indiens et Français dans le Pays d'en Haut, 1660–1715*. Sillery: Septentrion, 2003.

– *La Grande Paix de Montréal de 1701: les voies de la diplomatie franco-amérindienne*. Montreal: Recherches amérindiennes au Québec, 1992.

– *Histoire des coureurs de bois: Amérique du Nord, 1600–1840*. Paris: Les Indes savantes, 2016.
– "Les Pays d'en haut, un espace en mal d'histoire?" *Francophonies d'Amérique* 40–41: 19–54 (2015–16).
Hébert, Jean-Claude, ed. *Le Siège de Québec en 1759, par trois témoins*. Quebec: Ministère des Affaires culturelles, 1972.
Hébert, Robert. *L'Amérique française devant l'opinion étrangère, 1756–1960: anthologie*. Montreal: L'Hexagone, 1989.
Heidenreich, Conrad. *Huronia: A History and Geography of the Huron Indians, 1600–1650*. Toronto: McClelland and Stewart, 1971.
Henripin, Jacques. *La Population canadienne au début du XVIIIe siècle: nuptialité, fécondité, mortalité infantile*. Paris: Presses universitaires de France, 1954.
Henripin, Jacques, and Yves Péron. "La Transition démographique de la province de Québec." In Hubert Charbonneau, ed., *La Population du Québec: études rétrospectives*, 23–44. Trois-Rivières: Boréal Express, 1973.
Higginbotham, Don. "The Early American Way of War: Reconnaissance and Appraisal." *William and Mary Quarterly* (3rd series) 44(2): 230–73 (April 1987).
Hilliard d'Auberteuil, Michel-René. *Considérations sur l'état présent de la colonie française de Saint-Domingue: ouvrage politique et législatif; presenté au ministre de la Marine*. 2 vols. Paris: Grangé, 1776–77.
Hincker, François. *Les Français devant l'impôt sous l'Ancien Régime*. Paris: Flammarion, 1971.
Hinderaker, Eric. *Elusive Empires: Constructing Colonialism in the Ohio Valley, 1673–1800*. Cambridge: Cambridge University Press, 1997.
Horguelin, Christophe. "Le XVIIIe siècle des canadiens: discours public et identité." In Philippe Joutard and Thomas Wien, eds, *Mémoires de Nouvelle-France: de France en Nouvelle-France*, 209–19. Rennes: Presses universitaires de Rennes, 2005.
– *La Prétendue République*. Sillery: Septentrion, 1997.
Houllemare, Marie. "Procedures, Jurisdictions and Records: Building the French Empire in the Early Eighteenth Century." *Journal of Colonialism and Colonial History* 21(2): n.p. (2020).
Jacob, Annie. "Homme économique/homme sauvage, XVIe-XVIIIe siècles." PhD diss., École des hautes études en sciences sociales, 1992.
Jacquart, Jean. *La Crise rurale en Île de France, 1550–1670*. Paris: Armand Colin, 1974.

Jaenen, Cornelius J. *Friend and Foe: Aspects of French-Amerindian Cultural Contact in the Sixteenth and Seventeenth Centuries.* Toronto: McClelland and Stewart, 1973.
– "Inhuman Barbarism: Perspectives on French and American Violence in Colonial Times." Paper presented at the conference of the Canadian Historical Association, Calgary, June 1994.
– *The Role of the Church in New France.* Toronto: McGraw-Hill Ryerson, 1976.
Jennings, Francis. *The Ambiguous Iroquois Empire: The Covenant Chain Confederation of Indian Tribes with English Colonies from its Beginnings to the Lancaster Treaty of 1744.* New York: Norton, 1984.
– *Empire of Fortune: Crowns, Colonies and Tribes in the Seven Years' War in America.* New York: Norton, 1988.
Jesuits. Canada. *Le Journal des Jésuites, publié d'après le manuscrit original conservé aux archives du Séminaire de Québec.* Edited by Charles-Henri Laverdière and Henri-Raymond Casgrain. Montreal: J.M. Valois, 1892.
– *Lettres édifiantes et curieuses écrites des missions étrangères.* Compiled by Charles Le Gobien et al. Rearranged and edited by Yves Mathurin Marie Tréaudet de Querbeuf. Paris: Chez J.G. Merigot le jeune, libraire, 1781.
Jones, Colin. "New Military History for Old? War and Society in Early Modern Europe." *European Studies Review*, no. 12 (1982): 97–108.
Jouanna, Arlette. *Le Devoir de révolte: la noblesse française et la gestion de l'État moderne (1559–1661).* Paris: Fayard, 1989.
– *Ordre social: mythes et hiérarchies dans la France du XVIe siècle.* Paris: Hachette, 1977.
"The Journal of a Captive, 1745–1748." In Isabel M. Calder, ed., *Colonial Captivities: Marches and Journeys*, 3–136. New York: Macmillan, 1935.
Juchereau de la Ferté, Jeanne-Françoise, and Marie-Andrée Regnard Duplessis. *Les Annales de l'Hôtel-Dieu de Québec, 1636–1716.* Edited by Albert Jamet. [Quebec]: Hôtel-Dieu de Québec, 1939.
Kalm, Pehr. *Voyage de Pehr Kalm au Canada en 1749.* Translated by Jacques Rousseau and Guy Bethune. Montreal: Pierre Tisseyre, 1977.
Keegan, John. *The Face of Battle.* London: Dorset Press, 1976.
– *History of Warfare.* New York: Knopf, 1993.
Kellogg, Louise Phelps. *The French Régime in Wisconsin and the Northwest.* Madison: State Historical Society of Wisconsin, 1925.
Kidd, Colin. *British Identities before Nationalism: Ethnicity and Nationhood in the Atlantic World, 1600–1800.* Cambridge: Cambridge University Press, 1999.

King, Titus. *Narrative of Titus King of Northampton, Mass.: A Prisoner of the Indians of Canada, 1755–1758*. Hartford: Connecticut Historical Society, 1938.

Knox, John. *An Historical Journal of the Campaigns in North America for the Years 1757, 1758, 1759, and 1760 by Captain John Knox, Published under the Direction of Arthur G. Doughty*. 3 vols. Toronto: Champlain Society, 1914–19.

Kopperman, Paul E. *Braddock at the Monongahela*. Pittsburgh: Pittsburgh University Press, 1977.

Krause, Eric, Carol Corbin, and William O'Shea, eds. *Aspects of Louisbourg: Essays on the History of an Eighteenth-Century French Community in North America*. Sydney, NS: The Louisbourg Institute, 1995.

Krusenstjern, B. von, and H. Medick. *Zwischen Alltag und Katastrophe: der Dreissigjährige Krieg aus der Nähe*. Göttingen: Vandenhoeck und Ruprecht, 1999.

La Roncière, Charles de. *Jacques Cartier et la découverte de la Nouvelle-France*. Paris: Plon, 1931.

La Tour, Louis Bertrand de. *Mémoires sur la vie de M. de Laval, premier Évêque de Québec*. Cologne: Chez Jean-Frederic Motiens, 1761.

Labat, Jean-Baptiste. *Nouveau voyage aux isles de l'Amérique*. Paris: G. Cavelier, 1722.

Lacelle, Claudette. "Monseigneur Henry-Marie Dubreil de Pontbriand: ses mandements et circulaires." MA thesis, University of Ottawa, 1971.

Lachance. André. "Le Contrôle social dans la société canadienne du Régime français au XVIIIe siècle." *Criminologie* 18(2): 7–18 (1985).

– "La Désertion et les soldats déserteurs au Canada dans la première moitié du XVIIIe siècle." *Revue de l'Université d'Ottawa* 47(1–2): 151–61 (January-April 1977).

– *La Justice criminelle du roi au Canada au XVIIIe siècle*. Quebec: Presses de l'Université Laval, 1978.

– *Les Marginaux, les exclus et l'autre au Canada aux XVIIe et XVIIIe siècles*. Montreal: Fides, 1996.

– *Vivre, aimer et mourir en Nouvelle-France*. Montreal: Libre Expression, 2000.

Lacour-Gayet, G. *La Marine militaire de la France sous le règne de Louis XV*. Paris: H. Champion, 1910.

Lacoursière, Jacques. *Histoire populaire du Québec*. Quebec: Septentrion, 1995–97.

– "La Tentative de colonisation, 1541–1543." In Fernand Braudel, ed., *Le Monde de Jacques Cartier*, 275–83. Montreal/Paris: Libre Expression/ Berger-Levrault, 1984.

Ladurie, Emmanuel Le Roy. *L'Ancien Régime*. Paris: Hachette, 1991.

Lahontan, Louis Armand de Lom d'Arce, Baron de. *Oeuvres complètes*. Edited by Réal Ouellet with assistance from Alain Beaulieu. Montreal: Presses de l'Université de Montréal, 1990.

Lanctôt, Gustave. "Les Troupes de la Nouvelle-France." *Canadian Historical Association, Report of the Annual Meeting* 5(1): 40–60 (1926).

Landry, Yves, ed. *Pour le Christ et le Roi: la vie au temps des premiers Montréalais*. Montreal: Libre expression, 1992.

Landry, Yves, and Rénald Lessard. "Les Causes de décès aux XVIIe et XVIIIe siècles dans les registres paroissiaux québécois." *RHAF* 48(4): 509–26 (Spring 1995).

LaPierre, Laurier. *1759: The Battle for Canada*. Toronto: McClelland & Stewart, 1990.

Laufer, Roger. *Lesage ou Le Métier de romancier*. Paris: Gallimard, 1971.

Lavallée, Louis. *La Prairie en Nouvelle-France, 1647–1760: étude d'histoire sociale*. Montreal and Kingston: McGill-Queen's University Press, 1992.

Le Beau, C. *Avantures du Sr. C. Le Beau, avocat en Parlement, ou voyage curieux et nouveau parmi les sauvages de l'Amérique Septentrionale*. 2 vols. Amsterdam: Herman Uytwerf, 1738.

Le Blant, Robert. *Histoire de la Nouvelle-France: les sources narratives du début du XVIIIe siècle* ... Dax: Prodieu, n.d.

– ed. "Le Livre de raison de François de Tapie de Monteil, capitaine au régiment de Poitou (1661–1670)." *RHAF* 13(4): 562–73 (March 1960).

Le Blant, Robert, and René Baudry, eds. *Nouveaux documents sur Champlain et son époque*. Ottawa: Archives publiques, 1967.

Le Bras, Yvon. "Les Relations de Paul Lejeune: aux frontières de l'historiographie." In Réal Ouellet, ed., *Rhétorique et conquête missionnaire: le jésuite Paul Lejeune*, 53–65. Quebec: Septentrion, 1993.

Le Clercq, Chrestien. *First Establishment of the Faith in New France*. 2 vols. Translated by John Gilmary Shea. New York: J.G. Shea, [1691] 1881.

Le Goff, V.J.A. *Vannes and Its Region: A Study of Town and Country in Eighteenth Century France*. Oxford: Clarendon Press, 1981.

Le Jeune, L. *Dictionnaire général du Canada*. Ottawa: Presses de l'Université d'Ottawa, 1931.

Leach, Douglas Edward. *Arms for Empire: A Military History of the British Colonies in North America, 1607–1763*. New York: Macmillan, 1973.

– *Roots of Conflict: British Armed Forces and Colonial Americans, 1677–1763*. Chapel Hill: University of North Carolina Press, 1986.

Lebrun, François. *Les Hommes et la mort en Anjou aux XVIIe et XVIIIe siècles: essai de démographie et de psychologie historiques*. Paris: Mouton, 1971.

– "Les Soulèvements populaires à Angers aux XVIIe et XVIIIe siècles." In *Actes du 90e Congrès national des sociétés savantes, Nice, 1965*, 119–40. Paris: Bibliothèque nationale, 1966.

Lebrun, François, and Normand Séguin, eds. *Sociétés villageoises et rapports villes-campagnes au Québec et dans la France de l'Ouest, XVIIe–XXe siècles*. Trois-Rivières: Centre de recherches en études québécoises, Université du Québec à Trois-Rivières, 1987.

Leclerc, Jean-François. "Justice et infra-justice en Nouvelle-France: les voies de fait à Montréal entre 1700 et 1760." *Criminologie* 18(1): 25–39 (1985).

Lefebvre, Jean-Jacques. "Les Officiers de milice de Laprairie en 1745, leurs alliés, leurs prédécesseurs à 1700, leurs successeurs à 1760 et leurs descendants." *Mémoire de la Société royale du Canada* (4th series) 7 (1969): 169–205.

Lemieux, Denise. *Les Petits Innocents: l'enfance en Nouvelle-France*. Quebec: IQRC, 1985.

Lemire, Maurice, ed. *La Vie littéraire au Québec*. Vol. 1, *1764–1805: la voix française des nouveaux sujets britanniques*. Quebec: Presses de l'Université Laval, 1991.

Lépine, Luc. "Les Stratégies militaires françaises et britanniques lors de la guerre de Sept Ans en Nouvelle-France (1755–1760)." In Bertrand Fonck and Laurent Veyssière, eds, *La Guerre de Sept Ans en Nouvelle-France*, 133–54. Quebec: Septentrion, 2012.

Lepore, Jill. *The Name of War: King Philip's War and the Origins of American Identity*. New York: Alfred A. Knopf, 1998.

Lesage, Alain-René. *The Adventures of Robert Chevalier Call'd de Beauchene, Captain of a Privateer in New-France*. 2 vols. London: Printed and sold by T. Gardner, 1745.

Lesage, Germain. *Manereuil, fondateur de Louiseville, 1665–1672*. Louiseville, QC: Presbytère de Louiseville, 1966.

Lessard, Denis. "Un chercheur aux cent préfaces, Luc Lacourcière." *Bulletin Mnemo*, online at http://www.mnemo.qc.ca/html/99(26).html (viewed December 2007).

Lessard, Rénald. "Les Soldats des compagnies franches de la Marine au Canada et à l'île Royale: le prix de la défaite (1750–1763)." In Bertrand

Fonck and Laurent Veyssière, eds, *La Chute de la Nouvelle-France: de l'affaire Jumonville au traité de Paris*, 62–89. Quebec: Septentrion, 2015.

Lesueur, Boris. "Les Mutations d'une institution: le corps des officiers des troupes de la Marine au Canada." In Marcel Fournier, ed., *Les Officiers des troupes de la Marine au Canada, 1683–1760*, 33–82. Quebec: Septentrion, 2017.

– *Les Troupes coloniales de l'Ancien Régime: Fidelitate per Mare et Terras*. Paris: Éditions SPM, 2014.

Letaconnoux, Joseph. *Le Régime de la corvée en Bretagne au XVIIIe siècle*. Rennes: Plihon et Hommay, 1905.

Levi, Giovanni. *Le Pouvoir au village: histoire d'un exorciste dans le Piémont du XVIIe siècle*. Paris: Gallimard, 1983.

Lhéritier, Michel. *L'Intendant Tourny (1695–1760)*. 2 vols. Paris: Librairie Félix Alcan, 1920.

Lotbinière, René-Louis Chartier de. "Vers burlesques sur le Voyage de Monsieur de Courcelles, gouverneur et lieutenant général pour le Roy en la Nouvelle France en l'année 1666." Reproduced in P.-G. Roy, "René-Louis Chartier de Lotbinière." *Bulletin des recherches historiques* 33(5): 257–82 (May 1927).

Lozier, Jean-François. *Flesh Reborn: The Saint Lawrence Valley Mission Settlements through the Seventeenth Century*. Montreal and Kingston: McGill-Queen's University Press, 2018.

– "Lever des chevelures en Nouvelle-France: la politique française du paiement des scalps." *RHAF* 56(4): 513–42 (Spring 2003).

– "Les Officiers de milice canadiens sous le Régime français: étude institutionnelle et sociale." MA thesis, University of Ottawa, 2004.

"M. Jean-Félix Récher, curé de Québec, et son journal, 1757–1760." *Bulletin des recherches historiques* 9 (1903): 97–122, 129–47, 161–74, 289–307, 321–46, 353–73.

MacLeod, D. Peter. *The Canadian Iroquois and the Seven Years' War*. Toronto: Dundurn Press and Canadian War Museum, 1996.

– "Microbes and Muskets: Smallpox and the Participation of the Amerindian Allies of New France in the Seven Years' War." *Ethnohistory* 39(1): 42–64 (Winter 1992).

Malartic, Anne-Joseph-Hippolyte de Maurès, comte de. *Journal des campagnes au Canada: de 1755 à 1760*. Dijon: L. Damidot, 1890.

Malchelosse, Gérard. "Faux sauniers, prisonniers et fils de famille en Nouvelle-France." *Cahiers des Dix* 9 (1944): 161–97.

Mandrou, Robert. *La France aux XVIIe et XVIIIe siècles*. Paris: Presses universitaires de France, 1967.

– *Louis XIV en son temps*. Paris: Presses universitaires de France, 1973.

Marie de l'Incarnation. *Lettres de la révérende mère Marie de l'Incarnation*. Edited by Pierre François Richaudeau. Paris: Tournai Casterman, 1876.

Marion, Marcel. *Dictionnaire des institutions de la France aux XVIIe et XVIIIe siècles*. Paris: Picard, 1969.

– *Les Impôts directs sous l'Ancien Régime, principalement au XVIIIe siècle*. Paris: Cornely, 1910. Reprint, Geneva: Slatkine-Megariotis Reprints, 1974.

Martel, Jean Baptiste. *Mémoire pour le Sieur Martel: écuyer, seigneur de Saint-Antoine & de Magesse, ci-devant garde-magasin du roi à Mont-Réal*. Paris: n.p., 1763.

Martin, Daniel. "La Maréchaussée au XVIIIe siècle: les hommes et l'institution en Auvergne." *Annales historiques de la Révolution française* 239 (January-March 1980): 91–117.

Martino, Gina M. *Women at War in the Borderlands of the Early American Northeast*. Chapel Hill: University of North Carolina Press, 2018.

Marx, Karl. *Contribution to the Critique of Political Economy*. Chicago: Charles H. Kerr, 1904.

Massicotte, E.-Z. *Répertoire des arrêts, édits, mandements, ordonnances et règlements: conservés dans les archives du Palais de justice de Montréal, 1640–1760*. Montreal: Ducharme, 1919.

Mathieu, Jacques. *La Construction navale royale à Québec, 1739–1759*. Quebec: Société historique de Québec, 1971.

– *La Nouvelle-France: les Français en Amérique du Nord, XVIe–XVIIIe siècle*. Quebec: Presses de l'Université Laval, 1991.

Mathieu, Jacques, and Serge Courville, eds. *Peuplement colonisateur aux XVIIe et XVIIIe siècles*. [Quebec:] CÉLAT/Faculté des lettres, Université Laval, 1987.

Mathieu, Jacques, and Sophie Imbeault. *La Guerre des canadiens, 1756–1763*. Quebec: Septentrion, 2013.

May, Louis-Philippe. *Histoire économique de la Martinique, 1635–1763*. Fort-de-France: Société de distribution et de culture, 1972.

McConville, Brendan. *The King's Three Faces: The Rise and Fall of Royal America, 1688–1776*. Chapel Hill: University of North Carolina Press, 2006.

Melvoin, Richard I. *New England Outpost: War and Society in Colonial Deerfield*. New York: W.W. Norton, 1989.

Mémoire pour Messire François Bigot, ci-devant intendant de justice, police, finance & marine en Canada, accusé: contre Monsieur le procureur général du roi en la commission, accusateur. Paris: Le Prieur, 1763.

Meyer, Jean. "La Course, romantisme, exutoire social, réalité économique: essai de méthodologie." *Annales de Bretagne* 78 (June 1971): 307–44.

– "De la guerre au XVIIe siècle." *XVIIe siècle*, no. 148 (July-September 1985): 267–90.

– *La Noblesse bretonne au XVIIIe siècle.* Paris: Flammarion, 1972.

– Jean Tarrade, Anne Rey-Goldzeiguer, and Jacques Thobie. *Histoire de la France coloniale.* Vol. 1, *Des origines à 1914.* Paris: Armand Colin, 1991.

Miquelon, Dale. "Havy and Lefebvre of Quebec: A Case Study of Metropolitan Participation in Canadian Trade, 1730–60." *Canadian Historical Review* 56(1): 1–24 (1975).

– *New France 1701–1744: A Supplement to Europe.* Toronto: McClelland and Stewart, 1987.

– "'A Supplement to Europe': Canada in the Reclaimed Empire, 1701–1744." *Journal of the Western Society for French History* 13: 261–70.

Mirabeau, Victor de Riqueti, Marquis de. *L'Ami des hommes, ou Traité de la population.* Avignon: n.p., 1756.

Mitchell, John. *The Contest in America between Great Britain and France.* London: A. Millar, 1757.

Moogk, Peter N. *La Nouvelle France: The Making of French Canada – A Cultural History.* East Lansing: Michigan State University Press, 2000.

Moore, Christopher. "Colonization and Conflict: New France and Its Rivals (1600–1760)." In Craig Brown, ed., *The Illustrated History of Canada,* 95–180. Toronto: Lester and Orpen Dennys, 1987.

– *Louisbourg Portraits: Life in an Eighteenth-Century Garrison Town.* Toronto: Macmillan, 1982.

Moreau de Saint-Méry, M.L.E. *Description topographique, physique, civile, politique et historique de la partie française de l'isle Saint-Domingue.* Philadelphia: n.p., 1797–98. Reprinted, Paris: Société de l'histoire des colonies françaises and Librairie Larose, 1958. Edited by Blanche Maurel and Étienne Taillemite. 3 vols.

Morin, Marie. *Histoire simple et véritable de l'établissement des religieuses hospitalières de Saint-Joseph en l'isle de Montréal.* Edited by Ghislaine Legendre. Montreal: Presses de l'Université de Montréal, 1979.

Morton, Desmond. *A Military History of Canada*. Toronto: McClelland and Stewart, 1992.

Mourin, Samuel. "Le Nerf de la guerre: finances et métissage des expéditions françaises de la première guerre des Renards (1715–1716)." *French Colonial History* 12(1): 67–86 (2011).

– *Porter la guerre aux Iroquois: les expéditions françaises contre la Ligue des Cinq Nations à la fin du XVIIᵉ siècle*. Montreal: Éditions GID, 2009.

Mousnier, Roland. *Les Institutions de la France sous la monarchie absolue, 1598–1789*. 2 vols. Paris: Presses universitaires de France, 1974–1980.

Murray, James. *Report of the State of Government of Quebec in Canada*. Quebec: Dussault and Proulx, 1902.

Myrand, Ernest, ed. *Sir William Phips devant Québec: histoire d'un siège*. Montreal: Beauchemin, 1925.

Nash, Alice N. "Captives among the Abenakis, 1605–1763." Paper presented at McGill University, February 1992.

– "Two Stories of New England Captives: Grizel and Christine Otis of Dover, New Hampshire." In Peter Benes, ed., *New England/New France 1600–1850*, 28–48. Boston: Boston University, 1992.

Navières, Joseph. "Un voyage à la Nouvelle-France en 1734." *Revue canadienne*, 1886.

Nerich, Laurent. *La Petite Guerre et la Chute de la Nouvelle-France*. Outremont, QC: Athéna Éditions, 2009.

Nicolai, Martin L. "A Different Kind of Courage: The French Military and the Canadian Irregular Soldier during the Seven Years' War." *Canadian Historical Review* 70(1): 53–75 (1989).

Noël, Dave. *Montcalm, général américain*. Montreal: Boréal, 2018.

Norton, John. *Narrative of the Capture and Burning of Fort Massachusetts by the French and Indians, in the Time of War of 1744–49, and the Captivity of All Those Stationed There to the Number of Thirty Persons*. Edited by S.G. Drake. Albany: Printed for S.G. Drake of Boston by J. Munsell, 1870.

Nutc, Grace Lee. *Caesars of the Wilderness: Médard Chouart, Sieur Des Groseilliers and Pierre Esprit Radisson, 1618–1710*. St Paul: Minnesota Historical Society Press, 1978 [1943].

O'Callaghan, E.B., ed. *Documents Relative to the Colonial History of the State of New York*. 15 vols. Albany: Weed, Parsons, Printers, 1853–87.

Osman, Julia. "Pride, Prejudice, and Prestige: French Officers in North America during the Seven Years' War." In Mark H. Danley and Patrick

J. Speelman, eds, *The Seven Years' War as a Global Conflict: Essays and Interpretations*, 191–211. Leiden: Brill, 2012.

Otterbein, K.F. "Why the Iroquois Won: An Analysis of Iroquois Military Tactics." *Ethnohistory* 11 (1964): 56–63.

Ouellet, Fernand. "Officiers de milice et structure sociale au Québec (1660–1815)." *Histoire sociale/Social History* 12(23): 37–65 (May 1979).

Ouellet, Réal. "Jésuites et philosophes lecteurs de Lahontan." *Saggi e ricerche di letteratura francese* 29 (new series): 119–64 (1990).

Ouellet, Réal, and Jack Warwick, eds. *Le Grand Voyage du pays des Hurons*. Montreal: Leméac/Bibliothèque québécoise, 1990.

Ozouf, Mona. "L'Opinion publique." In Keith M. Baker, ed., *The French Revolution and the Creation of Modern Political Culture*. Vol. 1, *The Political Culture of the Old Regime*, 419–40. Oxford: Pergamon Press, 1987.

Panet, Jean-Claude. *Journal du siège de Québec en 1759*. Montreal: E. Sénécal, 1866.

Panissié, Florian. "La Petite Guerre à l'épreuve des colonies, de la théorie à la pratique: le cas du siège de Québec en 1759." In Éric Schnakenbourg and Frédéric Dessberg, eds, *La France face aux crises et aux conflits des périphéries européennes et atlantiques du XVIIᵉ au XXᵉ siècle*, 155–68. Rennes: Presses universitaires de Rennes, 2010.

Paret, Peter. "Colonial Experience and European Military Reform at the End of the Eighteenth Century." *Bulletin of the Institute of Historical Research* 37: 47–59 (1964).

Parker, Geoffrey. *The Military Revolution: Military Innovation and the Rise of the West, 1500–1800*. Cambridge: Cambridge University Press, 1988.

Parkman, Francis. *Montcalm and Wolfe*. New York: Atheneum, 1984.

Parmenter, Jon. "At the Wood's Edge: Eighteenth-Century Iroquois Politics and Society." PhD diss., University of Michigan, 1999.

Pease, Theodore C., and Ernestine Jenison, eds. *Illinois on the Eve of the Seven Years' War, 1747–1755*. Springfield: Illinois State Historical Library, 1940.

Peckham, Howard H. "The Captivity of Charles Stuart, 1755–57." *Mississippi Valley Historical Review* 13 (1926–27): 58–81.

– ed. *Narratives of Colonial America, 1704–1765*. Chicago: Lakeshore Press, 1971.

– "Thomas Gist's Indian Captivity: 1758–1759." *Pennsylvania Magazine of History and Biography* 80(3): 285–311 (July 1956).

Penhallow, Samuel. *The History of the Wars of New-England, with the Eastern Indians*. Boston: Printed by T. Fleet for S. Gerrish at the lower end of Cornhill, and D. Henchman over-against the Brick meeting-house in Cornhill, 1726.

Perrot, Nicolas. *Mémoires sur les moeurs, coustumes et relligion des sauvages de l'Amérique septentrionale*. First edition introduced and annotated by Jules Tailhan. Leipzig and Paris: Librairie A. Franck, 1864.

Petit, Émilien. *Dissertations sur le droit public des colonies françaises, espagnoles et anglaises, d'après les loix des trois nations, comparées entr'elles*. Geneva/Paris: Knapen et fils, 1778.

Picaud-Monnerat, Sandrine. *La Petite Guerre au XVIIIᵉ siècle*. Paris: Economica, 2010.

Pichichero, Christy. *The Military Enlightenment: War and Culture in the French Empire from Louis XIV to Napoleon*. Ithaca, NY: Cornell University Press, 2017.

Pioffet, Marie-Christine. "L'Arc et l'Épée: les images de la guerre chez le jésuite Paul Lejeune." In Réal Ouellet, ed., *Rhétorique et conquête missionnaire: le jésuite Paul Lejeune*, 41–52. Quebec: Septentrion/Célat, 1993.

– *La Tentation de l'épopée dans les Relations des jésuites*. Sillery: Septentrion, 1997.

Plank, Geoffrey. *Atlantic Wars: From the Fifteenth Century to the Age of Revolution*. Oxford: Oxford University Press, 2020.

– *Rebellion and Savagery: The Jacobite Rising of 1745 and the British Empire*. Philadelphia: University of Pennsylvania Press, 2005.

Pluchon, Pierre. *Histoire de la colonisation française*. Vol. 1, *Le Premier Empire colonial: des origines à la restauration*. Paris: Fayard, 1991.

Poirier, Monique. "The Fortifications of Montréal, 1717–1744: The Development of the Plan." MA thesis in art history, Concordia University, 1991.

Porchnev, Boris. *Les Soulèvements populaires en France de 1623 à 1648*. Paris: SEVPEN, 1963.

Pote, William. *The Journal of Captain William Pote Junior during His Captivity in the French and Indian War from May 1745 to August 1747*. Edited by Victor H. Paltsits. New York: Dodd, Mead and Co., 1896.

Pouchot, Pierre. *Mémoires sur la dernière guerre de l'Amérique septentrionale entre la France et l'Angleterre: suivis d'observations, dont plusieurs sont relatives au théâtre actuel de la guerre, & de nouveaux détails sur les moeurs & les usages des Sauvages: avec des cartes topographiques*.

3 vols. Yverdon (France): [n.p.], 1781. *Editors' note*: Reprinted, Sillery: Septentrion, 2002.

Poulantzas, Nicos. *Political Power and Social Classes*. Translated by Timothy O'Hagan. [London]: NLB & S & W, [1973].

Pozzo-Laurent, Jeannine. "Le Réseau routier dans le gouvernement de Québec (1706–1760)." MA thesis, Université Laval, 1981.

Pratt, Mary Louise. *Imperial Eyes: Travel Writing and Transculturation*. London and New York: Routledge, [1992] 2008.

Pritchard, James S. *Anatomy of a Naval Disaster: The 1746 French Expedition to North America*. Montreal and Kingston: McGill-Queen's University Press, 1995.

– *In Search of Empire: The French in the Americas, 1670–1730*. Cambridge: Cambridge University Press, 2004.

– *Louis XV's Navy, 1748–1762: A Study of Organization and Administration*. Montreal and Kingston: McGill-Queen's University Press, 1987.

– "The Pattern of French Colonial Shipping to Canada before 1760." *Revue française d'histoire d'Outre-Mer* 231: 196–200 (1976).

– "Ships, Men and Commerce: A Study of Maritime Activity in New France." PhD diss., University of Toronto, 1971.

Proulx, Gilles. "Soldat à Québec, 1748–1759." *RHAF* 32(4): 535–63 (March 1979).

Rameau de Saint-Père, François-Edme. *Une colonie féodale en Amérique (L'Acadie, 1604–1710)*. Paris: Didier, 1877.

[Raudot, Antoine-Denis]. *Relation par lettres de l'Amérique septentrionale (années 1709 et 1710)*. Edited by Camille de Rochemonteix. Paris: Letouzey et Ané, 1904.

Rawlyk, George A. *Nova Scotia's Massachusetts: A Study of Massachusetts–Nova Scotia Relations, 1630–1784*. Montreal and Kingston: McGill-Queen's University Press, 1973.

Raymond, Charles de. *On the Eve of Conquest: The Chevalier de Raymond's Critique of New France in 1754*. Edited and translated by Joseph L. Peyser. Lansing: Michigan State University Press, 1998.

Récher, Jean Félix. 1959. *Journal du siège de Québec en 1759*. Quebec: Société historique de Québec, 1959.

Redlich, Fritz. *De Praeda Militari: Looting and Booty, 1500–1815*. Wiesbaden: Franz Steiner Verlag, 1956.

[Regnard Duplessis, Marie-Andrée]. "Lettres de mère Marie-Andrée Duplessis de Sainte-Hélène, supérieure des hospitalières de l'Hôtel-Dieu de Québec." Edited by A.-L. Leymarie. *Nova Francia* 4(1): 33–58 (1929).

Reid, John G. "Acadia or Nova Scotia." In *Six Crucial Decades: Times of Change in the History of the Maritimes*, 29–60. Halifax: Nimbus Publishing, 1987.

Revel, Jacques. *Logiques de la foule: l'affaire des enlèvements d'enfants: Paris 1750*. Paris: Hachette, 1988.

Rey, Alain, ed. *Dictionnaire historique de la langue française*. Paris: Le Robert, 1993.

Rice, James D. "War and Politics: Powhatan Expansionism and the Problem of Native American Warfare." *William and Mary Quarterly* 77(1): 3–32 (2020).

Richard, Jean-Olivier. "Bougainville à la lumière de ses lectures: les références classiques dans les *Écrits sur le Canada*." *Revue d'histoire de l'Amérique française* 64(2): 5–31 (2010).

Richter, Daniel K. *The Ordeal of the Longhouse: The Peoples of the Iroquois League in the Era of European Colonization*. Chapel Hill: University of North Carolina Press, c1992.

– "War and Culture: The Iroquois Experience." *William and Mary Quarterly* (3rd series) 40(4): 528–59 (October 1983).

Robert, Jean-Claude. *Atlas historique de Montréal*. Montreal: Art global/Libre expression, 1994.

Robichaud, Léon. "Le Pouvoir, les paysans et la voirie du Bas-Canada à la fin du XVIIIe siècle." MA thesis, McGill University, 1989.

Roche, Daniel. *La Culture des apparences: une histoire du vêtement, XVIIe–XVIIIe siècle*. Paris: Fayard, 1989.

Rogers, Robert. *Journals of Major Robert Rogers: Reprinted from the Original Edition of 1765*. New York: Corinth Books, 1961.

Roupnel, Gaston. *La Ville et la Campagne au XVIIe siècle: étude sur les populations du pays dijonnais*. Paris: A. Colin, 1955.

Rousseau, François. *L'Oeuvre de chère en Nouvelle-France: le régime des malades à l'Hôtel-Dieu de Québec*. Quebec: Presses de l'Université Laval, 1983.

Roy, J.-Edmond. *Histoire de la seigneurie de Lauzon*. 5 vols. Lévis: Mercier, 1897–1904.

Roy, Pierre-Georges, ed. *Édits, ordonnances royaux ... concernant le Canada, arrêts et règlements du Conseil supérieur, etc.* 3 vols. Quebec: Fréchette, 1854–56.

– *Inventaire des papiers de Léry conservés aux archives de la province de Québec*. 3 vols. Quebec: n.p., 1939–40.

– *Ordonnances, commissions, etc., etc., des gouverneurs et intendants de la Nouvelle-France, 1639–1706*. 2 vols. Beauceville: L'Éclaireur, 1924.

Roy, Pierre-Georges, and Antoine Roy, eds. *Inventaire des greffes des notaires du Régime français.* Vols. 18–19, edited by Antoine Roy. Quebec: Quebec, 1942–.

Ruggiu, François-Joseph. "La Noblesse du Canada aux XVIIᵉ et XVIIIᵉ siècles." *Histoire, économie & société* 27(4): 67–85 (2008).

– "Une relation tombée dans l'oubli? Le Canada et la Monarchie française entre 1759 et 1783." In Bertrand Fonck and Laurent Veyssière, eds, *La Chute de la Nouvelle-France: de l'affaire Jumonville au traité de Paris,* 533–61. Quebec: Septentrion, 2015.

Rushforth, Brett. *Bonds of Alliance: Indigenous and Atlantic Slaveries in New France.* Chapel Hill: University of North Carolina Press, 2012.

– "Insinuating Empire: Indians, Smugglers, and the Imperial Geography of Eighteenth-Century Montreal." In Jay Gitlin, Barbara Berglund, and Adam Arenson, eds, *Frontier Cities: Encounters at the Crossroads of Empire,* 49–65. Philadelphia: University of Pennsylvania Press, 2013.

Russell, Peter E. "Redcoats in the Wilderness: British Officers and Irregular Warfare in Europe and America, 1740 to 1760." *William and Mary Quarterly* (3rd series) 35(4): 629–52 (October 1978).

Sabean, David Warren. *Power in the Blood: Popular Culture and Village Discourse in Early Modern Germany.* New York: Cambridge University Press, 1987.

Saint-Félix. *Monseigneur de Saint-Vallier et l'Hôpital général de Québec: histoire du Monastère de Notre-Dame des Anges (religieuses hospitalières de la miséricorde de Jésus), ordre de Saint-Augustin.* Quebec: C. Darveau, 1882.

Saint-Vallier, Jean-Baptiste de La Croix de Chevrière de. *État présent de l'Eglise et de la colonie française dans la Nouvelle France.* Paris: Chez Robert Pepie, 1688. Reproduced in H. Têtu and C.-O. Gagnon, eds, *Mandements, lettres pastorales et circulaires des Évêques de Quebec,* 1: 191–265. Quebec: Imprimerie générale A. Côté, 1887.

Sanfaçon, Roland. "La Construction du premier chemin Québec-Montréal et le problème des corvées (1706–1737)." *Revue d'histoire de l'Amérique française* 12(1): 3–29 (1958).

Sayre, Gordon M. "*Michipichik* and the Walrus: Anishinaabe Natural History in the Seventeenth-Century Work of Louis Nicolas." *Journal for Early Modern Cultural Studies* 17(4): 21–48 (2017).

Schmalz, Peter S. *The Ojibwa of Southern Ontario.* Toronto: University of Toronto Press, 1991.

Selesky, Harold E. *War and Society in Colonial Connecticut*. New Haven, CT: Yale University Press, 1990.

Serjeant-major of Gen. Hopson's grenadiers. *A Journal of the Expedition up the River St. Lawrence: Containing a True and Most Particular Account of the Transactions of the Fleet and Army under the Command of Admiral Saunders and General Wolfe, from the Time of Their Embarkation at Louisbourg 'til after the Surrender of Quebeck*. Boston: Printed and sold by Fowle and Draper, at their printing-office in Marlborough-Street, 1759.

Sévigny, André. "'S'habituer dans le pays': facteurs d'établissement du soldat en Nouvelle-France à la fin du Grand Siècle." *Cahiers des Dix* 46 (1991): 61–86.

– "Les soldats des troupes de la Marine (1683–1715): premiers jalons sur la route d'une histoire inédite." *Cahiers des Dix* 44 (1989): 39–74.

Shy, John. *Toward Lexington: The Role of the British Army in the Coming of the American Revolution*. Princeton: Princeton University Press, 1965.

Silver, Peter. *Our Savage Neighbours: How Indian War Transformed Early America*. New York: Norton, 2008.

Slotkin, Richard. *Regeneration through Violence: The Mythology of the American Frontier, 1600–1860*. Middletown, CT: Wesleyan University Press, 1973.

Stacey, Charles P. "The British Forces in North America during the Seven Years' War." In *Dictionary of Canadian Biography*, ed. Ramsay Cook, 3: xxv–xxxii. Toronto: University of Toronto Press, 1974.

– *Quebec, 1759: The Siege and the Battle*. Edited by Donald E. Graves. Toronto: Robin Brass Studio, 2002.

Standen, Dale. "Politics, Patronage, and the Imperial Interest: Charles de Beauharnais's Disputes with Gilles Hocquart." *Canadian Historical Review* 60(1): 19–40 (1979).

Stanley, George F.G. *New France: The Last Phase, 1744–1760*. Toronto: McClelland & Stewart, 1968.

Steele, Ian K. *Betrayals: Fort William Henry and the "Massacre."* New York: Oxford University Press, 1990.

– "Governors or Generals: A Note on Martial Law and the Revolution of 1689 in English America." *William and Mary Quarterly* (3rd series) 46(2): 304–14 (April 1989).

– *Guerillas and Grenadiers: The Struggle for Canada, 1689–1760*. Toronto: Ryerson Press, 1969.

- *Warpaths: Invasions of North America.* New York: Oxford University Press, 1994.

Stevens, Sylvester K., and Donald H. Kent, eds. *Wilderness Chronicles of Northwestern Pennsylvania.* Harrisburg: Pennsylvania Historical Commission, 1941.

Sullivan, James, ed. *The Papers of Sir William Johnson.* Albany: State University of New York, 1921–65.

Sulte, Benjamin. *Histoire de la milice canadienne-française, 1760–1897.* Montreal: Desbarats, 1897.

Swanson, Carl E. "American Privateering and Imperial Warfare, 1739–1748." *William and Mary Quarterly* (3rd series) 42(3): 357–82 (July 1985).

Symcox, Geoffrey. *The Crisis of French Sea Power, 1688–1697: From the* guerre d'escadre *to the* guerre de course. The Hague: Nijhoff, 1974.

Tanguay, Cyprien. *Dictionnaire généalogique des familles canadiennes.* 7 vols. [Québec: E. Senécal, 1871–90].

Tarrade, Jean. *Le Commerce colonial de la France à la fin de l'Ancien régime: l'évolution du régime de l'exclusif de 1763 à 1789.* 2 vols. Paris: Presses universitaires de France, 1972.

Têtu, H., and C.-O. Gagnon, eds. *Mandements, lettres pastorales et circulaires des évêques de Québec.* 8 vols. Quebec: Côté, 1888.

Thévenin, Michel. *"Changer le système de la guerre": le siège en Nouvelle-France, 1755–1760.* Quebec: Presses de l'Université Laval, 2020.

Thwaites, Reuben G., ed. *The Jesuit Relations and Allied Documents: Travels and Explorations of the Jesuit Missionaries in New France, 1610–1791.* 73 vols. Cleveland: Burrows Brothers, 1896–1901.

Titus, James. *The Old Dominion at War: Society, Politics and Warfare in Late Colonial Virginia.* Columbia: University of South Carolina Press, 1991.

Tocqueville, Alexis de. *The Old Régime and the French Revolution.* Translated by Stuart Gilbert. Garden City, NJ: Doubleday Anchor Books, 1955.

Touzery, Mireille. *L'Invention de l'impôt sur le revenu: la taille tarifée de 1715–1789.* Paris: Comité pour l'histoire économique et financière de la France, 1994.

Tremblay, Yves. "Questions de méthode." *Bulletin d'histoire politique* 18(1): 247–61 (2009).

Trigger, Bruce G. *The Children of Aataentsic: A History of the Huron People to 1660.* Montreal and Kingston: McGill-Queen's University Press, 1976.

– *Natives and Newcomers: Canada's "Heroic Age" Reconsidered.*
Montreal and Kingston: McGill-Queen's University Press, 1985.

Troyes, Pierre de. *Journal de l'expédition du chevalier de Troyes à la Baie d'Hudson, en 1686.* Edited and annotated by Ivanhoë Caron.
Beauceville, QC: L'Éclaireur, 1918.

Trudel, Marcel. *L'Église canadienne sous le régime militaire, 1759–1764.*
2 vols. Montreal/Quebec: Institut d'histoire de l'Amérique française;
Presses de l'Université Laval, 1956–57.

– *Les Événements.* Book 1 of *La Seigneurie des Cent-Associés: 1627–1663,* vol. 3 of *Histoire de la Nouvelle-France.* Montreal: Fides, 1979.

– *Le Régime militaire dans le gouvernement des Trois-Rivières, 1760–1764.* Trois-Rivières: Éditions du Bien public, 1952.

– *Le Régime militaire et la disparition de la Nouvelle-France, 1759–1760.*
Vol. 10 of *Histoire de la Nouvelle-France.* Montreal: Fides, 1999.

– *La Société.* Book 2 of *La Seigneurie des Cent-Associés: 1627–1663,* vol. 3 of *Histoire de la Nouvelle-France.* Montreal: Fides, 1979.

– *Les Vaines Tentatives (1524–1603).* Vol. 1 of *Histoire de la Nouvelle-France.* Montreal: Fides, 1963.

True, Micah. *Masters and Students: Jesuit Mission Ethnography in Seventeenth-Century New France.* Montreal and Kingston: McGill-Queen's University Press, 2015.

Ulrich, Laurel Thatcher. *Good Wives: Image and Reality in the Lives of Women in Northern New England, 1650–1750.* New York: Alfred A. Knopf, 1982.

Varachaud, Marie-Christine, Michel Vergé-Franceschi, and André Zysberg.
"Qui étaient les capitaines de vaisseau du Roi-Soleil?" *Revue historique* 582 (April-June 1992): 311–8.

Vattel, Emmerich de. *The Law of Nations, or, The Principles of Natural Law.* Translated by Charles G. Fenwick from the 1758 edition.
Washington: Carnegie Institution of Washington, 1916.

Vauban, Sébastien Le Prestre de. *La Correspondance de Vauban relative au Canada.* Edited by Louise Dechêne. Quebec: Ministère des affaires culturelles, 1968.

– *Les Oisivetés de Monsieur de Vauban, ou, Ramas de plusieurs mémoires de sa façon sur différents sujets.* Edited by Michèle Virol. Seyssels:
Champ Vallon, 2007.

Vaughan, Alden V., and Edward W. Clark, eds. *Puritans among the Indians: Accounts of Captivity and Redemption, 1676–1724.*
Cambridge, MA: Belknap Press, 1981.

Vaughan, Alden V., and Daniel K. Richter. "Crossing the Cultural Divide: Indians and New Englanders, 1605–1763." *Proceedings of the American Antiquarian Society* 90(1): 23–100 (April 1980).

Verney, Jack. *The Good Regiment: The Carignan-Salières in Canada, 1665–1668*. Montreal and Kingston: McGill-Queen's University Press, 1991.

Veyssière, Laurent. "Louis-Antoine de Bougainville au Canada (1756–1760): la découverte et l'expérience de la guerre." In Bertrand Fonck and Laurent Veyssière, eds, *La Guerre de Sept Ans en Nouvelle-France*, 173–98. Quebec: Septentrion, 2012.

Vidal, Cécile, ed. *Français? La Nation en débat entre colonies et métropole (XVIe–XIXe siècle)*. Paris: Éditions de l'École des hautes études en sciences sociales, 2014.

Vigié, Marc. "Justice et criminalité au XVIIIe siècle: le cas de la peine des galères." *Histoire, économie et société* 3 (1985): 345–68.

Villain, Jean. *Le Recouvrement des impôts directs sous l'ancien régime*. Paris: Marcel Rivière, 1952.

Vo-Ha, Paul. "Le Sort des vaincus pendant les dernières guerres de Louis XIV: les limites de la culture de la reddition honorable." In Hervé Drévillon, Bertrand Fonck, and Jean-Philippe Cénat, eds, *Les Dernières Guerres de Louis XIV, 1688–1715*, 157–71. Rennes and Vincennes: Presses universitaires de Rennes and Service historique de la Défense, 2017.

Ward, Matthew C. "Crossing the Line? The British Army and the Application of European 'Rules of War' in the Quebec Campaign." In Phillip Buckner and John G. Reid, eds, *Revisiting 1759: The Conquest of Canada in Historical Perspective*, 44–68. Toronto: University of Toronto Press, 2012.

Way, Peter. "The Cutting Edge of Culture: British Soldiers Encounter Native Americans in the French and Indian War." In Martin Daunton and Rick Halpern, eds, *Empire and Others: British Encounters with Indigenous Peoples, 1600–1850*, 123–48. Philadelphia: University of Pennsylvania Press, 1999.

Weyhing, Richard. "'Gascon Exaggerations': The Rise of Antoine Laumet dit Lamothe, Sieur de Cadillac, the Foundation of Colonial Detroit, and the Origins of the Fox Wars." In Robert Englebert and Guillaume Teasdale, eds, *French and Indians in the Heart of North America, 1630–1815*, 77–112. East Lansing and Winnipeg: Michigan State University Press and University of Manitoba Press, 2013.

– "Le Sueur in the Sioux Country: Rethinking France's Indian Alliances in the Pays d'en Haut." *Atlantic Studies* 10(1): 35–50 (2013).

White, Bruce M. "Encounters with Spirits: Ojibwa and Dakota Theories about the French and their Merchandise." *Ethnohistory* 41(3): 369–405 (Summer 1994).

White, Hayden. *The Content of the Form: Narrative Discourse and Historical Representation.* Baltimore: Johns Hopkins University Press, 1987.

White, Richard. *The Middle Ground: Indians, Empires and Republics in the Great Lakes Region, 1650–1815.* Cambridge: Cambridge University Press, 1991.

Wien, Thomas. "Accumulation in a Context of Colonization: Rivière-du-Sud, Canada 1720–1775." PhD diss., McGill University, 1988.

– "Castor, peaux et pelleteries dans le commerce canadien des fourrures, 1720–1790." In Bruce G. Trigger, Toby Morantz, and Louise Dechêne, eds, *Le Castor fait tout: choix de textes présentés à la 5e conférence nord-américaine sur la traite de la fourrure, 1985,* 72–92. Montreal: Lake St Louis Historical Society, 1987.

– "Les Conflits sociaux dans une seigneurie canadienne au XVIIIe siècle: les moulins des Couillard." In Gérard Bouchard and Joseph Goy, eds, *Famille, économie et société rurale en contexte d'urbanisation (XVIIe–XXe siècle): actes du colloque d'histoire comparée Québec-France, tenu à Montréal en février 1990,* 225–36. Chicoutimi and Paris: Centre interuniversitaire SOREP and École des hautes études en sciences sociales, 1990.

– "La Conquête racontée en 2009." *Revue d'histoire de l'Amérique française* 64(1): 103–25 (2010).

– "En attendant Frégault: à propos de quelques pages blanches de l'histoire du Canada sous le Régime français." In Cécile Vidal, Thomas Wien, and Yves Frenette, eds, *De Québec à l'Amérique française: histoire et mémoire,* 65–94. Quebec: Presses de l'Université Laval, 2006.

– "Note de lecture: quarante fois la Conquête." *Revue d'histoire de l'Amérique française* 66(3–4): 441–54 (2013).

– "Selling Beaver Skins in North America and Europe, 1720–1760: The Uses of Fur-Trade Imperialism." *Journal of the Canadian Historical Association* 1(1): 295–6 (1990).

– "Les Travaux pressants: calendrier agricole, assolement et productivité au Canada au XVIIIe siècle." *RHAF* 43(4): 535–8 (Spring 1990).

– "Vie et transfiguration du coureur de bois." In Philippe Joutard and Thomas Wien, eds, *Mémoires de Nouvelle-France,* 179–86. Rennes: Presses universitaires de Rennes, 2005.

Williams, Alan F. *Father Baudoin's War: D'Iberville's Campaigns in Acadia and Newfoundland, 1696, 1697.* [St John's]: Department of Geography, Memorial University of Newfoundland, 1987.

Wismes, Armel de, ed. *Jean Bart et la guerre de course*. Paris: Julliard, 1965.

Woods, Patricia Dillon. *French-Indian Relations on the Southern Frontier, 1699–1762*. Ann Arbor, MI: n.p., 1980.

Zeller, Gaston. *Les Institutions de la France au XVIe siècle*. Paris: Presses universitaires de France, 1948.

Zoltvany, Yves F. *The Government of New France: Royal, Clerical, or Class Rule?* Scarborough, ON: Prentice-Hall, 1971.

– *Philippe de Rigaud de Vaudreuil: Governor of New France, 1703–1725*. Toronto: McClelland and Stewart, 1974.

Index